Meet Mr. Mistake

Luckiest Ordinary Man Alive

By Chic Perkins
aka Charlie Perkins

Meet Mr. Mistake

Meet Mr. Mistake is a work of non-fiction. For certain individuals referred, names were changed to protect their privacy. Generally speaking, last names of people the author knew on a personal level were left out for a matter of privacy, though last names were provided for individuals the author was associated with on a professional basis.

All photographs appearing in this work come from the author's personal collection, and were either taken by the author or by people associated with the author.

ISBN:978-1-66784-471-8

Dedicated
to the memory of Dan
and Janice

Table of Contents

Preface

There is nothing particularly special about me. I'm just an ordinary guy. I was just a better-than-average sportswriter. I was a much better job coach by comparison. I am just an average piano player. I've written some music that's pretty to listen to, but I'm no Beethoven. I wrote a couple of screen plays that were pretty good. But special? If they were, you would have heard about them.

I am a good storyteller. I've always enjoyed telling a good story. To be a good storyteller, however, you need good stories to tell, and while I may be an ordinary guy I have led an extraordinary life, an unconventional life that has manifested itself in an inordinate number of good stories. When I thought back on my life, and all that I had been through, I thought: 'Man, I've got to tell these stories.' They are stories that don't happen to everybody. They happened to me, and I've lived to tell them.

I've been very lucky in that way and boy, do I know it. In many cases, I'm lucky to be alive. Bullets have been dodged. That's why I've dubbed myself "Luckiest Ordinary Man Alive."

I've lived relatable experiences which transpired in extraordinary fashion. I've had my share of adversity. I had one boss tell me to look for another job, was fired from a job, demoted at yet another job, had my heart broken more than once, divorced four times, got ripped off, survived a major health setback, and experienced painful loss. I've also had a lifetime of loves and experiences that have made me feel like the richest man in the world. I have captured the essence of life in the smallest of moments.

I don't regret any one of the loves in my life, though admittedly I regret love lost with at least one, or two. Love is a double-edged sword. "Falling in love means you're one step away, from heaven or heartache, which way is hard to say," I wrote in a song.

I do have a few regrets. I missed out big-time on the day-to-day experience of raising my kids. I tried my best to be a part of their lives as much I was able. But that only partially filled the void.

I learned to live with the choices I made. Mistakes were made, and some choices were made for me, but I have no cause to complain. On balance, things have worked out very well for me.

Most of all, I've been lucky enough to tell many of these stories with a smile and, just maybe, bring a smile to those who read them. Or maybe my sense of humor is warped. I will let the reader be the judge. The luxury of finding humor in one's life in the process of reflecting back is blessing enough.

Meet Mr. Mistake

Luckiest Ordinary Man Alive

Chic Perkins, the sports writer

CHAPTER 1
Hello, My Name Is...

Hello, my name is Chic.

You heard that right. It's not Chip, or Skip. Or Chet, or Chuck.

But my name also happens to be Charlie. Chic or Charlie. I'm known by either name.

Now, you're not going to find in the story of my life a split personality between good and evil associated with the two names. Chic is not my evil twin. What you will find is a rich mixture of both very good and very bad (and often amusing) twists of luck. Ultimately, as luck would have it, most of the bad turned into good.

I was born into this world, specifically in Santa Monica, Ca., named Charles, after my father. My mother, in her infinite wisdom, figured I didn't want to be called Charles, so she decided on a nickname for me. Chuck is the most common nickname for Charles, but I guess Mom didn't want me to be confused with my Uncle Chuck. I guess she also didn't care to call me Charlie.

So she came up with Chic. Thanks Mom.

When I meet someone for the first time and say, "My name is Chic," they typically think they've heard anything but "Chic." You can see it in their faces, that puzzled look. The furrowed brow, the squinty eyes. That's where the Chips or Skips or Chets or Chucks get thrown up in the confusion. Then when they realize your name really is Chic, the more polite ones will say "Really?" The not-so-polite ones will stifle a giggle. The downright rude ones will just burst out laughing.

My worst experience with name confusion came one night while stopping in the old Fatburger on State Street in downtown Santa Barbara to get something to eat on my dinner break from work. A young Hispanic woman took my order, writing it down on an order slip. She asked for my name so that when my order came up, it would be announced over the intercom for pickup at the front counter. When I told her my name, I recognized that familiar puzzled look as she scribbled down the name she thought she heard on my order slip. Then she handed me a carbon copy.

When I looked down at my order slip, I could not believe my eyes. On the bottom of my order, she wrote, in shaky letters, "Shit."

No shit. As God was my witness, my life had sunk to a new low. My name was Shit at Fatburger. I decided to wait for my "name" to be called when my order was ready. You can just imagine how confused the guy at the intercom had to be when my order was ready and he tried to read the name at the bottom of my order slip: "Uhh… Sh… Shi…She.. Sheet? Aw shit, your order is ready."

"Oh, that would be me. I'm… Shit."

But I was primed for the abuse by then. Let me tell you what it's like for a boy growing up named Chic. Johnny Cash recorded this song called "A Boy Named Sue." That's what it's like, like that song. When I think back to the kids who teased me about my name, I recall Cash singing how he tracked down his father in a bar and challenged the sonoabitch who named him Sue to a fight that ended up with them rolling in the "mud and the blood and the beer." Likewise, I wanted to fight those teasing kids until we were rolling in the mud and the blood and the root beer.

Junior high was really tough. Thirteen and 14-year-old boys in the 60's just thought it was hilarious that a boy would be named Chic. I could have used years of therapy to suppress the buzzing in my head from the "Brrccck-brck-brck-brck" sound I routinely heard from my junior high male classmates, mimicking a stirred-up hen coup. It got pretty old answering their inquiries on what kind of eggs I had for breakfast.

It wasn't just my male classmates in junior high who had a problem with my name. So did my English teacher, Mrs. Jaubert, who instantly ruled out calling me Chic on the first day of class. She insisted on calling me Charles. "You don't mind, do you, Charles?"

Now, my dad was a Charles, too. But he didn't have the dilemma of going by a shorter nickname for Charles, because he went by his middle name, Wesley, or Wes. How convenient. Mom, not to be outdone by the torture inflicted by naming me Chic, decided to dip into our family tree to brand me with a family surname for a middle name. One could only hope that our family heritage would yield a family last name that middle school-aged males would think was cool, like Grant (as in Cary Grant) or Wayne (as in John Wayne). But nooooooo, not with my luck, no siree, The middle name my mother plucked from our lineage was Ebersole, which didn't come close to registering on the scale measuring adolescent coolness. When word somehow got out about my middle name, "Hey Eb," and "Hi, Eber" were the taunts that, metaphorically speaking, regularly turned my peanut butter and jelly sandwiches to mush during lunch recess.

But I grew to respect the Ebersole name I bore, having heard from my mother numerous times over the history of the seven Ebersole brothers who sailed to America from England in the 1700's. They got around, evidently.

My destiny-detoured and weirdly-bent buddy Dan, rest his soul, used to send me birthday and Christmas cards from his homes in Nevada and Washington, addressed to Charles "Rubbersole" Perkins. But I took no offense. In fact, association to John, Paul, George and Ringo rendered a little flair to Ebersole.

I learned to wear the name Chic with pride, too. It served me well as a sportswriter, starting in high school, when as a staff writer on the school newspaper at Hawthorne (Ca.) High, "The Cougar," I wrote a weekly sports column called "Chic's Kicks."

Girls started thinking the name Chic was cute in high school. As I grew older, I think some gay guys thought it was cute, too.

I wound up writing under the byline "Chic Perkins" as a sportswriter for two newspapers for 28 years, 13 with the Los Angeles Herald Examiner, and 15 with the Santa Barbara News-Press. I made a name for myself in my day. One of my proudest moments came when I was covering an L.A. Lakers game in the mid-1980s. After the game, I had the opportunity to introduce myself to the legendary Lakers broadcaster, Chick Hearn.

"Allow me to introduce myself, Chick," I said as I approached him. "I'm Chic Perkins from the Herald Examiner. From one Chick to another." He shook my hand.

It was my mother's idea to spell "Chic" without the "k," like the fashion magazine, "Chic." I have no idea why, but I'm reminded of my first day at the Daily Titan at Cal State Fullerton, when I introduced myself to Sports Editor Jim Ruffalo. I told him "I'm Chic Perkins, without the 'k.'" Jim responded on queue, "So, you're Chic Perins?"

The name Charlie popped up for me on a couple of occasions early in my life. My lifelong friend Rich was the first person to call me "Charlie" in high school. He wanted nothing to do with "Chic."

Then, at age 19, I got a part-time job through my buddy Dan where he was working, at the Children's Baptist Home in Inglewood.

I was hired as a recreation leader. Jerry, the rec staff supervisor with the Kodak smile, charisma, dashing looks and body-builder bod who had a knack for giving everyone a catchy nickname, hated mine. "No way, we're not callin' you Chic. The kids will brutalize ya."

"The kids" were the wards of the court who lived at the Childrens Baptist Home. I was sooo over-my-head. So Jerry ordained me as "Charlie" at the Home.

The name started to take on more permanence later in my life when I moved to Santa Barbara. I met a woman in Dargan's bar in downtown Santa Barbara, when I was still a sportswriter named Chic at the News-Press. When I introduced myself as Chic, she burst out laughing and blurted,

"I can't call you 'Chic'! Can I call you 'Charlie'?"

She batted those big, beautiful green eyes at me, and how could I say no? She became my girlfriend, and the second significant person in my life to call me Charlie.

That relationship didn't last, but the name Charlie eventually stuck. It took on a whole new life when my sports writing career ended. I was 54, out of work, with no future in the newspaper business, especially at my age. Destiny directed me in random fashion to a new career in social services working as a job coach supporting individuals with disabilities, with an agency called Work Training Programs.

I decided that the new career called for a new identity apart from my old career. Hence, Charlie replaced Chic. Work Training Programs eventually changed its name as well, to PathPoint. There is a whole community of individuals whom I've supported who know me as Charlie, the job coach. More than a few of them teased me by linking me to the cartoon character Charlie Brown. Just think what they would have come up with if my name was Chic.

I met my wife Cyndi at PathPoint. She calls me Charlie. My previous four wives all called me Chic. Maybe it was the name that wasn't a match with matrimony. The various divorce lawyers, arbitrators and judges all called me Mr. Perkins. The respective case filings called me Respondent.

In all other cases, pun intended, I'm called Chic or Charlie. The whole town of Santa Barbara that I've encountered as a job coach the past 15 years knows me as Charlie. But when I drive down to visit my friends in L.A, they all know me as Chic.

So I guess, that's how it was supposed to break. I really don't have a preference what people call me.

Just don't call me Shit. Or give me any.

Charlie Perkins, the job coach

---◆---

I've learned to appreciate just how lucky I am. But we all wonder when we might be pushing our luck. I certainly didn't think my time was up when I woke up on the morning of January 26, 2014.

---◆---

CHAPTER 2
Stroke Of Luck

I've lived long enough to know now that luck is relative. Bad things happen to everybody. You're lucky when you can see the good that comes out of the bad.

I've learned to appreciate just how lucky I am. But we all wonder when we might be pushing our luck. I certainly didn't think my time was up when I woke up on the morning of January 26, 2014. I was a 60-year old man who had managed to avoid any major health problem. I was an active tennis player in reasonably good shape. I had never so much as sat on a hospital bed. Ever.

I was sitting on the toilet at home that Sunday morning, getting ready to make the 100-mile drive from Santa Barbara to Azusa to visit my daughter at her college dorm. She was a freshman at Azusa Pacific University. It was a drive I had made countless times before.

Nothing seemed out of the ordinary. But a curious thing caught my attention. My left hand was curling involuntarily and turning over all on its own. I wasn't controlling the movement. I felt no pain, no numbness. I was sort of amused at first. How odd. Why was my hand doing that?

I finished my business in the bathroom and stumbled out into the hallway. Cyndi, my domestic partner who was off to the side watching me, was alarmed.

"Charlie, are you okay?"

I didn't think it was a big deal. I must have mumbled something to her and she repeated the question, with increased alarm, as I started to fall off to my left side.

Her voice rose. "You're not okay, Charlie. I'm calling 9-1-1."

Cyndi had always been a worrier. But I admit my thought processes were a little warped at the time and I really didn't know what was happening to me. The next thing I knew an army of paramedics was swarming into our living room and surrounding me as I sat in a recliner.

One of them beamed a flashlight in my eyes. Then others started wrestling my pajamas off me, stripping me down to my underwear and socks. They wrapped me in a hospital gown and taped an IV to my hairy left arm. Then I was hoisted onto a gurney and wheeled out into the ambulance parked in front of our house.

I was thinking, hold on a second. I had a big day planned with my daughter. Instead, I was taking my first ride in the back of an ambulance. We were zipping through the Mesa neighborhood streets I had driven for over 20 years as a resident. From the back window of an ambulance it all looked surreal.

Within a few minutes we arrived at the Emergency Center at Santa Barbara's Cottage Hospital. They rolled me into a room where they conducted a CAT scan on my head. Then a group of doctors and nurses huddled around me, and Cyndi, to discuss what to do next.

I was still in a bit of a cloud, but by then I knew something serious was happening to me.

Dr. Corraza, a neurologist, explained that the CAT scan showed that I had suffered a stroke as a result of a blood clot in the right side of my brain, which was affecting control of the left side of my body. Ahh, the curling left hand. Now I was getting it.

Dr. Corraza recommended something called a tPA treatment. which would effectively dissolve the clot in my brain. TPA, or tissue plasminogen activator, is a treatment for stroke caused by a blood clot interrupting blood flow to a region of the brain. Dr. Corraza said the treatment would effectively dissolve the clot in my brain.

He was straightforward. But the look on his face failed to disguise the gravity of the situation. He explained there was risk involved – the tPA had a 1 in 16 chance of causing hemorrhaging in the brain, which could be fatal. Cyndi's face turned ashen white.

I'm pretty good with numbers. A 1-in-16 chance? The room we were in wasn't very big, but it could hold 16 people. That meant if all 16 of us were experiencing a stroke and were being treated with tPA, one of us wouldn't make it. I would have felt a whole lot better if we were talking about a football stadium full of stroke victims and only one of us would be left lying on the 50-yard-line.

Dr. Corraza clearly wanted us to think about it, but explained that a decision had to be made soon, because tPA was a viable option only within 3-4 hours of the onset of stroke symptoms. After that the risk factor increased exponentially.

There was some hesitation in the doctor's voice, because dexterity tests on my left hand were showing signs of the stroke symptoms disappearing. A few minutes passed. Then I was asked to sign a release form basically stating that I understood the risks involved with the tPA treatment.

While I do most things right-handed -- throw, bowl, play tennis -- I write left-handed. It's a quirk in my makeup. As I started to sign my name on the form I lost control of my left hand and couldn't write. O...M...G.

I think that was the first moment I realized I was in real trouble. The look on Dr. Corraza's face changed. He told me then that any option other than tPA meant I stood a real chance of suffering permanent disability. I scribbled an illegible version of my signature on the release form and was whisked away to the Intensive Care Unit.

From a rolling gurney, the view of hospital hallways seemed very strange. The lights on the ceiling were very bright. The walls were very clean but bland. Left turns, right turns, an elevator ride, then a couple more left and rights. I lost track of direction.

Cyndi was my constant companion in my ICU room until late in the evening.

A very friendly nurse name Mark, with distinctive reddish hair and a goatee, said a lot of nice things to make me feel at ease, assuring me that they would take good care of me. He proceeded to tape two IVs to each of my arms – one to keep track of my vitals, and the other for administering the tPA treatment. Then — I'm not sure how many there were — maybe 10 half-dollar-sized contact patches with wires connected to the vitals monitor were applied to my hairy chest. Mark made a comment on how hard it was to make the contact patches stick.

Mark then explained that neurological tests had to be administered to me every 15 minutes for the first few hours. By early evening they would be cut back to every half hour.

The neurological tests began with a flashlight shined into each eye, followed by an assortment of rudimentary movements as commanded by the nurse: smile to show my teeth, shrug my shoulders, close my eyes and count how many times the nurse tapped my hands, hold my arms out, grasp the nurse's hands and push them away from me, then pull them toward me, straighten each leg and lift, and push and pull with each of my feet.

After an exhausted Cyndi returned home to get some rest, the longest night of my life lay ahead. Sleep wasn't really in the program.

Every hour on the hour I was awakened by a flashlight shining in my eyes, followed by the series of neurological tests. In between I tried counting sheep, but that didn't work. I just lay there trying not to focus on the splitting headache that got worse as the night wore on.

By around 2:30 a.m. I couldn't stand the pain anymore so I pushed the help button by my bed and summoned the overnight nurse, Maria. I told her how badly my head hurt and asked if I could take something for the pain. She said she had to call the doctor first to see if it was OK.

Within a few minutes Maria returned and told me the doctor required a CAT scan first, to make sure the headache wasn't the result of hemorrhaging.

So, at about 2:45 a.m. I was being rolled back to the CAT scan room. If I hadn't felt fear before I definitely was feeling it on that cart ride. Crap, was I going to be the one unlucky bastard out of 16? I never felt more alone than during those 20-plus minutes lying inside the CAT scan tube. I closed my eyes to avoid feeling overwhelmed by claustrophobia. For reasons I can't quite explain, an old Bee Gees song, "How Deep Is Your Love?", kept running over and over in my head:

"How deep is your love, how deep is your love,
I really need to know,
'Cause we're living in a world of fools . . . . . Da-da-da-dahh."

The song wasn't doing anything for my headache in that CAT scan tube, let me tell ya. But it may have kept me from losing it altogether.

Back in my ICU room, my head felt like it was going to explode as I waited to hear the results of the CAT scan. It was after 4 a.m. when Maria finally came in with the verdict—no hemorrhaging. I was so relieved I could have kissed her.

Finally, Maria was able to give me Vicodin™ for the headache. For a couple hours, the pain subsided, but I still couldn't sleep.

At around 7 a.m. Maria came in and asked if I wanted to order breakfast. My first order was a couple more Vicodin pills, as my headache was creeping back. I thought I finally felt like eating, but when the meal arrived I stared at it for about an hour.

Cyndi returned some time that morning. It was Monday and a work day for both of us. We both worked as job coaches for PathPoint, a non-profit agency that provides support services for people with disabilities. Cyndi called our boss Jaime to let him know what was going on with me. I imagined how word would spread at work about my situation and pictured the shocked reactions from our colleagues.

Meanwhile, the neurological tests kept coming, and I passed with increasing efficiency.

As the day wore on I was consulted a few times by Dr. Lemmon, who was encouraged by my progress. All my vital signs were positive. Dr. Lemmon said the second CAT scan, performed in the middle of the night, showed that the clot in the right side of my brain had dissolved, confirming that the tPA treatment worked.

A technician came in at one point to do a "bubble" test to see if I had a hole between the two compartments of my heart, which was a potential explanation for how the clot was created in my brain. But that test came up negative.

Mark, the red-headed nurse, was back on duty and he made it a point to stop in to see how I was doing. He was so impressed with the news of my progress that he dubbed me the "poster boy" for quick-recovery stroke survivors.

Other than a lingering headache, I was feeling pretty normal by late afternoon. Dr. Lemmon decided I could go home. The headache wasn't going away so the nurse checked with the pharmacy to see if I could take the Maxalt pill prescribed by my regular neurologist to treat my migraines.

The headache wasn't the worst of it as far as getting prepped to leave the hospital. All those contact patches attached to my hairy chest had to be removed. The nurse decided it would be less painful if I did it myself. So, left alone, I did an excruciating reenactment of the unforgettable scene from the movie "Forty Year Old Virgin," in which Steve Carell's character screamed bloody murder while lying on a table as a beautician ripped wax strips off his chest to remove the hair. If I could survive that, I could survive anything.

What next? I was dressed, so I figured I had already been cleared to leave, and I walked down some stairs and out of the hospital by a side exit. Hey, no one had told me that I was supposed to be escorted out of the building in a wheelchair. I felt kind of stupid when

Cyndi found me wandering around outside and asked me if I had been formally released. "Uhh, I guess not."

I have to say, though, Cyndi couldn't have looked any prettier than she did when I saw her outside the hospital after the last 40-something hours inside.

I considered myself a very lucky man that night after dodging a potentially fatal bullet. I survived a significant malfunction in my brain! Now, all that stood in the way of full normalcy was a week off from work and another neurological test to clear me for driving. My job required that I drive.

That migraine wasn't going away, though. Normally, one Maxalt did the trick, but this time I needed to take another one in the evening and then a third one the next morning when the pain was still lingering. I had never taken more than two in a 24-hour period before.

The headache finally went away by mid-day Tuesday. I rested, read a lot, and planned for my return to work.

That evening, while watching TV, I was having a tough time following the shows. I'd hear the words spoken but I couldn't connect any meaning to them.

The next day I called my boss, Jaime, and made a pitch to return to work for a half-day on Friday. The five-minute conversation did not go well. Jaime would ask me a question and I would stumble in my response. When I hung up I realized I hadn't made a convincing case with Jaime. He told me not to rush back, and to consult my doctor.

By evening a sense of feeling mentally trapped had crept up on me. It was very strange. Cyndi and I were sitting in the living room, eating dinner and watching "Elementary" on TV, and Sherlock Holmes' English accent was becoming increasingly more unintelligible.

Cyndi made casual conversation. She would ask me a question and I wouldn't respond. She asked me a few more basic questions and I stayed silent. With each question I felt increasingly uneasy and wanted her to stop. Cyndi looked at me quizzically. Then, she asked me one more question: "What is my name?"

The response was the same -- silence. I was frozen, because I couldn't think of the name of the woman I'd been living with for the past six years. The response from What's-Her-Name was resolute. "I'm calling 9-1-1."

Oh God, no! Not back to the hospital! I wanted to run out of the room. I wanted to go to the bathroom. But the paramedics arrived in a flash.

Second verse, same as the first. Flashlight beamed in each of my eyes. Stripped down to underwear and socks, a quick change into a hospital gown, and an IV taped to my arm. Then off for my second ride in the back of an ambulance.

Wait! I had to go to the bathroom. Did I fail to mention that? Or rather, I couldn't mention it. I couldn't formulate the words to say anything, but my thoughts were clear. With the increased adrenaline running through my veins, the pressure on my bladder increased exponentially.

Even more dire thoughts were racing through my dysfunctional brain. *Was this it? Was this the final curtain? Am I not going to make it to my sixty-first birthday? Or, if I live, will my life be permanently altered by living in a disabled state?*

I started thinking about all the things I still wanted to do in my life. I was in utter disbelief that this was the end. *Please, God, let me live.*

But first, God, please let me pee!

At first the fear of having suffered another stroke overwhelmed my thoughts during that ambulance ride. But the increasing pressure in my bladder gradually consumed me. I was dying.

This time, I was rushed into a holding room at the Emergency Center. Cyndi was by my side. A woman doctor flashed a flashlight in my eyes and did some basic neurological tests.

She held up a pen and asked me to identify it. I couldn't. Silence again. Then we waited. And waited. All the while my bladder was screaming for relief, but I had no way of telling anyone. Where the hell was that pen? If only I had been thinking clearly I could have used that pen to scribble a note about my urgent urge to urinate.

Cyndi kept telling me how much she loved me. I wanted to tell her I loved her. Words escaped me.

The wait extended well beyond midnight. At some point Yifat and Eyal, our caring Israeli friends, showed up. Yifat is a colleague of ours at PathPoint and Eyal is her husband. Cyndi must have called Yifat, who is her closest friend. I remember making eye contact with Yifat, who looked worried. But I had no words for her. My mind was blank.

Later, I was debating if I should just release my bladder while lying in the bed. For some reason, I couldn't bring myself to do that; I guess it was an illogical sense of propriety that stopped me. I don't know how I was able to bear the pain.

Then something miraculous happened. Holding a plastic container, Cyndi cupped my hand and said: "They want a urine sample."

May God have mercy!! There is a God!! When Cyndi handed me that plastic container and I lowered it to my genitals underneath my hospital gown it felt like I had died and gone to heaven. As I exulted in the longest pee of my life, hope was restored.

It wasn't until later, when Cyndi recounted events of this night, that I understood how dire my situation really had been. My speech challenges, signifying the onset of another stroke, had started hours ago. That meant the window of opportunity to implement the tPA treatment had passed.

I was finally transported to the main hospital, with the first stop in the CAT scan room again. No Bee Gees tune this time, but I closed my eyes and my thoughts drifted inside the scanning tube. I was getting somewhat accustomed to this.

This CAT scan revealed that I had an entirely new clot in the left side of my brain that was affecting my ability to speak and cognitively process words. This wasn't a reoccurrence of my first stroke. This was a completely different stroke event, with completely different symptoms.

I wound up in the neurological floor this time around, not ICU. Once again I had a bunch of contact patches attached to my hairy chest. *Really? OK God, I get it.* Since tPA was not an option, I was having blood thinner pumped in my veins through an IV.

The neurological tests administered to me this time included a booklet of illustrated objects that I was asked to identify. I felt like I was back in first grade at school. If they had handed me crayons and asked me to color and stay inside the lines, that would have been a really bad sign. The initial agenda was to get me just to verbalize. It was a struggle. I'd look at the illustrations, recognize what they were and their purpose, but could not think of the words. It was the strangest feeling I've ever experienced. It was frightening to think that as a professional communicator I had lost the ability to communicate.

14

This battle carried on all through the next day, but it got a lot better when I got a surprise visit from my daughter, Tessa, and her college roommate, Alex, who I was supposed to meet on that scheduled visit the previous weekend. Tessa brought me an APU sweatshirt. I was thrilled.

Seeing Tessa clearly lifted my spirits, but conversation was very minimal. Tessa could have freaked out seeing me like that but she remained calm.

By early evening I was showing some progress with my neurological coach, haltingly uttering descriptive words on cue. I remember thinking I was making some progress when she asked me to name our current President.

"O…O…O…ba….ma."

The neurological tests continued hourly through the night. But this time I slept better between tests. In fact, I remember dreaming, and when I awoke at about 6 a.m. I vividly remembered my dream. I had dreamed I was at a house party at somebody's very elegant home and I was with Eva Longoria, the actress from the TV show "Desperate Housewives," drinking banana daiquiris?

Banana daiquiris? Of course. Who among us wouldn't enjoy a refreshing banana daiquiri, after suffering a stroke? I think I may have had one banana daiquiri in my life, years ago, and Eva Longoria wasn't there. So why on earth would she pop up in my dream? In this moment, in this hospital bed? Drinking banana daiquiris? Only in my dreams.

I chuckled at the thought and a switch turned on in my brain. I whispered "Eva Longoria" to myself. I…remembered… her…name. Wow.

I think I laid in bed silently for another half hour or so, in a blissful dreamlike state. Reality reappeared when my nurse Adrianne stepped into the room to give me the next battery of neurological tests.

"I'm so sorry I have to keep waking you up like this," she said apologetically, and I responded, "You're only doing your job."

The look on Adrianne's face was priceless. "You're talking!" she exclaimed.

Indeed, that had been the first full sentence I had uttered since being admitted some 30 hours before. It was a sign of a breakthrough.

Several hours later, after a consultation with the doctor on duty, it was confirmed that I had made another full recovery from a stroke, my second one in four days. I was now able to verbalize and identify the illustrated pictures. A physical therapist came in and walked me through the lobby to see if my physical mechanics were fully functioning. They were.

By mid-day, I was released to go home again. This time they didn't leave me alone and I was wheeled out by a nurse. I was leaving with a few less hairs on my chest from contact patches being stripped off, but otherwise I felt great. This time no headache.

That evening was definitely celebratory as Cyndi and I went out to dinner with Tessa and Alex. I wore my new APU sweatshirt.

The next day was Super Bowl Sunday. I never felt more alive, quietly watching the Seahawks clobber the Broncos in the comfort of my home.

In the course of the following week I visited my regular neurologist, Dr. Karen DaSilva, who analyzed the medical data on my ordeal through the two strokes. She ordered cardiovascular tests for me to see if any clues could be found to explain the cause of the strokes. The tests did not show any signs of defibrillation or any other cardio abnormalities.

The most plausible explanation for the first stroke was my history of high cholesterol. I had been on a prescribed statin for a few years, but I had not been taking them regularly for several months. Un-huh, no more of that. In fact, Dr. DaSilva doubled my dosage.

In addition, I was prescribed Plavix, a blood thinner, and was told I would have to take it the rest of my life. And since I was on blood thinner, Dr. DaSilva said I could no longer take any other medication that thinned the blood, specifically aspirin and ibuprofen.

Then the subject of Maxalt, my migraine medicine, came up. I told Dr. DaSilva how I had taken three Maxalt pills over a 24-hour period for that persistent migraine immediately after my release from the hospital from my first stroke.

Dr. DaSilva was careful with her words. She didn't come right out and say it was a mistake for me to take Maxalt right after my first stroke. She said the cause of my second stroke was not conclusive, but the Maxalt may have contributed because its pain-relief effect is induced by constricting the blood vessels in your brain. Not exactly what

With Cyndi, whose name I haven't forgotten lately

you want to do right after suffering a blood clot in your brain. So Maxalt was added to my "banned" list.

I was back to work within two weeks. I was back on the tennis courts within a month. I was one lucky SOB. Two strokes, full recovery from each, no side effects, other than I'm a bit of a bleeder now, and get cold a lot easier because of the blood thinner.

Oh yeah, I also experience a little fear every now and then whenever I can't think of a word in my head.

Later, on Dr. DaSilva's recommendation, I underwent sleep tests that revealed I had moderate sleep apnea, which was another possible explanation for the first stroke. Welcome to the wonderful world of CPAP.

The good that emerged out of the bad in this story is my renewed appreciation for how precious life is, to make the most of whatever life I have left, and the hard lesson I learned to pay more attention to my health (Diet! Exercise!).

This life-altering experience served as a major motivation for me to write these memoirs, an in-depth examination of my life overall. I was given the gift of a new leash on life to be able to tell these stories.

Most of all, I was reminded again how blessed I am. How thankful I am for Cyndi's loving support – where would I be now if she hadn't called 9-1-1? For the support from my daughter Tessa and friends Yifat and Eyal in my time of need. For the professional expertise and care of Drs. Corraza, Lemmon and DaSilva, nurses Mark, Maria and Adrianne, and a few others whose names I can't remember (but don't worry, it's not stroke-related this time… I hope.)

Life is good. And to elaborate the point, life for me is like drinking a banana daiquiri—it's sweet, but not what I expected.

CHAPTER 3
Started Out Kinda Ordinary

What kid in junior high school knows what he wants to do with the rest of his life? That was the question my father posed to me at the breakfast table one day. I knew then that I wanted to be a writer. But I knew that wasn't the answer he wanted.

"Well, after I graduate from high school I'll go to college and get my degree, get a job in the career I studied for, get married, have kids, and buy a house like ours."

"Good answer, son."

I had no idea at the time that my life would not follow that idyllic path. There was nothing in my childhood to suggest my life would deviate from what my father would consider to be a "normal" transition into adulthood and family life.

I was the son of a nuclear physicist and a lab technologist but I showed no proclivity for the sciences, so I wasn't going to follow in their footsteps. I liked writing stories from an early age. I started almost as soon as I learned how to use a typewriter at age seven. I typed out these little one-page stories that I'd mail off to my Aunt Bee in Cincinnati. Aunt Bee was really my step-grandmother, married to my grandfather, but I called her aunt since my grandmother was still alive.

My story-telling paid a dividend in fourth grade when Mrs. Michelson assigned us to write prose using all the words on our weekly spelling lists. I loved those assignments and my imagination flew while trying to fit every word on those lists into some logical sense within the wild stories I devised.

My fifth grade teacher, Mr. Rivers, was a father figure who broke the tumultuous news of JFK's murder to the classroom. He allowed me to spread my wings as playwright, director and star of my own plays. These theatrical presentations were essentially Perry Mason courtroom drama rip-offs heavily influenced by my mother, who loved mystery novels and the popular Perry Mason TV show.

As a young teen I had a fascination for WWII stories. The first "novel" I wrote was a WWII story that was very similar to the movie "The Dirty Dozen." It chronicled how an earnest American Army captain assembled a bunch of misfits to embark on a dangerous mission behind enemy lines in occupied France. The misfits' mission was to free a U.S. general held captive in a German prison camp. There was a little romance involved, too, between the captain and a French farmer's daughter on the farm where the rescue squad took refuge for a while. And, of course, not everyone returned alive once the mission was completed.

My second attempt at a novel, which was never completed, was also a WWII story, but it was much more personal. It centered on three best friends growing up in Southern California (like me), enlisting in the army and going off to war. The story detailed their farewell from home, boot camp training, and deployment to some remote island in the Pacific to fight the evil "Japs," repeating the racial slur that my adolescent mind imagined some young soldiers commonly using back in the day. The three friends wind up stranded on that island and one of them doesn't make it home.

Of course, I based one of the characters on me. One of the cool things about writing fiction is that you can make your own fantasies come true in your story. My character had left behind his sweetheart, who was a classic blonde, blue-eyed beauty named Sheila. I confess that in real life I had a boyhood crush on a girl in my neighborhood who was a classic blonde, blue-eyed beauty named — can you guess? — Sheila.

———————•◆•———————

That brings me to my neighborhood and the la-la land of my youth. As mentioned, I grew up in the suburbs of Los Angeles in Southern California. Home was in the city of Hawthorne, just 10 minutes from Los Angeles International Airport and two miles from the beach. I attended Hawthorne High, the same alma mater as the Beach Boys, who preceded me by about nine years. How cool was that, to hang out at the same beaches that inspired the Beach Boys to write "Surfin' USA" and "California Girls"?

My father used a GI loan he earned by serving in the Navy during WWII to buy our home on a cul-de-sac called Rossburn. We were entering a community that, for the first half of the first century, had a dark history as a "sundown" town — where African-Americans were forbidden to live or even be within city limits after sundown without risking getting arrested.

Hawthorne was also home for a while to the famous Olympian, Jim Thorpe. That was at the start of the Depression in the early 30's, when even his family struggled to carve out a living. A little girl named Norma Jeane Mortenson also lived in Hawthorne until she turned nine, long before she became better known as Marilyn Monroe.

Growing up on a cul-de-sac imparted a sense of cocooned security. The enclosed street was our playground without the impediment and danger of free-flowing traffic. Rossburn Avenue was a keyhole-shaped cul-de-sac consisting of 15 homes, six lined up parallel on either side of the street leading to three at the wide curved end. Our home at 13707 Rossburn was one of the two homes on the "curve," meaning its lot was nearly double the square footage of all of the other homes on the block (and for that matter, the rest of the neighborhood). My crush, Sheila, lived in a house in an identical spot on an identical cul-de-sac one block over. There were three identical cul-de-sacs side-by-side-by-side with Rossburn in the middle.

My dad, who always made an impression on me by how smart he was, had an IQ in the 160 range. His intelligence was on full display when he took advantage of our 9,500-square foot lot and expanded our original three-bedroom, two-bath home. He added a huge 24X12-foot family room with fireplace, a den, another full master bathroom, a laundry room and yet another half-bathroom. He did all the construction himself. Even with all that, we still had a backyard big enough to play baseball in.

On the other hand, the 9,500 square feet wasn't nearly enough space to house the history of the over 100 people who wound up inhabiting the Rossburn house over the span of 62 years in family hands.

Our house's location had another distinct advantage as far as attending my junior high school. The school grounds were separated only by the eight-foot high cinderblock wall bordering our backyard. So every school-day morning I was scaling that wall at 8:25 to make it to class on time at 8:30. My classmates were jealous.

Rossburn Avenue was populated by families with kids. And boys ruled. The ratio was something like 22 to 5. There were the four Gerke boys who lived next door to us. I still cower at the memory of the boys shrieking in accompaniment to the sound of the belt being wielded by their mother, who was as big as a house. I was closest to

Bruce, the youngest of the four Gerke boys and one year younger than I. Our friendship survived the only (brief) fisticuffs episode of my life (not counting wives) when I was 6 and he was 5. Then there were the three Ely boys down the street. The oldest was Wayne, who was my age and my best friend in early childhood. I have a particularly fond memory of his dad, Forrest, who was a fun-loving, beer-drinking, bigger-than-life-character. I will always relate Wayne's father to the family pet mynah bird who could mimic phrases. Mr. Ely trained it to sing on queue, "How 'bout a beer, Dad?" The Elys were also huge dog-lovers. Their breed of choice was the Basset Hound, perpetuated by several off-spring raised by Betsy, their original hound.

Our other neighbor opposite the Gerkes had a teen-age son, Wally, who was in the same age group as the Beach Boys and apparently was friends with Brian Wilson. I remember listening from my bedroom window to a band jamming in my neighbor's garage. Later, Joel, one of the Gerke boys, told me the band I had been listening to was a primordial version of the Beach Boys.

The paucity of girls on the block was not a good situation for building social skills for my little sister, Pam, who was eighteen months my junior. Pam tried hard to keep pace with her best friend, Jody, who was a purebred tomboy. So Pam, shy and quiet as she was, had no choice but to integrate with a masculine-inflated upbringing.

My sister Pam and I, starting out mini-sized

Jody and Pam were constantly forced to put up with Wayne and I and our annoying antics. On the high end of the annoying scale was our favorite game, Spy, which involved sneaking up as close as we could to the girls before they noticed. No place in the neighborhood was safe for Pam and Jody. Our inevitable discovery would be announced by the girls with a resigned "We see you."

One of my earliest childhood memories was of coming down with chicken pox at age five, at the same time Wayne was afflicted, and we were allowed to play together during recovery. This was really a big deal for me at the time.

A not-so-fond episode with Wayne, which I remember in much clearer detail, is from our days together in first grade with the evil Mrs. Earrug. Doesn't that name sound like a witch? Wayne had convinced me that a classmate named Greg had given the OK for us to pinch him in the butt relentlessly during recess. The shocker to me was that it turned out not to be true. When we got back into class after recess, Mrs. Earrug hammered that message home loud and clear in front of the whole class, and that was truly humiliating. While absorbing that humiliation, all I could think of was how had I been so misled by my buddy Wayne, without any self-awareness of how gullible I was.

First grade presented a huge dilemma when I was being taught how to write in cursive. While I did everything else right-handed, I preternaturally held the pencil with my left hand to write. But I was slanting the pencil at the same angle as a right-hander. Because of that, my teacher tried to force me to write with my right hand, failed miserably, and to this day I write left-handed with that awkward wrist-bend that results in smearing the ink or pencil lead as my hand moves left to right across the page. I do only three other things left-handed — brush my teeth, eat (both hands), and play billiards. Everything else — throw, bowl, play golf, tennis —I use my right hand. There's no rhyme or reason for it, but explains why I describe myself as Not-Quite Ordinary.

———————————◆———————————

As far as marriages go, my parents' union was not idyllic by any means. They were classic opposites — my dad was the introvert, my mom the extrovert. Mom was a social butterfly -- active in the PTA, League of Woman Voters, bridge club, book club, Unitarian

Church group, yoga class. She liked being around people, Dad didn't like crowds and was the stay-at-home type.

They did meet socially through a folk dance group at UCLA, where Dad was attending school while working on his PhD in physics. There must have been something that clicked between them when they danced. The folk dance group stayed intact for decades and remained the one social outlet that my father cherished and shared a common interest with my mother.

They came from distinctly different backgrounds. My father was born into a Mormon family in Salt Lake City, the oldest of three siblings. The family moved to Venice, California, early in Dad's childhood. His father, who had been a cop, was also an alcoholic who eventually deserted the family at the height of the Depression. One story alleged that he did some bootlegging during Prohibition, which couldn't have boded well for his career as a cop.

In his father's absence, Dad at a very young age assumed the role of man-of-the-house to his younger sister Evelyn and younger brother Ray, helping out Grandma, who was stuck in a hapless single-mom role during hard times. Dad never spoke about his own father; what little I do know of him I learned later from Aunt Evelyn, with whom I forged a close adult relationship that had a profound effect on my life.

My Mom, an only child born in Cincinnati, Ohio, was spared the financial frailties of the Depression largely because of her paternal grandmother's diamond business. My mother's parents divorced when she was barely two years old; her dad was living with his mother, so he could provide Mom a reasonably comfortable living while growing up when the Depression hit. Mom was primarily raised by her grandmother. She did, however, spend summers with her mother, who was living in Evanston, Ill., which is home to the University of Northwestern, where Mom eventually chose to go to college.

Consequently, my parents had diametrically opposed views on money -- chiefly on how to spend it. More simply, Dad resisted it mightily while Mom had no problem spending it. That was the source of friction throughout their marriage. It's a minor miracle it lasted as long as it did. They divorced when Pam and I were in our early 20's. The breaking point came after they had gone on a driving tour of Europe. It was their first vacation without us kids and it evidently did not go well. When they returned they announced that the marriage was over.

My divorced Mom set her sights on travel, an interest kindled from the wonder and fantasy of the driving tour of Europe she had taken with her father and a business partner of his when she was an impressionable 13-year-old. It was September, 1939, and Mom loved retelling this story many times for anyone who would listen. Her dad rented a Duesenberg convertible to roam the picturesque countryside of France. They attracted quite a bit of attention, in each village where they stopped along their route, from the locals who weren't used to seeing a luxury car in their midst. But Hitler's Germany was stirring things up considerably and the threat of war was imminent, so they had to hastily flee the continent before they got caught up in it.

———————◆•••◆•••◆———————

I will forever be grateful for the way my parents raised me — a good education, a sense of open-mindedness and acceptance of all races and creeds, an appreciation for culture, arts and the finer things in life, an appreciation for travel, and a progressive (OK, liberal) political influence.

Both Mom and Dad played a part in giving me the gift of learning to play the piano, which would serve an incomparable role throughout my life. Dad never had a piano lesson in his life. But when he was growing up he had one of those old-time player pianos with the rolled-up scrolls, inserted in the bowels of the piano, which could be activated by pressing down on foot pedals. Dad had about a dozen scrolls of classical pieces by Beethoven, Chopin, Liszt, Mozart, and Schubert, and taught himself how to play by memorizing how the keys depressed when he activated the foot pedals. To hear him play, you would have never guessed that he never had a lesson.

As a child I often drifted off to sleep hearing him play after bedtime. That was a much more harmonious way to induce sleep than my routine method back then — pounding my head on the pillow for several minutes. (My sister was the only person who knew that odd habit of mine, but since I was older than her, who was she going to tell? I knew how to keep her silent.)

My dad was damn smart, I'm tellin' ya. I can't say we were that close until his final years, but I was always awestruck by the things I was told he had done. He built his own stereo set! Who does that sort of thing? My dad probably did it just to prove he could.

Mom, whose father was a classical concert pianist of some note, was the one who pushed Pam and I through piano lessons. I lasted five years, from 9 to 14, until I called it quits entering high school. Our teacher was a Jewish lady named Mrs. Rosenberg, who was so tiny she sat shoulder-to-shoulder with me at the piano bench. She was a good teacher, but to be honest, I was a marginal talent; Pam was so much better than I was in technique and form. Somehow, though, I was the one who ended up as the pianist in the junior high orchestra and jazz band (gotta love those Herb Alpert tunes), while Pam played cello in the orchestra. I once performed a solo of a Tchaikovsky piece I committed to memory before a packed auditorium of 100 or so. I have no memory of how well or poorly I played during those terrifying six or seven minutes.

I was a late bloomer as far as getting in the groove with the rock 'n roll craze of the 60s. The classical influence of my piano lessons probably retarded my conversion until I started listening to the radio in high school. The Beatles invasion in '64 certainly didn't sway me; I never did understand what all those young girls were screaming about. I remember my "nerd" stripes being woefully exposed during a music appreciation class in junior high — circa 1966 — when the teacher asked us to list our favorite band. I can still picture the smile on her face when I asked her, "Is it OK if I put down Andy Williams?"

As for the cultural arts, our parents exposed Pam and I to the live theatre experience, taking us to high-profile performances such as "Camelot" and "My Fair Lady" at LA's finest venues. Then there was the shocker, at the height of my sexual awakening at age 13, when they took us to see the Vietnam War - protest musical "Hair." There is just no describing the impact on a young male teen of seeing the entire cast completely naked on stage — the finale scene for which "Hair" was controversially renowned. It surpassed any wet dream I could imagine at the time. "Let The Sunshine In" opened my eyes. My parents, arguably more musically "hip" than their 13-year-old son/slash Andy Williams fan, had my undeniable admiration after that night.

There was no denying the open-mindedness that my

parents taught by their example. For what it's worth, considering the anti-semitic sentiment that existed in this country, many of their friends were Jewish, particularly in their folk-dancing group, with a repertoire consisting of many Israeli dances. Also, my parents' closest friends in the neighborhood were the Nathansons, a Jewish family, down the block on Rossburn.

Racism was another concept that was foreign to my sister and I growing up in lily-white Hawthorne, as it existed back then. There were no blacks within miles of us, but Mom hired Mary as our long-time house cleaner. Mary was a Louisiana-born Black woman who spoke with a molasses-thick Southern accent and who was like a nanny to Pam and I. I recall with considerable fondness how Mary would call me "Chickee" in that raspy voice of hers. We genuinely considered her family and never considered her any different because of the color of her skin.

We never did figure out how old Mary was — her past was cloudy enough that she herself didn't seem to know. Mom kept her on long after the divorce from Dad when she kept the Rossburn house. Mary stayed on well into her 80s and outlived her husband Chester, who had dutifully picked her up at the end of each work day for decades. Mary couldn't do much the last 10-12 years because of her age, but Mom paid her no less because that's just the way it always was; Mom's loose spending habits were matched by her generosity.

Our family vacations produced some memorable travel — trips to Vancouver, Canada, and Victoria Island; a campground on the Russian River in Northern California; all over Montana in a meandering drive before winding up in Missoula, where Dad attended a work-related conference; and Scandinavia, my first experience overseas.

Politics was a common topic in our household. Dad and Mom were huge supporters of JFK and Robert Kennedy. Dad was a big fan of political satire TV shows like "The Smother Brothers" and "Laugh-In." I recall my parents listening to the radio talk show hosted by Dorothy Healy, a spokesperson for the Communist Party in the U.S. during the early 60s. Dad was the more socialist-minded one of my parents, which fit his intellectualism. He was politically aligned with his best friend Tom, who moved with his wife to Canada in a subtle protest against the U.S. government.

I wasn't raised to scorn America or the red, white and blue. I was both a Cub Scout and Boy Scout for a good chunk of my childhood, assuring my appreciation and respect for our country.

As for church, we didn't go. Dad had declared himself an atheist, his scientific mind having rejected his Mormon upbringing long before I came along. Mom wasn't active with the Unitarian Church until after the divorce.

Grandma Perkins, however, rejoined the Mormon faith late in her life, in part due to the influence of her sister Gay. Grandma Perkins was a quiet influence in the family. She taught me how to be humble by the way she conducted herself. She eked out a living well into her senior years by working on the assembly line dipping chocolates for Sees Candies. Images of that classic "I Love Lucy" episode in which Lucy stuffs rapidly moving chocolates into her mouth come to mind. I heard a comedian once tell a joke about how his grandmother always managed to send him $5 in a card for his birthday every year, even well into his 50's. He stole that joke from me because he was talking about my grandmother. I have many classic memories of Grandma, a couple of which will pop up in stories ahead.

I was blessed with two great grandmothers in my life. "Mimi," the nickname Pam and I called our mother's mother, was distinctively different from Grandma Perkins. Mimi was the more flamboyant one, a true bohemian spirit. She had a much bigger presence in my life than my maternal grandfather, who I barely knew before he passed away when I was 9 years old. We called her the "Lavender Lady" because that was the favorite color she usually wore in her clothing and shawls. She was also the "cat lady" because she always had them around, and Mom followed suit. Mimi lived in a modest little cottage house in Montecito, in the foothills of Santa Barbara. She owned a beautiful acre of land with a forest of trees surrounding the property and a running creek through the front yard. Visiting Mimi in Montecito was always a treat. She was married to "Uncle" Bill when I was a kid; I'm not sure how many husbands preceded him. She worked for years as a social worker at an adoption agency, a past that would render one of life's many surprises to me much later.

If I was destined to be a writer, then I guess I was destined to write about sports. My youth shaped my love of sports along with my love of writing. I was a baseball nut in general as a kid, and an LA Dodgers fan in particular.

I latched onto the Dodgers at an early age, in the late 50s when they were still playing their home games in the LA Coliseum. My favorite Dodger from the start was Wally Moon, best known for his "Moon shots" into the left field pavilion at the Coliseum. I stayed a loyal Wally Moon fan long after his prime, as he began to fade badly when the Dodgers moved into their new home at Dodger Stadium in the early 60's.

It was Mom, not Dad, who nourished my love for baseball. She was the one who took me to Dodger games and taught me how to keep score. She kept score at every Dodger game we attended in the programs she bought at the gate. Her appreciation of baseball was cultivated by her dad, who took her to Cincinnati Reds games when she was growing up. Mom provided one of my biggest thrills by yanking me out of school one day to attend a '65 World Series game against the Minnesota Twins at Dodger Stadium. We were sitting in the right field pavilion when Joe Ferguson made his famous peg from the outfield to nail a runner at home plate.

The most memorable Dodger game I ever attended, however, was with Grandma, on Ringo Starr Poster Night in '64. We were sitting on the slim, exclusive VIP third deck —not sure how we rated getting seats there — which had a restaurant at the far end of the right field side of the stadium. Grandma and I arrived a couple of hours before game time. A Dodgers team function was happening at the restaurant, because Dodger players were sauntering right past us going to-and-from the restaurant well before the game started. My free, 10-inch X 20-inch Ringo Starr poster became a collector's item as I excitedly ran up to players like Willie Davis, Ron Perranoski, Willie Crawford, Maury Wills and Ron Fairly to get their autographs on the back of that poster. One player whose signature I wasn't able to get was pitcher Johnny Podres, who appeared to be inebriated as he was being assisted back to the clubhouse by teammates. Obviously, Podres wasn't slated to pitch that day.

It's fair to say I was a pretty "nerdy" baseball nut as a kid. I read lots of baseball books, on all the legends of the early days.

I'm pretty sure I was the only kid who played baseball by himself growing up. Our cul-de-sac street presented the perfect playground for my make-believe games. I would stand at the large circular sewer cap in the street; that was home plate. Then with a bat in one hand and a ball in the other, I'd smack the ball and note where it landed in my make-believe baseball diamond, and based on where and how the ball traveled I would rule whether it was a hit or an out. I'd keep track of the outs, runners on the base paths, runs, and innings for my two make-believe competing teams, until I reached a nine-inning conclusion. Somehow, I managed not to smack the baseball through any bedroom or car windows on the block. I'm sure this had to look rather peculiar to anyone who may have been watching, because I had only one ball. Which meant that every time I hit the ball, I had to retrieve it and bring back to home plate. I had a lot of energy to burn as a kid, so I repeated these at-bats tirelessly for hours. I know Pam saw me in action a few times, and thought I was certifiably nuts.

I also wiled away idle hours "pitching" make-believe games in my backyard, by throwing a baseball against the cinderblock wall. I went through the whole pitching wind-up on each throw, kept track of balls and strikes, outs, and so forth. Then, in true dork fashion, I obsessively would go around the house simulating the pitching motion, without provocation, which was also eye-witnessed by my sister and further confirmed her belief something was not natural about me.

I played out imaginary basketball games with my backyard hoop in similar fashion. I would create games with my imaginary friends and keep track of how many points each friend scored. I would play-act that Paul passed the ball to Wayne, who passed to me, and I then shot and scored. Of course, I always ranked among the scoring leaders in every game.

All of this keeping score at an early age was another sign that I was probably born to be a sportswriter. In fact, I was probably ordained to be a sportswriter considering the obsessive degree with which I loved keeping and calculating stats. And there's no sport that reveres stats more than baseball.

I had a baseball board game that consisted of hundreds of circular 4-inch-diameter cards representing real baseball players that you inserted in place around a spinning needle to determine what that player would do in a given at-bat. The cards were parceled by numbers that designated every possible variety of at-bat outcome. For instance, 1 was a home run, 3 and 12 were fly-outs, 10 was a strikeout, 9 a walk, 7 and 11 were singles. The cards were purportedly designed according to the players' real-life batting statistics. In other words, Babe Ruth's 1 for home runs was much bigger than Pee Wee Reese's.

I took this relatively simple board game to another level. I divided the player cards into 10 different teams, made out a head-to-head schedule for all 10 teams, played out entire games for a full season of 50 or so games per team, kept track of wins-losses in league standings, and kept batting stats on every single player in every single game throughout the season. Somehow, I still had time to do my school homework. I showed Wayne my reams of stats sheets one day and I think he was so stupefied that he didn't know what to say.

Of course, like most boys in my day, I dreamed of being a professional baseball player someday. One of the great tragedies of my life was that I was never that good of a baseball player. I was the classic all-field, no-hit type. I played Little League, languishing in the minors on the Cubs for all but my very last year of eligibility. Then at age 13, I moved up to Babe Ruth League for 13-14-15-year-olds, an experience that set me up for a cruel letdown.

After playing my first year of Babe Ruth in the minors, a fluky thing happened during tryouts before the start of my second season as a 14-year-old. Incredibly, I made enough of an impression to get drafted by the major-league Redmen, which was a tremendous boost to my ego and my waning dreams of being a big-league player. Just making it on the Redmen's roster turned out to be a dreadful experience as I disappeared to the end of the bench all season long. I think I got a grand total of 13 at-bats for the entire season as a sometimes late-inning replacement, struck out eight times, and eked out one wanky hit. I was miserable.

Then came my first rude awakening to how life can be so unfair. I supposedly was guaranteed a spot on the Redmen the following season as a 15-year-old and wasn't required to go through tryouts again. But right after the tryouts were completed the league made an unusual ruling on a kid who evidently was close to turning 16 to determine that he was still eligible to play in the league. The Redmen "owned" the rights to this kid, so they had to make room on their roster for him. As it was explained to me, I lost in a coin flip with another bench player to determine the luckless player to be dropped back to the minors, without being given the chance to try-out to make another major-league team.

I didn't believe this explanation for a second. My gullibility quotient evidently vanished after Mrs. Earrug's shaming for my butt-pinching escapade back in the first grade. My suspicions were aroused considerably by my awareness that the other player supposedly involved in the coin flip was the son of one of the Redmen coaches. Hmm, yeah, right. Oh well, I didn't want to be on a team with a racist name anyway.

During my final year in the minors my manager tried an experiment with me that provided some qualified success— he turned me around to bat left-handed. He must have noticed that I wrote left-handed. I could see the pitches better from the left-side of the plate, my swing felt like it had a little more drive to it.

This entire episode proved to be a valuable lesson for me for a string of setbacks, disappointments, and life's cruel twists that I would have to overcome as an adult. But as the Luckiest Ordinary Man Alive, I neither seek nor warrant any sympathy. My blessings far outweigh the bumps in the road I have encountered.

------◆------

My love for sports was fueled further by my intense competitive nature — I hated losing. So it was my karma to forge a life-long friendship with Phil, who shared my competitive spirit. We met when we were in the same fourth-grade class and our friendship was cemented on the playground when we started a very intense rivalry built on beating each other in that highly masculine sport of... hop-scotch.

I'm not exactly sure how we gravitated to this particular competition. It wasn't like we were playing hop-scotch with girls and then branched out on our own — yecch! Heck no, I hated girls in the fourth grade. But I wanted to beat Phil very badly in hop-scotch.

The trouble was, Phil was just so much better at hop-scotch than I, which made it all the more maddening. This pattern persisted when we graduated to other sports — hand ball, kick ball, basketball, football, softball. The problem was physical; Phil was taller, sleeker, had an arm-span about a foot wider than mine, a leg stride about a foot longer than mine, and was quicker and faster. He was a natural athlete; anything he attempted came effortlessly. I had virtually no natural ability. Any athletic skill at all came from sheer determination and focus to overcome my shortcomings, which were many; I was short, with small hands and stubby legs.

As we got older and our friendship grew, Phil and I were perpetually matched against each other as opposing team captains in whatever sport we were playing at the time. In a straight head-to-head matchup, this gave Phil's team an automatic advantage before we even began choosing sides. That was not exactly satisfying for someone who hated losing as much as I did. But somehow, after many years I resigned myself to my fate. Again, another life lesson, learning how to accept losing. That was a tough one.

Meanwhile, Phil was learning his own life lesson by dealing with me. Patience. I drove him crazy with my deliberate style. It was that focus I mentioned. The one sport in which I enjoyed some relative success against him was tennis, in part because I simply wore him down with my long, drawn-out serves; I had to bounce the ball about 30 times before finally hitting it. "Just serve the damn ball!" was Phil's common lament, which of course broke my focus and I'd have to start over with my bounces, which tested his patience even farther.

The friendship managed to withstand our legendary arguments on the field of battle during our games with friends. The arguments typically were over some ruling that may or may not have had little effect on the outcome of the game — "That ball was fair!" "Hell no! It was foul by a mile!" Typically, our friends had to sit around on the grass waiting for Phil and I to finish jawing at each other, as the competitiveness in each of us didn't allow either one of us to back down. Looking back, I think it's fair to say I was the more hard-headed one and maybe got my way more often because, once again, I just wore Phil down.

I still sometimes wonder what Phil saw in me as a friend. But deep down I've always admired him, and not just because of his athletic prowess. I found out very early in our friendship that Phil had a way with animals and birds. He could have been a great veterinarian if he had put his mind to it. This was revealed to me by an incident instigated when I was standing in my backyard, and noticed a beautiful hawk perched on the TV antenna high on our rooftop. It had a leather strap attached to one of its claws, a clue that it belonged to somebody as a pet. It wasn't going anywhere and I suspected it was hurt. The first person I thought of calling was Phil, who knew exactly what to do. In no time he had corralled that hawk, which was indeed injured, took it home and nursed it back to health over several weeks. Then he let it go free. I thought that was so cool.

———————◆———————

Phil, and other friends who have known me a long time and made the normal transition into adulthood and family life that my father had hoped for me, often wondered why I didn't follow suit. They had heard enough of my stories to wonder if, maybe, the circuitry in my head wasn't exactly right. I have been known to be a little dingy, spacy, perplexed, confused, absent-minded or forgetful, at various random moments. That generally would lead to odd choices and/or ill-timed bad luck. Or, sometimes, remarkable good luck despite myself.

So when I pondered that hypothesis it occurred to me that I survived a few disturbing head-banging incidents in my youth that might explain the behavior patterns that many considered to be not quite ordinary later in life.

The first such incident occurred when I was only four years old. Back then Mom was driving a tiny Nash, which was no bigger than an enclosed golf cart. I was sitting in the passenger seat. This was way back in ancient times, before there were seat-belt laws, before cars even had seat belts, so I was unencumbered in my seat. Mom was driving about 30 mph in the right-hand lane on a pretty busy street and I must have been leaning against the door because suddenly the door cracked open and I rolled right out of the car!

My memories of this incident are very vague and probably cobbled from my mother's recollections, but I guess I rolled directly into the street gutter, out of harm's way. I don't know what my mother's reaction to this was and I couldn't tell you if she rushed me to the hospital to get checked out. For all I know, I dusted myself off, maybe passed Mom's inspection with a few nicks and bruises, and we continued on our way. But maybe there was some head trauma inflicted that day that we didn't know about and there you go — that's why I'm so crazy.

34

Or maybe it was that one fine day during my third-grade school year that my head might have been inexplicably altered. I was home, playing outside, when this girl named Kim who was a classmate came waltzing down our street with a friend. She came specifically to tell me that she liked me. Well, I handled this extraordinary admission with the calm and coolness you would expect from someone as suave and debonair as I was at the time. Just kidding.

Speechless, I immediately turned in embarrassment and dashed straight for home at 100 mph, not bothering to slow down as I approached the two steps leading up to our front porch. I slipped on the first step, which sent me crashing head-first into the wall below the front window like a cannon shot. I'm sure this made an indelible impression on Kim and her friend. As for me, it made an indelible impression in the form of a bruise above my right eyebrow and a bloody scrape on my chin. My pride was pretty bruised, too. As for my head – well, who knows? If that didn't make me dorky on its own, it certainly advanced me considerably toward that stage.

Further cerebral damage could have been suffered in a very controversial incident that occurred when I was about 10. It was a topic of considerable debate in our family for several years whether Pam deliberately did this to me as an act of revenge or it was really an "accident"? The key to understanding this controversy is what transpired a few days before, when Pam and I were playing baseball in our backyard with friends. I stood at home plate as the batter and Pam was squatting directly behind as the catcher. I warned her: "Pam, you're too close. You need to move a little farther back so I don't hit you with the bat." She ignored my advice and didn't move. The pitch came, I reared back and swung, the head of the bat hit Pam square in the face on my follow-through, and well, I broke her nose. I felt bad, of course, after I got in my "I told you so."

That didn't spare me from retribution a few days later when Pam and I were playing in the backyard of the Nathansons down the street. In this instance, I didn't get any warning from Pam, who was armed with a golf club and decided to take an uppercut swing with it. (For the record, there was no golf game going on at the time.) The club caught my forehead on its way up, opening a significant gash that sent blood running down my face. Jan Nathanson, the mom watching over all us kids at the time, rushed to stop the bleeding and get me to the nearest ER for stitches. Mom didn't know what to make of my sister and I after that week, but we got a stern lecture on how we needed to be nice to each other.

How many more blows to the head could I take? Well, for those of you keeping score, there was at least one more doozy in my youth. It occurred sometime during my high school years in a pick-up football game with my friends. We were young and foolish enough to play tackle football without any pads, which was an open invitation for serious injury for anybody on the field. But I managed to bring harm to myself without anyone laying a hand on me. The incident came on a pass play in which I was an intended receiver. I was making a beeline full-speed for the end zone on what is described, in football jargon, as running a "post pattern," which took me straight up the middle of the field toward the goal post.

Somebody forgot to tell me you're supposed to watch out for the goal post when you're running this particular route. So as I ran past my defender, I looked back with my sights on catching the long pass in my outstretched arms for a spectacular touchdown. Instead, I ran head-long into the goal post, smacking it so hard that it rang out with a loud bong and vibrated for several seconds as I hit the ground with a thud. I laid there motionless for I don't know how long as my friends all gathered around me, searching for some sign of life. Finally, when I began rubbing my throbbing head, I heard my buddy Wayne's distinctive, deep belly laugh. I'll never forget that laugh that broke the tension. Then everyone joined in the laughter as I slowly picked myself up, woozy but determined to finish the game, no matter how much my head hurt.

So, evidence of brain damage? The court rests its case.

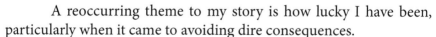

A reoccurring theme to my story is how lucky I have been, particularly when it came to avoiding dire consequences.

In that context, I recall one experience in my youth that, when I think about it, I still can't believe I did what I did and got away with it. I had to be about 13 at the time and at the peak of my sexual awakening. I considered that to be a big deal because I am acutely aware of how sex played a significant role in shaping my life. I was an active masturbator at this point in my life, serving pretext to how the act of sexual release made me feel so good. Maybe I was just turned on after seeing "Hair."

I must have felt aroused by my body awareness, my naked body in this awakening phase of my life. That was heightened by the element of risk attached to this particular incident. My bedroom window faced out on the front of our house, offering me easy access to the street. Late one night, long after I had gone to bed and my parents had retired, I was still awake. I stripped naked, climbed out my bedroom window and took off running *au natural* down the street. I turned left onto 138th Street for a block or so, then finally turned around and ran back home and climbed back through my bedroom window. I remember my heart beating incredibly fast from the adrenaline rush I was feeling. Amazingly, no one saw me.

I think back to that moment now and wonder, my God! Was that really me that did that? Looking back, it feels now like an out-of-body experience, or more plausibly, an adolescent hormonal thing I couldn't fully control. What would have happened if I had been caught? What was I thinking? What would I have said to my parents? What would have been the consequences of my actions?

A guardian angel was watching over me that night. I believe in guardian angels, because I've encountered more than my share over time.

My Hawthorne High School senior Class of '71 yearbook photo

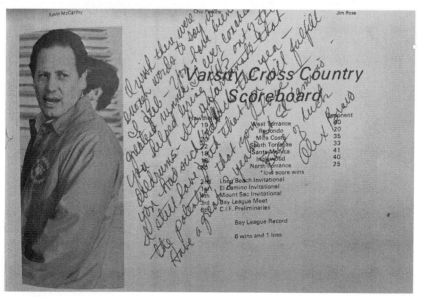

My high school cross country coach Alex Bravo, with the emotional message he wrote in my senior yearbook

CHAPTER 4
High School: Off and Running

Retribution was mine when I entered high school. That is, I finally found a sport that I was better at than Phil – long-distance running.

This was back in 1967, long before running had become such a popular form of fitness in the U.S. In fact, people spotted running on the side of the road in that day were often the subject of scorn and/or taunting.

Regardless, running had become my redemption for my utter failure as a baseball player.

I got some inkling that I might be good at running a couple years before entering high school, quite by accident. Rick, a boy three years older than I who also lived on Rossburn, started an impromptu clinic by timing any willing kid on the block in running one mile. He measured out the distance over the sidewalks snaking inside the three side-by-side cul-de-sacs. Then he lined five of us youngsters up, one by one, and put a stopwatch on us for the full mile. I was the fastest.

Then, in eighth grade as part of PE class, everyone had to run a 660-yard race around the massive grass field that housed a couple of Little League baseball fields, soccer fields, and unused space left over. Astonishingly, I finished first in the entire school and Phil finished second. It started to sink in that I was really good at this running thing.

So during the summer prior to entering our freshman year at Hawthorne High, sign-ups for the school's cross-country team were open for the fall season. Encouraged by our showing in that 660-yard run, Phil and I signed up.

High school cross country consisted of two-mile races back then. It seems the longer the distance, the better I was. Phil and I were both good enough to make the seven-man varsity squad. I ranked No. 4, behind two seniors and one junior. Phil was No. 5.

The cross-country coach, Alex Bravo, took a shine to us. He became another father figure for me. Coach Bravo, who taught Spanish in addition to coaching, was an ex-pro football player who had spent a few years with the LA Rams. He had a burly build like a football player but he didn't choose to coach the highly-popular football team, he chose to coach the "black sheep" of sports — cross-country, the skinny guys with bony knees wearing skimpy running shorts.

Coach Bravo's coaching style tended to be a bit gruff — "Suck up your purple belly guts!" was one of his favorite call-out phrases to urge us on during the races.

Because of nagging injuries to the junior teammate, I ranked as the No. 3 runner on the team most of the season. That junior wasn't around for the following season, so Phil and I ascended to No. 1 and 2 on the team as sophomores. We held the top two spots unchallenged for three straight seasons through our senior year.

I often thought that Phil stayed in cross-country for all four years just to try to beat me. I had played opposite him in enough pick-up football games to know he would have been a stand-out high school player if he had chosen football over cross-country in the fall season. Instead he got stuck in a lifelong friendship with me because of that decision.

High school buddies forever: Me, Jim, Rich W., Phil and Rich B.

In fact, lifelong friendships were forged with three other guys through that high school cross country team — Rich W., a sophomore I befriended in the very first summer practices as an incoming freshman; another guy named Rich (Rich B.); and Jim, Phil's younger brother. To differentiate between the two Richs we had to call them by their last names. The five of us have remained friends and gotten together at least once a year over the past five decades for a poker game and dinner with our respective wives (although I was going through too many wives to include mine.)

In the spring came track season, and that's where Phil found his glory exclusive from me. With his long legs he was more suited for the shorter 880-yard distance and excelled as a three-year varsity letterman.

On the track team I stayed with the two-mile event, and sometimes doubled up on the mile, but I was better at two. In fact, I caused a bit of a stir in my freshman season when I became the first runner in school history to run a sub 10-minute two-mile on the track in competition— 9:59. I was on a two-mile high after that feat. Coach Bravo felt I was something special. Little matter that my school record held up exactly one week; a senior ran two seconds faster in a meet the following week. The big deal was that I was the first to crack 10 minutes, and I was a *freshman*.

————————◆————————

It took a little bit longer for me to blossom when it came to girls. I lied when I said I didn't like girls in fourth grade. I've always liked girls, ever since my first-grade crush on a girl named Nancy. In sixth grade it became much more pronounced because of my crush on my very pretty teacher, Mrs. Brett. My sixth-grade class was dominated by girls — they outnumbered the boys by about 24-12, I think. I remember a cute girl named Teresa who liked me, but I was too shy to do anything about it. I decided I liked her in junior high, but couldn't figure out how to clue her in.

That shyness carried on through my first two years in high school, when I wanted a girlfriend so bad. It was in my sophomore year when this shortcoming denied me what would have been an unforgettable high school memory. The Beach Boys, who were at the height of their rock and roll fame in '69, somehow were lured into performing at our junior-senior prom! As a dorky sophomore, my only hope of attending was if a junior or senior girl invited me to the prom. In those days, girls didn't ask the guys, much less younger guys who had zero experience with girls. I heard that "Good Vibrations" were happening' that night.

———————◆———————

My junior year served witness to a meteoric rise in my personal profile, as far as girls were concerned.

The initial breakthrough was spectacular, dazzling. In other words, I was in way over my head. Her name was Doris and she was a beauty, every bit as blonde and beautiful as Sheila was, except that Doris was brown-eyed. She was a child beauty queen. And this girl thought I was cute? Oh my God, this couldn't be happening.

I met Doris at a church bible study class I was invited to by one of my cross-country buddies. She was the aggressor, for sure. This was just the start of my junior year and I still hadn't experienced my first girlfriend. She wanted to be it.

We were hand-holding boyfriend-girlfriend for about, oh, three weeks. We never kissed once. But hand-holding felt like kissing back in those days. I went to her church with her parents on a couple of Sundays. It was when we returned to their house after the second church visit that Doris' assertive mother, cornering me alone in the kitchen, asked me this rather imposing question:

"You don't have much experience with girls, do you?"

I shyly shook my head. I wasn't able to fake it. I wasn't that far removed from that third grader who ran away from Kim and headlong into the front porch wall with respect to timidity. Doris's mother nodded knowingly. The die was cast. Two days later Doris broke up with me, over the phone.

I was only mildly crest-fallen by the break-up, and one especially important benefit emerged from that relationship. I resumed playing the piano because of Doris. She had been a virtuoso violin player, a child prodigy of — are you ready for this? — Jack Benny, the comedian who had his own TV show in the late 50s and early 60s. He played the violin, usually deliberately badly, in some of the skits on his show. He was, in fact, Doris's godfather. A photo of her as a child and Jack playing the violin together on stage before an audience was prominently displayed in their living room. I had told Doris I knew how to play the piano, even though I had stopped playing after lessons had ended two years earlier. I started playing again, just to impress her.

The relationship ended, but the piano playing continued.

———————◆———————

The star status I gained in cross country and track seemingly put me on track to a certain destiny. But simultaneously an alternative path was being laid out when I signed up to work for the high school newspaper. It was called The Cougar, named after our school's sports teams' name. I worked on the paper all four years of high school.

I had two great counselors over those four years — Mrs. McGinty for the first two before she retired, and Mrs. Krislock, a much younger, spunkier mentor who guided me toward choosing Cal State Fullerton for college.

I served in all sorts of roles for the paper over those four years — reporter, columnist, editorial writer, news editor, sports editor, chief editor. I pretty much made up my mind then that newspaper work was what I wanted to do professionally after college.

Serving on the newspaper staff made me innately aware of world events and nothing was more prominent then than the Vietnam War. It wasn't hard to guess my sentiments on the war based on my upbringing with my liberal parents. There was an anti-war rally held during my senior year and I gave a speech that reflected all my impressive historical research — the French involvement in Vietnam prior to the U.S. engagement, Eisenhower's warning about the "military-industrial complex." I gave a great history lesson that no doubt put the crowd into a deep snooze. I had the anti-war, liberal hippie look going — my wavy, sun-streaked brown hair was always kinda long as I let my freak flag fly. I had a mustache and long sideburns for good measure. But while I had the look, I wasn't sucked into the hippie lifestyle of doing drugs. I was a clean-cut athlete and didn't mix in with the drug crowd.

Through my experience on the Cougar staff I formed one meaningful friendship that extended long beyond high school. Teri was two grades younger than I so I didn't meet her until my junior year. Teri and I just *clicked*. We shared the same sense of humor and I respected how smart she was. She was my co-conspirator on our favorite long-running gag during my high school days, one we played out on naive Mr. Anderson, the humble print shop teacher who printed our Cougar editions on a very old-fashioned cold-type machine. We convinced Mr. Anderson that we were half-brother and sister (same mother, different father, hence different last names), and kept that myth alive the entire two years we worked together on the Cougar. "You do kinda look like each other," Mr. Anderson would say repeatedly, in earnestness, which would make Teri crack up while I grinned knowingly.

As I mentioned, I had resumed playing the piano again about this time. But I was more interested in composing my own music than in just performing classic or contemporary pieces. Teri was that rare friend who would listen to my compositions. My early pieces were simple, with some classical influences, from melodies that sprang from my mind that I had transferred to the piano keys with basic bass rhythm accompaniments. Teri listened to me play and liked what she heard; she was probably my first fan. She validated my music.

The thing was, I acted and felt like a big brother toward Teri. I wasn't physically attracted to her. She may have been somewhat self-conscious about her weight, judging by her significant weight loss years later when our paths crossed. By my junior year I had broken through my shyness with girls and chose girlfriends who weren't Teri. I genuinely cherished her endearing friendship, but I was blind to the possibility that Teri might have had a crush on me in high school. Clues surfaced when our friendship extended into adulthood, and then took an unfortunate turn.

———————◆———————

While the brief Doris experience had been an upsetting setback, it did boost my overall confidence with girls. How could it not? The mere idea that someone like her could be attracted to me did wonders for my self-image. So it did not take me long to rebound in my junior year. Very quickly, I found myself in the middle of a tug-of-war between two attractive freshman girls who thought I was cute. Now, this really went to my head.

I was obviously still fixated on blondes, as both Jennifer and Lizette fell in the fair-haired category. Jennifer was the shy, sweet, naive type. I remember we went to a movie together and we could barely muster enough nerve to do anything more than touch hands when the sexual tension was ratcheted up.

I wound up choosing Lizette, who was the more aggressive one, and naturally I allowed the choice to be made for me. Jennifer more or less conceded to Lizette, as if it was her "right" to do so. Lizette had the inside track, in part due to the fact her parents were members of my parents' folk-dance group.

Lizette was smart, and a little more "out there"— dreamier — in her view of the world. She was playful and was definitely the more flirtatious one during the courting competition with Jennifer. We stayed together for the remainder of my junior year. She was my date at the junior-senior prom, for my first experience with that whole scenario. Our favorite pastime was walking home from school together and stopping every 100 feet or so to make-out. That's as far as we got as far as intimacy went. She probably was being suggestive with the little game she played when she stuck her hands in my front pants pockets, but I didn't have the wherewithal to initiate anything further.

Lizette definitely advanced my experience quotient with girls. I think she finally got bored with me and moved on by the end of the school year.

I moved on, too, to a sweet, short summer romance with Laura, a platonic friend of my buddy Rich W. I spent most of that summer partaking with lovely Laura in make-out sessions on beautiful seasonal nights on the beach. By summer's end that had run its course as well.

———————•◆•———————

As if my junior year wasn't eventful enough, it also included my first foray into gainful employment.

I got my first job delivering pizza for HiLo Pizza, a local pizzeria on Hawthorne Boulevard. I worked there during the winter months between cross-country and track seasons. It was a tiny place that strictly catered to delivery service only; there was no in-house dining area. The business was owned and run by an extremely eccentric German man named Richard, who was assisted by his wife Trudy.

Richard was a gruff, imposing boss. He had a growl to his voice. He was a 40ish tall, lanky man with jet black hair combed back who had a streak of meanness in him. That was on display one harrowing night targeting his poor wife. Trudy, who was also German, had the plump, round-faced, stereotyped look of a woman who worked in the kitchen with an apron around her waist. She was also very sweet with me; I loved her sing-song-y German accent when she spoke to me.

I was intimidated by Richard from the start and didn't like him very much. He often smoked a cigar while he worked. He did most of the pizza prep himself and I occasionally witnessed his cigar ashes falling on pizzas he was dressing. Disgusting.

I delivered pizzas driving my first car, an old Chevy Nova that my grandmother Mimi handed down to me. I experienced my first major car accident during one delivery. I was waiting at a red light on a side street near the pizzeria with a steaming hot, boxed pizza on my passenger seat. When the light turned green, I started making a left turn onto the multiple-lane Hawthorne Boulevard and was broadsided on the passenger side by an elderly man behind the wheel of an old Mercedes.

I found a phone booth and called Richard right away. His only concern was the pizza I was delivering. I assured Richard that the pizza was OK, and oh yeah, I was OK too. My car had a significant gash on the door but otherwise was still drivable. The other driver took full responsibility, so his insurance took care of the damage to my old car.

My opinion of Richard had been damaged, however, and became irreconcilable not long after. When I showed up for work at 5 p.m. one day, Trudy was weeping in the kitchen and Richard was sitting in the tiny front waiting area, watching a tiny TV suspended high in one corner. He was watching a beauty pageant, puffing on a cigar. Work was obviously slow.

As soon as I arrived Richard began making remarks about how beautiful the women in the pageant were. I glanced back to Trudy, who was in the kitchen dabbing her tears with her apron. Trudy's agony only seemed to egg Richard on as he began to elaborate on the beautiful women on display on his tiny black-and-white screen.

Then he said, "Hey Chic, did you know today is Trudy's birthday? Say happy birthday to Trudy." He blew smoke from his cigar.

I stood aghast at what I was hearing. I could not bear to look at Trudy, who let out a soft sob in reaction to Richard's pronouncement.

The rest of the night was unbearable. It ended in a scene pierced forever in my memory. Returning from a delivery and driving my car into the back parking lot, I was blocked by four police cars with headlights illuminating the brick wall at the rear entry to the pizza shop. As I got out of my car, I could see that all the attention was directed at Trudy, who was sitting slumped against the brick wall, wailing into the night. My heart broke for her.

That was the last time I saw her. She never returned to work. I gave my two-week notice a few days later.

———————— ◆ ————————

While my love life had taken its first running steps in my junior year, my running career made great strides. I was still unchallenged as the No. 1 runner on varsity cross-country in the fall, with Phil a solid No. 2. The rest of the squad was filled by a pack of promising sophomores, led by Kevin, who was pushing Phil and I for top status. Also included in that sophomore pack was Phil's brother Jim, who was competing for the sixth and seventh spots on varsity. We had the potential to be championship contenders the next season,

To gain a head start on our junior season, Coach Bravo took us to a summertime running camp at June Lake, near Mammoth. He had never done anything like that before, and it served to build team unity in addition to our long-distance conditioning. Our team improved considerably that junior year. We were still a year away from our prime, however, failing to advance beyond the preliminaries in the California Interscholastic Federation (CIF) Southern Sectionals. Back then CIF lumped every high school in the southern half of the state in a single division. The CIF Southern Section wasn't splintered into a dozen or more divisions like it is now.

Individually, I was on a different track from the rest of the team. I qualified as an individual runner for the CIF-SS semifinals, which were held at Mt. San Antonio Community College, a k a Mt. SAC.

From 1971 Hawthorne High Cougar Yearbook: Phil and I leading the way in a high school cross-country event ("Sexy from Ape" note added by my high school sweetheart April, a k a "Ape")

That semifinal race provided a prelude to my potential. Coach Bravo couldn't believe his eyes when he saw me in the lead as I entered the track for the final 300 yards. I swear I could hear his screaming amid the throng on the other side of the track near the finish line as I opened up my stride for my final kick entering the far turn of the quarter-mile track circling the last 200 yards to the finish.

My final kick was not my strong suit. I usually beat runners over the long haul with room to spare at the finish. Against the creme-de-la-creme on this day, two runners passed me in the final 100 yards. Another runner, Bruce Johnston of Mira Costa High, our fierce school rival that had beaten us for the league title, was fast approaching me 15 yards before the finish line.

I needed only to finish in the top 10 to advance to the finals. So did Bruce, who was a year older than me as a senior and would become my teammate at El Camino College two years later. I will never forget his gracious gesture within a few strides of the finish line.

He had me beat; he was quickly closing on me and was ready to pass me. Instead, he gently pushed me so that I could finish ahead of him in third place.

I would go on to finish eighth in the CIF-SS final the following week. Six seniors, including Bruce, and only one junior finished ahead of me. With the unlikelihood of some phenomenal freshman emerging the following season, I potentially had only one guy to beat as the fastest cross-country runner in the entire Southern Section as a senior.

My progress continued in the spring of my junior year during track season, in which I lowered my school record in the two mile (9:28) and recorded an impressive 4:25 mile. It was all laid out for a spectacular senior year, and who knows where that would take me afterward?

Laura wasn't the only highlight of the summer of 1970. That was the summer our family went on our Scandinavian vacation to Copenhagen, Denmark; Stockholm, Sweden; and Oslo, Norway.

I had to leave our cross-country team's summer running camp in Big Sur a few days early for that family trip. We were joined in Big Sur by our Mira Costa High rivals, who were likely to compete with us again for the league title. Rivalry aside, we were fast becoming friends with our Mira Costa comrades in running camp. (This connection would eventually link me to wife No. 1.)

I didn't let the Scandinavian trip interrupt my training. I nearly got lost running on the crooked streets of Copenhagen. In Stockholm I had to battle my way through a crowd of Swedish navy officers to gain entrance through a side door of the hotel, all sweaty from my five-mile run. In Oslo I had to stare straight ahead to avoid getting distracted by all the naked statues I was running past in the park.

The Big Sur running camp kicked off a summer that bonded us as a team. We trained together all summer and mixed in some crazy fun along the way.

One night a bunch of us ran down to Hermosa Beach at midnight to play volleyball by the lights of the pier, and cooled off afterward by jumping off the pier into the water. Phil and I took another night run during which we took a long break by climbing over a fence at a drive-in movie theatre to watch an entire movie squatted by a vacant speaker.

I also ran my first marathon, the Palos Verdes Marathon, early on that summer. For the first 18 miles I ran like an animal, clocking in under two hours on a demanding, hilly 26.2-mile course. But two miles later, I quickly learned that a marathon was a completely different animal than anything I had run before. I hit the proverbial 20-mile wall when the course began a consistently gradual climb for the next five miles. I cramped up badly and had to alternate between running and walking. I felt humiliated watching a 10-year-old kid pass me by.

It took me over an hour-and-a-half to finish the final 8.2 miles. My overall time was 3 hours, 31 minutes, 45 seconds, not bad for a first attempt, but I had expected something a lot better at that 18-mile mark.

By the end of the summer, I was tested at a distance that was much more in my comfort level — 10 kilometers (6.2 miles). Coach Bravo entered us in a 10-K race that was part of a coordinated nation-wide competition designed to gauge high school long-distance running talent. I posted the sixth-fastest time (32:52) in the nation. *In the nation*. I was stoked. So was Coach Bravo.

———————◆◆◆◆◆◆◆———————

Something was in the air at the start of my senior season. You could feel it. It was going to be a momentous year. I was in the best shape in my life and I was in my fourth year on the Cougar staff, with my budding journalism career in line to take off.

Most significantly, love was in the air.

I was a big-shot senior, a cross-country and track star. It was September, and a new crop of impressionable freshmen girls was roaming the campus. I was feeling my oats. I was looking around. But I wasn't sharp enough to notice who was looking back at me. It took a brazen scheme by a beautiful freshman girl with shimmering long, straight blonde hair down to the middle of her back and deep blue eyes locked in on me to get my attention.

"I forgot the combination to the lock on my locker. You wouldn't happen to know how to pick a lock, would you?"

I was looking at this gorgeous face I had never seen before posing this question to me. I was bemused. I was smitten. I was a senior,

I was no longer that inexperienced, shy guy who couldn't make the grade with Doris.

"Do I know you? What's your name?"

"April."

The ruse over the forgotten lock combination was momentarily dropped as we exchanged smiles. I played along and made a feeble attempt to pick the lock to her locker, but it didn't matter. We made the connection.

April, or "Ape" as I affectionately called her, became my high school sweetheart. And I can say, in deep earnestness, this was the first time I had fallen in love. It was real. it was the kind love you have for a high school sweetheart that never truly goes away. And April never went away in my heart.

It was April with whom I shared my first true intimacy. She was just a freshman, but she was such a level-headed girl for a 14-year-old. She had an innate sensibility about right and wrong, maturity beyond her years. Our intimacy evolved to heavy, heavy petting, and after about six months together it escalated as far as bare-naked pelvic humping, but she wouldn't let it advance to actual penetration. She had much more self-control than I did.

All said and done, it was intense, it was emotional, it was love. It was all so pure and innocent. It was our mutual baptism into real sex. I think it helped shape my general sensitivity toward sex in future relationships. Not that I fell "in love" with everyone I had sex with, but I craved that feeling I had with April and wanted to emulate that in the act of lovemaking. It probably was a big contributing factor to the pattern of entanglements I always seemed to be getting myself into and the consequential messes I had to get out of.

Our trysts usually took place on the living room couch at April's house, where she lived with her Italian-born father (divorced from her mother) and older sister Joy, who was a sophomore. I think April preferred doing it in the living room rather than run the risk of getting caught in her bedroom upstairs. In the living room she could react quickly enough to get dressed and pretend we were just watching TV if her father or sister suddenly arrived home. Smart, because there were a couple close calls.

April and I were a couple my entire senior year. I think we were perceived as one of the "cool" couples on campus. She went to all my home meets for cross country and track. She had a group of girl-friends that we hung out with and did things that high school kids did for fun back then — go to the movies, burger and pizza joints, bowling, miniature golf, the beach. My cross-country buddy Rich B. dated Joy for a few months.

April and I loaded up on young love memories —frolicking in Tuna Canyon in Malibu; huddling under a blanket together overnight on Colorado Boulevard in Pasadena on New Year's Eve to watch the Rose Parade on New Year's Day; doing the whole prom scene; and spending a glorious Grad Night together at Disneyland that trickled into the wee hours of the morning.

April and I dressed up for Christmas dance

April felt like a soul mate. Our paths would cross numerous times over the decades. Some fifty years after we met, she shared with me her own "epithet" she wrote in eighth grade to fulfill an assignment handed out by her teacher, who was a nun in a Catholic school:

"Here I lie, April C.
With peace all around me
I met my death with happiness
Went surfing, slipped and fell in
A 20 ft. wave
The wave collapsed on me
Then it was over.
I traveled everywhere enjoying
myself
I didn't sit around watching my
Life go by the way some people do
I enjoyed my life
So why can't you?"

I don't know what grade April got on her epithet assignment from the nun. But that, right there, says everything you need to know about April. The epithet proved to be poetically prophetic prose on how she has lived her life.

It's no wonder that my ultimate Beach Boys California Girl would pop up in my dreams for years. I can't tell you how many "April" dreams I had. They were happy dreams, a few of them sexual; and I always woke up from them with a glow. Those dreams made me wonder If I had let the best thing that ever happened to me slip away.

At the end of my senior year, Ape wrote in my yearbook about how she would always love me. But that innate sensibility of hers was telling her my graduation meant a natural break, with me going on to college while she had three more years of high school. Her yearbook note declared that she felt like she would be "holding" me back from the experience of being with other girls, and that we both needed to be free at that point in our young lives. So, we parted with heavy hearts, but that would not be the last we saw of each other.

Rolling into my senior year, I was ready for a banner cross-country season. So was our team. In the very first meet of the season, the Long Beach Invitational, competing against about 30 schools, we showed we were for real. Competing against over a couple hundred runners, I led a 1-2-3 sweep at the finish with Phil and Kevin right behind me. Unfortunately, we finished only second as a team with sub-par performances from our fourth and fifth runners. We knew we were better than that.

We bounced back by handily winning the next scheduled event, the El Camino College Invitational, which was conducted on eight laps around the track instead of a spread-out two-mile course that typified cross-country, due to street restrictions in the vicinity of the campus. I was the race winner in a two-mile time of 9:15, shattering my school record of 9:28 set during my junior year. It didn't count as a school record, though, because it came in a cross-country event. Nevertheless, the fact I had exceeded my best track two-mile time by 13 seconds wearing cross-country shoes instead of track spikes early in the fall projected to something spectacular for track season in the spring. A two-mile time nearing the 9:00 mark was within reach.

Momentum picked up as our cross-country team headed into head-to-head competition in league. With Phil, Kevin and I representing a formable trio, we swept past our Mira Costa rivals and every other team in our way.

———◆———

Life was grand the autumn of my senior year. I was on top of the running world, I was in love, there was every reason to party. Somehow, our parents allowed my sister and I to host perhaps the biggest house party of the year at our humble abode on Rossburn.

We did all right with the party we threw the year before, but the bash during my senior year topped it big-time. This time we had a live band setting off some maniacal dancing in the family room; Pam was dating one of the guys in the band. The backyard patio was hopping with the ping-pong table and kegs of beer. Add in the prevalent BYOB, and it turned out to be a raucous event.

54

Word must have gotten out that 13707 Rossburn was the place to be that night. Party crashers poured in to push the attendance to — I'm guessing — nearly 200 from start to finish. Popular football players and their cheerleader girlfriends joined in on the party that was otherwise populated by the cross-country crowd and Pam's artistic, drug-happy friends. Even Scott Laidlaw, the biggest football star at school who went on to play at Stanford and for the Dallas Cowboys, deemed it worthy of his presence. Everybody who was "somebody" at our school was there.

Obviously, our parents were out for the evening. But when they got home, at 11ish, oh boy, I had some 'splaining to do to my dad, whose stern look said it all. I sheepishly told him that I lost control of the flow of party crashers. Quietly, he drew me aside and directed me to ask the non-invitees to leave. My parents had demonstrated extreme leniency by allowing us to throw a party of this magnitude with a live band, and beer to boot, so I felt extremely lucky that my dad let me off easy. Fortunately, the only damage done was a huge clean-up the next day, collecting lots of discarded plastic beer cups and empty Boone's Farm wine bottles.

⸻ ◆ ⸻

My luck, and our cross-country team's championship dream, was headed for a crash landing. About midway through the season I began experiencing some pain in my right foot just as I crossed the finish line of each race. The foot wasn't slowing me down, but it would act up as soon I stopped running. The pain would quickly dissipate after finishing a race, so I didn't worry about it.

Then came the Mt. SAC Invitational, a huge event late in the season involving about 40 schools that served as a precursor for the upcoming CIF prelims. The weekend event utilized the same course on which I ran my promising eighth-place finish in the CIF finals the year before. Mt. SAC was our second-to-last regular scheduled event, one week before our big showdown with North Torrance High on our home course. That dual meet stood to decide the league champion, as we were both undefeated. Comparable scores against all other league foes projected us as the odds-on favorites to beat North.

About halfway through the hilly two-mile course at Mt. SAC, I stepped on a rock with my right foot and felt something snap. But I felt no pain and kept on running, leading the pack at the time. Just two strides away from winning the race, I got nipped at the finish line by Purcell Keating, a runner from Morningside High in Inglewood who had distinguished himself as one of the elite runners of the Southern Section. There was no shame in a second-place finish.

As soon as I stopped running and made my way through the roped-off finishing corridor, I started limping. The right foot was hurting badly and this time the pain wasn't going away.

On the following Monday, five days before our showdown against North Torrance High, I went in to have a doctor examine my right foot. X-rays showed a fracture of my right baby toe. The doctor explained that it most likely was a distressed fatigue crack initially, causing the minimal pain I was experiencing after races. Then it finally became stressed and gave way to a clean break in the Mt. SAC race.

The news was devastating. A broken bone in my right baby toe, perhaps the smallest bone in my entire body, was going to prevent me from competing against North High. as well as League Finals and CIF. The timing could not have been worse. When Coach Bravo announced the news to the team the next day, the gloom that consumed the locker room hung in the air like a 10-ton wrecking ball.

That Friday, upon North High's arrival for our dual meet, I suited up as if I was going to run. We wanted to hide my injury from the enemy as long as possible to delay the psychological lift they would derive from knowing I wasn't running. I was our team's No. 1 runner and my absence would create a huge discrepancy in the team scoring. But just before the runners were called to the starting line, I flung my running shoes in utter despair, as April helplessly looked on and then gathered my shoes for me.

The ruse was over. Without me, we lost. If I had been able to run and had an off-day, my worst race of the year still would have been enough to beat North. But North ran away with the league championship that was meant to be ours. Our three-year dream that began when we were all sophomores and freshmen ended in a flash, on a bad break with a baby toe.

The toe didn't heal in time for CIF. So, the team faded in prelims and I was denied a chance to see where I ranked among the best cross-country runners in the entire Southern Section. North finished third overall in the CIF finals, and we were good enough to finish two spots ahead of them if I was fit to run.

I still had track season in the spring to redeem myself. The toe took about eight weeks to sufficiently heal, which set me back in my conditioning, but I got back into my training right away.

My two-mile times in the first couple of track meets showed that I still had some catching up to do. In the third meet I finally ran a decent race and felt like I was back on track.

Then unbelievable misfortune struck again. It was a beautiful spring weekend day, in the middle of track season, and I was playing basketball with my teammates in the driveway at Phil's house. I was dribbling the ball, looking to make a move on Rich W., who was defending me. As I crossed my right foot to make a cut, Rich accidentally kicked that foot. It started hurting right away.

I could not believe what I was hearing from the doctor Monday morning when results of the X-rays came in. He said I had suffered a completely new fracture of that same baby toe — not a re-fracture of the previous break but a new break in a different location.

I need to pause here to explain that the bone in my right baby toe — to this day some 50 years later — is the only bone I've broken in my entire body. Twice, in two different places, in my senior year of high school, at the height of my running career, wiping out both my cross-country season in the fall and my track season in the spring. I guess bad things happen to me in pairs, whether it's broken baby toes or strokes.

Way back in my freshman year, when I was the first runner in school history to break the 10-minute barrier over two miles, it was a foregone conclusion that I was destined to receive a track scholarship at a four-year college once I finished my senior year of competition. But my baby toe changed all that. I had no impressive season-ending results in my senior year to attract any offers.

My life had been redirected to another course.

My sister Pam, who alway thought I was nuts, questioned my sanity after the cat-food eating episode with T

Team photo of El Camino College's 1971 Community College State Champion cross country team. I'm in the first row, with the longest hair on the team. 'T' is in front row, far left; No. 1 runner Bruce is in second row, directly behind me

CHAPTER 5
College Daze and Confused

Cross country carried me all the way across town to El Camino Community College, in nearby Torrance, 10 miles from Hawthorne. With no athletic scholarship to any four-year college in the country, my local community college was the prudent next step to take after high school.

I signed up for the college cross country team in the fall. Baby toe had healed up. I was back in excellent shape. I gave the Palos Verdes Marathon another shot over the summer. This time I set out to run at a slower, even pace and vowed not to take a single walking step, no matter how much it hurt. I succeeded in that goal, but I improved on my previous time by a stinking 37 seconds — 3 hours, 31 minutes, 8 seconds. Very disappointing; I was expecting something like a 10-minute drop.

In community college cross country, the events were run on 4-mile courses. That suited my style of running just fine.

I was the No. 3 runner on the team, but the top freshman. My friend Bruce Johnston was the No. 1 guy. We were guided by Coach Bob Myers.

It was a memorable season. But the memories that stayed with me the most were related to the teammate we called "T", whose real name was Mike.

T was battling to make the seventh and final scoring spot on the team. But he stood out in every other way. T's zaniness kept us loose and stress-free from Coach Myers' intense training drills. It was T who suggested our fight song – "Wild Thing," an early 60s song by The Trogs. T had us singing the song in unison, like a battle cry, and everything was "groooovy."

T was a surfer, and after every practice when it was time to shower he would shout "Surf's up!", then carry a locker room bench into the shower and pretend to "hang-10" on end of the bench while showering.

Any taunts from drivers passing by us while we were on training runs along the city streets didn't go unanswered by T. He was the most vocal at shouting barbs back at the offenders and he stirred the rest of us to join in as a united front.

Pam and I threw another of our big parties at our Rossburn home during my freshman year at El Camino and T established himself as the life of the party. He and I got drunk enough to challenge each other to a cat food-eating contest, which was just as gross as it sounds, and elicited plenty of "Eeew's" from the girls when T and I tried to give them kisses after consuming said cat food.

T took it a step farther by challenging me to a one-mile race later that night, when our alcoholic consumption had peaked. We were driven (we were in no condition to drive ourselves) to the track at Hawthorne High, with a bunch of party goers in tow, well after midnight. T and I stripped down to our underwear and ran four laps around the track, much to the screaming delight of our audience. As far as I can remember, T beat me in the race.

There was this fearless "live life to the fullest" spirit about T, but there was one moment when he may have pushed it a bit too far. Our team was down in San Diego on an overnight road trip. We were staying at a hotel that was near the freeway. T and I decided to go for a casual late afternoon run. On the way back to the hotel, T talked me into taking a shortcut — by running across the freeway. As I was standing on the freeway median halfway across, anxiously waiting for a clearing in the traffic so I could make it safely to the other side, I was thinking to myself that this was truly nuts. We made it across, luckily, and laughed about it the rest of the way back to the hotel. But inside I was thinking, "Hmm, maybe I won't try that again."

T was hampered by injuries through most of the season and wasn't a factor for our team's post-season run after winning our conference title.

In the state semifinals, which included all conferences in the southern half of the state, we finished in a disappointing third place. But we advanced to the State Finals to live a better day. We won the whole damn thing that day. We were state champions! We had three runners in the top 10, including me as the 9th-place finisher overall.

For me, it was the crowning achievement of my running career. I can't say it made up for the huge disappointment of my senior year in high school, because the four years of hopes and dreams I had shared with my closest friends were dashed by the freaky broken baby toe. But to win the state championship, after our dull showing in the southern semis, was tremendously satisfying.

I was the ninth-fastest community college runner in the state as a freshman. I fully expected to top that in my sophomore year.

At our season-ending team awards banquet, I was honored as the team's top freshman. But the school's athletic director wasn't particularly impressed. He was more focused on the length of my hair, which was in violation of the sports department's strict grooming rules. I cut it short at the start of the season to comply with the rules but didn't bother with a haircut after that, so it got kinda long. Which drew this loud reaction by the athletic director at the banquet: "I wasn't aware we had allowed *girls* to run on our *men's* cross-country team."

Kathy couldn't wait for April and me to break up so she could spring herself on me.

Kathy was openly flirtatious with me for months during my senior year of high school, when I was still very much with April. Kathy knew it. She knew April; she was a freshman, too.

Kathy was trouble, and troubled. She was the daughter of the Chief of Police for the City of Hawthorne, for starters. That was a red flag that I didn't pay attention to.

Since I was unattached starting my freshman year at El Camino College, Kathy lured me in. She was extremely cute, I had to admit. She was hard to resist. She had short-cropped reddish blonde hair that set off her hazel brown eyes like a lighthouse in a storm.

I found out she had some serious daddy issues. She was the youngest of three siblings and the only daughter. I would find out much later that she was bipolar. She had her manic ups and downs.

When she was up, she liked sex. A lot. I found that when we spent one day together in Pam's little shack in the back of the garage. The shack was where Pam hung out with her artistic friends, who collaborated to paint colorful designs and star constellations on the walls and ceiling blanketed by black paper, so the paint glowed under the ultraviolet light to cast a panoramic psychedelic kaleidoscope. Pam and her friends usually did drugs in the shack and their artwork reflected that.

Kathy and I had sex all day in that shack. I stopped counting how many times. All I remember is that I was pretty wiped out at the end of the day. I was 19; it took a lot to wipe me out at 19.

Sex was the major recreation we shared in the short time we were together — maybe three months. Then she was done with me and set her sights on… Phil.

Oh God. It was as if she was using me to get to my best friend all along. If it sounds like I took the break-up badly, it's because I did. I was really pissed. She flaunted it in front of me. I remember eating my heart out one day, watching her sit on Phil's lap while we were riding in a bus. We had just broken up a few days before. I can't remember where we were going on that bus. I was so fixated on that image of her on Phil's lap, smiling, rubbing his cheek softly.

All my anger was targeted toward her. I absolved Phil of any blame. I knew what he was dealing with. She was irresistible. He would wind up living through a much, much longer, impactful history with Kathy.

I wrote a short story that symbolized how I felt about the break-up, and Kathy's treacherous move on my best friend. The story set out to be an adventurous would-be cross-country road tale about two young guys — obvious stand-ins for Phil and me — aboard motorcycles. In the real world I was riding my first motorcycle, which represented "Easy Rider" freedom for me. I was kind of passionate about it. In the story, as the two riders were approaching Baker, the last small desert town in California on the highway to Las Vegas, one of the bikes breaks down. They get stuck in desolate, isolated Baker for a few days while waiting for delivery of a part needed to repair the bike. During their stay they make acquaintances with a tavern owner and his beautiful young daughter. A competition ensues between the two guys for the affections of the daughter. The guy who wins her over was obviously a reference to Phil in real life, and he decides to stay in Baker. The guy representing me loses out in love, but he rides out of town solo on his motorcycle, his freedom intact.

Back in real life, after a few months even Phil decided he didn't want to be stuck in Baker with Kathy, so he broke it off. Kathy really did love him. She wasn't ready to let go. Phil wanted to move on. He had ideas on hooking up with an old girlfriend, Terri.

It was summertime and time for a beach party. We planned a big bash at El Porto Beach. I was home by myself late in the afternoon, packing up things for the party, when Phil came knocking at the front door. He had Kathy in his car with him. He had a favor to ask me.

He told me Terri was going to be at the beach party and he wanted to be with her, and he wanted to be free of Kathy. He asked if I could take Kathy to the party to get him off the hook. I obliged him. So, Phil dropped Kathy off at my house and took off for the beach.

Kathy was holding a big purse when she quietly entered the house. She had a curious smile on her face as she glanced at me, then looked around.

"Are we alone?" she asked.

"Uhh, yeah. I was just going to grab a couple of beach towels and chairs, and then we can head on down to the beach. Uhh, are you OK?"

"Oh, I'm fine," she answered assertively, again with that smile fixed on her face. She started to head down the hallway, as if she was looking for a place to hide. Then she held her purse out to me. "Feel how heavy my purse is," she said.

She handed the purse to me and it felt like she had a bowling ball inside.

"What the hell do ya got in there?" I asked as I struggled to hold the purse up. I handed the purse back to her. Kathy then reached in and pulled out a gigantic pistol and pointed the barrel straight up in the air.

"Jesus!! Where'd you get that?!" I shrieked.

"Oh, this belongs to my Dad. He's got so many guns he won't even notice it's missing."

That would be her dad, the Chief of Police of Hawthorne.

"Oh, great! What the hell do you plan to do with that?!"

Now her smile transformed into a mischievous smirk. "I thought it would be fun to use it at the beach party, by blowing my brains out in front of Phil and Terri."

She let out a hearty laugh in reaction to the horrified look on my face. "Can't you just see it, my brains splattered all over the sand!"

"You can't be serious, Kathy. Come on, a joke's a joke, but this is carrying it a bit too far."

"Oh, I'm not joking." Her smile vanished as her hazel eyes darkened in an intense stare. "I'm dead serious."

For the next twenty minutes, I tried every psychological tactic in the book — I reasoned, begged, joked, philosophized, begged some more — to get Kathy to hand that gun over to me.

I kept wishing one of my parents would pop in and resolve the situation, or maybe my sister would appear and break the tension. But I was completely on my own and completely out of my element. I was genuinely afraid that Kathy was capable of carrying out her threat.

Finally, Kathy gave up the gun, and I received it with immense relief. Now that I had it, what the hell was I supposed to do with it? I didn't want to freak my parents out. I went into my bedroom looking for a place to stash it. It was a big gun. I decided to empty the bullets from the cartridge just to be safe. Scanning my closet, I deposited the six bullets in a shirt pocket. Then I shoved the gun into the deep pocket of a big, brown wool winter coat hanging in the closet. I thought, there, out of sight for now and out of danger from Kathy. So, we were good to go down to the beach party.

The party turned out to be a blast. Everyone had a good time. Evidently, Terri didn't make it to the party, so Phil wound up with Kathy anyway, and with enough alcohol consumption he was feeling romantic all bundled up on a blanket with her.

Pam, who was notorious for arriving late at every social event she ever attended, got to the party late as usual. She was accompanied by Tony, a friend and "maybe" boyfriend with my sister. I saw them in the distance in the dark, walking toward our gathering on the beach. As they drew nearer, I focused on Tony and shook my head to make sure I wasn't hallucinating. When they got within a few yards of me, my worst fear was confirmed. Tony was wearing the brown wool coat in which I had hidden the gun! *Really!?*

I dashed up to them in a state of panic. "Uhh, hi guys, glad you could make it. Uh, Tony, uhhh, I see you're wearing my coat!"

"Yeah, hope you don't mind. I thought it might be kinda chilly down here, and your sister said it'd be OK."

"Well-l-l, yeah, except for one small detail. Did you happen to find … something in one of the pockets?"

"Yeah, man! A gun! That was weird!"

"Yeah, pretty weird!" I laughed off nervously. "I bet you were surprised! Gotta ask, what the heck did you do with the gun?"

"Oh, well, I wasn't sure… just left it on …on the top of your dresser."

"On the top of my dresser. Ahh, that's just great. Pam, were you aware….?"

"No! I didn't know anything about a gun! What were you doing with a gun?!"

Aw shit. I threw my hands up in exasperation. There was no point in explaining it to my sister. The bigger problem would be explaining it to my parents if they wandered past my bedroom and happened to see a gun lying on top of my dresser, in full view. I was trying to picture the interesting conversation awaiting with my dad when I got home.

"Son, who does that gun in your room belong to?" I imagined him saying.

"Oh, well, that would be the Chief of Police of Hawthorne, Dad. I can explain, really. You see, his daughter had this funny joke in mind ..."

Fortunately, my parents never saw the gun.

It would all seem like a funny joke now, if you didn't know the rest of the story. Phil wound up joining the Army a year later. He was stationed in Germany and Kathy went with him. They got married and had three kids, then Kathy's mental health deteriorated over the years and they divorced, Phil got remarried and wound up with the three kids, and Kathy tragically wound up taking her own life sometime in her mid-40s.

I guess it could be argued that I dodged a bullet with Kathy, no pun intended. How different would my life have been if I had remained under her lure, instead of Phil, and wound up having three children with her at such a young age?

But don't think for a minute that Phil felt like he wound up on the tragic end of this tale. He would not trade anything in the world for the experience of fathering his two sons and daughter, who are all devoted to their father, and parents to the bevy of beautiful grandchildren whom he cherishes.

He did go through a few rough years with Kathy, but given a second chance, his fate was to meet the love of his life in Sharon, his second wife who became the real "mom" of those three kids.

Phil ended up living a life that resembled the life I described to my dad in junior high when he asked me what my life would be like when I grew up.

Phil fulfilled his service in the U.S Army, then enjoyed a prosperous career working as a grip at Universal Studios. He worked on television shows like "The Rockford Files, " Knightrider," "Murder She Wrote," and "Desperate Housewives" over the years. Now he's happily retired.

His dad was a studio union head who paved the way for studio careers for both Phil and his brother Jim. It's kind of funny how Jim's life mirrored his older brother's. Jim worked at Paramount Studios ("Happy Days," "Cheers," "Frasier," "How I Met Your Mother"), and wound up exchanging vows with the love of his life, Diane, in his second marriage. Diane was one of Sharon's closest friends. Jim and Diane have two beautiful daughters and, following Phil and Sharon's script, live in an elegant home in the 'burbs.

It somehow didn't quite work out that way for me.

I recovered quickly from the Kathy heartbreak and actively dated several girls for a while. Then I settled on an extremely sweet, innocent girl named Sandy, with whom I *didn't* have sex. The romance with her was all very sweet, and innocent and lasted about five months.

I also made a momentous decision that altered my career focus. I decided not to go out for the El Camino track team in the spring, much to the chagrin of Coach Myers, and turned all my attention to working on the school newspaper staff.

While that provided the push toward a newspaper career, it came at the expense of my once-promising running career. My training fell off for those idle six months during the spring semester and I wound up putting on nine pounds by the time cross-country season rolled around again in the fall of my sophomore year.

With the extra poundage, I basically gained no ground on my running times in my sophomore season. I was beaten out as the No. 1 runner on the team by a freshman from Mira Costa High who I had regularly beaten in high school. The team was not a contender to repeat as state champions, but we did qualify for the State Meet. I finished 10th in overall, one place lower than my freshman year. For me, that felt like one dreadful step back, and I was totally discouraged.

That was the last official cross-country race I ran. When I graduated from El Camino and transferred to Cal State Fullerton, I was done with competitive team running and completely focused entirely on working for the school paper, The Daily Titan.

As for T, our friendship could not out-run the cross country connection. He had some psychological hang-ups with his father, a Bible-thumping minister, that seemed to sap his spirit. After our sophomore year, T jumped in on a get-rich quick scheme of selling Amway products and vainly tried to get me to join him. Within a couple of years I lost track of him.

When Phil enlisted in the Army, he avoided the draft that would determine who would end up fighting our dirty little war in Vietnam.

I was 19 my freshman year in college, which plunged me square into draft eligibility. All 19-year-olds in the country had to sweat it out to see if their birthdate got called in the lottery for an all-expenses-paid trip to 'Nam. It was a matter of fate. My stand against the War was no secret. It was a damn scary time in my young life. I saw "Hair." I wasn't just gawking at naked bodies, I followed the story of the lead character, the long-haired, freedom-loving, free-love-preaching, pot-smoking hippie who gets drafted, has his head shaved, is shipped off to Vietnam, and tragically dies in battle.

I composed a song that I entitled "Song of My Youth" when I was 16. I didn't like the lyrics I wrote to the music back then. I took a shot at re-writing them 50 years later shortly after visiting D.C. and seeing the Vietnam War Memorial for the first time. This is what I came up with for "Song Of My Youth":

"One/One life to live/One life to give/Who will you die for
Son/You're number one/ Now here's your gun/Set your aim on our war

"Fate/It's a matter of fate/Tied to birthdate/Hear my mother's prayer/
Wait/Why must I wait/On dreams I create/ What say the soothsayer

"Kill/Why should I kill/To further the will/Of those who feel no sin
Why/ Why must I pause/To fight for a cause/That I don't believe in

"Drum/The drum still beats on/Sing a new song/Men, women of honor
Wars/Glorious wars/Heaven restores/What the hell do we fight for

*"Wealth/Born into wealth/Here's to your health/You won't have to serve, sir
Poor/Pity the poor/We'll show you the door/We've no other offer*

*"Drum/The drum still beats on/Sing a new song/Men, women of honor
Wars/Glorious wars/Heaven restores/What the hell do we fight for*

*"I/ I missed the call/ I avoided the fall/Of fifty-eight thousand
Now/Now I am old/ I pray for the souls/Of youths whose dreams
en-DEAD"*

My birthdate drew a lottery number of 221 at age 19. I got lucky. I was well within the clear of the odds of likely getting drafted, which affected the top 95 birthdays selected.

With Phil off to Germany for a couple years in the Army, it felt like I had lost a best friend.

Soon, another best friend appeared in my life.

———————◆·•·———————

I met Dan in my junior year in high school as a teammate on the track team, after he had transferred to Hawthorne High from Morningside High. He knew Sandy, who went to Morningside as well. He was a good-looking guy with curly locks and a mustache, and a muscular build. As I would get to know him, I learned that he possessed a peculiar and off-kilter sense of humor. No one could make me laugh like Dan did.

We really didn't start becoming friends until the latter part of my freshman year at El Camino College. It was ice hockey that united our friendship. The Gerke brothers who lived next door on Rossburn, invited me to play ice hockey with a group of guys at the Torrance ice rink late on Saturday nights after it closed to the public. The group rented the rink out after midnight. It was very informal. We laced up skates, went out on the ice wearing street clothes and without any pads, and banged the puck around until about 2:30 in the morning, after which we stopped at a 24-hours-open Denny's for food. We gave ourselves an unofficial club name — "The Mother Puckers."

When I casually told Dan about the ice hockey, his eyes lit up. Turned out, he was a huge hockey fan and was very interested in joining. A lasting friendship was born.

But it appeared that the U.S Army snatched away another

friendship. After a few months of Mother Pucker comradeship, Dan decided to join the Army. I don't know if it was by design, but Phil's deployment in Germany surely saved him from combat in Vietnam. Dan, meanwhile, seemed destined to wind up in 'Nam, having signed up for the tank division.

<hr>

Dan had a parting gift for me — his job at the Children's Baptist Home in Inglewood. CBH, as we fondly called it, was home to about 90 kids who were placed there as wards of the court. They all came from broken homes due to divorce, abuse, drugs, parents in jail, abandonment, you name it. The kids ranged from ages 5 to 14, about 55 percent white, 30 percent black, 10 percent Hispanic. They were hard-luck kids, with a lot of emotional and psychological issues playing into their psyches.

Dan had the inside connections to get me into CBH. He was dating Sharon, the daughter of the director. Dan was a recreation leader, supervising on-ground activities and games, and off-ground outings like the zoo, movies, Disneyland. Taking over his job, I was about to begin a working experience that left a lasting imprint.

I was just 19, with no experience working with troubled kids. When I interviewed for the job, I was taken aback when Jerry, Dan's boss, emphasized that the main qualification for the job was that I had to be "rotten" enough to handle the kids. In other words, I had to be tough with them or they would rip me apart.

Overall, Jerry painted a pretty cynical picture of life at CBH. He callously characterized the kids as "hopeless." His favorite expression for anything that applied to the job was "Mickey Mouse." 'We have this 'Mickey Mouse' rule for that," he would say, in an off-handed way, which left me wondering if I should take anything he said seriously.

I wasn't prepared for such a harsh welcome. To top it off, Jerry insisted I change my name from Chic to Charlie because "Chic" wasn't going to command any respect.

I got an introduction to "rotten" my first day on the job, from Dorey Mac, another recreation leader who was scary looking. He was a huge, menacing presence, standing 6-foot-5 and about 260 pounds. He was an albino, with pure white hair, a ghostly white face, absolutely no facial hair, including no eyebrows, and piercing, blue eyes. He never smiled; his countenance was fixed with an expressionless stare. It was after dinner on my first day, while I was observing him supervising kids at play just outside the Game Room, that I witnessed how he handled a 12-year-old boy who was behaving badly. Dorey grabbed the boy with one hand around his neck, hoisted him up in the air, pinned him against the building wall, and screamed in his face. He got the petrified boy's attention and the bad behavior ceased. Ok, so that's how it's done.

There were several means of discipline to deal with kids who warranted it. Dan, the hockey nut, was credited with implementing the first option, which he identified in hockey jargon as "the penalty box." The idea was to make the kid sit out the supervised activity for a few minutes for CBH versions of "high-sticking," until the rec leader decided he or she had calmed down enough to return.

That was the most common, benign, option available. Option two was more severe and would never be allowed in today's society — the "swat." It was as bad as it sounds. We would haul the out-of-control kid into the recreation supply office and administer a "swat" to the behind with a wooden paddle. Thank God I only had to do this a few times, and I cringed every time.

In the most severe cases, when no other options were effective, there were the "lock-up"or isolation rooms in the administration office. These were self-explanatory, and available for very extreme circumstances. I never had to resort to banishing a kid to a lock-up room, but I witnessed others being taken away and it never was a pretty sight.

All that being said, I couldn't bring myself to be "rotten" as prescribed by my supervisor. I exercised my authority when I had to, but generally I was a soft touch. I felt bad for these kids. The circumstances that brought them to the Home were heart-breaking and I felt true compassion for them.

I admit I picked out a personal favorite among the kids who won me over right away. Her name was Lizette, a seven-year-old girl who was half-Black and half-Puerto Rican. She had long frizzy black hair, which was usually gathered up at the ends with a rubber band. She spoke with a slur that I found endearing.

My introduction to Lizette was audio, sight unseen. It was my first week on the job and I was walking outside the grounds late one afternoon before dinnertime. The swimming pool was open for kids to swim, but the opaque, rubber bubble cover was raised because it was cold at dusk. I could hear Jerry's loud, booming voice inside the bubble where he was supervising the swimming. He barked out a peculiar command that immediately caught my attention.

"Lizette, if you don't stop hitting him with your leg, I'm going to take it away from you!"

Did he say "hitting him with your leg?" Did I hear that right? My curiosity was instantly piqued hearing that proclamation. I found out later a logical explanation — Lizette had an artificial leg, which of course she had to detach when she was in the swimming pool. Jerry was letting her know it was not OK to use it as a weapon on another kid.

The next night I formed an instant bond with the feisty Lizette over a game of billiards in the Game Room. She won me over with her smile and raspy slurred speech that melted my heart.

There was a story behind each kid at CBH, and Jerry had a nickname for just about every one of them. He was big on nicknames. To recall a few:

- Kenny "Whiz-Bang Boomerang," 10, was a freckle-faced butch blonde kid with a pig-squeal for a laugh. He loved playing HORSE on the basketball court with the rec leaders and had a knack for nailing shots from half-court. He also had a reputation for being a pyromaniac because he once set his grandparents' house on fire. This was a kid who used desperate means to gain attention.
- Steve "Squirrel," another unruly 10-year-old, had a disturbing habit of flushing his tennis shoes down the toilet. He was acting out some kind of aggression.
- Scott "Goliath", at 12 was the biggest kid in the Home at 6-3 and 225. He was a gentle giant most of the time, but one day he lost it during a basketball game I was supervising, and took a punch at me, a glancing blow to my jaw. He was the only kid who made an attempt to hit me. I had to react quickly to show I was in control, so I immediately pounced on and restrained him until another leader came to help.
- Mike "Pilot," an 11-year-old with a terminal brain tumor, was a loner, and in his literal flight of fancy thought he was an airplane,

as he liked to spread his arms like wings and fly across the room. We'd have to watch him carefully to make sure he didn't make a crash landing. He was smart, too, often talking about airplane engines and jet propulsion.

- Glen "Wartman" was a cute little six-year-old who spoke with an adorable lisp. Dan and his girlfriend Sharon were so taken by him that they wanted to adopt him as their own.

- Kyle "Crybaby" was a 10-year-old who had a disturbing habit of crying or screaming when he got upset. Kyle missed out on a special outing to the circus because he went into a crying fit that he couldn't stop. As we drove off to the circus and left him behind, we could hear him screaming in an isolation room. Three hours later, when we returned home, he was still screaming.

- Ricky "Dodo" was a nine-year-old Hispanic who picked out his own nickname when Jerry asked him what he wanted to be called. The name fit his goofy personality, and it carried over to his six-year-old brother Victor. Dan jokingly offered Victor a dime if he would run head-on into the wall. Dan didn't think he'd have to pay up.

- Jody "Polar Bear" was a plump, blonde-haired kid whose nickname was fitting for the way he clumsily lumbered around the grounds like a polar bear.

- Roger "Dodger" was a seemingly innocent little six-year-old, with that pip-squeak voice of his. But he would sound totally out of character when he'd suddenly launch into a tirade of curse words for no apparent reason.

- Tony "No Love" was a 12-year-old Black kid who elicited no love from the staff as the most sullen kid at CBH. I was warned not to turn my back on Tony, because you never knew what he was capable of doing. He held the record for the most frequent banishments to the isolation rooms.

- Shane wasn't given a nickname, but her reputation belied any need for one. She was 12, physically mature beyond her years, beautiful, and trouble. All the other girls looked up to her and all the older boys looked at her lustfully, with the wrong idea in their heads. She was subtly flirtatious, even with the rec leaders. We were on alert to occasionally patrol the "Bowl" area, which was an obvious hideaway with its heavy vegetation and large trees, located in the far corner of the property next to the fence that separated CBH from the cemetery grounds next door. The Bowl was where Shane reputedly liked to rendezvous with various boys for unapproved activities.

I made an impression with these kids with the motorcycle I rode to work every day. They had all sorts of questions: "Can I have a ride?" "How fast do you go?" "Have you ever crashed?" I think my motorcycle gave me the credibility that gained their respect.

The CBH job turned out to be the first of three jobs I had working with kids during my college days. The other two were considerably less challenging and in more normalized settings. I worked one summer at a day camp, then a whole year as an after-school playground supervisor at a Montessori school. Collectively, I genuinely enjoyed working with them, and gave me reason to seriously consider going into teaching.

———————◆———————

Pam and I had another one of our house parties on New Year's Eve during my sophomore year. One unexpected guest was a young woman who would eventually become my first wife.

David, one of my teammates on the El Camino cross-country team, was a Mira Costa High grad. He brought a bunch of ex-Mira Costa cross-country guys with him to the party, including his younger brother Mark. Tagging along with Mark was this adorably cute young woman named Dorrean, who was a 17-year-old senior at Mira Costa.

Evidently, Mark and Dorrean were just platonic buddies. I was introduced to her, and well, there was instantly a mutual attraction between us.

When the clock struck midnight to usher in the new year, she was the one sitting next to me on the living room couch, so I planted a kiss on her. I got her number.

I was really attracted to her — she had a cute, roundish doll-like face, with long, Prell-perfect brown-blondish hair, and a perky personality. I must have made an impression on her at the New Year's Eve party, as I later learned she drove by my house after the party before I built up the nerve to call her.

Ours was a sweet courtship, befitting Dorrean's sweet and innocent nature. I was accorded a few insights of our early days from a couple months of entries in a diary of Dorrean's, circa 1973, that I somehow still possess after all these years, dug out of an old box full of memories. It was so strange to read her words about me decades later. She drove by my house six days after we met. She was hoping I would call, and I finally did two days later. On our first date we saw the movie "Deliverance," which *"wasn't as bad as I thought it would be."* Then she added, in a broad hint about how long ago this date took place: *"As a matter of fact they were both very good movies."* Ahh, such were the good ol' days when you could watch two movies for the price of one.

Dorrean

I obviously made an impression on her that night, and I mean that quite literally. She wrote, verbatim: *"But, who was it that said Chic(k) was shy? Debbi maybe? Well, in this reporter's opinion that guy isn't shy. He isn't horny or anything but he sure isn't shy. The whole think turned out to give me the biggest hickey you've ever seen before."*

The romance skyrocketed after that. We went on quite a few motorcycle dates in those first couple of months. Bowling was also big with us, and I dragged her to basketball games I was covering for the school newspaper. By February 1, a month after we had met, she wrote: *"I really love being with him because I really love him. My whole life revolves around him."*

And I really fell in love with the sheltered ("partially spoiled"— her words) lone daughter and youngest sibling in a family that was respectable on the surface, but troubled on a number of fronts underneath. Her mom was petite, sweet like her daughter, and domestic, who always had her adorable pet poodle at her side at home. Dorrean was devoted to her mother, always checking in with her. Her father was an amicable alcoholic who drank himself to sleep every night with a bottle of whiskey. Dorrean had two older brothers. The oldest brother was a rebel, had a drug problem, and often disappeared for weeks. He committed suicide many years later. The other brother typified the middle sibling — often overlooked, but really a decent guy.

74

With my annoying habit of arriving late for dates, my self-absorption with my own interests, and maybe the fact that I turned out to be a little more "horny" than she expected, the relationship with Dorrean got tested over my final two-and-half years of college. By then we had reached the point of — break up? Or get married? It could have gone either way.

<hr>

I needed a fifth semester to graduate with my AA degree from El Camino. Then I enrolled at Cal State Fullerton, because Mrs. Krislock, my high school newspaper adviser, had touted the university's media communications department. It was conveniently an hour's drive away from home. I joined the Daily Titan newspaper staff right away and worked on it in some capacity every semester.

Fullerton was too far to commute from Hawthorne, so that dictated the decision to move out of my parents' home and live on my own for the first time, close to the campus. I worked out a budget plan with my parents, each of whom contributed one-third of my total living expenses. I had to cover the other third.

I came across an ad for a room to rent in an owner-occupied condo in nearby Yorba Linda. I was just 20 years old, still very naive, and was completely clueless on what I was getting myself into.

I was moving into a two-bedroom condo with the owner, Rick, who was just a couple years older than I, and another roommate, Paul, who was 29. To repeat, this was a two-bedroom residence, one room occupied solely by myself and the other occupied by both Rick and Paul.

Did I mention how naive I was? Rick, who displayed some devious tendencies right from the start, satisfied my curiosity about the shared bedroom in an off-handed way. He explained that Paul wasn't around very much, and they had worked it out so they could co-exist in the same bedroom. He colored his story further by mentioning an old girlfriend whom he nearly married, which had given him the impetus for buying the condo in the first place. I took him at his word with this explanation, because who was I to doubt him? Did I mention how naive I was?

Meeting Paul was another story. He was tall, slender, handsome, intelligent, Jewish, and well-traveled, having visited various places around the world, including eight months living in an Israeli kibbutz. He was into yoga and health food, neither of which was in vogue at all in the early 70s. And very quickly, he was into *me*. When he found out I was a writer, he immediately expressed an interest in reading my stuff. I took the bait and showed him all my writings, and he was very generous with his gentle critiques and praise. I ate it up.

He found one short poem of mine that he really liked. The poem seemed prescient at the time, but I was still too naive to realize it. That was probably why he liked it so much:

If you tell me what your secrets are
Then perhaps I'll tell you mine
We may find out that our inner selves
Correspond on different lines
For what we perceive to be our truths
As we seek out one another
May be buried deep within our hearts
So might we not know each other

I admit I was very impressionable and taken with Paul. I was fascinated by and envious of his world travels and his stories about living in a kibbutz. He was where I wanted to be in terms of life experience when I reached his age. He inspired me to be a better writer. Chiefly because of him, and all sorts of conflicted feelings brought on by my relationship with him, I wrote a novel about this first experience living away from home. It was a work of fiction, but I drew a lot from the real deal.

The novel was entitled "Last of the Orange Groves," which was a dorky metaphor in reference to the orange groves disappearing from Orange County due to urban sprawl, representing life's inevitable changes, whether we like them or not. I was writing about the changes I was experiencing in my life at the time, of course.

Things got a bit crowded in the condo a couple months after I had moved in when two more people, Clint and Karen, crashed, supposedly on a temporary basis. While I was oblivious to the true nature of Rick and Paul's relationship, I started to get suspicious because Clint was so outwardly swishy in his mannerisms; I was starting to think, *"Ya think maybe he's gay?"* Karen, meanwhile, was just a tagalong. I wasn't sure what her connection to Rick was, other than she liked to drink his liquor.

Clint and Karen extended their stay too long for Paul, who moved out.

I often went home to my parents on weekends, and like any spoiled college kid, I often took my dirty laundry with me. One Sunday night, when I returned to the condo from my parents' house, I was going upstairs to my bedroom, carrying a laundry basket of clean clothes. As I approached the top of the stairs, I noticed my bedroom door was closed but I could see through the crack at the bottom of the door that a light was on in my room.

With my hands full, I kicked the door open. To my shock, I saw Clint and a guy I had never seen, both shirtless but wearing shorts, thank god, sitting on my bed, drinking beers. The light from the lamp on the nightstand was dimmed by a towel draped over it—for "atmosphere," perhaps? They instantly jumped off the bed at the sound of the banging door.

They apologized profusely, quickly gathered their things, and high-tailed it out of the room. But I was left standing there, thinking, *"Eewww, what just happened here? In my bed?"*

The next morning, I had a conversation with Rick. That's when all was revealed to me. Rick and Paul were gay lovers. But the relationship was waning when I moved in and Clint's presence in the house gave Paul the excuse he needed to move out.

It was a couple weeks later when I received a letter from Paul. It was a sweet letter, in which he finally admitted that he was attracted to *"my mind as well as my body,"* which was meant to imply that his interest in my writing was genuine. He also wrote a short poem for me.

The letter struck me in an odd way. In no way was I put off by it. In fact, I was flattered by it. But Paul knew that I was heterosexual. He knew about my relationship with Dorrean. And as for me, while I genuinely yearned for Paul's friendship, it never translated to anything sexual. There was no latent homosexual feeling attached to my fondness for Paul, even though I did think he was handsome. And his feelings for me would in no way alter my fondness for him.

All of that held true when Paul stopped by the condo to say good-bye. He was headed back to Israel. It remained true even when he surprised me by kissing me on the lips before departing.

*In the company of Dan, I was exposed to the whims of
whatever came off the top of his head*

CHAPTER 6
Dan, Part 1

Dan lasted all of four months in the Army.

They must have found some defect in his twisted personality in boot camp. Or maybe it was medical. It could have been mental. Or maybe it had something to do with the fact he was adopted and the only son of his widowed mother.

Whatever the reason, he returned home and was welcomed back at CBH with open arms. It wasn't at my expense. I was allowed to stay.

I mentioned that Dan had connections through his girlfriend Sharon, the daughter of the pastor who ran CBH. I don't know how, but Dan knew everything that went on at that place, and he filled me in with every dirty detail. Sharon's father wasn't exactly a devout pastor who lived by the Ten Commandments. This was especially disturbing considering how he coveted CBH's "Director of Education," who, according to Dan, had no teaching credentials and whose only qualification for her position seemed to be that she was sleeping with the boss. Dan's contempt for the man was considerable, given that he knew and respected Sharon's mother, who still was very much married to the devout pastor.

Dan viewed the world in a cynical fashion, generally speaking. His knowledge of Sharon's father's carnal misdeeds only further colored his perspective of CBH. But we worked together as rec leaders for nearly an entire year, and the stories that evolved from that shared experience fueled our friendship.

Despite his negativity, Dan had a way with the kids with his skewed sense of humor. There was just something about him that commanded the respect of the kids. This was a trait that served him well later, as a teacher in which he specialized in tutoring students nobody else wanted to deal with, kids much like those at CBH.

His first teaching "job" after college encompassed two years serving in the Peace Corps. He enlisted with girlfriend Kathy, who had succeeded Sharon in his life and would later become his first wife. They taught English to native kids in a remote village on the Solomon Islands, off the shores of New Zealand. Service in the army hadn't worked out, so Dan had signed up for the Peace Corps instead, which earned my admiration. The Peace Corps was a much better fit than the Army for his resistance-to-authority personality.

It was at CBH that I first witnessed Dan work his magic with kids. I recollect one incident that epitomized his inventive tactics. It happened one night after dinner when Dan and I teamed together to supervise the huge Game Room, which was overrun by about 40 kids that particular night. We had an hour to kill and Dan had this crazy idea. He brought out a bunch of bean bags and proposed a free-for-all bean bag fight — Dan and me versus 40 wild kids.

In the ultra chaos that ensued, many of the bean bags split apart and beans were scattered all over the place. It was a minor miracle no one got hurt, but Dan and I were the targets of the kids' unfiltered aggression, so the damage was contained. But one 11-year-old boy, Joe, got a little carried away toward the end of the session, so Dan had to sit him down in the penalty box.

When play time had ended and the kids returned to their dorms, a major clean-up remained with spilled beans everywhere. Joe had not served sufficient time in the penalty box to complete his punishment, so Dan wasn't about to let him off the hook. He instructed Joe to pick up as many beans as he could in five minutes. But the catch was, to avoid any further penalty box time that would carry over to the following day, he needed to pick up more beans than Dan and I combined in the same time span.

Joe scurried about, scooping up as many beans as he possibly could, while Dan and I casually did the same. Two piles of beans were laid out on a table for a final count by Dan.

To the naked eye, it was obvious Joe's pile of beans was larger than ours. But that didn't account for who was doing the counting. Dan started on our beans first: "One, two, three, five, eight, ten…"

"Hey, you're skipping numbers!" Joe protested.

"Hey, buddy, who's doing the counting here? This is what you get for making me do all this extra work."

Dan finished counting our beans. "Sixty-eight, sixty-nine. OK, we'll just round that off to eighty."

Joe shrieked. Dan was showing no mercy. He then started counting Joe's beans.

"One, two, three… that one doesn't count, four, five, that

one's no good, six, seven, oh-there's another one we're throwing out."

"Why aren't you counting all of my beans?! That's not fair!" Joe was beside himself with the injustice of it all.

Dan offered a very logical explanation. "I forgot to mention, you were supposed to pick up only *male* beans. We're not counting the female beans. See the difference? This bean is round, that's a male bean. Those we'll count. But this bean is curved, that's a female bean. That bean is no good."

I busted out laughing. So did Joe. He knew by then that Dan was just teasing him. Dan let him go. But I marveled at how Dan came up with that male-female bean concept off the top of his head. I was too young at the time to consider the sexist implications of rejecting the female beans.

It's stories like those that I took away from my experience working at CBH. Dan and I would reminisce for years about CBH. Stories like: the time "Squirrel" tried to run away by jumping the fence into the cemetery grounds next door, and Dan and I assembled a posse of about eight kids to chase after him, which only served to unleash the kids for too much fun hopping over tombstones while freaking out cemetery security guards; like how all the blonde kids at CBH had their hair turn green from the heavy chlorine in the swimming pool; like how on "Movie Night" in the Game Room, the kids preferred watching the movies projected completely backwards; like how I lived to talk about my harrowing overnight stay subbing for a wing leader; like how the publicity-seeking pastor brought in a "model" kid from outside to make a short public service film on life at CBH, instead of featuring the real kids; like how Shane got pregnant (no surprise there); like how Whiz Bang Boomerang cut his wrists; like the field trip to Catalina Island and how we managed to beat the odds by not leaving any kids behind when we headed back to the mainland; like how swatting was finally banned and we had to temper the pervading mentality of being "rotten"; like how we felt pretty rotten for the few kids who had no family to pick them up for holiday visits at Christmas time.

My days at CBH ended in all sorts of infamy. Sharon's father wound up leaving both his wife and the job over the scandal of his affair. Dorey Mac and another rec leader quit, leaving us short-handed. Acrimonious work relations broke out on a number of fronts, with workers trying to form a union. Jerry lost his job over a contract dispute. Finally, I was let go, with the lame explanation that I was being laid off because there weren't enough hours to justify keeping me employed.

So, it ended. But it was a life-expanding work experience that opened my eyes in so many ways.

———————————◆———————————

Our exploits didn't end at CBH; they were just beginning. Dan and I decided to rent an apartment together during my last year at Cal State Fullerton. Dan was attending school at Long Beach State, so we found a place midway between the two campuses in Garden Grove, or as Dan called it, "Garbage Grove."

As my roomie, Dan introduced me to pot, and it was mind-blowing. I was a virtual virgin when it came to any drug experience at the time. We smoked a lot of pot, and I never laughed so hard. Steve Martin was the funniest human being on the planet when we listened to his debut comedy album while under the influence of a bong cloud. Those were good days.

It's a wonder I got through my senior year of college with my BA degree. Pot did have one lasting positive effect on me. From the influence of marijuana I always had melodies playing in my head. Over four decades of composing music, I'd estimate at least 80 percent of the inspiration was cannabis-induced.

We shared one inside joke that Dan wasn't ever going to let me live down. He teased me incessantly over the excessive body hair I used to leave on the shared bar of soap in the shower. (There's a reason why I describe myself as the missing link to the Neanderthal Man.) Dan had the right zany personality and sense of humor to put up with my quirks; excessive body hair was one of them. It couldn't have been easy. The hairy soap cemented our friendship.

———————————◆———————————

Dorrean and I got through our wedding *despite* Dan, who was my Best Man. It was a big, formal church wedding and Dan added his touch to the occasion by showing up wearing this ridiculously tall, black top hat. That was a bad sign.

As weddings go (and I've had a few), this one had more than its share of stress. One of the tuxes for our wedding party, intended for Rich B., didn't arrive on time with the other tuxes and had to be hurriedly shipped out on the morning of the wedding. Rich showed up at the church dressed in a non-matching suit (Dorrean's choice of color for the wedding tuxes was dark green, not the easiest color to match). Dorrean was stressed out over the mix-up. Her mother was frantic, her father was drunk.

Then the wedding was held up for 30 minutes because my poor grandmother got lost on her way to the church. She was so upset by the time she arrived, that she could have benefitted from a sedative.

Dan had the perfect remedy for the pervading anxiety in the breast pocket of his tux — a joint, which was his intention to be shared with me. He only had my best interests at heart, of course, and wanted to help calm my nerves through all of it. So, while we were waiting for Grandma's arrival, he led me off to the back of the church for a few tokes. I had to admit, it did help get me through it.

"Ya sure you want to go through with this?" Dan asked between hits.

"Oh hell, I don't know. I've come this far, so I might as well."

Pam's performance of one of my piano compositions during the ceremony was a nice touch. It wasn't enough to mask the olfactory evidence of our pot break during the wedding vows, no doubt having some impact on my overall lack of coherence. Unfortunately, my bride noticed, and was not pleased. You could tell when it came time for the post-ceremony group photos. Dorrean was not smiling. The furled eyebrows were a dead giveaway.

That beginning probably didn't portend to matrimonial bliss. I might as well point out here that Dan was my Best Man at my first four weddings. With his track record for mischief, I could easily lay blame on Dan for none of those marriages lasting.

I made a reference at the start of this chapter to a possible mentally-related reason Dan was discharged from the Army. I wrote about the blows I've taken to my head, but I've got nothing on Dan when it comes to that.

He went on to play ice hockey for 25 years after our Mother Pucker days, and he chose to play goaltender. It takes a certain type to want to play goaltender; Dan said as much. I don't know how many concussions he suffered from hockey pucks crashing into his forehead at 100 mph. Even with his face mask on, his bell got rung numerous times. The problem was, I think Dan liked it. He got off on the sensation of getting his bell rung.

I'm ashamed to say, as his best friend I may have been guilty of exploiting that little kink in Dan's personality. We played pick-up tackle football games with no pads for years during and after high school. We were the skinny cross-country geeks who challenged ex-varsity high school football players to grudge matches, and usually beat them because we were faster and in better shape. Dan, who possessed the bulkiest upper body in our huddle, was a key participant for us.

Playing without pads, we all took a pretty good beating. No play in football is more punishing than that hard-fought, suicidal one-yard plunge you need for a first down. Everyone on the field knows it's coming, and everyone converges on the guy carrying the ball. For us, that guy was Dan. He wanted the ball on those plays; it took a certain type to want the ball for those plays. And I, his best friend who usually called the plays, kept calling on him and handed the ball off to him. I may never live down the shame.

———————◆◆◆◆◆———————

Dan always said he liked dogs more than he liked humans, and after our college days I never knew Dan to be without a dog.

Dan always picked his dogs out of the shelter – rejects like him, he would say -- because he was adopted by his mom, who became a widow when Dan was 12. So, he went through his developmental teen years without a father. Dan wouldn't have been able to find out who his birth father was if he had wanted to. He used to talk about how his birth certificate listed his name as "John Doe," with father listed as "Unknown."

Dan bonded with every dog he owned. The first dog I associated with Dan was Rogie, a huge, dumb St. Bernard. Dan named him after Rogie Vachon, the legendary goaltender for the LA Kings ice hockey team. He linked his kinship with dogs to his fondness for goaltending.

84

The two dogs who lasted the longest with Dan were Solomon and Godiva. Solomon, a black lab, was the smart one, the alpha dog who got the not-so-smart Godiva — a massive St. Bernard-Great Dane mix — into all sorts of mischief. Godiva was 120 pounds of sweetness who considered herself a lap dog, and I provided the sacrificial lap whenever I came to visit.

Me with Dan's lovable "lap dog" Godiva

———————◆———————

Deep Creek was a special place early in our friendship. Dan loved the outdoors; it was his way of escaping urban existence. His two years living in thatched huts in the remote Solomon Islands had ingrained that yearning in him. We went camping several times at Deep Creek, which was a flowing, clear-water creek located midway between Running Springs and Big Bear in the San Bernardino Mountains, east of the greater L.A. basin.

Deep Creek wasn't the easiest place to find. It required a five-mile drive over a bumpy, rain-grooved dirt road, then an hour-long hike down a steep trail to get there. It was all worth it once you made it. The crystal clear, snow-melting water rendered a mind-altering shock to the system when you waded into it, but it was bliss drying out in the sun while laying on the smooth, flat boulders bordering the creek.

On one camping trip at Deep Creek, Dan made a sobering proclamation. We were in our mid-20's at the time, in the prime of our lives. Maybe Dan felt some sort of spiritual connection at Deep Creek that inspired him to share this eerie thought he had about his own mortality.

"I don't think I'm gonna make it to 50," he said soberly.

I was stunned. The pot may have been an influence, but we were mellow, and there was nothing in the wonderment that surrounded us to precipitate such a doomsday mood.

"Why? Why would you think such a thing?" I asked. I had no reason at this point to have any concerns about his mental well-being.

"I just don't see myself getting old," was all he would say.

Then he took it one step further. "When I do go, I want you to bring my ashes up here and spread them out around here. Can you do that for me, buddy?"

"Yeah, sure, Dan. I can do that."

He was serious and so was I. With that pact, Deep Creek had been ordained a sacred place for us.

———————◆◆◆◆◆———————

More than once, I feared Dan's prediction about his mortality would come true a lot sooner than he was expecting.

The Truckee River in the High Sierras very nearly proved to be Dan's undoing. He got this wild idea for six of us to pair up in three rented canoes on the Truckee at the tail end of April. The fearless half-dozen included Rich B., one of my lifelong buddies from high school cross-country, and Fred, who was Dan's best friend during his childhood. Fred was also a member of the high school cross-country team. The other two on board for the canoe adventure were named Ralph and Jim.

Our goal was to canoe 80 miles down the river from the town of Truckee to Reno, Nevada. It was mid-spring but still winter-like, with three feet of snow on the banks of the river. When we were checking out our canoes, the guy at the rental store warned us about how cold the water was.

"You don't want to fall in," he told us. "Get out as soon as you can. You've got maybe three minutes before you freeze to death."

We only fell 76 miles short of our final destination.

In the beginning, I was paired with Rich. Dan and Fred were

in another boat, then Ralph and Jim. Things went smoothly for the first couple of miles. The river was full and raging, fueled by the melting snow.

Rich and I struggled in the turns, zig-zagging from one shoreline to the other. We were not in sync and could not keep a straight line in the strong current. So, we switched it up. Jim and Rich swapped places, pairing me with Jim, Rich with Ralph.

At mile four, we could hear the roar of a waterfall in the distance. We banked on shore to sneak a peek farther downstream to see what all the commotion was about. Sure enough, we scouted a treacherous 'S' curve just ahead that flowed through a washed-out bridge. The bridge stood at the midway point of the 'S' with only four concrete pillars spread about 15 feet apart left standing.

The river presented three fast-moving lanes to shoot past the four-foot-wide pillars before quickly adjusting to negotiate the second part of the 'S' curve. Just beyond the second bend was a calm tide pool off to the right, which was where we needed to land on shore. A few feet farther the waterfall descended about 25 feet at a 60-degree angle over huge boulders. We would have to carry the canoes on land to get past the waterfall.

Dan and Fred, who were easily the most adept pair, went first and made it to the tide pool. Jim and I went next and made it past the concrete pillars, but we swung too wide left on the ensuing right-hand curve. We careened into the left bank on the opposite side of the tide pool, parking our canoe there to contemplate our next move.

Looking around, we could see we were in a tough spot. We were completely engulfed by vertical cliffs to the left, so the only way out was to paddle over to the right side, where the safe tide pool lay. It was about a 20-foot crossing, but the tricky part was navigating a vicious, swirling whirlpool circulating just before the waterfall.

My boots were soaked from plunging into the water when we hauled our canoe on to shore. My feet were freezing, the air was gray and cold, and we were surrounded by blankets of snow. Just as I removed one boot to change my wet sock, I could see snowflakes falling on my bare foot. Just what we needed — more snow.

Ralph and Rich never made it past the first curve, so Dan and Fred hiked back upstream to bring their canoe down for them. Jim and I had front-row seats for their valiant effort, which started out spectacularly and ended up disastrously. They shot past the pillars like a rocket and swung into the second curve like a bat out of hell. But as they plunged into the whirlpool, the canoe nose-dipped precipitously. Dan, who was in the front of the boat, was slung into the water by the momentum. Jim's pack, which was also in the boat, followed Dan into the water and sank. Fred managed to hang on in the canoe, swinging it off toward the tide pool and scrambling safely to shore.

Jim and I watched in horror as Dan floundered in the center of the whirlpool. He had three minutes, we were thinking. Fred was thinking, too, seeing his childhood friend listless in the freezing water. Dan called out, "I can't move."

Fred sprang into action, grabbing a large six-foot-long tree limb he found on the ground. He extended it out toward Dan. It was barely long enough to reach Dan's shoulder so Fred could nudge it. That caused just enough sensation in Dan's rapidly freezing body for him to grab hold of the limb, which enabled Fred to pull him ashore.

Relieved to see Dan safely ashore, Jim and I then refocused on our plight. Having just witnessed Dan nearly drown in the whirlpool we had to cross, our task seemed much more daunting.

I put my soaked, wet boot back on. Jim and I each took a deep breath and went for it. We had no recourse other than to guide the canoe at an angle directly into the eye of the whirlpool, which immediately spun the boat full-circle and directed it straight toward the waterfall. Jim, at the rear of the boat, hastily cast the long rope tied to the bow over to Fred, standing onshore. Fred was able to pull us in just as I got a bird's-eye view directly down the gut of the waterfall. Another couple of seconds and we would have tumbled over.

It took several hours to thaw Dan out with a makeshift bonfire. Jim lost everything in his pack that we never recovered from the river. We realized how lucky we were that Jim's pack was the only thing we lost. Our Truckee River adventure was over.

————————◆◆◆————————

You'd think the Truckee River experience would be enough for us to swear off ever coming near a river rapid again. But you wouldn't be Dan if you thought like that.

Dan was only encouraged to try again. Only this time, he built his own boat. He built a two-man kayak, all from scratch, layer by layer with fiberglass, and painted it dark green. Then he and I launched a series of river trips over the next decade in quest of perfecting the river rapid experience. This was Dan's and my deal together, a two-man kayak for the two of us. Each trip over the years had varying degrees of success.

We utilized my Ford camper van and little Honda 90 motor scooter to carry out logistics for our river trips. Committing to a goal of kayaking about five miles downstream per day, we dropped off the motor scooter at each day's designated stop. We drove the van carrying the kayak back to our planned starting point, then kayaked down the river all day to where we left the motor scooter. Then I rode the scooter back to get the van, loaded the scooter into the van, and drove the van back to where we ended up on the river. Camping overnight, we'd repeat the same pattern each day.

Our first river adventure was on the Merced River, just below where it flowed out of Yosemite Park. We went in summertime, when it was much warmer than it had been for our doomed Truckee trip. But it was also a drought year, and the river was running very low. We had to do a lot of "tracking" — manually carry the boat through water because it was too shallow to paddle through.

Bad luck prematurely ended that trip. Wearing simple deck shoes, I slipped on a rock while we were walking the boat through shallow water and suffered a large, jagged cut just above my ankle. I was thinking I could patch it up and plug on, but Dan made the call after inspecting the cut, which was deep enough to require stitches. "We're done," he said.

The next trip was on the American River, which traversed through California's gold country. We covered a considerable distance on the river, particularly through a mellow stretch backed up by a dam that turned it into a virtual lake. That was an arduous task to paddle without any momentum from the river current to carry us along.

We got our fair share of rapids action further downstream -- a little more than we bargained for. In one wild stretch the boat flipped over and we were thrown overboard, hanging onto the kayak for dear life as the river carried us head-on into thorny branches of river bush that poked like knives. In the course of being flipped out of the boat, Dan alertly grabbed our daypack, which contained the van and scooter keys, saving it from sinking to the bottom as a sacrificial offering to the river.

On our next trip we finally found the ideal river, the Eel River. The Eel, the only river in California that flows downstream in a northern direction, starts in Humboldt County, redwood forest territory, and winds up emptying into the Pacific at Eureka, in the northern tip of the state.

The Eel was a perfect match for our relative novice skillset and the vessel carrying us, which weighed a lot more than a typical one-person kayak. The Eel had long mellow stretches that carried us at a leisurely pace with minimal effort, and an occasional adrenaline-pumping rapid patch here and there to satisfy our thrill quotient without tossing us out of the boat.

The Eel turned out to be so ideal that we went back for an encore trip, which was easily our most memorable river trip of all, notably because of the passenger we collected on our way downstream.

Dan and I were floating along through a peaceful, remote neighborhood peeking between the shadows of a splendid forest when we heard the shrill barking of a dog from shore. It was, I repeat, a dog, and Dan was never one to turn away from a dog in need, so he pointed us toward shore. We didn't have to look far — a red-haired Doberman pup, no more than four months old, was desperately trying to get our attention.

We parked the boat and made our introductions to the poor dog, whose visible ribcage was clearly a sign he hadn't eaten for days. His incessant barking also let us know how hungry he was. We offered him some of the food we had packed in our day pack, and he wolfed it down as fast we could wave it in front of his frantic nose.

He had a noticeable collar line around his neck, so we knew he probably belonged to somebody. There were a cluster of homes nearby, so we gathered him up and knocked on a few doors nearby in search of his owner. No one claimed him.

"I guess you're coming with us," Dan told him.

The pooch was all too willing to jump into the boat as we pushed back into the water. It was all we could do to contain him. He was so excited, jumping up and down, rocking the boat from side to side. It was a good thing we were in calm waters for a good stretch to give us time to get him settled.

Food was the best way to settle him. Barking was his way to let us know he wanted more food. This was in the late 70s, when the craze over the first Star Wars movie and all of its popular characters was in full force. The adorable robot R2D2 came to mind when Dan, ever the punster, chose a name for our new passenger. Since the pup's two favorite things to do were bark and eat, Dan named him Bark Too Eat Too.

Bark Too Eat Too became the stowaway in our version of a Huck Finn river raft adventure. To say that he won our hearts would be an understatement. At first he was gratified to get his stomach filled, then he was gratified just to be with us.

Dan in two-man kayak he built for all of our river trips

Me and Bark Too Eat Too

That night, as Dan and I were settling in our tent, we could hear Bark Too Eat Too playfully growling away. We opened the tent flaps and shined a flashlight out to see what he was fussing over. The light caught him in the act of vigorously chewing on one of our shoes that we had left outside the tent. We should have realized then Bark Too Eat Too was up to no good.

When we woke in the morning and climbed out of the tent, our shoes were missing. It took a half-hour search before we found them scattered about some 40 feet away in the bushes.

Bark Too Eat Too rode it out the rest of the way down the river, and that made the trip an unqualified success. When we packed up to return home, we returned to the neighborhood near where we picked him up, for one more search to find his owner, No luck. Now what do we do?

We had no choice but to take him home with us. At the time, we were both living in apartments that didn't allow dogs. But Dan figured he could temporarily house him in his Long Beach apartment until he found somebody who would give him a home.

On the drive home, it was obvious Bark Too Eat Too had never seen a freeway before. My camper van had a raised engine cover between the two front seats on which Bark Too Eat Too sat and gazed in wonderment at the flowing traffic in front of us and the blurred landscape on the periphery.

When we arrived at Dan's apartment several hours later, Bark Too Eat Too was totally wired. Dan's apartment had two floors. When he opened the front door, Bark Too Eat Too eagerly dashed in and made his way up the stairs to the second floor while we tried in vain to keep up with him.

Dan had a balcony on the second floor with a mere two-foot high perimeter wall. Bark Too Eat Too made a beeline for the balcony, leaped right over that wall, and fell two stories down to the concrete below! With our mouths gaping open, we dashed back downstairs, expecting to find a broken pup, or worse.

Instead, Bark Too Eat Too was jumping up and down, happy to see us again. *Hey guys, got any more food for me?* I'm telling you, in that moment I wanted to keep him so bad. So did Dan.

It took Dan less than a week to find a great home for Bark Too Eat Too — somebody who lived on a ranch with lots of wide-open space. It was a perfect ending to my favorite river story.

———————◆•◆•◆•◆———————

Not every story has a perfect ending. This one is an addendum to the Truckee River Adventure. It's about Fred, Dan's best friend growing up.

Fred was a quirky little guy. I still picture his photo in our Hawthorne High senior yearbook, with his long, wavy, golden brown hair parted on one side, a big loop of hair dipping close to one eye. Come to think of it, he had hair very similar to mine. He was a member of our cross-country team, but he was never quite good enough to crack the varsity line-up, so he ran JVs.

Dan's friendship with Fred drifted after Fred got married at a fairly young age and moved to San Jose.

Fred was always a quiet, meditative, reserved type who displayed keen strokes of humor once in a while. I'm sure Dan made him laugh like he did me. Fred had some distinguishing interests, like his rose garden and mountain climbing.

Fred still had connections to LA, where his brother lived and ran a vacuum repair business. Rich B. worked briefly for Fred's brother.

When the phone rang and I answered, I could tell right away by the tone of Rich's voice that he had bad news. Rich was always very direct, so he got straight to the point.

"Chic, I've got some bad news. Fred... is dead. I found out yesterday from his brother."

"Oh my god!" I exclaimed. I was numb.

"The way he died — you're not going to believe this, Chic — he fell off a cliff in Yosemite while mountain climbing."

"Jesuz!" Trying to conjure up an image of Fred falling off a cliff in Yosemite was almost inconceivable. Instead, my thoughts turned to Dan, who was living in Washington state at the time. "I... I've got to call and tell Dan."

"Yeah, Chic. I don't envy you having to make that call."

It was the hardest phone call I've ever had to make. I knew what a "best" friendship with Dan felt like, and he had that with Fred when they were growing up. He did not take the news well at all.

I was calling him every night for at least a week to console him. We talked about the Truckee trip, and how Fred saved him from freezing in that whirlpool.

"I'm alive today because of Fred," Dan said. Fred was only in his early 30's, too young to die.

The follow-up calls from Dan kept coming, with more information on Fred's death that he was getting from Fred's widow, with whom Dan had been in constant contact. Fred was climbing on the face of Yosemite's famous Half Dome, with an expedition group of eight. He was chained to another climber, who was climbing about 10 feet directly above Fred. Fred's partner lost his grip and fell directly onto Fred, knocking him loose from the rock.

"Between the two of them, they had four safety ties in place that, had any one of them worked, should have saved them," Dan intoned over the phone. "All four of the safety ties gave way. They fell 800 feet."

Listening to Dan's description brought chills to my spine. I was trying to picture Fred floating downward, with his long wavy hair that resembled mine blowing in the breeze.

"Fuck it, when it's your time to go, it's time to go," Dan declared.

Then he softened. "I imagine Fred was at peace when he was going down," he said. "He just closed his eyes and waited 'til he hit bottom."

"Going down" and "hit bottom" could be interpretive phrases for someone losing their grip on life, but I'm sure Dan was aiming for irony.

Dan went to the funeral in San Jose. He stayed there for a couple weeks comforting Fred's widow, helping her sort through what Fred left behind.

I made a trip up to Washington shortly after Dan had returned home from the funeral, to try to give him comfort in the face of this horrible tragedy.

What I remember most about that particular visit was Dan holding up a soiled, bright Irish green tank top that he kept to show me. It obviously held great significance for Dan.

"This is what Fred was wearing when…" he stopped in midsentence, but I completed the thought.

CHAPTER 7
Beginnings and Endings

I was only 22 when I married Dorrean. She was only 20. We were too young to be getting married. We were literally at a breaking point in our relationship when we decided marriage was the best thing to try to save it. Here's some advice to any young couples in a similar situation — marriage doesn't magically solve relationship problems.

But we were young and we had our whole lives ahead of us. I was a few months away from graduating from Cal State Fullerton with my BA in English, ready to take on the world. Dorrean had her part-time job at a bank.

We got married in January, 1976, and waited until I graduated in June to embark on an ambitious honeymoon trip — a month-long drive crisscrossing the country in my Ford camper van. The van was equipped for just such a trip. It had a full-sized double bed in the back that was easily disassembled, or could be reassembled into a dinette table with cushioned seats on either side. It had a full sink with water tank, and a gas stove that folded out from the side door. The interior was fully carpeted and fully paneled with shellacked birch wood. It had an auxiliary gas tank that could hold an extra 20 gallons of fuel along with the main tank with the same capacity.

We managed to get all the way to… Bellflower, 10 whole miles, before the van started acting up. It was fine when the highway was flat or going downhill, but on uphill climbs it would sputter, chug along, and lose speed. It was very disconcerting.

It was just the start of a rocky road trip, metaphorically speaking.

We stopped in Las Vegas for one night. I wound up $1 on the plus side after hours playing at the blackjack table. I was a winner!

Then we continued to our first planned extended stop — a couple of days in Aspen, Colorado, to visit my sister. Ascending into the Rockies, the van really struggled. Our goal was to make it to Aspen, where we hoped Pam could recommend a good mechanic. Pulling into Aspen, we wandered for five hours to find the trailer park Pam was living in because knucklehead here didn't think to get her phone number from Mom.

We finally found Pam, and her girlfriend Linda. By girlfriend, I mean they were romantically involved. This was a revelation for me, finding out my sister was… gay? Or was she? Because for years she had a boyfriend named Louis, with whom she lived for a year in Connecticut, before winding up in Aspen. She and Louis parted ways because, yes, it turned out he was gay. It was all very confusing, and I don't know if that experience had anything to do with Pam seeking comfort in the arms of Linda. But Linda was very nurturing, and presumably very good for Pam at this point in her life.

Pam seemed happy in Aspen, playing on a softball team, working at a ski lodge, and studying at the Aspen School of Music. We had a lovely visit with her and managed not to catch the infectious mononucleosis she had. Pam had enough energy to do some hiking with us. She showed us the three beautiful, snow-capped Maroon Bells mountain peaks that cast maroon hues off the sun's reflections. She showed us Snowmass Village, where she was working. We ate dinner at Little Annie's with Pam's rowdy softball teammates, patronizing the business that sponsored the team.

When we departed Aspen, we thought we had had our van problem solved by a mechanic Pam recommended. He replaced the plugs, points, condenser, and rotor.

But as we headed up Independence Pass at a maximum speed of 15 miles an hour, it was obvious the car problems had not been solved. The car's woes somewhat spoiled our enjoyment of the stunning views from the top of the Pass, where it felt like we were on top of the world as we stood on snow-covered ground in June.

We didn't make it nearly as far as we intended that day, our car problems forcing us to pull into a gas station in Georgetown, Colorado., a tiny, four-gas station town outside of Denver. The lone repairman at the gas station diagnosed the problem as a faulty fuel pump, but he wasn't able to order the part until the following morning. We had no choice but to stay overnight in the station's parking lot.

Surprise! The fuel pump didn't solve the problem. We chugged into Denver, this time pulling into a Ford dealership. Their assessment revealed a problem with the carburetor, which was clogged up from sediment that had collected at the bottom of the auxiliary tank. Evidently, about a quarter-gallon of old gas had been festering in the tank forever because I never had used the auxiliary tank before this trip.

We spent the day watching a movie and going bowling in Denver while the car was being fixed.

We decided to drive through the night to make up for lost time. We were doing OK for a while, even surviving a spectacular lightning storm while driving through Nebraska. But at 3 a.m. we heard loud, intermittent thumping noises coming from the rear of the van. We stopped for a short rest about 20 miles outside Lincoln, Nebraska. When we resumed driving the thumping grew louder and more persistent.

I stopped, got out, and discovered the tread on one of the rear tires had peeled off —we were literally burning rubber on the highway— so we had to limp into Lincoln to buy a new tire. The salesman convinced us that at least two other tires were in bad shape, so we bought three new tires. They added a front end alignment for good measure.

Getting the hell out of Lincoln with all its downtown road construction and one-way streets was a bitch. I nearly had a nervous breakdown. But we finally escaped, made good time through hot and windy Iowa, cruised over the Mississippi River sometime in the night and made it to Illinois by 1 a.m. We found a campsite where we were able to take showers, and stayed overnight there.

The terrain turned greener, with more rolling hills, as we rolled into Ohio. The rolling got bumpy again as the remaining old tire blew, which meant buying another new tire in Akron. But we managed to cover more than 600 miles that day, winding up at a motel in Dubois, Pennsylvania.

The next day took us through the beautiful Allegheny Mountains of Pennsylvania with their wide variety of green trees and endless fields of green grass. We were headed for Philadelphia, where Dorrean's grandmother lived. It took some doing to find her, driving through neighborhoods that looked hapless and hopeless. We had an address but needed to stop to ask a cop for directions. We finally found her grandmother among a row of old, brick two-story homes. But inside her cramped abode, she lived comfortably among her ornate furniture and array of ceramic knick-knacks.

The next day Dorr's cousin Buddy and wife Linda played tourist guides for us, taking us to Washington's Crossing at the Delaware River. We also bought one more new tire for a spare, after I wired my mother to send us some much-needed money.

Our second day in Philly was spent visiting Independence Hall, the Liberty Bell, and Betsy Ross's home with Dorr's grandmother. It was 1976, so it felt especially apropos to visit these landmark sites in honor of our country's bicentennial celebration. The heightened activity for the occasion was a bit overwhelming.

It also felt apropos to gorge on a fantastic turkey dinner at the home of Dorrean's Uncle Bud and his wife. I was amused by Uncle Bud's accent; "piano" would come out as "pie-ann-ah."

The following day Dorr and I, accompanied by Buddy's 15-year-old brother Bobby, decided to take a bus into New York City. We fell behind schedule by missing the 9 a.m. bus by a few minutes — in perfect Perkins fashion. The time lost eventually cost us time to catch the boat ride out to the Statue of Liberty. But we did take in Rockefeller Center, watched the movie musical "1776" at Radio City Music Hall, and took in the spectacular view of three different states from the top of the Empire State Building. It was a delightful day.

We headed for Washington, D.C., the next day, driving through five states— Pennsylvania, New Jersey, Delaware, Maryland, and Virginia. We passed through "Balteemore," as Uncle Bud pronounced it.

In D.C. we stayed at the home of my friend Paul, who I had known since high school. Paul was a skinny little guy when I knew him during our pick-up basketball games. He had a late growth spurt and now stood 6 feet tall, towering three inches taller than me.

Paul was serving in the Army. He drew the plum assignment of serving on the White House Communications Agency directly within the White House. Lucky for us. That got us an insider's tour of President Ford's White House. We also took in the Smithsonian, the Washington Monument, and the Lincoln and Jefferson memorials with Paul as our personal guide.

Paul allowed us into the Old Executive Building where he worked. He got us a pass to Betty Ford's "open house" to the White House gardens. He let us make some long-distance calls free-of-charge at his office, which enabled me to call my Great Aunt Betty, who we planned to visit, along with my Aunt Bee, in Cincinnati. Aunt Betty was my late grandfather's sister, and Aunt Bee was my grandfather's widow.

The drive to Cincinnati landed us in the middle of vicious rain storms in Pennsylvania and West Virginia. The rains subsided by the time we hit Cincinnati at 2 a.m. After futilely searching for Aunt Bee's house, we had to call her at 2:45 a.m. We slept well at her place after traveling 520 drenched miles.

Both my aunts were relics from a bygone era. Both of their homes were filled with antique furniture and lots of ceramics and Rookwood china pieces passed down from mothers, uncles, great grandfathers, and second cousins of years gone by.

Dorrean with Aunt Bee and Aunt Betty with Cincinnati skyline in background

Dorrean and Paul in front of White House fountain in front lawn

Together, they enthusiastically showed us around town, their tour including 35 different views of the Ohio River. Aunt Betty said that Ohioans were just as proud of the Ohio River as Californians were of the Pacific Ocean.

Aunt Bee was a patron of the Cincinnati Art Museum, which we visited, and a longtime member of the University Club, where we had a robust dinner one night. An old black waiter named Roscoe who served us knew my grandfather way back when. "He used to sit over there and play bridge every day for lunch," he told me.

Aunt Bee and Betty took us to the cemetery where my grandfather's gravesite was located. It was a large family plot, with lots of Ebersoles buried there, descendants of my middle namesake. Bee pointed out the spot next to my grandfather's that was reserved for her.

My Great Aunt Betty was someone to behold. Well into her 80s, she had the energy of someone half her age. She was a proud woman, and she told us the story of how she was still teaching kindergarten well into her 70s, and still *walking* the mile to and from the school in which she taught. She proudly heralded her membership in the Daughters of The American Revolution, which was my cue not to bring up any politics with her.

Then, Aunt Betty tipped her hand as to why she was always so perky. "My doctor prescribed these little white pills to give me energy," she said perkily. "They made me feel so good that I kept taking them even though my doctor told me to stop years ago because supposedly they weren't so good for my heart. The only bad thing that I could tell is that I have trouble sleeping at night!"

Dorrean and I looked knowingly at each other with the realization that my Great Aunt Betty had an amphetamine habit and didn't know it. Wonder how that would fly with her fellow Daughters of the American Revolution?

We finally pulled away from dear Aunt Bee and Aunt Betty, crossing a bridge for our 36th view of the Ohio River before leaving town.

We made it to Wisconsin on my birthday (June 23), the 18th day into our trip. We took a boat ride in the Wisconsin Dells that featured interesting rock formations with line-patterned limestone and sandstone along the river route. We crossed the Mississippi River into Minnesota, and made it to South Dakota by nightfall.

The following day featured a slight detour to take in the Badlands National Monument, which offered spectacular views of wind- and water-eroded rock. Closing in on Mount Rushmore, we passed through the Black Hills National Forest, characterized by beautiful dark green trees set off by rich red soil.

Mount Rushmore was everything the standard postcards promised with the magnificent stone faces of Washington, Jefferson, Teddy Roosevelt, and Lincoln. From afar, I found myself wishing I could climb over Washington's nose or across Roosevelt's mustache to get a clearer sense of their dimension.

Making our way toward Yellowstone National Park, we had to climb 8,000 feet over Granite Pass to the eastern slopes of the Rocky Mountains. We found a campsite in Yellowstone, where we pitched a tent to sleep in on a near-freezing night. Dorrean woke up the next morning with a cold.

That didn't stop us from driving a 100-mile loop through Yellowstone on a crisp, beautifully clear day. Magical sites abounded — Yellowstone Lake with majestic snow-capped mountains in the background; a grazing mother moose and her calf alongside the road; steamy, colorful hot springs emitting sharp light blues for the deeper springs, murky yellow, orange, beige and brown for the muddy run- offs, light green where the run-offs ran into the dark blue lake, and purple flowers popping up everywhere; the famous Old Faithful geyser, shooting off a 40-foot sprout after a 10-minute wait; a couple of bison napping in the fields.

And, finally, breathtaking Yellowstone Grand Canyon and the Lower and Upper Falls, viewed from Inspiration Point. I nearly killed off my new bride by making her hike down a narrow, steep trail for a closer view of the Lower Falls. We drove to another spot along the Canyon just above the Upper Falls, where we could feel the incredible force of the water crashing at the bottom.

We continued on through Montana, Idaho (Coeur d' Alene was pretty), and arid western Washington on the way to the Seattle area. We stayed at the home of my high-school "Half-Sis," Teri, her husband Kirk, and their 13-month-old daughter Katie. They were managing a church home where four elderly residents lived. Teri still had her giggly personality that I adored, with some motherhood maturity in the mix. We had been keeping up a letter correspondence since high school.

Then we ventured on to remote Fox Island off the Puget Sound, near Gig Harbor, where we hooked up with my dear friend Rich W., from the high school cross-country team. He lived with his brother Bob, wife Linda, and young daughter Mandy in an utterly cute white house on a grassy knoll on the edge of water.

Rich and I spent a lot of time playing chess and talking 'til 3 a.m. one night, mostly about his dreams for Bob and Linda's bluegrass country band and their newly-released single that was getting some local radio play. He also talked about his hopes and dreams, which really solidified our long-lasting friendship.

Our last few days were spent driving down the Pacific coast, through the foggy Oregon coastline, across the Golden Gate Bridge into San Francisco, and our last night of the long trip in Montecito, at my grandmother Mimi's house. After 30 days on the road together, our nerves must have been frayed, because Dorrean and I got into our worst fight on the whole trip that night.

But we made it back home. The time had come to start living real life.

————————◆————————

I had built a fairly decent resume for a newspaper job, having spent a couple of years as a stringer covering sports for a couple of local papers, along with my extensive newspaper experience in high school and college.

So, I was ecstatic when I got hired as a copy clerk at the LA Herald-Examiner in the fall of 1976. My foot was in the door for the start of a real newspaper career. The part about getting a job in the field I studied in college was the only part I got right in the answer I had given my father on what I was going to do with the rest of my life.

The pay was horrible but the experience was invaluable. I was working in a real living, breathing newsroom, housed in a historic building on the gritty corner of 11th and Broadway in downtown LA. The Her-Ex was a Hearst family-owned paper, and the Her-Ex building was a wonderful relic designed and built in the early 1900's with some of the same design flairs as the much more famous Hearst Castle. The four-story building was pink, with a blue-and-yellow-checkered, circular dome tower and a lookout deck on the top floor.

The walls were distinguished by sweeping 20-foot tall arches that had once been glass windows, until they were paved over with concrete during the never-ending strike that had crippled the paper from its heyday in the mid-1960s, when it topped the LA Times in circulation. The glass was taken out because strikers were tossing rocks through it. When I was hired in '76, nine years after the start of the strike that never officially ended, the paper's circulation had shrunk to about 360,000, a steep decline from its peak of nearly 900,000.

I was in awe when I first stepped into the lobby, which resembled that of a museum. Any sound or voice in the lobby echoed up to the high ceiling that extended to the top of the median floor between the lobby level and the newsroom. A stairway that used to extend all the way up to the newsroom dead-ended into a brick wall, leading to nowhere. It was symbolic of the paper's destiny. The only way up to the newsroom from the lobby was in an ancient elevator that creaked and groaned on every painful trip upward and gave the impression it would stop in mid-flight between floors at any time. Which it did on a few occasions.

Historic Herald Examiner building at 11th and Broadway in downtown LA

I was part of a young, seven-person copy clerk staff led by a long-haired, prematurely-balding young man named Dean. We operated out of a tiny cubicle on the newsroom floor. An everlasting symbol of our newsroom status was represented by a dead, three-inch-long cockroach mounted on the inner wall of the clerk cubicle by super glue we used to stick multiple sheets of news copy together.

The copy clerks were the low-lives of a vibrant, irreverent newsroom headed by News Manager John Lindsey, who set the tone with his long blonde hair, beard, and the Hawaiian shirts that he wore daily. There was no pretense of formality or stuffy company dress code dictating "proper attire."

We were at the beck and call of News Editor Bill Ryan, an elf-like, bespectacled elderly man with thinning white hair and a mutton-chop beard. Ryan would shout out "Boy!" whenever he had hard copy or photos for us to run downstairs to the galley room where the pages were pasted up. I always wondered how the "Boy" proclamation went over with the one female on our staff.

One of our basic duties was to monitor the wire room, which housed six black boxes on three-foot-high stands. The black boxes spit out continuous strands of half-inch thick, yellow ribbons of paper tape with punched-out holes. The holes were code that converted to type for the news stories provided by the national wire services.

The yellow tape would fall to the floor and bundle up in a pile until we, the lowly clerks, came in and separated the individual stories, which were sequentially numbered on the tape. We had to tear off each individual tape whenever a new number popped up signifying the start of a different story. Then we spiked the separated pieces of tape onto Captain Hook-like spikes on the wall.

I think I was haunted by that yellow tape. I experienced a dream that Dorrean had to tell me the next morning; she said that I jumped out of bed and dashed to the bicycle we had standing at the foot of our bed. It had a basket attached to the front handlebar. According to Dorrean, I was frantically acting as if I was repeatedly pulling something out of the basket, shouting, "Gotta get the tapes! Gotta get the tapes!"

Over the years I've frightened, annoyed, terrified, or caused grave concern for various wives and girlfriends with whom I shared a bed because of dreams or nightmares that I acted out in my sleep. I rarely remembered what I did in the middle of the night, entirely reliant on my partner to describe my bizarre behavior the following morning. Poor Dorrean, unfortunately, was subjected to too many of these episodes triggered by the stress of my job. On one occasion I woke her up in the middle the night pulling on her leg at the foot of the bed. That annoyed the hell out of her.

Copy clerk duties in the Her-Ex wire room also included monitoring a half-dozen typewriter machines that typed out stories on carbon-copy paper with corresponding numbers matching those on the yellow tapes.

We bundled up and presented the wire stories to the news desk, which selected which ones would run in the next day's editions. Responding to the "Boy!' command, the clerks were handed corresponding rolled-up yellow tapes of those stories. We then carried the tapes over to a wall housing a long plastic vacuum tube, in which the tapes were deposited and channeled down a chute to a control room downstairs, where a prehistoric "computer" would convert the tape to newsprint columns for paste-up. Boy, I gotta admit, conjuring up that whole process sounds prehistoric.

Paste-up on page layouts in the galley room had replaced the old-fashioned hot type machines. Now we were venturing into the modern era of newspapers! Except this was still pre-desktop computer days, as reporters were still using typewriters to type out stories on double carbon-copy yellow paper. Typewriters... copy paper...yeah, I'm old enough to relate to these long-ago out-dated tools of the trade.

Early on, I had to pay my penance by working the graveyard shift for a couple of months. The newsroom was empty except for myself and the overnight news desk guy, Jim Brezina. Jim was a grizzled old-timer who spent most of the time asleep at his desk, with frequent gulps from the bottle of vodka I saw him withdraw from his desk cabinet; he didn't bother to hide it.

With Jim passed out most of the time, I had the run of the place. Curiosity drew me to the large desk of one of the top news editors, Tom Cates, another old-timer. His desktop was covered by a large glass plate that anchored a dozen notes and business cards for easy reference. One note, slightly grimy by age, caught my eye. It stated:

"If anybody calls saying they are holding Patty Hearst, ask them these questions:

1. *What is Patty's mother's maiden name?*

2. *What is the name of Patty's grandmother's cat?*
3. *What is the name of Patty's favorite doll as a child?"*

It was barely two years after Patty Hearst's infamous kidnapping by the left-wing terrorist group Symbionese Liberation Party had taken place, and just over a year since her release. Her legal problems over her alleged involvement in the group's series of bank robberies were still very much in play, so the note still held significant relevance. The Her-Ex was a Hearst paper and calls related to her abduction were coming in to our office.

The graveyard shift had a lot of down time, other than the requisite "gotta get the tapes" routine in the wire room every 20 minutes or so. I took advantage of the idle time by working on my great American novel, "Last of The Orange Groves." That kept me sufficiently energized throughout the shift that ended at 6 am.

———————◆———————

My 11 months as a copy clerk at the Her-Ex were heady times. While the copy clerk job itself wasn't all that inspiring, I was offered some actual writing opportunities that were absolutely golden and probably would never happen in today's corporate-heavy atmosphere. The opportunities presented me also were undeniably created in part because the paper was in decline. There was no sense of elitism in the newsroom that would lead to any animosity toward a young upstart like me, giving me a chance to show my chops.

The first chance came from an unlikely source — the entertainment department. Bob, the entertainment editor, was easily the biggest stoner in the entire newsroom. He was 30ish, with sleepy eyes, long, wavy brown hair over the ears, a big nose, and he wore glasses. Bob must have detected my eagerness to please when he started handing out assignments to me. These weren't bottom-of-the barrel stories nobody else wanted; these were interviews with big-name stars in the music industry.

The very first assignment was a helluva starter -- Kenny Rogers. He had just broken off from the band First Edition and his first solo single, "Lucille," had become a huge hit. His agenda for the interview obviously was to promote his first solo album.

His publicist arranged for me to interview Kenny in the waiting room — officially called the Green Room because the walls were painted green — before he was to appear on "The Merv Griffin Show," a popular daytime TV talk show in its day.

Kenny was affable and friendly during the interview; I was nervous. Kenny's friendliness didn't end with the interview. He was so gracious that he gave me a free pass to see him perform live at the Palamino Club in the San Fernando Valley the following week, and then invited me to a post-concert, post-midnight party at his Brentwood home that same night.

The Brentwood home Kenny shared with his then-wife Marianne was over-the-top in its extravagance. There was no hesitation in showing off its luxury with its chandeliers, golden-paneled walls, and assorted other shiny objects.

I hung out at the top of the three-tiered backyard, where a couple of chefs were preparing omelettes for guests, with a variety of ingredients to choose from. My attention was immediately drawn to the backyard pond housing a huge school of large koi fish; there had to be at least 100 fish swimming around. I was silently watching the fish leisurely float by, then stuck my hand just below the surface of the water where one of the fish puckered up and laid a gentle smooch on my palm.

"Her name is Cecelia," I heard a woman's voice with a distinctive southern drawl intone behind me. I turned around to see a beautiful, statuesque woman with wavy, shoulder-length blonde hair standing before me.

"Hi! I'm Marianne," she said in a very friendly voice. I instantly realized she was the lady of the house.

"Hi, I'm Chic Perkins from the Herald-Examiner."

"Oh, you wrote that very nice story on Kenny! Kenny was very pleased."

"He made it easy for me. He was easy to talk to."

"Oh, that's Kenny alright. He has no problem talking about himself."

She laughed, so I did, too.

"So, are you enjoying the party? Did you help yourself to an omelette?"

"Yes, ma'am. It was excellent." I turned my gaze back to the fish. "So, do you have names for all the fish here?" I asked.

"Oh, yes. See that big fat gray one?" she said, pointing. "We call that one Kenny."

I laughed again.

Marianne excused herself to circulate among other guests. But she had made me feel at ease and welcome. I later learned that she was an ensemble cast member on the TV show "Hee-Haw." I tuned in on the show once and recognized her popping up out of a fake cornfield on stage reciting corny jokes.

Bob followed up by giving me several interviews over the next six months. Frankie Vallee was another big assignment. He was launching another comeback with four new Four Seasons, and his latest hit, "December, 1963 (Oh What A Night)" was getting a lot of radio play.

I also interviewed John Lodge of the Moody Blues, Thelma Houston (who looked like she just crawled out of bed for the interview), Melvin Franklin of the Temptations (a phone interview in which his deep bass voice was unmistakable), William King of The Commodores, Gene Clark of The Byrds, and Blondie Chaplin, who was a protege of Brian Wilson of The Beach Boys on their big hit, "Sail On Sailor."

———————◆————————

During my copy clerk days, I also ingratiated myself to the sports department by covering high school football and basketball games — on my own time — that netted byline stories in the paper. I teamed up with another copy clerk, John Sevano, on these assignments.

John was a burly guy and a big character who filled the room and attracted attention to himself just from the several gold chains he wore around his neck. He got hired on charm alone, because he had no college degree, and the charm card was played to the max with Larry Stewart, the easily impressionable Assistant Sports Editor who was handing us the assignments. John and I were consciously focusing all this hard work on the singular goal of getting promoted into the sports department.

The high school basketball games customarily took place in primarily black neighborhoods of LA, where racial tensions were always high. There were a few games I covered where I was one of only a handful of white people in attendance. I was conscious of that but not intimidated by it.

I'll never forget one game I covered at Crenshaw High. I was sitting at the press table at court side. It was an intense game between two schools that were bitter rivals. The fans for each school sat on opposite ends of the court. The predominantly Black crowd was very loud and boisterous.

Suddenly, near the end of the game, the lights went out, plunging the entire gym into darkness. Immediately, screams rang out from both sides and commotion reigned as people were frantically trying to find the exits. My heart was racing as I felt fleeing shadow figures run precariously close to me. The only thing I could think of to protect myself was to jump up and stand on the press table to evade the flow of human traffic.

A die-hard journalist supposedly accepts the risks involved in pursuit of a story. I don't know if this incident earned my stripes in the sports department. I think John's BS with Larry had more impact, to tell you the truth. But all the hard work we put in paid off, as John and I were simultaneously promoted into the sports department.

John and I were beside ourselves when we were given the news.

"Can you believe it?!" John exclaimed. "We're actually going to get paid to watch sports and write about it!"

It was darn near hard to believe. We were joining a sports staff that was truly legendary — columnists Melvin Durslag, Doug Krikorian and Diane K. Shah, NFL writers Jack Disney and John Czarnecki, baseball writers Ken Gurnick and Tom Singer, NBA writers Lyle Spencer and Rich Levin, college sports writer Bob Keisser, hockey writer Rick Sadowski, horse racing writer ("Professor") Gordon Jones, boxing writer John Beyrooty, and the incomparable Allan Malamud, who covered everything.

———————◆———————

Allan Malamud was Sports Editor of the Her-Ex at the time of my promotion. Winning over Assistant Sports Editor Larry Stewart was one thing, Allan was quite another. Allan was one of the most respected L.A. sports columnists in his day. His succinct, craftily-written Notes On a Scoreboard column was one of the most widely read sports columns in LA throughout the 70s and 80s. He was a master of his craft.

Personality-wise, he was difficult to get to know. Deep down, Allan was a shy man. I never knew him to be in a relationship of any kind with a woman. Sports was his whole life. He was an odd-looking man, overweight, with a round face enveloped by kinky, Afro-like black hair that wasn't a pleasant look on an overweight white guy. He was constantly battling with his weight; he had eating problems. His Achilles heel was chocolate cake; he couldn't resist a slice of chocolate cake, or two. A legendary chocolate cake story related to Allan will appear in a later chapter.

There was no one on the sport staff whose approval I wanted more than Allan's. He usually kept his feelings to himself, and his thoughts about you. But inexplicably, Allan offered me the motorsports beat within a couple weeks of being promoted. I'm guessing the only reason why he offered me that opportunity was because he saw me carrying a motorcycle helmet into the office every day. Something he said to me made me believe he thought I knew something about cars and engines. I knew nothing about cars. It was the helmet.

It was an opening for the taking and I jumped at it. The person I was replacing as our de facto motorsports writer at the time was a woman in the entertainment department; I think she was some kind of "groupie" who liked to hang out with race car drivers.

Allan evidently sought a change, and he was giving me a crack at it, which I ultimately found rather ironic. Here I was, a true sports nut who enjoyed playing just about any sport you could think of. But I distinctly recalled watching an auto race on TV as a kid, scared out of my wits at the speeds the cars were going, and thinking, "There's no way I'm ever trying auto racing." Now, as a matter of fate, I was covering auto racing.

My first assignment was the California 500, a big Indy car event at Ontario Motor Speedway. I had no time to prepare. I mean, Allan offered me the motorsports beat one day, qualifying for the race was the very next day. I knew nothing about auto racing.

Allan offered me a great tip — talk to Deke Houlgate. He was the public relations director for Riverside International Raceway and used to free-lance for the Her-Ex covering motorsports events. I gave Deke a call right away and spent a good hour on the phone with him. He was the nicest guy and gave me a quick-study course on the basics of auto racing, and more specifically Indy car racing.

From then on, I immersed myself in the beat, made myself a student of the sport. I had a weekly motorsports column to share and expand on what I was learning. I learned from my subjects and tried explaining what I learned in layman's terms in my columns. That first weekend at the California 500, I covered the 500-mile race that Johnny Rutherford won. Deke was there in the press box to hold my hand.

My weekly column, which ran with a little boxed photo of me, forced me to come up with topics to write about every week. That never seemed to be a problem. It started with Ben Foote, the publicist for Ascot Park in Gardena, which put on racing events almost every Friday, Saturday, and Sunday night with everything from sprint cars and midgets to figure-eight track and destruction derby stock cars. Ben had this deep, gravelly voice that was instantly recognized over the phone by everybody on the sports desk — "May I speak with Chic Perkins, please." He filled me in every week on his venue's events and pitched me interviews with local drivers anytime I needed a column idea. I don't know what I would have done without Ben in the pursuit of filling out 12 years of weekly motorsports columns.

I was given virtually carte blanche control of my column. I wrote on both national and local topics in the motorsports world.

I was allowed to cover a number of major motorsports events throughout the country, starting with the granddaddy event of them all, the Indianapolis 500 every Memorial Day Weekend. A few years into the beat I was sent off to Daytona Beach, Fla., to cover NASCAR's premier season-opening event, the Daytona 500. The Long Beach Grand Prix, which started as a Formula One event in the late 70s and then switched to Indy cars in the mid-1980s, was a much-heralded event on my calendar every season. Riverside International Raceway hosted several big races, including the Good Ol' NASCAR boys, the Six Hours of Riverside Endurance Race for Grand Prix sports cars, and Mickey Thompson's off-road extravaganza. Mike Goodwin introduced motocross to enclosed stadiums at both the LA Coliseum and Anaheim Stadium and the races became so popular they were must-cover assignments. Pomona Raceway was the site of the National Hot Rod Association's (NHRA) season-opening Winternationals and season-ending World Finals for nitromethane-burning, eardrum-shattering dragsters.

There was no shortage of publicists in the sport who made sure they knew me — wining and dining me — to gain publicity for their respective drivers and teams and, most importantly, team sponsors. I formed memorable friendships with the irreverent NHRA press relations duo of Steve Earwood and Dave Densmore, whom I have more to say about later. Likewise, Penny Nicolai, Mickey Thompson's class-act, chain-smoking media liaison, became a dear friend and confidante with whom I shared sordid details of my love life. I harbored a secret crush (which put me in crowded company with all other LA male motorsports writers) on Penny's attractive partner, Nancy Wager. I openly flirted with the adorable Nancy Hubbell, a blonde, blue-eyed beauty with the irresistible smile. Tom Blattler, Hank Ives, Susie Arnold, Joe Sherk, and of course, Deke Houlgate, were just a few other notable names in the motorsports press relations field whom I heavily leaned on.

Motorsports wasn't in the same league as the major stick-and-ball beats for football, baseball and basketball. But if any of my co-workers had had any idea how much fun I was having, they would have been envious.

I had gained some notoriety as one of the Big Five among LA motorsport writers. Shav Glick of the LA Times was the undisputed king, but rounding out the top five were Tim Tuttle of the Orange County Register, Jim Short of the Riverside Press-Enterprise, Allen Wolfe of the Long Beach Press-Telegram, and me. I would be remiss if I neglected to add that Louis Brewster of the San Bernardino Sun outlasted all of us on the beat.

I also became a respected member of the American Auto Racing Writers and Broadcasters Association, which was presided over by the legendary flaming red-headed queen of Southern California motorsports journalism, Dusty Brandel.

———————◆◆◆◆◆———————

Corky's Bar will forever be linked to the legacy of the Her-Ex. They were separated only by the width of 11th Street, where both were located.

Corky's was a dark, dank bar owned and operated by a tiny, *tiny* Japanese woman named Betty. I'm pretty sure she adopted an American-sounding name to integrate into American society. Corky's was divided into two distinct rooms. The room nearest the entrance was where the Her-Ex gang hung out and generally dominated after-work hours. Off to the right of the entrance was a larger, darker room occupied by Japanese clientele, mostly older Japanese men, who tipped cash to mingle and slow-dance with scantily-clad young Japanese "hostesses." The dance music typically was familiar American pop songs that were crooned by Japanese singers in Japanese. You haven't lived until you've heard "Feelings" sung in Japanese. The Japanese music provided an odd mix with the 60s-70s rock and Motown songs the Her-Ex crowd cranked out of the front-room jukebox.

Working in sports wasn't all that glamorous. I worked nights and weekends. Seventy-five percent of the time I worked the night sports desk, editing copy, writing headlines and photo captions, compiling agate — box scores, standings, all the small-type stuff you see on the sports section's scoreboard page — and supervising the paste-up of pages in the galley room. The shift ended around midnight, and it was usually stress-packed trying to make deadline (which we frequently missed) getting all the pages "to bed" ready for print.

Corky's became the place to unwind after a stressful shift. Jay Christensen and Mark Gears were my two drinking buddies from the Her-Ex staff. Jay worked exclusively on the sports desk as a copy editor. Mark worked on the night news desk, and he was a big sports fan. Jay was a gentle, bearded, fair-haired Paul Bunyan-esque (6-foot-4, 260) figure of a man born and raised on an Iowa farm, but a true-blooded liberal politically with whom I felt a kindred spirit. Mark was a lean Midwesterner from Ohio with dark hair and a receding hairline, a pleasant face, and a warm, down-to-earth sense of humor.

Betty took inordinate care of we Three Amigos, often offering us free food like chicken wings and fried tempura veggies. She frequently kept the bar open way past closing time of 2 a.m. because a handful of the patrons — well, mostly Jay, Mark and I — weren't ready to go home.

Corky's had its share of regular patrons, none more prominent than a crusty old barfly named Henry, who presided over his own "Cheers"-like stage in his nearly permanent alcohol-induced blur. Jay, Mark and I befriended this funny little Black guy, who loved the attention we bestowed on him. Henry, who was 50ish, had a big patch of frizzy hair graying on the edges, one false eyeball that was slightly cocked to one side, and spoke with a scratchy, weary voice in a Southern accent. He had a meager job as a janitor at one of the downtown buildings nearby. We often talked about how much of his paltry paychecks he spent on booze at Corky's.

Whenever we entered Corky's after midnight, Henry would always be there. When he'd see us, he'd raise his glass and shout out, "Asante'!" in bravado fashion. With my longish light brown hair, he thought I resembled the actor Patrick Swayze, for some reason, so he'd great me with a gleeful "Pat Swayzee!"

Henry had this classic statement he often recited to sum up his existence: "I was once a super-stah, until I went astray, and fell into the gut-tah, where I remain."

Jay, Mark and I tried to get more detail out of him to explain how and why he fell from superstar to gutter status, but he'd only answer with another swallow of whatever he was drinking.

——————————+·•·◆·•·+——————————

As one of the new guys working on the night sports desk, I often got stuck with making the dinner run for the whole staff, which was generally a nightly routine.

We had a short list of favorite stops in the nearby downtown area that were iconic eateries in the LA scene — Langer's Deli on Alvarado, a classic Jewish deli, and Philippe's on Alameda, renowned for its French-dip sandwiches, to name a couple.

I've mentioned my belief in guardian angels before. I truly believe I had one looking over me on a dinner run one night.

I stopped at a liquor store for sodas on the way back to the office from Langer's. It was a dark, seedy part of town and I was driving my camper van. I had parked in a parking slot right next to the sidewalk, some 30 feet from the street corner. When I got out of my van, I noticed a young Black man with unkempt hair dressed in ragged clothes standing on the corner, closely watching me head for the liquor store entrance. I couldn't help notice his gaze and turned my head to lock in on him for a couple of beats as I strolled toward the store.

When I re-emerged from the store with a bag of sodas and made my way across the parking lot to my car, I noticed the young man suddenly break from the street corner, making a beeline for me. I got very nervous. Something instinctively told me he had some bad intent in mind.

I hastened my stride, eyeing the front door to my van as I walked with my back to this guy. I couldn't see him but I could feel his presence as he was closing in on me. My heart rate sped up as I briskly removed my car keys from my pants pocket and, all in one swift, sequential motion, inserted the door key, unlocked the door, opened the door, and jumped inside the van. I swear I could feel him breathing down my neck just before I jumped in.

When I returned to the office, I removed the suede jacket I was wearing and flung it on the back of my chair. That's when I noticed two distinct, thin, crisscross slices directly in the middle of the back of the jacket. I stared at the slices, thinking that they had to have been cut by a razor blade. Or maybe a knife sharp enough to make clean cuts that wouldn't fray the fabric.

Either way, the thought of that guy approaching me with a razor blade or a knife in his hand and slicing at my jacket just as I jumped in the van sent chills up my spine. What the hell would have happened if he had had a couple seconds more, or if I had fumbled with my car keys trying to unlock the door? With my back to him, I was defenseless.

Except for the Guardian Angel watching over me.

<hr />

The inordinate amount of time I spent at Corky's after work may have been one sign that my marriage was headed for a crash. Judging by my dubious marital record, it could be said that life as a sports writer can be hard on marriages.

Obviously, the work hours weren't conducive to domestic tranquility at home. Six months into my job on the sports desk, I was regularly taking calls from my lonely wife at home. As the routine progressed, the more lonely and unhappy she became. There were a few calls in which she broke down and cried, and I felt helpless trying to comfort her.

When we did have time to spend together, we often were in the company of my friends, which became an issue with Dorrean. She often complained that I was more interested in being with my friends than being with her, that we lacked common interests. There may have been some truth to that.

To make matters worse, I pursued interests that didn't involve her at all.

One was the bowling league the Gerke clan had recruited me

to join during my college years and continuing after Dorrean and I exchanged vows. The clan, all of whom were better bowlers than I, included all four Gerke brothers— Wayne, Doyle, Joel, and Bruce -- as well as their father, Spence. I will be forever grateful to Spence, the kind, quiet patriarch, for keeping my junkyard-destined Nova running all those years by doing car repairs and charging me nowhere near what a car repair shop would have charged. Bruce, the only Gerke brother who was younger than I (by one year), was my closest friend among the bunch. Bruce and his wife Shirley lived in the same apartment complex as Dorrean and I and we often socialized together.

My other sports hobby was baseball. I managed to re-live my childhood dream through a "D" League team organized by my Her-Ex colleague Bob Keisser. Our team was called the Grey Sox. Bob recruited John, Dean and me from the copy clerk staff. I primarily played shortstop and second base and was a better fielder than hitter.

So I encouraged Dorrean to pursue other interests with her friends, especially when I worked at night. It was only fair. She gradually started going out with her girlfriends, which helped.

I was no angel. I did cheat on her once. It happened one night when I accompanied John and Larry for a drink at a bar in Chinatown, which was about a mile away from the Her-Ex. Picking up women at bars never was my style. But on this night…

All three of us initiated a casual flirtation with a slightly older Hispanic woman who was sitting at the bar with a couple of girlfriends. She was intrigued when we told her we were sports writers. Ironically, when I told her my name was Chic, she claimed she was called Chic, too. I had been presented with an assortment of reactions to introducing myself as "Chic," but this was a new one for me. I don't know if she was putting one over on me or not, but that was the only name I knew her by. I think the name connection gave me the inside edge on John and Larry in the flirtation competition. When our eyes locked at one point, I knew the connection went beyond the name.

It finally came down to who was going to give her a ride back to her car, which was parked about 12 miles away in a plaza parking lot in Montebello. The clincher was when I told her I was riding a motorcycle — that sounded exciting to her.

So, she climbed aboard, despite the fact she was dressed in a short skirt and skimpy sweater. It was a chilly November night and I gave her my jacket, knowing she was going to need it. Then I froze my ass off on that ride to Montebello. It got so bad that my hands were shaking on the handlebars. The only elements that kept my senses intact were the warmth of her soft, supple breasts pressed against my back and the smell of her strong perfume.

It was after 2 a.m. when we got to where her car was parked. I had to take a pee right away, so I found a dark corner. I was shaking badly from the cold as my urine splattered on the ground and echoed conspicuously, as if it were being broadcast over loudspeakers. The next thing I knew headlights beamed on me. It was lucky my fly was open or else I might have peed in my pants because it was a cop car! I saw "Chic" talking to the cop, and whatever she told him, it was good enough to persuade him to drive off.

Then "Chic" suggested taking a short drive to a Winchell's Donuts for coffee. That sounded like a helluva idea, so I followed her to the donut shop. We climbed into her car, a tiny Chevy Vega, where we drank our coffee. Once we thawed out, we had sex in the crammed back seat. Then I rode my bike home, guilt rapidly creeping in, as I wondered if Dorrean would notice how late I was arriving home.

Why did I do it? Why did I cheat on Dorrean? Why is a young man who marries too young, who hasn't had much experience with women, not able to resist temptation when it's looking at him from just a barstool away?

I knew it couldn't go any further, though. I had lied to "Chic" when I told her I wasn't married. She called me a couple of nights later at work. She wanted to see me again, but the guilt in me forced me to tell her I didn't think that would be a good idea. I don't think Dorrean ever suspected. She never confronted me about that night.

Feeling guilty doesn't get me off the hook for what I did. But it did give me a renewed sense of appreciation for Dorrean over the next couple of months, and I attempted to express it by buying her flowers and writing a little poem for her in a card. These were the types of things I wasn't doing enough before then.

Too little, too late.

Dorrean announced that she and her girlfriends were planning a weekend ski trip in the local mountains. I had to work and had a Grey Sox game that weekend. So, I wholly encouraged Dorrean to go on the ski trip without me. Have fun with your girlfriends, I told her.

My whole life changed on that weekend. When Dorrean returned home, she solemnly told me she had met someone. A guy named Ernie. She just came right out and said it — she and Ernie fell in love. She was asking for a divorce. There was no debate about it. Her mind was made up.

———————◆•◆•◆•◆———————

I don't think I realized just how much in shock I was over Dorrean leaving me. It happened so suddenly, just bam! no warning. I was in a world of hurt.

The effect the separation had on me showed at work. It was hard enough when Allan started occasionally scheduling me on the early morning desk shift, which started at 6:30 a.m., spelling the regular early desk guy. I was never a "morning" person. It made it even tougher having a couple of 6:30 a.m. shifts in the same week I was working night shifts until midnight. It played havoc with my sleep routine.

Then throw a divorce in the mix. While the legal proceedings were stifling and drawn out, there was no haranguing or bitter disagreements between Dorrean and I over our meager mutual belongings. I got to keep the waterbed. She didn't ask for any support. But I was emotionally wrought, and my mind was messed up. I was screwing up, making silly mistakes in my desk work. This went on for a couple of months until Allan called me into his office one day.

"I think you better start looking for a job elsewhere," he told me bluntly. "I don't think it's working out for you here. You're at the bottom of the staff, and I don't see any hope of advancement for you in the foreseeable future.

"You are due for a raise. Right now, I'm not recommending one for you."

This was the kind of gut-punch I had never experienced; the air was just sucked out of me. My initial reaction was intense anger toward Allan; I felt he was judging me so unfairly. But when I got home to my empty apartment I was in tears. I was shattered.

I stewed for a couple of weeks, plotting my next move. I hated Allan. *Bottom of the staff*, he said. That hurt. I felt alienated from the rest of my colleagues, thinking I was a goner. I kept to myself and wouldn't talk to anyone.

Then, I don't remember what got into me but I mustered enough intestinal fortitude to walk into the office of the Managing Editor, Ted Warmbold, to request a meeting to make my case with him. He was a warm personality, much warmer than Allan, and I felt my only chance for a re-start was to plead my case with him. He agreed to meet me in a week.

The following week, when my scheduled meeting with Ted came up, he surprised me. He invited Allan to the meeting. A sense of dread permeated the room when I saw him, but I had no choice but to suck it up.

So, with some measured restraint, I opened up to both of them about the ordeal I was going through with my divorce.

That's when Allan surprised me. The expression on his face softened. He was a man of few words, but his meaning was succinct. "I had no idea that's what you were going through," he said.

The mood of the meeting instantly changed. Both Allan and Ted gave me reason for hope. "Your trip to Indy is next month," Allan said. "We'll meet again after your trip."

I was always inspired when I was at Indy. I was even more inspired that year. Rick Mears won his first of four Indy 500 races, three of which I wound up covering over the next 12 years.

When I returned to the office after that Indy trip, Allan looked up at me from his desk, his face, as usual, expressionless. Again, he uttered few words to get his message across, but I'll never forget it.

"Great job at Indy, Chic."

Dad and Mom, before they got divorced

I served as escort for Nipa, our Thai sister foreign exchange student, to her high school prom

Pam and Janni, our German sister foreign exchange student

CHAPTER 8
Rebounding at Rossburn

When Dad and Mom divorced in the early 1970s, Dad relinquished all rights to the family house on Rossburn to Mom. In her hands, the legacy of that house instantly changed.

Dad wound up remarrying within two years of the divorce, finding another bride, Gloria, in the same folk dance group where he had met Mom. Dad and Gloria moved into one of two side-by-side homes his sister, Evelyn, owned in an exclusive neighborhood in Santa Monica. Aunt Evelyn lived next door for a couple of years, waiting it out until Dad finished building a unit behind the house he and Gloria were living in. The unit had a spectacular ocean view from the spacious kitchen, as per Evelyn's specifications. When it was finished Evelyn moved in while allowing her daughter, Bebe, briefly move into the house she vacated. Many years later, that double-unit, gold-mine house in Santa Monica would belong to me.

As for the Rossburn home, Mom had no problem filling the void my Dad left. It was a big house and she was too much a people person to live alone. Whether it was by design or not, her resource to fill the void expanded internationally.

The international connection had been established years before my parents' divorce. I suspect it was more Mom's idea than Dad's to invite foreign exchange students to live with our family. Janni, from Germany, was the first to come live with us, during my freshman year in college. Nipa, from Thailand, followed suit the next year. Both stayed for the full school year.

I have kept in contact with both Janni and Nipa ever since. I love them both like sisters. They could not have been more different in personality. Janni was very Germanic – stoic, highly intelligent, serious-minded. She went on to become a doctor and married a Japanese man named Tetsu, with whom she has settled in Germany. Nipa was also smart, but she was more nurturing and loved to laugh. I loved to make her laugh, which was easy to do because we shared a similar sense of humor. She wound up falling in love with a Black gentleman named Harrison, who she met at the U.S. Embassy in Bangkok, Thailand, and they eventually settled in his native South Carolina. Over the years, I have made visits both to South Carolina to see Nipa and Harrison, and Germany to see Janni and Tetsu. Janni also has visited me in Santa Barbara.

Mom was very close to both Janni and Nipa. After divorcing Dad, Mom took a number of globe-trotting excursions that included trips to Germany and Thailand to visit each of them. Mom had been set free by the divorce and she made the most of it.

International travel was expensive, however, so Mom figured out a way for international travelers to come to her. After Dad left, she worked for several years as a volunteer at the information desk in the international terminal at LAX. The Rossburn home turned into a respite for international travelers Mom had met at that information desk. Typically, the conversation would be initiated by travelers asking Mom about places to stay in town. She lived a convenient 10-minute cab ride from LAX and had plenty of room so, "Hey, you can stay at my place." This started a procession of foreign visitors at the Rossburn home.

Pam also funneled a string of European travelers to the "Hotel Perkins." My sister had gone on a wanderlust trip to Mexico for several months after she moved out of Aspen, and often ran into European vacationers who mentioned they were making their way to LA. So, Pam, taking her cue from our mother, told them they could always find a place to crash at 13707 Rossburn.

Over a few years there was a steady stream of primarily European travelers staying with Mom in her three vacant bedrooms for extended stays that ranged from a week or two to a year-and-a-half. One guy who kept finding excuses to stay was a handsome, fair-haired young German fellow with a prominent mustache named Michael, who may or may not have been a romantic interest of my sister's.

A visit by an odd pair of Italians left a lasting impression. Marcello, 40ish, was utterly charming, and he was accompanied by an incredibly adorable, but naive, 18-year-old Italian named Francesca. She was stunningly beautiful, with an amazing shock of curly reddish-brown hair. We all wondered about their age difference but they seemed comfortable with each other. The household was abuzz during their entire two-week stay. On their final night, Marcello prepared an Italian feast, making fresh fettuccine from scratch.

I also recall a lanky young Canadian man with long hair to his waist who stayed for about six months dawdling through repairs on his old VW van that he slept in while it was parked in the driveway. There were two young comely women from Switzerland who stayed for a couple weeks, as well as a bunch of French visitors, including one young woman from Paris who I would wind up marrying.

I don't know if it had anything to do with Mom's influence, but the next three women I married following Dorrean were all foreign-born.

———————◆———————

My parents' divorce preceded mine and Dorrean's, which transpired in 1978, by a few years. I guess it's fair to say that divorce unleashed a turbulent streak over the next decade or so that crushed the mold my father had hoped he had set for me.

As stated, I was devastated by the break-up of my marriage to Dorrean. I was still only 24 and significantly too immature to make sound choices in relationships. Maybe because of the hurt I suffered from my divorce, I became a bit callous in the manner I broke off a number of relationships that followed, and consequently hurt more women than I care to count.

It should be a surprise to no one that shortly after my divorce I thought about April, my high school sweetheart. Those "April" dreams I mentioned earlier were occurring regularly and it was only a matter of time before we got in contact with each other.

She was married at the time and had a four-year-old son named Sheldon. She had been thinking a lot about me, in part because she was unhappy in her marriage to Terry. He was boorish, had gained a lot of weight, and the romance in their relationship had completely died.

Their marriage was headed for divorce. At first I was providing April emotional support during those hard times. I was someone she could easily talk to; we could tell each other anything. One of our discussions drifted into the subject of sexual fantasies.

Fantasy eventually crossed over to reality between us. Sex felt so natural and uncomplicated with her. But for reasons I can't quite explain, it wasn't enough to bring us together. It may have had something to do with Sheldon, who wasn't comfortable with us being together when he met me. Then he told his dad, who April hadn't officially divorced yet. I think that unsettled her.

My high school sweetheart April and I, reunited years later

She would go on to divorce Terry, time passed and we drifted on different paths again. April met another man she would marry, a man twice her age who had money and a sailboat, which became a passion of hers and paved the way for world-wide travel coveted by this California Girl. Our paths would cross again several times. In the meantime, I would go through a maze of relationships that set my personal life adrift on an ocean of uncertainty.

———————◆———————

My buddy Rich W. and I were out at a bar one night when I exchanged smiles with a cutie named Karen. That led to a six-month relationship. Karen, who had moved south from Seattle, had a sweet smile, perfectly coifed, short-cropped blondish hair, a slender physique, and a perky personality that made it very easy to converse for someone like me, who usually got tongue-tied at the bar scene.

At the time I met Karen I was living with Rich B. in a two-bedroom apartment just a block off the ocean in Manhattan Beach. These were the good ol' days when a low-paid sports writer and a somewhat better paid bug and pest exterminator could afford a two-bedroom apartment just a block off the beach. We were enjoying the good life as bachelor beach bums in our mid-twenties.

I brought Karen around to meet my mother. Mom liked Karen; she was the type that moms usually liked. I think the whole dynamic was giving Karen false hope. She was definitely looking for a real commitment and marriage down the road. I was still in rebound mode from my divorce and not eager to go down that road anytime soon. This would lead to an inevitable downfall of the relationship.

Mom's house was filled with all sorts of interesting people from other countries, laying fruit out on the table that was ripe for the picking. Karen deserved much better, but I unceremoniously dumped her for somebody else I met, courtesy of Mom.

———————————◆◆◆————————————

Jocelyne, the girl from Paris I mentioned previously, had come to live at the Rossburn house on a teacher exchange visa. Her straight, jet-black hair was cut and styled to curl just above the neckline. Her dark hair set off her big, beautiful blue eyes. She spoke fluent English, as well as Italian, Portuguese, and Japanese. She was undeniably intelligent, and intense about advancing her career, which she aimed for the international diplomatic field in the hope of utilizing her linguistic skills.

Her exchange visa was good for about six weeks. During that time, we fell in love. When the visa expired, she had to return to Paris. We maintained a correspondence (love letters) and tried to figure out a plan to get her back to the states on a more permanent basis. Our

Jocelyne

letters were passionate exchanges, a fair amount of desperation expressed in anticipation of being reunited. Love was wonderful but the distance between us was painful.

This may have been my first passionate affair with being in love. Robert Palmer had me in mind when he wrote his hit song "Addicted To Love." I loved being in love. I was addicted to it like a drug. Unfortunately, that feeling didn't have a sense of permanence with a number of partners in my life, so I kept feeding my addiction, leading me from one relationship to another.

While Jocelyne was stuck back in Paris, Rich B. and I were forced out of our first beach apartment, but lucked into an awesome upgrade. It was a three-bedroom apartment just six blocks south of our first rental. We needed another roommate to afford the rent, so we recruited Randy. Randy and I didn't always get along.

I think back to our brief occupancy of that apartment and pinch myself, because nowadays you couldn't rent it for less than $5,000 a month. For starters, the place was perched at the apex of the hill that overlooked Manhattan Beach, just two-and-a-half blocks up from the "surf and sand where the girls all get so tanned," as the Beach Boys sang. The living room was spacious and surrounded by windows that offered a sweeping, panoramic view of the beach, ocean and horizon beyond. Paying a little more than Rich and Randy for the privilege, I had the largest bedroom, with a balcony facing out at the same view as the living room.

We lived like three beach boy bachelors, but it was a constant battle to contain the sand brought in from the beach. Occasionally Randy and I would have small roommate-type disputes like, "Hey, did you use up my spaghetti sauce?"

Jocelyne managed to secure an extended visiting visa to return to California, and Mom was accommodating her again back in the Rossburn house. The romance immediately picked up where it had left off a few months before.

Those first few months of Jocelyne's return to the States felt carefree. I took her up to Deep Creek for camping, which was glorious. We had the idyllic hideaway that Dan had introduced to me all to ourselves, freeing us to skinny-dip in the water, sun-bath nude, and make love on the rocks with no threat to our privacy.

Approaching the holidays, we ventured across the country to visit one of my closest motorsports buddies, Steve Earwood, at his home in Alpharetta, Georgia. Steve was the public relations director for the National Hot Rod Association that presented drag races at Pomona Raceway twice a year. Steve invited Jocelyne and me to visit him during the racing off-season. Steve, ever the Southern gentleman with his grace and charm, made the perfect host in a gentle, southern-style pace of life that distinguished quaint Alpharetta. As a native Parisian, Jocelyne was fascinated by this quiet, semi-rural part of the states, in striking contrast to LA's urban sprawl.

—————————◆—————————

The clock was ticking on Jocelyne's temporary visiting visa. She didn't want to have to return to Paris, wait a few months, and come back again like we had tortuously gone through before.

The apartment in Manhattan Beach was ideal for three bachelors. But with the frequency that Jocelyne stayed overnight, it made for an awkward foursome. Randy's grumbling over her presence was growing louder. But his grumbling was drowned out by the very loud shrieks Jocelyne customarily made whenever she and I made love in our bedroom.

One afternoon, after she and I took a shower together that involved a lot more than just soap and water, I emerged from the bedroom drip-drying my hair while seeking something to drink in the kitchen. I got a disdainful look from Rich.

"Chic, do we have to call the paramedics?" he asked sarcastically. "Is she all right in there?"

"I guess we were a little loud, huh?"

"Well, Randy stormed out of here a little while ago. He couldn't take it anymore."

It became evident a decision had to be made. Within a couple of months, I had moved out of that dream beach apartment and into a crummy, cockroach-infested one-bedroom apartment in Hawthorne with Jocelyne.

An even bigger decision was reached regarding Jocelyne's vexing visa issue. We decided we would get married so she could stay in the U.S. longer and apply for gainful employment.

Jocelyne and I filed for a confidential marriage certificate. Then we had an intimate little wedding ceremony at a small park with a gazebo in Palos Verdes, attended only by Dan and my mother. That was by design because we really didn't want people to know we were married.

Well, we did want the INS to know it. Jocelyne wanted a green card to show prospective employers. So, we went to the INS office in downtown Los Angeles to apply for permanent resident status for her as my legal spouse.

Luckily, Jocelyne was able to find a job long before her green card arrived in the mail, working as a tutor for a couple of kids parented by a rich French couple in Long Beach.

The green card process was arduous, as expected. It took months to get an appointment for an interview, then hours of waiting before we actually sat down for that interview. The interview itself obviously was a test to see if we were really married and living together; questions like which side of the bed we slept on, what was your partner's favorite color, name a food your partner doesn't like.

Then it was a 10-month wait for the green card to arrive in the mail.

———————◆———————

When Jocelyne and I made the move into matrimony the romance waned and stress started to build in the relationship. She was extremely frustrated with her situation and her frustration spilled over into wacky lines of logic that drove me crazy.

Ever ambitious, she felt handcuffed by the slow-moving immigration system. Her tutoring job with the little French kids wasn't doing it for her. She constantly complained about how bratty they were. She didn't seem to have much patience for children in the first place. Jocelyne was so career-oriented she made it clear that she didn't intend to have children of her own. This was troubling for me, since I knew I one day wanted to become a father and raise children of my own.

Honestly, this affected my attitude toward the marriage. It warped my attitude about the union, which I considered it merely to be a legal maneuver to help Jocelyne out with her situation. I didn't see it as a real, binding commitment, because I could foresee the issue of children evolving into an irreconcilable issue.

My sudden divorce from Dorrean may have also diminished my perspective of marriage as a permanent, death-til-we-part proposition. My parents' divorce, which preceded my first divorce by a few years, didn't help.

So, it was inevitable that, in time, I began to stray from Jocelyne.

———◆———

When Carolyn was hired as a copy editor on the news desk at the Herald Examiner, it was inevitable that we would hook up. We weren't strangers; we had been acquainted with each other years earlier in college as co-staffers on the Daily Titan newspaper at Cal State Fullerton. We barely knew each other back then, but it didn't take long for us to get to know each other better at the Her-Ex.

Carolyn was a study in contrasts with her book-worm look dominated by her large-lensed glasses, her amazingly slender, curvaceous body, and her stylishly long, wavy brown hair. Her sex appeal was subtle and irresistible. Her demeanor was quiet, enigmatic, controlled, but when the relationship turned sexual, it was as if her inhibitions had been unleashed. She was a wild one. Her favorite form of foreplay was to engage in an aggressive nude wrestling match, which she would ultimately lose in submission and succeeded to work both of us up to a frenzied lather.

We both worked the night shift. I drove my camper van to work to facilitate our after-shift rendezvous in the dimly lit company parking lot that was a block and a half away from the office building. It was no secret in the office. The guys on the sports desk all knew what was going on and were wondering how I was hiding it from home. Jocelyne, I hate to say, was so self-absorbed that it was easy to carry on this affair behind her back.

Carolyn knew I was living with Jocelyne and I think one of the reasons she was attracted to me was because I was with a French woman. But at the same time, she resented me for it, which weirdly played into our sexual dynamic. She would get even with me by telling me about other men in her life, which, of course, I had to accept because of Jocelyne. At the time, it all seemed like a game to me and I was willing to play along for as long as it was going to last.

On one of our late-night escapades we encountered a really weird scene. Carolyn and I drove back to the Rossburn house, in search of a change of venue to have sex. The European traveler invasion that my mom welcomed had subsided, so rooms in the house were vacant at the time, and I had my old bedroom in mind. Instead, I got a shocking reminder of why we hadn't tried this before.

The presence of my mom in the house portended potential awkwardness, but nothing prepared me for what we nearly walked into that night. As we approached the front porch, the living room was lit up and the curtains were drawn open from the front window. Just before reaching the front door, I peered through the window and gazed on the naked buttocks of a prone elderly man on the floor between the outstretched naked legs… that I presumed were attached to my mother.

Mom, God bless her, had been enjoying the companionship of a nice man named Phil for a few months. I thought I recognized his bald head, so I had concluded it must have been them. I was clearly embarrassed by this unsavory image of my mother, but it wouldn't be the last time my mother would shock me with an ill-advised lesson in modesty. Surely there were more discreet places they could have chosen for their amorous activity, but it was Mom's house and she could do as she pleased in any room she wanted. Carolyn and I made a hasty retreat to the camper van, where we shared a good laugh and had perfectly satisfying sex.

Alas, the spark between Carolyn and I burnt out after about three months. Amicably, we called it quits. If only all my break-ups were this easy.

————————————→•••◆•••←————————————

I have to credit my mother for demonstrating the ability to adapt to life's changes. She adeptly made those changes in her own life.

The run on foreign guests at "Hotel Perkins" had to end sometime, for financial reasons. Mom made the transition to renting out her vacant bedrooms to tenants because she needed the money.

One of her first roommates was Janice, a bedazzling, soft-spoken wonder from Mississippi who would grace my life in so many ways. By chance, Mom met Janice at a NOW (National Organization of Women) convention in downtown LA. Janice, with her delicate, breathy, sensual Southern drawl that would have fit perfectly in a Tennessee Williams play, charmed her way into Mom's life just like she did into mine. Mom brought her home from the convention and she moved in.

Janice was not one for dramatic entrances; she had a quiet presence and would sneak into the conversation. Then, as soon as she opened her mouth and you heard that soft, mesmerizing voice, she would subtly captivate you. To say nothing of her alluring physical features — her curly, floppy brown hair, encompassing a pretty face set off by her soulful, blueish-green eyes. She had the graceful, curvaceous body of a dancer, which she just happened to be. She was a serious ballet student.

Janice moved into the Rossburn home — and my life — nearly two years into my relationship with Jocelyne. She would become a much bigger part of my life long after Jocelyne and I split up.

Janice befriended Jocelyne and was sympathetic to Jocelyne's plight of trying to defy the odds in a man's world by becoming a successful career woman. Janice wasn't driven that way; she was more interested in cultural pursuits and enjoying life at a leisurely pace, with no definitive plan in mind, come what may.

Janice was the perfect antidote to stress. We became friends, and she became a confidante to whom I could express my frustrations from my relationship with Jocelyne, whose unhappiness was all-consuming. Janice and I often held our tete-a-tete's with a joint that took the edge off the everyday stresses we were trying to resolve.

The piano had always been my go-to for stress relief. Without a piano of my own, I would frequently drop in and play my own music on the piano at the Rossburn house. It was an excuse to see Janice, too, and she loved listening to me play. I was composing a lot of my early piano pieces during this period of time. Janice had a favorite among my compositions — the first time she heard it, she told me she could dance to it. That became her song.

A lot of my music was classically influenced, which appealed to Janice because of her exposure to classical in her ballet classes. Her life was heavily influenced as a student in the West Hollywood studio of one of LA's most prominent ballet teachers — Carmelita Maracci, who was heralded as a phenomenal soloist who created her own choreography that mixed ballet with Spanish-style dancing. One biographer described Carmelita's unorthodox style of dancing as taking "the girdle off ballet." As a self-described anarchist, Carmelita's promising performing career was cut short by her volatile hostility toward the dancing establishment.

When I met Janice, Carmelita was in her 70s, with dramatic gray-streaked hair. Carmelita wasn't just a ballet teacher to Janice, she was educating her on life. Teaching while sitting in a chair because of debilitating arthritis, the fiery Carmelita gave lectures in a booming voice, often focusing on art, literature and politics. Her students were extremely devoted to her, as was Janice, whom Carmelita treated like a daughter.

Framed photo of Carmelita Maracci, Janice's life mentor and renowned ballet dancer, in her prime in the 1930's

I distinctly remember visiting Janice one day at her dance studio. I was taken by the image of her gracefully going through the motions of her ballet routines — I could have framed her in a painting. Listening to classical music that a student once described as so beautiful it made you weep, I felt enriched merely from breathing the air while watching her.

Janice was a long way from home, which was Vicksburg,

Mississippi, an old Southern town that still pined for its Confederate glorydays. Her dad had passed away but her mom was still alive, living a quiet life in Vicksburg. Janice was the only girl in the family, with three brothers, two older and one younger.

Not long after I met Janice, one of her older brothers committed suicide. When she shared her grief with me, that was my first soulful connection with her. We were sitting in a parked car at night, down near the beach, when she bared her soul to me. Janice was the type of person who grieved quietly, with silent tears. It touched me deeply to feel her pain. It brought us closer together. That closeness turned naturally to a sweet, tender intimacy that left an indelible mark on my heart.

I often talk about my addiction to love and the women I have loved. Janice was one of them, maybe the purest love I shared with any woman, but flawed. We would become off-and-on lovers over many years, in-between — and during — my string of relationships.

Czech author Milan Kundera wrote the novel "The Unbearable Lightness Of Being," which spoke to the heart of my love life. Wikipedia noted: *"The 'unbearable lightness' in the title refers to the lightness of love and sex… Kundera portrays love as fleeting, haphazard and possibly based upon an endless string of coincidences, despite holding much significance for humans."*

That hit close to home. Except my problem often was struggling to differentiate between love and sex.

I was engrossed by the movie version of the book that came out in 1988, directed by Philip Kaufman, and starring Daniel Day-Lewis, Lena Olin, and Juliette Binoche. I often thought a good title for my life story could be, "The Unbearable Lightness of Being Me." But I digress.

When I saw the movie, I was profoundly reminded of Janice and me in the portrayal of the relationship between Tomas and Sabina, played by Day-Lewis and Olin. The story, which takes place in 1968, mostly in Czechoslovakia during the Russian invasion, revolved around a triangular love relationship that Tomas balanced between Tereza (Binoche) and Sabina. But his relationship with Sabina had no strings attached. Supposedly, they were lovers but not in love; it was just about sex and sensuality. If Tomas openly felt love for anyone, it was Tereza.

133

Kaufman's abundant use of erotic scenes, which were a turn-on for me, drew this comment from film critic Roger Ebert in his review of the movie for the Chicago Sun-Times: *"He has made a movie in which reality is asked to coexist with a world of pure sensuality, and almost, for a moment, seems to agree."*

It's no wonder I associated Janice to this movie. Sensuality superseded the sex between us. But our No-strings-attached bond really represented a pure form of unconditional love that we shared. That's how I interpreted Tomas and Sabina's relationship in the tragic end.

It took awhile, but eventually Janice confided in me what she was running away from in Mississippi. She was escaping from a husband who wound up in prison on drug charges and was soon to be released on parole. She had divorced him, but she knew he would try to get her back and lure her back to the drug world. She took off for California where he couldn't find her. Somehow, she found Carmelita and my mother. And then me.

My long-time paramour Janice

Janice soon served an important role for Mom. My grand-mother Mimi was diagnosed with breast cancer, which eventually spread through other organs. While undergoing treatment, Mimi reached a point where she could no longer take care of herself living on her own in Montecito. That forced her to move in with Mom, where she could get round-the-clock personal care. Janice became an in-house nurse of sorts for Mimi over the last couple of years of her life. That role sealed Janice's bond with our family forever.

In one of those life decisions we lived to regret, Mom sold Mimi's Montecito property because she was cash-poor and needed the money to help pay for Mimi's ongoing treatments. This was 1980; Mimi's dumpy little house on its huge lot commanded a selling price of a mere $145,000. Ten years later, the land alone would have been worth 10 or 15 times that amount if Mom could have figured out a way to hold onto it. Mimi's little house was razed and a mansion was constructed. Most of the trees were cleared out and the creek that had run through her property was diverted. Whenever I drive by the property nowadays it doesn't remotely resemble the cozy, peaceful habitat when Mimi resided there.

Mom managed to go through that $145,000 in less than a decade. I'm sure her globe-trotting adventures gobbled up a good portion of that.

------◆------

There was another red-headed beauty I was in love with who resided at the Rossburn house for years, and she loved me unconditionally. Her name was Trig. She was my beautiful, sleek Irish Setter who wound up at Mom's house because I wasn't allowed to have a dog where I was living at the time. I had gotten Trig from a friend of mine looking for a home for her.

Mom gave Trig her name, short for "trigonometric." Mom somehow related the triangular white patch on Trig's chest to trigonometry. Mathematics was not her strong suit in school, but I just took her word for it she knew what a trigonometric patch would look like. I looked up "trig" in the dictionary, first to see if such a word even existed. It did, and the word's original roots are Scandinavian, as an adjective meaning "faithful." That fit Trig to a "T".

Mom often would tie Trig on the front porch waiting for my anticipated arrival. Trig lived for that moment when I walked up to greet her.

I found more and more reasons to go by Mom's house. Over the years I planted a vegetable garden in the backyard, with limited success, largely due to a fierce streak of jealousy from my red-head. I had to put up a chicken-wire fence to keep her out of the garden because she kept digging up the veggies, like carrots and onions, and knocking over the corn stalks. The fence didn't hold her back; one day I found the underpinning of the fence bent upward with red hair caught along the bottom. Trig was busted; the dug-up carrots and onions and broken corn stalks were undeniable evidence of her mischievousness.

Trig, graying in her face in her elder years, lived until the ripe old age of 12. She died on Christmas Day, her stomach terribly bloated from an inner organ explosion. It was my fault. I should have never given her that chicken bone the night before.

———————— ◆ ————————

Mom always had at least one cat at the house, dating way back to our childhood to Typsy, a long-haired back and white beauty who was the first family pet I remember having.

In my junior year in high school, two kittens came into our lives and were together for 16 years. Ebony was the slender, all-black, finicky female, and Musty was the big, fat, lovable, orange-and-white-striped mellow male. Musty would out-live Ebony by two years, until age 18.

I brought Ebony home as a kitten I inherited from a friend. Mom, Pam and I hid her from Dad in Pam's artsy clubhouse behind the garage, buying time until we could get up the nerve to tell him we had brought home a kitten, violating his declaration of no more cats because of his supposed allergies. We kept Ebony hidden from him for a week, but then we double-downed on Musty, who Mom brought home from somebody giving away kittens. We basically sucked at hiding the two kittens. Dad, left all alone in the kitchen during breakfast one morning, wandered out to find all three of us in the clubhouse tending to the two kittens.

After the big secret was out, Dad took it well. Take one wild guess who doted on and played with them the most after that. My Dad was the man of the house and he set the rules, which didn't apply when it came to adorable kittens.

Ebony and Musty lasted a lot longer than my parents' marriage and started a long string of cats that Mom had over the years, cats who seemingly lived forever.

The Rossburn house was home for many characters who rented out rooms over the years. Mom never lived alone the rest of her life for over 30 years. Pam eventually moved back home sometime during the 1980s and converted the garage into her own eclectic, funky room. She effectively took over as Mom's financial manager.

Overall, the number of foreign visitors and tenants who lived with Mom and Pam over three decades-plus came darn near close to 100. Jocelyne and Janice weren't the only women among them whom I got to know better.

Neither Mom nor Pam were very good at handling money and the rent they collected was never enough to sustain them. Together, they would refinance the house over and over again, cashing in on equity and falling deeper and deeper into debt. Years after Mom's passing, I had to take extraordinary steps to resolve the situation, which was the basis of one of the more tumultuous chapters of my life.

Familiar faces from my motorsports coverage for the LA Herald Examiner over 12 years: (counter-clockwise, starting top left): Mario Andretti receiving a smooch from the Queen of Auto Racing, Linda Vaughn, before the start of the Indy 500; Formula One hunk and 1976 world champ James Hunt of Great Britain in a casual moment at the Long Beach Grand Prix; Bobby Allison, winner of the 1-2 father/son finish at NASCAR's 1988 Daytona 5oo on Valentine's Day; Two of Indy's four-time winners, A.J. Foyt and Al Unser Sr., exiting the driver's meeting the day before the big race; and Danny Sullivan, winner of the 1985 "Spin and Win" Indy 500

CHAPTER 9
Racing and Racy Stories Part 1

The motorsports beat opened a whole new world to me, and the Her-Ex allowed me to cover an array of major motorsports events. The stories that evolved from that coverage were numerous and incomparable.

I didn't just write about motorsports, I actually got a chance to experience time behind the wheel for a couple of the wildest rides of my life.

The first chance came when I had the beat for less than a year. I had an opportunity to participate — for free — in a four-day racing school at Ontario Motor Speedway (OMS), as a prompt to write about the experience in the Her-Ex.

The cars were open-wheel Formula Ford cars, junior versions of Formula One, in which the driver sat about six inches off the ground in the cockpit while driving hair-raisingly fast. For the bargain of writing an article about it, I was prodded into participating in the one sport I vowed I'd never do.

It wasn't just the four-day class. An invited field of 13, including the six journalists who were invited to the racing school, would actually race against each other in a 10-lap exhibition as an added event to a Formula Ford series weekend at Ontario.

Holy shit.

There were nine students in the racing class, including Craig Breedlove, the former land speed record holder. Our school instructor was a French Canadian named Jacques Couture, former Formula Atlantic champion. He was dashing, manly and bearded, just what you would picture a racing instructor to look like. The four-day class consisted of classroom lecture for most of the first day and almost exclusively on-track driving on the final three days, for which we wore a full racing uniform and helmet. We were taught the basic tricks of the trade to maximize speed on the 3.2-mile, 19-turn road course laid out inside the 2.5-mile banked oval at OMS. We were taught all about how to hit the "apex" of each turn, which basically meant trying to navigate the turns in as straight a line as possible.

The scariest part of the course came when we'd swing up on the high bank between turns three and four of the oval for the 19th turn before heading back into the infield. We would climb that bank and swerve parallel to within 12 inches from the wall at about 130 mph. *Gulp!* The 45-degree bank was what braced our momentum and (hopefully) prevented us from kissing the wall. We practiced avoiding calamity on that bank at least a couple dozen times over the four days. It was all I could take not to swallow my tongue each time.

I experienced one adrenaline-boosting, high-speed spin-out in a cloud of dust. I came in too fast on a turn in the infield portion of the track, slid off-course in the dirt, and spun full circle at least four-five times. I was trying to slow down to about 80 mph heading into the turn, but didn't quite get there. Fortunately, this was a solo spin; I didn't collect any of the other drivers.

Our objective was to improve our practice lap times, and I was nowhere near the head of the class. I couldn't even beat out four of my journalist colleagues, who were all from racing magazines. I was the only writer from the LA Big Five newspaper beat in the group. There was one woman in the class. She wrote for Penthouse Magazine. She looked like she could have appeared in the magazine a few years back. She was the only driver turning slower practice times than I was.

When it came time for the exhibition race I felt like I knew what I was doing after four days of racing school. But they shortened the course, taking out a couple of hairpin turns, making it faster than what we were used to.

My article recounting my participation in a racing school at Ontario Motor Speedway in 1979, which included a photo of me in a Formula Ford race car

I qualified 12th out of the field of 13, 12 seconds slower than the pole sitter. I thought I was ready, but nothing prepared me for the bare-knuckle start of that race, gripping the steering wheel for dear life, all of us heading into the first turn in a bunch so tight that we could reach out and high-five each other. The collective wheezing of the 13 Formula Ford engines drowned out the loud pumping of my heart.

What I ultimately learned from that 10-lap race was that I sucked at being a race car driver.

I was second-to-last off the start, ahead of only the Penthouse gal writer. One driver spun out in the dangerous Turn 6 in a cloud of blinding dust, creating a moment of panic. But we all got through it OK.

The Penthouse writer passed me on the back straightaway on the first lap. I snuck past her on the front straightaway on Lap 4, which put me in the 10th spot only because two guys had spun out. Both those guys eventually passed me but I held off the Penthouse writer for my unspectacular 12th-place finish.

I decided I didn't have what it took to be a good race car driver. I wasn't able to push the car to the limit, to that ragged edge where you feel like you're floating on air, which is where you needed to go to gain that milli-second advantage over the other drivers. I was lifting my foot on the accelerator pedal ever so timidly in those turns.

But I wrote a helluva story for the paper.

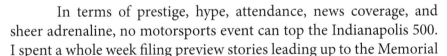

In terms of prestige, hype, attendance, news coverage, and sheer adrenaline, no motorsports event can top the Indianapolis 500. I spent a whole week filing preview stories leading up to the Memorial Day weekend race every year for 12 years between 1978-1989.

Covering the Indy 500 wasn't easy. Just acquiring a press credential may have been equivalent to getting a press credential to a White House briefing. Requesting a credential had to be done way in advance; it was usually on my "to do" just before Christmas. But once you were on the "list," you were in. I made the list.

Lodging was also a consideration to think about way ahead of time. Every hotel vacancy in Indianapolis got booked months in advance for Memorial Day weekend. Luckily, I managed to reserve a room at the same hotel every year on the "guest list" with one of the major Indy-car teams, Patrick Racing. Dick Rutherford, a distinguished gentleman who I met through my connections as the Her-Ex motorsports columnist, was the personal manager for Patrick team owner, Pat Patrick. He personally made sure I had a room every year at this same hotel. Bill Center, an acerbic, funny-as-hell sports writer from the San Diego Union, was also on Rutherford's guest list. Bill and I bonded every year at the same Indy hotel.

I made another memorable connection of a certain sort a few years into my stay at that hotel. I was checking out the day after the race, bags packed for my flight home, when I caught the prettiest smile from the young lady at the counter handling my checkout. She was a cute, short-haired blonde named Debi, and within a two-minute conversation we exchanged phone numbers and addresses with a nod toward my return the following year. We sent each other holiday cards, and when May rolled around the following year, I checked into the same hotel and was greeted by the same smile. Long story short, we made full use of my hotel room, in the biblical sense, and it had nothing to do with Gideon.

I watched the city of Indianapolis grow from a sleepy mid-level, midwestern city to a major metropolis in the 12-year span that I covered the race. The whole town was one big party the entire month of May. The party started with qualifying on back-to-back weekends and carried through Carburetion Day, the last day of official practice on the Thursday before the race. Indianapolis Motor Speedway was the hub of much of the partying. That was evident just from the thousands of crushed beer cans piling up at the corner of 16th and Georgetown where the IMS entrance was located. Judging by the variety of license plates on the vehicles roaming in the vicinity, race fans came from throughout Middle America for the show.

And what a show it was. "The Greatest Spectacle In Racing" had earned its moniker, attracting over 400,000 spectators annually on race day. An estimated 100,000 of those would be packed into the infield area. That was a younger, raucous crowd that camped overnight and partied. Those who overindulged and slept through the race the next day crashed out on blankets spread out on the dewy grass. I'd arrive at the track several hours before the race, parking in the infield, and take in the scene as I made the long stroll to the press room. The smell of booze, BBQs and body sweat in the Indy humidity was overwhelming.

The sights and sounds of the crowd were entertaining. One year as I was wandering through the infield, a throng of young males had hovered around two scantily-clad young women perched atop a car rooftop, relentlessly chanting "Show us your tits!" One of the women cheerfully obliged them. Men are so easily entertained.

The logistics of covering this event were challenging. I parked my rented car inside the immense racetrack, which is large enough to contain a nine-hole golf course with a small lake. One time I had to park on the golf course, which took a good half-mile hike to reach the Press Room. The hike felt so much more laborious carrying my heavy typewriter, dating back to the pre-computer days. Wrapping up my work day around 9 p.m., I found myself trekking back out to my car in pitch darkness. After a futile search, tugging that burdensome typewriter that sagged nearer to the ground with every step, I realized with utter dismay that my car had been towed away. Cussing up a storm, I eventually found my car stored elsewhere on the premises, lugging my !#?*$!@ typewriter the whole way.

One year I skipped the bother of parking inside the racetrack on race day, choosing instead to walk in with my colleagues Shav Glick of the L.A. Times, Tim Tuttle of the Orange County Register, and my hotel bud Bill Center, from the Howard Johnson's motel where Shav was staying. The HoJo was about a mile away from the corner of 16th and Georgetown. We gathered at 7 am, four hours before race time, to start the walk-in. Along the way we passed rows and rows of RVs and campers, with smoke wafting in the air from barbecues and race fans imbibing in their own tailgate parties, Indy-style.

My favorite part of the Indy experience was taking in the pre-race lineup of the 33 cars at the start line. I loved standing on the two-foot wide strip of brick marking the start-finish line. That strip remained as the last remnant of the original brick layout over the entire 2-1/2 mile track, which explained IMS' original colorful moniker "The Brickyard." I'd check out each of the 33 exotic, low-lying race cars, bearing the bright colors of its primary sponsors and numerous names of its subsidiary sponsors on the side panels. Over a thousand people would loiter around the cars — race-team crews adorned in their matching team uniforms, the tony-dressed owners, sponsors, their respective wives, family members and guests, and, of course, numerous media members. I'd be among them, snapping photos of everyone and everything.

The most photogenic of the crowd would be the army of about 20 beautiful young women clad in identical, summery cotton outfits — short-shorts and button-down shirts — to add glamour to the proceedings. Then, there was the unofficial "Queen of Racing," Linda Vaughn, who seemingly appeared at every major auto racing event in the country. You couldn't miss her — a big-busted, wavy-haired blonde lady dressed in the tightest outfits possible on her outrageously curvaceous figure.

As the race start approached, the 33 race-car drivers would emerge from the garage area, sucking up the attention of the throng. Momentum built up as the drivers prepared to climb into their cockpits and the loiterers were cleared out from the track.

Reporters watched the race from a long press-designated stretch of seats above the field level section, offering a full, unobstructed view of the banked oval.

All the pomp and circumstance prior to the race —Jim Nabors singing "Back Home In Indiana," the military presentation of "Taps" to memorialize every fallen soldier on Memorial Day, a color guard presentation of the National Anthem, the release of hundreds of colorful balloons, and finally the proclamation of "Gentlemen, (and Lady

Press row view of Indy cars roaring down the front straightaway at Indianapolis Motor Speedway

added in, if a woman driver, such as Janet Guthrie, was entered) start your engines!" — lent an anticipation unrivaled in sports, especially with the roar of 400,000 spectators.

Standing in front of the race position tower at the start-finish line at Indianapolis Motor Speedway

I'll argue that there is nothing more exhilarating in the world of sports than to watch the start of the Indianapolis 500 from press row. To see 33 of the world's fastest race cars accelerate past the start-finish line in one long colorful bunch roaring toward the first turn of the track simply takes your breath away, no matter how many times you see it. The roar of the crowd rises in a coordinated orchestration, because everyone knows that the slightest jiggle of any one of those land rockets could potentially trigger a violent disaster of epic proportions. It has happened a few times in the over 100 years of the "Greatest Spectacle in Racing."

Tragedy hangs on every lap of the 200-lap race, with cars exceeding 200 mph and often racing side-by-side inches apart while waging war for position heading into the turns. Reporters are kept apprised of all developments from reams of race notes that flow down press row throughout the race. While we could see the entire action from our seats, closed-circuit TVs monitored the leaders for closer views. I still took copious notes, which was my usual custom for any event I covered.

When the race ended, there was the mad rush to get across the track to Victory Circle in front of the Garage Alley. The race winner was made available in the Press interview room roughly 30 minutes after the race. But if you wanted to talk to anybody else, you would have to scramble to their respective garages in the historic brick-laden Garage Alley to get the quotes you wanted that nobody else got. But bless those team publicists, they always had quotes from their respective drivers that they typed out on releases and handed out to the press, looking for any kind of publicity for their team.

My first Indy 500 was in 1978. I remember being blown away by all of it the first time. That race was won by Al Unser Sr., one of his four victories at the Brickyard. I saw his record-tying fourth win in '87, when he was a surprise last-minute sub for the injured Danny Ongais and even more surprising race winner.

Rick Mears won the following year in '79. He was a young driver out of Bakersfield whom car owner Roger Penske took under his wing. Mears went on to match A.J. Foyt and Al Unser Sr. as the only four-time winners at Indy. His '79 win came in the year in which I was fighting for my job in the wake of my divorce. I watched Mears win twice more in '84 and '88.

Johnny Rutherford, who won the very first race I covered at Ontario Motor Speedway back in '78, won at Indy in 1980.

Bobby Unser, Al's older brother, won the infamous '81 race. It was a very controversial result. Mario Andretti had crossed the finish line first on race day and gulped down the customary splash of milk in Victory Circle. Five months later, an appeals panel rendered an appalling decision that Andretti had committed a pit lane violation that warranted a one-lap penalty, which took the victory away from him and gave it to Unser, who was the second-place finisher on race day.

Gordon Johncock, driving for the Patrick Racing team, survived several incidents to win one of the closest races in Indy history in '82. That was the year pole-sitter Kevin Cogan took out both Mario Andretti and A.J Foyt, two of the biggest names to ever race at Indianapolis, in a first-turn crash that eliminated the entire front row on the opening lap. It took Cogan years to live down that bit of infamy.

Tom Sneva won his lone Indy race in '83. I'll never forget that race day. I had pulled an all-nighter the night before in my hotel room with two local young ladies, Trina and Jane. How I ended up with

146

those two lovely ladies in my hotel room, I'll never know. I think they were just mischievous enough to hang with me all night — we drank a lot of booze and stripped down to our underwear — but that's as far as it got. I think if Trina, the dark-haired beauty, and I had been alone, it might have gone farther, but Jane's presence kept the hanky-panky to a minimum. I do remember that the TV was on at 5 a.m., and we were all in a daze, squinting at an old black-and-white episode of "The Phil Silvers Show," featuring the Army base antics of the character Sergeant Bilko. We're talking vintage, late 1950's TV. I finally drifted off to sleep at 5:45… and got my wake-up call from the front desk at 6!

Bidding the girls a hasty good-bye, it was time to go to work. The shower and morning coffee wasn't enough to get me through race day on 15 minutes of sleep. After hearing my story and seeing what condition I was in, my empathetic press colleagues at the race track kept pouring Cokes down my throat all day to keep me awake. It's a wonder I had any recollection that Tom Sneva won the race, much less being able to render any kind of focus to write a story. Then even more miraculously, when I returned to the office the following week, Allan Malamud praised me for my work at Indy, singling out *my race-day story.* The wonders of Coca-Cola.

The '85 race featured the famous 360-degree "Spin and Win" by the dashing, good-looking Danny Sullivan. The spin came on the front straightaway at 200 mph midway through the race. Somehow Sullivan overcame bad luck and the law of physics and managed to steer the car away from the wall and all oncoming traffic, then point it in the right direction and keep going. He went on to take the checkered flag. That was a fun race to write about.

The interview I had with Sullivan on the Friday before the race will always stay with me. I was hoping to catch him alone in his garage, but it's all in the timing. When I made my approach, this guy from the LA Times arrived at the same time. The guy happened to be Jim Murray, arguably the most famous sports columnist in the world. I assumed that ended my chances of talking to Sullivan.

LA Times writers, as a rule, were snobs who generally looked down on their LA Her-Ex rivals (motorsports writer Shav Glick was a superlative exception). Jim Murray could have wielded his considerable clout to squeeze me out of the opportunity to interview Sullivan in that moment, and Sullivan's availability was precious. Instead, after

I sheepishly identified myself as the writer from the Her-Ex, Murray graciously suggested we talk to Sullivan together. He was a genuinely nice man.

We won't debate the point on who wrote the more brilliant prose on Sullivan in print the following day.

The 1986 race is remembered for being the first-ever Indy race postponed by rain and not held on its traditional Sunday on Memorial weekend. Postponing the Indy 500 is a logistics nightmare when you take into account the 400,000 race fans who traveled from all corners of the country and had to be given rain checks. But the biggest entity that had to be pacified was ABC, the network that invested a ton of money and procured hefty TV ads to broadcast the race. The network held everyone hostage in the track for hours on Sunday hoping, praying, for a break in the clouds that would enable the race to take the green flag. Hundreds of sports writers were hunkered in the press room loudly grumbling, as the holdout played out all day. The sun never broke through.

ABC tried again the next day, Memorial Day Monday. Local weathermen were sweating bullets trying to give the network bigwigs the forecast they were betting millions of sponsor dollars on. But alas, Mother Nature wasn't giving in. So, after another few hours of futility, the race was postponed again until the following Sunday.

That meant I had to stay an extra week in Indianapolis, a town that was already up to party speed and primed for more. I filed stories all that week leading up to the race. There was plenty to write about with the fiasco caused by the week's delay. It was a sports writer's dream come true.

My last Indy race was 1989. Emerson Fittipaldi held off Al Unser Jr. in a famous last-lap duel in which they touched wheels heading into the third turn and managed to stay in control through the final banked turn and into the front straightaway roaring to the checkered flag.

Watching that race, I had no idea then that would be my swan song at Indy, which would bring an end to a 12-year run that made an indelible mark on my life.

———————————◆———————————

The Long Beach Grand Prix could not be more different from the Indy 500. But it was just as much of a blast to cover, especially in the early days when it was a Formula One (F1) race, with acclaimed international stars like Austrian Niki Lauda and Englishman James Hunt. After 1983, the Indy-car circuit replaced Formula One as the featured event.

The LBGP is a street race carved out on the streets of downtown Long Beach, a dream-come-true hatched by flamboyant, transplanted British entrepreneur Chris Pook. Formula One is the world's most elite racing circuit, and it was a coup by Pook to sway the international F1 gang to stage an event in Long Beach, which isn't LA but offered proximity and marketing opportunities.

Long Beach was a mere 20 minutes down the 405 freeway from where I grew up, so it was in my neighborhood. I watched the downtown Long Beach area that surrounded the temporary street circuit develop from a sleepy, coastal poor cousin of massive LA into a glitzy, fashionable metropolis with swanky, high-rise hotels, night-life attractions and restaurants worthy of a Formula One global destination.

In the early years the race was run among ongoing construction. That made for unsightly dirt patches blocked off by chain-linked fences along the track route headed into the first turn and facing out to the harbor and Queen Mary. But race organizers, in their infinite wisdom, camouflaged the look by allowing race fans to park along the fence and watch the race, which offered a better view than the VIP seat section along pit row at the start-finish line.

One year, I boldly took advantage of this scenario with my coveted press parking pass that gave me vehicle access inside the racing premises. I drove my camper van down to the race circuit at midnight before the race, flashed my parking pass to the overnight security guards, and drove on in, where I parked in a prime spot along that chain-linked fence. That's when it was safe for my buddy Dan, and my then-third wife, Lizamara, to come out of hiding in the back of the van. They were set up to watch the race the next day from beach chairs atop the van. Within a couple years, the chain-linked fence — and the view for fans— was gone. Paradise was paved over.

Even with its unkempt beginnings the event had all the trappings of the glamour and conspicuous lifestyles of the rich. I got a literal taste of it at the annual press luncheon on the Wednesday before the three-day racing weekend. The F1 luncheons were hosted by Moet Chandon, the very expensive French champagne, which was served in copious amounts throughout lunch. The luncheon, attended by the press, drivers and celebrities taking part in the Toyota Celebrity Race, a companion event that ran on Saturday, featured a spectacular presentation put on by the Moet people. The presentation was set up with hundreds of slim, crystal champagne glasses stacked in a circular, 12-foot-high pyramid, held up by a base of about 50 glasses ascending to a singular glass at the top. A French gentleman from Moet stood atop a ladder, tilting an over-sized bottle of champagne over the top glass, continuously pouring the sparkling golden beverage to allow a cascade flow into the glasses below. Waiters in white tuxes then carefully removed the filled glasses one by one from the top on down and served them to the luncheon guests.

In one incident that would live in infamy, an actor named Robert Hays was invited to the luncheon as part of the Celebrity Race cast. Hays is best known for his role as the clueless passenger on a plane in peril in the movie spoof "Airplane," in which he is unwittingly placed in the position of taking over control of the plane from the cockpit in an attempt to save it from crashing. In the movie, there was a running gag about his character having a drinking problem. Well, at the luncheon, he obviously drank a bit too much champagne that clouded his judgement. He thought it would be really funny to callously remove one of the champagne-filled crystal glasses from the center of the pyramid, which caused about 100 of the glasses to collapse and shatter onto the floor. Those weren't cheap glasses. The luncheon gathering looked on aghast, while the horrified look on the Moet guy's face said it all. Let's just say, Hays wasn't invited back for any future celebrity races.

This was part and parcel for the Grand Prix in its F1 glory days — outrageous behavior was the norm. One example— immediately after one race, I went into the indoor garage area looking for driver quotes. Each team had a roped-off area, side-by-side open to public viewing. One driver, Jody Scheckter of South Africa, did not do well in the race and was obviously feeling uncomfortable in his driver's suit. So he removed his driver's suit, drawing oohs and ahhhs from the on-looking crowd by displaying his well-conditioned young physique stripped down to undershirt and boxer underwear. Playing to his adoring audience, Scheckter then whipped off the underwear and threw it into the hands of one shrieking female fan, exposing a bare moonshot for all to see, as he was wearing a mere jockstrap underneath.

You never knew what you could wind up witnessing in this bawdy atmosphere. During a long dormant stretch after qualifying had concluded on Friday, I had my head down typing out my story in the near-empty press room, which had an inner circuit TV displaying all manner of scenes from the track and beyond. The street course through downtown was lined by high-rise hotels occupied by the rich Fl followers from around the world who could afford the over-inflated rates on race weekend. The cameraman for the inner circuit telecast was passing time since there was no track activity, casting his camera in search of anything that caught his eye. He panned up to one of the high-rises, a fancy, circular building with balconies, and boy, did he ever catch something with his eye. I happened to look up from my typewriter in mid-thought and my eye wandered over to the TV suspended from the ceiling in a corner. My jaw dropped and my eyes widened and zoomed in on the cameraman's focus of attention — a big-busted naked woman leaning over the railing of the balcony, with a naked guy pumping her from behind. I lost all focus on that story I was writing.

The aforementioned Celebrity Race was always a source for interesting interviews. Toyota was the sponsor for that race, the celebrities raced identical Toyota Celicas, and their publicist set me up with a celebrity interview every year. To name a few, this included acclaimed actor Gene Hackman, Jon Schneider of the "Dukes Of Hazzard" TV show, singer/songwriter Christopher Cross ("Sailing, Take Me Away"). One year I was invited to participate with the celebrities in their three-day driver training course out at Willow Springs Raceway in Rosamond, about 80 miles northeast of L.A. That class included Jay Leno, who, to no one's surprise, was the class clown cracking jokes all the time. Chicago Bears football star Walter Payton was also part of that class.

Another occasion found me driving all the way out to Willow Springs in an attempt to track down Eddie Cheever, the lone American driver in the F1 field that particular year, for an exclusive interview. He was racing for the French Ligier team, which was running some tune-up laps out at Willow Springs early in the race week. I drove a long way to try to get that damn interview. When I ventured out on the track, one of the Ligier cars was running practice laps. I assumed Eddie was the driver. I waited a good 40 minutes for him to come in for a break. When the helmet came off and I saw long hair fly from underneath I realized it wasn't Eddie, but rather his dashing French teammate. So I asked one of the crew members where Eddie was.

"Eddie Cheever?" The crew member repeated in a French accent. "He's on holl-ee-day." On holl-ee-day, my ass.

Hank Ives, the publicist for the Grand Prix main event, was the guy who sent me on that wild goose chase. But I cut Hank some slack because he was about the nicest, easiest-going publicist in the business. A tall, lanky, silver-haired, distinguished gentleman, Hank served me well in getting just about any driver not on "holl-ee-day" that I wanted to talk to. And more often than not I talked to Mario Andretti, the most popular driver of that era, who Hank set me up with at least three or four times. Andretti, to date still the only driver to win the Indy 500, Daytona 500 and F1 world championship, ruled at Long Beach, winning it four times, including three times over four years in the mid-1980's. I had interviewed Mario so often that he stunned me by remembering my name, greeting me with a "Hi Chic" at one Grand Prix luncheon.

One year Hank presented me with a choice of venues to interview Mario. "You can join a bunch of LA sportswriters for lunch with Mario Tuesday in Chinatown in downtown LA, or you can fly up to San Francisco with us on Wednesday for lunch with the Bay Area press."

Well, duh, flying to San Fran with Mario Andretti for lunch — the choice was easy. I just assumed a band of other sports writers were given the same choice. But much to my surprise, the traveling party consisted of only four of us — me, Hank, Mario and Miss Long Beach Grand Prix, a stunningly beautiful, dark-haired young lady named Candy. I had a suspicion that wasn't her real name.

On the plane, with three seats wide, Mario and I sat on either side of Candy. I was in a captivated daze the entire flight while Mario and I both engaged in casual conversation with Candy. At one point when she got up to use the restroom, I was exchanging quips with Mario Andretti on what a beauty she was. It's scenes like this that usually only pop up in dreams.

152

'Candy': Miss Long Beach Grand Prix

We arrived in San Francisco Airport, which was a good 45-minute drive to the downtown restaurant where the press luncheon was taking place. Candy and I felt like outsiders among this gathering, so we stuck together off in a corner during lunch. That was nice for me as she seemed to be genuinely enjoying my company. Again, the dream scenario applied.

When it was time to leave we all piled in a taxi. It was mid-afternoon, and we didn't have much time to catch our flight back home, with another 45-minute or more ride back to the airport, depending on how badly traffic had accumulated.

In Mario's world, though, no flight was important enough to catch when there was an elite Italian shoe store in the neighborhood, just a few blocks from the restaurant. In a moment of spontaneity, Mario asked the taxi driver to stop so he could jump out of the cab and hustle into the shoe store; it was an opportunity that the Italian-born driver couldn't pass up. We waited in the cab a few minutes, until he walked back out with a handsome pair of Italian leather shoes.

Now we were really cutting it close for making our flight. Hank, who was sitting in the front passenger seat, alerted the taxi driver that we had a plane to catch and anything he could do to get us to the airport as quickly as possible would be appreciated. Mario, Miss Long Beach Grand Prix and I were all piled in the back seat.

On the freeway, the taxi driver took Hank's request to heart, driving as fast as he could in the dicey traffic, constantly changing lanes to advance his position. Hank took notice, and turning to Mario, quipped: "Maybe we've got a budding talent here that a racing team might want to check out."

The taxi driver propped up with pride when he heard this. "Yeah! I've always wanted to be a race car driver, like Mario Andretti!"

Hank smirked, and pointing to Mario sitting directly behind the driver, told him, "Well, you've got the one and only Mario Andretti sitting right behind you."

That cab driver was no fool. "Yeah, right!" he snarled sarcastically, not believing it for a second.

Hank shrugged, Mario smiled, Candy and I exchanged slight giggles. Hank and Mario proceed to talk about racing stuff — qualifying that was scheduled for Friday, Indy, Lemans. The talk went on for a good 10 minutes before the cab driver started catching on.

Finally, the driver took a long, hard look at the man sitting behind him in his rear view mirror. "Oh my God! You are Mario Andretti!"

That triggered uproarious laughter from everyone in the cab.

———————◆———————

Riverside International Raceway managed to last a little longer than Ontario Motor Speedway, which was modeled after Indianapolis Motor Speedway and was supposed to rival IMS for prestige on the West Coast, until its premature demise and razing to make way for a giant mall in the early 1980's.

As mentioned before, my motorsports mentor, Deke Houlgate, was the publicist for RIR, which was located in the cacti-populated, arid region on the outskirts of Riverside. Deke saved my ass more than a few times, particularly since I had a penchant for arriving a few laps late for races I was supposed to be covering. My reputation for lateness had reached the point on one race day on Sunday, when Deke passed a hat around the press room to collect money for the "What Time Will Chic Arrive?" pool. The writer predicting the time closest to my actual arrival was awarded the pool money. One smart-ass writer had the temerity to write down, "3 o'clock Monday."

Unlike OMS, RIR was strictly a multiple-turn road course that hosted NASCAR, sports car, and off-road buggy races. NASCAR, of course, was its flagpole event, the only road course that NASCAR raced on in the entire country at the time.

The immense popularity of NASCAR at RIR, and my coverage there, eventually convinced Her-Ex management to send me to Daytona to attend NASCAR's premier event, the Daytona 500, which kicked off the season in February. I covered the Daytona 500 for six years in the 1980's.

I became immersed in the stories of NASCAR'S big names in those days — Richard Petty, Dale Earnhardt. Bobby Allison, Dave Pearson, Cale Yarborough, Bill Elliott, Neil Bonnett, Darrell Waltrip.

NASCAR stock cars winding through the road course for a race re-start at Riverside International Raceway

But the one NASCAR driver that I remember the most from the 80's was Tim Richmond. He was a young, charming, driver with the matinee-idol good looks who had a legendary reputation from the race-groupie women who swooned over him. Then mysterious, vague reports started surfacing of an "Illness" that sidelined Richmond from racing. The NASCAR public relations machine went completely mum on the subject, which was a challenge the longer Richmond remained out of action. Richmond's absence at Riverside was the topic that reporters asked about the most, and NASCAR turned a deaf ear. The mystery lingered for well over a year, until the unthinkable happened — Richmond passed away, in the prime of his life in his 30's. It had become all-too obvious by then that the "illness" that claimed his life was the dreaded disease that was just beginning to gain devastating notoriety in the 80's— AIDS. That reality seemed inconceivable, given Richmond's reputation.

Neil Bonnett was another NASCAR driver I fondly remembered who died prematurely. During the interview I had with him, he genuinely came off as a really nice, aw-shucks Southern gentleman from Alabama. So, the experience only deepened my sadness when he died in a practice crash at Daytona six years later.

My biggest NASCAR-related assignment didn't take place at RIR. Instead, it took place at Atlanta's NASCAR venue in the mid-1980's when I was sent to cover the NASCAR debut for Willy T. Ribbs. This was a big deal because Ribbs was attempting to become only the second black driver to race in NASCAR, which was heavily rooted in the Deep South and its fan base was almost entirely white red-necks.

Ribbs' debut, unfortunately, never took place in the Atlanta race. I wound up writing an in-depth article on Ribbs' mighty struggle to get *thisclose* that weekend. His saga literally hit a wall during Friday qualifying when he crashed and destroyed his car. Without a back-up car for the Atlanta race, his NASCAR race debut would have to wait for a later date on the calendar. But it still made for a good story.

My favorite Daytona 500 race I saw in person was the '88 race in which the father-son duo of Bobby and Davey Allison finished 1-2 on Valentine's Day. Bobby was 50 at the time and the oldest driver to win a 500-mile race. The Allisons duplicated the only other father-son 1-2 finishes in auto racing history, by Al Unser Sr. and Jr. and Lee and Richard Petty.

It was that same '88 Daytona race in which Richard Petty, proclaimed "The King" of NASCAR racing as the all-time winningest champion, survived a horrific crash. As a reporter, I watched with that gut-wrenching dread of writing an obituary on a legend. Petty's car became airborne down the front straightaway across the start-finish and somersaulted a hundred yards across the chain-link fencing that protected the crowd before landing upright back on the track. His car immediately was T-boned by another car at a high speed. Petty's car spun wildly down the track until it finally settled to a stop. Incredibly, he climbed out of the driver-side window and limped away, suffering a couple of cracked bones in his foot. Petty was racing in the very next race on the schedule the following week. I gladly wrote about the miraculous outcome.

RIR was the scene of the most horrendous crash —with another miracle result — that I witnessed. It came during the 1986 IMSA GT sports-car race and the crash happened right at the start-finish line of the counter-clockwise, nine-turn track, directly in full view of the press room. The crash involved three cars, one driven by female driver Lyn St. James, with Skip Robinson and Doc Bundy in the other two cars.

Coming off the famous ninth turn that circled back toward start-finish, Robinson and St. James were side-by-side, with Robinson on the outside, and Bundy was closing in from behind. It was common sense among drivers that at start-finish the track was barely wide enough for two cars to safely pass abreast. But inexplicably, Bundy made a move on the inside, forcing all three cars to race side-by-side-by-side past the start-finish at about 160 mph, with St. James pinched in the middle. Bundy's car made contact with St. James', instantaneously sending both Robinson's and St. James' aerodynamic vehicles airborne, while Bundy spun out like a whirling dervish behind the chaos he triggered. Robinson's car flew straight up and high into the dirt off to the right in front of the chain-link fence shielding the crowd in the grandstands. His car obliterated on impact with the retaining wall. St. James' car, meanwhile, landed back down on top of the two-foot high concrete pit-row wall, somersaulting over the wall several times, spitting off brick chunks in its path, before settling upside down on the track, and then bursting into flames. Miraculously, we watched St James crawl out of her upside-down car and walk away from the fiery wreckage. The cars' amazing safety cockpit design — and God's mercy — allowed all three drivers to survive.

Another driver in a different GT race that I covered at RIR was not so fortunate. Rolf Stommelen was a German driver competing on a three-car team in a six-hour endurance event on April 24, 1983. He was running in second place after 96 laps around the racetrack's longer 3.27-mile configuration when he lost control of his Porsche Turbo entering the hairpin ninth turn at about 180 mph. The car exploded into the retaining wall, somersaulted a couple times over the wall and burst into flames. He was extracted from the car unconscious, and pronounced dead at the hospital. His death was announced while the race was still in progress, which meant his teammates, John Fitzpatrick and Derek Bell, were well aware of his fate. Fitzpatrick was so upset that he discontinued driving. Bell went on to win the race, leading to a very somber post-race interview in the press room.

I covered plenty of race crashes, but Stommelen was the only fatality I personally witnessed. From both a professional and personal standpoint, that was one too many. I was really shaken.

"I was drawn like a magnet to her dripping sexuality."

CHAPTER 10
Crime and Debauchery

At a time when my professional life was accelerating full speed, my personal life was spinning out of control. Turning into the 1980s, I was married to a woman I didn't want to be married to. Heck, it was officially filed as confidential and we were keeping it a secret from most of my friends. The relationship was sliding off the rails; Jocelyne and I were on different tracks. As a result, I was straying.

It came to a head when I met Lizamara. I noticed her right away when I approached her teller station at my bank. Tall, with a model-like, slender figure, she was a commanding presence. She had wild, long, frizzy-curly dark hair cascading down the elegant curvature of her back. Her olive-colored skin exuded an exotic look, accentuated by a perfectly round face set off by dark, beautiful, crescent eyes, a small, doe-like nose, and pouty, voluptuous lips.

I was drawn like a magnet to her dripping sexuality. But I detected that she was sad, almost near tears, when I stepped up to her window.

"Are you OK? You look sad," I said.

She wiped a tear from her eye. "Oh, I'm just thinking about my country. I miss my country."

Now I was enchanted by her husky voice and her thick Hispanic accent. I asked her what country she was from.

"Nicaragua."

The answer projected a dreamy image just by the way she said it: *"Nee-ka-ra-gu-a."* I was intrigued. I was also smitten. The fact she opened up about her feelings to me like that felt like an invitation. I wanted to console her. I asked for her number. With a smile, she readily scribbled it down on a bank withdrawal slip.

The courtship moved *very* quickly. Sex was wild with Lizamara. I had no idea in the beginning just how wild this woman was, but I was hooked. It felt like love. I abandoned Jocelyne quickly and it was messy. It was becoming very apparent that I was not good at breaking up with someone. It always involved my finding someone else I'd rather be with, so the break-ups tended to be abrupt.

In Jocelyne's case, I disclosed that I had "met someone new." I didn't want to go through hiding another affair from her like I had with Carolyn. She was hurt, of course. I felt bad about hurting her, but I was caught up in a tizzy over Lizamara that made me somewhat emotionally detached from Jocelyne. In a word, I was an asshole.

On our second or third date, when I drove Lizamara home to her apartment, she was presented with a rude surprise — her roommate had locked her out and changed the lock. A note was left at the door regarding a dispute over an unpaid utility bill. My mother happened to be out of town, so we wound up sleeping in her bedroom that night.

The next morning, Jocelyne made a surprise visit to the Rossburn house, suspecting that I would be there with Lizamara. Jocelyne waltzed into the house to make sure I knew she was there. I greeted her in the family room while Lizamara stayed out of sight in Mom's bedroom. The conversation was brief, but it was awful.

"Do you remember that we are *married*?" Jocelyne intoned loudly enough for Lizamara to hear. Oh yeah, I had forgotten to mention that to Lizamara,

Jocelyne made her point and left. But I had some 'splainin' to do to Lizamara. She wasn't upset, accepting my explanation that the marriage was intended to help Jocelyne get a green card. She was in a forgiving mood. But she had her own agenda.

Because of the sudden fallout with her roommate, Lizamara needed to find another place to live, quickly. All of a sudden, we were apartment hunting together. Within a couple of weeks, we found a cute house in Manhattan Beach and moved in. She had been able to stay with another friend in the interim.

Meanwhile, I had consoled Jocelyne with the promise that we wouldn't dissolve our marriage until she had received her green card. Just to complicate matters, we were called in by the INS for another interview. *That* was awkward, but we passed without raising any suspicions. Jocelyne, it turned out, had some acting ability, and managed to mask her bruised feelings in front of the INS agent.

Jocelyne and I had some heart-to-heart talks during this awkward period. She told me she really liked being married to me, which added to the guilt I was already feeling. Until then I was under the impression she felt like I did, that our marriage wasn't real, that it was marriage of convenience to mitigate her immigration status. I was wrong, which wouldn't be the first.

160

As Lizamara and I settled into our new, cozy home in Manhattan Beach, her dream world began to spin. She was in America, living the good life. Considering where she had come from, this was a major change for her.

I was caught up in a romanticized facade. The more I learned about Lizamara's story, the more I became fascinated by her. She basically told me her life story that I recorded on cassette tape — covering several hours. She remorsefully recited the details to me as if it were a confessional, as if she wanted to make amends for an amoral life. The truth was, she was so conflicted between following her heart and a compulsion to do what's right, and a passionate yearning to live life to the fullest.

She was the oldest of five daughters from what would be considered an upper middle-class family, by Third-World standards. Her family lived in the nation's capitol, Managua. She had been sent to the U.S. in 1978, at age 21, at the height of the Sandinista revolution that sought to overthrow the repressive, U.S.-backed Somoza family dictatorship that had reigned in Nicaragua for over a half century. I met her three years later.

As the oldest, Lizamara was expected to serve as a role model for her four younger sisters. She tried to be the brave oldest sister during the most terrifying moment of their lives — in the dawning hours of Christmas Day in 1972, when the great Managua earthquake struck. In its wake the city was leveled, destroying Lizamara's school and the Christmas card shop where she was working. Friends and neighbors were buried under the vast rubble. The beautiful city that had been the center of her world had been permanently scarred, and it symbolized the instability that would become her life.

She had already displayed some rebelliousness by then, smoking cigarettes and losing her virginity to her childhood boyfriend Naio by age 12. She ran away from home at age 16 to live with her paternal grandfather, who was something of a rebel himself, a product of a scandalous broken marriage. He had a son, Billy, who was about 10 years older than Lizamara. She quickly idolized Billy.

Her grandfather ran an elite casino in Managua. When her grandfather suddenly died, her "Uncle" Billy took over as manager of the casino and hired Lizamara to work there as a dealer. She mixed in with the fast crowd quickly, meeting a rich, married man who whisked her away to Europe (Spain, Italy, France and England), for three months, and she picked up some work as a model. While in Italy she met an older woman who seduced her, which appealed to her sense of adventure. All of this transpired before her 18th birthday.

Upon her return to Managua, Uncle Billy installed her as co-manager of the casino, along with Joey, Billy's sleazy American side-kick. One of her primary responsibilities was to take care of the live cheetah that was on display in a cage in the center of the casino. That symbolized Lizamara's wild life — while most teenagers have cats as pets, she had a *cheetah*. She had continued her affair with the married man, accompanying him on another trip, to Puerto Vallarta, Mexico. But the wife became suspicious and *that* cat fight abruptly put an end to the extramarital affair.

Meanwhile, the Sandinista revolution was heating up. Naio, the boy to whom Lizamara lost her virginity, had joined the Sand-inistas and was a devoted Marxist who tried to sway Lizamara to his way of thinking. He persuaded her to visit a couple of revolutionary camps with him. But at the same time she was having too much fun with the other side, hanging out at the Intercontinental Hotel and at the beaches with the rich and powerful who were sympathetic to the Somoza regime. She was drawing suspicions from that crowd with her continued contact with Naio. He showed up at her doorstep on one awkward occasion with a leg wound from battle. She nursed him back to health for a couple of weeks.

The casino catered to loyal followers of Somoza, and Lizamara, now 20, caught the eye of Somoza's 18-year-old son. He was smitten and started courting her with flowers every time he visited the casino. Soon they were dating over the next five months, during which she met his parents, the despicable dictator and his wife. "Dates" evolved to trips to Colombia for weekend-long cocaine parties, fostering a habit she found difficult to resist.

Naio learned that Lizamara was dating Somoza's son and showed up at her place enraged, threatening to kill her. They wound up making love. But he was arrested shortly after that, and Lizamara had drawn the attention of the government. Naio was actually a neph-ew of Somoza, the man he was fighting to throw out of power.

The family connection got him out of jail, but with the stipulation that he leave the country. Naio left Nicaragua briefly, but soon returned and was arrested again. This time, he disappeared and was never seen again. Lizamara was devastated.

The revolution became really intense as Somoza started bombing his own people. Billy closed the casino, set the cheetah free, and left the country. Lizamara's father decided she should leave the country too, so he sent her to Los Angeles to a school where she could learn English. In LA she joined a Sandinista support group. Finally, in July of 1979, the Sandinistas succeeded in overthrowing the Somoza regime.

The transformation of her country to Sandinista control left Lizamara disenchanted with the whole scene. She moved to Miami, where she was reunited with Lorena, an old friend from Nicaragua. Lorena was an older professional photographer who became her lover. They developed a scheme in which they took advantage of unsuspecting male victims for a while. But Lizamara started spending more time with some of these men, which made Lorena jealous. Lizamara grew tired of Lorena's possessiveness and returned to LA, where she found work at my bank.

Lizamara had not been back to her country over three years when she met me. That's why she was missing it. Meeting me, an American, had given her inspiration to return to her country, and had given her an idea that would put her back in the good graces of her respectable parents. She was well-versed on how to manipulate unsuspecting men.

"I would like to do something that my parents would be proud of me," she said to me in her earnest, guttural voice that dripped with emotion. "They would be so happy for me if I were to marry an American man and establish a new life in this country! And they would be so honored if we got married back in my country!"

Lizamara knew I was still legally married to Jocelyne. I had explained to her that I had promised not to dissolve the marriage until Jocelyne had the green card in her possession, which could take another six-to-eight months, minimum. She seemingly was sympathetic to that idea.

I also intrinsically understood that Lizamara, deep down, was jealous of Jocelyne being my wife. So, what was I to do in this dilemma, as the proverbial knight on the white horse? How could I satisfy the woman to whom I had professed my love for such a noble cause as wanting to please her parents, and pull it off in a timeline that would accommodate Jocelyne's green card agenda?

Lizamara's proposal was contingent on a wedding in Nicaragua. So, I thought well, if we got married in *another country,* especially a war-torn Third-World country like Nicaragua, maybe, just maybe, I could get away with being married to two women at the same time. I was young, and this would certainly not be the last utterly foolish decision I made in my life.

So, gulp!, I agreed to marry Lizamara in Nicaragua. What could possibly go wrong?

She was so, so excited that she immediately announced our plans in a phone call to her parents in Managua. It was spring, and we projected a wedding that summer. But life with Lizamara would prove to be just one twist after another. A month later, after another call to her parents, Lizamara announced a change in plans.

"My father told me that we shouldn't come to Nicaragua, because it is too dangerous right now," she said. Then her face brightened, as only her face could. "But he said for us not to change our plans to get married. They can come here for our wedding!"

The stunned look on my face could not have masked the corner I had painted myself into. There went the idea of getting away with international bigamy by getting married in another country! I should have said right then, *hold on, this won't work; you're just going to have to wait to be my wife, sweetie.* But being young, and foolish, I came up with an alternative solution — get married in *another state.*

It was a gamble, for sure. But that's what Las Vegas is all about.

———————————————◆•••———————————————

The trip to Nicaragua was canceled. But Lizamara talked me into a spring vacation getaway — to Miami.

Lizamara had plenty of friends and family in Miami with whom she wanted to reunite. I think introducing me to them was her way of validating our decision to get married.

She had one sister living in Miami — Cristiane, who was married and had a couple of toddlers. She was the second oldest among the five sisters. Lizamara was excited about Cristiane meeting me.

Like Lizamara, Cristiane was very attractive, with curly, shoulder-length brown hair, a thin figure, and doe-like brown eyes. Her personality was much more bubbly than Lizamara's; she was excited to meet me. She and her husband prepared a big dinner for us. I think I earned her approval for marrying her older sister.

The one person in Miami whose approval meant the most to Lizamara was Lorena, her girlfriend and former lover. I met Lorena, who was a couple years older than me. Her approval took a lot more effort to earn, as she cast a wary eye toward me at first. She projected a protective, big sister-like instinct toward Lizamara. At least I did not detect any sense of jealousy on her part, so that made it easier. But Lizamara presented herself as a changed woman who had put her mischievous past behind her, and marrying me would brand her with a measure of respectability. By the end of the trip, I think Lorena accepted this concept.

In Miami, I met some of Lizamara's old friends who had fled Nicaragua with the Sandinista takeover, which included Alexis Arguello, the three-weight world champion boxer who was regarded as a national hero in the home country. He knew Lizamara dating back to primary school when they were young kids. We went out to dinner one night with the extraordinarily handsome Arguello, which was an extraordinary meeting. They obviously knew each other well. He called her by her childhood nickname, "Flacca," which meant "skinny" in Spanish. He was very gracious and respectful with me.

But one topic in the conversation stayed with me. It was regarding fidelity in Arguello's marriage. Lizamara had brought up the subject in a flirtatious manner, of course. With no reservation, Alexis stated that he was free to be with any woman he wanted, and that his wife had to accept it because he was providing all the prosperity enjoyed by the family. But as to whether his wife would be permitted the same freedom with another man, that was out of the question. I didn't think Lizamara was going to accept those terms in any marriage she entered.

Overall, the Miami trip was a lovely and romantic experience, capped off by our excursion down to Key West. It was my first time seeing the Keys — the breathtaking 180-mile drive from Miami down to Key West that marked the southernmost spot in the continental states. I loved that drive; crossing miles of bridges and tiny spits of land with ocean on both sides made you feel like you were gliding on water in a speedboat. I enjoyed my first slice of tangy key lime pie on our drive through the Keys.

Hanging out in Key West was laid-back personified, mingling with the locals decked out in bright-colored, flowery shirts, shorts and sandals. I bought a shirt in Key West that drew compliments every-time I wore it. Set against basic black, the shirt dazzled with color-ful red and gold-chested parrots perched on large, lavender, fern-like flowers, and emerald green leaves. Not known for my fashion sense, I finally wore out the shirt that lasted over twenty years. But I still have a remnant of it for silly, sentimental reasons, which tells you how special it was to me.

Key West was a special place. We visited Ernest Hemingway's charming Spanish Colonial house, home to dozens of cats. We drank cocktails at Sloppy Joe's Bar, Hemingway's favorite in town. We basked in the sun at the beach and swam in the mellow, warm water. We watched a brilliant sunset that expanded over three-fourths of the sky, as if it was an opening to heaven.

This could have been a honeymoon trip. The wedding was to follow soon.

———————◆◆◆◆———————

No one was more amused by my impending bigamy than my Best Man, Dan. He made the trip to Vegas and brought the mandatory pot to help me get through it. We didn't even bother with requisite conversation on whether I was ready to face that impossible situation.

Dan liked Lizamara, and she adored him. But he recognized trouble when he saw it. When we took refuge in a Vegas bar the night before the wedding, he likened marriage to Lizamara to a wild rapids ride on the Truckee River. As usual, Dan's metaphor was appropos.

Flying in from Managua were my in-laws, Mr. and Mrs. Pa-sos. Lizamara got her olive skin from her mother, who was pleasingly plump in middle age. Her father was lighter skinned, but Lizamara got her roundish face from him. Lizamara's parents were humble, gracious people who treated me with the upmost respect. They liked me from the get-go and welcomed the opportunity to call me their "hijo." They made it clear that I would be welcomed in their home in Managua, when the time was right, when conditions made it safe to travel there.

Mr. and Mrs. Pasos also brought their 15-year-old daughter Vilma with them for the wedding. Vilma was not like her older sisters — plain-looking, a little chubby like her mother.

Lizamara sprang another caveat for which I wasn't prepared. Vilma, the second- youngest sister among the five, was about to turn 16. Under Sandinista rule, every male and female reaching the age of 16 was eligible for *mandatory* service in the army. Her parents, who weren't big supporters of the Sandinistas in the first place, wanted no part of sending one of their daughters off to military service.

"My parents asked if Vilma can come live with us," Lizamara told me with her soul-searching eyes focused on mine.

How could I say "No" to that? So, marriage would make three.

The wedding took place in one of those cheesy Vegas chapels. Lizamara wore a classic, Nicaraguan white wedding gown — simple, elegant, cotton, floor-length, with tiny colored dot patterns embroidered throughout — and a simple white halo wreath. She was very pretty. I wore a classic, faded pastel Nicaraguan dress shirt — short-sleeved, side pockets, embroidered stitches throughout, worn untucked hanging a few inches below the belt. I was pretty stoned.

Lizamara and I at our Vegas wedding

As planned, Vilma didn't return to Managua with her parents, staying on to live with us in Manhattan Beach. Since we were fine with bigamy, we were also comfortable with bending the rules governing high school enrollment. Manhattan Beach was not within the boundaries for enrollment at my alma mater, Hawthorne High, but the Rossburn house was. So we used my mother's address as Vilma's address of record so she could attend Hawthorne High. In the back of my mind, the address was one less link to her sister that the INS might scrutinize.

I got along great with Vilma. I don't know if it had anything to do with the fact our birthdays were three days apart near the end of June, but I felt a connection with her. I felt affectionately paternal toward her. While she may not have been considered as attractive as her sisters, she was easily the smartest. She was a shining star in class, a straight-A student. She was the quiet type, very serious, always did her homework. We didn't have to worry about her hanging out with the wrong crowd. I couldn't have been prouder of her if she had been my own little sister.

From left to right: Janice, Lizamara and Vilma on the beach in Manhattan Beach

In the first year of the marriage, I tried my best to please Liza-mara. She had aspirations of pursuing a modeling career and, like I said, she had a model's physique. So I put up the money to help her put together a portfolio. She got a couple of fashion runway gigs, but nothing after that, so the modeling career never took hold. Lizamara got discouraged and felt her Hispanic ethnicity was a liability.

Life with Lizamara proved to be difficult and Janice, who tried to talk me out of marrying her in the first place, became heavily involved. Lizamara bonded with her right away. I think Lizamara related to Janice's free spirit, which, in a sense, may have been counterintuitive to the marriage bond. They became close friends and, unbeknownst to me at first, lovers. They hooked up a couple of occasions while I was working nights.

That didn't change the special bond I had with Janice. Marriage No. 3 with Lizamara felt like a protracted, tenuous fling, and it was a marriage she had pushed me into in order to please her parents. Janice served to fill whatever void existed in the marriage, for both of us.

Janice's role as a lover in the marriage expanded in one special night. Vilma was staying over night at a friend's house. We were smoking pot at home that night, the three of us together, having fun. Lizamara was very relaxed. And turned on.

As the night wore on, the two of them slipped into very sexy lingerie. Now we were all turned on. They posed for some very provocative, black-and-white photographs that I took with my expensive Canon camera.

At some point, Lizamara and I made love. Then, in the afterglow, she softly said to me, "I want to see you make love to Janice." So, we did. In the moment, the whole experience felt so tender and loving, from all sides. I felt like the luckiest man on earth.

So, what did it mean? Did it mean our marriage had turned a new leaf? With Lizamara, it was hard to tell, more like a leaf blowing in the wind.

The free spirit in Lizamara wasn't as expansive when she caught Janice and I in bed on another night, when we both thought we had Lizamara's blessing. We argued. I wasn't sure if it was because she felt betrayed or because of jealousy for Janice.

Lizamara got over that transgression. Coincidentally, the camera became an instrument that brought us closer together, for a while. She liked to pose for the camera, and she was more than willing to pose for provocative nudes that served as a turn-on for both of us. We went wild with the camera on a weekend in a Santa Barbara hotel for my 29th birthday.

But Lizamara's inner demons were starting to surface — the struggle within her over whether she wanted to be good or bad. A major test was about to arrive at our doorstep.

——————————•·•·◆·•·•——————————

Like a Managua earthquake, our lives got a jolt by a surprise visit from Lizamara's notorious Uncle Billy.

After fleeing Nicaragua, Billy wound up in Miami, where he found employment in the drug business. He was the go-between from the East to West coasts for both drugs and cash for some Miami-based drug cartel. Oh my.

When I first set eyes on Billy, my gut was telling me that he couldn't be trusted. Hell, just the way Lizamara greeted him, with a big smooch and way-too-cozy hug at our door was enough to raise my suspicions on so many levels. He had that pearly-white smile that suggested he was up to no good. His slick-backed, greasy salt-and-pepper hair was the perfect metaphor for just how slick and greasy he could be.

Billy brought a large mystery bag inside which he snuck in and stored in our bedroom closet. I had no idea what was inside the bag until later that night, when Lizamara drew back the closet curtain to

Lizamara and Uncle Billy

170

show me. My mouth fell agape at the sight of a large white sphere the size of a football sitting on a large platter.

"That's pure cocaine — 100 percent," Lizamara cooed.

She retrieved a razor blade that she started using to shave off a line of the powder onto a small plate. Her mood swings were about to change.

"He'll never notice. It's too big for him to notice."

So, just to get this straight —We had pure cocaine belonging to a Miami drug cartel, worth probably hundreds of thousands of dollars at street value, in our bedroom closet, and my illegitimate wife was scraping off a sliver, essentially stealing from the drug cartel, and assuring me, "He won't notice."

Uncle Billy's visit extended for over three weeks, and I was a basket case the whole time. The cocaine lightened Lizamara's mood and we weren't fighting so much. I was glad to see her happy again, so I joined the party and snorted some, too. It was a helluva high.

Then I got a little carried away and shared a dash of Billy's stash with a couple of my colleagues at the Her-Ex sports department. Definitely poor judgement on my part. Next thing I knew, they were stoked over the pure cocaine high and begged for more, asking if they could purchase one gram each. I went back to Lizamara and — what the hell!— she was all-in for making a little money on the side. Billy had a weight machine to measure out a gram and, I'll be damned, Lizamara knew how to use it. Nervously, I delivered the goods on this one transaction and that was the extent of my drug-dealing.

She did say Billy wouldn't notice what we scraped off the "football." But I think Billy just chose to look the other way. I think he was used to spoiling his favorite niece.

After experiencing pure cocaine, I was spoiled after that, as the cut stuff normally sold on the street never did much for me. In fact, the cut cocaine only seemed to clog my sinuses because of whatever was being mixed in with the real powder. My experience with pure cocaine through Uncle Billy was short-lived. I briefly engaged in cut cocaine when it was offered at parties; I never bought the stuff. But my sinuses couldn't take it anymore, and eventually I declined from doing it altogether.

———————◆•◆•◆◆•◆•◆———————

My crime spree hadn't ended, as long as I was still a practicing bigamist. But I officially divorced Jocelyne after she finally received her green card in the mail. She was relatively content with everything by then and was well on her way to making connections toward her career goals. I was happy for her. We parted on relatively good terms.

Soon after, Lizamara and I went through another brief wedding ceremony at the courthouse. We used that wedding date to apply for Lizamara's new INS status as my lawfully-wedded wife. Now she had some legitimacy. I guess there weren't any cross-references to my just-annulled marriage to Jocelyne in the INS files to raise any suspicions. I quite likely dodged a bullet there, just on sheer luck.

Legitimacy didn't necessarily translate to good behavior, because of undue influence. Billy came back, for a few months.

Billy wound up renting a high-rise apartment in Marina del Rey, rooming with Joey, his American, old-fart sidekick from his Managua casino days. So Billy was splitting time between coasts. He and Joey would pop over to our place every once in a while, driving up in a big, white Cadillac that Billy had bought. He wasn't storing anything in our bedroom closet.

The lure of cocaine got Janice's attention, but I was too caught up in the excitement of the drug's presence to recognize this as a red flag with my "Unbearable Lightness" paramour. The charismatic Billy set his eyes on Janice, she returned the look, and soon they were engaged in an affair.

Jealousy never fit into the dynamic of my ongoing, unorthodox relationship with Janice. But I was surprised to see that her affair with Billy made my wife jealous. This only cast further suspicions on the nature of Lizamara's relationships with her uncle. She liked Billy pampering her, and God knows what else he was doing with my wife. I knew he was trouble the moment I laid eyes on him.

Janice was also selling some of Billy's cocaine to friends, which has troubling. But who was I to judge, since I had done the same thing?

Then one day, the problem suddenly went away. Billy left us this chilling voicemail message, relating that he and Joey had to leave town in a hurry and abandon their Marina del Rey apartment. Why the sudden vacancy? Because Billy was going on the run and taking about $300,000 of the cartel's money with him. *Are you shitting me?!*

Then he left this parting gift in the message: "You can have the

Cadillac, if you want. You can pick up the car in the apartment lot, I left the keys on the front tire."

I gave Lizamara the sternest possible look I could muster. "No way in hell are you taking that car," I told her. I had visions of that Cadillac blowing up at the turn of the key in the ignition.

A couple of weeks later we got a call from Miami. I think this was the point in my life when my hair started thinning out. They were asking Lizamara about Billy's whereabouts. She told them she knew nothing, which was the truth. I prayed that they believed her. Thank God, the Miami people never paid us a visit with an ominous knock at our door. And we never saw Billy again, though he did call Lizamara once about six months later from god-knows-where.

————————◆————————

Billy may have been gone but problems mounted between Lizamara and I. Our fights grew and became more intense. The effect from cocaine had something to do with it. With Billy gone, Lizamara substituted alcohol for the white powder.

We discussed a remedy to our relationship problems that was completely illogical. Maybe having a baby would make everything good between us. We tried like hell to conceive one. Then we'd fight again over something stupid.

Then the unthinkable happened. Lizamara suffered a medical setback that required the removal of one of her tubes. It cut her chances of getting pregnant in half, and she was having a hard enough time as it was with two tubes.

"My operation," she would often refer to it, glumly, as her prospects of motherhood seemed to diminish as time went by. This was a source of depression for her and it was not good for our relationship. It led to more drinking.

When I needed advice on my relationships, I ran to my Aunt Evelyn.

My special relationship with my Aunt began to evolve shortly before I met Lizamara. Our bond began to crystalize at a point in her life when her estrangement from her two daughters, Linda and Esther, (who also was called Bebe), started to develop. I will have much more to say about Evelyn in a later chapter.

But as it related to Lizamara, Evelyn took on a role as a marriage counselor of sorts for me, drawing from her experience of three failed marriages. Lizamara met her and in her open-hearted manner she charmed Evelyn, which wasn't easy with someone as reclusive as my aunt was. Evelyn took a crack at counseling both of us in a few meetings. Evelyn may have had her own psychological need in play; she may have been trying to fill a void with Lizamara that had been created with her own daughters. But in counseling me independently, she recognized that Lizamara was deeply troubled, especially with her dependence on alcohol and drugs. This was a topic near and dear to her heart because her own father, my grandfather who deserted the family during the Depression, was an alcoholic.

◆ ◆ ◆ ◆ ◆

Lizamara made an earnest attempt to get her booze habit under control, going several months without a drink. That ended on Christmas Eve, 1982, with disastrous results. Maybe because it was the holidays, Lizamara decided she could imbibe that evening. The combination of alcohol and the memory of the Managua Earthquake that had shattered her life on Christmas Day just 10 years earlier, was a recipe for disaster.

While preparing dinner, she was sipping wine throughout. As the evening progressed, a slow simmer was seeping into her overall mood.

We had a gathering of about a dozen people at our home that evening. Dan was there. So was Lorena, Lizamara's former paramour, visiting from Miami. Another unexpected guest was a handsome young man named Bill, who Lizamara had befriended just a couple of weeks before in a random meeting at the beach; a nice guy, really. So she invited him to our Christmas Eve gathering — hell, why not?

As was customary in Hispanic culture on Christmas Eve, a big feast was planned, followed by the opening of gifts. Lizamara was preparing beef tongue, a Nicaraguan delicacy, as the main course. Yes, she had coerced me to eat tongue, which I never did quite acquire a taste for. She delayed the meal to accommodate my habitually late sister, who still had not arrived well past 10. A slow boil was gradually consuming my wife.

174

She and I retreated into the bedroom, where I thought I could calm her down with reasonable logic, but she was quickly disintegrating. I was taken aback by her reaction, not quite understanding why this was so important to her. I tried to reason with her. Why not proceed with our meal without Pam? This tactic failed spectacularly.

Lizamara had reached her boiling point, and I'm sure the effect of the alcohol had kicked in. She erupted by grabbing a high-heeled boot on the floor and flung it at me. The boot missed my head by a couple of inches and struck the wall, leaving a sizable hole in the wall poked through by the heel.

I bailed from the bedroom, hoping to avoid further intervention with her. But she followed me into the living room, where our war of words escalated in front of everybody for a few seconds. Then Lizamara just lost it. With a cocked fist, she pulled her arm back, ready to unleash a wild swing at my face. But nice-guy Bill, bless him, gallantly stepped in-between us in an attempt to be a peacemaker. Lizamara's swinging fist landed squarely on his jaw, a one-punch knockout as he dropped to the ground, evoking shrieks and gasps from our guests.

I immediately made a beeline across our living room to the kitchen, a good 15 feet away, trying to seek refuge from the maniac that my wife had become. As Bill rose from the floor and rubbed his assaulted jaw, her rage was still focused on me. So she reached up and pulled down a potted plant hanging from the ceiling, then heaved it across the room, again missing my head by a few inches. Bedlam broke out among the gathering.

I believe Pam arrived a few minutes after that.

My head had narrowly avoided two flying projectiles that evening, courtesy of my wife. But the emotional harm I had suffered was irreparable. Our marriage was on the brink.

------------------◆------------------

Over the next six months, things got a little crazy with Lizamara and I… as if Uncle Billy wasn't enough. With the strain in the relationship, we were both playing fast and loose with our marital vows.

Lizamara started going to AA meetings. Through that group she made "friends" with a guy named Volker. He was handsome, charming, a foreigner from Germany. I met him, and I was pretty sure Lizamara was having an affair with him. It would have made sense at the time.

AA was just the start of Lizamara doing things on her own. Volker may have had something to do with her landing an appearance in a dubious music video, in which she wore racy, R-rated lingerie. She got paid for laying around on the floor, showing some skin, while a punk rock band performed.

April drifted back into my life shortly after the infamous Christmas Eve blowout. My high school sweetheart was still married at the time, so she had re-emerged as a support for me through a hard time as a friend.

But Lizamara had her radar way up during this period. So, when April and I, with nothing to hide, dropped in at the house after a lunch date, Lizamara happened to be home. I introduced her to April. Lizamara knew who she was, and what she meant in my life. Pleasantries were *not* exchanged.

"I hope you're enjoying fucking my husband," she said bluntly to April.

April burst out laughing, taking it all in stride. For the record, she wasn't fucking me at the time.

But that painted the portrait of the tension between my wife and I those days.

It was during this tumultuous period in the spring of 1983 that my drifting tendencies came into play on my annual work trip to Indianapolis for the Indy 500. That was the week in which I stayed up all night on the night before the race, partying with two lovely young ladies in my hotel room, culminated by watching "The Phil Silvers Show" at 5 am.

Lizamara approached me with a bizarre proposal one day. It may have been an attempt on her part to put some excitement back into our marriage, months after the Christmas Eve fiasco.

"How would you like to do some porn photos with me?"

"Porn? You mean sex?"

"Yes. In front of the camera."

Well, since she was asking me and not somebody else, I went along with it. I had to admit, it was a titillating proposal. I don't know where the hell she met these people. I asked, but Lizamara had a way of giving vague answers. My guess was that Volker was the contact again.

However we got linked, this led us to a dank studio somewhere in the San Fernando Valley run by a Hungarian photographer with a thick accent and his platinum-blonde, heavily made-up girlfriend.

This guy shot photos of Lizamara and I having sex. I tell you, there was no experience that compared to this. He moved in for some close-ups, barked out directions in his thick Hungarian accent for us to move into different positions, moved in for a few more close-ups, and then commanded the requisite climatic shot.

For me, having the camera on us wasn't necessarily intimidating, but it wasn't a real turn-on either. It did feel unreal, however, like an out-of-body experience. We did all right for amateurs. I think I got paid $100 and Lizamara $300. But then she was photographed in a second session with the girlfriend, one-on-one.

Somewhere in Europe, I presumed, was a magazine floating around with photos of Lizamara and I having sex. We never saw the publication. It was probably just as well.

As for what it did for our marriage, it didn't feel like love, or intimacy. It was a show for the camera, posing. It didn't have the same effect when it was just the two of us, with our own camera.

The picture would get clearer a couple of months later, when our marriage would face its ultimate test.

From San Juan Del Sur, Nicaragua, Summer '83 (From top): Hanging out in a hammock at the beach; Mom displaying her fascination with a pig freely roaming on a street; Gathering at the dinner table (from left): Lizamara, me, Papa Pasos, Katya II, Katya, and Mama Pasos

CHAPTER 11
Santiagatita

The Summer of '83 changed my life. "What I Did on My Summer Vacation in 1983" was one of those unforgettable stories, an unimaginable experience.

My summer vacation that year was a trip to Nicaragua.

Lizamara and I had purposely gotten married on the same day as her parents — July 23. The summer of 1983 would mark their 25th anniversary and Lizamara wanted to return to her native country to celebrate joint anniversaries with her parents; it would be our second.

Five years had now elapsed since Lizamara had not returned to Nicaragua. There was no question she had a strong yearning to return to her country. It was under full Sandinista control by then. Mr. Pasos, Lizamara's father, had determined that it was safe for us to visit.

"Safe" was a relative term, depending on who was coming to visit. This time, one of those moments you wish you could have taken back in time to prevent consequential events from happening occurred when Lizamara and I were telling my mother about our plans to visit Nicaragua in a few weeks.

Mother, who was in the midst of the world-traveling phase of her life, chirped, "Oh, I want to go!"

Now, as soon as the words escaped her lips, I knew it was a bad idea. But I didn't snatch the moment quickly enough, before Lizamara fell right in step by responding, "Why don't you come with us? My parents would love to see you!"

Oh God, no!, I thought. *Please, Mom, have the common sense to say No.*

"I'd love to! It sounds like fun!" My mom was beaming that wide smile of hers that masked the impending disaster to follow.

So, there we were, the three of us— myself, Lizamara, and my mother — in a plane, eventual destination, Managua, Nicaragua. It wasn't a direct flight from LA; we had to change planes in San Salvador, El Salvador.

If I could name one place on the planet that sounded scarier than Nicaragua in the summer of '83, it would be El Salvador. There were horrible headlines on reports of government death squads marauding around that country committing senseless killings at the time. So, a two-and-a-half hour layover in the San Salvador airport to change planes sounded a bit dicey, if you asked me.

The airport was very small. And when we arrived there at night, it was nearly deserted, with the exception of about a half-dozen El Salvadoran soldiers with machine guns on their backs, loitering in the airport lobby. Dealing with the jitters of entering a Third World country for the first time in my life, I imagined a death squad looking a lot like those soldiers in the lobby.

We were pretty much the only passengers around at that time of the night — two American gringos and a Nicaraguan woman married to an American. The soldiers seemed to be checking us over. I felt pretty nervous. I remember the scene distinctly — we were sitting in these simple, wooden chairs, in front of an old black-and-white TV set that was showing an episode of the old "Flintstones" cartoon, dubbed in Spanish. The only thing I could understand was when Fred Flintstone yelled out his famous "Yabba-dabba-doo!"

My mother was an attention magnet for those soldiers with her orange-dyed hair that stood out like a neon sign. But Fred Flintstone wasn't holding her attention, so she started swaying to the Mariachi music playing over the airport intercom and stepped out into the lobby walkway into a full dance. Now she had the full attention of those soldiers. They snapped up like they were seeing an alien. It was clear by the look on their faces, they didn't know what to make of my mother.

Thinking that having my mother get shot by soldiers in the San Salvadoran airport would create bad karma for the rest of our trip, I nonchalantly wandered over to her, tapped her on the shoulder, and pointed discreetly at the soldiers.

"Hey Mom, I think you're making them nervous," I said. I clearly meant "me" when I said "them."

I got Mom to cool her heels in San Salvador. But evidently Third World country airports seemed to elicit questionable antics from my mother. When we arrived at the Managua Airport, we were passing through Customs and Mom stopped to admire the large "Bienvenidos a Nicaragua" banner on display at the entrance. She thought that would make for a great photo, so she took her camera out of her carry-on bag and snapped a shot. That prompted a woman customs security guard to rush at Mom, shouting, *"No foto! No foto!"*

Mom stood petrified while the guard snatched the camera from her hand, popped open the back cover and ripped out the film. Oh…my…God. This was going to be a fun trip.

————•••◆•••————

We managed to get through Customs without getting arrested and made it to the baggage claim area, where we were greeted by Lizamara's parents. We all piled into a little old Datsun automobile to escape from the pack of kids offering to carry our bags for loose change.

Mr. Pasos began driving us to their Managua home, which was not far from the airport. Within minutes we were abruptly stopped by a pair of soldiers with machine guns slung on their backs. This was a fine "bienvenidos" to Nicaragua. I was nervous as hell. They asked Mr. Pasos a couple of questions, glancing at Mom and I in the back seat a couple of times, then waved us on.

From the back seat of that Datsun, I was getting my first view of a Third World country. My eyes were wide open. I felt like I had been transplanted into scenes from a Mel Gibson movie I had recently seen, "The Year Of Living Dangerously," which would have been a fitting title to describe the past year being married to Lizamara. The movie took place in the Philippines, but it presented a similar intensity to what I was witnessing in Nicaragua. We drove past colorful murals painted on building walls of martyred Sandinista soldiers, with proclamations glorifying the revolution that had succeeded in overthrowing the Somoza dictatorship four years before. *"Todas Las Armas Al Pueblo"* ("All the arms to the people") was a predominant slogan on display. Nearly every street corner appeared to have a couple of soldiers — a few of them were barely teenagers — standing around with machine guns on their backs.

We passed several blocks in town in which buildings had been laid bare with missing walls from the massive earthquake that nearly destroyed Managua 11 years ago on Christmas Day. In the aftermath of that earthquake baseball legend Roberto Clemente was killed when a rescue flight he had organized tragically plunged to earth. Eleven years later, buildings stood as reminders of the quake with little sign of any reconstruction. People were living in those decrepit buildings.

The quake remnants also triggered a flood of memories of herself as a 12-year-old that continued to haunt Lizamara.

There were very few signs of American businesses in Managua— a couple of Shell and Esso gas stations, Coca-Cola and Pepsi signs, one McDonald's. Otherwise, I hardly noticed any American influence, other than the Bank of America office where Mr. Pasos worked as manager.

Signs of abject poverty were prevalent. The Pasos were considered "upper middle class" by Nicaraguan standards. They owned a spacious, nice home, and they could afford to employ a cook, Heidi, and a house servant, Bayardo. Heidi had a 21-year-old daughter, who lived with her and already was mother of four children. Bayardo, who was 19, had lived with the Pasos since he was 8. He came from a very poor family of 12. Lizamara told me he was "given" to her family as a gift after Mr. Pasos had found his father a good-paying job as a gardener.

Heidi and Bayardo lived next door, in stark contrast to the Pasos' home, in a makeshift shack composed of wood shingles, aluminum sheets, and cinder blocks. The divide between the "haves" and "have-nots" in Nicaragua was non-existent. The common ground was the street they lived on —a poorly managed dirt path, with deep ruts in spots that made it barely drivable.

Under Sandinista rule, Mr. and Mrs. Pasos' comfortable way of life was tenuous. Mr. Pasos worked for the only remaining Bank of America branch in all of Nicaragua in Managua. But because of the political tension between Presidente Daniel Ortega and President Reagan, BofA was pulling its business out of Nicaragua. Soon Mr. Pasos would be out of a job.

Mr. Pasos took me to his BofA office branch, showing it off as a source of pride. I asked him if he was worried about losing his job. Mr. Pasos, who spoke English fairly well, quipped, "Senora Pasos is," hinting at a crack in their marriage.

Before we left for Nicaragua, Lizamara had told me about her concern over her parents, that she was worried they might split up. Their marriage mirrored ours, evidently.

I think Mr. Pasos was trying to bond with me. He was genuinely grateful that I had married his rebellious daughter, and he felt she was secure under my wing. He literally offered me the shirt off his back, so to speak, because when we arrived in Managua, my checked-on luggage with all of my clothing didn't. It took a week for my luggage to finally arrive, so until then I was wearing borrowed clothes from Mr. Pasos. It was summer and very hot and sticky, so I required very little clothing — shorts, tank tops, and for going out at night, the customary Nicaraguan shirts similar to the one I had gotten married in in Vegas.

Later, I met two of his daughters — Katya, who was 21, and married to Roberto with a three-year-old daughter, and Maria Mercedes, the youngest at 14 who still lived at home. The fifth sister, Cristiane, who was the second oldest to Lizamara, was married and living in Miami.

Speaking of cracks in marriages, when Katya and I first cast eyes on each other there was an immediate spark. When there's a spark, there can be fire to follow.

—————— ◆ ——————

Mr. and Mrs. Pasos were very amiable and accommodating hosts. They were eager to show us the best this strange Central American country had to offer, despite undergoing immense political and social change.

We were given a tour of downtown Managua, where you couldn't escape the shadow of Sandino, the legendary revolutionary from whom the Sandinistas derived their name. Sandino was the ultimate martyr of the revolution, leading the resistance against the Somoza regime during the 1930s until his assassination. A giant mural of Sandino adorned the front of the fenced-off huge Cathedral in the public square.

Downtown also featured the Teatro Nacional Ruben Dario, founded by Somoza's wife Hope, in honor of the revered Nicaraguan poet whose works rose to prominence at the turn of the 1900s. A statue of Dario stood in front of the Teatro. Lizamara loved his poetry. Her voice got serious and full of emotion when she talked about him. Dario's statue, and my wife's reaction to it, gave me a glimpse of her passion for art and beauty, and how she could embrace the humanity in the words of a poet.

It was hot, so to cool off we didn't have to drive far out of town to reach Jilua, an idyllic lagoon with waters warm and blue, surrounded by plush green vegetation. Grass huts dotted the meadowy shore, which offered a tranquil setting just an echo away from the poverty of the nation's capital. This used to be the playground of the privileged under Somoza, and the Pasos enjoyed that privilege in those days. On this day, we had the place virtually to ourselves on a Saturday morning. I was Katya II's playmate for a day, as the youngster couldn't get enough of being in the water.

In the afternoon of that same day we took another short drive above the town of Masaya, to visit the most fascinating site of the entire trip — Santiago, the active volcano overlooking Lake Nicaragua. It was less than an hour's drive from Managua.

I had seen nothing quite like this. We drove to the top of the volcano, a flat mesa with an open mouth a couple of hundred yards in circumference. For something as spectacular as that, I would have expected a touristy park with an entrance fee and lots of people around, but we had the place all to ourselves. We walked up to the very edge of the mouth, where a two-foot-high brick border wall was all that stood as a barrier to the mass of spewing, spitting, red-hot lava lurking about 100 yards below. That little brick wall wasn't high enough to prevent a fall from one small misstep. I kept that in mind as I leaned ever so slightly to gaze in awe at the red glow below. It felt like a sneak peak into hell.

We climbed some stairs to a wooden cross that towered above the volcano. The cross stood in memory of a Nicaraguan general who was put to death by being thrown into the volcano in the late 1960s because he knew too much. Lizamara speculated that Somoza's army also disposed of Sandinista prisoners in the same manner at the height of the revolution.

"I'm sure this is where Naio died," she said softly, as we meditated on the gurgling lava.

My breath was taken away by the story Lizamara was telling. The thought of her first boyfriend meeting such a horrendous fate was unimaginable.

I was so taken by that story that years later I developed a screenplay with a central plot point around Naio's mythic fate at Santiago. The screenplay had many elements of this summer trip mixed in. But at the core was Lizamara's story. I entitled the screenplay, "Santiagatita," which was a reference to Lizamara herself.

"Santiagatita" implied a miniature version of Santiago, which was a volcano. Yes, you read that right, I named my wife after a volcano. In other words, metaphorically speaking, Lizamara was a small volcano primed to blow at any moment.

Uncle Billy was the villain in the screenplay. The fictitious story reveals in the end that his character nefariously turned Naio over to Somoza's troops, and that led to his ghastly death. Retribution comes in the climatic scene, when Billy is holding both Lizamara and I at gunpoint, terrified,

Cover page for my screenplay, "Santiagatita"

at the edge of Santiago. In a brief moment when he's distracted, Lizamara manages to charge Billy in a volcanic-like rage and push him into the mouth of Santiago and down to the red-hot hell below.

◆

We spent a little time in Masaya, the first town the Sandinistas successfully took control of in their gradual overthrow of the Somoza regime. What I remembered most about Masaya were the myriad of yellow, pink, turquoise and white adobe buildings throughout town distinguished by their bullet-riddled walls.

We also stopped in a tiny rural town called San Juan del Oriente, which was off the main road on a winding dirt road. The town could best be described as "earthy;" the smell of clay was overwhelming. Even the people looked "earthy." It was fitting that the town's specialty was clay ceramics.

Those two stops were on the way to San Juan del Sur, a magical beach on the Pacific Ocean side just a few miles from the Costa Rica border. San Juan del Sur encompassed an intimate, picturesque azure bay with gentle waves lapping at the pure white, palm tree-lined sand beach. The water changed colors, depending on the depth.

We stayed at a quaint, rustic inn just a few steps from the water. The wooden window shutters to our adjoining rooms opened to a breathless view of sand and water. The rooms themselves were crude — one sagging double bed and cot per room, with a few chairs and a wooden table. It was BYOTP— bring your own toilet paper. The bathroom/shower was down the hall. Chickens scampered freely all over the premises.

I vividly recall one scene that crystallized the image illustrating that this was a different world than I was accustomed to. With the beautiful bay at dusk as a backdrop, I watched a cauldron of piglets following mother pig down a side street, passing by a row of simple, stucco, pastel-colored buildings. The pig patrol continued past a man asleep in a hammock strung between two palm trees, and finally crossed the street to avoid a pair of young soldiers armed with machine guns, standing at a corner while passing a cigarette between them.

The traveling party consisted of Lizamara and I, Mom, Papa and Mama Pasos, and Katya and Katya II. No Roberto. Mr. Pasos would have nothing to do with Roberto. In addition to Lizamara's tainted opinion of him, my father-in-law's disdain further influenced my general lack of respect for Roberto.

In the intimate setting of San Juan del Sur, the attraction between Katya and I fermented.

Katya was the direct antithesis to Lizamara. They looked nothing alike. Katya was much lighter skinned. She had short-cropped, dark hair that was a far cry from Lizamara's long, wild mane, exposing her delicate neck. Her face was much more angular; Lizamara had a roundish face. Katya's eyes were round, dark olives, in contrast to Lizamara's which were more crescent-shaped. She was thin like Lizamara, but about three inches shorter. And her voice had a sweetness to it, not at all like the rough, husky quality of Lizamara's. Then there was her sweet, hearty laugh, which came easily when we were together.

Lizamara had encouraged me early on to "be nice" to Katya, because "Roberto treats her so bad." Katya had been a teen-age bride and very quickly became a teen-age mother, subservient to her dominating husband. Roberto, a doctor by profession, likely saw himself as intellectually superior to Katya, who had no advanced education. Lizamara had talked about Katya wanting to move to LA with her little girl, and hinted at the idea of them living with us.

An innocent flirtation between us was almost instantaneous when we met. Katya knew almost no English, but we somehow managed to communicate through a jumbled *Spanglish* that we developed between us. I gotta say, it was precious. Despite the cultural divide, there was a natural ease to our interplay. That just made the attraction between us all the more magnetic.

At San Juan del Sur, our playful flirtation got more physical. I playfully carried her over my shoulder and threw her in the water at one point. There was an extra charge in the body contact with her. We frolicked in the water probably longer than we should have. Lizamara was watching.

Later that evening, when we were sharing a moment alone strolling along the shore in the moonlit night, Lizamara surprised me by saying, "I'm glad to see Katya happy. This is good for her. She is so unhappy with Roberto."

I looked at Lizamara's face, lit up by the moon, and reflected on our own marital aftershocks. "I'm sorry to hear that."

"She deserves to be happy," she said.

"You're a good sister," I told her.

"You like her, don't you," she said, purposely vague.

"Oh yeah, she's sweet. I like to make her laugh."

"I mean, you like her as a *woman*."

I hesitated, caught off guard. "Now, Lizamara, I admit Katya is an attractive woman. But I would never…"

She laughed. "Just remember, Chic Perkins. She's married."

"So are we. Aren't we?"

After two days in San Juan del Sur, we drove back to Managua on July 18, the day before the Sandinistas' "independence day" from Somoza rule.

This marked the fourth anniversary of that glorious triumph, so it was still very fresh. Tensions were still extremely high, considering the fighting going on with former Somoza guards, known as "Contras," in the northeast region of the country.

A huge celebration, with military marches, music, and a grand speech by Presidente Daniel Ortega, was scheduled the next day in

Leon, a major city about 60 miles outside of Managua.

Security was ramped up. On at least a dozen occasions on our drive home, we were stopped by Sandinista soldiers. Each time we were ordered to step out while they searched the car. Mr. Pasos later explained they were searching for guns, on high alert that Contras might try to instigate an armed uprising to disrupt the celebration in Leon. An agitated Mrs. Pasos, who knew I was keeping a journal during the trip, made a point for me to write down, *"Puta Sandinistas."* It was not meant as a compliment.

We finally made it home that night. But just before midnight, I could hear from our bedroom window a crowd of people marching down the street, chanting revolutionary slogans. They were headed to the bus station, making their way to Leon.

<hr />

We didn't bother going to Leon for the July 19 celebration. Instead, Lizamara and I, Katya and Roberto, and Lizamara's cousin Mimo and wife Francis spent a lovely day at Jilua.

With Roberto present, I cooled it on the flirting with his wife. My wife seemed more at ease with her cousin around, teaming up with him in a little game of water football against Katya and I. But as the sun started to set, Lizamara took action to show that she and I were still a team. The two of us were alone, wading together out in the calm lagoon, when she surprised me by initiating lovemaking under the cover of water. It was truly a beautiful moment that rekindled the romance that had drawn us together in the first place. The mood carried over when we spent that night in Mimo and Francis's air-conditioned home.

For a few days, all was good between Lizamara and I. A couple of days later she and I took a drive alone on a winding road through plush green hills to another beach called Pochomil. We took refuge from the hot, humid sun under one of the many new grass cabanas the Sandinsta regime had put in as part of overall improvements for the beach. We ate lunch at a nice hotel on the beach, where we befriended two couples from Masaya. One of the men tried to get me drunk and talk me into joining him to watch some cockfights scheduled in Masaya in a couple of weekends. I wasn't near drunk enough to accept his invitation.

Later that day, we wound up in an old town called San Marcos, situated in the mountains where it was cooler than Managua. This was the birthplace of Somoza, and Lizamara also considered it her second home, where an uncle of hers and a bunch of cousins still resided. Taking a break from the relatives, we took a stroll that evening through the streets of San Marcos, bringing back memories for Lizamara. We ended up at the house where her deceased grandmother had lived. She had just passed away six months earlier, so Lizamara's emotions over her loss were still high.

The house was unoccupied, so we went inside. What a house. "If these walls could talk, they would have a lot to say," Lizamara said softly. It was an old, old house. The living room had a very high beamed ceiling and was divided by a partition to set off sleeping quarters. The kitchen looked like something out of the 1800s — a stone, wood-burning stove and thick wooden doors with removable boards latched horizontally to lock them. Outside, in the backyard, my eyes were drawn to a structure with wooden drains to funnel rain water for practical use. Lizamara was moved to tears, as if she could still feel her grandmother's presence.

It started to rain intermittently on our walk back to her uncle's home through an extremely poor section of town. As we walked past a young man lying in his hammock on the front porch of his shack-for-a-home, it seemed so unreal, like we were walking on a movie set. I felt like I was walking in a bubble, somehow separated from it all.

On the night of July 22, the day before Mr. and Mrs. Pasos' 25th anniversary and Lizamara's and my second anniversary, we were all invited to dinner at the gorgeous ranch home of a married couple who were friends of Lizamara's parents. Everything about the house was plush and ornate, easily the nicest house I had seen in Nicaragua. It was surprising that the Sandinistas hadn't seized ownership of it. Neilo, the husband, was obviously wealthy. He owned a car repair business, but he must have had connections. He and his wife Marita were a handsome couple. Lizamara said that Neilo looked a lot like Naio, her boyfriend who had been killed in the revolution.

There was plenty of music and dancing. Mom, the San Salvador Airport dancing sensation in the lobby walkway a week earlier, had a great time moving her feet with her dance partner, an invited guest named Rafael.

I skipped on the dancing. I was dealing with a bout of diarrhea and woeful lack of sleep.

At some point during the party, in which a lot of alcohol had been consumed, cross words were exchanged between Mr. and Mrs. Pasos. She was obviously upset. Lizamara tried to intervene and it didn't help matters. Papa Pasos sat silent.

On the drive home, Mama Pasos' rage was building like a flash fire. With Lizamara sitting in front between her parents, Mama Pasos lit into both her husband and daughter in a swirl of Spanish that I couldn't understand. Mom and I were in the back seat, dumbfounded.

It only got worse when we got home. Outside the house, Mama Pasos was intent on letting the entire neighborhood know there was a domestic fight in progress. Evidently, the heart of the matter was Mr. Pasos' extramarital activities. Lizamara desperately tried to calm her mother down, but that only made Mrs. Pasos turn her attack on her daughter. I learned later that Mama Pasos was accusing Lizamara of calling some guy named "George" in LA behind my back. That would have been Serge, the Canadian guy who was house-sitting for us along with a friend named Lison while we were gone. Her mother drove Lizamara to tears.

So, to shut her up, Lizamara started spraying her with a garden hose in the front yard. Oh boy, that didn't work.

Papa Pasos left. We didn't see him for days.

———————◆———————

It was tough facing a very distraught Mama Pasos the next day. She and Lizamara weren't speaking to each other. Needless to say, our anniversary celebration with Lizamara 's parents did not go as planned.

We made the most of what we could that day. We saw some children and teenaged dance groups perform traditional Nicaraguan dances at the Ruben Dario Theatre. Then we watched the Goldie Hawn movie "Private Benjamin" with Spanish subtitles. That night Lizamara and I went out with Katya and Roberto to a discotheque, where we felt way over-dressed. We did a lot of dancing and drinking and we all got drunk. Katya claimed it was her first time being intoxicated. She hadn't developed a drinking problem yet, like her oldest sister.

God bless Mom, who provided more than her share of comic relief.

For starters, Mom didn't speak Spanish. But she knew how to speak some French and, oddly, she got the idea that Nicaraguans would understand her better if she spoke French rather than English. Every time she broke out in French, I'd try to discreetly shake my head to make her stop, while the Nicaraguan she was speaking French to would smile politely in bewilderment. This was just so goofy, but just so like my mother.

We thought we lost her on the Sunday following our anniversary. That day marked the occasion for "tope," which was a celebration of the saints representing the three neighboring sister cities of Jinotepe, Diriamba and San Marcos. We went to Jinotepe to watch a procession that included three colorful, five-foot tall, wood-carved replicas of each saint. Seemingly, everybody from all three towns either joined in the procession or watched on the sideline as the parade snaked through all three towns. Some were in costume, some were on horseback, many were drunk.

The procession ended in Jinotepe, where a host family had food for everybody, and I mean *everybody*. A long line formed for some kind of unappetizing mush being scraped out of large barrels into wooden bowls. The Pasos were evidently related to the hosts, so

Ominous, ever-present armed Sandinista soldiers bringing up the rear of the "tope" parade. Mom took this photo at the risk of being admonished again with "No foto!"

we didn't have to wait in line. Mom passed on the mush and wandered off somewhere.

We missed out on the hosts' planned show featuring the slaughtering of the pigs in preparation for the main course, because we had to go look for my mother. It was a bit nerve-wracking wondering how much trouble a middle-aged, orange-haired, camera-toting, French-speaking American woman could get herself into around a drunken Nicaraguan crowd. But we managed to spot her and corral her.

We wound up at the home of a friend of Katya's where a party was going on; it seemed every home in Jinotepe was having a party that day. I sauntered into the living room and was drawn to the portrait photo of a young Nicaraguan man surrounded by memorabilia on a display table. The woman of the house saw me and explained her son had died in the war. I asked her what she thought of the Sandinistas. "*Muy difícil,*" she said.

————————◆————————

The scars left from the revolution were everywhere. The fighting wasn't over. It continued with the U.S.-backed Contras — mostly composed of ex-Somoza army guardsmen — who had staked out camps in the heavily forested region in the northeast corner of the country.

We set out for an ambitious adventure that required a drive directly through the region of conflict with the Contras, traversing virtually the only road across Nicaragua that connected Managua, which was near the Pacific, to the Caribbean coast.

The traveling party consisted of just four of us — Lizamara and I and our respective mothers. My mother managed to resurrect "Cameragate" on this day.

Our eventual destination, hopefully, was Corn Island, located off the Nicaraguan Caribbean coast. The way Lizamara and her mother described the island, it sounded idyllic, a tiny paradise hideaway that very few people knew about.

The drive was about 180 kilometers (112 miles) and it didn't even go all the way to the eastern coast. It dead-ended in a small town where we were expected to board a small riverboat for a four-hour ride down a river through a monkey-populated jungle, taking us to the coastal town of Bluefield. At that point we were planning to stay overnight with an uncle who lived there, then set sail the next morning on another boat for about a six-hour ocean ride to the island.

That 180-kilometer drive across the country took us nearly four hours. The one-lane road was pocked so often by giant holes from bombs, remnants of the war, that we had to take it slow. Then, on numerous occasions we had to stop for large herds of cattle crossing the road. They were in no hurry, brushing up against the car as we were marooned in their path.

When we reached the river boat dock, we were in for a rude surprise. The guard at the entrance to the boarding plank stopped us, asked for my and my mother's passports, then denied us going on board because we were Americans. The region had recently become ultra-sensitive, especially for Americans, because President Reagan had deployed U.S. aircraft carriers off Nicaragua's Caribbean coast a week earlier, in a show of intimidation to the Sandinista regime because of its close ties with Cuba and Russia. That sucked.

So, Reagan's ploy ruined our plans for Paradise on Corn Island and we had to turn around to drive back home.

Driving so deep into the eastern countryside placed us precariously close to battle grounds with the Contras. The lone road crossed several bridges over rivers.

The bridges were heavily guarded at each end by clusters of Sandinista soldiers. As Mrs. Pasos explained in Spanish and Lizamara interpreted, the soldiers were there to make sure the Contras didn't blow up the bridges. That road was strategically important for transport of supplies and mobility of military vehicles.

We started to cross an expansive bridge that spanned about a quarter-mile long. At about the midway point, Mom wanted Mrs. Pasos to stop the car so she could take a "foto," looking out toward the water.

She got out of the car. As she was setting up her shot, I looked back and noticed a soldier started running from the end of the bridge, about 100 yards away. He was running directly to Mom, wildly waving his arms.

Mom saw him coming and quickly jumped back into the car. Then she tucked her camera into her handbag. The soldier kept coming.

"Oh, mi Dio!" Mrs. Pasos shrieked.

Lizamara glared at Mom. "Let us do the talking," she told her.

The soldier pulled up to the passenger window, which Lizamara rolled down for him. She started a casual conversation with him, trying to deflate any tension. He was pointing to Mom in the back, which made her nervous. Lizamara and her mother were both addressing the soldier, trying hard not to mention anything about any camera or photo. Mom, evidently not understanding the concept "Let us do the talking," felt compelled to say something. If she had to say something, saying it in French would have been preferable at this point. Unfortunately, she remembered the Spanish word for "photo" from her airport experience, which was "foto" and pronounced exactly the same in English.

"No foto, no foto," Mom blurted out.

That got the soldier's attention, triggering eye darts from both Lizamara and her mom directed at my mother in utter disbelief. Luckily for Mom, her camera was hidden out of view. But it was my misfortune that I was sitting there with *my* camera and its fancy strap around my neck. "No foto, no foto" instantly got linked to my camera by the soldier, who immediately demanded that I hand it over. Very reluctantly, I complied. I had paid a lot of money for that Canon camera.

At the San Salvador Airport on our flight in, I had feared for my mother's life thinking those El Salvadoran soldiers were going to shoot her just for hell of it. On that bridge in the Nicaraguan war zone, with my camera in the possession of that Sandinista soldier, the greater fear was that I was going to grab his machine gun and shoot her myself.

Lizamara and her mother did some really fast talking in Spanish to get my camera back from the soldier, thus sparing my mother from my tragic act of retribution. But, oh boy, subtract a few years from my life expectancy, thanks to my dear mother.

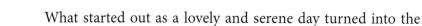

What started out as a lovely and serene day turned into the most explosive day of the trip.

Packing up two cars, the entire Pasos clan came along to show us Granada, easily the most charming city we had visited in Nicaragua, about 40 miles east of Managua. With its Spanish-style red-brick roofs, columns, towers, plazas, fountains, statues, and horse-drawn carriages, it felt like stepping back into the 19th century.

Granada was also very scenic because it bordered the shores of Lake Nicaragua, with the mighty Santiago volcano standing tall in the distance. We took a short boat ride out among the hundreds of tiny islets that were formed by a volcanic eruption in ancient times. For lunch, we ate fish caught the same day from the lake and cooked on the grill by a simple family living a simple existence in a hut for a home.

We spent the afternoon lying on the white sand and sun on one of the islets and swimming in the warm waters of the lake. We swam at our own risk under the warning that Lake Nicaragua was inhabited by the only known fresh-water sharks on the earth. We were drinking beers in the warm sun. Lizamara drank a few beers. That was the precursor for the volcanic eruption forthcoming from Santiagatita. I don't know what got into her. She suddenly became very despondent after asking me for a kiss. She complained that I didn't show her enough affection, that she had to ask for it, that I showed more affection toward Katya. I thought we had gotten back on track together, but her parents' split in recent days conflicted her perspective of us. *Ahh, dancing with Katya,* I then thought. That recent night in which Katya got drunk for the first time when we all went out dancing, was factoring in Lizamara's emotional spin. I could sense how the alcohol effect was twisting her logic. She suddenly announced that she might be pregnant, and that she wanted me to understand that the baby was exclusively hers. Then she began verbally attacking me, blaming me for our failing marriage. Then she declared, "It's over."

I was unhappy and mad. I gave her the silent treatment as she drove us home. She resumed the verbal attack, getting so upset that her mother asked her to stop the car so she and Katya II could get out and ride in the back of Roberto's truck. That left Mom and I alone with Lizamara; I sat in the front passenger seat, and Mom in the back.

Lizamara kept at it, her voice rising in anger the longer she talked. There was plenty I could have said in response, but I kept my mouth shut. The more she talked, the harder it was for me to bite my lip. She was obviously goading me to say something.

Finally, I did. "You can sure dish it out, but you can't take it," was all I said.

With that, she swung her right hand out and slapped me across the face with a stinging blow. The volcano was bubbling.

I froze, holding as still as I possibly could. So, she swung and slapped me in the face again.

Again, I didn't stir. Then she slapped me a third time.

I couldn't withhold it anymore. It was an instant reaction to her third blow. I allowed my hand to fly out and slap her across the face.

Santiagatita went into full eruption mode.

"I'm going to turn you in to the Sandinista police and tell them you are an American spy, you sonofabitch!" she shrieked.

I was shellshocked by what I was hearing, mortified because I was on foreign turf and had no idea if I could count on being on safe ground. I looked at my maniacal wife and the rage on her face was frightening.

All I could think of in that moment was to escape. I wasn't going to try to call her bluff. So, I swung the passenger door open and jumped out of the moving car. You're thinking, *can it get any worse?* Yes it can, and did.

As I collected myself on the sidewalk of a major street that cut through downtown Managua, Lizamara made a u-turn in the middle of the street to circle back to where I was standing. She stopped in the center lane, stared at me for a moment, and I flipped her off. She made another u-turn and drove off, leaving me stranded. Flipping her off made me feel too good to worry, at first, as I watched her drive away.

I stood there for I don't know how long, trying to get my head back on straight. Slowly, I started to assess my situation, and getting nervous. The first thing I realized was that I had jumped out of the car without either my wallet or passport. Well, that was inconvenient.

I was dressed in shorts, a bright orange tank top, and wearing flip-flops. It was late afternoon and the sun was starting to dip. It would be dark in less than two hours. I decided I certainly didn't want to be wandering in this city in the middle of the night. That didn't project to being a safe predicament for an under-dressed, undocumented, cash-poor American.

I decided I had better start walking. I took a few steps, and one of the flip-flops broke. *Aw shit, just pile on the misery,* I thought. So now I was down to one flip-flop and walking barefoot on the other foot. Add the bright orange tank top and petrified expression on my face, and I couldn't have looked more conspicuously ridiculous to Nicaraguans.

I recognized the street; we had driven down the street numerous times before. I knew that the Pasos house wasn't far. I knew that I had to take a turn off this street at some point. But I was so disoriented that I wasn't sure if it was a left or right turn. So I walked with the hope I would recognize *something* that would clue me in.

This was a Third World country. This was a look so different from anything I had experienced that nothing was familiar to me. As I kept walking and the sun was sinking lower on the horizon, I passed a cemetery on the other side of the street. My thought then was, *you would think I would remember a cemetery if I had any idea where I was.* But that cemetery wasn't triggering any memory of location for me. Shit, that's when I realized I was in real trouble. Maybe it was a sign to start digging a hole for me in that cemetery.

I was feeling fairly desperate as the sun was beginning to disappear behind a hill. All I could think of was that I had to make a turn off this god-damned street to get to the street the Pasos resided on. I could guess left or right turn, but there was a 50 percent chance I could be wrong. I didn't like my chances. After all, it hadn't exactly been my lucky day.

Suddenly, a thought became clear in my muddled head — I remembered the name of the street the Pasos lived on. It was "Del Munich," kind of a strange name for a street in Nicaragua. Maybe that's why it stuck in my head.

My Spanish was pretty poor. But as I entered a crosswalk on the street, two young Nicaraguan women were passing me. Frantically waving at them with the broken flip-flop in my hand, I decided to take a crack at asking them, in terrible Spanish, "*Tu sabes a donde a calle que nombre Del Munich?*"

Of course, the young women both started jabbering at me simultaneously in Spanish. I strained hard to listen, but I wasn't deciphering any of it. It was a feeling of utter helplessness. But after about a minute of chatter, one of them *finally* pointed to the left. That's all I needed.

"*Gracias!*" I screamed at the two women. At the next street, I turned left. I walked about four or five blocks down and came across the street I identified as Del Munich. I recognized a huge clock sign, frozen in time because it wasn't operable, at a street corner. I knew I was only about three blocks from the Pasos' home.

I made it to the Pasos' home as dusk settled in. Lizamara was asleep in our guest bedroom, sleeping off her hangover. I mellowed out in the living room, rubbing the bare foot that I had to walk on without a flip-flop. About a half-hour later, Mom and Mrs. Pasos came through the front door. They had gone off in the Datsun in search of me and were happy to see me. Mama Pasos immediately served me up some food in the kitchen. I was glad to be alive and safe.

———————◆·◆·◆·◆·◆———————

When Lizamara sobered up the next day, she was contrite. We decided we needed a couple of days alone together at a hotel. We laid low for a day before heading out to the hotel. I made a concerted effort to be more affectionate toward her.

Papa Pasos finally resurfaced and invited me out — alone — to one of his favorite hangouts, the bar at the lavish, pyramid-shaped, gleaming-white Intercontinental Hotel that hovered over its quake-traumatized neighborhood. On our drive to the hotel, a three-week old Yankees-Orioles baseball game was being re-broadcast on the car radio. The Orioles had a Nicaraguan pitcher named Dennis Martinez whom the entire country had an intense interest in following.

At the bar, Papa Pasos told me an interesting story about how Howard Hughes once inhabited the entire top floor of the hotel for nearly a year. What held greater immediate intrigue was the story behind the potential rift I witnessed in the Pasos' marriage at the bar. A fashionably dressed young woman sauntered up to Mr. Pasos. Quickly, he told me to call him "Orlando," not "Mr. Pasos." The woman plopped in his lap and affectionately wrapped an arm around his neck. He casually put his arm around her waist. Obviously, they were well acquainted. I decided, out of respect for my father-in-law, that discretion was the better part of valor, and I kept the knowledge of this scene to myself.

While Papa Pasos still had not reconciled with his wife, Lizamara and I had. We booked a room in the nearby Camino Real Hotel, woke up to breakfast in bed and made delicious love. We had booked Mom her own separate room.

We then went for an outing in Leon, the birthplace of the revolution. This region was dryer than most other places. Instead of sugarcane, coffee, corn and wheat that grew in most other parts of Nicaragua cotton was the main crop near Leon.

There was a "Nuevo" Leon and a "Viejo" Leon, the red-brick remnants that remained from the Momotombo volcanic eruption of 1918. The mostly poor residents of this section of town now lived in grass huts. The new, modern Leon was being groomed to possibly replace Managua as the nation's capitol. The "Viejo" section of town is where most of its 82,000 residents lived. The most prominent structure in town was the massive Cathedral, surrounded by several statues of lions standing guard. "Leon" translates to "lion" in English. The outside walls were blackened from war bombs, but inside it was exquisitely palatial, displaying numerous memorials commemorating Nicaragua's long line of poets.

From Leon we embarked for Poneloya, a gorgeous beach with rough but bath-water-warm water. We had the beach all to ourselves. Nearby was a cliff point jetting out to the sea, with a resort standing on top, and people were drinking and dancing on balconies. By late afternoon we climbed to the top of a gigantic rock, directly below the resort, that offered a view of the entire beach in both directions. Massive waves crashed into the rocks below, sounding like a sonic boom each time they crashed and sending far-reaching sprays toward the sky. We watched a brilliant sky show commanded by the setting sun. Not far from us, enjoying the same scene, was a foreign family, speaking a language that we deduced was Russian. Russian tourists in Nicaragua implied the underpinnings of political tension between our two countries, in the face of Russian influence on Nicaragua as a threat to our national security.

On the ride back to the hotel, we incurred a flat tire. It was Saturday night, around 8:30, and we were lucky to find a repair place open. When we got back on the road again, we were stopped twice by Sandinista police. The second duo included a kid who couldn't have been more than 12 years old, with a rifle slung on his back.

The next day we relaxed at the hotel, enjoying a poolside barbecue and mariachi band. Mama Pasos, Roberto, Katya and Katya II drove out to join us. On the way home that afternoon we stopped at the Managua Fair for the first day of the annual 10-day celebration of Santo Domingo. The 10 days commemorated the length of time that saint Santo Domingo needed to travel between newly-established Catholic churches in Las Serritas and Santo Domingo when Spaniards first settled in Nicaragua in the 1700's.

A family band that included an old boyfriend of Lizamara's was playing music that had people dancing, including my mother. Gradually, the crowd stopped in amusement to watch my mother's "unique" style of dancing.

* * * ◆ * * *

The party mood for Santo Domingo not only set the stage for reconciliation between Mama and Papa Pasos, but also between Papa Pasos and Roberto. Well, for a couple of hours anyway.

Papa Pasos made a point to include Roberto in the family get-together at the Intercontinental Hotel, for a poolside dinner. We arrived at about 2:30 p.m. for drinking and dancing. Dinner was delayed another hour, which was really bad, because that meant more drinking.

I had already witnessed Roberto drunk on a couple of occasions on this trip. This time he started getting belligerent, making comments to Katya that were intended to upset Papa Pasos. When Papa Pasos decided to shift the entire family to another table in the shade, out of the sun, Roberto refused to move. Comments were being thrown back and forth, across the pool, between the two men.

Lizamara, who had been drinking, too, decided to get involved, arguing with Roberto. Katya separated them. After a momentary truce, Lizamara stepped up again, objecting to how Roberto was treating Katya II. Roberto hit my wife. Not good. As he made his way back to the table, Lizamara tried to push him into the pool. He turned and took a swing at her, which got Papa Pasos out of his chair, and he tried to hit Roberto. A beer glass shattered on the ground. In the ensuing melee, Roberto's glasses flew off, blinding him. As he frantically scrambled to find his glasses, I spotted them at the bottom of the pool and pointed them out to him. So he dove into the pool to retrieve them. Ai-ya-yai!

Thankfully, a dripping wet Roberto, Katya and their daughter left. But there were more drunks at this gathering. One of them, an old man, started shouting at Papa Pasos. Lord have mercy. Lizamara, totally out of control, stepped in between them. I'm sorry, but the scene was just too comical to take seriously — seeing my wife, towering a a good four inches above this little old man, challenging him to a fight, defending her father. Viva la Santo Domingo!

———————◆———————

We had one last full day before our three-week "vacation" would end. After the family fireworks at the Intercontinental the night before, Lizamara and I sought privacy at a nearby seedy hotel. We had a memorable love-making session, not knowing when we'd be doing it again.

On our final evening at the Pasos home, the family gathered to say goodbye to Mom and I. Lizamara was planning to stay longer. She and Roberto made peace, believe it or not. We had a beautiful dinner with the entire family. I got up to make an emotional speech. So did Mom, Katya, and even Bayardo, the house servant. Tears were choked back.

Lizamara was in a touchy mood when she helped pack my bags that evening. She wasn't sure how long she was going to remain in Nicaragua.

We had an 8 a.m. check-in time for our flight out of Managua the next morning. Papa and Mama Pasos were truly sad to see Mom and I leave. Lizamara and I hugged each other as long as possible before I entered the customs station.

Lizamara wound up staying a lot longer than we thought — five months. I knew part of her motivation for staying was to make sure her parents were back in good stead, but the longer she stayed, the greater the toll was on our own marriage.

I had returned home to find the house in good shape under the watch of our Canadian friends Serge and Lison. Vilma and I got along fine in Lizamara's absence. I started seeing a lot more of Janice.

Meanwhile, I had no idea what Lizamara was up to those five months in Nicaragua. Her country had changed dramatically and it was an emotional shock for her. I knew she wanted to reconnect with old friends and family to try to recapture her past. But I couldn't help wonder how much of her past she wanted to rekindle. She had confided on our last night in Nicaragua that at the Intercontinental Hotel, where all the fighting broke out between her and Roberto and her father, she had seen the married man with whom she had had an affair when she was 18, when they traveled through Europe and Mexico.

They had exchanged glances and a nod, but he was with his wife, and they didn't stick around. I'm sure he knew how to get in contact with her if he wanted.

When Lizamara finally returned home, a lot had changed between us in five months. We didn't talk about what we had done, or with whom.

But my mind was made up. I told her I wanted a divorce. I had decided I needed to get out of this marriage before it killed me.

Parting shots of Nicaragua (From top): Church in downtown Managua with huge poster of Sandino on the wall; Local store with a sign displayed everywhere in the country, proclaiming the Sandinista revolutionary slogan: "Todas Las Armas al Pueblo" ("All Weapons to the People"); View from the unbuffered edge at the mouth of the Santiago volcano

CHAPTER 12
Racing and Racy Stories, Part 2

Steve Earwood had a natural wit that never ceased to make me laugh. He was amused by my stories about Uncle Billy and my involvement with his two nieces, Lizamara and Katya. In his typical inappropriate, Good-Ol'-Boy-humor manner, he summed up the whole scenario with a precise moniker to label Lizamara and Katya: "The Coke sees-ters."

Then Steve, more than once, told me, "Next to Densmore, you're the craziest sonofabitch I know."

For the record, Katya is guilty only by familial association with her uncle and oldest sister. My flirtations with her in Nicaragua in no way implied that she had any connection with coke.

Earwood, and his cohort Dave Densmore, were the main reasons why I looked forward to visiting Pomona Raceway twice a year to cover the NHRA season-opening Winternationals and season-ending World Finals.

The price I paid for the 12 years of covering the eardrum-shattering engines of the Top Fuel and Funny Car dragsters at Pomona is the 30 percent hearing loss I'm dealing with in my senior years. Those suckers were so loud they made the whole press tower shake violently when the engines were fired up and the vehicles blasted off from the start line. You didn't dare stand too close to the windows in fear that they might shatter from the reverberations.

Earwood and Densmore, better known as "Denswood" as a bonded team in friendship and the motorsports world, made the sacrifice to my hearing worthwhile.

Earwood was the national publicist for the NHRA. He was a dark-haired, good-looking Southern charmer from Alpharetta, Ga., who had the easy-going, smooth talk down to a science. Densmore, who wrote PR releases for the NHRA as well as publicity work for individual drag-racing teams, was Earwood's short, stocky, bearded, quirky, unpredictable sidekick from Amarillo, Texas. They both spoke with the Southern drawls of their respective roots.

They were hilarious together; I was brought to tears with laughter from so many moments shared with these two guys. I regarded both of them as true friends.

Steve set me up for interviews with all the big names in drag racing in the 80's — Don "Big Daddy" Garlits, Don "The Snake" Prudhome, Tom "Mongoose" McEwen, John Force, Kenny Bernstein, and of course Shirley "Cha-Cha" Muldowney. The nicknames were gimmicky names tagged by radio announcers in their loud, tacky, on-air promos for drag-racing events.

Muldowney was my favorite, and Steve obliged by arranging several interviews with her over the years. She was a genuine sensation in her in-the-face challenge of the male-dominated drag-racing circuit, driving her outrageous pink Top Fuel dragster as the well-respected "First Lady of Drag Racing." She won the NHRA's elite Top Fuel championship three times during the 70's, the first woman to win a title in any major category. Her story inspired a movie in 1983 entitled "Heart Like A Wheel" starring Bonnie Bedelia. Shirley was an attractive lady with long black, curly hair, slender figure and make-up; she had no problem playing up her feminine looks in a grease-smeared, masculine sport. She was always accommodating with the press, at least with me. I think she and Earwood were genuine friends; she would hardly have been the first woman turned on by his charms.

NHRA Publicity Director Steve Earwood, a k a "Unknown Confederate Dead," in Alpharetta, Ga.

It was an Earwood-arranged interview that resulted in the second most-embarrassing moment in my sports writing career (the most embarrassing is re-told at the end of this chapter.) Steve set me up to speak with a drag racer from Georgia by the name of Roy Hill. The Southern accent was laid on thick when Hill talked, and I admit I had trouble understanding.

It is obligatory that all drivers mention the primary sponsors of their cars to reporters interviewing them. For Hill, as I heard it, his sponsor was a "food company," and that's how I reported it in my feature story on him.

Steve called me up on the day the story ran in the paper. "Good story, Chuck," he said, very politely. "Chuck" seemed to be the name both he and Dave preferred calling me, just for the sake of spite. "There was just one minor error, though. Roy's sponsor actually is a 'boot' company, not a 'food' company."

No matter how often Steve insisted it was "no big deal," I felt god-awful about that mistake as a professional journalist who took pride in reporting accuracy. Steve, of course, wouldn't let me forget it each time we sat down at a restaurant together and ordered "boot."

On the subject of restaurants, a couple of Dave's classic screwball antics come to mind. Dave was especially funny when he was drunk. Steve customarily treated a contingent of the press to a post-event dinner after NHRA events at the Pomona Valley Mining Co., a renowned steak restaurant located just a couple miles from the Pomona drag strip. With Dave in attendance, and with the wine pouring in generous amounts, these gatherings had a tendency to degenerate into raucous and bawdy affairs. Dave set the tone at one gathering by biting a chunk off his wine glass and vociferously crunching it with his teeth in a public display of disobedience (bad dog!). On another occasion he got a little more creative with his mischievousness — he grabbed a large serving bowl of sour cream off the table and vanished. There were 12 of us seated at a large dining table, and we were all fairly blitzed, too. So we were oblivious to the fact that he was crawling underneath the table. By the time we realized what was going on, most of us had been treated to this moist sensation in each of our laps, where Dave was serving up dollops of the sour cream.

When he was sober, Dave was sweet and harmless and a lovable, big-hearted guy. He resided in the LA area in the '80s, and he and I had a gym racquetball gig going for a while. Dave displayed some pretty good athletic ability, whether it was quick footwork on the racquetball court or balancing a bowl of sour cream without spilling while crawling in tight quarters under a dining table.

Group shot autographed by newly-crowned NHRA Funny Car champion Kenny Bernstein (kneeling, holding trophy) at Pomona Raceway. The group includes members of Bernstein's race crew and supporting staff, plus members of the media, including four of L.A.'s Big 5 motorsports writers of the 1980's: Shav Glick of the L.A. Times (2nd from left of Bernstein), me (between Glick and Bernstein), Tim Tuttle of the Orange County Register (2nd from right of Bernstein), and Jim Short of the Riverside Free-Press Enterprise (far right, sitting.)

My favorite "Denswood" story occurred on an unforgettable Daytona trip. They were in the Florida town on the week of the Daytona 500, schmoozing it up with racing sponsors. They invited me to stay at the large suite they rented at a hotel along the beach. The suite was large enough to accommodate one other sports writer from Fort Worth, Texas, a young man in his mid-20's who everybody called "Gunner."

Gunner was an odd sort— short, chubby, balding, thick glasses, and for reasons that defied appearances, possessed of an especially obnoxious cocky attitude. He was the consummate "BSer", in part, I assessed, to boost his own self-esteem. He could talk the talk, but he wasn't fooling anyone — everybody could see right through him. I was stuck in the same room with him all week, so I heard more than my share of his talk. Not to mention his extremely loud snoring at night, too, unfortunately.

The story began on a night the four of us went out to a Daytona strip club — a "titty bar," as Steve colloquially described it. We collectively engaged in friendly conversation and flirtation with a comely blonde stripper named Tammy. Gunner, in his cocky manner, overplayed his hand, convincing himself that he and Tammy were connecting. Tammy, ever the sweetheart, was being nice with him.

Meanwhile, I managed to make a connection with her when she told me she was from Kokomo, Ind., which is in the suburbs of Indianapolis. The Indy 500 was three months away, I was going to be in town to cover it, and I told her I could get her a ticket to the race. I got her phone number in Indiana on the prospect of hooking up.

When it came time to call it a night at the strip club, Gunner decided he was going to stay longer because supposedly he and Tammy had a "date" after closing. Steve, Dave and I returned to the hotel, and Gunner and Tammy showed up hours later, near 3 a.m. He was wearing a jacket with the name of the strip club emblazoned on the back that Tammy had given him. She also gave him a Polaroid photo of her sitting by a pool in a scanty bikini, which only inflated his head way out of proportion.

Sharing a room with Gunner, I was wakened by their arrival. Tammy gave me a knowing look, quietly told me aside to call her in Indiana, then left. Gunner then started bragging about how she had —ahem — "taken care" of him, and somehow the photo he had of her in a bikini was proof.

Three months later, when Tammy and I rendezvoused in Indianapolis, she had a good laugh over Gunner's fantasy about their "connection" that night in Daytona. Tammy wasn't that kind of girl. I could vouch for that. She slept with me for two nights in my hotel room at Indy, but we never had sex. Yep, I slept with a stripper and we didn't have sex. We cuddled, and I did give her a full-body massage in the buff (her, not me). But, despite all appearances from what she was willing to bare working at a titty bar in Daytona, Tammy was just a wholesome girl from Indiana.

However, she did like to dress provocatively. She created a stir when I brought her in the Indianapolis Motor Speedway press room on the quiet Friday before the race. Dressed in a form-fitting, skimpy mini-skirt, she definitely turned heads, and there were a few looks of envy cast my way.

Gunner was in Indy for the race that week. So was the Denswood duo as guests through sponsor connections. A couple of nights before Tammy arrived, there was a buffet dinner/live music/dancing affair for the press in a large hotel conference hall. Gunner was flashing the photo of Tammy in a bikini and bragging about his "score" in Daytona back in February to anybody who could stand hearing his obnoxious story.

Steve and Dave had heard more than they could stand. They launched a plan for Gunner's comeuppance, recruiting the help of a tall, handsome young sports writer named Joe from the St. Petersburg, Florida, newspaper. The set-up was sprung when Gunner and Dave were returning from the restroom in the hotel lobby. Joe, a stranger to Gunner, suddenly appeared and charged toward Gunner from about 20 feet away.

"Are you the sonofabitch who's going around bragging about sleeping with my wife Tammy in Daytona?!" Joe screamed, pointing a discriminatory finger at Gunner.

Steve and I stood off the side to witness the carnage. It was ugly. Poor Gunner seemingly shriveled before our very eyes. In desperation, Gunner's first instinct was to get rid of the incriminating evidence — the photo of Tammy. Steve and I started cracking up watching him try to shove the photo into Dave's pants' back pocket.

"Oh, no, no!! That wasn't me! I'm just a guy from Fort Worth!" Gunner pleaded, staring at Joe's cocked fist, ready to strike. "Never been to Daytona!" Never. Why would a guy from Fort Worth be in Daytona, so goes the logic.

"You better stay away from her if you know what's good for ya!" Joe snarled.

Steve and I quietly applauded the Oscar-worthy performance.

Gunner's bragging about Tammy ceased. "Tammy? Tammy

who? Don't know anybody named Tammy." The Denswood duo succeeded in silencing the mouth that wouldn't shut up, earning my eternal respect.

Another opportunity to participate in a racing event was presented to me — the 1985 Mint 400 off-road race held in the desert just outside of Las Vegas.

The folks at Nissan who were in the business of sponsoring off-road teams and events came up with a wild idea. How about putting two sports writers in one of Nissan's stock trucks in the grueling Mint 400, to prove how tough and rugged the vehicle was? The idea was presented to Jim Short, the motorsports writer from the Riverside Press-Enterprise, and myself to procure a couple of first-person stories exhorting the off-road prowess of the Nissan truck.

The Mint 400 was run on a nasty, bumpy, hilly, unpredictable 100-mile loop, four times around. Jim and I were given only a scant few miles of pre-run time the day before to gain any familiarity with the course. There wasn't anything "trick" on the Nissan truck to beef up its suspension for the punishment it would have to absorb, so this idea was doomed from the get-go. Jim and I were in for one continuous string of calamities that resulted in an unmitigated disaster of hilarious proportions.

The race called for a staggered start, shortly after dawn at 7 a.m., at 10-second intervals for several hundred vehicles, ranging from motorcycles, race-enhanced dune buggies, and trucks (except our stock mini-truck class) modified for off-roading.

While waiting in line at the start, I became engaged in an open flirtation with an attractive, statuesque, dark-haired, olive-skinned woman who approached me out of nowhere. Jeri, who worked for off-road entrepreneur Mickey Thompson, was patrolling the lineup of vehicles looking for something, and she found it with me.

Finally, we were nearly the last to get waved off the start line, which was just as well because it kept us out of the way of everybody else for a short while.

Jim drove off the start and I was buckled in the passenger seat. Within the first few miles we had to cross a long stretch of bumpy whoop-de-doos that rattled my inner organs like shooting the rapids on the Truckee River. That made me have to pee so bad that I begged Jim to stop after about 10 miles so I could get out to relieve myself.

I jumped out of the car, unzipped my all-white racing suit, and let it all hang out. That's when I heard a chorus of "We see you!" from a throng of spectators sitting in beach chairs, perched atop nearby sand dunes. "I don't care!" I shouted back, because, really, I had no choice under the circumstances.

I took over the driving from there. About twenty miles into the loop, we reached a dry lake bed consisting of soft soot about two feet deep in some spots. The challenge was to keep the foot on the gas to power the truck through the soot and avoid getting buried in it. To complicate matters, the faster dune buggies that had started the race way ahead of us were already circling on their second lap and roaring past us. Every time one of those buggies whizzed by, a blanket of dust was heaved across our front windshield, completely obscuring my vision. I had no choice but to drive completely blind at full throttle for several seconds each time in their wake.

On the fourth or fifth dust-bathing I peeked through the dirt-covered windshield to determine the truck was headed directly into thick brush. I took evasive action by slightly lifting off the accelerator and veering right, but the truck suddenly swerved in the soot and the wheels planted. I floored the throttle in an attempt dislodge the back tires, but they just furiously spun, spitting out a soot cloud from behind and digging deeper. We became hopelessly stuck.

Jim and I climbed out of the truck, coughing and wheezing from the hovering soot cloud. When the dust settled, every strand of our hair and every inch of our faces and body — except for our goggled-covered eyes — was coated with soot. As we wiped the soot from our clogged nostrils and scratched our dusty heads, we assessed how deep the rear tires were dug in.

Then we noticed the lone, tiny, two-foot-long shovel that Nissan attached to the bed of the truck. That was all we had to dig ourselves out of this mess. We took turns shoveling, sinking our knees into the two-foot-deep soot in a scene of humiliation.

For 20 minutes this went on and we weren't making much progress because the soft soot kept sliding right back around the tires. Meanwhile, parked about 50 yards off course was an old Cadillac belonging to a grizzled, long-haired, bearded, near-toothless spectator.

He was sitting in a beach chair, guzzling down beers, completely enjoying our futility. Finally, the guy let out a cackle and shouted out to us:

"Hey, you wanna tow? I gotta line."

"Hell yeah!" Jim shouted back.

The guy's thick line was long enough to reach our truck, so that his car could stay out of danger from the soot bed. He attached the line to the rear bumpers of both vehicles, which enabled him to successfully drag us free. We thanked him profusely and told him if he made his way back to start-finish and found the Team Nissan pit, they would reward him with a couple six-packs of Budweiser, courtesy of the official sponsor of the Nissan team.

Jim resumed driving from that point. We escaped the dry lake bed, but within a few miles we encountered our next laughable calamity. Entering a section of tall dunes, we came upon a steep hill about 60 feet high looming directly ahead. Jim floored the truck to give it momentum in an attempt to reach the top of the hill. The engine wheezed angrily as the Nissan tried in vain to climb to the top but gradually lost acceleration and, pitifully, started sliding back down the hill. Jim floored the engine again for another try. And another try. And another, with the same result each time. The truck simply didn't have enough horsepower to reach the top.

Perched atop perimeter hills were about 100 spectators taking in this hilarious spectacle. Their laughter echoed through the chambers. Finally, in the distance was the sound of a dune buggy approaching. Jim and I watched, with utter disbelief, as the dune buggy roared past us off on a path that went around the base of the hill.

"Aw shit," Jim muttered. "I guess we're supposed to go that way."

Humility had no limits on us on this day.

This is what happens when you put two inexperienced sports writers in a race vehicle who have no business being in a professional race. Two sports writers who don't know anything about the inner workings of a car engine, which would have come in handy a few miles further down the road when the dang throttle stuck wide open. It took all I had to press down on the brake pedal to keep the truck from veering off-track. That wasn't working, so finally I shut the engine off and coasted to a stop.

We got out again and opened the hood, scratching our sandy heads, and helplessly looked at each other for a solution. More head scratching. Again, a Good Samaritan spectator stepped in, tinkered with something connected to the carburetor, and we were off and running again.

Our next misstep somehow landed us in a spot we didn't want to be — inside a 10-foot deep ditch, hopelessly stuck as Jim vainly tried powering the truck back and forth to get us out. Back and forth we swung, like a see-saw. This went on for a good 10 minutes before spectators came to the rescue once again with a tow. What would we have done if there were no spectators? We were pitiful.

About 75 miles into the 100-mile loop we were driving through another stretch of treacherous whoop-de-doos. The truck started bouncing around more violently than it should have and Jim struggled to keep it from veering toward the right. Once again, we were forced to stop and take a look. We discovered that the right rear tire had completely shredded and the mangled rubber tread was wrapped tightly around the near-bare chrome wheel.

We searched the back of the truck for a tire jack to mount the spare tire — that much we knew how to do. The problem was, the Nissan folk evidently didn't think it was necessary — or forgot — to supply us with a tire jack; there wasn't any to be found. Well, that was just fine and dandy.

Now, Jim was my senior by about 10 years. He was presumably the smarter veteran between the two of us and naturally predisposed to cynicism. So this was the moment in which he threw up his hands and intoned: "What the hell possessed us to take this assignment in the first place? What the hell were we thinking? This is exactly the way we knew this would go for us."

We looked around to assess our situation. What was I just saying about if there were no spectators? We were in the middle of nowhere. There wasn't a soul within sight of us for miles… except for that one RV parked about 50 yards off course from where we stopped. Just out of sheer luck those folks were parked there, obviously succeeding in finding a place of solitude, because there was nobody else around. Otherwise we would have been stranded, drawing only the attention of vultures circling overhead.

Sheepishly, we slogged across those 50 yards. Again, we were pretty pitiful.

It took some muscle to free up that nasty wad of shredded tread off the wheel. Jim and I gratefully admired the strength of the young man who did all the work for us.

With the fresh spare on, we were on our way again. But not for long, and you knew this inevitability was coming. Mercifully, our day came to an end, 80 miles into the 100-mile loop, when that poor Nissan truck shouted "uncle!" The A-rod suspension on the right side gave way, effectively rendering the truck un-drive-able. We radioed in to the Nissan pit to come and get us. Once we got back to the pits, it was time to start sucking down some of those Budweisers.

We must have presented a sight to behold, two soot ghosts from head to toe, save for around our eyes shielded by our racing goggles. But Jeri sauntered by and my Pigpen appearance evidently didn't change whatever the hell she saw in me. She wound up in my hotel bed that night. She was exactly what I needed that night.

Me and the Nissan truck are both thrashed at the conclusion of 1985 Mint 400 off-road race outside of Vegas

I didn't get the chance to cover major off-road events like the Mint 400 or Baja 1000 for the Her-Ex. But I wrote a few feature stories on local drivers competing in those races.

One year I wrote a feature story on a celebrity who tried his hand racing a dune buggy — James Garner, the handsome actor who played the cowboy sheriff Maverick and the laid-back private investigator Jim Rockford in the TV shows "Maveriick" and "Rockford Files," respectively. He also had a starring role in the racing movie, "Winning." He told me about his extensive experience racing stock cars in the early days of Baja racing before race-engineered buggies took over.

I did a phone interview with Garner, who was coaxed into driving in a celebrity off-road race at Riverside Raceway during his "Rockford" run, which precluded him from racing on a regular basis anymore. The interview happened at the time I was sharing an apartment with Rich B. at El Porto Beach. I don't remember the conversation with Garner much, but I do remember coming home one afternoon with Rich excitedly greeting me with, "Chic, you've got a call. He says he's James Garner!" It's not every day that you get a phone call at home from a famous actor that'll impress your roommate.

I also interviewed "Walker, Texas Ranger" TV actor Chuck Norris and his brother Aaron when they tried their hand at Baja racing

⸺ ◆ ⸺

I never covered Baja as a sports writer, but one year I joined up to help with the chase crew of a driver in the Baja 1000 race, courtesy of an invite from Bruce of the Gerke clan, my next-door neighbors as a kid.

The driver was Bruce's boss, Ron, who ran a business installing telephone systems. Ron, like most off-roaders, took up racing as a hobby and built his own racing dune buggy. Bruce, who inherited some of his father's mechanic abilities and had done some odd jobs on my old Chevy Nova, back in the day, helped build his boss's vehicle.

Traditionally, the Baja 1000 (kilometers) ran the entire length of the Baja peninsula, starting in Ensenada and finishing near the southern tip at La Paz. For this race, the 1000-kilometer course didn't go all the way to La Paz; instead, it circled back up to Ensenada in a 1000-kilometer loop.

Bruce and I were part of a four-man crew who were to "chase" Ron's progress along the race loop in trucks, meeting up at various checkpoints along the way. We would provide gas for refueling, and any maintenance work/repairs to the race vehicle as needed. Bruce and I were to be paired up in one truck, with the other two crew guys in the other vehicle.

We stayed overnight in Ensenada the night before the start of the race. Lordy, we came dangerously close to not making it to the race because of our shenanigans that night.

The trouble started when we hit the local strip bar in town. We were drinking lots of beer and getting pretty loud. The local women putting on a show for us were "very" friendly. The atmosphere was raucous, we were drunk, the women were loose. Before long, we were all getting treated to five-dollar blowjobs in separate stalls in the men's restroom.

One of the crew members, a kid who I don't think was even 20 yet, evidently was being treated to more than a blowjob. We had to drag him away from the girl he was with, pulling him outside the bar with his pants halfway down to his knees.

He was really drunk, loudly babbling away that he wanted to marry the girl. We slapped some sense in him, got his pants back on and piled him in the truck, where he passed out.

That's when we noticed the Mexican *Federales* about a block away, across the street. They were standing outside a building, checking us out.

"Oh shit," Bruce said when he saw them. "Let's get outa here."

We quickly got in the truck, with Bruce driving, and pulled away. Bruce drove cautiously to the next stop light and looked in his rearview mirror. He could see the *Federales* vehicle about 100 yards behind us, coming for us. Bruce stepped on the gas.

"Damn it! If you guys got any drugs on you, get rid of it now!" he barked.

Bruce wasn't heading for our hotel, he was heading for the border. He started talking about horror stories of Mexican jails and how *Federales* threw American visitors in jail on the smallest of pretenses.

He was soon on the open highway and increasing his speed. The *Federales* were gaining on us from behind.

"Shit! We're not going to be able to outrun them," Bruce said. He rolled down his window and tossed out the bag of cocaine he had. Bruce had a pretty bad coke habit. I had a tiny bit of pot in a baggy, which I threw out my window.

The *Federales* were drawing nearer. "All right guys, look, give me any cash you can spare," Bruce barked. "If we play it right, we can bribe our way out of trouble with these guys."

I handed Bruce some cash, as did the other young crew guy who was still awake.

Bruce slowed down and let the *Federales* vehicle pull up to our left. The vehicle's red lights were flashing so Bruce pulled over to the side of the road and stopped in a cloud of dust. The *Federales* car parked in front of us, and two officers got out and approached us with flashlights pointed at us. Bruce rolled down his window again.

"Hello, officer. Did we do something wrong?" Bruce asked anxiously.

I was in the passenger front seat. I could barely make out the officers, who appeared as shadowy figures at the driver side of the car. My heart was racing.

"Why are you in such hurry? What was going on back there at the bar?" one of the officers dryly asked.

"Our buddy in the back here got sick. We just wanted to get him some air," Bruce coughed out.

"How much did you have to drink?"

"Oh, I'm good, I'm good." Bruce nervously rubbed his thighs with his hands. I froze with morbid fear, conjuring up images of being stuck in a disgusting Mexican jail for days.

Bruce finally held out the wad of cash, about $40, and pitched an offer to the officer. "We don't want any trouble."

The officer took the money, thankfully, and they drove off, leaving us visibly shaken. The young guy who had passed out let out a moan in the back seat. I let out a huge sigh of relief.

We headed back to town and back to our hotel. We caught a few hours' sleep before the 5 a.m. wake-up call.

It was a beautiful morning as dawn broke over the Mexican desert on the outskirts of Ensenada, where the throng of race vehicles gathered for the start of the race.

One of Ron's two other co-drivers suffered minor injuries in a pre-race run crash a week earlier. So Ron had to alter the driving strategy, limiting his injured driver to just one 99-mile stretch, and assigning himself to run a huge chunk of the course, the middle 422 miles of the 822 miles himself.

As soon as Ron's remaining healthy co-driver was waved off the start, Bruce and I took off down the highway in one of the chase trucks, heading for the first checkpoint some 65 miles away. The adrenaline pumping in our veins and coffee we gulped down for breakfast had washed away the trauma and hang-over from the previous night.

For the first 110 miles into the race, we were hightailing it through Mexican desert, trying to keep ahead of the team's pace on the course so we could beat the race car to the first two checkpoints. It was exhilarating.

After the second checkpoint stop, Bruce and I drove 80 miles across the Baja desert terrain to San Felipe, a little sleepy fishing village on the Gulf of California side of the peninsula. San Felipe marked the end of Ron's long driving loop, so we had a lot of time to kill, which was my favorite part of the day. I daydreamed on the beach there for a long while, meditating on the handful of tiny fishing boats sitting in the sand and the gentle lapping of waves nipping the shore. I was thinking I'd like to return there someday just to hang out.

When Ron rode into town well into the night, he had the lead in his class. But unfortunately, he went to the wrong checkpoint and lost precious time. When he double-backed and finally found us, another buggy driver was precariously close to overtaking the lead by the time he exited the checkpoint.

Ron's co-driver took over for the final 184-mile leg. Bruce and I drove through heavy fog and high winds to reach the final checkpoint 65 miles from the finish, at El Alamo. We beat the race car at that checkpoint by less than three minutes. The driver, complaining that his goggles and glasses kept fogging up, left El Alamo about 30 seconds behind the class leader.

We made it back to Ensenada and anxiously waited at the finish line, only to see another buggy in Ron's class cross the finish in first. Word via radio reported that Ron's co-driver had crashed into a guardrail about eight miles from the finish, possibly due to foggy goggles. Ron and his third driver chased the race car down at the crash site and worked on the smashed front end so he could finish the final eight miles as the second-place finisher in the class. With only one more race left on the schedule, Ron virtually needed to win the Baja 1000 to have any chance for the season championship.

I wrote an epic first-person account of the whole experience for the Hex-Ex. Needless to say, some of the details about the night before the race were left out of the story.

We were exhausted after nearly 20 hours of race-chasing. As we re-crossed the border, looking back to how close we came to possible Mexican jail time, getting back on U.S. soil felt like a sweet, awesome reprieve. That Guardian Angel was along for the ride.

———————◆———————

Mickey Thompson was the founder of the sanctioning body SCORE International, which presented the Baja races. He imported his off-road events to stadium venues such as the LA Coliseum, and Anaheim Stadium. He followed the lead of fellow promoter Mike Goodwin, who introduced motocross to the same two Southern California stadiums in the early 1970's to rousing success. Both the off-road and motocross events packed in the crowds.

Thompson and Mike Goodwin were a pair of flamboyant personalities who quickly clashed as rivals and eventually engaged in a very public, very ugly feud. Since they were basically competing for the same audience and its entertainment dollars, it was inevitable that their destinies would eventually collide, given both of their enormous egos.

I got to know both Goodwin and Thompson well in my coverage of their events and intense rivalry. They were both exceedingly charming men, a characteristic that served them well in drawing publicity for their events.

Goodwin was in his 30s and much younger than Thompson. He was a handsome playboy from Orange County who exuded supreme confidence in the way he talked and conducted himself with the press. I was blown away by one junket Goodwin arranged for a select few members of the press that included myself, in which he took us out to sea on a small dive boat. We set anchor off the shores of Santa Cruz Island for lunch. Lunch turned out to be fresh abalone hauled up from the ocean floor by a diver hired by Goodwin. The fresh catch was then battered and fried before our very eyes on the boat deck. We washed the abalone down with champagne. Goodwin was feeling very lucky that day in advance of his Anaheim motocross event, which was his biggest cash cow.

Thompson, in his mid-50's, had been a fixture in the racing scene much longer. He made a name for himself some 20 years before pursuing land speed records with his own custom-built cars. He was known as the first American to break the 400-mph barrier. He then tried his hand designing and entering cars in the Indy 500 a few times in the 60's before he ventured into off-road race promotion. As an old-school type, his methods with the press were a bit more old-fashioned than Goodwin's — his idea of treating the press to lunch trended more toward tacos than fried abalone. He was married to the sweetest woman — Trudy, who was considered his partner in running the Mickey Thompson Entertainment Group, which hosted off-road events at RIR and in stadiums.

It was in the stadiums where Goodwin and Thompson met their cross to bear. In a union that could only be classified as unholy, they inexplicably negotiated a partnership that attempted to merge their motocross and off-road events together. It all ended up getting tied up in knots. And it did not end well at all.

I covered the Thompson-Goodwin alliance extensively. Within a year, the acrimonious divorce wound up in court with both suing and counter-suing each other with accusations of being swindled. Hundreds of thousands of dollars were at stake, but more importantly the court would determine who would retain the rights to both the Coliseum and Anaheim Stadium venues. These were two bitter men who didn't like to lose.

The big winner in court, to no one's surprise, was Thompson. Goodwin's somewhat shady reputation faded badly against Thompson's. This was a huge financial blow to Goodwin and, more likely, a bigger blow to his ego.

Then, early in the morning on March 16, 1988, came the shocking news that Mickey and Trudy Thompson had been brutally murdered, shot down in the driveway of their gated home in Bradbury. Two hooded men were seen riding away from the home on bicycles early in the morning. But it was clear in the minds of everyone familiar with the Thompson-Goodwin feud, there was no doubt who was responsible. My stomach sickened at the thought when I heard the news.

I got a call at 7 in the morning to get cracking on a local reaction story to the murders that ran with the top story splashed on the front page of the Her-Ex. It was an unbearable shock across the board. The Her-Ex front page stirred up quite a controversy by displaying a gruesome photo of Thompson's body, lying on the driveway in a pool of blood, from the vantage point peeking through a nearby tree. He was next to the SUV where Trudy's body was found, as she was shot moments after guiding the vehicle out of the garage.

I wrote a tribute column to Mickey a few days after the murder, relating how he had cheated death so many times in his racing career. Mickey had so many crashes in everything he drove –- land-speed cars, motorcycles, dune buggies, snowmobiles, powerboats — that he used to brag about having broken more bones in his body than famed motorcycle daredevil Evel Knievel. Mickey was proud of that. He walked away from a 200-mph crash after his car flipped 60 feet in the air and rolled like a tumbleweed. He momentarily lost consciousness while topping 400 mph because his oxygen mask came loose near the end of the run. In the early 1950s he drove a buggy over a short cliff in a Mexican off-road race and killed 17 spectators. He was OK. In 1961 he severely broke his back and was partially paralyzed after crashing a powerboat and was told he'd never walk again. Seven months later he was back on his feet.

A lengthy investigation of the Thompson murders couldn't link Goodwin to the hooded bicyclists nor identify who they were or lead to any arrests. Colleen Campbell, Mickey's sister, kept calling me for years at the Her-Ex sports desk with supposed updates on the investigation, swearing as God was her witness that she knew Goodwin hired the killers. She was going to nail him, if it was the last thing she did.

It took 13 years, but Goodwin finally was charged with two counts of murder. His case didn't go to trial until 2006 and he was found guilty and sentenced to two consecutive life-without-parole terms on January 4, 2007, based on overwhelming circumstantial evidence.

————————————◆————————————

I will forever link Mickey Thompson to wonderful Jeri, the angel of love I met at the 1985 Mint 400.

Since Jeri worked for the Thompsons, I saw her over the years at Thompson off-road events working the press box, and we carried on an open flirtation with references to our hook-up in Vegas.

Then there came a time in my life when the timing was right for us. We started it up again, and again, and again, until it became a thing. In today's parlance, you would call it "fuck buddies." That's what Jeri and I had become for about nine months.

It's weird that I have a hard time placing the timing of when we finally came together (sorry, no pun intended) sometime just after the Thompson murders in March, 1988. The tragedy must have unleashed something between us that we could no longer hold back. I have hard evidence, which is a dated memento I kept all these years: a lavender-colored "coupon" that Jeri designed which stated:

"**This Coupon Good For**
ONE (1)
NIGHT OF WILD SEX
(Notice: 6 hour minimum)"

In the upper right-hand corner of the coupon it stated: "Expires July 15, 1988." Is it weird that I kept that coupon all these years?

I received quite a few notes and cards from Jeri promising more "nights of wild sex." Then we'd book a room at a hotel. Sometimes it was wrapped around a racing event, sometimes it was just to get together.

We didn't always need a hotel room. With new housing and urban sprawl of an expanding Riverside creeping in on RIR that eventually doomed the race track, one of our more daring rendezvous was at an incomplete construction site a few miles from the track prior to a race. The framework of the building walls barely (this time, pun intended) concealed our naughty play.

My favorite moment with Jeri is crystalized in my memory bank, occurring on a full-moonlit night in Phoenix. A NASCAR race was in town. It was late at night, after a lovely dinner at an expensive restaurant that somebody else paid for, and in search of a romantic spot we drove down to a dry lake bed. Jeri disrobed and stepped out of the car, wearing only her golden high heels. The moon shined onto the dry lake bed, spotlighting it like a stage. Jeri bent over the front hood of the car and spread out those high heels. I don't mean to sound crass, but climaxing under that full moon was pure bliss. You don't get moments like that very often.

Jeri filled a void in my life at the time. I was very grateful for our moments — they felt so decadent, so pleasurable. It was out of character for me, because I typically wanted the security of a more evolved relationship when I was having sex with someone. Jeri never asked for that. She was a gift.

———————◆———————

I saved my best racing story for last. It's usually the first story I tell people in relation to my experience as a motorsports writer. I typically identify the experience as the "most embarrassing moment of my (sports writing) career."

A major component to the embarrassing aspect of this story is who it involved — *Paul Newman*. Yeah, legendary, Oscar-winning actor, Paul fucking Newman. Butch Cassidy and Cool Hand Luke himself.

Newman had caught the racing bug, much like his co-star James Garner, while making the racing movie "Winning" in 1969. Newman, in his late 50's, launched a legitimately serious racing career in the early 1980's in IMSA GTO sports car racing.

Newman was a natural draw for interview requests from the motorsports press in advance of his first appearance in an IMSA GTO endurance race at RIR. Publicist Tom Blattler, handling press relations for Newman's team, arranged an interview session for the LA "Big 5" in the privacy of Newman's RV in the garage area in the quiet of post-Friday practice.

Blattler gathered Shav Glick of the LA Times, Tim Tuttle of the Orange County Register, Jim Short of the Riverside Press Enterprise, Allan Wolfe of the Long Beach Press Telegram, and myself in the press room to escort us across the race track to Newman's RV. It would take a good eight minutes to make the trek to the garage area and on the way, Blattler briefed us on Newman's expectations for the interview.

"You can ask him anything you want," Blattler began. "Just

don't ask him, 'Why do you race?' He gets that question all the time and he's sick of answering it."

As I absorbed Newman's request through Blattler, I was conjuring up a much more complicated question to ask the acclaimed actor. Given a few minutes to think about it, I decided that it was too long and wordy, so I started editing it down in my head. As we approached the RV, the question was shrinking.

Finally, we entered the RV and assembled in a semi-circle, facing Newman in the flesh. He was seated in a relaxed pose, one leg drawn up on the cushion seat at the kitchenette table. After Blattler made introductions, he opened it up for questioning.

None of my colleagues were speaking up so I ventured into the void, prepared to ask my carefully-thought-out question.

Instead, inexplicably, I uttered, "So Paul, why do you race?"

As soon as the words rolled off my tongue, I knew I was a dead man. *Oh my God! I just pissed off Paul Newman!* As surprised as I was to hear myself say those very words that Blattler explicitly told us *not* to say, it didn't begin to compare to the shock of my comrades, who stood with mouths agape and eyes wide open in fear. How would Newman react? Would he walk out on us? Blattler, I imagined, was muttering under his breath, something to the effect of "Don't invite Chic Perkins to next interview."

As for Newman, he sat stoned silent. Those famous blue eyes were *cutting... me... in half.* The awkward silence hung in the air for a good 15 seconds, but it felt like an eternity. I was wishing I was anywhere else but inside that RV.

Nobody was saying anything so I had to say *something* to salvage the situation. Finally regaining my composure, I rephrased the question to: "What is it you get out of racing that you don't get out of acting?"

That, thankfully, broke the ice. The scowl on Newman's face vanished as he gave a thoughtful response, something to the effect that competition was the main component he thrived on in racing that he didn't derive from acting. That was consistent with his reputation for disdaining the endless gauntlet of awards events associated with the theatrical arts.

I would cross paths with Newman many times after that monumental guffaw. Newman later became active in Indy-Car racing as a part-owner of the Newman-Haas Racing team. Mario Andretti raced for Newman-Haas for years.

I recall sitting next to Newman in the VIP section for a good portion of the Long Beach Grand Prix one year, watching the race from the closed-circuit TV hanging from the rafters. I was tempted to bring up that embarrassing moment in that RV at Riverside a few years earlier. I doubted Newman had any recollection of it, but I did.

But nahhh, I decided against it. I thought that one through.

Paul Newman at Indy, answering the question, "Why do you race?"

CHAPTER 13
Unbearable Lightness of Prosperity and Love

I have been blessed to have known so many extraordinary women in my life. Lizamara was doubly so, both extraordinarily good and extraordinarily bad. You take the good with the bad and chalk it up to life's experiences; to me, that's what makes life worth living.

I wouldn't trade my experience with Lizamara for anything, given all the illegal stuff and poor judgements on my part. I did love her and I am richer for the experience. Lizamara undoubtedly was the second-most extraordinary woman I have ever known, in terms of utter complexity.

The most extraordinary, I'd have to say, was my Aunt Evelyn.

My father's sister was every bit as smart as he was. The depth of her intelligence was extraordinary, and she educated me in ways I'm not sure I can translate on these pages.

In her younger days, she was an extraordinary beauty. My father was very good-looking, too, so it was genetic. I have a recollection of her when she was young from an 8X10 black-and-white studio portrait photo. She had a strikingly angular-shaped face and jawline, with pencil-thin eyebrows that arched over her dramatic eyes. Her nose was slender and appealing. Her hair was dark, wavy, set to curl just below her shoulders. Other photos of her showed off her hour-glass figure.

Her good looks attracted three men who married her. She had two daughters with two of those husbands — Linda and Bebe. She raised four step-children from her third marriage and retained the surname from that marriage —Christoffersen —until her death.

Evelyn was incredibly smart with her money. She never had a high-paying job, that I was aware of. To my knowledge, the only job she held was working as a telephone operator; I think she reached the rank of a manager. But somehow she parlayed the modest wage from that job into purchases of two homes in Santa Monica and another home in Orting, Washington, where she moved Grandma in her later years.

As I explained in a previous chapter, she bought the two Santa Monica houses side-by-side on Bryn Mawr Avenue. She lived in the corner house for a couple of years while Dad and Gloria resided in the house next door and he built an upper unit in the rear that Evelyn eventually moved into.

The house she moved into was perched high on a hill. The rear unit, hovering over the front house, afforded a gorgeous ocean view from the extra-large kitchen that Dad had customized as her main room. The master bedroom was expansive, too. A side door from the bedroom opened onto a beautiful brick-laid courtyard. The unit had one bathroom and a tiny sitting room big enough for a sofa and TV. A stairway led down to a small, half-bedroom on the bottom floor. The kitchen served as the de facto "living" room.

The front house consisted of two bedrooms and one bathroom. Below was a huge basement attached to the garage. The basement housed a shared laundry room and extra space that eventually was converted into another bedroom.

In her later years, Evelyn lived a hermit's existence in the rear unit. Age robbed her of her youthful beauty. She developed a crooked back, her dark hair turned gray, and she wore simple, comfortable clothes around the house. She didn't venture out much. She had large dramatic eyes, which were magnified by thick eyeglasses that presented a constant glare.

Somehow, I was one of the few people she allowed into her inner world. Evelyn, who was naturally predisposed to distrust anybody and everybody, trusted me, and I offered her companionship that she truly cherished.

She trusted me enough to share her pain. Her biggest burden was over her father, trying to reconcile his desertion of the family when they needed him the most during the Depression. Evelyn felt deep resentment toward her father. She subjected herself to a very intense therapeutic process that was popular in the 1970s, called EST.

. Then she launched a long search to find out what happened to him. She finally found her father's gravesite in a New Orleans cemetery. She made a pilgrimage to New Orleans and implemented the EST "primal scream" that brought her to tears at his gravesite. She shared the whole experience with me.

I was truly invested in her companionship because I was

fascinated by her world. Politics connected us from the start. Evelyn was well informed on the various conspiracy theories floating around in the 70s and 80s. She was always researching, digging into stories that weren't mainstream. She listened to public broadcasting news. She was a rabble-rouser at heart, constantly writing letters to her congresspersons and senators, espousing her thoughts on domestic and foreign issues in fluid detail. And she had plenty to say.

She was also keenly drawn to philosophy. She religiously listened to the radio broadcasts of Alan Watts, who was a practitioner of Buddhism and one of the early scholars of Zen in the Western world. She recorded scores of Watts' broadcasts on cassette tapes. I have the whole collection in a box collecting dust in my garage.

Evelyn loved writing letters. She corresponded for years with my Great Aunt Mina, one of my grandmother's younger sisters. These were typically long letters, four or five handwritten pages, that ranged from daily observations on life, deep-felt experiences on pain and spirituality, and matters of the heart. Evelyn made carbon copies of every letter she ever wrote and collected them in binders, all of which I kept. Her letters were written in exquisite cursive.

Her handwriting was emblematic of her gift as an artist. I have one of her oil paintings that I love, a cubic, socially thematic piece depicting a man pointing an accusatory finger at a woman with eyes cast down in shame. But most of her art was sketches of faces. She once told me she would draw faces that appeared to her on her ceiling. I kept a whole portfolio of her face drawings.

On the left, self-portrait pencil drawing Aunt Evelyn drew of herself when she was young and beautiful. On the right, the one full-sized painting of my Aunt Evelyn's that I have in my home

Evelyn had a very analytical brain that greased her curiosity in human behavior.She studied biorhythms, and mapped out biorhythm charts for the entire year for me. Briefly, biorhythms purport to track a trio of frequency waves — mental, physical and emotional — set in motion in each of us at birth that perpetually rise and drop between "high" and "low" levels. The cycles are fixed on specific spans of 23 (physical), 28 (emotional) and 33 (mental) days, each crossing the median which are neutral or "critical" days. I know I've experienced more than my share of mentally "critical" days.

I can't say I knew exactly why Evelyn took a liking to me. Maybe because I didn't prejudge her and accepted her the way she was. But I was very lucky in that way, because she made it difficult for most people to get close to her. I think she intimidated most people when they first met her. Those magnified eyes behind her large eyeglasses were scary. Her directness also made people feel uncomfortable.

And Evelyn had anger issues. The two people most affected by her anger, sad to say, were her two daughters. Evelyn wore her emotions on her sleeve, particularly when it came to her daughters. She felt immense hurt from what she perceived to be their lack of respect for her.

Generally, the main friction point with her daughters was over money. Evelyn helped both of them out financially over the years. She expected some kind of respect and consideration in return, and, as she told it, received a sense of entitlement and resentment instead.

Evelyn was remarkably kind and generous with me. She signed over a Deed of Trust on a parcel of land she bought in the Salton Sea area. She bought the land on the prospect of development in the region that would turn a potentially sizable profit on her investment. But the politics over water, rising desalination levels of the dying lake, and the perpetual limbo of developmental plans threatened to turn the area into an environmental disaster if the lake dried up and converted to a big dust bowl. Evelyn made the calculation that any profit on the land wasn't going to be made in her lifetime, but maybe in mine, so she signed the property over to me. Ownership would cost me about $85-$95 a year in property taxes. I'm still waiting on that investment to cash in.

Later, when I had a few thousand dollars to invest, she also linked me to her Treasury Bonds account. That would prove to be fortuitous for me down the road.

I learned a huge lesson about Evelyn with respect to her

attitude toward money — and her generosity in lending it out. She bought me a gift for which I will forever be grateful— an upright Baldwin piano. Most of my piano compositions were drawn from this piano. Evelyn wasn't just "giving" me this piano — our agreement was that I would pay her back on a lenient payment plan that I could afford. The point wasn't about the money for Evelyn. It was about me living up to the commitment I made with her, which I did — and for which I would be richly rewarded.

This was a lesson that was lost on her daughters. Evelyn felt "used" by her daughters, which led to a bitter rift between them. Eventually, after too many arguments, Evelyn and her two daughters had a falling out that was never resolved. So Evelyn wrote both of them out of her life.

I hate to say it, but the one person who benefitted the most from this was me. One day Evelyn sat me down and asked if I'd agree to be Executor of her Will. She showed me her Will. To my astonishment she was bequeathing to me everything she owned, with the exception of $1 to each of her daughters.

This wasn't just an in-a-moment-of-rage decision. Evelyn had given this a lot of thought. We had become close enough that she regarded me as a son.

She looked me directly in the eye, and with the seriousness that only Evelyn could convey in her countenance, said, "Promise me you will carry out my wishes conveyed in my Will, to the word, and not give in, out of the goodness of your kind heart, anything more than what I've bequeathed my daughters!"

I gulped, and gave her my promise. It was a hard promise to make, knowing that it could put me in an uncomfortable position with my two cousins, with whom I had only a passing acquaintance.

I was clearly aware that Evelyn's estrangement from her daughters could put me in a compromising position that would eventually determine the fate of the goldmine that was her Santa Monica home. But as things turned out, control of the Bryn Mawr house eventually fell out of my hands, and not exactly as Evelyn's Will dictated.

———— •·•◆•·• ————

Evelyn bought a home in Orting, a small town located about 30 miles from the base of mighty Mt. Rainier in southwestern Washington. She bought the house specifically so Grandma could live there. Grandma's sister Gay lived nearby, as well as my cousin Jeff, so the proximity of family had something to do with the purchase. And I had an excuse to visit my extraordinary grandmother in Orting.

My dear friend Rich W. had already been living in Washington for a few years, which prompted me to make a few summer visits. He lived on quaint, remote Fox Island with his brother Bob and wife.

My Grandma may have been quiet and reserved, but she had some spunk in her. She was all in when I proposed we take a drive to the top of Mt. Rainier. Rich lent me his family's spare car, an old Audi. The adventure turned out to be a little more than my Grandma and I had bargained for, but the memory of it still makes me smile.

We took a meandering drive up the long, winding mountain road to reach the highest point on pavement on the 14,411-foot snowy peak. We stopped at vista points, which were numerous and glorious.

It was late afternoon when we started our drive back down the mountain. A few miles down, we stopped at a parking area for a short hike to a small waterfall. Grandma was using a cane to walk, so it was a very short hike.

When we got back in the car, I turned the key in the ignition — and nothing; dead battery. It was dusk. We were stranded in that parking lot. We had no battery cables, and there was no sign of any car around to help us out.

This was the early 1980s, pre-cell phone days. I had no idea where the nearest pay phone could be to call for help. But I came up with an idea. With Grandma behind the wheel, I pushed the car into position to get it rolling down the fairly steep mountain road. The hope was that we would coast down the road until we found some sign of civilization where we might locate a pay phone.

Sign of civilization was the operative phrase, because it was getting dark fast and there were no street lights on the road. The car was rolling down the road at a pretty good clip, but as we plunged into the pitch black of night I had to navigate almost completely blind. There was no juice left in the battery, so the headlights were out. We were reduced to dim light from the emergency bulbs on the front bumper that illuminated a few feet ahead, which was no help at all.

With unexpected turns in the winding road, we were in for a wild trip. Grandma could have gone into cardiac arrest but she stayed perfectly quiet and calm in her passenger seat. Meanwhile, I wasn't anywhere near any state of calm. It was intense; my hands were clutching the steering wheel for dear life. At one point I nearly crashed into a gate blocking entry to a side road. At another juncture a jogger suddenly emerged out of nowhere and I jerked the steering wheel to avoid hitting him. He disappeared quickly, heading upward in the opposite direction, and we quickly lost contact with him as we rolled on our merry way.

Grandma and I in front of her home in Orting, Wa., in the shadows of Mt. Rainier

We were the last damn car on that mountain that day. We kept coasting down that lonely road for several miles before finally coming across the first sign of civilization — a small lodge. We stopped, hope abounding as we approached the front door. The lodge was dark, closed for business, but it had a small lobby accessible from outside, with a night light and, thank God, a pay phone.

I called my cousin Jeff, who had to make the hour-and-a-half drive from Puyallup to rescue us. Poor Grandma had to be tired and hungry by then, with every reason to grumble while waiting for that ride. But she never uttered a single negative word throughout the entire ordeal.

So, we turned that hour-and-a-half wait into one of the sweetest moments I experienced with my dear grandmother. In a Norman Rockwell moment, we passed the time playing the word game "Hangman." We were having so much fun, that hour-and-a-half went by in no time. It wasn't how I envisioned we'd finish our day, but after our harrowing ride down the black abyss, Hangman made for the perfect ending.

———————◆◆◆◆◆———————

To quote a line from lyricist Bernie Taupin in the Elton John classic "Your Song," there were many moments when another extraordinary woman in my life, Janice, was my "How wonderful life is while you're in the world" girl.

I wasn't the only guy who felt that way about her. That was the challenge presented in the unbearable lightness of loving Janice. None was more prominent and enduring than Brian. I never totally understood the dynamics of Janice's relationship with Brian. His devotion to her was unwavering and unconditional, but I often wondered if they ever had sex.

As far as I could tell, Brian never married and was childless. From what I could recall, for most of his adult life he lived with and provided personal care for his elderly, disabled mother. Brian was a pleasingly plump, mild-mannered man whose glasses gave him a studious look on a Pillsbury boy baby face. I think Janice loved him like a brother who would give her money every now and then when she needed it.

She did have other lovers. I saw her with a couple of them. There was one young Latin guy, all of 19, whom Lizamara introduced to her. Then there was Uncle Billy, for which I forgave her, no matter how unbearable that thought was.

But after the divorce, Janice and I made some inclinations toward acting like a couple, although we could never quite verbalize that concept.

Then, one day over the phone, she casually presented me with the news that she was pregnant. Her implication was that I was the father. But I had to ask:

"Are you sure I'm the father?"

In that soft, demure manner that only Janice could pull off, she simply said, "I'm sure."

I believed her wholeheartedly. But there was never any debate about what we were going to do about the pregnancy. She had decided she would abort it.

All she asked of me was to pay for it. This wasn't something she could run to Brian to pay for. Of course I'd pay for it. I offered to go to the clinic with her. She said she had Elspeth, Carmelita's faithful assistant, to accompany her.

Afterward, Janice healed herself by staying a couple of weeks at

Sea Sprite Motel on the Strand in Hermosa Beach, in what became her favorite chill-out place over the years. Brian typically paid for those stays.

I paid for the drinks at the Lighthouse Cafe near the Hermosa Beach pier, where Janice and I loved to hang out during that "almost couple" phase we were going through, listening to jazz artists perform. I distinctly remember seeing her face illuminated in the soft light of the famed Lighthouse insignia on stage and thinking how wonderful life was with her in the world.

I didn't think it was coincidental that Janice shared the same birthday as Dan — September 5. They were the male and female — yin and yang, if you will — counterparts to whom I felt the closest during my young adult life.

It was all so very sweet one night when, with the softness of Lighthouse Cafe booze setting in, Janice wistfully gave me that look with her blue-green eyes and gently said, without any remorse, "I wish I had kept our love child."

———————◆———————

Near Misses (No Near-Mrs.)

I'll start out by saying that some people might hear my stories and think I've been unlucky in love. Maybe in the conventional sense, I have. Because it didn't work out for me, falling in love with the right person at the right time, when everything fell in place because we were meant to be and we lived happily ever after.

I kept wanting to believe in that fantasy; I was a hopeless romantic. I wanted to follow the script my father so wanted for me. But after my third divorce, I took a deliberate pause to reconsider whether marriage was right for me. I looked at my first three marriages and realized I had been coaxed into all three of them; none of them was solely my original plan. It also occurred to me that my first three wives all had birthdays 10 days apart in April. That was ironic, since my high school sweetheart who I should have married was named April (and her birthday was in March).

In the moment, I didn't see myself as being "unlucky" in love. I've never felt sorry for myself. Yes, it made for a lot of drama and stress, but it also made me feel alive. But in retrospect, especially with respect to this memoir, regrets have grown as I have reviewed some of my romantic relationships.

In my search for love, I've had more than my share of "near-miss" relationships with some extraordinary women, but there are no real regrets attached to those experiences. I rated a couple of the near-misses as "spectacular," which, in other words, made me wonder, "What could have been?"

The next set of stories occurred sometime during the mid-1980s, spanning mostly from my post-Lizamara days to just before the birth of my first child. I may not be telling the stories sequentially, because I don't exactly recall.

———————◆———————

The absolute weirdest near-miss encounter I experienced came during one of my trips to Indy. It was a sensational flame-out that made me wonder, "What the heck just happened?"

It was a few nights before the big race and I was out for a drink at a tiny bar in the hotel where my sports-writing colleague, Tim Tuttle, was staying. Had I been staying there this might have been a completely different story, but my hotel was a good 20-minute drive away.

"Tuts" and I were sitting at the bar when this gorgeous redhead with the biggest blue eyes walked in, and she and I made instant eye contact from about 20 feet away. We locked in on each other.

She approached the bar and sat two chairs away from Tuts and I, with Tuts sitting closer to her. She ordered a drink and gave me another long look as she sipped. I had never experienced a woman who I had just set eyes on having such an overt reaction to me.

Tuts glanced at her and started up a conversation with her. She slid over one chair next to him. We introduced ourselves. Her name was Nancy.

Tuts had the gift of gab, so he was pretty much carrying the conversation. But the communication between her and I was unmistakable — the eyes said it all. Tuts sat between us, but we didn't let that stand between us.

Finally, a slow-dance song popped up on the juke box. Nancy leaned back in her chair to get my attention behind Tut's back and gestured toward the tiny dance floor.

I got out of my chair and led her to the floor, and wrapped an arm around her slender waist. We slowly started to sway to the music.

The smell of her perfume was intoxicating. The body heat between us was palpable. Within seconds, she said to me:

"I think I'm in love with you."

My heart nearly jumped out from my throat. As a heart-pounding, hopeless romantic, I was hooked. So of course, I professed my love for her. This was the singular most exhilarating moment in my life shared with a perfect stranger.

That slow dance could have gone on forever. Our bodies were locked in, her hips nestled around my thigh, the music rhythmically holding sway over us.

Tuts, sitting alone at the bar, got the message loud and clear. "I think I'm going to call it a night," he shouted out when we stayed out on the floor for another song.

"Do you have a room here?" she asked me when we were finally alone.

I shook my head no. I tried to convince her my hotel wasn't that far, but we got only as far as my rental car in the parking lot. We started making out like crazy outside the car, then carried on in the front seat. We were furiously groping and grabbing each other. It was over-the-top passion.

I begged her to let me take her to my hotel.

"I can't. I'm…married," she said. "I really want to, but… I can't."

Shit. Love went unrequited that night.

———————◆———————

Another road trip, another bar, another near-miss.

This time it was Phoenix. I think I was covering a NASCAR race. I met Cindy at a nightclub. Cindy was long and slender, and like the folk-rock group America described in their classic '70s song, she was a "golden hair surprise" lady who looked awesome in blue jeans.

Cindy was also married. I was getting divorced. She sounded unhappy in her marriage. We didn't dance in that nightclub. We just talked, a good long time. She was a down-to-earth type, no BS. I liked her a lot.

We corresponded by letter over the next six months after that chance meeting. She was thinking about leaving her husband, which gave me reason to think this could lead to something meaningful. I had an occasion to return to Phoenix for another event and we met again for a drink. Maybe this time…

But ultimately, when it came to leaving the marriage, she pretty much echoed what Nancy said. "I really want to… but I can't."

Out of all the women who made my "what might have been" list, Lison is the one whom I've known the longest, surprisingly.

Lison was a young, French-speaking Canadian woman from Quebec whom I met through Serge, a young, French-speaking Canadian man from Quebec. Serge and Lison were touring LA as platonic friends when they somehow crossed paths with Lizamara. My wife recruited them to house-sit at our Manhattan Beach home during our Nicaragua trip in the summer of '83. They took good care of our house and were respectful. Of course they were respectful, they were Canadian.

Months later, I wound up visiting Lison and Serge in Quebec after riding a train for four days across Canada, starting on the West coast in Vancouver. Dan, who was living near the Canadian border in Bellingham, Washington, at the time, drove me across the border to the Vancouver train station. Dan was always doing those sort of favors for me.

I fell in love with Quebec. Serge and Lison showed me all over the city, which reminded me of a quaint European town with its narrow cobblestone streets and lots of potted flowers. The weather in early September was ideal.

Serge and I hit it off. He spoke English well and shared my goofy sense of humor. So we traded jokes and cracked each other up.

We created a "crack-up" line that became our mantra during a visit to a charming castle. We had labored up a very steep trail alongside the outskirts of the castle to reach the top. Only then we noticed some steps parallel to the trail that would have made the climb much easier. *Merde!* After pondering our misguided choice, we reconciled it with a simple explanation: "Because we are young, we are strong, and yes, we are stupid." Endless scenarios abounded over the next several days in which we applied this mantra, which cracked us up every time.

Poor Lison hardly understood any English, so she kept wondering what was so funny. Lison was a cute, petite, shy gal. Not knowing English inhibited her even more.

But that didn't spare her from Serge and I having a little fun at her expense. She was anxious to learn to speak English, and she was particularly having trouble with "f" and "th" words. So Serge and I created a tricky phrase to help her practice her English pronunciation: *"I thought I felt a feather from a faggot."*

Lison would repeat this line over and over again, and she sounded so cute in her sweet, soft French accent. She had a real tough time with the word "thought," so by the time she got to "faggot" it didn't matter that she had no idea what she was saying.

Meanwhile, Serge and I were stifling ourselves from laughing out loud, having too much fun with the phonetics to fret over the offensive nature of the phrase. Occasionally we would offer Lison pronunciation tips, particularly on "thought," and "faggot."

"Listen Lison, it's 'Fag-gut,' 'Fag-GUT.' Don't swallow the 'G's."

Finally, she did get up the nerve to ask what "faggot" meant, and we shamelessly gave her a vague, false answer: "Someone who likes feathers."

I think Lison may have had a little bit of a crush on me; don't ask me why. That's the only explanation I can offer as to why she has made the effort to stay in contact with me as a friend over the years, sending Christmas cards and birthday greetings every year. Her birthday was during the holidays, the same as my dad's (December 20), so I sent her combined birthday and Christmas greetings every year. This continued long after she married a guy named Alain and raised a family together in Quebec. I adored the effort she initiated to remain in contact and was grateful for her friendship.

Meanwhile, Serge and I remained friends for a while. He returned to California on his own for a visit a couple of years after his initial trip. We exchanged letters for a few years after that. In the last letter he sent he told me about a woman he had fallen in love with. That effectively ended our correspondence .

—————— ◆ ——————

Another dear friendship that lasted for years evolved from a spectacular "near-miss." I met Ana through Dan when I accompanied him to turn in his rent check at a property management office where she worked as a secretary. Dan was living in Bremerton, Washington, at the time with his second wife Elizabeth. The Lizamara nightmare had just ended, and Ana fell in my wheelhouse as the type of woman I'd fall for — a petite, stunning, dark-haired, Spanish-born beauty.

I was smitten. Ana spoke with a flowery Spanish accent, and had a hearty laugh that I could easily elicit. It started out with a harmless flirtation. She was living with a guy named Bill, but the way she talked about him sounded like she was fed up with him. So, on a whim, she accepted my invitation to dinner one night.

It was one of those romantic, soft, candlelight dinners and she looked as beautiful as ever in the flickering flame. That date served as the inspiration for one of the more romantic songs I've written, called "Candlelight," capturing the emotions I was feeling that night.

"In the candlelight,
I want to stay with you all …night
In the candlelight
I can see that it's all… right"
Oh yeah"

The lyrics seductively move from *"We sip on wine, and share a thought that is so sublime,"* to *"The candlelight whets my appetite, What I'm craving eats away all doubt."* There was no doubting how the date in this song was going to end.

But it didn't pan out that way with Ana and me. I had been on a roll, and this near-miss kinda burst my bubble. She wound up marrying Bill, in part because he was the father of her son, Lance.

But she and I remained dear friends for years, through letters, postcards from Spain, and phone calls for her birthday in May. Lance was near my son's age, so the various challenges of raising a son was a common topic of conversation. But our conversations mostly were laced with laughter. She laughed at all of my corny jokes.

Ana came to visit me while I was living in Hermosa Beach. She was intrigued with a beach called "Hermosa," which means "beautiful" in her native Spanish tongue. She booked a room at a hotel on the beach strand for a week, and we had a wonderful time as I served as her personal tour guide. The romance never advanced beyond "playful" flirting. Lord knows I tried. I couldn't coax her into joining me skinny-dipping in the ocean at night near the Hermosa Pier, but she got a good laugh out of watching from shore.

I saw her many times over the years during my annual treks to Washington to visit Dan. I saw her grow older and a little plumper.

I tried to keep up on the phone calls. But one day she announced she and Bill were moving to Mexico and I lost touch. I miss her.

My Spanish lady friend Ana whom I met through Dan — a classic "near-miss" romance, indeed

———————————•◆•———————————

Topping the "spectacular" near-miss list would have to be Sasha. It was February 1984, just after Lizamara and I had officially separated, when Sasha and I first met. I was flying to Daytona Beach, Florida, for the Daytona 500 and had to change planes in Denver. Sasha also boarded the plane in Denver, headed to Daytona to work as a model in a photo shoot for a Coppertone Tan magazine ad. Our seats were next to each other and we talked for the entire flight.

Sasha was knockout gorgeous. She aced the blonde, bouncy, curly Farrah Fawcett 'do. She had the requisite sparkling blue eyes, was every bit as pretty as Farrah without the makeup, and well-shaped, everywhere. Her only drawback as a model? She was short in stature.

She was exquisitely engaging in our flight conversation. She lived in Aspen, Colorado. I told her about visiting my sister there on the honeymoon trip I made with my first wife. I may have told her some of my Nicaragua stories; they were still very fresh in my mind.

We got together in Daytona Beach. She invited me out to the beach house she was sharing with a half-dozen other models working on the photo shoot. We sun-bathed for a couple of hours on the sun-deck fifty yards from the ocean. I was daydreaming of her sunbathing topless, but in reality she loosely covered up her considerably well-rounded breasts with an untied, skimpy bikini top.

I'm a little hazy on recollecting anything else we did in Daytona Beach. It's what happened five months later in Aspen that I'll never forget.

It was July 1984, three weeks before the 1984 Olympic Games that Los Angeles was hosting. This was a huge deal for the LA Herald Examiner sports department. One of the sports I was assigned to cover was cycling, both the track and road events.

Cycling has always been tremendously popular in the state of Colorado. In the '80s the most prestigious road cycling event in the U.S. was the three-week-long Coors Tour through various towns across Colorado in July. Nearly every member of the U.S. road cycling team was using the Coors Tour as a final training event for the Olympics. The Her-Ex dispatched me to Colorado for a few days midway through the Tour to write some feature stories on the American road cycling Olympians. I picked up the Tour on the night before the stage scheduled in Aspen.

Oh, wherefore art thou, Sasha?

When I checked into my Aspen hotel that night, I combed the local phone book in my room to see if Sasha was listed. She had an unusual Austrian-sounding name that would have stood out. I didn't find her listed.

The next day, which was a Wednesday, the Aspen stage race was set to start in the center of downtown. I was standing on a raised press photographer's stand for a prime view of the start. I happened to glance down at the grassy, tree-shaded town square directly behind the photo stand when I saw this short, bombshell Farrah Fawcett loo-kalike striding across the lawn.

My gut was about to burst. The race start was only a moment away, but that didn't stop me from dashing off that photo stand and madly running to cross her path.

"Sasha!!" I screamed when I intercepted her.

"Chic!!" She was beaming. I received one of the best hugs of my life.

I got back to covering the race, which was won by one of the U.S. Olympians, Alexi Grewal. But I couldn't wait to get back to Sasha.

I pinch myself every time I think about how fortuitous it was to see Sasha that day, and the experiences that played out from that chance meeting.

There was no denying a strong mutual attraction between us. I could feel it; I felt it in that hug. She invited me over to her apartment that night, where I met her feisty, red-headed roommate, Rebecca.

Another "near-miss" Sasha, right, with her roommate in Aspen

Sasha and I got to talking again, catching up. I told her about my divorce, which had been filed and was a mere formality by then. So I was unattached. Sasha was sorta unattached. She told me about this relationship with a guy who had recently been diagnosed with lupus, an autoimmune disease. It sounded like that had given the relationship a pause.

Sasha took me to a party later that night. She had connections from a gig she was working for a catering company providing the buffet spread for a celebrity-laden party. The party was a preview social event for a pro-celebrity tennis tournament scheduled at the local Aspen tennis club that coming weekend. ABC was televising the event live.

The party was held at an Aspen bar owned by Jimmy Buffet. It was wall-to-wall people, and if you paid close attention some recognizable faces would pop up. At one point I found myself gazing up at a large man with a big pot belly as I was rubbing bellies with him while trying to squeeze by in the shoulder-to-shoulder crowd. I recognized him as a well-known character actor, with receding reddish hair and a handlebar mustache. His name was Pat McCormick, who was probably best known for his role as Burt Reynolds' sidekick in the "Smokey and The Bandit" movies.

Venturing further into the bar, I focused on two gentlemen engaged in conversation, sitting at a booth across the room. There was no mistaking who they were — "Chinatown" detective Jack Nicholson, and "Superman" Christopher Reeve. It was a bit surreal seeing them in this setting. I recall it like a dream.

That party turned out to be just a tease to my celebrity gazing, as my plans for the rest of the week took a dramatic turn. The following morning, breaking news emerged from the Tour. Every stage winner was routinely given a drug test immediately after the stage and Alexi Grewal, the winner of the Aspen stage, had failed his test.

This was big news because Grewal was considered one of the U.S.'s best hopes to win a medal in men's road cycling in LA. Failing his drug test meant an immediate 90-day suspension, which effectively knocked him out of the upcoming Olympics.

But Grewal immediately filed an appeal in hopes of restoring his Olympic eligibility. This became the big story I needed to pursue, taking priority over any feature story I might come up with by following the Tour to its next stop, in Boulder. It just so happened that Grewal lived in Aspen, so he wasn't going anywhere while waiting out his appeal, which would take a few days to run its course.

That meant I had to extend my stay in Aspen, doggone it. I was so upset that I couldn't wait to tell Sasha.

"So, you're going to be around this weekend?" she asked.

"Yeah, it's lookin' like it."

"Well, if you're interested, I could get you a press photo pass to the celebrity tennis tournament. You are a member of the press."

I could not believe my ears. I did happen to bring my Canon camera that I almost lost in Nicaragua. This offer was just icing on the cake to gaining a few extra days to spend with Sasha.

I had to pinch myself to make sure I wasn't dreaming this stroke of luck. The next three days, I was filing updates on the Grewal appeal and spending quality time with Sasha (think: picnic in a park). Then, with exclusive press access as a photographer at a swanky tennis club hosting the pro-celebrity tennis tournament on Sunday, I made the most of it.

I don't mean to sound like a star-gazer, but it was a jaw-dropping experience. As the crowd mingled before settling into their seats, I went around snapping candid shots of famous faces— singer Dionne Warwick, boxer Ken Norton, Mick's ex Bianca Jagger, pop artist Andy Warhol, and eight-year-old Emmanuel Lewis, the cute sensation in Oscar Meyer Weiner ads running on TV at the time.

Catching Andy Warhol with a lady companion at celebrity tennis tournament in Aspen, Colorado.

Then came the action on the courts. I had the best view in the house crouched at the side of any net of my choosing. A few of the celebrities I caught in action were Donna Mills, a blonde actress from the TV soap opera "Knots Landing"; Barbi Benton, one of the better known Playboy Magazine playmates and Hugh Heffner girlfriends; and Lloyd Bridges, star of the 1950s TV show "Sea Hunt" that popularized skin diving and father to movie star sons Beau and Jeff Bridges. I would cross paths with Lloyd Bridges years later in another fanciful twist in my life.

The televised event was hosted by Howard Cosell, Billy Jean King, and Arthur Ashe, and the Master of Ceremonies was "Dynasty" TV star John Forsythe. I caught photos of all of them with mics in hand, court-side before ABC's cameras.

Then came the showcase exhibition match between John McEnroe and Vitus Gerulaitis. Crouched near the net, I caught some really terrific action shots. My favorite captured McEnroe turning his back to the net and returning a shot between his legs.

Both players were loose and playing to the crowd. I caught one comical moment on camera after a controversial call by the referee. Gerulaitis approached the ref and reached into the pocket of his tennis shorts as if to pull out cash to offer a bribe.

These photos were for my personal collection, making for some great memories.

John McEnroe goading on the crowd while Howard Cosell tried to interview him in Aspen

That Sunday night was my final night in Aspen with Sasha. We had been teetering on romance the previous four days and it was coming to a head on that final night. Sasha was definitely conflicted over her relationship with the boyfriend, who I met. He was very nice, dang-it, a good-looking guy. I'm sure he was wise to what was going on between Sasha and I, but he never confronted me.

The moment of truth finally came when Sasha and I were alone in her apartment, having that "serious" discussion on whether we were going to take the next step. We hadn't even so much as kissed up to that point, we were just hanging out as friends.

The big question she posed came down to this — Was I a Christian? She basically said she couldn't be romantically involved with a man who wasn't Christian. If I was horny enough it would have been so easy to lie in that moment. "Praise the Lord, in the name of Jesus!" I had definitely been exposed to Christianity — way back in high school when I met my very first, short-lived girlfriend Doris at that Bible study class. There was a lot about Christianity that appealed to me. I wholeheartedly embraced Jesus's teachings that laid out a moral foundation for how all of us should live our lives. But I couldn't wrap my head around the concept of accepting Christ as the one and only path to salvation. My beliefs were influenced by my mother— Jesus taught me to forgive her for all of her wackiness. She was a member of the Unitarian Church for most of her adult life. Unitarians hold a basic belief that all religions can claim validity and no single faith held exclusive rights to eternal peace. Christianity, to me, seemed to challenge that concept.

So I told Sasha something like that, in so many words. Alas, Sasha and I parted as friends. But yeah, there was some regret tied to that one.

Here's the kicker to this real fairytale; Grewal won his appeal of his suspension. The verdict came down over the weekend after the Aspen stage and I reported on it, justifying my extended stay in Aspen.

Grewal's eligibility for the Olympics was reinstated. A couple of weeks later, the men's road cycling event was held on the first day of Olympics competition in Los Angeles, and I was there covering it for the Her-Ex. After a grueling ride of more than 100 miles through the urban sprawl, Grewal beat Canadian rider Steve Bauer by a half-bike length in a dramatic finish to win the gold medal.

My article that ran Mar 6, 1984 in the LA Herald Examiner on Steve Young signing the largest contract in sports at the time with the LA Express football team

CHAPTER 14
Career Blooms As Train Wreck Looms

While my personal life was veering off the tracks, the newspaper business was modernizing and my professional life was taking off.

The newsroom was advancing into the computer age in the early 1980s. We discarded our typewriters for these dinky, prehistoric computers that were pretty basic in function. Underneath our desks was a spiderweb of wiring connected to the computers, and if you accidentally kicked the wires with your feet, chances were the whole row of computers would be short-circuited. The computers were so sensitive that they were prone to start buzzing on their own, causing the screen to wobble. The immediate, common remedy was to give the computer a good whack on the side. This became so commonplace that every couple of minutes or so the newsroom would echo with the sound of someone smacking their hand against their computer. Such was the sound of progress — smacks against the computer replacing the clacking of typewriter keys.

We eventually had portable computers to file our stories from the road. The computers were equipped with phone couplers used to transmit the stories directly into our newsroom via a phone call. This replaced the old press room service provided by attendants (for a small fee) who operated these spinning cylinders in which typewritten pages were transmitted over the wires to the reporter's phoned-in newsroom at a rate of about three minutes per page.

Early in 1984, when my marriage with Lizamara was ending, a nice man named Jim Perry was hired as Sports Editor at the Her-Ex. I had long escaped Allan Malamud's doghouse, but my role rarely expanded beyond my motorsports coverage and weekly columns and nightly desk duty. Once in a while I was given a bone to cover — a college track meet or college basketball game, or assigned an occasional off-beat feature story like, say, yachting.

But Jim's hiring effectively gave me a clean slate. And Jim, who I described as a "nice man" for a reason, saw something in me. He started giving me more writing opportunities.

A couple of new sporting vistas sprouted in LA within the span of a few months in 1984 and Jim handed me the lead in both. The first was with the Los Angeles Express, a fledgling franchise in the newly-established United States Football League. The Express broke out with a big splash by signing quarterback Steve Young to what was then the largest contract given in any professional sport.

That was a front page story with a banner headline. It was huge. It was a big story because Young was spurning the NFL to sign with the Express. And it was an all-time record amount of money. We reported it as exceeding $35 million over four years, which was a lot of money back in 1984.

Funny thing about that money figure — the LA Times was reporting a slightly different figure, as was the Long Beach Press Telegram, as was the Orange County Register. We were all dealing with Young's agent, Leigh Steinberg, and he was purposely handing each of us a different figure so no one could claim exclusively reporting the accurate amount. It didn't matter. It was still a helluva lot of money.

After that, I was assigned the Express beat for their inaugural season. They played their home games at the LA Coliseum, which held about 100,000 seats. But the Express played in front of a lot of empty seats, barely drawing 10,000 spectators per game.

Still, it was a fun season to cover. Young made it fun with his scrambling ability and left-handed spunk. He earned his money, pulling out victories with come-from-behind finishes all season long and guiding the Express to the first USFL Western Conference championship game.

To get there, they had to beat Michigan in what was then the longest pro football game in history, a four-hour, four-minute marathon spanning three overtimes, in which LA prevailed, 27-21. Mel Gray scored the game-winner with a 24-yard TD run on which he broke his arm on the tackle in the end zone.

It was one of the most incredible games I ever covered. The Express sent it into overtime with a touchdown in the final minute of regulation and a miraculous two-point conversion run in which Young reversed course in yet another desperate scramble to avoid would-be tacklers and reach the end zone. LA then had to survive two botched, easy field-goal attempts by Michigan's kicker in the first two overtime periods before finally closing it out in the third OT.

LA then had to travel to Tempe, Arizona, to play the George Allen-coached Arizona Wranglers in the conference title game in early July. The Express had earned the home date but had no place to play because the Coliseum and Rose Bowl had commitments for the upcoming LA Olympics and ABC couldn't agree on a compromise time to televise the game around a Rams fan event at Anaheim Stadium. There were no other LA-area options. So the game was moved to Tempe.

One small problem— it was July in Arizona. The scheduled 12:30 p.m. kickoff time on game day in Tempe was drawn into question because of a dangerous, no-end-in-sight heat wave. Temperatures as high as 126 degrees were recorded at field level at noon at Sun Devil Stadium a couple of days before the game. Facing the fear of players collapsing from heat stroke, USFL officials negotiated with the network to move the starting time to 8:30 pm, when it would be much cooler and safer.

That was great for the players, but it was hell for us West Coast sports writers who had deadlines to meet. I had a midnight deadline to file my story. The game ended a couple of minutes after midnight (the Express lost a close defensive battle), which meant I was writing play-by-play in my story with the game in progress and waiting until the very end to make sure I had the final score right. That was stressful.

The Express season was over. But the Olympics followed immediately after my extended Sasha-surprise trip to Aspen for the road cycling Coors Tour and reports on Alex Grewal's drug suspension appeal.

Covering the LA Olympics was definitely a career highlight, starting with Grewal's fairytale gold medal in the men's road cycling event on Day 1. I also covered the women's road cycling event (a gold-silver finish for the U.S. with Connie Carpenter and Rebecca Twigg), all the track cycling events at the Olympic Velodrome at Cal State Dominguez Hills, the U.S. Men's water polo team that advanced to the gold medal game (playing Yugoslavia to a 5-5 tie but losing on the tie-break), and some track and field events (gold for the U.S. women's 4X400 relay team.) It was a magical two weeks.

I think my work covering the Express and Olympics impressed Perry because the next opportunity was the biggest yet. San Diego's NBA franchise, the Clippers, was moving to LA. in the fall of '84. Perry assigned me the Clippers beat.

I was ecstatic. It wasn't the Lakers, but it was still the NBA, so it was a major beat. The Clippers hit town with some LA "cred" with ex-Laker Norm Nixon and ex-UCLA stars Bill Walton and Marques Johnson on the roster.

Unfortunately, I wasn't given free rein to cover the beat like our Lakers writer, Lyle Spencer, was afforded. I covered all of the Clippers home games at the Inglewood Forum, but only spot coverage of their road trips. I was still tied to desk duty and still had to carve out time to write my motorsports column, in addition to the usual motorsports events that warranted coverage. This left little time to put the focus on the Clippers that they deserved. But heck, I wasn't complaining.

I traveled on one east coast trip to New York, New Jersey and Cleveland. It was late November and it was snowing back east. I remember looking out of my hotel window in New York City and watching the snow fall. To a native Southern Californian, this was a rare treat, especially in the heart of the Big Apple. I felt alive, on top of the world, like I had really made the big time. Then, to cover an NBA game in Madison Square Garden, one of the Mecca arenas in the world, drove that feeling home.

I got to travel with the team on a West coast trip, too. One of the stops was Phoenix. I have a vivid recollection of going out to dinner with Don Greenberg, the Orange County Register beat writer, and Walton, the 6-foot-11, redheaded Clippers center. The three of us sat at a small circular table, and I had to make room for him to stretch out his legs, which extended way beyond the table. Then it came time for ordering food. First, Walton ordered a huge, family-sized bucket of mussels for an appetizer, then followed that up with a full, 16-ounce steak dinner entree. That was a lot of food, but there was a lot of Bill Walton to feed.

The other tic I remember about Walton was that he struggled with a stutter when he talked, so he was a difficult interview. Trying to get a usable quote out of him was virtually impossible. He seemed uncomfortable during interviews because of the stutter. When his playing days were over, he obviously worked hard on getting rid of the stutter to become a very successful TV commentator.

The Clippers came to LA with a lot of promise, but they weren't very good. Besides Nixon, Walton and Johnson, they had some other good players, like Junior Bridgeman, who came to the team in the same trade with the Milwaukee Bucks that landed them Johnson. Michael Cage and Derek Smith were also pretty fair players on that team. Both Walton and Johnson were hurt a lot, so they didn't contribute much. The Clippers wound up with a mediocre 31-51 record.

One surprise assignment I drew during the NBA season was covering the Lakers for one West Coast trip while Lyle Spencer traveled with the Clippers on an East Coast trip. This was during the "Showtime" era headed by Magic Johnson, Kareem Abdul-Jabbar and James Worthy. I traveled with the team to the Bay Area, Portland and Seattle. Lyle, who was our weekly NBA columnist, wanted to make the swap so he could get more acquainted with the Clippers players. I had no problem covering the better, more popular LA team for a week.

I also covered the NBA All-Star Game that season. It was hosted by Indianapolis, a city with which I was quite familiar. That was a blast, seeing all the NBA's best in action on the same court. Seven-footer Ralph Sampson of the Houston Rockets was named the MVP of the game.

My days of glory were short-lived. After less than a year, in early March of 1985, Jim Perry was replaced as Sports Editor by Leslie Ward, who had spearheaded our Olympics coverage the previous summer and was accorded accolades from management for her efforts. We did produce a spectacular daily, tabloid special section on the Olympics for its full two-week run. Leslie provided the leadership for what was a great team effort.

When she came on as Sports Editor, she carried out a brainstorm regarding the Clippers beat that screwed me over. Ailene Voisin was the Clippers beat writer for the San Diego Union when the team was playing down south. Leslie saw an opportunity for another female hire in the sports department by luring Voisin away from the Union specifically to cover the Clippers for the Her-Ex. Ailene's educational background in law was perceived to be an asset as well, insofar the Clippers were immersed in lot of legal problems. The concept sounded good on paper.

When Leslie dropped the bomb on me that Ailene was replacing me on the Clippers beat, she gave me some weak BS about how I wasn't scoring enough "scoops" as the beat writer. Well, I felt it was unfair to judge me on that count since I was routinely relegated to desk duty, unlike every other major beat writer. Of course, when Ailene was brought on board, she didn't have to work the desk.

I was pretty bitter and even thought about quitting. I was no fan of Leslie Ward. And I won't quote my buddy Bill Center from the Union on what he thought of Ailene. Suffice to say, he wasn't going to miss her in San Diego.

———————◆◆◆◆◆◆———————

When I was in Seattle on that Lakers road trip I had a very strange reunion with Teri, my dear friend in high school who played along as my half-sister in our running joke with Mr. Anderson, the press room teacher.

Teri and I had kept a consistent letter correspondence long after high school. Her letters were always addressed to "Half-Brother." They were airy, stream-of-conscious diatribes on details of her mundane life, which she managed to express in an amusing way that made them a great read. She maintained the same basic sense of humor that made us click in high school. She heard about my three marriages and divorces and she often had something to say about them, pretty much siding with me and wondering why any woman would divorce me. When she married Kirk and had a daughter with him, she went through a Christian phase —a lot of PTL ("Praise The Lord") references in her letters. But she wound up getting divorced after a few years. The divorce was hard on her and the struggles of becoming a single mother weren't easy. But it was like we had never left high school, as far as our correspondence went. She was a really good friend.

She moved back in Seattle after her divorce (she and Kirk last lived in Missouri together) and we met up on my Lakers work trip that culminated in Seattle. I was surprised when I saw her because her physical appearance had changed dramatically — she had lost a lot of weight. I never thought she had a weight problem to begin with, but she dropped a good 50 pounds, which resulted in making her look very thin.

She looked good, but she looked different. I really liked her stylish, curly, bouncy haircut.

I had a free night on the night before the Lakers game I had to cover. We hung out at the original Starbucks and Peats Market down at the Harbor. It was a brisk, fall night, but clear; no rain, no snow. We grabbed a bite to eat at one of the restaurants at the harbor. We were reminiscing and feeling good.

We wound up back at my hotel room. After an awkward, subdued start, we made love. I sensed that Teri had been waiting since high school — nearly 20 years — for this moment. It may have been too brief a moment to warrant a 20-year wait.

Come morning, I had to leave quickly to catch the Lakers practice at a hotel gym. I thought we parted on good terms. But 10 days later, when I was back home in LA, I received a terse, one-sentence letter from Teri.

"I never want to see you again," was all it said. It felt like a punch to the gut when I read it. It was such a shock after our years of correspondence and sharing our lives together.

What had I done? I asked the question, just like the typical, empty-headed guy who doesn't know what's going on, not knowing what he did to piss her off, but guilty as hell. I thought back on the events that transpired— was I too subdued during love-making? Did I leave too soon that morning? Did I say something about her appearance that offended her? Maybe I acted a little surprised at first — it was a bit of a shock. But she still went to bed with me; maybe that was the plan, to even the score with whatever the heck I had done. It bothered me for months that I screwed up somehow with Teri and messed up a beautiful friendship. We should have never had sex. That was a mistake; it changed the dynamic of our friendship.

As far as her weight change, in retrospect I have to say I preferred her old look, how I knew her in high school. The bottom line was, it should have never become a physical thing between us. She was my Half-Sis.

It took a whole year for Teri to finally write back, seemingly she had gotten over whatever happened between us that night in Seattle. By then she had moved to North Dakota, of all places. But it was never the same between us. We eventually lost touch, which mystified and saddened me.

———————◆———————

Over the bulk of two-and-a-half years after the split from Lizamara, I tried to avoid committed relationships — out of my comfort zone. It was during this time when I was free-lancing with Sasha, Ana, Cynthia, Nancy, Tammy, and Debi —all on the road, no ties —came into play.

Jeannette, who I met at a wedding, broke the pattern. We had an exclusive relationship for about seven months. The best part about being with Jeannette was that she could make me laugh. She had the best-sounding laugh of any woman I dated and just the sound of it made me want to laugh. The laughter was there, but the passion wasn't, so the relationship didn't last. I hurt her when I broke it off.

Flirtation with Gail ended it between Jeannette and I. Gail was yet another tenant I met at my mother's house who I fell into a "relationship" with that was hard to define. She was a divorcee, having escaped living on a farm in Wisconsin. She lived in Minneapolis for a couple of years before heading west for California. She was originally from Boston.

We started out as just friends and should have stayed friends. Gail was dark-haired, petite, thin, with a fair resemblance to the actress Mary Steenburgen. She was soft-spoken but stubbornly opinionated. She was a Catholic-raised Bostonian who became immersed in the New Age, metaphysical wave of spiritual belief. She was a devoted student of astrology.

"When's your birthday?" she asked me, using her standard icebreaker with anyone new whom she met.

"Ahh, you're a Cancer, on the cusp with Gemini," she immediately informed me when I answered. I should have known right then that she was sizing me up to determine if I was a good astrological match for her. She was a Leo. I knew next to nothing about astrology and everything I now know about astrology I learned from her. I learned that Leos generally aren't a good match for me.

Gail offered to map out my astrological "chart" and I was curious enough to accept. The "chart" showed how all the planets were aligned at the moment I was born, which meant I had a different sign for each planet that colored my overall astrological palette. I also had a "rising" sign, which is "the zodiac sign and degree that is ascending on the eastern horizon at the specific time and location of an event." I quoted that from a Google search, but that's exactly how Gail talked about astrology, which I found very fascinating at the time.

Of course I did. I was flirting with her. But with both of us coming off divorces there was a reluctance on both sides to dive into a relationship, so we were just friends, at first. Playing chess became the activity that brought us together most often. We'd sit for hours dueling it out on the chessboard; we were an even match.

Besides astrology, Gail was also a devotee of meditation, which was tied to her strong spiritual belief. It was a practice that she shared and bonded with another tenant at the Rossburn home, Merrie.

Merrie was an interesting woman. She lived as Mom's tenant for 10 years, so she essentially became "family." Pam and Merrie became very close. Merrie, who kept her dark hair short, stood six feet tall, and had ample breasts that were hard to overlook. She was very gregarious and had what I would call a very "friendly" face — large blue eyes that made direct contact when she spoke with you — and a large mouth. Merrie was very much into all the New Age beliefs — chakras, astro-planing, past lives —and her planets were aligned with Gail's on all of those subjects.

Gail influenced me to try practicing meditation. We'd go down to the beach, lay out towels on the sand, sit with eyes closed and cross-legged, with open-palm hands spread out in the standard meditating pose, and remain still for 20 minutes with the sound of the ocean waves serving to block out all thoughts. It was just the antithesis I needed for the drama I had lived through with Lizamara, as well as the deadline stress I lived with daily from my job.

Naturally, sex eventually complicated our relationship, not long after I broke up with Jeannette. It just sort of happened one day. Weeks went by, then it happened again, and it would pop up at infrequent intervals. What I wasn't picking up in the early stages of our intimacy was that Gail wasn't all that "into" sex. This certainly made her an incompatible companion for someone like me, who had a highly-charged sex drive. Gail recognized the hold sex had over me, so she pretty much controlled when and how often we had sex. It wasn't very often, which frustrated the hell out of me.

Gail camouflaged her indifference to sex with her choice of contraception. While she was no longer an active member of the Catholic Church, she relied on the Church-validated rhythm method as her preferred means of birth control. That generally accounted for long gaps in her cycle when she wasn't ovulating.

I didn't think we were in an exclusive relationship. I realized this was an issue with her when she "accidentally" read a journal entry in which I described meeting and swooning over Ana, my Spanish lady friend, on one of my trips to Washington. Gail got jealous. That was a signal that maybe we should back off.

I was going through this period of sorting out my feelings and it took me a long while to come around to accepting an exclusive relationship with Gail. Janice and I were dangling; she was seeing other guys. My relationship with Jeannette ran its course.

Janice briefly drifted back into the picture, moving in with me in my Hermosa Beach apartment when she needed a place to stay. It was intended to be temporary. I may have gotten nervous with the idea that she was looking for me to replace Brian as her source of financial support. I think I was also having trouble handling a live-in arrangement in an open relationship such as ours. I now wish I had given Janice and I more time together at this juncture.

But one day, that all changed when Gail was looking for a cheaper place to live. She wanted to cut her work hours so she could make room for classes she had enrolled in at an acupuncture school. I invited her to move in with me as a cost-cutting move for her. Sheepishly, I asked Janice if she could move out to make room for Gail. Janice complied, staying true to our no-strings-attached understanding.

I guess I was ready to be exclusive with Gail.

———————◆———————

I never stopped running. While my running career ended in college, I kept on running to stay in shape. I typically would go out on a four-mile run either at mid-day before my night desk shift or at night after a writing day. I was running three or four times a week consistently. It was in my blood. I got off on the runner's "high."

So when Los Angeles announced months in advance of its plans to hold the first LA Marathon, scheduled for March 1986, I decided to enter the race. It had been eight years since I had run my last marathon, but was still in good enough shape to try again.

Once I committed to it I had to step up my training. It meant gradually increasing my mileage so I could finish the 26.2-mile distance required in a marathon. I was already aware of the challenge, from my first three attempts when I was younger. Now I was in my early 30's. My body hadn't changed that much, but it needed the conditioning to take on the punishment of a marathon.

Then, in a stroke of genius that boosted my sportswriting career, I told my boss I was running in the first LA Marathon. Leslie

Ward was no longer that boss; she had been replaced as Sports Editor by Rick Arthur, giving my career another lease on life.

I pitched Rick the idea of writing a first-person story for the Her-Ex from a runner's perspective. This wouldn't have been the first time; I had written a similar first-person story for the Her-Ex eight years earlier, running the Palos Verdes Marathon, when I was still a lowly copy clerk trying to get promoted into the sports department. But the inaugural LA Marathon was a much bigger deal. Rick was all for it.

I don't know what was harder — finishing a 26.2-mile race or writing a story after surviving the race. It was definitely a career highlight for me. First, there was the challenge of completing a marathon; no small feat, even if I had done it three times before. But my competitive running days were long gone, so it was no slam-dunk.

Then there was the historical aspect of the event. I was one of over 11,000 runners entered in the inaugural race. Tens of thousands of spectators came out to cheer us on along the race route that snaked through the city.

The race started and finished in downtown LA on Figueroa Street in front of Exposition Park. The weather was perfect — cool and overcast. The atmosphere was electric. Thousands were gathered along the sidewalks to watch the start. When the start gun blasted, it set off a huge human wave stampeding forward like a river rapid.

Snapshots: Running through Little Tokyo, where diminutive Japanese-American women waved mini-American flags as we passed by; through Skid Row, where the homeless stood and urged us on; through Chinatown, where firecrackers popped and a Chinese dragon danced in celebration of the Chinese New Year.

Heading uphill on Sunset Boulevard after six miles, the longest climb of the race; crossing the Hollywood Freeway at Mile 12 and seeing so much traffic on a Sunday morning — it wouldn't be LA without traffic.

My right knee started to stiffen after the 12th mile — a bit of a concern, especially since I had never had knee problems. I saw my support crew — Gail and buddies Rich W. and Serge, who was visiting from Canada — for the first time at Mile 16 at Sunset and Vine.

Breakout quote from my story in the paper related to when I approached Mile 20: *"Oh, the pain. People are passing me left and right. Only ones I passed were either walking or dropping out. From here on out, the mental strain to stop only increased, sometimes becoming unbearable."*

After the 20-mile mark, my ex-roommate Rich B. surprised me by jumping in the race to pace me the rest of the way. With six miles to go, it wasn't going to be easy.

From that point, I struggled along at a forlorn 10-minute-a-mile pace, with Rich practically running in place next to me, traversing miles 21 through 26 along Exposition Boulevard.

Somehow, I achingly made it to the corner at Figueroa, turning right for the final 200 yards to the finish. I gave it everything I had to stretch my stride in those final yards. I crossed the finish line in a time of 3 hours, 28 minutes, 20 seconds, a full hour and 13 minutes behind race winner Ric Sayre.

At the finish, my legs were in so much pain I could barely stand it. Gail tried to massage some life back into them. Somehow, I got myself cleaned up and limped into the office to write my story later in the afternoon. I gave high marks across the board for the first LA Marathon — volunteers, abundant water and ERG stations at every mile, profuse spectator support.

The headline that ran with my story read: "He missed out on the thrill of victory, but not so the agony of the feet."

My article on running the very first LA Marathon in March, 1986

Approaching Memorial Day weekend and my annual trek to Indianapolis to cover the Indy 500, my relationship with Gail was beginning to grow sour again. So I began to stray.

The 1986 Indy 500 was postponed due to rain, forcing me to stay an extra week for the rescheduled race. It was during that prolonged stay that I experienced my passion-charged encounter with the red-headed Nancy in the bar of the hotel where my colleague Tim Tuttle was staying. I was in dire need of romance at the time, with the embers at home with Gail cooling off to barely a flicker.

I must have been on some kind of magic carpet ride, because the night following the Nancy encounter in Indianapolis was equally memorable. I wrote it down to remember the moment. It felt like a fairytale worth savoring at the time.

For the record, I was high on pot that night and I was definitely feeling it. I was on the streets of downtown Indianapolis, which was in peak party mood with an extra week to celebrate The Greatest Spectacle in Racing because of the postponement.

It all started with a casual drive-by on a bustling downtown street, where I spotted an incredibly beautiful, dark-haired woman at the reins of a horse-and-carriage. Rock-n-roll 60s music was blaring out of a nightclub called Ike and Jonesy's. I was near Union Station, the downtown train depot, which clamored with amusement park atmosphere. I parked in the station parking lot, took another hit off my pot pipe, and drew a suspicious look from the parking lot attendant from afar.

I set out on foot and wandered downtown with the memory of Nancy the night before still very alive in my mind. I was hoping against hope that I might "by chance" bump into her, since it seemed everybody else in town was there.

I had walked several blocks when The Lady Driving the Horse Carriage passed by again, headed in the opposite direction. She moved on at a leisurely pace and had drifted a couple blocks away when I stopped, thought it over, reversed direction and ran back to catch up to her. Breathlessly, I asked her, "How much? Where do I go for pickup?" She flashed me an unbelievable smile, and answered, "Union Station, in front." Then she continued on with her riding party aboard.

I made my way back to Union Station. I stopped briefly to listen to a band playing outside next door to the station. I saw someone eating an ice cream cone, which made me crave one. I found the ice cream shop on the station's third floor and bought a rocky road cone.

I looked at my watch and saw it was 11:45 pm. I decided I needed to find the carriage by midnight before it turned into a giant pumpkin. Walking to the end of the third floor, I looked out the window and saw The Lady Driving the Horse Carriage pull up at the curb directly below.

I rushed downstairs and out the door to where I had spotted her on the street, but she wasn't there. I waited for about five minutes, and, suddenly she pulled up again.

Approaching her and seeing her up close for the first time, I thought she looked more beautiful than I initially believed — dark eyes, curly dark hair worn shoulder-length, dressed in black clothes, black cowboy boots and a long gray cape.

I asked the price again and she said, "$25, for up to 4 people."

"Can I go alone?"

"Yeah," she replied with a laugh.

I struggled to remove my credit card from my wallet with my free hand that wasn't holding onto the ice cream cone. I nearly dropped the cone, and my bumbling made her laugh again. She asked for my address and phone number for the credit card form she was obligated to fill out. So she knew I was from LA. I was introduced to Blue, the horse who was doing all the hard work.

I then climbed onto the front seat and sat next to her. When the meandering ride commenced, we talked. Her name was Michelle and she lived in nearby Plainfield. She owned a horse, a Tennessee Walker. She was a Gemini, with a birthday in June.

The conversation was interrupted when I heard a guy's voice on the street say, "That looked like Chic." I turned around and recognized Joe, the sports writer from the St. Petersburg, Florida, newspaper who we — Steve Earwood, Dave Densmore, and I — had enlisted to pretend to be the husband of the Daytona Beach stripper Tammy to scare the bejeezus out of Gunner a couple of years earlier.

As we pulled away, Joe called out louder, "Is that you, Chic?" I turned again, waved, and said "Yeah." Michelle was cracking up.

The conversation continued. Yes, she had a boyfriend, who

built hot-rod dragsters. She was at the rained-out Indy 500 last Sunday — her first time at the race —in seats located at the third turn. She was a small-town gal who couldn't stand the thought of living in a big city where she "couldn't yell out something without disturbing somebody." A couple of guys on the street yelled out something to her; she said she heard that all the time from luckless guys and let it go "in one ear and out the other." We discussed movies; the last one she saw was "probably something stupid."

I finally introduced myself as "Chic," which made her laugh, recognizing that was the name Joe had called me, and she thought he was referring to her. She said her nick-name used to be "Pickles" when she wore her hair in two ponytails. Her last name was of Spanish origin, reflecting her ethnicity, which instantly made me think of my spectacular near-miss Spanish lady friend, Ana, in Bremerton, Washington.

I asked Michelle if her boyfriend was the jealous type who would get mad if I bought her a drink sometime. "Yeah, he'd get riled up just to see you sitting like this next to me." That's when Blue offered up what he thought of my question by stopping to empty his bladder.

As every cherished moment must, this one came to an end. When we climbed off the carriage she removed her glove and shook my hand. There was an awkward pause, as if neither of us wanted to say good-bye. But another customer was waiting for a ride.

So, I sauntered off, looking back to see if a glass slipper had been left on the ground.

———————◆———————

I believe my marathon story made a favorable impression on Rick Arthur, who was a decent man. I started getting more diverse assignments over the next three years, a sign that I was in good stead with Rick.

The LA Marathon became one of my bigger yearly assignments, but I was just covering it as a spectator. It got banner headline treatment on the sports' front page.

I covered some UCLA basketball games, a couple of major track and field events at the Coliseum, and was sent to Denver for a Rams preseason football game one summer.

But topping them all were the baseball assignments that came my way — harking back to my first love in sports. I was feeling like a kid — memories cascading — while sitting in press row on the narrow third deck of Dodger Stadium to cover a Dodgers-Cubs game during the 1989 season home opener. This would be the same narrow deck where I sat with my Grandma as a young teenager, using the back of the Ringo Starr poster that was handed out at the ballpark that evening to collect autographs of Dodger players waltzing by our seats before the game.

I was given spot major league baseball assignments starting with the Angels' 1988 season-opening game. The Angels' opponent was the Chicago White Sox, whose lineup included the oldest pitcher-catcher combo ever to start in a season-opener — ex-Dodger left-hander Jerry Reuss and Carlton Fisk. They were both over 40 years old at the time. Chicago easily won the game, 9-2, which gave me the false sense of confidence that I could approach Fisk in the visitors' locker room afterward to ask him about the age distinction he and Reuss represented in baseball lore. But he evidently didn't like being reminded how old he was, and he brushed me off with a very rude response. If I was capable of pissing off Paul Newman, it was no stretch to think I could do the same to Fisk.

In 1989, I was asked to cover an Angels road trip for our Angels beat writer, Tom Singer. I went to Arlington, Texas, Kansas City, and Detroit. I got to see Hall of Famer Nolan Ryan pitch against the Angels for the Texas Rangers in Arlington.

Intimate Tiger Stadium in Detroit was the highlight of that trip. I think at the time it was the second oldest ballpark in the majors, topped only by Boston's Fenway Park. Press row was on the third level at that stadium, but the trajectory from home plate was almost straight down, as if we were looking from the lip of a bowl. That explained how a foul ball off the bat of Tigers star Alan Trammell flew straight up and landed right in my lap. After all those years of disappointment in my youth leaving Dodger games with my glove empty-handed, I was gifted by the baseball gods on that night in the press box at Tiger Stadium.

That nearly became a longer night than I bargained for at Tiger Stadium. I was one of three West Coast writers— along with beat writers from the LA Times and Orange County Register — who were the last to vacate press row because we had the luxury of West Coast deadline times to file our stories. We all filed our stories within a few minutes of each other and collectively headed for the nearest exits. The dozen or so doors were all chained up, so we walked on to the next set of exits. Same story — all the doors were chained up. We kept on walking, and it became apparent we were the last people in the whole damn stadium to exit and all the doors had been chained up. As we continued to circle around the stadium and panic began to set in, we finally crossed paths with a janitor who had keys to let us out. Whew!

I saved clippings of every article I wrote for the Her-Ex. The clippings are folded up and bundled by year, held by rubber bands. The clippings have turned yellowish brown, showing their age. They represent a throwback to a time gone by, the good ol' days when it was a great time to be a sportswriter. I was so lucky. My articles were real stories, with beginnings and endings, and depth and breadth of human experience expressed within the realm of athletics. Back then writers had so much more freedom to write, and we rarely faced the indignity of having our stories cut. We weren't force-fed to fit a pre-designed template of a specific length. Back then editors usually yielded discretion toward the writers on length of stories, and page layout followed accordingly. It helped that I was writing in an era when most of the public was still reading newspaper stories. My writing was allowed to blossom in this environment. I was surrounded by the best sports writers in the business, from whom I learned the craft by editing their stories when I worked the desk — Durslag, Krikorian, Disney, Spencer, Malamud. I was very lucky, indeed.

———————◆———————

From a large stack of short stories, notes, lyrics and novel outlines, I dug out five pages that I had forgotten about. They were a mix of type-written and hand-written pages, on which I recorded a conversation I had one night with Gail. I read it over in wonderment; it was a clear illustration of how dysfunctional our relationship was. The situation: it was the night of my 33rd birthday (June 1986), and Gail announced that she didn't feel like making love with me. Here's the rest of it, verbatim:

Me: Is it me?

G: You mean your performance?

Me: No, your feelings toward me.

G: Chic, I feel a lot of affection for you and I care about you a lot, but I don't have that passionate feeling towards you anymore.

Me: But you did once (starting to feel a little hurt.)

G: Yes.

Me: What happened, Gail? How did you lose it?

G: I don't know exactly. I… I've started feeling that feeling towards someone else. (Sees me start to react hurt and withdraw.) Now Chic, that person doesn't even know it. I haven't told him. Nothing's happened between us. We haven't even dated or anything. It's a situation where he's not available to me. He's married. It's an impossible situation.

Me: (Silence. I'm starting to feel mad again; how dare her do this to me, I'm thinking.)

G: I'm just infatuated by him and I can't get him out of my mind. I can't hide the way I feel. Gosh, I can't believe I'm telling you this, especially tonight, on your birthday. (I swallow hard.) But I have to be honest with myself.

Me: (I'm mad) So where do we go from here?

G: Ultimately, I hope we can be friends.

Me: (Oh my God, it's worse than I thought. I'm thinking, I'm getting my due; I'm thinking, 'God, you planned this. This is for the times I did the same thing to Jocelyne, Jeannette and Karen.' Yes. Now I know how they felt. And I'm surprised I didn't do it to Gail first. But I knew it was going to come to this. I just KNEW it! I started to pull away from her. I'm hurting, and I don't want it to end.) So, you just want to not see me at all for a while?

G: We can … date periodically.

Me: Well, what do you expect of me?

G: I think you should date other people.

Me: With the understanding that I'm going to go to bed with them?

G: (Doesn't answer).

Me: What if I were to tell you I went to bed with another woman? How would that make you feel?

G: It would really shake me up.

Me: It would shake you up? Now what in the hell is that supposed to mean?

264

G: I would want to have the same freedom.

Me: Of course. Absolutely (What a liar.) Would you want to be told if I indeed go to bed with someone else?

G: Is this a hypothetical situation, or are you trying to tell me something?

Me: (quickly) It's hypothetical. Strictly hypothetical. (It's the truth, but I don't think she really believes me.) I want you to know, Gail, that despite all your suspicions about me, I've been true to you.

G: Yeah, but I don't think you can be forever... that it's a matter of time. (Ah-hah, she wanted to beat me to the punch.)

Me: And a matter of time for you, too?

G: Like I say, it's an impossible situation. The situation is... I hate to describe it this way... but it's fucked.

Me: (I laugh out loud but cut it short.) Yeah, I know that feeling. I know exactly how you're feeling. (It's starting to dawn on me who she's talking about— her acupuncture instructor, Paul.)

G: I just can't help my feelings toward this man.

Me: That's pretty obvious, knowing that you want to invest your money in his Ojai project.

G: How did you know? (I caught her off-guard on that one.)

Me: I just put the pieces together. It was easy.

G: Yep, he's the one.

Me: (I'm starting to feel benevolent, and I also think it might eventually be a way to win her back.) Well, let me tell you, Gail, (I'm speaking very gallantly now, with strong emphasis) my love for you is such that I think you should go for it. Go for it all the way.

G: But I can't. It goes against everything I believe in.

Me: But I want you to know that it's all right should you change your mind, should you be able to convince yourself to do it.

G: That's sweet of you (she touches my brow affectionately.) I think this is just something I've got to go through. I mean, this type of thing happens to married couples all of the time.

Me: (thinking about that statement) Yeah... who knows? Infatuations have a way of fading away. (I don't sound entirely convincing this is where the situation will head. There's a brief pause. I sit up in bed, away from her. I'm starting to make it OK for this to be happening to me.) You want to hear a funny story? I was seriously thinking about...um,... calling Dr. Ruth Westheimer to talk to her about our problem. I actually pictured myself doing that.

G: *Maybe that's a good idea. So you know what to do in the next situation... if it happens again.*

Me: *(I start to laugh. I start to realize that I'm accepting the situation, and it's all because of Aunt Evelyn. I'm starting to think about all the possibilities my sudden freedom open up. I'm bowled over at how quickly I went through the process of making it OK.)* Wow, I'm going through the process.

G: *What process is that?*

Me: *The process of making it OK for this to happen to me.*

G: *(She starts to smile.) Are you picturing me sitting on a toilet?*

Me: *(This question really throws me for a loop. I give her a funny expression.) No, not really. What... what do you mean by that?*

G: *The process I'm thinking about is a process I read in a book called "How to Fall Out of Love." You picture the lover you're breaking up with doing abnormal or unflattering things, like sitting on the toilet, or in awkward situations...*

Me: *(I realize that she's putting ME through this process, and it immediately depresses me. I don't want to be thought of like that, and again, I'm hurt.) Gail...(I cut her off quickly) I don't think I want to hear this.*

G: *(She reaches for me as if to comfort me.) OK, I'm sorry.*

Me: *That wasn't even close to the process I was thinking about.*

G: *So what process were you thinking about?*

Me: *(Trying to grasp the right words) Realizing all the emotions I went through; first I acted ... desperate. Then hurt. Then mad. Then benevolent. Ver-ry benevolent. (She and I laugh.) Then mad again, then hurt again. Then finally... accepting it. Realizing that that's part of life. That it's OK to feel all those feelings. It's normal to feel all those feelings.*

G: *Did you think out each feeling? (She sounds impressed.)*

Me: *Yeah, and then I'd turn off immediately. (Pause.) Instantaneously (that was the original word I was searching for.) And I went through all those emotions (I glance at the clock to figure out how long we had been talking.) in about 15 minutes. Fifteen minutes! Oh, wait until I tell Evelyn. She won't believe it. That's what she taught me. (Another thought flashes across.) Of course, if I didn't have it inside me in the first place, it wouldn't have been there for me to bring it out. She brought it out of me.*

G: *(Nodding in agreement.) That's right.*

Me: *(I'm starting to feel a little smug about myself. I then start thinking about how Gail's going to be sorry for letting me get away. Yeah, I'll show her.)*

G: You're really a sweetheart (She snuggles up to me.)

So, after *all that,* of course, we agreed to be platonic room-mates. I get it now; she just wasn't all that into me. But the platonic roommate status made it kinda weird, because it was a one-bedroom apartment, so we were sleeping in the same bed, and the 's' word was never mentioned. I have to say, that felt very strange for me, and from what I had already experienced in life, I knew what "strange" was. But Gail seemed perfectly fine with it. It was a perfect fit for her.

Gail had this peculiar theory about us after she consulted a "psychic." She told me the psychic told her that she was my *mother* in a past life. Well, that explained everything.

So we were on board, headed down the tracks, in the direction of that train wreck just around the bend, up yonder.

Gail sitting pretty at Vazquez Rocks, in Antelope Valley. Sustainable intimacy loomed too lofty of an expectation with Gail

---◆---

She tilted her head to kiss me and I took her into my arms while Maria held onto her hand. The kiss lingered for several seconds. It was intensely passionate, an electrifying moment frozen in time, a kiss that had waited three years to happen. We had crossed the line, but it empowered us with a sense of fearlessness.

---◆---

CHAPTER 15
Michelob Quenches A Thirst

It was the summer of 1986 and I was on the phone with Lizamara. It had been two-and-a-half years since we had split up and, believe it or not, we had gotten past the hard feelings of our divorce. She had hired an attorney back then and tried to get spousal support out of me, but got *nuthin'*.

Then she moved to Miami, where her sister Cristiane was already living. Vilma, who had graduated from Hawthorne High in the top five percent of the class, moved back to Miami as well. All five sisters were reunited in Florida. Making the move from Managua were Maria Mercedes, the youngest sister, and Katya and Roberto. Mr. and Mrs. Pasos remained in Nicaragua, presumably still married.

Since I had last seen her Katya had given birth to two more kids— a boy and another girl. So, a *lot* had changed with her circumstances.

Lizamara and I had been keeping in touch. On this call in the summer of 1986, she was telling me about Vilma getting married. Then we started talking up the idea of my flying to Miami to visit. Lizamara offered the sofa in the living room in her apartment for me to sleep on. She assured me that her boyfriend wouldn't have any problem with me staying at her place.

"It would be nice to see you," she said. "Everybody would be happy to see you. Everybody in my family thinks you're Mr. Perfect, Mr. Wonderful."

I had to admit, I thought about seeing Katya again and felt my heart racing. But now she had *three* kids; I quickly dismissed those feelings I had felt for her three years earlier in Nicaragua. Three kids. Of course, it wouldn't be the same. I wondered if she was happy.

"Katya would be happy to see you," Lizamara tossed out.

"How is she?" I asked.

"Miserable. She's married to a monster."

I didn't push the subject further. I just felt sorry for Katya.

I decided to go to Miami. It would be nice to see Vilma again, I thought. Gail and I were now platonic roommates, so I had no problem telling her my plans. I could handle the boyfriend. The question was, could I handle Lizamara? I had sensed in our phone conversations that she had changed over the past two-and-a-half years. This did not deter the concerns of some of my closest friends who thought I should have my head examined when I told them I was going. I tried to assure them I had everything under control.

But when I was on the plane headed east, the thought of seeing Katya was causing those heart flutters again.

———————◆———————

The reunion with Lizamara in Miami was pleasant. She looked good and she greeted me warmly when I arrived at her apartment. I met her boyfriend, who was a nice fellow, but I thought he was kind of an odd match for her. He was a little chubby and may have been a few years younger than Lizamara. She treated him like he was a big teddy bear.

A family reception for me was planned at Cristiane's apartment. Newlywed Vilma would be accompanied by her new husband, so I looked forward to meeting him.

But when I entered Cristiane's living room and was greeted by a gathering of a dozen or so, my eyes were riveted on Katya, who gave me the same look she had when we first met three years ago. Her face lit up; she gave me a brief hug. I could barely swallow. She looked exactly the same as she had three years ago; hadn't changed a bit.

I met her two little ones — Robertito, who was 2 1/2, and Maria, who was almost 1 1/2. Robertito's age suggested Katya might have been carrying him when I first met her in Nicaragua. I reacquainted myself with Katya's oldest daughter, Katya II, who was 6.

I tried to focus on everyone else. Roberto shook my hand firmly. Vilma was all aglow as a new bride; she looked beautiful. I gave her a warm hug. Maria Mercedes was turning into a beautiful young lady — she was now 15, much taller and her slender figure filling out; she had changed dramatically from when I had last seen her in Nicaragua.

After making the rounds around the room, I drifted back towards Katya. Her eyes were open with anticipation. She was beaming with a warm smile, bearing no pretenses in view of a wary husband watching. I was struck, like a thunderbolt, by how beautiful she looked.

270

We started talking in our *Spanglish* way. Her English hadn't improved at all. But I had her laughing within a minute. The amazing thing was, it felt like we were back in Nicaragua in an *instant*. It was as if the three-year gap hadn't happened. How many women had I met/flirted with/become romantically involved with over those three years? Maybe a dozen? Didn't matter. With Katya standing before me, they all receded in my memory. Despite the language barrier, we were connecting on a deeper level. It was an astonishing feeling.

That moment reminded me of a song receiving a lot of radio play at the time — Howard Jones' hauntingly beautiful "No One Is to Blame." Every time I heard it I couldn't help thinking about Katya.

"You can look at the menu, but you just can't eat
You can feel the cushion, but you can't have a seat
You can dip your foot in the pool, but you can't have a swim,
You can feel the punishment, but you can't commit the sin

"And you want her, and she wants you
We want everyone
And you want her and she wants you
No one, no one, no one ever is to blame"

———————◆———————

Later that night Lizamara and I wound up at a classy, art-deco bar just off the beach. It was a balmy evening, with a brisk, warm, off-shore breeze blowing in, whisking Lizamara's long-flowing hair back, as we sat at a glass-top table on the front patio sipping on drinks out of long, tall glasses. Music from jazz musicians inside floated through the air. We could talk above it and had our first real, face-to-face conversation.

"I can't believe you're here," Lizamara started. She said it with a smile.

"It was great to see everyone," I returned. "I'm glad I came."

"I can't believe Vilma is going…to have a baby already." Her voice turned soft.

"Yeah, that really took me by surprise. Vilma having a baby. Little Vilma."

"She isn't the one who should be having a baby. It should be me. (Pause.) You know, Chic, the one thing I regret about our marriage is that we didn't have a baby. I think we would have had a beautiful child."

"We … never got the chance, because of your…"

"Operation," Lizamara interrupted. (With contempt.) "My operation. Because of my operation I may never be able to have children. Because of my *operation* I have to pretend I have children through my sisters."

"I do remember how you were with little Katya in Nicaragua three years ago. You treated her as if she were yours."

"I am the same way with Robertito and Maria. I do wish they were mine. Katya needs all the help she can get with those three kids. I wish I didn't have to work. She needs to get out of the house, stuck there all day while Roberto works. What about you? If you have no other plans, you could do something with her during the day."

"She's invited me over to dinner tomorrow night."

Lizamara cared for her sister. She wanted her to be happy. The sense was that Roberto kept impregnating Katya and she was hopelessly bogged down taking care of the kids. She wasn't happy.

With the air blowing in from the ocean, I felt a sense of clarity. I turned toward Lizamara and asked her directly:

"What would you think if I *did* something with Katya?" I purposely used her words to phrase it.

Lizamara paused before answering. "You better not tell me."

———————◆———————

The next day I accompanied Katya and the two little ones while they shopped, before picking up Katya II from school. Then I joined them for dinner in the evening, along with Roberto, the husband, after he came home from work.

I made an effort to play with the three kids during most of my visit. Robertito was repeatedly shooting a toy machine gun at me. That gave me a headache.

I tried to show some attention to Katya II, the oldest daughter. She needed it. She had some tough competition getting any attention with the two little ones around. She never complained.

Roberto was quiet during dinner. I talked to him a little bit about his job. He was putting in long hours as a nurse's aide at a hospital. He was a doctor in Managua, but his doctor's license wasn't applicable in the U.S.

He asked about Lizamara and I, as if there was any chance we could get back together. I deftly gave him an evasive answer to avoid any perception that I was in Miami for any ulterior motive.

Katya listened attentively, not offering any clue to what she was thinking.

———————◆◆◆◆◆◆———————

The next day, I decided to "do something" during the day with Katya and her two little ones, as Lizamara had suggested. We went to a local beach. We had the bulk of the day until it was time to pick up the oldest daughter at school.

It was an overcast day, with rain clouds building up. Katya appeared to be cold, sitting on the beach towel on the sand. In a bold move, I maneuvered behind her and wrapped my arms around her. She melted into my arms. I started to think about "doing something," when I felt raindrops on my head. Quickly, we gathered up the beach towels and kids as the rain started to come down harder. We ran for cover under a beach hut, just as a downpour erupted.

Katya looked up at me with a smile and I noticed mascara running down her face from one eye. I reached to wipe the mascara away, which startled her at first. Then she relented to my gentle touch.

Somehow, I summoned the nerve to say to her, "*Damen un beso* (Give me a kiss)".

"OK, *solamente uno* (OK, only one)".

She tilted her head to kiss me and I took her into my arms while Maria held onto her hand. The kiss lingered for several seconds. It was intensely passionate, an electrifying moment frozen in time, a kiss that had waited three years to happen. We had crossed the line, but it empowered us with a sense of fearlessness.

I glanced around quickly and saw an ice cream store nearby.

"*Quierres* ice cream?"

"*Si, Cheek* (her pronunciation of Chic). *Il quierre.*" She pointed to the two little ones.

The downpour stopped as we started toward the ice cream store. Halfway there, she grabbed my arm to pull me toward her and kissed me again.

We went a little further the following day, when I drove Katya and her two little ones down the coast to picturesque Key Biscayne Beach. It was a warm day. There was an irresistible pull toward Katya that I could no longer fight. It was overwhelming. I knew I was playing with fire. I was feeling those same butterflies in my gut that I felt with my high school sweetheart April when I was first experiencing the sensation of being in love. I was — dare I say it? — falling in love with Katya!

We were sitting in the shallow water together, with my arms around her, while Maria sat in her lap. Robertito was playing nearby. I couldn't resist nuzzling Katya's neck.

"Katya, I wanna make love with you," I whispered quickly, nervously, in her ear.

Katya's face was hidden from me, but she appeared puzzled and didn't respond. I winced. *"Oh no, I've gone too far now,"* I thought. I've blown it. I've insulted her. I felt uneasy and withdrew my arms from her.

"Uhh, *so tienes hambre* (are you hungry)?" I asked, purposely to change the subject.

"No. *Tienes sed* (are you thirsty)?" she asked.

"Que?" I asked.

Katya gestured as if she was drinking. *"Tienes sed?"*

"Am I thirsty? No, no."

Now I was puzzled. I rose out of the water, creating an awkward pause.

Katya looked up at me. *"Como se dice Mick-ee-laub?"*

"How do you say Mick-ee-laub? You mean Michelob?

"Si. Esta cerveza, no?"

"Si, esta cerveza. Beer."

"Como se dice?" (How do you say?)

"Mick-eh-lobe."

"Mick-eh-laub."

"Lobe."

"Laub."

"Lobe."

"Laub."

"Lobe, lobe. Mick-eh-*lobe*." I pulled on my earlobe, as if that was going to help Katya in any way on how to pronounce it correctly, since she likely didn't know the English word for ear-lobe, much less how to pronounce it.

She looked puzzled, as to be expected, but pulled on her ear-lobe anyway. "Mick-eh- (pulling on her earlobe again) lobe?" Seemingly, pulling on her earlobe magically helped her pronounce "lobe" correctly.

"Right! You've got it!"

Katya paused, reflecting on a thought.

"*Porque, si tu no tienes sed* (Why, if you are not thirsty), you say you want a Miche- (pulls on her earlobe) lobe with me?"

I had to think for a moment. Oh gosh, this was embarrassing. I probably rushed and mumbled through it when I said it, so she thought she heard me say "Michelob." I stifled a laugh with the realization that *this* was a classic moment to treasure.

"Ahh, I wasn't saying I want a Michelob with you. I said I want to (pause) ahh... (embarrassed) you know, ahh (pause) *make love* with you."

Michelob.. Make-ee love...it was understandable how those two phrases could get mixed up when you're speaking Spanglish. Her tendency to throw in an extra syllable for silent "E's" speaking English did confuse the translation. Hey, what *really* mattered here was that she finally learned the correct pronunciation of "Michelob."

There was another pause and for a brief moment I braced with the fear that I had pushed it too far again. Until Katya said,

"*Quando, Cheek?*"

"You're asking me when?" I happily responded.

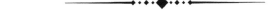

The question of "when" did not linger long. The next morning, after Lizamara and her boyfriend both had left for work, I was just barely stirring from my sleep on the living room sofa when I heard a knock at the front door. It was Katya, with baby Maria in tow.

She sauntered in with her little girl. As soon as I closed the door behind her, we embraced in another deep, passionate kiss.

All self-control vanished from that point. We clutched each other in a frenzy. Quickly, we pulled the sheet on which I had been sleeping on the sofa and spread it out on the living room floor. Katya then searched the room and found a pen and paper, which she presented to Maria in a corner to keep her occupied.

Clothes were whipped off in seconds and then we were rolling on the sheet making wild love in the living room of my ex-wife. The danger of the moment only intensified our love-making. How could something so forbidden feel so good? This was what making love was intended to feel like. Anyone who's ever been passionately in love and has experienced one of God's greatest gifts that expresses the ultimate feeling of being alive knows what I'm talking about. She kept screaming, *"Mi amore!"* I have no idea what I was screaming. Maria was the only one keeping quiet, taking notes with that pen and paper; she was a good little girl.

This was pure emotion on display; it went way beyond physical gratification. Katya and I had found something together that gave profound meaning to shared human existence. This would explain every decision we made together from here on out.

Katya with her beautiful baby, Maria

There was no stopping us from that point. We were emboldened, we felt no fear. Later that afternoon, with the heat emanating from the baking sun outside, I felt no fear standing in Katya and Roberto's kitchen when Roberto arrived from work. The look on his face was expressionless when he saw me, signaling no sign of suspicion.

Katya and I glanced at each other, feeling our secret was safe.

When Roberto disappeared into the bedroom and I was getting ready to leave, Katya cornered me in the kitchen and silently stole a kiss with me one more time.

When I returned that night to Lizamara's apartment, she asked me about our day. Playfully, she asked me if anything happened "yet" between Katya and I.

I told her no.

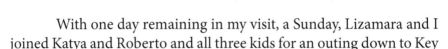

With one day remaining in my visit, a Sunday, Lizamara and I joined Katya and Roberto and all three kids for an outing down to Key Largo.

It was a perfect day in paradise. The water was a crystal-clear turquoise, the sand was sun-bleached white, the palm trees were ever so gently swaying in the soft breeze.

It was in this setting that Katya and I found a private moment to profess our love to each other.

How much were we pushing our luck? It was hard to say that day. But there might have been a telling sign when I emerged dripping from a dip in the water with an anguished look on my face.

Katya, looking up from the beach towel she was laying on, asked, *"Que pasa?"*

"Oh, no big deal. Robertito pulled on my chain in the water…" I held out the broken golden neck chain that used to hold an Italian good luck charm that Lizamara had bought me. Lizamara came walking up just at that moment, carrying Maria.

"…And it broke and I lost my good luck charm."

"Oh, I buy *anotre*," Katya offered.

"No, no, that's OK. *No quieres.*"

Lizamara chimed in, "Maybe your next wife will buy you one."

"I don't want one," I replied.

"You don't want what? A new chain or a new wife?" my ex-wife playfully queried.

"I'm not sure what the difference is," I quipped back with a smile.

The real question was, would losing the charm spell the end of my good luck? Even the Luckiest Ordinary Man Alive has limits on luck.

———————————•◆•————————————

Lizamara and I said goodbye on the Monday morning that I was to return to LA. Katya, having left the kids with one of her sisters, came by after Lizamara left for work to take me to the airport. We made love one more time. We wondered if it would be the last time.

I got back home on the West Coast, barely escaping hurricane season in Florida — reports of developing Hurricane Lizamara fizzled.

I told Gail everything that happened. I had no problem telling her.

"Do you think you're… in love with her?" she asked.

I paused before answering, with hand resting on chin. "Maybe."

OK, I didn't tell her *everything*. I kept that one for myself. I wanted that feeling all to myself. I was feeling over-the-top. I know it sounds crazy — and I know it is crazy — but there was no "maybe" about it; I was in love with Katya.

There was no logic to it; there's no logic to being in love. We were both just swept up in the emotion and carried away by the feeling. It was exhilarating and inescapable.

I called Katya within a week of my return home.

"*Te quiero, mi amore,*" she said to me in her angelic-sounding voice.

"*Te quiero,*" I repeated back to her, meaning it wholeheartedly.

Katya then initiated an intimate exchange of memories of favorite parts of each other's body. There was a sense of urgency as to when we'd see each other again, not that those memories were fading anytime soon.

We were calling each other every few days, like a pair of excited teens in love.

A few weeks later, I got a call from Miami of a completely different sort. It was from Lizamara. Those storm warnings popped back up suddenly.

"I've got some news that might interest you," she announced. "Katya is pregnant."

There was dead silence on the phone for — I don't know how long, because I was too stunned.

"Are you there? I said Katya is pregnant."

"Gosh... that's too bad," I finally stuttered. Hearing it twice didn't diminish the shock. "That's just what Katya needs."

"So, here's the thing," Lizamara began suspensefully. "Katya is about five weeks along in her pregnancy. I believe you were here five weeks ago."

"Five weeks?" I replied incredulously. "Uhh, it seems a lot longer than that."

"No, it was five weeks. I checked the calendar." Of course, she did.

Another pause. Then she abruptly jumped in again, "So, I wanna know, did you do something with my sister?"

"Well, uhh, yeah, I did a lot of things with your sister. We went shopping, we went to the beach..."

"You *know* what I mean. Did you do something with my sister... that could make her pregnant?"

"Now Lizamara," I started, with that uncomfortable feeling of being backed into a corner. I kept thinking back to the first time I mentioned to her the possibility of *doing something* with Katya and she told me not to tell her. "How long has she known this?"

"She just found out a couple days ago."

"Does, uhh... Roberto know?"

"I think so. I don't know for sure."

"So, how is Katya taking the news?"

"She's OK, she's been through it three times before." Lizamara's patience was starting to break. "Come on, Chic. Why don't you tell me?"

"Tell you what?"

"Tell me if you did something with my sister," she hesitated, softening her voice. "Come on, you can tell me. We're *friends* now, remember? We can tell each other anything."

"Well, I do want to be honest with you. I'm just, uhh, sort of, uhh, surprised by the news. I just feel bad for Katya. I mean, she has three kids already, and one more kid is just going to be..."

"I know, Chic," she cut me off. "That's why I want to know if you did anything with her."

"Well, I, uhh, I…"

"Just tell me the truth, as a friend, yes or no. Did you sleep with my sister?"

My mouth was agape as I vainly tried to keep the word from escaping from my lips. "Y-e-s-s-s."

Dead silence returned for a moment. Then Lizamara's voice reverberated in my ear, in a much lower, darker tone.

"As far as I'm concerned, *tu morte*."

"Tu morte" means "You're dead" in Spanish. Evidently, my good friend Lizamara was not responding to the truth very well. Shouldn't have told her.

In the face of desperation, my next phone conversation with Katya was intended to calm her. I was decisive, with a little help from work. As luck would have it, I had the season-ending Indy car race in Miami — a street race — to cover in a few weeks. Management felt it merited coverage because the championship battle was to be decided between two drivers— Bobby Rahal and Michael Andretti.

So, I told Katya I would come to see her during that trip to help her decide what to do about the pregnancy. There were options.

When I told Gail about my plans to return to Miami, she offered very "Gailonian" advice: "Be careful back there. The stars aren't in your favor."

Then I came around to the subject with Janice. I visited her to check out the new apartment she had moved into in the Fairfax district. There was a young man with long blond hair named Steven that she was dating who "crashed" at the apartment quite a bit. I was pretty sure he was helping her out with the rent.

The apartment was on the top floor of a three-story building and it had access to the rooftop. That's where we wound up during my visit, lying on a blanket, smoking pot, and gazing at the stars.

"I want to go someplace excitin," Janice declared in her airy way. "Let's go on a trip, Chic. Like maybe Mexico. I've always wanted to go to Puerto Vallerto (she mis-pronounced it.) Or better yet, let's go to Nicaragua! We could have some f-u-n there. Don't you want to go back and see what's really going on?"

"Well, yeah, it would be interesting to go back," I half-heartedly agreed.

"Lizamara could go with us!"

"Mmm, I don't think that would be a good idea. She's not real happy with me right now."

"Oh God, Chic. What did you do now?"

"She told me Katya is pregnant."

"Well, Lizamara doesn't have to go with us to Nicaragua." Janice was visibly upset.

"Janice, I believe the baby is mine."

"Of course you do." Now she was sounding hurt.

"I'm going back there to help her decide what she wants to do. See if she wants to get an abortion."

Janice shook her head. "She won't get an abortion."

I probably had said more than I should have. And Janice was offering insight into the psyche of a woman whom she didn't know that was dead-on.

———————◆———————

Katya was anxiously waiting for me at the Miami airport. When our eyes met, we rushed together into an intense embrace and kissed passionately.

Through our Spanglish vocabulary, I was able to understand that her kids were at her sister Cristiane's house, and that her husband thought she was at her new job, in training. The table was set for our momentous rendezvous. I was very apprehensive, with no idea what to expect.

I had both a rental car and a hotel reservation, on the Her-Ex economy budget, waiting for me. I was in for surprises on both accounts. At the airport car rental station, I was told that they had no compact car available like I had reserved.

"But we do have a Cadillac 5th Avenue that we can give you, at the same compact rate," I was told. "Would that be satisfactory for you, sir?"

Holy crap. The 5th Avenue they had was a luxury car awash in burgundy with plush, crushed-velvet seats and state-of-the-art dashboard. Not a bad upgrade.

Then we drove to the hotel where I had my reservation. I was told they were overbooked. "But we have a brand new hotel that notified us that they would take in customers whom we couldn't accommodate," I was told. I was given the address and we drove there with the anticipation of finding a dump.

Instead, we walked in with eyes wide open to the luxurious, five-star Hotel Sofitel, dazzled by the golden-paneled walls and glistening chandeliers hanging from the ceiling. We were escorted to our room by a young Hispanic bellhop, who opened the door to a jaw-dropping luxury suite.

"Oh my God!" I cried in joy while Katya shrieked "Oh, *mi Dio*" in unison. This was too good to be true. For Katya, considering the Third World where she had come from, this was something way beyond her experience.

In a matter of seconds we were on the pillow-soft, king-sized bed with the silk sheets, re-enacting our first encounter on Lizamara's living room floor. The encore was worthy of the wait.

This catapulted me into maybe the best week of my life. I had come to Miami to help Katya make a monumental decision. As soon as I touched ground, everything turned magical, starting with the 5th Avenue rental car, then the five-star hotel with the silk sheets. How were we supposed to make a rational decision after that prelude?

"I want to keep the baby," Katya said to me sweetly in the aftermath of our love-making. She cupped my face and kissed me softly.

"OK," I said, the wheels in my head spinning. "What will you tell Roberto? Will he *piense el nino es este*?"

"His baby? No *amore, es* your baby."

"I believe you. I mean, will he *piense* (tapped my head to indicate "think") it's his baby?"

"*Si.* I take care of Roberto. Don' worry."

Her face then turned serious as she looked deep into my eyes. "*Yo no quieres* you feel press-sew-er, *mi amore*."

"Pressure, no, no. I don't feel pressure, my sweet. We'll work this out, together."

I don't know if she understood every word I said, but my earnest look into her eyes conveyed the feeling and she seemed at ease. What pressure?

I had race qualifying to cover the next day. Then that night, Katya and I met up again. That work training for her new job that she was telling her husband was very intense. This time we went for a drive in the 5th Avenue on a full moonlit night and parked by the water in Key Biscayne. I have this image of Katya forever burned in my memory, of her wading barefoot in the water, lifting up the hem of her flowery sun dress, with one foot slightly raised out of the water. With her head slightly tilted, she's looking at me taking a photo of her, flashing her impish smile that I adored.

Then we made love in the back seat of the 5th Avenue, on the crushed velvet. I'm reminded of one of the all-time classic romantic movies ever made that came out 11 years later, "The Titanic." We were Jack and Rose, re-enacting the scene where they were making love in that vintage car parked in the bowels of the ship, with Rose's hand jutting suddenly up against the precipitation on the window created by their body heat. We were Jack and Rose, on opposite ends of societal status, falling in love aboard the Titanic, headed for that iceberg.

I covered the race (Bobby Rahal clinched the championship) and did my job, then stayed an extra four days in Miami to spend solely with Katya. There has never been a more romantic week in my life than that week in Miami. Handholding over a candlelight dinner... making love while standing by the hotel window... kissing in the hotel elevator until the doors open, with the same Hispanic bellhop who showed us our room standing there and giving us a knowing smile... kissing and laughing in a slithering embrace during a bubblebath in the hotel room... taking a serene walk along hotel row at the beach at sunset, palm trees swaying in the ocean breeze... slow-dancing and kissing on a nightclub dance floor, oblivious to the attention we were attracting... Katya pulling on her earlobe to signal what she had in mind, and it had nothing to do with being thirsty for beer.

The week totally shaded my world in rose hues. I left Miami committed to the idea that, once the baby was born, I would take in Katya, the baby, and her three other children and find a way to support them in LA — an instantaneous family of six. I dismissed the idea that I would be taking Roberto's three kids away from him. I was hoping for some sort of sign during my week in Miami to guide us to the right path. I would say we got a humongous, flashing neon sign, after the week we experienced.

I knew Katya was desperate to escape a loveless marriage that had trapped her in a thankless, mundane role of motherhood. I offered an impossible dream escape for her, embraced in passionate love with the promise of true happiness. This was the role I was born to play — that of the knight riding in on the white horse to save the day.

But by the time I got home, the idea of having five dependents to take care of suddenly had me scared shitless.

Gail was not happy when I told her. In fact, she got angry, questioning what would happen to her once the baby was born.

I was surprised by her reaction.

"I thought we had an understanding about our relationship," I said.

"I know. I guess I always knew it would come to this," she responded despondently. "I can accept what's happening intellectually. But I can't accept... (her voice started to crack)... the thought of losing you yet."

I stared at her intently. Now I was really surprised.

The call coming in from Miami at my work desk sounded urgent. It was Katya, telling me, "*No bueno.*"

I asked her in Spanish, "What is it?" She said "sangre," which I didn't understand.

I looked around at my colleagues in the sports department and decided to call her back from a pay phone in a back hallway, where I could have some privacy.

"What is *sangre*?" I asked over the pay phone.

"Blued."

"Blued?" I repeated. "You mean blood?"

"Si."

"*Porque* blood, Katya?"

"*Esta es problemo con el nino.*"

"Problem? With the baby? What problem?"

"Doctor say *yo tango dos.*"

"*Tu tango dos* what? I mean, *tu tienes*".

"*Dos niños.*"

I stopped to briefly consider what she was telling me.

My voice rose. "*Two babies*? You're pregnant with two babies?! Twins?!!"

At this point, I just lost it and broke out in uncontrollable laughter. I just didn't know any other way to react. It was just so ludicrous, the situation I found myself in. It was just... beyond belief.

Katya was freaking out on the other end of the line, asking me *"Que pasa?"* I collected myself, making sure no one was near the hallway to hear my psychotic outburst.

"We'll just deal with it, that's all. Yeahhhh." Make that family of seven. Ok, now there was pressure.

Then we talked about the blood. She explained that it was probably due to the stress from her job, taking care of her three kids, and now carrying two more. I suggested she should quit her job, but she said they needed the money.

"Es muy dificil para mi," she said in a desperate tone. "I need *Cheek* here in Miami. I no stop think about you. I... (she stifled a cry), fear, *Cheek."*

"Fear? Fear what, Katya? About the babies?"

"No. *Para que Lizamara me dice."*

"Lizamara? She say something about us?"

"No. She say, *tu vives con anotre muere."*

"Muere?"

"Anotre woman."

"Whew! You're full of surprises today. (Pause.) Yes, Katya. It's true. It's *verdad*. Her name is Gail."

I convinced her that I didn't feel the same way about Gall as I did about her. I loved her, and she was going to be *"Madre de mi nino. Err, ninos."*

"OK, *Cheek*. I believe you," she said softly, surrendering. I wasn't going to let her down.

———•◆•———

Maybe Dan wasn't the best friend in the world to rely on for sage advice on the predicament I found myself in. He was generally crazier than I was. But he had heard all my stories up to this point, including my Nicaragua stories, which only cracked him up. He could afford to laugh because I survived them all, and he was cracking up over my current predicament, because he figured I'd survive this one, too.

With the holidays approaching, he sent me the perfect gift — a 12-pack of Michelobs.

Janice, on the other hand, wasn't seeing the humor in the situation. She had a different take.

"Lizamara will *kill* you. If Roberto doesn't do it first."

———◆———

The Christmas holidays were approaching. It was the season for holiday cheer. But the call I received from Katya in early December was anything but cheerful.

Katya didn't know the right English word to use, but the word was "miscarriage." All the air sucked out of me when she said "lost *los ninos.*" She was going to undergo an operation to remove the fetuses. She sounded very depressed and very afraid. My entire body ached for her.

This was crushing news. I had concluded this pregnancy was predestined to bring Katya and I together; all the signs were showing that this was meant to be. This was the point in my life where I met the love of my life, and three years later everything fell in the right place so we could live happily ever after. I accepted the fact that nothing came easy for me, so the standard fairy tale would figure to have a few kinks in it when it came to my story.

But this…this just sucked. Devastating. But the question had to be asked: Did we avoid running into that iceberg?

———◆———

I stopped calling Katya for the rest of the holidays, knowing she was having her operation and was bound to be too depressed. What could I possibly say to make her feel better? It felt like it was over between us. Destiny, all of a sudden, seemed derailed.

I told Gail about the miscarriage. She seemed buoyed by the news. She was feeling especially cheery for the holidays. We picked out a Christmas tree together for the apartment and decorated it together. We talked about having a gift exchange, so I asked her what she wanted. At first she said a purse, then stunned me by changing it to "lingerie."

"You… want lingerie?" I had to ask.

Gail seemed a little uneasy by my open-mouthed reaction.

"Sure. Why not?" She shrugged. "I haven't worn any… for a long time. It might be… (half-smiling) fun."

On Christmas Day, when we opened our presents under the tree, she seemed to like the lingerie I bought her.

A few nights later, when I was playing the piano and Gail was quietly listening on the sofa, she disappeared into the bedroom, and came back out wearing her new lingerie.

This was a different look for her. She looked sexy. I followed her back into the bedroom.

I was not expecting this. The train was starting to slip off the tracks.

This was the crusher. This was the point where I realized I was going to crush a heart in Miami. But I was forced to finally realize that I shouldn't be breaking up that family, for better or worse.

CHAPTER 16
Paternal Instinct, Part 2

To celebrate New Year's Eve, Gail and I attended a party at the Rossburn house. The theme of the party was to dress in "bad taste," which was the grand idea of Merrie, Mom's longtime tenant and Pam's close friend.

So, we were appropriately dressed in tacky outfits, in very bad taste, and we were acting like a cozy couple, in the spirit of the New Year. Janice was at the party, too. She drew me aside and expressed surprised by Gail's and my demeanor.

"Are you like, *together* again?" she asked with purposeful disdain.

"Well, for tonight, anyway," I said, coyly.

"If you ask me, *that's* in bad taste," she said, and walked away.

Our romantic interlude was a momentary blip, a step out of time. It didn't change what I was really feeling in my heart. Within the first week of the new year, I was back on the phone talking to Katya, mapping out a plan to see her again. I couldn't just abandon her after her crushing miscarriage.

This did not sit well with Gail. She saw the phone bill and noticed all the calls to Miami. The ice in our relationship returned, and within a couple of weeks we were back to being strictly platonic again, no longer *together*. The chemistry just wasn't there between us.

That was as it should have been in the first place. Katya's miscarriage had thrown me for a loop. I was despondent during the holidays when I rushed for comfort into the accommodating arms of Gail, dressed in her seductive lingerie. That was a mistake, a moment of weakness on my part when I was caught up in the heightened emotions of the occasion.

Mr. Mistake had struck again and the mistakes were piling up. The fact of the matter was that I was in love with Katya. Still.

Things had deteriorated so quickly between Gail and I that she announced that she was going to move out at the end of the semester in June. I was relieved by her decision. The platonically-sleeping-in-the-same-bed scenario was just a little too weird for me.

Katya's pregnancy and my willingness to dive into parenthood — five-fold — had inspired me to write a screenplay I entitled "Paternal Instinct." I was ready to become a father and my passion for Katya was enough to persuade me to take on the responsibility of (gulp!) five kids all at once, if so be it.

The miscarriage ended that noble gesture. But our feelings for each other hadn't changed. We weren't exactly sure where that left us but we both knew we wanted to see each other again to find out.

The Daytona 500 was coming up again in mid-February and I was assigned to cover it again. Miami was less than a four-hour drive down the coast from Daytona. That provided an opportunity for me to make that drive after the business trip to see Katya.

So, when the Daytona 500 had concluded and I filed my race story, I started south down Highway 95 toward Miami.

◆ ◆ ◆ ◆ ◆ ◆ ◆

Katya worked at a large retail store at night. I arrived in town close to the end of her shift. I walked into the store and located her in the women's apparel section. She was with a woman customer. I watched from afar until I finally caught her attention. I pulled on my earlobe. She broke out in a wide smile and briskly walked up to me.

"Five more minute," she said. Then she returned to her customer.

Her English had noticeably improved during our recent phone conversations, probably from working this job. I patiently waited. The five minutes turned into twenty.

When she finally finished, we embraced in a passionate kiss outside the store. It felt good to feel her in my arms again.

She had the drill down by now on what story she told at home to free herself up to be with me. I had a compact rental car — no 5th Avenue this time — and she followed me to my hotel in her own car. No five-star hotel with silk sheets this time. It didn't matter. We didn't waste time jumping into bed together.

I pulled out a packet of condoms.

"No worry," Katya said, waving off the condoms. "I take peel now."

Our love-making was frenzied, passionate, loud, and quick. She quickly showered, then had to rush home.

This visit felt rushed. It didn't feel at all like my previous visit. Katya and I were fighting it, against all odds. The mood for this trip was set while we were parked in my car at Key Biscayne at dusk, the rain coming down, beating against the front windshield, as I clutched her in my arms in the front seat.

"Vilma have her baby," Katya announced softly.

"Really? Boy or girl?"

Her voice started to crack as tears welled up in her eyes. "Boy."

"Katya, don't cry," I said tenderly, cupping her face. "I think about our babies, too."

"*Cheek*, I love you so much, *pero*…I… no see… hope for us. We are so deeferent. You have your life, I have my. *Tu vives* in Los Angeles, I in Miami. I…. *Mi ninos. Tu vives con* Gail. I no see… how…"

I gave Katya the speech I had been rehearsing in my mind, how I had felt something special with her when I met her in Nicaragua and then how that feeling only intensified when we met up again three years later. It felt so *right,* that we were meant to be together. The pregnancy was proof. But now, without the pregnancy to consider, we had time to think this through. I told her I still wanted to be with her and her three *ninos,* but I just needed some time to figure out how to make that happen.

"*Yo quiero*…make you happy, *Cheek. Pero,* I have think my children first."

I had no pat answer for her for that.

———————◆•••———————

Weeks later, there was another development at home. One morning, after showering, I headed for the bedroom in my robe and stopped at the door, which was cracked open. I peaked inside and saw Gail standing in front of the dresser mirror, topless, tenderly fondling one of her breasts. I was aroused at first, but then focused for a closer look.

Gail suddenly noticed me in the mirror, hastily covered herself up with a blouse, and turned toward me in anger.

"Chic! Are you watching me?!"

I quickly turned away and closed the door, embarrassed.

"I'm sorry, Gail. I just got caught off-guard."

"Caught off-guard," she smirked. "Oh, sure."

"I swear to you, I didn't mean to gawk. I was about to walk in when… I don't know how to say this…unless my eyes were deceiving me, your breasts… they looked…bigger!"

Gail had always had smallish breasts, but now they appeared to be fuller and rounder in shape.

After a moment of silence, Gail reappeared, full clothed, opening the door wider.

"Maybe that's it," she began in a speculative manner. "I felt something different about my breasts and maybe it's because they are bigger. Do you suppose the weight-training class I'm taking at school could have … developed that area?"

I shrugged. "I suppose it's possible."

"I've never worked out much, so now that I am, maybe it's starting to show results."

————————◆————————

Dan was cracking up again over the phone.

"Larger breasts from weight-training? Maybe if she was pounding the beers down, that might do it. At least, that's what it does to me, before it works its way down to my gut. Did she help you finish off that Michelob 12-pack that I sent you?"

"No. She doesn't drink beer."

Dan cut right to the chase.

"I hate to break it to ya, buddy. But, given your luck… I'll bet she's *pregnant!*"

"No! No way!" I was adamant; I couldn't fathom the thought. "We only had sex that once; well, maybe there was a second time."

"It only takes one time, buddy. You're on a streak. I remember when you knocked up Janice, then Katya, hell, Gail why not?. In baseball, you're allowed up to three swings before striking out. Janice and Katya were Strike one and two. You better hope you struck out. But I think you've made contact on your third swing."

"Not if it's a curveball," I countered. "I was always a good contact hitter, but I've always been a sucker for a curveball."

————————◆————————

By late April, life was pitching me that curveball. I could not believe what I was hearing from Gail in our living room…that I had made contact. Lucky me. On a curveball, no less.

"I was in total shock! When they told me it came up positive, I told them, 'There must be a mistake!' I couldn't believe what I was hearing!"

"*God-damn it, Dan was right,*" I was thinking to myself.

"And you're sure it's mine," I said glumly.

"Chic, I haven't had sex with anyone but you."

"But we haven't had sex for over three months!"

"They told me I was fourteen to sixteen weeks along."

"Fourteen to sixteen weeks!!" I stopped to calculate. "Well, that would place it just before New Year's." I grew agitated. "Did you have *any* clue in the past three months that you were pregnant?"

"That was the furthest thought from my mind! I didn't feel any morning sickness, like my mother and sister did when they were pregnant. I wasn't having my normal periods, but I was having some spotting that led me to believe...It's... only when I started feeling a pain right here... (she touched the left side of her pelvic area) that I began to wonder if I might be pregnant. But I was sure it was going to turn out to be something else. I didn't think I could get pregnant after all these years. I was married for six-and-a-half years and couldn't get pregnant when I *tried!*"

After we both shook off the shock, the discussion focused on what we were going to do about it. At fourteen to sixteen weeks along, abortion was *not* an option. Not that that would have been an option at any time; there was still a trace of Catholicism in Gail. So much for the rhythm method.

So, that's what it came down to — I was going to become a father. Crap.

———————————◆◆◆◆——————————

This was the crusher. This was the point where I realized I was going to crush a heart in Miami. But I was forced to finally realize that I shouldn't be breaking up that family, for better or worse. I couldn't take his kids away from Roberto. It took *this* to finally convince me. The miscarriage wasn't enough. So God had to take it one step further.

That's how I easily summed it up in my head, over 33 years later. I had blocked out the extremely complicated manner and whirl of events that resulted in Katya finally finding out about Gail's pregnancy. Nothing ever goes down easy in my life and this story got real messy. This is how it all went down:

It took me a couple weeks to call her. I was all set to tell her, until she gave me pause with the news that she might have cancer and she was going to have another surgery — a hysterectomy — as a preventative measure. I was literally speechless. The good news was, Roberto couldn't get her pregnant anymore.

Then Gail walked in when I was on the phone with Katya. I told her I'd call her back.

"Did you tell her I was pregnant?" Gail angrily demanded.

"No."

A couple weeks went by before I even thought about calling again. But in early June I got distracted when my dad suffered a heart attack. I got a call from Lizamara, who evidently had called Aunt Evelyn out of the blue — what were the odds of that?— and Evelyn told her about my dad. So Lizamara was calling me to express her condolences. Dad was out of the hospital and rehabbing back at home, so in a moment of brilliance, I told Lizamara, 'He'd love to hear from you.' I didn't think that one through.

Lizamara must have called Dad, and his wife Gloria answered the phone. Gloria casually mentioned about Gail being pregnant to Lizamara. I found this out in roundabout fashion, when I arrived home and Gail announced that Lizamara had called me again after Gloria told her about the pregnancy. I asked Gail if she knew if Lizamara told Katya about the pregnancy.

"Hell no!"

Ok, just askin'.

I tried calling Katya again about a week later, but Roberto answered the phone. All of a sudden, calling wasn't a reliable option.

Honestly, my memory is clouded on my next move, a bit of a blur between fact and fiction from my script outlines for the eventual screenplay I wrote, "Paternal Instinct." But I do remember, in an act of pure insanity, that I went back to Miami in an attempt to tell Katya in person.

I didn't have a clear-cut plan. I just wanted a moment alone with her. In one of the crazier moments of my life, I recall staking out Katya's house in my rental car on a Sunday morning and following her to church. I waited outside the church for over an hour for her to appear after the service. I was standing outside the car parked on the street in front of the church and leaning against a tree when I saw Katya emerge from the church walking side-by-side with…can you guess? Lizamara.

Katya didn't see me but — yeah, Lizamara did. Hastily, I ducked behind the tree. But I already had gotten a good look at her ugly glare directed right at me.

I was so spooked that I flew back home, deciding the whole trip wasn't a good idea. There should have been guys in white frocks waiting with a straight-jacket when I got off the plane back in LA.

Katya had her surgery on June 18. I found this out when she called me for my birthday a few days later. Surgery went well. I chickened out and didn't bring up Gail's pregnancy. It was just too damn hard!

Then I got one more call from Lizamara. She wasn't calling me to wish me Happy Birthday. She had some advice for me, telling me if I tried to see Katya again, "I'll make your life miserable." She then made it clear, in no uncertain terms, that Katya didn't want me to call or write to her. I'm pretty sure she finally told her about Gail's pregnancy.

I hung up. It was over.

Despite what Lizamara said to me, I did write Katya an impassioned letter, stating at the start that it was "the hardest letter I have ever had to write," and worse yet, "I don't know if you will ever read it." I didn't expect forgiveness. I laid it all out to her, Gail's pregnancy resulting from my period of "confused feelings" after Katya's miscarriage during the holidays, which I had confided to her at the time. It didn't change anything; Gail was having my baby and I still loved Katya. I told her I felt our love was not a mistake. She did not write back.

In retrospect, I underestimated the sister bond between Lizamara and Katya. I think among all of her sisters Lizamara felt closest to Katya and most protective of her. There was some comfort in knowing that with her big sister, Katya was going to be OK.

In my screenplay, "Paternal Instinct," I had a purely fictitious, much more dramatic ending to Katya's and my affair. She and Roberto, and their three kids, wind up returning to Nicaragua in the screenplay, because Roberto could find better work there and she had no real reason to stay in the states, in her heart and mind. My character travels to Nicaragua in a desperate attempt to woo her back, with disastrous results. I set the scene so that Roberto happens to see me on a street in Managua, hails a Sandinista soldier standing at a corner, and identifies me as an American spy. As I try to flee, the soldier opens fire on me with his machine gun, reality mirroring the seemingly innocent scene months earlier at Roberto and Katya's home in Miami when little Robertito was playfully shooting at me with his toy machine gun. No metaphor was needed in that Managua street scene; I was *literally* dodging bullets while running for my life.

Sometimes, fact is better than fiction.

Trying to get back to some sense of normalcy, I reached out to my high school sweetheart, April. She, for one, wasn't buying Gail's excuses for not knowing she was pregnant.

"She had to know," April was telling me.

April's life was in a state of flux. She had become widowed nearly a year earlier when her husband, who was twice her age, died in her arms of a heart attack. She was just starting to date another guy who had a sailboat, who she would eventually marry.

But she remained a true friend to me. When I told her about Gail's pregnancy, and how it happened just after Katya's miscarriage, it sounded too fishy to her. Gail's reliance on the rhythm method as her form of birth control didn't make her trustworthy, from April's perspective.

April had been through a pregnancy and I trusted her common sense. She had given me reason to suspect Gail may have thrown caution to the wind with respect to her "rhythm" during our holiday tryst. Then, when her periods weren't coming around as usual, was she hiding the truth from me? April forced me to consider that question.

Then there was Janice. I was about to lose her altogether. She had decided that she was planning to move back to Mississippi. Her life mentor and ballet teacher, Carmelita Maracci, had just passed away, so I think Janice felt a need to be closer to her real mother. I don't think she wanted to be around when Gail finally would give birth to my child. Not with the memory of aborting my child that she was carrying. Janice was not fond of Gail.

"Oh, darlin,'" she said to me, "you've got yourself in a mess with that woman."

Despite the best intentions of two women who I loved and who loved me, I decided to give Gail the benefit of the doubt and try to make the best of the situation with her. Maybe a newborn baby would somehow bring us closer together. With the Katya matter finally resolved, our relationship was on much firmer ground by Gail's birthday in early August.

I accepted my responsibility to this unborn child, and deep in my heart, I always wanted to be a father. Clearly, this was not the way my father envisioned I would bring his grandchild into the world. But he would approve of my decision.

We were eventually given a due date of October 7 (1987) which, coincidentally, was my mother's birthday. Given the normal gestation period for a full pregnancy to be about nine months plus one week, the calculation was that the baby was conceived on that first coupling a few days after Christmas.

Gail and I carried on like a normal expecting couple. We signed up for a Lamaz birthing class. Gail wanted me to be an active participant in the birth. I was all in.

We eventually learned the gender of the baby — it was a boy. We decided that it would be better if he wasn't circumcised. Gail more or less made that call, on the basis that circumcision was a painful experience for a newborn, and I went along with her decision. Any objection on my part just wouldn't cut it.

My mother's take on the whole scenario was nonplussed. I think after my three marriages and divorces, she just more or less figured I'd come out of this all right, too. She was fond of Gail — she had lived with her for a few years after all — and she was excited about the impending arrival of her first grandchild. She squealed with joy over the prospect of sharing a birthday with her grandson. I was probably her only hope for grandkids; Pam didn't show any indication that she would likely have any.

I digress to expand a bit on the woman who gave birth to me.

I loved my mother, no question. My relationship with her was a paradox. I made light of the fact that she branded me with the name

"Chic" I think in some way the name "Chic" shaped my personality. The comical connotations attached to that name predisposed me to not take myself too seriously, for which I credit my mother. I wrote about how I became romantically involved with various women, including Gail, by way of their living with my mother at our family home. It wasn't by design on Mom's part to fix me up with partners that met her approval, but I could see how that assumption could be made by the casual observer. I've written how she could drive me crazy;

Mom

Exhibit A: Our trip to Nicaragua. "Cameragate" will forever reign in infamy in the annals of our family's legacy.

I wrote about how Mom became a free spirit after she divorced Dad. It wasn't just in her world-wide travels, her love affairs (including one with a married man), the expansion of her social life by becoming active in the Unitarian Church, and her participation with a book club. She also eventually hung up the white frock she always wore as a lab technician, quitting that job to work as a licensed masseuse well into her senior years.

But here's where my mother's free spirit veered into unorthodox territory. She was a practicing nudist. Mind you, I had no desire whatsoever to see my mother sans clothing. I carried no subliminal Oedipal complex. But I discovered her *au natural* practices by accident one night.

I was allowed to drop in on the Rossburn home anytime I wanted, as the son of the owner, even with a houseful of tenants. Much like an occasion years earlier, when my Her-Ex colleague and paramour Carolyn and I nearly walked in the front door and came *thisclose* to interrupting a very private endeavor between my mother and boyfriend on the living room floor, I experienced an awkward moment crashing a party in progress. This time the front door was locked, but I gained entry through the back door, which was always unlocked. The back door opened up to the laundry room, leading to the kitchen. As I wandered into the kitchen, my eyes widened on a scene involving about 16 people in the family room engaged in, as best as I could tell, one of my mother's massage parties. The catch was, everyone was bare-ass naked.

Mom was leading the party with demonstrations on massage while everyone was paired up, with one person lying on a mat and a partner administering the massage. At least that's what I thought I had discerned in the 1 1/2-seconds I loitered in the kitchen before offering a meek "Oh, sorry," and making a quick retreat into the living room. I don't even recall what the purpose of my visit to the house was that night. I think I just rushed out the front door in a cloud of distraction.

It was some time after that massage party that Mom disclosed to Pam and I her membership in a nudist colony hidden in the hills of Malibu. This was highly revealing. She wasn't sheepish at all about it. In fact, she seemed proud of it. Then she double-downed and asked us if we would like to join her at the colony on a Sunday afternoon, as her guests. You know, just your regular, fun, family outing at a nudist colony.

Pam immediately shouted out "Sure!" and for reasons that defy logic, I chimed in with a "Why not?" I've got some good advice to pass along from this experience: if your mother ever invites you to go with her to a nudist colony, *don't go*! Now that I'm older, I can think of at least a dozen reasons for "Why not?" For the record, let me just state that what I said about having no desire to see my mother in the nude applied to my sister as well.

But there I was, on a beautiful Sunday afternoon, in the company of my mother and sister, bare-ass naked on the grounds of a nudist colony nestled in the secluded hills of Malibu. The three of us laid out in the sun on beach towels on a well-trimmed grass lawn, surrounded by dozens of fellow nudists.

Pam and I, each in our early 30s, were likely the youngest adults partaking in the clothing-free environment that day. Most were my mother's age — late 50s — or older.

I managed to cast my gaze away from my mother and sister on

that lawn. Instead, caught in the crosshairs of my stare was a very attractive older woman, maybe early 40s, improving on a beautiful tan, lying on her back in the sun, eyes closed behind sunglasses, slender legs drawn upward. I could tell she was in her own world. I was about to turn away when she started to sway her drawn-up legs. Then she began slightly parting her legs, letting the sun in. I had a straight-on view, about twenty feet away. That's when the staring kicked in; it was, in a word, very provocative and utterly sensual. I had to make sure I didn't suddenly become aroused; that would have been embarrassing.

This story served to illustrate the extraordinary dynamic I shared with my mother. By going with her to that nudist colony, I'm betting I did something with my mother that a lot of guys wouldn't be able to do with their mothers. It's not like I had any particular lingering hangups over it. I never went back for a second visit, but I at least allowed myself to experience it once. It was exactly as it sounds on the page — a weird, but very out-of-body experience. Mom was out there, you could say, in terms of experiencing life, and I was a willing participant and protege.

So, with the anticipation of the arrival of Gail's and my son, I found myself wondering what kind of dynamic between mother and son would result from this birth. Gail had her own unconventional ideas on how to live life, also *out there,* but way different from my mother's. She would carry undue influence on her son that I could not foresee. Years later, I'd have a clear answer on the effects of that dynamic.

—————————•◆•—————————

I think everybody measures themselves up against their closest friends on the occasion of entering parenthood for the first time. My closest competitive friend Phil, married to Sharon, was way ahead of me with three kids from his first marriage to Kathy (the ex-girlfriend who wanted to blow her brains out at the beach party.) My longest friend Wayne, who grew up with me on the Rossburn cul-de-sac, married his high school sweetheart, Jeannie, and they were in midstream, raising a son and a daughter, before I entered the fray. Jim, Phil's younger brother, and wife Diane were a few months ahead of Gail with the expectation of their first child, a girl. They would eventually introduce a second daughter into the world a couple of years later. Rich W. married and adopted a couple kids up in Washington, but that didn't work out, and he eventually tried the marriage thing again and hit pay dirt with Emily. They mutually agreed to have no kids so they could be free to travel around the world together. To which Rich would react by shrugging his shoulders and mumbling, "Yeah, that's us." Rich B., my ex-beach-bum roommate, whose wife was also named Sharon, was a relatively late bloomer as a parent to two boys who were a few years younger than my son. As for Dan, he never fathered any kids.

———————◆———————

Before baby's arrival, Gail and I moved into a new home. The distinction was, I was part-owner of this home. I was lured into my first foray into home ownership by my friend Rich B., who was in the early days of applying his adept instincts in real estate investments.

I put down $7,000 for a 25 percent share on a house that Rich and I bought together in the quaint seaside town of El Segundo, bordering LAX. The sale was contingent on owner occupancy on the property by at least one of us, and Rich needed me to fulfill that contingency. I met that contingency by moving into the separate one-bedroom back unit attached to the garage, along with Gail. Rich needed time to sell the house that he and wife Sharon were residing in before moving into the main house we co-owned, which he was renting out in the interim.

That $7,000 investment netted me a $13,000 payout after two years when Rich and his wife were ready to move in. I turned that $13,000 over to Aunt Evelyn, who added it to her U.S Treasury Bond account, boosting that balance to over $90,000. That money would pay off in a big way for me down the road.

———————◆———————

That August, in Gail's seventh month, we ventured on a road trip to Washington to visit Dan and his second wife Elizabeth in Bremerton. They were renting a large house in the woods, away from people. Dan was forever trying to recapture the isolation he enjoyed living in the Solomon Islands during his Peace Corps years.

301

Dan was a bit of a revelation in how well he treated Gail. He knew of the heartbreak I had been through with Katya and privately he shared some of the same suspicions that April had about Gail's pregnancy. But he couldn't have been more accommodating with Gail. He treated her with respect and doted on her, actually. With me, he acted like my big brother, excited about becoming an uncle for the first time.

Gail had never been to Washington before. Dan, the nature lover, exposed her to the beauty of the Northwest, taking us to an easy trail along the Colombia River. It was a far cry from LA — lush greenery, the rush of an ice-cold stream, clear blue skies in summertime. August was always my favorite time of year to visit Washington.

On our drive back down the Pacific coastline, Gail and I made another planned visit in the tiny coastal town of San Gregorio, just south of San Francisco. We stopped there to visit Pam's old boyfriend, Louis, and his partner, Steve, at their utterly charming cafe-slash-antique shop, located on Highway 1 that ran along barren, breathtaking beaches.

Louis was the guy who — I guess — broke my sister's heart by proclaiming he was gay. Pam still loved him and remained close friends with him and embraced Steve as well.

They were a handsome couple. Louis, who had an Italian last name, definitely possessed some Italian good looks with his boyish, angular face set off by a distinguishing thin mustache. He had a big mop of curly dark hair crowning his tall frame. Steve was shorter, stockier, but he also had a well-trimmed mustache and neatly cut dark hair that framed his pleasing, roundish face.

Louis ran the cafe and Steve the antique shop. Louis, who attended a cooking school, was a fabulous chef. He prepared the best omelette I had ever eaten, even better than the omelettes served up in Kenny Rogers' backyard at that after-concert midnight party I attended after writing a feature on him for the Her-Ex.

I was quite fond of Louis. He was a gentle spirit, sweet-natured. I could easily understand why my sister, and Steve, would fall in love with him.

Louis and Steve were the only two people I personally knew who eventually died from AIDS. Louis was afflicted first, showing symptoms sometime in the early 1990s. Pam visited him often and supported Steve in the care of Louis, particularly when his final days approached. Pam maintained contact with Steve after Louis had passed away, and it was a few years afterward that Steve eventually succumbed to the same disease. I fondly associate both of them to that wonderful visit Gail and I spent in the summer of '87, in their picturesque cafe-antique shop, when Gail was carrying our child.

Gail's water broke right on schedule in the wee hours of October 7 and we — my Mom and I — rushed her to the hospital. That's where Gail remained over the course of the day, struggling through the perils of labor. Petite in stature and carrying a large baby weighing over 10 pounds, Gail was a candidate for a Caesarian C-section birth. The longer she labored, the greater the odds were for surgery.

The decision was finally made to go the surgery route sometime before midnight on October 7. The surgery didn't take place until two hours later, so the official delivery date was October 8. The baby just missed Mom's birthday by two hours.

I sweated it out in the waiting room during the surgery. When it was done, I was able to set eyes on our beautiful boy for the first time. He had a nice crop of dark hair, kinda like I did when I was born, and the squinty eyes that Mom and I shared.

It was a bit of a shock to finally see my first newborn child. It really happened. I was subdued on the outside but bursting with pride inside. Gail, meanwhile, was a wreck, totally wiped out. She bled quite a bit. That was a bit of a concern, but it was a minor issue that was brought under control.

Baby was perfectly healthy, had all ten fingers and toes. We agreed on a name for him — Kasey Michael. Gail had originally wanted to name him Julian or Justin, but I ruled out any "J" names because I thought "J" names were too much in vogue. So she went along with my choice on Kasey. I had the classic "Casey at the Bat" baseball story in mind when I came up with the name, but insisted on spelling it with a "K" to deviate from the common spelling.

I also had an ulterior motive for using the "K" spelling. I am about to reveal a secret that I have never disclosed to anyone before. I will always associate Kasey's birth with Katya, given the juxtaposition of Kasey's conception to her miscarriage.

Katya's married surname at the time of Kasey's birth began with a "C." To honor the love I shared with Katya, I surreptitiously came up with the idea of naming my son "Kasey," which is pronounced exactly the same as "KC," the initials for Katya C.

Cradling my newborn son Kasey

CHAPTER 17
Changes Every Which Way

I loved my baby boy. I loved being a father. I felt a lot of pride holding that little guy in my arms.

I loved showing him off. One person I wanted to introduce my son to was Mary, our lifelong Black housekeeper who had served as a nanny for Pam and me as kids.

Kasey was barely four months old when I drove him to the home of Mary and her husband Chester in the Watts section of LA. Mary welcomed us into her home with open arms and I felt safe.

Her eyesight wasn't all that good — she had to be well into her 80's; remember, we didn't quite know when she was born. But she was beaming when she took Kasey into her arms and cast a loving gaze at him. She cackled that loud cackling laugh of hers and exclaimed: "He looks just like a little Chickee!" She always called me "Chickee."

Kasey did have somewhat slanted eyes like my mother and I, so Mary was right about his family resemblance.

My life had come full circle as it related to Mary. This was my last memory of seeing her.

————◆————

Fatherhood, and the immense responsibility that went with it, did change me. I did accept the responsibility, as promised. I covered my baby shift in the morning hours when Gail returned to work on her part-time job as a receptionist at the acupuncture center. As the night owl in the household, I handled my fair share of late-night feedings. I changed diapers.

We didn't have insurance to cover the cost of delivery, so I took the responsibility of paying off the major medical bill owed. Evelyn loaned me some money to help pay this off.

Even under the best of times while Gail was pregnant we had an understanding that our living arrangement would be temporary. But after Kasey was born, I gave careful consideration to the idea of making our coupling work.

To that extent, Gail and I got along for a little while as a three-some. But our relationship continued to struggle with respect to to intimacy. The glow from the birth was short-lived, and the strain was beginning to show within a few months. I knew Gail was frustrated because she had to put off her acupuncture classes.

Working nights didn't help matters. I wasn't stopping by for after-shift nightcaps at Corky's Bar nearly as often as I used to with my co-worker buddies Jay and Mark, but I didn't cut them out entirely. I needed the occasional stress relief. Gail had no outlet for her stress, other than her infrequent attempts to meditate.

It took me years to finally realize that the underlying conflict in my relationship with Gail was a covert power struggle. It probably incubated in the early days of our friendship when we played chess. Chess is a very cerebral, competitive, ego-driven game that inherently creates a hard-line acceptance with losing. I know that I hate to lose a game of chess, to be outwitted by my opponent. I know that Gail had always possessed a strong sense of self-pride, and she enjoyed beating me in chess almost as much as I did her. That competitive edge carried over to the relationship in a manner of asserting dominance. Gail was all-too-familiar with the various other intimate relationships I was in-volved in during the early years of our "friendship," and intimacy be-came the predominant means to establish dominance, or control. Gail would never allow herself to feel subservient to her feelings toward any man.

When our son came into the world, his mere presence magni-fied that dynamic, providing Gail with all the leverage. I grew to resent that weakened position more and more. It was only a matter of time when our relationship would come to a breaking point.

That moment finally came on the morning of March 16, 1988, when Kasey was just over five months old. That was the morning I received a 7 a.m. phone call from work about the Mickey and Trudy Thompson murders. My mind was spinning from the shocking news and it was a struggle trying to focus on the task at hand — making phone calls for the local reaction story I needed to write. It was darn near impossible to focus on the baby.

But Gail handed me the baby and asked if I could tend to him for a few minutes. I held him for a couple of minutes, but then I laid him on the living room couch, briefly to get my bearings straight as I stressed over planning my hectic day. Suddenly, Kasey rolled off the couch and fell to the floor, screaming in terror when he landed.

Gail rushed out of the bathroom, screaming at me. "How could you leave him alone on the couch like that?!"

She was angry and I was upset. I got very defensive, as I tend to do. The words between us escalated, as they had been tending to do in those trying times. I became so frustrated that I kicked at an empty plastic laundry basket lying on the floor. The basket flew up in the air and hit Gail in the arm.

The act was purely accidental, but in the heat of the moment Gail didn't see it that way. She saw it as an act of assault.

She over-reached by pulling the exceedingly excessive power play. She called the cops.

I was still trying to wrap my brain around the fact that Mickey and Trudy Thompson had been brutally murdered on their driveway less than two hours earlier. I could not believe that Gail had the temerity to call the cops in that moment, that she couldn't cut me some slack knowing the incredible duress I was experiencing. I already felt like shit about the baby rolling off the couch; I didn't need the added stress she was causing.

Now I had to explain all of this to the cops that came knocking at our door minutes after her call? This felt like a betrayal of trust in our relationship. It did not sit well with me.

The two officers showed me the compassion that Gail couldn't. They assessed the assault weapon — the empty laundry basket — and determined an arrest was not necessary. The baby was fine. Gail's arm was fine. The officers politely drew me aside outside, away from Gail, and basically assured me that I wasn't the one who was out of order here.

I managed to write my local reaction story to the Thompson murders after all that. But the rift between Gail and I had been split wide open.

I crossed paths again with my Mint 400 angel, Jeri, in the wake of the Thompson murders. My utter discontent at home rendered Jeri's charms irresistible, and I crossed the line again to the point of no return with Gail.

————•·•·◆·•·•————

Life at the Her-Ex had been feeling pretty shaky for some time. The paper had been losing money hand over fist for years. It was no secret. The Hearst family was keeping it running for sentimental reasons, not for any rational business reason. There were some whispers that the paper might be sold.

To make matters more unsettling, the employees' union contract was up for renewal in the summer of 1988. We hadn't received raises in ages. Negotiations with management were going poorly. Talk of a possible strike began circulating.

As the situation heated up, this was a hot topic for our after-shift gatherings at Corky's among Jay, Mark and myself. Henry, our constant barfly companion, often chimed in with his two-cents worth.

The paper's wobbly financial status figured prominently in the conversation. There was a clear divide in union membership on what tactic should be used in negotiations with management. The newsroom staff upstairs was unified in taking a militant stand against management's meager offering, which the union was resisting in the early stages. Meanwhile, the vast majority working in the downstairs departments — composing room, marketing, advertising — was fearful of losing their jobs and wanted the union to accept whatever pittance was put on the table.

The matter finally came to a head with a strike authorization vote meeting called at a large conference room in the LA Biltmore Hotel. Over 300 employees showed up for the raucous affair. A three-member union panel sat at a table on stage to present management's supposed final offer and gave a tepid recommendation to accept it. There was a perceptible divide in the crowd with respect to opposing viewpoints on the issue. The vociferous newsroom participants were very loud, and at various intervals began chanting "Throw back the bone!" Most of that crowd occupied the rows of seats closest to the stage, making its presence known. Further back, silently listening in horror, were the downstairs folk. It was intense.

Then, the voting started, with each employee called up one-by-one to cast a vote in a curtain-partitioned booth. Andy Furillo, a news reporter who was one of the more radical proponents pushing to reject the proposal, tried handing off a large replica of a bone — as a symbol of unity — to each voter who entered the voting booth behind the curtain. But there weren't a lot of takers of the bone among those rising from the rear rows.

Mark and I had decided at Corky's that we were going to side with the downstairs folk and protect our jobs. Jay, a hardcore union guy, was voting against the proposal.

When the votes were added up, the union panel announced the verdict — the vote to strike was defeated by a two-vote margin. Mark and I gasped.

"If we had voted like Jay, our two votes would have turned it the other way," Mark duly noted.

The union wound up accepting an insulting 3 percent wage increase over two years.

———————— ✦ ————————

In the fall of 1988, at the start of the NFL season, Jay recruited a bunch of sports junkies in the Her-Ex newsroom to join in on a fad that was emerging from its incubation stage — fantasy football.

The inaugural season of the Her-Ex Fantasy Football League was launched with 10 original members. As of 2020, the league was still going strong after 32 years, with 12 members. There were only two original owners among that dozen — myself and Gary, who had eventually succeeded Jay as the league commissioner. Jay got burned out after about a dozen seasons.

Fantasy football allows grown men to act out their completely obnoxious obsessions with football and carry on as fantasy "owners" of a football team. One of the first responsibilities of a fantasy football owner is to come up with a creative team name. Sometimes creative clashed with class, with a couple despicable team names in our inaugural season called "I Love Dead Cats" and "Sandy Duncan's Eye."

My team's name the first year was "Perkins' Psychos," a word play on my last name, the same as that of actor Anthony Perkins, the star of Hitchcock's classic movie, "Psycho." In Season 2, I decided having my last name in the team name was lame. So I changed the name to "Psychotic Genes," a vague nod to my newborn son, genetically speaking, while retaining a tie to the "Psycho" origin. That name stuck for a few seasons until, after a particularly bad season, it became "Psuicidal Genes." Then another bad season made me feel blue, so I changed the name to "Blue Genes," sticking to the "Genes" theme with a word twist on "Blue Jeans." That name carried on for many years, until the start of the Trump Era, when I had another terrible season. I got so pissed off at my team that I decided to quote then-Secretary State Rex Tillerson and renamed my team "Effing Morons," deciding that "Fucking Morons" would be too crude (even though the standard was set real low by my friend Sean's shameless team name 'Sloppy Seconds"). After a couple of weeks I decided to reinstate "Genes" to re-establish some continuity, so the team name became "Effing Genes." That could conceivably be interpreted as another nod to conception.

There's a bit of insanity to keep at it after 32 years of fantasy football. I won the championship five times out of those 32 years. That translated to 27 years of "effing" bad luck.

———————◆◆◆◆◆◆———————

The fall of 1988 stands out in the memory of any LA sports enthusiast and diehard Dodger fan, which apply to me. I'm referring to the 1988 World Series, of course, and one of the most iconic moments in LA sports history — the Kirk Gibson home run in Game 1 at Dodger Stadium.

For those who neither care for sports nor the Dodgers, the Gibson home run was so memorable primarily for the sheer magnitude of its miraculousness. Under the circumstances, it had a profound impact on the rest of the best-of-seven Series, which the Dodgers went on to win against improbable odds in five games over the heavily favored Oakland A's. The Gibson home run was one of those moments sports fans die for to see in person. I could have been there.

The Dodgers were down to their final out in the bottom of the ninth inning against the best relief pitcher in baseball that year, Dennis Eckersley. Eckersley was protecting a 1-0 lead in a game in which the Dodgers had exhibited no offensive threat. Eckersley gave L.A. a hint of hope by walking pinch-hitter Mike Davis with two outs.

Dodger Manager Tommy Lasorda summoned Gibson from the bench to grab a bat as a pinch-hitter. As a last gasp, this was pure desperation, because Gibson was too hobbled to start the game. He had an injured knee on one leg and pulled hamstring on the other.

My friend Paul, the anti-Dodger and big Giants fans who was rooting for the A's, was in the stands that night. He turned to his buddy attending the game with him and said, "Lasorda is looking for a fairytale." Paul was prescient.

A low murmur spread out over the crowd as Gibson limped up to home plate. He could barely walk, let alone run if he had put the ball in play in the field. He was easy pickings for Eckersley, who had been so dominant all year long with his devastating slider.

Gibson worked the count full (three balls, two strikes), and Davis had stole second to place himself in scoring position. Here came the patented Eckersley slider, slicing downward about knee-high at a devastating angle. Somehow...*somehow*... Gibson got all bat on the low pitch and sent a rocket over the right field wall for the game-winning home run.

After pausing nearly a full minute to listen to the raucous, continuous roar of the crowd, the legendary, elegant voice of Dodger broadcaster Vin Scully intoned on the network broadcast: "In a year of the improbable, the impossible just happened!"

The Dodger Stadium crowd went absolutely nuts as Gibson hobbled around the base paths, fist-pumping along the way. Everybody in that stadium knew they had just witnessed one of sports all-time iconic moments.

Every respectable Dodger fan knows where they were when Gibson hit his immortal home run. I was watching the Gibson Game from the Her-Ex sports desk. As I watched Gibson's home run sail over the wall on the sports staff TV, my heart soared. But later, I learned from my sports desk colleague Bill, who had the night off, that he would have been willing to switch nights with me so I could go to the game. My heart sank.

I could have been there. Paul, who was the high school buddy whom I visited at the White House where he was working under President Ford while serving in the U.S. Army, had two tickets to the game and had asked me first if I wanted to go. I didn't think I could get out of work.

Shit. All I had to do was ask. Even by Mr. Mistake's standard, this one ranked really high.

———————◆———————

Kasey's first birthday in October of 1988 was an occasion to herald, which we did in a small gathering at Mom's home. Photos were taken, Kasey was dazzled by lots of presents. We had cake.

As for Gail and I, we were no longer living together. She and

Kasey had moved out a couple months before that birthday event.

She found a small apartment to rent. We agreed on the child support that I would contribute — $350 per month. She was counting on me to take care of Kasey on weekday mornings when she worked. I wasn't trying to escape from my fatherly duties.

Jeri and I had a good thing going for many months. But then, on one lucky night at Corky's, I met a wonderful woman who worked at the Her-Ex. Her name was Sofia (not her real name.) She was one of those downstairs workers who had voted against the strike.

Sofia was a beautiful young Mexican-American — with long, straight, jet-black hair cascading down the back of her skinny, big-busted, tanned body. She had magnetic, dark eyes that stood out on an angular, high-cheek-boned face, with the cutest little over-bite under perfectly shaped lips.

She was hardly a Corky's Her-Ex regular. She was a single mother of two living in East LA and getting major assistance from her mother. So, this night at Corky's was a rare night out for her, indeed.

We got acquainted over drinks. She was sooo sweet. She had the softest voice, with a hint of the innocence of a teenager. She talked about her kids — 8-year-old Gabby and 5-year-old Miguel. The boy was named after the father, who was in jail on drug charges. She had a tough time talking about him.

I didn't prejudge Sofia on her past for a minute. She didn't pre-judge me for my three failed marriages and one child out of wedlock. On the contrary, I felt she was a cultural victim and a brave woman trying to raise two kids without a father, with the odds stacked against her. She was grateful for her job at the Her-Ex; she was just hired bare-ly a year earlier.

We were strongly attracted to each other. Sofia became the woman for whom I finally ended the good times with Jeri. I think Jeri took it well enough; she knew it wouldn't last forever.

Sofia and I went out to dinner on our first date and, and the strong sexual impulse drove us to a room in a low-rate hotel for a heavenly nightcap. But only after Sofia got over the shame of showing me a small tattoo just to the left of her collarbone. It was supposedly a symbol representing the gang to which her now ex-boyfriend in jail had belonged. I assured her the tattoo didn't bother me. I thought it was pretty. It was tasteful body art that didn't scream for attention.

It didn't take us long to skip the dinner part. Sex became her escape from her home life.

The more we got into it, the kinkier the sex became. Sparing the details, I sensed that Sofia had been mistreated sexually by her ex-boyfriend. She vaguely alluded to some abuse. She really wanted to please me, but my heart ached from the perceived backstory.

Love leapfrogged from the physical attraction, obscuring reality. I had played up the romance — flowers, candlelight dinners, a memorable Phil Collins concert. I had swept Sofia off her feet.

Sophia paid to publish a personal note to me on a special Valentine's Day page in the Her-Ex that was an unabashed public proclamation of her love. I was overwhelmed when I read it. I loved her, too, and wanted to make her happy. It fit my knight-on-a-white-horse role.

It was a Westside-story romance, two figures from the opposite sides of town swept up in love. But it was a somewhat tenuous relationship, strained by Sofia's two kids. I went on a few outings to the neighborhood park, but otherwise had very little interaction with them. Sofia clearly wanted time alone with me most of the time. Perhaps my experience with Katya and her kids had made me a bit gun-shy about projecting myself into a supportive role for someone else's children, particularly since I now had one of my own to support.

Sofia and I were together for nearly a year. I did love her, until I broke her heart. To this day, I feel big-time regret at letting that one go. Changes were happening quickly at the time of our break-up and someone else entered my life.

———————◆———————

Someone from my past popped up in the most unexpected place — the B section of the Her-Ex newspaper. The B section focused on stories primarily related to the greater LA area.

It was just by chance that I happened to glance at Jane Birnbaum's left-hand column on the front page of the B section published on June 10, 1989. It started off with: *"A woman named Jocelyne Del Monaco called and outlined a terrible plight."*

I did a double-take. Jocelyne Del Monaco was my ex-wife No. 2, my French connection. I then read the headline and thought, *"Oh no!"* It read: *"Shoplifting trial gives court a case of the giggles."*

So I read on. The story sounded soooo Jocelyneish. As

Birnbaum reported: *"She had been charged with shoplifting two au-diocassettes — "Hawaiian Bells" and "The Velocity of Love" — from the Tower Records store on Sunset Strip. She'd been handcuffed and interrogated."*

Oh God.

Then she insisted on her innocence, of course, claiming she had a receipt for the cassettes, but *"It was lost in court."*

Hmm-hmm.

She could have paid a $100 fine, had the arrest expunged from her record and been done with it. But no, not Jocelyne. She insisted on a jury trial. She sent the court a letter with suggestions on selecting a jury. As Birnbaum explained it, Jocelyne preferred jurists who *"were to be well-traveled, well-educated, know the names of world leaders and enjoy the music of Julio Iglesias."*

Oh, I see. This is where the giggles kicked in.

Birnbaum wrote, *"Oddly, a number of deputy district attorneys and public defenders had found time in their busy schedules to attend the final day of testimony in the trial of Jocelyne Del Monaco."*

Jocelyne spoke five languages fluently, including English. In fact, she spoke English better than I did. But in court, she requested to have a French interpreter. *Bien sur!*

Birnbaum described Jocelyne as *"tall and auburn-haired,"* appearing in court wearing *"dark-tinted glasses and a flower-splashed dress."* She always had a flair for fashion. It reminded me of how theatrical she could be, breaking into character at any moment with a dramatic change in her voice.

In the courtroom, she flashed a smile every once in a while at her fiance, who was identified as a worker for the New Zealand consulate.

So, I learned something new about my ex-wife. I was happy for her and felt just a tad less guilty for divorcing her.

Evidently, after a long and hilarious exchange with Jocelyne on the stand, regarding the tear in her Tower bag from which her receipt had allegedly slipped out somewhere in court, the jury was driven to loud laughter, but wasn't persuaded to render a not-guilty verdict. The judge gave her probation, ordered her to perform 60 hours of community service, and undergo psychological counseling.

Presumably while listening to the crooning of Julio Iglesias.

John Beyrooty, of Lebanese descent, was the boxing writer, fellow night desk colleague, and class comedian in the Her-Ex sports department. He was armed with a sharp wit and had a sarcastic response for every occasion. He was a character with his own peculiar tics, known for his habit of smoking thin, brown Shermans (brand of cigarettes), constantly munching on carrot sticks to — he claimed — improve his eyesight, and the big bags of sunflower seeds he routinely brought in to share with his night sports desk buddies. By the end of the night shift the sports department would be littered with a disgusting display of spit-out seeds spread all over desks and floor.

"Bey," as we all called him, found my parade of relationships a source of amusement. He referred to me as the "Dobie Gillis" of the sports department, in reference to an old TV show from the late 1950s-early 60s called "The Many Loves of Dobie Gillis." Dobie was a teenager who was a hopeless romantic lost in poetry and literature, an ordinary student who was always pondering his bewildering love life in front of the Rodin sculpture "The Thinker."

"The many loves of Chic Perkins," was Bey's inference.

It was October. The Bay Area World Series between the San Francisco Giants and Oakland A's was underway. The nights were getting cooler, the days were getting shorter.

At the Her-Ex, all the talk was about the gorgeous "new girl" downstairs in ad paste-up, a Hispanic young woman named Maggie. Bey was the first in sports to get a first-hand look.

"Now Chic…" he cautioned me with a wagging finger after returning upstairs to report his first sighting of Maggie. "Don't even go near this woman if you know what's good for you. She is just your type. I forget what South American country she's from. But she is trouble. With a capital 'T'. And you seem to have a knack for finding trouble, Dobie."

Well, Bey nailed it. It didn't take long for me to get my own look at Maggie and Bey was dead right. It was hard for any guy not to take a long, hard look at her. She was positively beautiful, with a voluptuous, 36-24-36 hour-glass figure that she put on display in a tight-fitting, leopard-skin top and black skirt. Her face was very attractive, her black hair stylishly cut in curls resting on her square shoulders, and her soft, ivory skin was elegantly pretty.

I kept my distance from her as long as I could. I was still dating Sofia, after all, although lately our time together had been limited.

But temptation — and fate — stepped in, in the oddest fashion, as it turned out. One night, while I was working the night shift, I was approached by a Hispanic guy named Richard who worked paste-up in the composing room. He evidently knew Maggie.

"Do you know the new girl, Maggie, in ad paste-up?" he casually asked me while I was downstairs supervising sports-page paste-up.

"Well, I know about her. But can't say I know her," I said.

He waved his arms to illustrate the shape for her shapely body.

"Oh, well, I've seen her. I know what she looks like," I said. Boy, did I.

"Well, she asked me to talk to you. She said she wanted to meet the guy in sports with the long brown hair and beard. She wanted to know if you'd like to meet her for a drink after work tomorrow night at Corky's."

"Uhh, well, sure! I can be there tomorrow night. Tell her I'll see her then."

As the sports guy with the long brown hair and beard, I showed up at Corky's after the next night shift.

Maggie was sitting in a booth with maroon naugahyde seats, sipping on a drink in a tall glass. In the dim light of Corky's, she looked dreamy. I clued my Corky's buddies Jay and Mark about the meet-up beforehand, so they stayed anchored at the bar to let me give her my full attention. They sat back on their bar stools and were likely observing with considerable envy.

She seemed a little quizzical when I told her my name was "Chic." But we settled into a very nice conversation. I learned she was from Honduras, another Central American country that bordered Nicaragua, and she spoke with a fairly thick accent. She had been in the U.S. legally since age 12, so there were no immigration issues.

She had been married once before, no children. Her real first name was Zoila, but she went by a nickname derived from her middle name, Margarita, which was her mother's name. I told her about my three marriages and one kid, and I briefly mentioned my relationship with Sofia. As the conversation drifted, I think she was developing a

316

growing attraction to me. It might have partly been the effect of that drink she was drinking.

We parted that cool night with a warm feeling between us. For me, to have a woman like that set eyes on me was one huge ego trip.

Here's the catch! Our initial meeting was all set up based on a mistaken identity. There was another sports guy with long brown hair and a beard by the name of Jeff Bonior. He was about six inches taller than me and a heckuva lot better looking. Maggie would later confess that he was the sports guy she had intended to meet and her messenger, Richard, had passed on the message to the wrong guy. That dim light in Corky's worked to my advantage, hiding my false identity. It helped that I was sitting in the booth with her, so she couldn't tell how short I was. All of this contributed to her eventually becoming my fourth wife.

Jeff Bonior and I in our respective column mugs, representing two guys on Her-Ex sports staff who had long brown hair and a beard

A week after our fateful meeting, on October 17, the Bay Area Earthquake struck. Game 3 of the World Series between the Giants and A's was just about to start when the quake hit and forced postponement of the game. That was a precursor to an earth-shaking event just two weeks later, and this time I'm not talking about a personal matter.

Since meeting Maggie that night at Corky's, I had been avoiding Sofia. Clearly, my attention had been diverted. Maggie and I met up again a week later at a salsa dance night club in Hollywood. Maggie was dressed that night in a stunning, tight-fitting, velvet red dress that had every guy in the club staring at her. When we were on the dance floor dancing cheek-to-cheek, it brought to mind the smash hit on the radio from a few years earlier, by Chris de Burgh, called "Lady In Red":

The lady in red is dancing with me, cheek to cheek
There's nobody here, it's just you and me
It's where I want to be
But I hardly know this beauty by my side
I'll never forget the way you look tonight

I was having my own "Lady In Red" moment in the flesh. My fate was sealed that night. I was smitten. Maggie made it clear that night that if I wanted to continue seeing her, I would have to break up with Sofia. Maggie was direct, she knew what she wanted. She wanted Jeff Bonior, but she had to settle for me.

So I called Sofia the next day and broke up with her, trying my best to soften the blow and not succeeding at all. She knew something was up, she could see it coming. I had broken another heart and like all the others, she deserved better. I sucked at being a knight on a white horse.

Maggie was just too much for me to resist

The Bay Area Earthquake served as a prelude for what was to come on November 1. I'll never forget the scene of a Hearst Corporation executive, Robert Danzig, standing on top of a desk in the newsroom, delivering the stunning news that the Los Angeles Herald Examiner was going out of business after 118 years of existence. Its roots dated back to 1871, when the evening Herald Express began publication, evolving into the afternoon Herald Examiner in 1903.

Our last edition appeared the next day, November 2, 1989. Like everyone else on the sports staff, I wrote a farewell column for that historical edition, relating some of my fondest memories as the motorsports writer that I've elucidated in this memoir.

The announcement was sudden and an incredible shock, but not all that surprising given that the paper was rumored to have suffered losses averaging $12 million a year for the past decade. The paper's prestige had shrunk from its heyday of nearly 800,000 in circulation in the mid-60s to around 238,000 at closing. But for all of us in that newsroom, it was a labor of love trying to put out the best newspaper in the business and keep it afloat for as long as we could.

That night, tears and beers were pouring at Corky's well into the wee hours of the morning. Her-Exers packed the bar for a mad love-fest in which we mourned the loss of the paper that we had given our blood and guts, all for the measly 3 percent raise to our substandard wages we had voted on in the union contract just one year earlier. We were all wondering where our next jobs would be, knowing that the LA Times couldn't hire all of us.

Both of my Corky's drinking buddies, Jay and Mark, would wind up getting hired by the LA Times. But my future was very uncertain. Shav Glick, the Times motorsports writer, wasn't retiring any time soon, so my prospects looked dim. The Times hired Allan Malamud to write his "Notes On A Scorecard" column for them. A couple of our desk guys got hired on the Times sports desk — including Steve Horn, who would go on to reach legendary status for his brilliant pun-laden, topical sports headlines. "Purple Reign!" was a Horn original when the lavendar-and-gold-clad Lakers, led by the Kobe-Shaq duo, won the NBA championship.

Things got pretty maudlin at Corky's, as no one knew that night if we'd ever see each other again. Chuck Culpepper, one of our brightest young stars on the sports staff, surprised me by planting a full kiss on my mouth in an inebriated expression of fond farewell. Chuck, who may have been the most talented writer not named Karen Crouse on our entire staff, would go on to an illustrious sportswriting career at the Washington Post. Ditto Karen at the New York Times.

Our esteemed sports editor, Rick Arthur, made me feel like shit when everyone was in a drunken, touchy-feely mood. With everything that was going on that night, I didn't expect Rick to look earnestly at me and say,

"Sofia really loves you, man."

Word must have circulated about our break-up from downstairs, where she worked, and carried up to the second floor. It just deepened the sadness of the occasion for me.

Group shot of Her-Ex staffers on the last hours before the paper closed for good on Nov. 2, 1989. Notables mentioned in related stories include Sports Editor Rick Arthur (far left, front row.), Jeff Bonior (behind Rick, with beard), John Beyrooty (center, back row, with mustache), Karen Crouse (front row), Mark Gears (my Corky's buddy, back row, behind Beyrooty).

Herald Examiner

SO LONG, L.A.!

In closing, the Herald staff has one last word: Goodbye

Front page of the very last edition of the Los Angeles Herald Examiner, on Nov. 2, 1989

A change in relationships, a pending change in jobs. What next?

A change in residence was in the making.

I applied for unemployment compensation for the first time in my life to tide me over until I found another job. But I couldn't afford to string it out too long.

I remained unemployed for two-and-a-half months. As luck would have it (and luck always seemed to smile at me at the most dire moments), I learned of a job opening on the sports department at the Santa Barbara News-Press. Joe Eckdahl, who was a news editor at the Her-Ex and a good friend of my Corky's buddy Jay, had interviewed for the job but decided against it. He told me about the opening, so I went for it.

Honestly, I didn't think it was possible that even I could get this lucky. Santa Barbara? The paradise enclave on the coast a mere 100 miles north of LA, where my maternal grandmother Mimi had resided in nearby Montecito during my youth? While growing up and making all those visits to Mimi's house, never in my wildest dreams did I ever think it would be possible that I'd wind up living in Santa Barbara.

I made the drive to personally interview with the sports editor, John Zant, who was just about the nicest guy you'll ever meet. Oh, and he would be my boss, too? He seemed really impressed with my LA credentials. He saw some potential in using me to cover some LA teams, like the Lakers and the Raiders, who were in LA at the time.

I didn't tell him what the Her-Ex had been paying me. The News-Press was offering me a salary about 30 percent more. Living in Santa Barbara wasn't cheap.

John, who was about eight years older than me, was laid-back in his demeanor, but was a really smart sports enthusiast. As I got to know him better, I grew to respect him as a really talented sportswriter.

He introduced me to the Managing Editor, which was a good sign. I was hired.

So, now all I had to do was move to Santa Barbara. I asked Maggie if she wanted to come with me. We had been dating for a couple of months and our relationship had heated up pretty quickly. She said "Yes."

I still had to make frequent drives down to LA to see Kasey— at least twice a month. I became very familiar with the 101 freeway — "Ventura Highway" as America crooned — that linked Santa Barbara to LA. The drive was about 100 miles, approximately two hours if traffic was good and much longer if it wasn't.

I occasionally opted for the far more scenic and less stressful drive home via Pacific Coast Highway — Highway 1 — through Malibu. Often I would stop for a dinner break at sunset at the iconic, quirky Neptune's fish restaurant, a popular hangout for bikers. Fish and chips and beer at Neptune's made the drive home more palatable.

I started work at the News-Press on January 10, 1990. For my first two weeks I slept on the living room couch in the Ventura apartment of a Her-Ex colleague, Jim Logan, who also got hired by the News-Press on the news desk. Ventura was a 35-mile drive to Santa Barbara.

Jim tolerated me just long enough for me to find my own place in Santa Barbara — a back duplex unit on the east side of town owned by a quirky, old Italian couple. Maggie and I moved in as soon as I put a deposit on the place.

I brought along Dingledork (shortened to 'Ding'), my gray and white cat whom I had taken in as a stray when I was living in Hermosa Beach. Dingledork, the name in which I admonished her from her annoying habit of jumping onto the edge of the toilet to watch me pee, surprised me by giving birth to six kittens under a bush in the backyard of my Hermosa Beach apartment. I had to find homes for those kittens before I got evicted by the landlord, who was not pleased.

The old Italian couple who were our landlords in the Santa Barbara duplex were OK with the cat. But they were nervous about Max, the brindle boxer pup we adopted from Maggie's brother George.

With cat and dog in place, we were taking root in Paradise. It was an exciting time. And yes, Maggie and I were in love.

CHAPTER 18
Prospering and Procreating in Paradise

I could not have landed in a better place a mere two-and-a-half months after the closure of the LA Herald Examiner, with the uncertainty I faced.

I wound up with a gorgeous woman moving to Santa Barbara with me as I started my new job on the sports staff of the Santa Barbara News-Press. Both professionally and personally, my life was in sync on high notes.

But, I admit I was saddened by the phase of my life that I was leaving behind. My days as motorsports writer for the Her-Ex were filled with such adventure, travel, sex, and laughter that could never be duplicated in my wildest imagination. I had the responsibilities of fatherhood facing me, with some degree of normalcy settling in. But it was taking root in Paradise.

In my new job, new opportunities awaited. My new boss, Sports Editor John Zant, assigned me an exciting beat right out of the gate. Santa Barbara was awarded a franchise in the Continental Basketball Association (CBA), which was considered a developmental league for the NBA. The local team was called the Santa Barbara Islanders.

The Islanders brought a lot of excitement to Santa Barbara. Local investors lined up to support the team as it tried to get a profitable foothold in the city. That wasn't going to be easy because there wasn't a large enough facility to hold a sufficient amount of paying fans. The Islanders played their home games in the tiny gymnasium at Santa Barbara City College, with a maximum seating capacity of just over 1,000.

Nevertheless, the News-Press gave the Islanders major coverage treatment. Maybe not on the scale of UC Santa Barbara (UCSB) men's basketball, which was the biggest show in town, or even UCSB women's basketball, which was climbing in national prominence in the early 1990s. But I covered all of the Islanders home games and a few of their road games that didn't require too much travel, or expense.

The Islanders were a winning team. They were division leaders throughout the season. They were coached by Sonny Allen, who had very respectable college credentials. Their best player was Leon Wood, who had been an All-American and NBA first-round draft pick out of my alma mater, Cal State Fullerton. They had some other respectable players, such as Larry Spriggs, Rory White, and 7-footer Juan Oldham.

They weren't winning economically, however. Midway through their first season, signs of financial trouble started to surface with reports that creditors' bills for services and goods were not being paid and checks were bouncing. Rumors started circulating that even the players were not getting paid.

Howard Schneider, who owned and operated Craig Motors, a local Ford Motors car dealership, stepped in to resolve the crisis by buying into the team as owner. He wrestled control of the team from General Manager Craig Case, who was known in town for his private investigation and security business. Schneider's interest in the team came solely as a fan, and as a devoted father to his young teen-age son, Craig, for whom Howard named his car dealership. Craig fell in love with the Islanders when his father started taking him to home games.

Schneider's "ownership" of the Islanders lasted all of three weeks before the crisis imploded, and he backed out. I extensively interviewed Schneider, who lambasted Case and described the entire Islanders franchise as a fiasco. Investors were crying to be compensated for the money they invested in the team. It was an utter and complete mess.

With Schneider's sudden departure, league officials had to assume ownership of the team just so it could complete the season. As division leaders, the Islanders were playoff-bound, so the league had no other choice than to keep the team going or else face the public humility of having one of its most successful teams on the court flop spectacularly off the court.

Amid this major distraction, the Islanders meekly finished the season. They bowed out in the first round of the playoffs, having been forced to play their home games on the road. The franchise quickly dissolved after that one forgettable season.

I wrote a lengthy, three-part investigative piece on the demise of the Islanders franchise for the News-Press. It stands as the singularly most explosive, detailed and researched, investigative reporting of my career, engaging the most sources interviewed, by far. It was a piece of work I took a lot of pride in, and it was an auspicious start to my 15-year career at the News-Press.

During those first few years at the News-Press, I hadn't left LA completely behind. John Zant, and then Mark Patton, who succeeded him as Sports Editor, employed me for coverage of some sporting events down south.

My motorsports days didn't vanish completely. A classic David-versus-Goliath story involving a brother duo out of Santa Maria allowed me to reunite with my buddies Steve Earwood and Dave Densmore at Pomona Raceway for two annual National Hot Rod Association (NHRA) events. Brothers Blaine and Alan Johnson, with some help from their father, formed a team that completely dominated the Top Alcohol division with four straight seasonal championships from 1990-93. Blaine was the driver, Alan the crew chief. Then in 1994, they built a fire-breathing Top Fuel dragster in their family-run shop on a nickel-and-dime budget to compete against the big boys armed with major sponsorship money in the NHRA's premier racing division. They were competitive in the Top Fuel division, finally winning an NHRA event in the 1995 season finale at Pomona. They backed that up by winning again at Pomona to open the 1996 season. That launched a season that glowed with sky-high promise as Blaine led the division championship standings most of the year. The outcome of that season is the subject of a story covered in a later chapter.

Earwood also set me up with one more interview with Shirley Muldowney when she launched a comeback in the mid-90s. I also covered the Long Beach Grand Prix through the early and mid-90s. Other than the Pomona drag strip, Long Beach was the only race track in the LA area for a while. When California Speedway (now Auto Club Speedway) in Fontana opened in June of 1997 with NASCAR roaring into town, I was there reporting for the News-Press and saw Jeff Gordon take the checkered flag.

I wrote all sorts of feature stories on locals connected to the motor sports scene, none of them bigger than Montecito resident Andy Granatelli, saluting his induction into the Motor Sports Hall of Fame in 1992. Granatelli, who earned his fortune as the STP oil additive entrepreneur, was a legendary Indy car owner for whom Mario Andretti won his lone Indy 500 race in 1969. I interviewed Granatelli at the beautiful mansion that housed his vast vintage car collection in his warehouse-sized garage.

But my LA moments for the Santa Barbara News-Press weren't relegated to motor sports.

I had a few shining moments covering NBA basketball for the News-Press. The first was when I covered Game 6 of the 1991 Western Conference Finals between the Lakers and Portland Trail Blazers at the Fabulous Forum in Inglewood. Magic Johnson grabbed the rebound off of Terry Porter's missed jumper with three seconds left and rolled the ball downcourt to run the clock out. The timekeeper accidentally stopped the clock for about a half-second before re-starting it, leaving 0:01 remaining for one last gasp by the Trail Blazers. They couldn't get a shot off, preserving the Lakers' series-clinching 91-90 victory that sent them into the NBA Final against the Chicago Bulls and Michael Jordan.

The Bulls were vying for their first title and had the Lakers on the ropes with a 3-1 series lead. The wounded Lakers, missing both James Worthy and Byron Scott with injuries, were desperately trying to hold them off. I was sent down to cover Game 5 at the Forum.

About an hour before tip-off I was in the press hospitality room. I found myself standing at the coffee machine next to the No. 1 Laker fan, actor Jack Nicholson.

Nonchalantly I asked the iconic actor, "Are the Lakers going to do it?"

"I tell ya, I'm going to do it," Jack said. If only they allowed Jack to suit up.

I used that brief exchange in my lead for story coverage of Game 5 that ran under the banner headline, "Bulls fly Air Jordan to the top" on June 13, 1991. Nicholson couldn't save the Lakers. I followed the Bulls into their mad, celebratory locker room with a crush of other reporters, passing by Robin Williams and Billy Crystal standing in front of the hallway crowd cheering them on. The Bulls closed out the series with the clinching 108-101 win that night.

Jordan had tears in his eyes in the locker room when he blurted, "I never thought I'd be this emotional publicly." The first one is always the hardest, even though the Bulls made it look easy with a 15-2 run throughout the playoffs. That launched the Jordan-Scottie Pippen dynasty that went on to capture six NBA titles and marked the end of the Lakers' Showtime Era with Magic, who retired six months later under the cloud of his HIV diagnosis.

I covered one more Lakers game the following season. It was a late-season victory over the Clippers that was a "must-win" for the Lakers to make the 1992 playoffs. But without Magic they didn't go far in the playoffs, and that ended my run of NBA coverage assignments.

LA baseball fell onto my radar when I got to cover the Dodgers' home opener for the 1993 season. That game was highlighted by a special guest— Rodney King, just one year after the LA riots had erupted following the highly controversial acquittal of the police officers who had beaten him during a routine traffic stop. King was not made available to the press at the game, but I wrote a sidebar on Dodgers player Eric Davis, who purported to be a friend of King's.

Finally, the NFL became a major slice of my LA coverage for the News-Press, with the Raiders playing their home games at the Coliseum. Marcus Allen was the star Raiders player for a couple of seasons. It was a privilege to cover a class act like Allen, who patiently answered every question of every reporter who huddled around his locker after each game. Allen was the story even when he played in the Coliseum against the Raiders, in a Kansas City Chiefs uniform during the 1993 season. Reliving his glory days starring for the USC Trojans and Raiders, he called his return to the stadium "absolutely, positively, indubitably great." He led the Chiefs to a 31-20 victory. During the post-game interview, he had too much class to comment on the bad blood with Raiders owner Al Davis that had led to his unpopular trade to the Chiefs.

The Raiders and Chiefs played again in the Coliseum the following season, on December 24, 1994, and I was there. The Chiefs beat them, 19-9, to knock the Raiders out of playoff contention. A year later they moved to Oakland, effectively ending my coverage of the Raiders.

The News-Press assigned me to the only Super Bowl of my sports-writing career — the 1993 Super Bowl XXV11 at the Rose Bowl in Pasadena between the Dallas Cowboys and Buffalo Bills. The assignment started off with a couple of trips down to LA for the circus-atmosphere, pre-game interview sessions leading up to the big game.

The game itself was a dull blowout won by the Cowboys, by a 52-17 score. "It's as great a feeling I've ever had in my life," I quoted Super Bowl XXV11 MVP Troy Aikman, the Cowboys quarterback. "I wish every player could experience this."

The Bills players, of course, were wishing they could experience that feeling after losing their third Super Bowl in a row. Turning the ball over a record nine times was no way to accomplish that.

The most talked-about turnover by the Bills resulted in a spectacular gaffe by Cowboys defender Leon Lett Jr., who recovered a Bills fumble late in the game in Cowboys territory and ran it back 60-plus yards toward what should have been a sure touchdown. But inexplicably, within a few yards from the goal line he held the ball out in a premature celebration. That allowed Bills player Don Beebe, in hot pursuit, to swipe the ball out of Lett's hands and send it rolling out of the end zone for a non-scoring touchback. That play denied my colleague John Zant from winning the $200 News-Press Super Bowl office pool. The money slipped right out of John's hands the moment the ball slipped out of Lett's hands.

Whatever suspense was lacking in that game was compensated for by the dazzling halftime show put on by Michael Jackson, who raised the bar for Super Bowl halftime shows that night with a performance that threw the crowd into a frenzy. I was entranced, ignoring the halftime stats that passed by my press-row seat while MJ classics from "Billie Jean" to "We Are The World" filled the stadium. Colorful flashcard images of children spreading through the stands, a large inflated globe consuming center stage, and 100,000 fans partaking in singalongs made one momentarily forget that a football game was being played.

Halftime show during the 1993 Super Bowl XVII at the Rose Bowl in Pasadena

As my career started to blossom, so did my relationship with Maggie. It was the best of times for us, a fertile environment for love to grow.

Maggie quickly began furnishing our home with glitzy furniture and furnishings. We bought a fancy bedroom set — shiny black surface and large mirror — that added dash to our bedroom activities. And we were doing a lot of that. We were definitely in a honeymoon stage.

Max, our beautiful, well-chiseled, wild-child brindle boxer, basically represented the first child that we were rearing. He was adorable, very sweet, very loyal and obedient to me as his master.

I loved taking Max out for walks, and runs, along the beach. It cracked me up how passers-by were routinely intimidated by Max's muscular look; he looked ferocious. I'm pretty sure he was being mistaken for a pit bull. He got so excitable around strangers that passed by, all he wanted was to play, but his incontrollable body language often scared people. If only they knew how docile and sweet he really was.

One person who didn't fear Max was Kasey. Kasey bonded with Max, as only a young boy and dog can bond. Max loved to play with Kasey and showed enough body control not to hurt Kasey. He was so good with my son.

I had arranged with Gail to have Kasey up for weekend visits at least once a month. I drove all the way to LA to pick him up and bring him back to Santa Barbara. Maggie was on board in her "step-mom" role, in the beginning. She helped Kasey dress up in a Ninja Turtle costume and went trick-or-treating with him for Halloween. Then, she included him in the professional family Christmas photo we sent out to all of our family and friends in a holiday card.

This was an idyllic time, worthy of the scenario my dad always had in mind for me. There were a few minor challenges and obstacles. Our old Italian landlord couple often complained of the dog poop around the yard that I wasn't scooping up fast enough to satisfy them.

Maggie, ever ambitious with a strong work ethic, always managed to find a job. Her first job in Santa Barbara was with a photo development company for which she worked in processing and packaging. After a year she found a better paying job working in the administration office at the Samarkand Retirement home.

She liked her job at Samarkand, but she clashed with her plain-Jane supervisor, who I think felt threatened by Maggie. Maggie had this effect on women in general. She liked dressing in tight-fitting outfits that accentuated her well-rounded figure. Let's call it what it was, she was a show-off, and not embarrassed to admit it. Her supervisor admired Maggie's hard-work ethic, but ultimately Maggie's ambition wasn't being rewarded with any advancement, or increased pay.

But we were doing fine financially. We were building toward a future that obviously included marriage. Maggie had no qualms about becoming wife No.4.

———————————◆————————————

Talk of marriage led to my indoctrination into Maggie's very large family. She was the youngest of six siblings, with three sisters and two brothers, all living in LA. They all migrated from a modest existence in Honduras and found the good life in America.

Both brothers, George and Victor, established profitable auto body shops that fueled the American lifestyle they craved. They both were married with kids, with beautiful homes in the suburbs.

Nora, the oldest sister, was married to Sergio, a Hispanic man who had a decent job that afforded them a respectable life in Pasadena. They had a little boy, Oscar. Lucy, the second oldest sister, made good money handling immigration cases, but her personal life was a mess as a divorcee with a young daughter caught in the middle. The third sister, Gina, was the only sibling who never learned English. She was a housewife in a low-level apartment with her husband and three young daughters.

Maggie's mother, who was an avid church-goer, lived in her own modest apartment and helped Gina out in the care of her daughters. Maggie's father was estranged from the family living somewhere in Southern California. Maggie hadn't seen him or wanted to have anything to do with him since her early teens, when he and her mother first split up.

———————————◆————————————

In June of 1990 Maggie and I traveled to Honduras. We stayed a week in Tegucigalpa, the nation's capitol. It's funny that I don't recall much about that trip like I had about the trip to Nicaragua. I remember it was unbearably hot. I was not that impressed by Tegucigalpa as a city and we did not venture much out of the city. We mostly were visiting family — lot of cousins, aunts and uncles. We were there only a week.

What I remember most about that trip was the return flight home on June 27. When we landed back in LAX at around 11 p.m., local news channels on TV screens throughout the terminal were broadcasting live coverage of Santa Barbara ablaze from the destructive Painted Cave Fire.

Paradise was under siege. Temperatures had reached 100 degrees in Santa Barbara that day. High winds fanned the fire into a frightening frenzy. The pictures on the TV screen were horrifying. The fire roared down San Marcos Pass, paralleling Highway 154, engulfing homes in its path, all the way down to the 101 freeway. That line of demarcation didn't hold up, as the fire jumped the freeway and destroyed condos on the other side.

Two gentlemen on the same flight from Honduras to LAX lived in the Santa Barbara suburb of Goleta. We saw them in the terminal reacting in horror to the news on TV intercoms, wondering out loud if they still had homes standing.

Our home was safe. We lived on the east side of town, out of range from the fire. But that was still a heckuva homecoming.

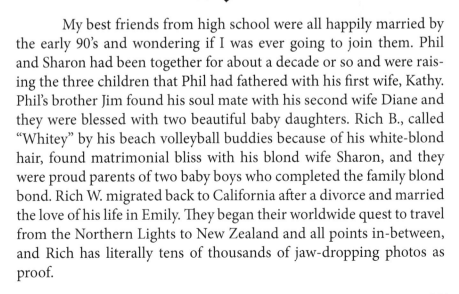

My best friends from high school were all happily married by the early 90's and wondering if I was ever going to join them. Phil and Sharon had been together for about a decade or so and were raising the three children that Phil had fathered with his first wife, Kathy. Phil's brother Jim found his soul mate with his second wife Diane and they were blessed with two beautiful baby daughters. Rich B., called "Whitey" by his beach volleyball buddies because of his white-blond hair, found matrimonial bliss with his blond wife Sharon, and they were proud parents of two baby boys who completed the family blond bond. Rich W. migrated back to California after a divorce and married the love of his life in Emily. They began their worldwide quest to travel from the Northern Lights to New Zealand and all points in-between, and Rich has literally tens of thousands of jaw-dropping photos as proof.

We have all customarily gathered at least once a year for a poker-dinner party at somebody's home, either one of the brothers in Simi Valley or Rich B.'s in El Segundo. While the guys played hours of poker, the wives played their own games and prepared the dinner. Through my first three marriages, none of my wives attended for these gatherings.

Maggie was my best hope to change that.

My high school pals at the poker party in the backyard of my house in Santa Barbara. Jim lost his shirt in this game. (So did I)

The poker wives — Emily, Sharon R., Diane, Sharon B. (My wife didn't make it.)

We had to get married first. That was the easy part. On February 16, 1991, we tied the knot in a ceremony attended by about 60 guests at a swanky restaurant in Burbank. We chose the location to make it easier for Maggie's family members, all of whom resided in the LA area. Dan made the trip down from Washington to stand in as my Best Man for the fourth time. Phil, Jim and the two Richs were all there, duplicating their roles as members of the wedding party from my first marriage. This time, this one was going to stick, right guys?

Aunt Evelyn also attended the wedding. She liked Maggie. She did a biorhythm chart comparison for us as a couple and said that Maggie and I were 100 percent compatible physically. That sounded about right. But Evelyn added that we were opposites mentally. That also sounded compatible with real life. Maggie saw everything in black and white. I saw everything in gray.

I think Evelyn was more approving of Maggie than either of my parents, whose not-so-fond memories of Lizamara were still too fresh. Maggie was nothing like the wild and rebellious Lizamara, but I think Mom and Dad, despite their progressive views, may have been guilty of making a judgmental connection purely on the basis that they were both Hispanic. Evelyn wouldn't harbor any prejudicial feelings toward Maggie on the basis of her ethnicity, given that Evelyn's first daughter Linda was half-Hispanic from her first marriage.

I paid a lot of money to marry this gorgeous woman. If you had seen her that night in her sleek, satiny white wedding dress, with her stylishly cut, short hair dyed red, you would have thought it was worth every penny. I did.

We cut a pretty wedding picture. I looked swell in my tailored black tux with my shoulder-length, curly brown hair and beard, a shorter version of Jeff Bonior.

We partied hearty all night. My in-laws all liked me. My friends were all still trying to figure out which country Maggie was from, because it got confusing differentiating from my previous wives.

Then Maggie and I were off for our honeymoon, on a Mexican Riviera cruise to Puerto Vallarta, Mazatlan, and Cabo San Lucas.

I gotta say, the only disappointment on the whole trip was when I lost the hairy chest contest on our ship's deck en route to Mexico. The contest was conducted by a young female cruise staffer who rubbed each contestant's bare chest in front of a large, boisterous, drunk crowd. I can tell you, I should have won the contest, hands-down; Maggie would agree. There's a reason I tell everyone I'm the missing link from the Neanderthal Man. The fix was in!

Other than that, we lived it up like honeymooners, Maggie and I.

Puerto Vallarta was charming. It is the sister city of Santa Barbara. Walking around the cobblestone streets and quaint shops, we felt a kinship toward the town we called home.

I had my first experience paragliding in Mazatlan. I was lofted 100 feet in the air on a line attached to the back of a little motorboat. I soared around over the ocean for about fifteen minutes before being dropped gently onto the sand.

Then there was Cabo. We only had a half-day to spend on land, and Maggie and I made the most of it. We paid for a ride on a tiny motorboat out to Lovers Beach, which was a secluded cove on a dot of an island about a mile off Cabo's shore. We had the beach all to ourselves, so what would a couple in love possibly do on Lovers Beach under such tempting circumstances? The prelude to our passion play was a photo I took of an exquisite, statuesque Maggie in the buff, leaning into a giant, voluptuous, golden boulder that provided cover for our lovemaking.

The honeymoon feeling lingered for months. Our sex life got very adventurous. There was something about doing it in nature, in the open air, that turned us on. We pursued similar amorous adventures on other trips to Lake Tahoe, Monterey, and the Sequoias.

But when the chips were down for poker with my lifelong friends and their wives, Maggie didn't fit in. She wasn't afraid to say what was on her mind and her directness was a bit startling. I really didn't have high expectations that this was going to be a good mix.

I got my hopes up when Maggie agreed to co-host a poker party with my friends and wives at our Santa Barbara home. Maggie didn't exactly integrate with the other women. For starters, she focused her attention on her sister Lucy, who just happened to be in town and visiting us at the house during the party. The wives, ignored for the first couple hours by my wife, decided to take a short group walk in the neighborhood.

When they returned from the walk, they were surprised — oh dear — to find that they had been locked out at the front door. *So nice to see you, ladies. Drive home safely!* Suffice to say, this was the last poker party that Maggie attended.

While my poker friends found Maggie — shall we say — perplexing, Aunt Evelyn held Maggie in high regard. Maggie earned Evelyn's respect on Christmas, 1992, when she invited the family — Mom, Dad, Gloria, Evelyn, Pam, Kasey — for a holiday dinner at our Santa Barbara rental home owned by the Italian couple. Convincing Dad and Gloria to come up to SB was a major coup.

Evelyn wrote about that dinner, and Maggie, in a letter to me a couple weeks later:

"I hope Maggie won't stress herself out planning anymore get-togethers for our bunch. She worked so hard for a family Xmas and she got very little reward. I think she achieved a greater respect for herself tho — and I think she surprised everyone. I was very proud of her — but my heart ached a bit as I experienced the day. While she projected grand manners and airs, I still wanted to cuddle her like my "baby," she has such great emotional needs, and I just absolutely hate it when others can't see her struggles."

A few weeks after writing that letter, in early 1993, Evelyn was in the hospital. She was suddenly struck down by a brain aneurysm that landed her in intensive care. She was clinging to life for six weeks with that magnificent brain of hers under siege. She had suffered a massive stroke that disfigured one side of her face and slurred her speech.

I made frequent trips to see her at St. John's Hospital in Santa Monica, which happened to be where I was born nearly 40 years earlier. Despite her slurred speech, Evelyn appeared to be as alert as ever.

Dad constantly visited her as well and was sometimes accompanied by his wife Gloria. But can you guess who never bothered coming to see Evelyn as she was fighting for her life? Neither of her daughters. I took note of that, recalling the promise I had made to Evelyn to honor the wishes spelled out in her Will as Executor of her estate. For me, her daughters forfeited any claim to her estate by not making any effort to check on her. Turns out, neither of them made any such claims.

Her daughters missed their chance to say goodbye to their mother. I got the call from Dad on the morning of March 22. Evelyn had passed away at the age of 71. She was preceded in death by only a couple of years by her own mother, Grandma, who had passed away at the age of 91.

I was thunderstruck by the news, as my eyes flooded with tears.

Dad and I led a small memorial gathering at the Santa Monica house, where we spread Evelyn's ashes in her precious garden. Aunt Mina, Evelyn's longtime letter companion, was too old and fragile to attend, but she sent a letter that was read at the memorial, a poignant tribute which I could not have put in better words:

"Evelyn and I had an intimate correspondence going in certain periods of our lives and especially in the last several years. Through these letters I got to know and love her very much. She had a gift in the use of words to express her thoughts and feelings which made her letters very interesting and stimulating. She was a deep thinker and through much reading and research and asking questions she made independent decisions about important issues in life, not always conforming to popular beliefs.

"Evelyn's ideal of how society should function was one of cooperation not cutthroat competition. Good government meant the poor and underprivileged would be protected from exploitation and oppression by the rich and powerful of the world.

"As her friends all know, Evelyn had a professional skill in art and especially drawing portraits. She recently shared with me some drawings of what she called her "ceiling people" because the inspiration came from shadows in the ceiling of her bedroom. They are skillfully done and very imaginative and amusing. When I asked her about this talent she wrote that a compulsive urge to draw people had been with her since childhood. She never received professional training. The skill developed through persistent and patient practice working on details until she felt satisfied with the result.

"Evelyn realized her habit of outspokenness had caused problems in her relationships but she believed she could only be true to herself by being honest about her feelings.

"In her poetry she had the same gift of words as in her letters. An ability to express strong feelings. I think they were truly inspired.

I am including one of them in this tribute. It was written when she lived in a remote mountain area in Washington state where she felt so close to nature and the spiritual side of life. I am saddened by her sudden death and will miss her thought-provoking letters very much.

"Good-bye Evelyn. Love, Mina.

"We look at the beauties in nature, trees, flowers, mountains and
We marvel at the wonders and wax ecstatic
At the intricacies and details in a rose, a passion flower, and orchid.
But we, who are doing the looking and the wondering,
Hesitate not to find fault, to downgrade the most
Magnificent, detailed, intricate formation in existence…
Our human body.
Nothing has ever been devised, invented or
Engineered to duplicate it.
See the blood surging through the veins, notice the
Breath breathing itself without assistance, look at a
Hand, a finger, a wrist and witness the
Tremendous machinery at work. No man can conceive
Of anything greater than himself, his body… the
Proof positive of the existence of the Ultimate Creator."

Evelyn's written words were captivating. I kept all of her letters she wrote to Aunt Mina, as well as all her correspondence to politicians all the over the years.

I found one short essay she wrote to herself, on a pink piece of paper, in her exquisite handwriting, that I had separated from the rest for a reason. It was meant to be republished in this memoir, She wrote it four years before she died, obviously in a time of despair. It was a heart-wrenching read. To wit:

December 23, 1989 1:00 A.M.
"Me. I am all these things around me. Everything is here because I am. Yet they could all be here even when I'm not. Scraps of paper I've written on, books I am reading, those I plan to read.
"I could take an old photo of me and set a match to it and watch it burn. That image of me would start to turn brown, the edge blacken and curl up. Then my image blackens and curls up, then cools off and

crumbles. That is me. The ashes disintegrate into black specks and blend into the surroundings. That will be me.

"This sheet of pink paper may last awhile. Maybe somebody will pick it up someday and read the words. Whoever you are, are you reading this in a fleeting moment? Will this paper get rumpled up and thrown away? It really would not make any difference — really.

"Would you care to know about this person? Would you wonder at all about me? I can't imagine any reason why you should. After all, you are just another Me.

"One day, a photo of you may get burnt. Will you have written down any words for someone else to read after you have gone?

"See this....(Form of a finger print on the page) That's my right index finger print. Maybe it will still be here for you to see long after I am gone.

"All the passions inside me, the rages over injustices, the loves I couldn't hold onto, missing the bonds I never had, that space inside me that holds gallons of tears that could overflow at a moment's notice... all this will disintegrate when I do.

"Why does everything seem so vital in life, when in the end, nothing really matters.

Evelyn May Perkins, Luera, Morrical, Christofferson
A daughter, sister, mother, wife, aunt, grandmother, etc.

Family gathering Christmas 1992, at our Santa Barbara home (from left to right): Pam, Aunt Evelyn, Gloria, Dad, Mom, Maggie and Kasey. Evelyn, quite suddenly and unexpectedly, died less than three months after this photo was taken

338

Series of Evelyn's ceiling face sketches

I am that "somebody" who picked up that pink paper and read it someday. But it wasn't in a fleeting moment, and I certainly didn't rumple it up and throw it away. I kept it. It made me think. It made me think of the moment Evelyn must have been going through to write that piece. Two days before Christmas, and she was alone. It made me think about why I'm writing the memoirs I'm writing — will anybody care long after I am gone? They are stories worth telling, triumphs and defeats. But it also made me think how I wished I could have comforted her in her moment of despair during the holidays, how much I miss her, and how blessed I was to have her in my life.

———————————◆◆◆◆◆———————————

It turned out that I didn't have to carry out the duties as Executor of Evelyn's Will, as she directed. Dad took that responsibility on himself.

So I was off the hook, as far as bequeathing $1 each to Bebe and Linda, Evelyn's two daughters. I don't know how my father dealt with them. Clearly, their ties with their mother had been severed long ago.

With respect to settling Evelyn's estate, Dad quietly hired a paralegal and had the deed to the Santa Monica house transferred to him. I suppose I could have raised a stink about this action if I had wanted to. But the last thing I wanted was to get into a legal battle with my father over the Santa Monica house.

For starters, I could understand that he would want to protect his and Gloria's interest in the house they were living in. The prospect of my taking ownership of the house and possibly selling it, thereby forcing them to move, could have been perceived as a threat to him. Not that I would have done that. Except there was Maggie, who I'm sure Dad didn't trust not to take matters into her own hands and use her influence on me.

All of that is conjecture. In my mind, I reconciled the matter by concluding that Dad probably would have been Evelyn's first choice as Executor of her Will if she had thought he would outlive her. But he was older, and his quintuple bypass surgery in 1989 laid odds that he would precede her in death.

Dad and I had a conversation about the Santa Monica house shortly after Evelyn's death. He assured me he would leave the house to me when he passed, which was reassuring. The only complication to that scenario would be if Gloria survived him and claimed spousal rights to the house that she could conceivably pass on to her children. I adored Gloria, but funny things happen when the dearly departed change dynamics in the family.

Dad, nevertheless, did not leave me empty-handed from Evelyn's estate. He transferred all of her Treasury Bonds account worth about $90,000 over to me. In addition, the next-door neighbors, Sandy Rios and her husband, still owed money to Evelyn on the sale of the house next door and were making modest monthly payments. Dad assigned those monthly payments over to me. How could I possibly complain? Sandy, with whom I would forge a respectful business relationship over the next few years, and I worked out a payment plan.

So, Maggie and I had a nice little nest egg. Just for the fun of it, we decided to look at homes for sale in the Santa Barbara area, just to see what was out there. And hey, we could dream, couldn't we?

An open house viewing of a modest home on a corner lot in the Mesa neighborhood proved to be too tempting to pass up. The deal-clincher was the redwood hot tub in the backyard. The house was priced to sell — it was the spring of 1993 and it was a buyer's market at the time. That $90,000 in the Treasury Bonds account was just enough to cover the 20 percent down payment and closing costs.

We made an offer. It was accepted. Just like that, we became homeowners in Paradise.

The move came just at the right time. Our Italian landlords had become fed up with our rambunctious boy Max and his persistent dog-poop problem and wanted us out. We moved into our new home on the Mesa when escrow closed in August.

Evelyn had made this all possible. I was truly blessed.

———————◆———————

We now had an even bigger home to fill, including two spare bedrooms. For a few months Maggie's 14-year-old niece, Katherine, occupied one of the spare bedrooms. She was Gina's oldest daughter and a very sweet, pretty girl. Gina was overwhelmed at the time, so we took Katherine in until her mother could get things a little more settled. I felt a little paternalistic toward Katherine during her brief stay.

When Katherine returned home, symptoms of empty nest hit us a bit. But Maggie and I were already thinking in terms of converting one of those spare bedrooms into a nursery.

Maggie had already gotten pregnant once prior to our move into the house, ending in a sudden miscarriage. That was a momentary setback, but Maggie wasn't easily discouraged. She got pregnant again shortly after we had moved into the house.

By Thanksgiving she had suffered her second miscarriage. She was a little further along with this pregnancy, nearly through the first trimester, which only added to the devastation.

Two misses was enough to shake even my unshakable wife. Maggie started to have serious doubts that she was capable of carrying a pregnancy to full term. When she got pregnant a third time a month after our second anniversary the following March, we were nervous. Maggie tread softly during the first trimester; she purposely curtailed any strenuous activity to give this pregnancy a chance.

Getting past the first trimester was a huge psychological hurdle. That had to take priority over a dramatic event — disclosed in the next chapter —that arose during the first trimester, forcing me to deal with it later than I wanted.

Maggie made it past the first trimester, and then the second, and the third. Our daughter was due on December 20 — my father's birthday. Funny how my son was due on my mother's birthday and my daughter was due on my father's birthday.

But our daughter was anxious to enter the world. Maggie went into labor four days earlier than expected. Complications forced a Caesarian C-section.

Tessa Marguerite Perkins arrived healthy on December 16. Tessa was a name Maggie picked from a character on one of her favorite TV shows, some princess warrior. Marguerite was a derivative of Margarita, Maggie's middle name and her mother's name. It was my idea to change the name to the French version.

It was a blessed event. I only wished Evelyn had lived long enough for my daughter to have known her.

My baby daughter Tessa wrapped in a furry, warm coat

CHAPTER 19
Dan Part 2

Dan couldn't wait to escape "Hell-A," his name for LA.

Somewhere between serving in the Peace Corps together on the Solomon Islands and returning to the U.S., where they resided in Long Beach, Dan and Kathy got married. Love had blossomed in the primitive thatched hut they had lived in.

Kathy was very quiet, reserved. She looked smart — blue eyes behind glasses framed by her shoulder-length blonde hair — because she was smart.

But I hardly knew her because she was so reserved.

While living in Long Beach, Dan cemented a close friendship with a guy named Leo, who had a sailboat. Leo was a cool guy; he liked to get high, which fit right in Dan's lane.

But Dan and Kathy weren't long for Long Beach, because Dan wanted out of "Hell-A." He found a teaching job in Coalville, just inside the Nevada border and east of the Tahoe area. Coalville was a tiny town. The high school where Dan taught had maybe 300 kids for all four grades.

I don't know what happened with Kathy. Maybe Coalville was too tiny for her. I don't really know the circumstances, but she quietly left Dan by the spring semester at the high school.

Then I figured out it might have had something to do with Lana (not her real name.)

Lana was a senior student in one of Dan's classes, attractive, with reddish-blonde curly hair. By June, she was 18 and graduating from high school.

Dan was available. She wanted to celebrate her graduation in a big way.

They lured me into their plans. I was unattached at the time, in the aftermath of divorcing Lizamara. Dan talked me into meeting Lana and him at a hotel in Reno. Lana wanted to fulfill a lurid fantasy with the two of us.

I won't provide any more detail. But I will tell you something about Dan that I had already known before that night in the Reno hotel. It was knowledge gained from sharing an apartment with him in college, from bathing in rivers during camping trips, and from skinny-dipping at Deep Creek. Dan was well-hung. We're talking, foot-long size. I think that made him a magnet for a lot of women.

Dan's against-the-grain attitude toward authority lasted all of one school year in Coalville. He decided it was time to move on, so he migrated to the state of Washington and found another teaching job in Bremerton, about 20 miles north of Tacoma along the Puget Sound.

Dan met Elizabeth, who became his second wife at some point in the mid-80's. They moved in together in a weather-worn house in Bremerton, along the water in the Sound. During one of my visits, I accompanied Dan when he dropped off the rent check at the property management office. That's where I met Ana, my enchanting Spanish lady friend.

For all his faults — and Dan had a few — I loved him like a brother because of the way he took care of me and overlooked all of my faults. A clear example came on our kayak trip on the Merced River when I opened a huge gash over my right ankle on a jagged edge of a rock. When I wanted to keep going, Dan made the decision that we were done and he had to get me to Urgent Care.

Another example stood out on one of my visits to Bremerton. I wasn't known for my punctuality; OK, I had a reputation for always being late. On this visit, I had a return flight home out of Sea-Tac Airport, which was sorta important for me not to miss. Maybe because I was a little stoned, I departed from Dan and Elizabeth's house for the airport a little later than I should have. I hadn't planned for the extra time I needed to drop off my rental car. Dan followed me there to drive me the rest of the way to the airport.

I was exceeding all posted speed limits on the highway high-tailing it to the rental place. I had rented a car from an agency called "Ugly Duckling Car Rental," which offered exactly what the name implied — butt-ugly vehicles for rent at a budget price. The cars were older models, with a few minor surface blemishes, but purportedly in reliable mechanical shape. You didn't rent these vehicles to impress anybody, you just wanted something that could get you around, on the cheap.

Dan thought it was pretty funny that I rented a car from this place. "You're just the kind of guy who would rent a car from a place called Ugly Duckling," my best friend assessed.

I roared into the Ugly Duckling lot in a cloud of dust (the lot was a dirt patch; pretty ugly, too). I had come in so hot that I swerved recklessly to a stop, nearly slamming into a parked rental car. When I turned the engine off, steam immediately escaped from under the hood, followed by water dripping out of the overheated radiator.

I hurriedly settled my rental car bill and jumped into Dan's car. Looking at my watch, my flight was less than an hour from takeoff. We had about 45 minutes more just to drive to the airport. It did not look good.

Dan got us to the airport in something less than 45 minutes; he always drove faster than the speed limit. But clearly I had not arrived in time to check my big duffle bag; I was given a boarding pass at the ticket counter and told to take my bag to the gate and see if they would accept it there.

It goes without saying that the boarding gate was at the very end of the terminal. These were pre-9/11 days, when security was much more lax, so the duffle bag got through the security check.

You measure a friendship by what lengths your friend will go to aid you in a time of need. I still can vividly picture how Dan lugged my heavy duffle bag down the entire length of that terminal to my boarding gate, in a mad dash, arriving in a sweat just before the doors were about to close for boarding. Dan was used to carrying heavy loads; carrying the football in the pickup games of our youth, with most of the opposing team piled on his back trying to bring him down made him pretty sturdy. But he could have made me carry the duffle bag. He may have made the calculation that my chances of making the flight were better if he carried it.

I had no right to be allowed on that flight. But my Guardian Angel —and Dan — saw to it that I was, as the boarding agent accepted my duffle bag and let me in before closing the door to board the plane.

———————————— ◆ ————————————

After a couple of years in the house along the shores of the Sound, Dan and Elizabeth retreated to a remote chalet-type home in the woods above Bremerton. The home was so remote it had a dirt driveway about a hundred yards long before reaching an exit road.

This was more to Dan's liking, as far away from the city as possible.

This was the home a pregnant Gail and I stayed at when we came to visit in the summer of '87.

Dan and Elizabeth were together for a good stretch of years, the longest of Dan's three marriages. It was with Elizabeth that Dan picked up Solomon, the ultra-smart black lab, and Godiva, the ultra-sweet Great Dane-St.Bernard mammoth mix, from the dog pound. They were a legendary pair in Dan's long line of canine associations.

I started a trend of summer visits every year to Washington with Dan and Elizabeth, carrying over to Dan's multiple relationships while living in the state. No matter where Dan lived, or with whom, he always made sure he had a spare room for me to stay whenever I visited.

Elizabeth and Dan both wear tuxes on their wedding day, with Dan in bridal white. They are accompanied by their wedding party of dogs

I was quite fond of Elizabeth. She was down-to-earth and very cute, brown-eyed, brown-haired, with a sleek figure. She was a preternaturally level-headed woman, but Dan incited a little bit of her wild side.

But something went awry in their relationship. Elizabeth tried to privately confide in me about her struggles in the relationship. There were problems in the bedroom. Elizabeth wouldn't specify, but I was starting to get a hint of Dan's darker side.

346

I saw the breakdown in their relationship develop over time. Dan had become sullen and cold toward Elizabeth. I was hearing it from both sides. To simplify, he felt his needs weren't being met after all he had done for her. She felt hurt from his insensitivity. I tended to side with Elizabeth and felt she deserved to be treated better.

This was transpiring at the time Maggie and I were settling in Santa Barbara.

Finally, Elizabeth left Dan. She accused him of mental cruelty and couldn't take it anymore. The tranquility they had found in their isolated home in the woods had been shattered.

Dan and the dogs moved to a house in Kent, east of Seattle. Living alone did not go well for him. He soon became very despondent over the marriage break-up. He was frequently calling me in utter despair. The tone of his calls became increasingly worrisome.

Then one night he called me late. He had been drinking heavily. He was talking about having lost the will to live. He was begging me to come up to see him. He was exhibiting all the signs of someone acting suicidal.

I caught a flight to Seattle as soon as I could.

I stayed with Dan for four days. He was a wreck. I was seeing him at his lowest point. He was angry at Elizabeth for leaving him, feeling betrayed. He drank a lot, cried a lot in his beer. Solomon and Godiva were very worried about him.

I couldn't help but think about what Dan told me at Deep Creek, that he didn't think he'd make it to age 50. But I didn't think he meant that he'd go out this way. He was still in his 30s, way too young to give up on life. It was too soon for his self-prophesy to come true.

The best thing I could do was just stay with him, hang with him, make sure he did nothing to harm himself. It was touch-and-go for a couple days. We didn't go anywhere. I wouldn't let him drive.

Gradually, he drank less and smoked more pot. That helped lighten his mood. Before long he was cracking jokes; he was coming around again to being the Dan I knew. I think the big, sloppy tongue kiss from Godiva was the turning point.

By the fourth day, I felt it was safe to leave him and return home. He was still feeling sorry for himself, but at least he assured me he wasn't going to check out and leave me behind. I got him to promise he'd be available to serve as Best Man at my next wedding, which

347

Maggie and I were in the planning stages. I was counting on him.

———◆———

Dan had friends in Washington who were looking after him. He had a bunch of good buddies in the adult ice hockey league that he had hooked up with. He played out his lifelong dream that had been awakened during our college days with the Mother Puckers. He was the goaltender, and he took some shots to the head that may or may not have had some effect on his mental capacity over the years.

He pulled himself out of his malaise, moved out of Kent and gravitated further north up the Sound where he found another teaching job.

He met a young divorcee named Becky who had two small boys. The break-up with Elizabeth was at least a year behind him. Dan was smitten with Becky. She was another slender blonde lady who had long legs, like a dancer.

While I was working on my fourth marriage, Dan was working on his third. Maggie and I sent out invitations for a February 16, 1991 wedding date. Dan sent his RSVP with a bunch of added comments written in sprawling fashion inside the invitation, displaying his twisted sense of humor. It also mixed in a big announcement:

"Becky and I got married two for the road, I mean 2/4/91."

A sampling of his other comments:

"I'm changing districts, moving to Sequim, and we just bought a house, even has a spare room. Please don't take that as an invitation to visit."

"Hi Chic, I haven't heard from you in a long time, I appreciate it. You could call me sometime, in fact call me anything — I'll answer unless I know it's you."

"Did you hear about the hitch-hiker that was standing beside the road, he had 3 ears, 1 leg, and no arms?"

"Remember, you can lead a horse to water— but don't crawl under him afterwards."

"I hope everything is going well — you know: job, marriage, hair control."

Dan then wrote on the back of the invitation: *"All kidding aside I miss you my friend."*

He signed it like he signed all his correspondence to me:

"Normal, Daniel (signed upside down)."

Then he added: *"P.S.: Reality is only a convenient measurement of perception."*

Dan was back in top form. I was pleasantly surprised by the marriage announcement. And they bought a home, too. Sequim was located way up north in what was considered the "banana belt" of the Puget Sound because it didn't rain as much in that region as in the rest of western Washington.

Dan was all in with Becky's boys. He enjoyed his role as a father to them because there was a lot of little boy in Dan. And the boys loved him. There were some minor skirmishes with the boys' real father over child support and visitation. Dan stood by Becky all the way through four years of turmoil with her "ex." He was wholly committed to this domestic life.

He became inspired to open up an after-school daycare center for kids in a closed-down church building he found in town. Dan, who was an artist, designed elaborate arts and crafts projects for the children. He had a knack for turning anything he found off the ground — rocks, shells, broken glass, and limbs and twigs— into objects of art creatively utilized in projects for the kids.

He named his daycare center Atlantis, after the mythical lost ancient city.

There was excitement in Dan's voice when he talked about his elaborate plans for Atlantis, which took him at least a year to put together. He had this surge of energy that you could just feel listening to him talk. Then when he brought it all to fruition, it sounded so idyllic, like he had found his true calling.

He seemed so happy. I visited Dan and Becky in Sequim every summer and stayed in that spare room of theirs, continuing the pattern I started when Dan and Elizabeth were together.

Atlantis appeared to be a big success. It was, for a couple years. Dan was totally consumed by it.

Then it all came crashing down, early in 1994. Becky, for whatever reason, strayed. Dan found out she was cheating on him and it destroyed him. They broke up.

The break-up didn't just end the marriage, it ended Atlantis. Dan immediately fell back into the dark hole that had nearly swallowed him before he met Becky.

He hid it from me in the first few calls I received from him. But I could tell he was slipping.

A few weeks passed and I hadn't heard from him. Instead, while at work on the News-Press sports desk, I received a call from Ben, a friend of Dan's. I had met Ben about seven months earlier, in my last visit to Sequim. He was an older gentleman and a private plane pilot who took Dan and I for a spectacular flight in a tiny four-seater all over the Sound that felt like floating in heaven. I have an 8 x 10 photo that Ben took of Dan and I in the cockpit of that plane

That was a much happier time. The tone of the impromptu call from Ben was much different. Ben explained the depths he went to try to reach me. He didn't have a phone number for me. He didn't even know my last name. All he knew about me was that I was a guy named Chic who worked for a sports department at some newspaper in Santa Barbara.

"I had to find a way to reach you," Ben said, with a sense of urgency in his voice. "Dan is in a really bad way. You've got to get up here to see him. I'm really worried about him."

There was one small conflict holding me back. Maggie was pregnant, on her third try after two miscarriages, and she was still a few weeks away from getting through the first trimester. I knew there was no way I could leave her to travel up to Washington until she got past the first trimester. I couldn't risk it.

"I can't leave my pregnant wife right now," I told Ben. "I can come up there in about four weeks. How bad off is Dan?"

"Pretty bad," Ben said. "I don't know, man. I don't know if he can hang on."

The fates of Dan and my daughter Tessa would intersect in a manner I could not have possibly foreseen before her birth

350

I was torn. My wife needed me to see if this pregnancy would make it through the first trimester, after two disheartening miscarriages. My best friend, who already had threatened suicide once, needed me again to persuade him not to go there.

I called Dan that night. He was really fucked up. He had mixed a lot of alcohol with some pills, which scared the shit out of me. I frantically called him again the next night. Thank God, he answered the phone. But he was wasted again.

Somehow, I strung him along with calls every day over the next four weeks, assuring him that I was coming, but I had to wait to make sure Maggie was OK with our baby. He was barely hanging onto hope with the thought of my coming up to see him. Back at home, Maggie rolled her eyes when I told her about Dan, but she accepted my compromise.

Four weeks later, Maggie and baby were still good. An ultrasound signaled a strong heartbeat. She gave me her blessing when I flew up north to be with Dan. By the time I was able to make that flight, I had lost phone contact with Dan. His telephone was out of order because he had put a bullet through it with a gun.

Yeah, this time, Dan's heart had really been broken and he did not respond well. Becky had done him wrong. She shattered his dream enterprise that was Atlantis.

But this time, it was easier for me to build him back up with a heightened sense of empathy, compared to the first suicide alert over the break-up with Elizabeth. I helped him write his impassioned court statement for his impending divorce from Becky.

Ben was there to help out, too. I needed all the help I could get. Dan eventually sobered up. He had given us a helluva scare, but he survived this one, too.

We got him a new phone, too.

———————————◆———————————

Rebounding is always an interesting journey; you never know where it will take you. Take it from someone who knows a little bit about rebounding, and I'm not talking about Shaquille O'Neal.

Dan knew a little bit about rebounding too. His rebound off Becky took an unexpected ricochet with a familiar face. Somehow Lana, his old high school student in Coalville who gave us that memorable night in a Reno hotel, drifted back into Dan's life.

They must have renewed contact with each other after Lana graduated. Then, after Dan found the will to live, post-Becky, he found her number and they hooked up.

Meanwhile, Maggie didn't suffer a third miscarriage and Tessa came into the world just in time for Christmas of 1994. Dan called me and let me know he was driving down to California for the holidays to see his mother in Long Beach, and Lana was accompanying him. Then he wanted to come up to Santa Barbara to celebrate the New Year with us.

Dan and Lana booked a hotel room in Santa Barbara for New Year's Eve. Maggie's mother, Margarita, had just moved in with us to help with the baby, so the plan was for the four of us — Dan and Lana, and Maggie and I — to hit the local bars to usher in 1995 and celebrate our new status as parents, while my mother-in-law stayed home with the baby. Ultimately, Maggie didn't feel like going out.

"You remember Lana, don't you Chic?" Dan said coyly when I greeted them at our door.

Then the three of us, the Reno trio, headed out to the bars to celebrate the New Year. We hopped around several bars on downtown State Street in Santa Barbara, and wound up downing quite a few tequila shots along the way. Midnight rolled past sometime during the night and we managed to mix in some food to sober up a little bit.

It was close to 2 a.m. when we started heading back home. Dan was driving. On the main road back to my house, a cop standing in the middle of the street waved us over to get in line for the sobriety check that a battalion of police officers was conducting in a closed gas station.

"Shit," Dan muttered. Since he was driving, he was the one who would be tested. We all knew how much he had been drinking. Lana and I were looking at each other, calculating how long of a walk home we would have after Dan was arrested and the car was impounded.

There were about six cars ahead of us. Dan was sweating it out, contemplating his fate as we waited. Dan chewed some gum to try to dilute his alcohol-tinted breath.

We waited a good thirty minutes to reach the front of the line. Then it was another tortuous ten minutes watching the driver ahead of us go through a series of arduous sobriety exercises that the officers instructed him to perform. We were a captive audience, held in suspense over that guy's fate.

We were all in agreement that the driver being tested did pretty well; surely he would pass. But when the verdict came in, we were in for a surprise — an officer slapped handcuffs on him and led him to the back of a police car.

"Holy shit! If that guy didn't pass, what chance do I have?" Dan exclaimed.

An officer approached our car and waved for Dan to get out. Dan scowled at Lana and me as he opened the car door and stepped out. It was looking like the New Year was getting off to a bad start.

Lana and I sat glumly inside the car waiting for the inevitable. After a few minutes, Dan opened the car door and sat back in the driver's seat, ready to drive away.

"You passed?" Lana shrieked.

"Yep. I just barely passed the breath-test under the limit. I guess I sobered up all that time we waited."

He shifted the car in drive and turned the car toward home. It was going to be a good year.

———————◆———————

Lana was a short-lived romance for Dan. By the summer of '95 he had reached into the teen pool once again to find the woman he was meant to be with. The shocking part was, Tami was not quite 18 when Dan first met her. Dan was 42 at the time. I admit I was a bit taken aback by how young Tami was when I first met her, before I got to know her.

Dan's nomadic journey through Washington had led him further north to Bellingham, where he met Tami. They moved in together in a big old house. Dan seemed to have a knack for finding funky dwellings to reside in. Every house Dan lived in had to have a dog; that requisite was filled in by Agnes, their sweet maroon-haired laberdinger.

Dan and Tami met in an art class at Western Washington State University. Art was a shared passion that obviously brought them together. Dan's artwork flourished in his bond with Tami.

Tami was a work of art in a naturalistic, innocent manner — very pleasing to the eye. She possessed the slender physique that always attracted Dan. Her hair was very yellowish blonde, thin in texture, straight, shoulder-length, nothing fancy. Her angular face was distinguished by her dark brown eyes and eyebrows, a stark contrast to her hair and soft complexion, features emblematic of her Slavic ethnicity. She never wore make-up; she didn't need to. She was a natural beauty.

Come to think of it, none of Dan's wives or girlfriends wore makeup. But Tami was the prettiest.

She was mature for her age. As young as she was, I picked up on a dysfunctional family dynamic Tami may have been escaping by hooking up with Dan. You could see how he lured her into his world. She was an innocent, he was her mentor. Together, they blossomed as artists. Their union belied their age difference.

Me, Tami and Dan at Mom's house during the holidays

After a couple of years in Bellingham, they were on the move. Dan found another teaching job in the small town of Mt. Vernon, about 25 miles south of Bellingham.

He asked me to fill out a "Character Reference Form" for the position. I had a little fun with the first draft of responses that I sent him:

In what capacity have you known the applicant? *"Fellow inmate."*

What was your title at the time you knew the applicant?: *"4-time loser at marriage."*

354

Outstanding Qualities: *"Tells good dirty jokes; Nickname is 'Louisville Slugger,' if you catch my drift; Exhibits excellent aim shooting out telephones; Rolls a perfect joint; Knows the difference between shit and shinola; When you need a guy to run the ball up the middle on 4th-and-1, he's your man."*

Weaknesses: *"Has taken too many pucks to the head over the years; Weak backhand in tennis; Complains about trivial things such as a little hair on the bathtub soap; Has fleas; Close supervision recommended when he's around teen-age girls; Has greasy fingernails from working on cars so much; U.S. scientists still haven't figured out what social disease he brought back from the Solomon Islands; (Can I request second page for this category?)"*

General Behavior: *"Prefers dogs to humans; shameless punster; thinks his farts smell like perfume; drinks beer for breakfast; thinks he can beat me in pool when he can't; has a huge poster of Alex Rodriguez in his bathroom."*

Dan got hired anyway (I submitted a second form with straight answers.) He taught at a middle school and became something of a legend there. He took on the special ed and problematic students who were considered lost causes — the students that none of the other teachers wanted any part of — and got them to respond to his unorthodox teaching methods. Many of these were the type of kids we used to work with at the Children's Baptist Home back in our college days — social misfits. That experience way back then had prepared Dan for this job and these students that he purposely chose to take on as his own. His own sense of child-like fun and resistance to authority, along with his ability to gain their respect, had an appealing effect with these kids.

Dan and Tami found a home to rent just a few miles from the school, in the tiny town of Sedro Woolley, tucked away just off a rural road that meandered past sprawling horse farms, nestled among pine trees on the shore of a small, scenic lake. They had a little dock off their backyard where the green kayak we used for all of our adventurous river trips was parked off to the side.

It was a little slice of heaven.

Their two-story home served as a gallery to display all of their artwork. Paintings hung on all the walls. Dan's art was abstract. My favorites of his included an eclectic painting of his first Bremerton house by the water; a six-foot long blob of dripping paint that looked like toxic waste with a dark reddish-black center faintly resembling the face of the devil; and a weird conglomeration of tubular shapes in blue, lavender, mauve and green that spelled out an obscure message in descending order: f...u...c...k....u. Another impressive piece was an eight-foot by three-foot assemblage of blocks of wood in blues, pinks, yellows and browns, laid out in a structured grid, with long, thin, blue streaks of wood spanning out like a web.

Ceramic, wooden and glass sculptures were placed all over the house on shelves, fireplace mantle, end tables, and coffee table.

At the top of the stairs leading to the second floor stood a half-mannequin wearing a hockey mask and jersey. Another life-like mannequin that resembled Dan was stationed by the ceiling-high window looking out to the deck and lake beyond. This distinguished fellow wore a tattered straw hat, sunglasses dangling over the nose, a navy-blue velvet sweater, and had some sort of stuffed marsupial with long arms draped around his neck.

I loved visiting Dan and Tami at their Sedro Woolley home every summer. We spent endless days and nights getting high, listening to good music, taking Agnes out for walks, and sharing a lot of laughs. Dan and I often paddled out on the lake in his kayak. I experienced some of the most idyllic moments of my life on those visits.

I wrote a song entitled "Inspiration in Dan's Bathroom," which was literally inspired in a bathroom at their Sedro Woolley home. It's a happy, triumphant tune.

I have three pieces of Dan's art in my Santa Barbara home. Two of them are wooden frames housing 8X10 photographs of mine that I asked Dan to design, and he honored my request in unorthodox "Dan" fashion. One photo was a shot of Lake Tahoe taken above from the level of the highway, looking down between trees onto a hideaway cove. The left side of the frame is an actual wooden branch resembling a tree trunk, tying perfectly into the photo. The other framed photo was a dramatic sunset at Hendry's Beach in Santa Barbara, which I shot through the lens of sunglasses, rendering dark yellow sunlight set off by black shadows along the shore. The yellow light reflected off the water, rocks and wet sand in the foreground. Dan designed a heavily shellacked black frame shaped by gentle curls, like lapping waves. The clear sheen brought out the contrast of the sunset. Tami said Dan

356

applied eight coats of shellack to draw out the intensity of the sheen.

But the most significant piece of art I received was a gift Dan created as a birthday present. This ceramic artwork, depicted as pieces of a puzzle, represented my and Dan's friendship and how it fit in my complicated life. In one grainy puzzle piece Dan faintly etched out the names of all the significant women in my life that Dan's friendship outlasted — Maggie, Gail, Liza (short for Lizamara), Jocelyne and Dorrean. In another puzzle piece he spelled out milestones of our friendship in barely legible muted colors as if the memories were fading in time — Mother Puckers, HHS (Hawthorne High School), Deep Creek. Another puzzle piece contained seven photos that subtly blended in to the surface, including three shots of the two of us together, and one featuring the gang from the fateful Truckee River trip. Then another puzzle piece displayed an inscription from a screenplay I wrote in which the main characters are based on Dan and Tami. It's a fictitious murder mystery in which the character that was based on me mysteriously winds up missing. The inscription Dan selected in the puzzle piece was kinda cryptic, reading: *"I don't know what to think, I'm hoping he just…flipped out. Maybe I drove him over the edge with all my stories about you and me. Maybe if I hadn't opened my mouth he would have never ….and gone to New Orleans. That's not all that's bothering me."*

Pieces of a puzzle — that's how acutely Dan saw my life. There are a thousand different pieces to the puzzle that, assembled together, present a whole. Those pieces have been scrambled all my life, and I'm just getting around to fitting all the pieces to fill the whole picture.

Dan inserted six holes along the bottom of the puzzle where he hung miniature symbols of our friendship: 1, a miniature football symbolizing the tackle football games of our youth that we survived; 2, a ragged blotch of hair, representing the hair I routinely left on the bars of soap we shared in the shower as college roommates (this gag was immortalized by another birthday "present" —a soap-on-a-rope coated with hair that Dan glued on); 3, a tiny replica of the green kayak that was the vessel for our epic white-water river trips; 4, a round black puck representing our Mother Pucker hockey days, on which Dan inscribed the word "You," by way of messaging "Puck You;" 5, a hole that was left empty, presumably to be filled by a future adventure yet to happen; 6, a remnant piece of the lime green shirt that Dan's childhood friend Fred Yenny was wearing when he fell to his death off Yosemite's Half Dome cliff, a fragment of fabric that froze an iconic moment in our friendship.

Dan added one final dig to the piece — he glued on a pair of screws. As he explained it, they were "loose screws" representing me.

I was being set up by a best friend who clearly believed I would outlive him and wanted me to have something to remember him by.

Dan's painting that spells out F...u...c...k...u, on display at his and Tami's home in Sedro Woolley, Wa

The ceramic puzzle art that Dan created to illustrate my puzzled life

CHAPTER 20
Art, For Art's Sake

I chose the name "Art" for the character who represented me in "Last of the Orange Groves," the novel I was writing during my college years. It was a purposeful name, admittedly a bit of a cliche, for someone who thought of himself as an "artist."

To that extent, I have always been driven to express myself creatively. For sure, I have always seen myself as a writer, from the days I wrote silly little stories for my Aunt Bee in Cincinnati, to my Perry Mason-style courtroom drama plays in Mr. Rivers' fifth grade class, to the World War II novels of my early teens, and so on.

I can't say the real-life "Art" grew up to realize the promise as a budding writer that "Jackson," the gay roommate who was infatuated with Art in "Orange Groves", saw in him. I did make it as a sports writer, but that wouldn't qualify as "art."

While I never saw myself as a poet, I tried my hand at poetry during a high school creative writing class. Here is one short piece I wrote that exposed my uncool, nerdy personality, but I liked it, coming from an adolescent perspective:

Somethin' Else

Man, you're somethin' else,
You think you're really big
With that long, white paper tube
Hanging from your
Cocky lips.
And all the girls crowded around ya,
'Cause they think you're cool
With that smog-contributing device,
And here I sit
With nothin'
Yeah!
I'm green with envy
And when we're in our 40's
I'll still envy ya,

'Cause while I'm doin' something dumb,
Like playing golf
Or bowling
Or enjoying a party,
With a cute wife
Of course,
You'll be sittin' there
Feelin' really cool,
Really big,
In a hospital bed,
With lung cancer
Or coronary disease
Or emphysema
Or whatever.

———————◆•◆•◆———————

Short stories was another form of writing I took a crack at in my youth. Reading them now, I'm reminded of the idealistic way I used to think, focused on the promises of youth contrasted by progressive themes raging against the evils of the world.

One short story that emerged from that high school creative writing class, was what I would describe as a valiant reach. In the story I make a very naive attempt to write from the perspective of a young, college-aged black man and his mother. As a white person, I wholly embrace support for the Black Lives Matter movement and the cause to overturn the racial injustices that have pervaded in this country, but I have no clue what it's truly like to be a black man in America.

The story, entitled "Futile Hope," was structured through a chain of letters between a mother and a son who had moved away to college, circa 1960's. While neither the college nor the predominantly black (poor) "home" base where the mother still resided are identified in the story, it's clear that the son's move is presented as a location improvement in terms of racist tendencies. The optimistic, wide-eyed son writes how he is going to be a success and lift his mother out of poverty. When I read the story now, his optimism sounds like it emanates from a wide-eyed young white guy. The son shares with his mother about how much better he is perceived at the college, marveling how the college allows black teachers. He tells his mother about a

360

young woman he has met and started dating, but he leaves out the part that she is white, until he is arrested by police falsely accusing him of raping her in a confrontation on the street. Hope is shattered in one tumultuous moment.

The voices in this story are cringe-worthy, a bit stereotypical, especially for the mother, whose letters are littered with misspellings that are supposed to reflect her uneducated background.

I was young then. Now, I'm thinking I should have left writing about the black experience to the likes of James Baldwin and Toni Morrison.

———————•••◆•••———————

Music is a universal language where I felt more at home to express myself creatively.

When I started piano lessons at age nine, I showed more interest in making up my own music from the start than in playing somebody else's music. I remember writing out the notes of my very first composition and proudly writing at the top of the musical page, "Written When I was 9 Years Old." I was well-acquainted with Mozart at the time and very impressed by his reputation for writing piano masterpieces at age 4. I was no Mozart, not even close, but I wished I was.

I still have the book of classical music entitled "Famous Piano Solos," from the piano lessons I received as a kid under the tutelage of my little Jewish teacher, Mrs. Rosenberg. The book is tattered, with loose pages falling out and pages 29 through 34 torn out from my dog Max when he got hold of the book. I held onto what remained of that treasured book from the Max attack and still practice about 20 compositions that I can play with some degree of competency, although I'll never quite master Chopin's "Nocturne, Op. 9 No.2," no matter how hard I try.

Turning through those pages is, for me, a fascinating turn back through the pages of time. Dates are written in pencil all over the title pages of pieces Mrs. Rosenberg assigned for me to work on. Multiple dates were an indication I struggled longer to learn those pieces. She wrote out instructive notes on some pages, such as *"Keep left wrist down," "Very Legato," "Fingering,"* and *"Dying away."* A couple of pieces, Beethoven's "Moonlight Sonata," and Souza's "The Stars And

Playing an old-time piano at the antique shop run by Louis and Steve in San Gregorio located along the Bay Area coast

Stripes Forever," still have star stickers on the title page, which was Mrs. Rosenberg's method of validating that I aced them. I'm just going to assume there were a bunch more stars that fell off the pages over the years.

Debussy's "Reverie," which I can still play, was always one of my favorite pieces, in part because it was one of the classics my dad had memorized from his old Depression-era player piano. Debussy is one of my favorite classical composers. Nothing quite can match the supreme elegance of his "Clair de Lune," which is another one of those pieces that I was never able to master.

The fact of the matter is, I was never close to becoming a master pianist. I listen in awe when I hear someone like the amazingly gifted Jon Battist play the piano. And as I stated before, my sister Pam was the gifted one in our family.

So I wasn't cut out to be a classical concert pianist. But my classical training did give me an appreciation for the classics, which influenced my own compositions. I may have my limitations, but what it comes down to is that I enjoy playing my own music. It gives me a sense of accomplishment, a place of calm, a means of meditation.

I marvel at some of the pieces I composed way back when I was a young teen, and wonder, where did those come from? It feels odd now, to reflect back on creations evolving from my youthful state of mind. I have a vague recollection of the process in which I worked on those compositions, purposely trying different rhythms, different chords at unexpected moments, experimenting with discordant tones, maybe throwing in an extra beat in a stanza every now and then. In one epic piece, I improvise a three-minute stretch riffing on the same three chords, never quite playing it the same way each time I try. It's a little scary, because improvising is literally a stretch for me, not my strong suit.

I took some improvisation classes as a young adult, from a kind, talented teacher by the name of Jai Josef. He taught me some basic music theory on chord structure. While I may have widened my skills as an improv player ever so slightly, it did expand my use of chords by breaking away from the basic 1-3-4 chord pattern.

Jai did a demo on one of my compositions, an elaborate project in which he expanded on and played the intricate piano part, brought in a female vocalist (at my request), a bass violinist, a flute player, and a clarinet player. What he did with the piece, entitled "Only Love Is," was nothing short of magical.

I wrote lyrics to about one-third of my 50-plus compositions. Like much of my poetry, I never thought my lyrics back then were good enough. Over time, I threw a bunch of old lyrics out and rewrote some of them. My lyric writing has improved as I got older.

In the '80s I took a semi-serious crack at songwriting by joining a weekly seminar in Hollywood. The seminar was designed for aspiring songwriters who wanted to pitch songs in the music business. The classes were structured so that writers could present songs either by live performance or recording, then the class would critique them. The feedback was helpful, and often brutal.

Through the seminar, I met a top-notch guitarist named Robert who did some demos for me. He put out a quality sound, laying out multiple tracks with synthesizer, drums and his own guitar licks. It was kind of cool to hear my piano pieces converted to a guitar accompaniment.

I had exactly only one indirect connection to the music business. Ben Foote, the legendary publicist at Ascot Park racetrack in Gardena who called me weekly to publicize his events in my Her-Ex motorsports column, was my link to renowned songwriter/

producer Mike Curb, who owned an LA-based record company. Curb, who also served as California's Lieutenant Governor under Gov. Jerry Brown in 1979-83, was a man of many talents and interests, and auto racing was one of them. In the 1980s he joined forces with Cary Agajanian, proprietor of Ascot Park and Ben Foote's boss, as co-owners of a widely successful racing team on the national sprint car circuit that competed regularly at Ascot.

I wrote a motorsports column on Curb, which gave me an "in" to submit a couple of demo tapes to Curb Records. Nothing came out from those submissions.

I eventually gave up on the idea of making it in the music business and just played my music for myself. It wasn't until years later, after I turned 60 and survived my pair of strokes, that I decided to record my music.

——————————•◆•——————————

You're not a writer in LA if you don't take a shot at screenwriting. I bought books to read up on screenwriting formats; learned all about three-part story arcs.

Then I took a stab at writing a few. My first screenplay was "Paternal Instinct," which contained elements of the wild, real-life stories related in chapters 15 and 16. I changed my character's profession in the screenplay from sports writer to professional photographer. It explored the whole Lizamara-Katya-Janice-Gail quagmire that had been my life in my early 30s and led into my first foray into parenthood, whether I was ready for it or not. I learned that love and parenthood don't always meet in the same place.

My second screenplay, called "Final Edition," told the story of the Her-Ex's gradual demise in its final years, based on my experiences working on the sports staff. I plugged the script with a bunch of quirky side stories, including scenes from the Corky's bar across the street where my drinking buddies Jay and Mark and I frequented after work and were joined by our lovable barfly Henry. Mark was the mastermind behind another sidebar in the script, a Corky's-inspired tale in which he enshrined an unbelievably gorgeous woman news reporter we admired from afar in the newsroom as "The Franchise." In sports terms, "The Franchise" is a very complimentary tag for any player on a team who is deemed indispensable, and this young, exotic-looking Black woman knocked it out the park. The script finishes with the sentimental closing of the Her-Ex, re-enacting the Corky's farewell, signaling the sad end of an era in LA journalism; ergo, the "Final Edition."

"Santiagatita," my epic tale based on my misadventures in Nicaragua in the summer of 1983, wrapped around Lizamara's quixotic biography, was my third screenplay attempt. It had all the drama of real-life events that occurred on our summer visit, with fictional fireworks added in the mix that paralleled Lizamara's past. In the screenplay I made a villain out of her Uncle Billy, who faced a fitting fate at the bottom of the Santiago volcano that immortalized her moniker. I was totally fascinated by Nicaragua, the places I had been and seen. To witness life in a Third World Country for the first time was such a shock to me. I wanted my screenplay to convey that feeling, a young American guy thrust into a world he didn't quite understand, dealing with a wife he didn't understand on her turf.

Finally, my fourth and final screenplay, entitled "The Big Lie," featured a character based on Dan as the protagonist. This was the script Dan quoted in one of the puzzle pieces in the ceramic artwork he gave me. His intimate relationship with his very young girlfriend Tami is a central part of the story, a dynamic that admittedly fascinated me. As I mentioned, it's part-murder mystery with scenes set in LA, Washington and New Orleans. The sad-sack character that stands in for me as Dan's best friend has a Black mistress in New Orleans and becomes a murder victim. I'm not sure what that said about my self-image at that point in my life. Lies…deceit…betrayal…murder… Oh my!

Here's an excerpt from "The Big Lie" screenplay, a dialogue between Jake and Denise — the characters based on Dan and Tami — taking place in their bathroom. I have some fun with their age difference in this scene:

Denise: I guess I'm just not old enough to understand how all this middle-age crisis stuff justifies Marty lying to his wife.

Jake: I think when people get older, they learn how to lie. It's part of that gray area that old farts like me notice a lot. When you're young, it's easier to see things in black and white. As you get older, you see more of the gray (runs his hand through his partially gray hair). You see a lot more gray.

Denise: *I see less and less gray on you.*
Jake: *(Laughs) Even that's a result of a lie!*
Denice: *Why's that a lie?*
Jake: *I don't know. I guess I consider any unnatural alteration of one's appearance to be a lie (applys a dab of Grecian Formula into his hair in front of the bathroom mirror), Not all lies are bad! (Laughs again.)*
Denise: *I don't know. If learning to lie is a matter of turning gray, and the ability to lie is a matter of seeing the gray, does it necessarily mean you're wiser?*
Jake: *More to the point, it means that the more gray matter you develop between the ears, the more gray matters.*

Both "Santiagatita and "The Big Lie" received some favorable reviews as entries in screenwriting contests conducted by the Screenwriters Association of Santa Barbara. "Santiagatita" earned second-place honors and "The Big Lie" garnered third place in a separate year.

For a couple of years in the '90s I actually had an agent, who supposedly was pitching my screenplays around Hollywood. I got a nice collection of rejection notes. After a couple of years with this guy I received a letter from a law firm. The "agent" turned out to be something of a scam artist. Me and a few hundred other screenwriter hopefuls each gave him $200, supposedly to cover mailing costs for scripts sent out to movie production teams. The letter stated that the agent's license had been revoked and he was out of business. Just like that, I no longer had an agent.

————◆————

I guess I've always been somewhat of a "ham." My sister could tell you stories from our youth to support that notion.

Acting always loomed as an interest. Those Perry Mason courtroom-drama plays I wrote for me to star in fifth grade were an early sign.

I took a couple of acting classes that were too much fun in college, one at Santa Barbara City College and another at Cal State Fullerton. I learned pretty quickly that acting classes tended to attract a fair share of pretty girls. I was able to interact with a bunch of them. Yeah, I could see me doing this acting thing for a living.

On a whim I signed up for another acting class at Santa Barbara City College in 1998, when I was 44. I was roughly twice the age of about everybody else in the class, except for the teacher. I was probably acting out some sort of middle-age crisis at the time. This was at a rough time in my life. Maggie and I had separated and I needed a creative diversion.

The acting teacher, Maggie Mixsell, was awesome. I eagerly responded to her creative assignments that tested all five of our senses — sight, touch, feel, hearing, smell. She gave me a lot of personal encouragement, helping me overcome the fear factor in performing before a live audience.

The fear started to fade with an assignment Maggie gave me to create a fictitious monologue explaining why I was eight minutes late for class. So I came up with this excuse about needing to stop to pick up a prescription for my 108-year-old grandmother.

Another improvised performance that was well received was my portrayal of a guy checking out a beautiful young woman in a bookstore. I was given one line to work with, repeating over and over: "I'm not staring." I mixed in every emotion I could think of using that line — startled, nervous, determined not to stare, staring intently, angry, pleading, distracted while holding a book upside down, embarrassed while conspicuously peaking around the corner down the aisle. I found it easy to relate to "I'm not staring" from real-life scenarios.

Among my classmates, I seemed to connect best with a young Black woman named Tammy. We acted out one assignment that had the class roaring with laughter. The repetition concept was applied to the performance, in that we each had one line we had to repeat, playing off each other, working it on as many angles as we could spontaneously come up with. My line was: "I just need to hear you say you still care for me." Hers was: "I'm not sure I can say that." I focused on her expressive eyes and responded accordingly. We fed off each other and it felt real. Afterward, when I analyzed what I had done, I found that I only had a vague memory of it; as if — duh! — I got completely into character. Then when I came out of it the moment was gone, as if it belonged to someone else. It was an extraordinary feeling.

My final monologue was a five-minute speech I had to memorize from Sam Shepard's play, "Buried Child." I was playing a young man harboring some very dark family secrets, who had been driving all night and was very drunk and very despondent. Maggie liked the prop I added, using a menacing knife that I held to my neck. She complimented me afterward for my "exposed vulnerability."

I think I needed that acting class to expose that vulnerability in me.

——————◆——————

I did have one flickering shot at Hollywood fame, at least in my ego-driven imagination. It all started with an 8x10 flyer posted on a bulletin board at the Las Positas Tennis Club where I was playing with my News-Press colleague, Dave Loveton. The flyer was announcing a casting call for local extras to work in the filming of the movie called "Steal Big Steal Little," set to be released in the spring of 1995. The casting call asked those interested to send in photographs of ourselves, which we did.

Nearly four months later, we both got calls from the casting company asking if we were available for a two-day shoot in the Santa Ynez Valley, starting "tomorrow." Each day required up to 12 hours of our time, and the pay was $5 an hour, which was minimum pay at the time. We were both in.

The obvious purpose of the film was to showcase the Santa Barbara area and feature some of its cultural flair. Director Andrew Davis, who lived in the Santa Barbara area, wanted to cinematically show off his hometown.

Davis had made his mark in the film business a couple of years earlier directing the movie "The Fugitive," the feature film version of the TV show. In the movie, Harrison Ford played the Dr. Richard Kimble part that David Janssen had made memorable in the long-running TV series.

"The Fugitive" was a good movie. "Steal Big Steal Little," not so much.

"Steal Big Steal Little" starred Andy Garcia playing twins — one good and the other evil — which was not the most original plot idea ever conceived. The best part of the movie was the closing credits, featuring Garcia in real life, dancing to salsa music while leading the way in Santa Barbara's extremely popular, colorful, irreverent Solstice Parade through the center of town on State Street.

The scenes for which Dave and I were recruited were being shot at Live Oak Park in the Santa Ynez Valley, recreating the annual Los Rancheros Vistadores involving real-life local horseback riders. I wrote a feature story about the Rancheros Vistadores for the News-Press, chronicling the annual week-long ride through the back trails of the scenic Santa Ynez Valley by its exclusively male club. The ride dates way back to 1930, and the hundred-plus riders it attracted every year had included a Who's Who of Santa Barbara County, such as Tom Storke, longtime News-Press publisher; and Dwight Murphy, name-sake of Dwight Murphy soccer fields in SB. Famous guest riders over the years included the likes of Walt Disney, Gene Autry, Edgar Bergen, Clark Gable, and Ronald Reagan before he became president.

Dave and I were told we would be portraying "food servers" at a wild cowboy bash during an overnight camp site at one of the ranches along the route. That ego-deflating notion dashed any dreams of instant Hollywood stardom, with the realization that the casting company took one look at my photo and immediately thought, "food server."

Dave L.. a k a "The Limping Cowboy," and me on the set of the film "Steal Big Steal Little"

Dave and I were instructed to show up the next morning at El Capitan State Beach, about 30 miles west of Santa Barbara off the 101 freeway. About 20 extras gathered there for the hour-long bus ride into Santa Ynez Valley at Live Oak Park. We were told to wear cowboy boots, if we happened to own a pair. I had a pair, but Dave didn't. At the last minute, he hastily stopped at a thrift store to buy himself a pair. Dave's a big guy— he stood about 6-foot-4 and 280 pounds then, with size 12 feet. He couldn't find a pair of size 12 boots at the store. He settled for a size 11 pair, which he lived to regret. For the entire one-hour bus ride to Live Oak Park, I watched Dave grunt and groan trying to force those size 11 cowboy boots on his size 12 feet, which was pretty funny. Now, if the script had called for a "limping cowboy" role, Dave would have been perfectly fit for the part by the time we arrived at the set.

The first day was scheduled for a noon-to-midnight schedule. Costume check-in was the first order of the day. I brought four changes of shirts as I was instructed to bring. But none of those shirts saw the light of day in front of the camera. Instead, we were handed identical, God-awful, flannel plaid cowboy shirts with burnt orange trim on the sleeves, collar and pockets. Burnt orange, yuck! Yet, I had to admit burnt orange made sense for food servers at a cowboy bash — it made you think of barbecue sauce. The final touch to our gauche attire were the lovely brown aprons.

When it was time for "Action!", Dave and I were split up. I was coupled with another food server, a young man named Vincent, who shared my predilection for mischievousness during the rest of the shoot. In our creative imaginations, stardom was within our grasp.

The set for the movie's cowboy party scenes included a makeshift wooden stage, a couple of campfires, hay bales spread out everywhere, three large, Old West-relic wooden carts, and plenty of beer kegs.

For the first scene, Vincent and I were handed an empty ice chest, and we were directed to carry it together across the set, pretending as if it was heavy. So, we were being asked to do some real "acting" with that make-believe heavy ice chest. Here was my chance to shine. Never mind that the focus of the camera was way beyond us, locked in on a pack of Vistadores riders charging in from an open field.

I thought I might catch the assistant director's attention with my over-the-top grunting and grimacing — Brando-esque improv acting on display — while carrying that really heavy ice chest. I did catch somebody's attention, but not for the reason I had hoped. After the first couple of takes, the costume designer pulled me aside and told me to hide the large comb sticking out of my back pocket.

I could just picture the assistant director throwing down his headphones in disgust and yelling out, "Cut! Damn it!! We had the *perfect* take ruined by that damned food server with the comb sticking out of his back pocket!"

I think the comb reprimand threw off my focus. For the second scene, Vincent and I were given a big, empty kettle to haul, replacing the ice chest, and evidently we forgot our initial instruction. This time we drew the notice of the assistant director, who drew us aside and quipped, "You know, that pot is supposed to be heavy." Take two!

Again, Vincent and I were mere background filler carrying that kettle. Instead, the camera was zoomed in on the boisterous arrival of hookers at the cowboy party.

With each succeeding take, it seemed that Vincent and I were placed further back, back, back into the background, gradually being reduced to burnt-orange specks on screen. We wondered just how far out of the scene we could be positioned in each succeeding take. By Take No. 8, we imagined the assistant director saying to us, "Here's two bus tickets to Solvang a few miles down the road. Take the pot with you. We'll phone you at the bus station when we yell 'Action!' That's your cue to start walking in with the pot. Walk fast or you may miss dinner."

Vincent and I were pretty sure we were miscast as food servers. We suspected Andy Garcia felt a little insecure with two good-looking food servers grabbing all the attention on the set, especially me with that scene-stealing comb in my back pocket.

For our own amusement, we created our own imagined scene for the movie— a wild orgy between the hookers and food servers in which those burnt orange-trimmed shirts would come flying off. Just our luck, we weren't allowed anywhere near Director Andrew Davis to pitch this great idea.

During shooting of the third scene, I got a chance at redemption when the camera guy asked me to pull a couple of cowboys out of view of the camera. After "Cut!" was announced to end the scene, the camera guy told me, "Thank you. You saved it." I saved it! I think that made up for the comb in my back pocket.

As nighttime arrived, I was allowed to put on a denim jacket and cover up that garish food server shirt. For the next couple of scenes I was instructed to parade around as an actual cowboy. For the record, that meant Andy Garcia, who was playing twins, wasn't the only one called on to portray dual roles; likewise, my talents were being diversified between interchangeable roles as food server and cowboy.

I liked playing cowboy. It didn't last long (sigh). I admit I got jealous of Dave in the final scene of the night when he continued his auspicious role of "limping cowboy," happily winding sparklers in the air as the party scene turned raucous. Meanwhile, I was relegated back to my thankless role as food server with Vincent, with the critical instruction from the assistant director: "Move pots." Vincent and I came up with a gimmick routine that didn't get the full appreciation it deserved — while I removed pots from a stove and loaded them onto a cart, Vincent would pick up the same pots from the cart and load them up back on the stove. It was a head-scratching circular skit straight out of the Laurel and Hardy playbook.

By all rights, we shouldn't have been invited back for the second night, but we were. The second 12-hour shoot was scheduled for 5 pm through to —gulp!— 5 am. Bring the No-Doze.

On the bus ride from El Capitan Beach to the set, Dave realized he forgot the long black coat he had worn through all the scenes shot on the first day. He worried incessantly that somebody would notice. Funny thing, but when we checked into costume design at the set, the costume supervisor looked us over and actually said, "Just checking to make sure you guys look exactly the same as you did yesterday." Dave, evidently, made quite an impression the first day in that long black coat. Meanwhile, I made sure I showed the supervisor the comb in my back pocket.

There was a lot of down time on the second night. Dave, Vincent and I sat around on some hay bales while the prop guys were setting up the first scene. As we sat there, a horse named Banana wandered over within an arm's length of Dave's left shoulder. Dave, looking to his right, was totally oblivious, until...

"Why does it smell like horseshit all of a sudden?" he announced.

I had to point out Banana hovering just over his left shoulder for him to take notice, clueing him in on the mystery of the sudden foul smell. That triggered a series of side bets among the three of us over who would be the first to accidentally step into Banana's contribution to the set. My money was on the limping cowboy.

With more time to kill, a stirring debate was instigated over the half-filled bottles of Corona and half-filled keg cups as requisite props in the hands of the partying cowboys — real beer or non-alcoholic beer? We concluded that since some of the extras were real Santa Ynez ranchers and cowboys, they were drinking the real stuff. We assumed that they understood that this was a BYOB party.

Finally, shooting of the first scene of the night was ready to go. Actor David Ogden Stiers, best known for his role as the snobbish Dr. Charles Emerson Winchester on the TV series "M*A*S*H," was playing a corrupt judge, and actor Charlie Rocket was playing a corrupt sheriff. They were both in full display on the makeshift stage, overlooking the campfires and Old West carts. The two actors were gaudily dressed in outrageous drag as a pair of slurpy drunks, spitting out really bad jokes for a rowdy, drunken cowboy crowd.

Vincent and I were allowed to play cowboys again for this scene. We were stationed on top of one of the old wooden carts, cavorting in all manner of drunkenness. After the first two takes, we were stunned when one of the "hookers" sauntered over and joined us in the cart.

"I was told to come over here and start flirting with you guys," she said as she cuddled up between us.

Vincent leaned over and whispered to me, "Maybe this would be a good time to suggest the orgy scene."

We wished we could have worked on that scene all night. But moving on to the second scene, Vincent and I were back to being food servers and told once again to "move pots."

One of the assistants actually came over to us and said, "The scene doesn't work without you. Believe me." In the world of make-believe, we believed him. For a couple of smart-asses like Vincent and me, we took some ad-lib liberties in our food server roles. We repeatedly re-enacted a Steve Young-to-Jerry Rice pass with a two-day-old, aluminum-wrapped baked potato in the background of the scene, which was, again, pure stroke-of-genius comedy going unnoticed.

At near midnight it was time to break for dinner. The pay may have sucked, but we were well-fed. A really long line formed at the buffet-row for food, which wasn't ready to serve right away, so there was a long wait.

As luck would have it, I was standing in line directly behind the star of the film, Andy Garcia, and one of the ladies playing a hooker.

Then, standing directly behind me, dressed in a floor-length maroon velvet dress and matching wig for the drag scene he just performed, was David Ogden Stiers, who stood an imposing 6-foot-3. The long maroon dress just made it all the more intimidating,

The line was at a standstill. Garcia noticed Stiers standing behind me and they struck up a conversation. It was very awkward because I was right in the middle, hearing every word they were saying as they talked about directors they had worked for, what so-and-so agent said about this and that, blah-blah-blah; industry talk. So I gestured to Stiers to move ahead of me in line.

"Oh no," he said, insisting on remaining behind me, Well, that was no good, because I was feeling increasingly uncomfortable as the conversation rambled on.

So, I took evasive action beginning with a very discreet side-step. Then, ever so slowly, I inched my way around Stiers' wide maroon dress without him noticing, until I settled behind him in line. I breathed a sigh of relief.

But relief was momentary. The line finally began to move forward, and when Stiers stepped ahead, much to my horror I realized that the hem of his dress was pinned under the toe of my cowboy boot, causing a tug that stopped him in his tracks.

Stiers whirled around, his eyes piercing down at my guilty toe, and with mock indignation, he growled, "How dare you!"

As a goofy, embarrassed look spread over my face, he then pointed at me and said, "Say, weren't you just ahead of me a few minutes ago?" God no, I didn't want to move back ahead of him!

Stiers and Garcia stared at me with grins on their faces to see what I was going to say to get out of this fix.

"Well," I stuttered, my mind racing. "I was admiring your dress so much that I wanted to get a view of it from the rear."

That drew a laugh out of them. What woman — or guy in drag — doesn't appreciate a compliment on what they're wearing? I was off the hook and allowed to stay behind them in line.

After dinner, it was back in front of the cameras. The next scene had all of us cowboys lined up in rows alongside an entry road, standing with hats off out of respect for somebody who had just died and was being hauled off into a waiting ambulance. Veteran character actor Kevin McCarthy, playing a corrupt rich guy, delivered a brief, irreverent, insincere eulogy, and then declared that partying could resume as soon as the ambulance drove away.

The clock ticked toward 2 a.m. for this scene, when temperatures dipped into the mid-30s on the brisk mid-March morning. This elicited some under-the-breath cursing and unflattering comments among cowboys about the dead stiff being eulogized.

The guy who had reason to curse the most was poor Stiers, who was required to vomit from drinking too much in the follow-up scene. During the first few takes he expended an impressive amount of saliva. But by Take No. 11, he was running dry. "Is it all right if I don't do this anymore?" he muttered to the director. He was expected to do it at least four more times.

After that, everybody huddled around the two huge bonfires in campfire pits to get warm. I felt especially bad for the scantily clad hookers.

Even Andy Garcia, the star of the movie, joined in with the rest of us, rubbing his hands in front of the campfire. He was gracious enough to pose with Dave and I standing behind him for a photo that another "extra" snapped on my camera.

Garcia's graciousness didn't end there. I made a ballsy move. I knew that Garcia was Hispanic, born in Cuba. So at 4 in the morning in front of that campfire, I stirred up the nerve to pitch my screenplay "Santiagatita" to him, explaining that it takes place in Nicaragua, and that the script offered an opportunity for numerous leading roles for Hispanics. He gave me an address of a production company he was associated with to send a copy of the script. I was so stoked and grateful. (I received a very polite rejection note in response.)

By 4:30 a.m., when every bone in our bodies ached from the night chill, we loaded up on the bus for the ride back to El Capitan Beach. For those of us still awake on Vivarin, we watched the sun rise over the horizon, basking in the burnt orange memories of ill-fitting boots, back-pocket combs, imagined orgy scenes, the smell of horseshit, stepping on maroon hemlines, and moving pots.

———◆———

Two 12-hour-day shoots amounted to about two-and-a-half minutes of screen time in "Steal Big Steal Little" when the final cut was released in theaters.

Actor Andy Garcia, sitting, enjoys the warmth of a cozy bonfire in the cold, wee AM hours of filming for "Steal Big, Steal Little." Dave and I are standing directly behind Garcia

And for about three seconds, I could be seen in one scene.

I was clearly visible in the scene in which Stiers was vomiting from drinking too much. I'm standing all alone, in cowboy hat and long hair and beard, reacting ever so slightly — not overplaying it in the least — to Stiers bent over and throwing up. Oscar-worthy performance, I have to say. I was talking about Stiers, of course.

I swear, there were about 15 or 16 takes of that one scene, and the one they chose for the movie was the only take featuring me in the background. I was a dark, undefined speck in all the other takes. Now, you tell me... well, there must have been some reason why they chose that particular take. Hollywood, your star-in-the-making was right there in plain sight.

————————◆————————

I recently rewrote lyrics to a song I composed in the late 1990s, which I think presents an example of how my lyric writing improved. These lyrics set the tone for the upcoming chapter:

376

The name of the song is "One Step Away."

Swe-e-e-e-t
Sweet memories of you
Dre-e-e-ams
Dreams were dreamt but never came true
Saw the white light
Then it turned blue
Love drifted out the door
But left its residue

Wh-e-r-r-r-e
Do birds in flight go to
Wh-y-y-y-y
Can't tides sit still for a minute or two
Passions rise then die
Must start anew
While trying to connect the dots
From what, why and who

Falling in love
Means you're one step a-w-a-a-a-y
From heaven or heartache
Which way is hard to say

L-i-i-i-fe
Life's a curious game
L-o-o-ove
Love is sweet but never the same
A what-went-wrong song
Same sad refrain
Then when the music fades
The search starts again

Falling in love
Means you're one step a-w-a-a-a-y
From heaven or heartache
There's always hope someday

---◆---

A few chapters ago, I alluded to a train wreck coming. No, it had nothing to do with Miami. This was it.

---◆---

CHAPTER 21
The Folly of Fatherhood
and Farewells

It's difficult to put a finger on it, but motherhood changed Maggie. And it wasn't in a good way, with respect to our marriage.

Having her mother live with us was a blessing. She didn't speak a word of English, but that was OK, "Mama" and I got along fine. She was great with the baby. We didn't ask her to, but she took it upon herself to clean our house. That's just what she did, she cleaned house, and she liked it.

That made life easier for Maggie. But the changes I'm talking about were subtle. She wanted everything for Tessa. She expected no less from me.

Therein lie the rub as applied with Kasey. He was coming up to Santa Barbara once a month, sometimes twice. I was making the drive to LA and back to pick him up and take him back home. I put in plenty of miles up and down the 101 on those drives.

Maggie and I proposed to Gail that we would be willing to take Kasey twice a month to give Gail an extra weekend free, in return for a $50 break on child support, reducing it to $300 per month. In Maggie's eyes, that was $50 more that could be spent on our daughter.

A few chapters ago, I alluded to a train wreck coming. No, it had nothing to do with Miami. This was it.

Gail categorically rejected our proposal. Our response was, in retrospect, a bad misstep. We —I — unilaterally reduced the child support by sending only a $300 check to Gail. I accepted full responsibility for that decision.

This really pissed Gail off. She responded by hiring a lawyer.

So now it was all-out war. I sought out a lawyer who specialized in representing fathers in child custody cases. He listened to my dispute over child support and was very sympathetic. Then he made the case to broaden the court battle over custody.

This is what lawyers do. They stoke the fires. But I was feeling the heat on the home front, too. My wife was ready for battle and encouraged me to dig in.

In a matter of a couple months, I was served papers filed in Los Angeles County Superior Court by Gail's lawyer to resolve child support. My lawyer, to be fair, didn't get carried away with wild promises. He advised me that the custody case was probably a long shot. But on the matter of child support, based on the court formula that would take into account Gail's total income from her two jobs, my income, and Maggie's income (which irritated the hell out of her, but those were the rules as applied to household income), we felt fairly confident that the judge would render an amount closer to the $300 per month that we sought. The formula also factored in the amount of visitation time with Kasey, which we were seeking to increase to validate the support reduction. The child support and visitation issues were linked.

Raise your hand if you think this did not end well for me.

This is where I present a picture of my ass, with life taking bite out of it. We had a September court date six weeks in advance, with all of the data we needed to present our case— everybody's income and expenses, cost and mileage of the drives from Santa Barbara to LA and back, records of child support payments to date, etcetera, etcetera.

When we walked into court for our much-anticipated hearing, my lawyer was summoned by the judge for a private meeting in the judge's chambers. After about forty-five minutes, my lawyer reappeared with a very glum look on his face. He handed me a court document that had bad news written all over it.

I read over the document in utter disbelief. A prison sentence was the only verdict I could conceive that could have been worse. The document, written out in barely legible, hastily hand-written words, spelled out a monthly child support order of $550 per month, good until said child turns 18, plus an additional $275 per month for 18 months to cover plaintiff's (Gail) attorney costs. The total sum of $825 per month would be automatically garnished from my wages over 18 months followed by garnishments of $550 to continue until Kasey's 18th birthday.

My lawyer meekly offered this explanation:

"This is the best offer I could get for you, under the circumstances."

My head was ready to explode. What had changed?

"Well…" my lawyer began, "It seems the plaintiff was laid off from her primary job just a couple weeks ago."

That completely changed the math in the court formula for

child support. Not to mention strengthening the hardship case to shift the burden of Gail's attorney costs to me. Gotta make sure her lawyer got paid.

I could not believe what I was hearing. Two weeks ago? And they didn't bother reporting that little piece of news to us until today? Hmm, this coming from the same woman who didn't disclose she was pregnant until she was 14 or 16 weeks along. I felt like we were absolutely ambushed, given no chance to prepare.

"But we can still appeal, and file for custody," my brilliant lawyer offered.

The "only" consolation out of the whole deal was on visitation. I was accorded one weekend per month, and Gail was ordered to make the drive halfway coming and going to hand Kasey over to me. Yahoo.

The war was over quickly, as quickly as Poland surrendered to Germany at the start of WWII. There was no "appeal." In fact, when I tried to call my lawyer a couple of weeks after our bitter court hearing, I was told he had come down with a "sudden, undisclosed illness," and that there was no determination if/when he might return to his practice.

"Sudden, undisclosed illness." Life is full of sudden, unexpected surprises. Kinda like train wrecks.

I won't say that Gail resented me for not marrying her, even when my track record suggested I appeared to be up to marrying just about anyone. But she definitely made it hard on my marriage to Maggie in the aftermath of our disastrous child support court battle.

Make no mistake, Maggie despised Gail as a consequence.

That sentiment reverberated in Kasey's monthly visitations. Maggie's affections toward Kasey tapered off conspicuously.

Kasey was already exhibiting signs of a troubled childhood. The child support court battle broke out in the aftermath of the school year, in which Kasey had to repeat first grade. He was held back a full year because he exhibited some learning disabilities, specifically with respect to reading. Seeing his parents engaged in open warfare couldn't have made it any easier for him at school. Then the sudden, cooling shift in attitude coming from his stepmother must've exasperated his fragile psyche. As his father, I did the best I could to make him feel loved and part of our home. But I could do only so much.

Meanwhile, Maggie was going through a tough postpartum phase. Three months after she had returned from maternity leave, she got fired from her job. Her female supervisor didn't like her. Maggie put up a stink, claiming discriminatory termination. I helped her write up her statement, her response to the termination. It wasn't pleasant. It did not end well for Maggie.

Gail and I set our designated meeting place for picking up and dropping off Kasey at a Wendy's restaurant in Newbury Park, which was calculated to be the halfway point between her home in Redondo Beach and mine in Santa Barbara. Gail didn't always live up to her end of the bargain, forcing me to make the full return trip on rare occasions, which bugged the shit out of Maggie. It didn't take much to do that at this point.

One weekend proved to be a sobering turning point. Once again, Gail was unavailable for the regularly scheduled pick-up on Saturday, so I agreed to make the full drive to Redondo Beach on Friday to get Kasey, thereby picking up an extra night with him. On this occasion she agreed to even things out by making the full drive to Santa Barbara on Sunday to pick him up.

This had all the makings of a combustible explosion, as Maggie was a very short fuse away from igniting. She was fed up with accommodating Gail's changing schedule.

When Gail showed up at our front door that Sunday afternoon, the match was lit on that fuse. I'm not sure how it started, because I was back in the TV room with Kasey when I heard the knock on the front door. Maggie answered.

I could hear some angry words being exchanged between the two mothers of my children. The next thing I knew, I heard one of them screaming outside the house. Mama, Max and I were all simultaneously running to the front door, which was left wide open. From the doorway, we all stood there with mouths wide open, Max with drooling tongue hanging out. We were witnessing a surreal scene — Maggie was dragging Gail by the hair across the sidewalk in front of our house, like a rag doll!

Desperately, I dashed out to the sidewalk, pleading for Maggie to let go of Gail. (Although, deep down, I was feeling some vicarious joy from this scene.) Max was in close pursuit, anxiously trying to help out any way he could. Maggie dropped Gail in a heap and stormed back in the house.

Thank God Kasey was spared the sight of his mother bearing the brunt of Maggie's rage. Gail rose from the ground, brushed herself off, and made some sort of threats that I don't even recall. I hurriedly gathered Kasey and his overnight bag and hustled him out of the house and into his mother's car.

It was so unlike Gail not to call the police. She drove off. I went back inside, where Mama was sitting next to her distraught daughter on the living room couch, gently rubbing her back, while Maggie stroked her forehead with her hand.

Suffice to say, the storm blew over. But clouds hovered in the air, and the weather pattern determined more storms were in the forecast.

———————◆———————

No question Maggie resented the repercussions on our budget from the added child support and attorney fees. Nevertheless, she doted on our daughter, and she spared no expense celebrating Tessa's first birthday in a house party that included Mom, Pam, and Tessa's godmother Patty, the big-hearted woman who was Maggie's closest friend from her job at Samarkand.

But the party guest list didn't include Kasey.

The hair-pulling sidewalk incident with Gail just a month earlier created a veiled strain on Kasey's subsequent monthly visits.

It led to a terrifying, hair-raising incident with Maggie on one of Kasey's visits in mid-February, nearing our fifth anniversary date.

Kasey was in the back room watching TV while Maggie and I were in the kitchen, in hot discussion over something about his mother. Maggie was getting hotter, which was a bad sign.

Finally, she blurted, "I don't want Kasey staying in this house any longer."

I was stunned at what I was hearing. "What?!"

"You can go down to LA to see him. But I don't want him here."

I stopped, concentrating hard on what she was saying. I was rapidly listing all the pros and cons to my measured response. Finally,

I responded:

"No."

There was no way in hell I was going to let Maggie dictate whether my son was allowed in our home or not. I was standing my ground.

What happened next nearly made my heart stop. Maggie grabbed a large steak knife from the knife cabinet hanging on the kitchen wall and turned to head down the hallway toward the back room. I followed in desperation. Then when she reached the back room, I stood my ground again between her holding that knife and Kasey on the couch.

I tried to gently talk her down. She backed off. But for a moment, I wasn't sure where her head was and I was scared.

I decided it was time to pack up Kasey's things and get him on the road to Wendy's in Newbury Park to meet his mother.

But the issue wasn't resolved. The knife incident was alarming enough to give me pause with respect to where Maggie and I were at in our marriage. I wasn't at the point of bailing chiefly because of Tessa; the last thing I wanted was to become a part-time father to her as I already was with Kasey.

But, as I had learned in more than one occasion in the past, some hard decisions are made for me. The Kasey issue — lets call it what it really was, the Gail issue — quickly evolved to rift level a few days later. Maggie reiterated her demand and basically made it a choice between my son and my daughter.

"It's my way or the highway," she said haughtily. "You choose, but I choose my daughter."

I told her that I couldn't choose. It was like asking me to choose which arm I wanted to cut off —my right or my left.

So she made the choice for me. By the end of the month, she, Tessa and her mama were all headed down the highway, moving back to LA.

———————◆———————

Something just died in me, having my wife take my daughter away from me. My heart was being broken in Paradise, in March of 1996.

We filed for legal separation and hired an arbitrator, a woman, to settle all related financial and legal matters. Maggie was getting full custody of Tessa; I would be given standard paternal visitation rights. We worked out a child support figure of $480 per month. She signed off on the deed to the Santa Barbara house for a payment of a few thousand dollars, amounting to half of the equity gained since we had purchased the house two-and-a-half years before.

The irony of this moment was not lost on me. Our union was a manifestation of mistaken identity — Maggie thought I was Jeff Bonior when we first met. Had she realized her mistake from the start, we would have never hooked up, and Tessa would have never been born. I realize now that I get caught up in these kind of life-twisting events in the moment they occur, as if they were pre-ordained to last forever, like in a fairytale. But life is not a fairytale.

So life moves on. Maggie and Tessa moved on to LA. I had already been rudely reminded that my connection with my kids was tenuous when Gail and Kasey moved to Tallahassee, Florida, to live with her brother for a few months. Kasey was in kindergarten at the time. Later I would be separated from my son for two whole years when they moved to Boston.

But the separation from my 1-year-old daughter was especially daunting. Fatherhood sucked. I was dying.

So it was, it seemed metaphorically fitting that death would emerge as a dark theme in my life by late summer in 1996. Two deaths, to be exact.

I had a story to finish on the climatic 1996 season of drag racer Blaine Johnson, the pride of Santa Maria. With the backing of his brother Alan as his crew chief, Blaine was well on his way toward achieving the impossible David vs. Goliath conquest. He had a comfortable points lead, beating teams with lots more sponsorship dollars to work with, in the seasonal championship race in drag racing's fastest category, top fuel dragsters. Entering the 16th stop on the 20-event schedule, the U.S. Nationals at Indianapolis Raceway Park on August 31, Johnson didn't have far to go to realize the dream.

That dream crumpled and went up in flames in a spectacular, fiery heap on the first day of qualifying. Johnson crashed after crossing the finish line at the end of his track record-breaking run, clocked at 4.61 seconds and 309 miles per hour. That almost equaled his NHRA record of 4.59 seconds on the quarter-mile strip. Eyewitness descriptions of the crash contained words like "disintegrated" with respect to the car, with Johnson inside. He was extracted from the driver's cage by the track rescue crew and helicoptered to the nearest hospital, where he was pronounced dead from massive head injuries.

He was 34, with a wife and nine-year-old son.

I was expecting to cover Blaine's crowning as king of the Top Fuel class at the season-ending World Finals at Pomona in October. Instead, I was assigned to cover his memorial service in Santa Maria. An overflow crowd of an estimated 1,200 attended at First Presbyterian Church in Santa Maria. It was easily the most emotional assignment of my career, the only memorial service I ever covered.

His older brother Alan, described as Blaine's "soul mate," told the congregation this of his brother: "He knew the risks of his sport, his chosen profession. He pursued a dream with me, our dad, our whole family, with great passion and commitment. He was on the gas all the time to be the best he could be."

Johnson's widow Kym led a 1,200-strong sing-along to the tribute song "One in A Million" for the gentle man she married.

The impact of Johnson's death loomed large on the NHRA circuit for the rest of the '96 season. Drivers in all racing categories displayed "In Memory of Blaine Johnson" stickers on their cars. When Kenny Bernstein won the Top Fuel title at the end of the season — Johnson still wound up fifth despite missing the last five events — Bernstein handed the championship trophy to Alan Johnson.

Interviewing Alan Johnson at Pomona Raceway after his brother Blaine made a 300-mph quarter-mile run in the family team's top fuel dragster

A little more than two weeks after Johnson died, another momentous passing led me to another memorial service — for Allan Malamud.

I don't think there has been anyone else in my life who has elicited such disparity of emotion toward them than Allan. When he called me into his office to advise me to look for another job early in my career, telling me he ranked me rock-bottom on the staff, I hated him with a passion. Then he pulled a complete turnaround a couple of months later, exhibiting sincere compassion for my anguish over my divorce, and gave me a new lease on life. I grew to respect and greatly admire him as someone I looked up to in my chosen profession.

So, I was sincerely saddened by the news that he had died of natural causes in his downtown LA apartment on September 16, at the age of 54.

I attended his service at Hillside Mortuary in Culver City and was accompanied by my not-quite three-year-old precocious daughter Tessa. I was exercising my visitation rights with her that day. Many of my old Her-Ex colleagues were in attendance. Numerous sports dignitaries paid their respects as well. Ex-Dodger manager Tommy Lasorda, ex-USC and LA Rams coach John Robinson, and boxer promoter Bill Caplan all delivered eulogies.

Malamud was a bigger-than-life figure, so it was a natural fit that he also blossomed as a part-time actor on the big screen, with credits in 17 movies. That included a small part in Martin Scorsese's classic "Raging Bull," on the life of boxer Jake LaMotta, which was right in Malamud's wheelhouse as an eventual posthumous inductee into the Boxing Hall of Fame.

But no one gave Malamud more screen time than his close friend, film director Ron Shelton, who cast him in cameo roles in many of his sports films, including "White Men Can't Jump," "Cobb," and "Tin Cup." Malamud's bit part in "White Men Can't Jump" was quite the gem. He played a rocket scientist appearing on the TV show "Jeopardy" who, when it came down to answering a crucial question to win the game, blanked out on a simple sports question. The correct answer, I believe, was "Who was Babe Ruth?" What do rocket scientists know about sports? The wink-wink joke was that the real Allan Malamud would have known the answer in a split second.

After the memorial service, Shelton, who had ties to Santa Barbara as a Westmont College grad, invited everybody in attendance to the spacious house overlooking the ocean in Pacific Palisades that he shared with his girlfriend, actress Lolita Davidovich. I chatted with Lolita for a few minutes. I think she was quite taken by my daughter climbing all over their patio furniture.

The memorial service was highlighted by classic stories about Allan and his love for food. He was always struggling with his weight and he often "tried" to go on diets that never lasted long. One story recalled a dinner order for the sports desk food run to Phillippe's, the downtown LA diner famous for its French-dip sandwiches. Allan asked if anybody wanted to split a sandwich with him. Everybody was thinking, wow, he was really sticking to his diet. Then he shrugged and decided, "Never mind, I'll have two sandwiches instead of one-and-a-half." The smirk on John Beyrooty's face said it all.

Allan had no love life that anybody knew about. His real passion was chocolate cake; he ate chocolate cake like it was his substitute for sex. For his 40th birthday, there was a large gathering at a restaurant in Chinatown in downtown LA, with about 50 people in attendance. Everybody was served a slice of chocolate cake for dessert. Every single slice of cake in that room was simultaneously passed down to Allan.

The highlight of the day at the memorial came when Beyrooty stepped up to the dais to re-tell a story about Allan that reached legendary status in the sports world. In my book, this may rank as the funniest story in this memoir.

First, some context. The story originated from a gathering by a bunch of sports writers, including Allan, at a restaurant one night on the road for some major sporting event. It was a large group, loosened up by a considerable consumption of alcohol. The topic going around the table was for each person to confess the worst thing they had ever done in their life. This was a chance for everyone to atone for their respective sin and wash away the shame.

Some pretty serious confessionals were offered from this bunch— cheating on a wife or girlfriend, cheating on taxes, pirating a video of a big league baseball game for public consumption without the express written consent of Major League Baseball. Scandalous! When it came to Allan's turn, the suspense was turned up a notch as everyone speculated on what despicable deed this shy man could have committed.

As Allan told it, shame was dripping off every word. He went for a walk in his downtown LA neighborhood. He came upon a bakery and his eyes latched onto a gorgeous-looking, decorative, chocolate cake in full view behind the large display window. Allan stopped in his tracks and stared at the cake, pining for it as if it were a beautiful woman.

Then he saw the white index card next to the base of the cake, with the written statement: "Reserved for Becky's 6-Year-old Birthday Party." Allan's shoulder's slumped in disappointment and he slowly turned away and began walking down the sidewalk.

Then he suddenly stopped, reversed course, and walked back to enter the bakery. He stepped up to the front counter and said to the attendant behind the counter:

"Hi, I'm Becky's uncle. I'm here to pick up her birthday cake."

— • • ◆ • • —

On the subject of people confessing sins, breaking Katya's heart felt like the worst thing I had ever done. I had not forgotten about her.

We had one phone conversation in November, 1989, shortly after the Her-Ex had closed. I was out of a job, and Maggie and I were still just barely acquainted. Out of the blue, I called Katya during this period. Two-and-a-half years had passed since we last spoke on the phone. She had forgiven me.

She had left Roberto by that time.

I could've gone back to Miami right then but the timing wasn't right. Not long after that call, I got the job in Santa Barbara. Then Maggie said "Yes" to moving with me, which, to be honest, I wasn't totally expecting her to say.

Nearly six years later, with Maggie and Tessa in LA, and I was left alone in Santa Barbara, I called Katya again. The tie between us had never been severed. This time, the timing seemed right. She was free to come visit me in Santa Barbara.

"Life's a curious game," I wrote in the lyrics of my song, "One Step Away." It's curious how life had made things feel so different in the nine years-plus that had transpired since Katya and I had last seen each other.

I think we both were hoping our reunion would recapture the magic of our magnificent Miami interlude nearly a decade earlier. But it was like trying to catch lightning in a bottle — rekindling the spark that had driven us to epic passion was nearly impossible to duplicate. After experiencing such an emotional high together, anything less than that would feel like a letdown.

For starters, she didn't look the same. She still had a slender physique, but her face appeared a little fuller. I know you're not supposed to let a change in one's appearance purportedly affect how you feel toward that person if you truly love them. They are still the same person inside and that is what you ultimately love about them, so the poets say.

Genuine affection did re-emerge. The sexual attraction was still there; we made love several times over several days. But it felt different, somehow. We had one memorable session that mimicked Maggie's and my favorite setting for love-making — in nature. We had gone for a hike up in the local mountains, along a stream on a typical, gorgeous Santa Barbara day, and we laid out a blanket in a secluded area off the side of the trail.

But that laid bare the underlying problem to our long-delayed reunion — Maggie. She was still very much in my thoughts and heart. So was Tessa. Our separation was still too fresh, and I was dearly missing my wife and daughter. Clearly, our "What-went-wrong song" hadn't fully played out.

Likewise, Katya's situation had changed. While she had divorced Roberto and had been free of him for a few years, she was free to date other men again. She clearly was still attractive.

Katya cut her visit to Santa Barbara short by a couple of days, which I took as a sign that something had changed between us. I was living with roommates by then, which probably made her a little uncomfortable. I think she also felt out of her element on the West Coast, and the idea of her moving there to live with me seemed daunting. She was eager to return home to her children. She asked for only one thing from me to take back to Miami with her — my photo album of our trip to Nicaragua in the summer of 1983, when we first met.

Katya returned to Miami and I never saw her again. She wound up marrying another man who was courting her. She did call to tell me the news, and she seemed very happy. That was that. I was happy for her. That's what mattered most — that she was finally happy. The happy ending didn't happen with me, like the fairytale ending I once envisioned.

Regrets? Maybe a few.

———————◆———————

I did some soul-searching after Katya's visit. I realized I wasn't in the same place I was nine years earlier, that I had changed, that I now had a daughter with a woman I loved. Separation hadn't changed that. The last thing I wanted to do was hurt Katya again with conflicted feelings toward another woman.

Maggie and Tessa may have been living down in LA, but the tie between us hadn't been completely severed. I was driving down to LA weekly to see Tessa. Nearly a year had passed since the infamous knife incident with Kasey, and the passing of time made it easier to forget all that. Maggie's "my-way-or-the-highway" attitude had softened since then.

Experiencing a little humility, which she wasn't used to, served to soften Maggie. In the beginning she and Tessa struggled mightily to take root in LA. For the first few months they were sleeping on the living room floor at the home of her sister Nora and husband, until Maggie found a job and could afford a modest apartment, in Burbank. Meanwhile, I had to rent out rooms to tenants in my home to cover the mortgage by myself and pay child support for both Tessa and Kasey.

Tessa was growing into that really cute stage. When Maggie worked in the daytime, Tessa and I spent a lot of time in nearby Griffith Park, riding the miniature train ride, the merry-go-round, and the gentle horseback rides in a small circle suitable for toddlers. Or I'd just let her loose, watching her in spurts of glee chase away flocks of birds grazing on grass. We hung out at the Park Observatory and took naps together in the Nissan Pathfinder that Maggie and I had leased together just before Tessa was born, intended as a family vehicle.

After about nine months, closing in on Christmas, Maggie and I were finding that absence had made our hearts grow fonder. The rift that had separated us — over Kasey — had not proved to be irreparable.

My kids Tessa and Kasey, posing in the backyard at the Rossburn house with our dog Max, were at the heart of the conflict that led to my separation with Maggie. For a short while, everything seemed squared between Maggie and I, until it wasn't

And Tessa was drawing us closer together. I sensed it when Maggie told me an amusing story that took place when she and Tessa were standing in line at the front counter of a thrift store. Maggie was holding Tessa in her arms when Tessa noticed a display of 4x6 framed pictures of Jesus at the counter. I still had the long hair and beard that I wore six years earlier on our wedding day. Tessa pointed to the picture of Jesus and shouted, "Daddy!"

Maggie and I realized we still longed for each other. At the turn of the new year heading into 1997, the still-palpable physical attraction between us kicked in, and we soon resumed as lovers, for a while. Now I was driving to LA to see both Tessa and Maggie.

When our relationship warmed up, the arrangement seemed to be working out better for me than it was for Maggie. I had my house filled with roommates paying me rent and I could make the drive to LA anytime I wanted to see Maggie and Tessa. Maggie got a slight upgrade in wages with another job, had her mother to help her care for Tessa, and was close to the rest of her family in the LA area. I was in no hurry to change my roommate situation, which would have been complicated.

Maggie and I were in limbo between LA and Santa Barbara. As time stretched to over a year-and-a-half from our initial separation, I was still content with how things were working out, and I thought Maggie was, too.

I was wrong.

With the holiday season approaching, totally out of nowhere, Maggie told me she wanted to finalize our divorce. The reason — she had met a guy who had asked her to marry him. She had accepted his proposal.

I was floored. Heaven flipped to heartache in one fell swoop. I had no idea that she was seeing another guy. His name was Bill. Evidently he was somebody she had known before she knew me. It was a fairly quick romance— they had become reacquainted about three months earlier.

So I was headed for divorce No. 4.

I met Bill. He was tall, about the same height as Jeff Bonior, minus the long hair and beard. He seemed to be a nice-enough guy. He owned a home in Alhambra, so he was providing a good home for Maggie and Tessa. In retrospect, I can say that *that* was what Maggie was angling for out of the marriage.

But I'm not going to sugarcoat it. When it was all said and done, I found myself bawling my eyes out in my car driving back home from LA, faced with the prospect of being a four-time divorcee before my 45th birthday.

(From top): Janice in the New Orleans hotel lobby where we stayed; Janice chatting with the saxophone player who serenaded her with a Barry White song in downtown New Orlean; Janice in front of the Robert E. Lee statue in New Orleans' Franklin Square

CHAPTER 22
We'll Always Have New Orleans

A couple years after Kasey was born, Janice gave birth to a daughter in Mississippi. Her name was Cori.

The father was some French guy who didn't hang around. I don't know anything about him, didn't want to know.

Janice may have been a thousand or so miles away but she never drifted far from me. She always yearned to return to California. In the summer of 1992 she did, and I briefly met Cori as a toddler during their stay at the Sea Sprite Motel in Hermosa Beach.

Cori was a *doll*. She was tiny and she had a wild set of reddish curls that would rival Shirley Temple. I was smitten.

Then in the summer of 1994, when Maggie was pregnant with Tessa, they made a return trip to California. This time Janice wanted to spend some time in Santa Barbara. Brian, the guy who carried an unrequited torch for Janice, was Cori's godfather. He booked Janice and Cori a room in the very expensive El Encanto Hotel. The visit was coordinated on a weekend when I had Kasey. Janice wanted to reunite Cori with Kasey from their California visit in '92, when the kids seemed to hit it off right away.

Janice adored Kasey, who was seven, and Cori was five in '94. We took the kids to the beach and they picked right where they left off from two years earlier. They looked so cute playing together. Janice and I smiled together watching them play.

"Can't you just see those two together when they grow up?" Janice mused. "I can tell Cori really likes Kasey. She's already told me she wants to marry him."

I gave Janice that knowing look for what she was hinting at. "What if" scenarios from the past resurfaced. We were bonding again through our children.

The problem was, I was already married, with another child on the way. But for one sunny day on the beach in Santa Barbara, Janice and I were allowed to dream on a pleasant "What if" that our kids brought to the forefront.

I didn't ask her any questions about Cori's father. I knew she didn't want to tell me anything about him. It just didn't feel right to bring it up, because what we had between us superseded everything else.

Janice was just so at ease, so at peace, to be in California again, to be by the sea. She had escaped Mississippi once; I could tell she wanted to escape it again. Deep inside, I wished that I was in a position to help her.

Young Cori and Janice at the El Encanto Hotel in Santa Barbara

———————————◆•◆•◆———————————

"New Orleans is a city of eccentrics. For those sons and daughters of the Confederacy who chose not to follow the traditional path of life, death, Junior League and Country Club, it's the place to be. New Orleans is a melting pot of food and mood, of mud and blood, and where the Caribbean begins or ends, depending on your point of view."

Sign in Jimmy Buffet's "Margaritaville" bar in New Orleans

New Orleans is a special town and it holds a particularly special place in my heart, because of Janice.

I uncovered a journal I kept of a trip we took to New Orleans, a journal I kept obviously because I wanted to bottle every magical moment for posterity.

It was the fall of 1996. Maggie had left me, and took Tessa with her, nine months earlier. Katya had come out to visit me that summer, but that didn't take hold. I was still drifting, aimlessly.

So it didn't take me long to circle back to Janice.

She was still in Mississippi, living in a farmhouse. We were talking on the phone. I had always wanted to see New Orleans. Janice wanted to show me New Orleans, and she was still harboring a desire to go someplace "excitin'" with me as we had talked about a decade earlier. We decided to meet in New Orleans in mid-November.

With the blessing of Julie, the mom with three kids of her own who lived next door and agreed to take care of Cori, Janice was freed up to meet me. I flew in from LA with an arrival time that coordinated with Janice's arrival from Vicksburg. I arrived on time, Janice was 25 minutes late, which was par for the course for Janice.

I rented a car. We headed for downtown. We wasted no time getting my first taste of beignets, washed down with coffee at Cafe du Monde. Is there anything more heavenly than a fluffy, powder sugar-coated beignet in New Orleans?

We cruised down Bourbon Street. I was dazzled by the aged, historic French Quarter architecture.

We stopped in a bar, where I got propositioned by a man in his 50s in the men's restroom. "Nothing better than a good pee" was his opening line. I hastily finished up my pee and got back to Janice.

We smoked a joint and walked around a bit on Bourbon Street. Along the way we ran into "Chicken Man," a skinny black guy with dreadlocks and missing teeth who was a lot higher than we were and tried to sell us one of his voodoo dolls.

We got back in our car to start our search for our hotel, the Olivier Hotel on Toulousse Street, located one block off of Bourbon Street. Smoking the joint did not aid our search, as we drove around the block four times before we found the hotel. That was OK. We were having fun.

Then when we checked into our very charming room, we took one look and it was an immediate turn-on. You can guess what happened next.

We slept in the next morning and were awakened by squawking parrots outside our bedroom window at 11:30 am. The parrots were part of the hotel decor.

When we finally decided to start our day, we walked to La-fayette Square. We went inside a cathedral at the Square. Inside the church, Janice lit a candle for Cori.

Lunch at Boulangerie consisted of spinach quiche, apple danish and coffee. Then we wandered into Jackson Square, where a saxophonist named Jay crooned a Barry White song for Janice: *"You tell me this, you tell me that..."* It seemed everywhere Janice went, she attracted attention.

We found ourselves by the river near dusk, where we gazed upon a floating sculpture called "Ocean's Song." It consisted of 15-foot-tall triangular mirrors as backdrops to four stainless steel rings, each four feet in diameter, suspended by wires with five three-foot-long steel rods per ring. When the wind kicked up, the rings rotated, but the air and rings remained still on this night. A sign below explained the "wave physics" of the sculpture, serving as a *"symbol of American dreams from sky labs to skyscrapers, dreams made of stainless steel."*

We drifted back toward town, where we were stopped by an energetic young black woman who read our palms. When she was reading my palm, Janice pointedly told her, "You can talk to him, but he's mine." I blushed and felt loved. Possessiveness never was in the equation between Janice and me, but I wanted to feel possessed by her on this trip.

You can't talk about New Orleans without talking about the food. Dinner at Tujaques that night was a meal for the ages — salad, crabmeat, spinach bisque, brisket of beef, a main entree of shrimp with cream sauce over rice, and almond bread pudding for dessert. We were pleasantly stuffed by the time we left.

We worked off the excess calories by going to two bars on Bourbon Street. The 554 Club featured 60s and 70s blues, including a rousing rendition of "The Saints Come Marching In." The bandleader introduced the song by making a crack about the pathetic Saints football team losing the rest of its games so the team could seal the No. 1 pick in the next NFL draft. This bar was just a warm-up as we sat attentively listening to the music, amused to be sitting next to a table of six quiet Japanese businessmen in suits. Our two tables was a study in contrasts.

Then we danced up a storm at "Voodoo Groove," which featured a 20-foot-long replica of a black spider suspended at the front entrance. Janice and I warmed up by each downing two shots of Jag-aermeister licorice liquor, which Janice referred to as "liquid vali-um." While we were out on the dance floor, a sexy brunette with two perfectly formed breasts that were nearly popping out of her tight, brown velvet strap dress was drawing attention with her sensual dance moves with her dorky boyfriend. She put on a show, knowing she was being watched. But she ditched the boyfriend and started dancing a seductive circle around — no, not me — Janice, of course.

We floated back to our hotel room and weren't ready to call it a night. I had brought a copy of my screenplay, "The Big Lie," and read the entire screenplay to Janice, all 124 pages. The story includes a murder mystery that takes place in New Orleans. Only Janice could indulge me like that; she was captivated. I rewarded her with a full-body massage, then we made love.

Day 3 started off slowly again, crawling out of bed at 11 with a bit of a hangover. Coffee and beignets were all we could handle for breakfast.

We finally ventured out to check out an art gallery. That turned out unpleasantly when the guy working at the gallery tried to hustle us into buying a time share near the Garden District. He completely lost us when he insulted Janice by asking her, "You're not inebriated, are you?"

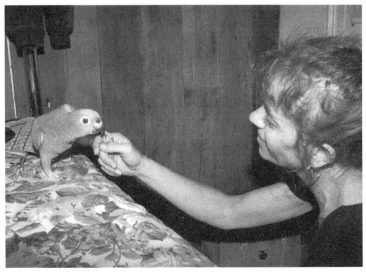

An "inebriated " parrot flirting with Janice in our New Orleans hotel room

We returned to our hotel room for a lazy afternoon and showers. The highlight of the afternoon was when a parrot came strolling through our room from an open window. Only in New Orleans. We asked the parrot, "You're not inebriated, are you?"

By nightfall we decided to cruise through the Garden District, Loyola University, and City Park, all lit up. We came upon the Robert E. Lee statue, behind which Janice elected to take a pee. Knowing Janice, she was making a statement on Lee's symbol to the Confederacy.

Janice was looking lovely that night in her flowery dress. I wasn't the only one who thought that. She had a of way of eliciting compliments all the time. "You look lovely," gushed a woman we encountered at the Old Time Photography Studio.

We chose to eat dinner that night at Arnaud's Remoulade, starting with the oyster bar with five different toppings to choose from — spinach, mushroom sauce, sausage sauce, Italian breaded, and one I forgot. Then the jambalaya was out of this world. Finally, dessert was a custard pecan pie with a coffee mixed with Baileys Irish cream. Yummmmm.

We went for another walk after dinner and came upon a small, round, covered wood stage. Janice was wearing her Spanish black boots. I was a captive audience as she broke out in an impromptu Spanish-style dance she learned from her ballet teacher/life mentor Carmelita, maintaining a hypnotic rhythm with her pounding boots. My heart pounded just from watching her.

We walked along the river's edge again and revisited the Ocean's Song sculpture. On this night the rings were revolving in the wind, effortlessly dancing like Janice was on that wooden stage. For a while we gazed in the haze of the joint we were toting.

On the way back to the hotel, we stopped in a novelty shop where I bought Kasey a real-life alligator skull.

Back in our room, Janice wanted to light up a cigarette, but couldn't find her ashtray. She looked all over the room for it and couldn't find it. It didn't help that we were high. We forgot about it, until a little later I was on the bed telling her another one of my stories when I laughed so hard that I dropped forward and my head landed right on the missing ashtray. "You found it!" Janice exclaimed. That's all it took, I just needed to use my head, which I'm not always accustomed to doing.

We left a wake-up call for our last morning in New Orleans. We got away from the hotel right away at 11:30, which was pretty good for us.

Another round of coffee and beignets at Cafe du Monde, a little Christmas shopping at the French Market, a stroll back to Bourbon Street, and po' boy roast beef sandwiches at Papa Joe's — it was all we could do to string out this unforgettable trip as long as we could.

Janice needed to buy hairspray and conditioner at a hairstyle shop. We struck up a conversation with the old guy who owned the shop. When we told him we were from California, he got the idea that we were part of the Disney production of the "Beauty and The Beast" movie being shot in town. We talked about Santa Barbara. He related a story of when he stayed at the same El Encanto Hotel where Janice and Cori stayed at two years earlier in Santa Barbara. The old guy saw Rita Hayworth dancing at the famous El Paseo Restaurant downtown in the '30s. Everybody has a story to tell.

We had just enough time before leaving town to see the old, old cemetery renowned for its huge tombstones and raised caskets above ground. We wanted to return to the Garden District once more, but ran out of time.

If only we had more time. But time couldn't take anything away from the magic of the last few days. No matter what would transpire between Janice and I from that day forward, we'd always have New Orleans.

———————◆•◆•◆———————

It was 2:30 pm when we pulled out of New Orleans. We had 200 miles, an estimated 3.5-hour drive, to reach Vicksburg, which gave us a half-hour to spare to make it in time for Cori's 2nd-grade class Thanksgiving show at the monthly PTA meeting.

It was really important for Janice to make it to that PTA meeting on time. She was in a near panic as we hit traffic leaving the city.

We stopped at a McDonald's for coffee and a strawberry sundae after crossing Lake Pontchartrain. I took over driving from there. I locked in on cruise control at 70, then 75, then pushed it to 80 as we were anxiously watching the time.

Janice resumed driving as darkness fell. We went from the

four-lane, divided Highway 55 to the two-lane Highway 27 the rest of the way to Vicksburg.

We arrived at Janice's farmhouse at 6:15 p.m., just five minutes before Julie was set to leave for the PTA meeting with her kids and Cori. I met Julie's twin 12-year-old daughters, Lisa and Georgia, and their seven-year-old brother Cody.

Cori was really happy to see her mom. She was happy to see me, too, remembering me from her visit to California two summers ago.

"How long are you staying?" she asked me.

"Three days. Hope that's OK with you. Tell me if it's too long."

"I was hoping you'd stay longer," she told me.

I'd be lying if I didn't admit there was a longing to stay longer. Since being separated from my own daughter, I felt a void that could have easily been filled by Cori.

Julie took the kids to the PTA meeting while Janice and I made a quick change of clothes. We arrived at the school nine miles away at 6:43 pm, five minutes before the meeting got underway.

"Damn!" Janice declared. The mere idea that we arrived *early* for anything was a near miracle. We were both thinking we could have squeezed in a stop at the Garden District back in New Orleans before leaving town, after all.

Janice and I mellowing out on a bench swing in Vicksburg

It was a packed house for the meeting, which was being held at the school cafeteria. I got my first close look at Mississippians. As a group, they did not look at all like Californians. You could tell just by looking at them that they were good, simple folk.

First there was a discussion on the PTA treasury, regarding a disturbing drop from an original accounting that was spelled out in the meeting notes thusly: "thirty-two thousand, three hundred thirty-six dollars and seventy cents." I don't know why I found that amusing.

Then came the event we were all waiting for — the Thanksgiving presentation by the kids. It was unbelievably touching. It started off with a song written by an Indian student about the importance of getting an education. While eight sixth-grade girls, including Georgia, one of Julia's twins, sang the song, the Indian girl who wrote it flashed corresponding Indian hand signs.

I took pictures of Cori in her performance in the skit "Turkey In Trouble." She said her one speaking line right on cue.

There was a sense of relief as we were driving back home, feeling good about making it on time for the show. Cori, sitting in the back seat, gave us a surprise, spontaneous encore performance, singing the hymn "What If God Were One of Us." What if, indeed.

———————————◆—————————————

Back at Janice's farmhouse that evening, I made a couple of calls. The first was to Gary in LA for vital fantasy football business.

Then I called Dan, and I surprised him by putting Janice on the phone. During the whole conversation he assumed we were calling him from Santa Barbara. They knew each other, of course. They were my two favorite people on the planet, two people who shared the same birthday.

When I got back on the phone with Dan, we had a good laugh over the first "Character Reference Form" I had filled out for him for the teaching job he was seeking with the Mt. Vernon School District (he liked the "Louisville Slugger" reference.) He had just received it in the mail at the Sedro Woolley home he was sharing with Tami.

Then we got an unannounced visit from Janice's neighbor, Deemo, who was "redneck" personified. He was in his mid-40s, but easily could have been mistaken for his mid-50s. Something about the two missing lower front teeth that camouflaged his true age. Speaking of camouflage, he was wearing a vegetation-camouflage jacket that he wore for deer hunting, which was "open season" that coming weekend, he gleefully announced. I thought, oh great, the area was going to be flooded with redneck deer hunters with guns.

Deemo was celebrating the opening of deer-hunting season with a "blow-out" cook-out with music and drinking at his house that weekend, and he invited Janice and me. Well now, that sounded like a lot of fun to me, hanging out with bunch of drunk redneck deer hunters with guns.

We got into a pleasant conversation about how many deer he was allowed to kill during "open season;" if I recall, the count was 10. He argued in favor of killing fawns, because "there's way too many of them." He claimed the deer population in Mississippi was over two million. So, thank goodness for all those deer hunters to weed out all those deer.

Then Deemo told us about this charming story he saw on a recent local TV news report. A 40-year-old deer hunter sprayed himself with "elk spray" to hide his scent while he snuck up on a nine-point buck deer. His wife caught everything on a video camera, which the TV news station decided it was a good idea to broadcast it. As Deemo told it, the buck "goes wild" from the scent, stood up on its hind legs, and punched at the guy like a boxer. The deer decked the poor sucker, who fell helpless on the ground. The video camera didn't miss a beat, remaining ever so steady, without a hint of the wife being the least bit concerned. Her perfectly calm voice providing commentary on the audio recording told the rest of the story: "This was not my idea. I told my husband, 'I suggest you do not do this.' So here I am, video-taping my husband being trampled to death by a deer." Well, chalk one up for the deer.

After Deemo left, Janice related the wife shooting the video of her husband getting trampled to death by a buck to the wife who plotted her husband's murder in my script "The Big Lie." Hmm, I've known a couple of wives capable of murder.

I slept through Cori getting off to school the next morning at 7. I woke up at about 11:30. Janice made me eggs and bacon for breakfast. I could have gotten used to this farmhouse living.

It was a beautiful day. I took a walk with my camera on the rural road, shooting pictures that caught my fancy. One was of the farmhouse, surrounded by a blanket of golden autumn leaves. Another photo was a group shot of eight big, fat cows at a water trough near the road, as they stared at me like I was some kind of alien.

The cows were no different from the strange looks from passengers in cars and trucks that passed me on the roads that I aimlessly wandered. One car made me nervous when it passed me and disappeared, then reappeared around the bend and headed back toward me. It stopped about 50 feet ahead of me, making my heart skip a beat as I thought of deer hunters with guns. The passenger door swung open, a teenage boy jumped out and asked me if I needed a ride. Well, dang, that was nice.

In early afternoon Janice and I took a drive to go pay her electric bill, then drove by one of the river casinos, and finally stopped by the house of Teri Jane, one of Janice's longtime girlfriends dating back to her childhood. Teri Jane wasn't home, but her dainty, 79-year-old mother Roberta was. I met Roberta and we talked about how she loved the gambling boats on the river, which were a big deal in Vicksburg.

Then we picked Cori up at school. Back home, Cori and I then went for another walk, down the road in the opposite direction from my earlier walk. I took more photos of a dilapidated wooden shack we stopped to explore. It was late afternoon and the sun was lowering in the sky, offering glittering, filtering light through cracks in the aged wood inside the shack. A near-full moon loomed overhead in the dimming daylight.

I focused for a close-up photo of a large knot in a wood post on the front porch of the shack. I was with Cori, so my state of mind came into play with the image I was seeing. The circular knot encapsulated a curved formation, remarkably resembling an undeveloped fetus inside an embryo.

Seeing that image, I couldn't help think about the aborted child that Janice and I could have had together years before Cori was born, if we had made that choice. In retrospect, I often wonder how different our lives would have been if Janice had carried that pregnancy through. I obviously would have chosen to stay with her, just like I had chosen to stay with Katya, then came around to eventually choosing to stay with Gail. Those choices would have never been presented to me if I was with Janice.

I easily could have immersed myself in the seduction of that soft, soothing, Southern accent of Janice's. But then again, Cori wouldn't have been born.

Like the line I wrote in a song, "Life's a curious game."

Knot in a wooden shack post that I thought resembled an embryo fetus inside a uterus.

———————◆·◆·◆·◆———————

That night Janice, Cori and I went to the movies, to see "Space Jam." We arrived, in Janice fashion, 12 minutes late for the scheduled start, but only missed the previews.

By the time we returned home at 9:30, Cori was asleep in the car. When we put her to bed, we discovered that her TV and VCR in her bedroom were missing. I remembered seeing both in her room that morning. We frantically checked the rest of the house —a much bigger TV and an expensive stereo set, both in the living room, remained untouched. My expensive camera, the same camera that survived my mother's "No foto" faux pas in Nicaragua, was left in full view in the living room. The front door had been left unlocked for the full four hours we were gone.

I was about to confront the darker side of Janice that gave me pause.

Teri Jane, apprised of the robbery, popped on over. I finally was meeting her for the first time. She spoke with a very heavy Mississippian accent. She was a petite woman, with short-cropped, very blonde hair.

I became engaged in a long conversation with Teri Jane about her concerns over a couple of shady characters that Janice was dealing with on a regular basis. Teri Jane went into detail about one particular nut case named Jerry. Teri Jane suspected he was bad news from the get-go. I wasn't told directly, but I assumed he was a drug connection.

Janice had overheard part of the discussion on Jerry. We were trying to formulate a list of possible suspects for the TV and VCR heist, so Jerry's name came up. I asked Janice what was the worst Jerry was capable of?

"Murder," was her response. Well, that didn't give me any southern comfort.

After Teri Jane left, Janice assured me that nothing bad would happen. But she speculated that the robbery was aimed at her, she was sure of that.

It was no less reassuring that we couldn't get the front door to lock. Jerry knew where Janice lived.

------------◆------------

I woke up late again the following morning, a Saturday. In renewing the conversation on possible suspects, Janice raised a new candidate — Teri Jane. She was convinced Teri Jane stole Cori's TV and VCR to get cash to buy drugs. That triggered my recall of the conversation I had with Teri Jane the night before, in which she asked me if I had done anything I regretted. Then she told me she had done a lot of things she regretted. Hmm, Janice's suspicions seemed plausible. Especially with the peculiarity of the robbery's limited scope, in which electronic components in Cori's room were all that was taken, leaving more expensive stuff in the living room untouched. That was very odd, like the action of a family friend who wanted to keep the theft minimal.

This was my last day in Vicksburg before returning home. Janice took me to see the Union Military Park, where the Vicksburg Siege

Battle in the Civil War culminated on July 4, 1864. The vast acres of green, rolling hills and sharp-dropping crevices were dotted with war monuments. The most intriguing on display was the resurrected Cairo Ironclad Classic gunboat that had sunk during the Siege. I've always been a bit of a history buff, so I was intrigued.

We followed that up with a drive-by tour of the four riverboat casinos docked on shore throughout town. We spent our final night together playing Monopoly with Cori.

Later in the evening another visitor came by — Sherrill Ann, Teri Jane's older sister. She was the same age as Janice and the closer friend between the two sisters. Sherrill Ann was looking "hot" — long, straight, reddish blonde hair, slender body in tight-fitting jeans. Janice left us alone for about 20 minutes to pick up a couple of joints from a local dealer. We had a nice conversation while she was gone. Sherrill Ann came off as more mature than her younger sister, more subdued. I had the impression she was the more trustworthy friend between the two sisters.

But the robbery, and Janice's association with someone capable of murder, left a cloud over Janice and me as I returned home to Santa Barbara. The glow from New Orleans still lingered — how could it not? But now that we were a couple of thousand miles apart again and I was still struggling with the separation from my wife and daughter, apprehensions about Janice crept into my conscience.

———————◆◆◆◆◆———————

I came upon another small piece of stationary— with a header entitled "Left-handed Genius!" — in which I scribbled some notes about Janice from her past. They were notes from a story she told about her husband — named Lee — from whom she fled when she came to California in the late 1970's. She must have told me this story when we returned to the farmhouse after our visit to New Orleans. I'm presuming the story took place when she returned to Mississippi sometime in 1987. I considered the notes to this story revelatory, told in sparse bits and pieces — Janice's voice coming through my interpretive words — that rang loud and clear:

(Janice)
Resolving a divorce after 8 years
Was 24 at time of separation. Stuck w/ police rap on dope. Hurt.

8 years later finally returns home, completes paperwork on divorce, makes mandatory court appearance (Oh God!), avoids Lee for 3 weeks, finally arranges (I crossed out "arranges" and wrote over it the very next word) choreographed to meet him at town fountain in middle of town. Tension.

He's balding. "You're skinny."

"Can we be friends?" (No.)

Uncomfortable. Tells him about divorce (Gulp!) (wasn't he expecting it?)

Lasted about 20-30 minutes.

Getting in car to get a Coke— real familiar.

The way he shifts gears — instant connection to past. Bitter feelings coming back.

"There's rural, suburban, urban."

(Voice changed over 8 years.)

Saw him later w/ older woman— typical redneck.

"Glad I'm not his partner."

I returned for another visit to Mississippi to see Janice, and Cori, about six years after the New Orleans adventure. The circumstances were much different then. They no longer lived in the charming farmhouse. They were sharing an apartment with Janice's brother Steven in the heart of Vicksburg.

Janice and 13-year-old Cori in Vicksburg

Cori was in middle school by then. A lot had transpired in my life since my previous trip to Mississippi. But I still loved Janice and still adored Cori.

Steven was very nice and accommodating. He worked as a captain on one of the riverboats, so he was gone for most of the time I was there. He basically was supporting Janice and Cori, who I could tell adored him. He loved and cared for his only sister, who was struggling financially. Janice had called and asked me for money prior to this second visit, a couple of hundred dollars to pay the electric bill, or so she said. Paying the electric bill seemed to be a chronic problem for Janice.

But the lingering suspicion in my mind was that she was spending money on drugs. She always had a craving for cocaine, dating back to the wild Uncle Billy days.

The visit had its sweet moments, as time spent with Janice always did. We made love a couple of times. But it ended on a sour note.

On my last night, Janice asked if she could borrow my rental car. She left me alone with Cori that night. Cori and I played games and watched TV. We were OK, for a while.

My expectation was that Janice would be gone for an hour, maybe two at the most. By midnight her absence had already stretched beyond three hours. Cori went to bed, but the longer Janice was away, the more restless I became. I had an early AM flight home the following day and needed to leave the apartment by 6:30. I was still awake at 3 am, and still no Janice. I was in utter despair.

I managed to doze off at some point, and when my alarm went off at 6 Janice was passed out next to me in bed. I never heard her come in. I was so wiped out from lack of sleep and stress.

She offered no explanation. But she knew I was upset. Just the mere thought that this was my last night there, and she went and disappeared like that was hurtful. I was certain drugs were involved, wherever she went, and whomever she was with. I was willing to give her the benefit of the doubt, that maybe she just passed out someplace.

But still…

The episode was troubling, the latest in a string of evidence that she had an ongoing problem with drugs. It dated way back to her divorce from her husband who had served time in jail on drug charges, and her attempts to avoid the same fate by escaping to California.

I knew about the drug arrest she faced when she returned to Mississippi for the funeral of the brother who had committed suicide. All that history came into play that night I waited wondering where the hell she was with my rental car.

So, we were a long, long way away from our unforgettable, sweet moments in New Orleans six years earlier, when we parted that second time in Mississippi.

I would come around to forgive Janice quickly enough. This was Janice we're talking about, after all. But it was a continuation of the price I paid for the Unbearable Lightness Of Being in love with Janice.

———————————◆•••———————————

The following is a poem Janice wrote to her young daughter Cori:

Sail into your dreams
My pretty child
Take a star
Follow it

Embrace youth's dew
Laugh, love
Dance in the moonlight
Sleep in the sun
Let the wind
Caress,

Move your Spirit
Know how precious
You are to me

Love, Mamma

Max loved playing tug-of-war, whether it was over a twig with Tessa, or over a slipper with Dan

CHAPTER 23
Roommate and Romance Roulette - Part 1

With one big mortgage and two monthly child support payments to cover by myself, I was forced to follow in my mother's footsteps to make ends meet. I had to adopt her Rossburn Roommate plan.

I was set on a course that would lead me to live with 26 roommates over an 11 1/2-year span between 1996 and 2007. It was everything I could do to keep from having to sell the house. It was well worth it.

Maggie and Tessa moved out in March of 1996. I had to wait only a couple of months for the ideal roommates — Lavelle, and her seven-year-old son Julian.

Lavelle and Julian were living next door at the time Maggie and I split up. They were renting out the house owned by Chuck and Sue, a pair of boomer school teachers who lived up in Seattle; Lavelle's lease was up at the start of the summer. Chuck and Sue needed her to move out for some planned renovation to the house.

This was convenient, as I needed a roommate. Lavelle jumped at the offer.

Lavelle, in a word, was a "trip." She evidently didn't have a last name, I only knew her as Lavelle. She was a few years older than me. She reminded me of Goldie Hawn, with her short, spiky blonde hair, blue eyes and sleek build. She had a Goldie Hawnish perky personality, full of vitality that fit her profession as a yoga instructor.

She was into eating healthy to keep her slender figure. She was using the blender quite a bit to make fruit and veggie smoothies.

She was very limber. I'd watch her get in these impossible yoga positions, wrapping her long, slender legs in all sorts of contortions.

Lavelle doted on her son, Julian, who was a cute, shy blonde boy. She enrolled him in Waldorf, the exclusive private school near the Santa Barbara Mission that was attended by all the rich kids in town.

Lavelle rolled with rich people. While she wasn't rich herself, she had connections and did OK. She always paid her rent in cash. She showed me the top shelf of her hall closet next door where she stashed a pile of cash, bundled up in sums of $200 each wrapped in rubber bands. She told me they were sent in from "investors." Details were murky, and I didn't want to hear anything more as a potential investor.

But she made good money as a private yoga instructor. Lavelle had some rich clients. One of them was Susan Bridges, wife of Jeff Bridges, the Oscar Award-winning actor.

One day, Lavelle announced that she was invited to the Bridges' 20th wedding anniversary party at their home in Montecito. She asked if I would like to go as her escort. Well, sure, I told her.

This wild idea came into my head. I asked Lavelle if Lloyd Bridges, Jeff Bridges' father, would be at the party. She assumed he would. This would be the same Lloyd Bridges who I had captured in a terrific action photo in Aspen during the celebrity tennis tournament that I attended 12 years ago with the press photo pass I acquired through my Farah Fawcett-lookalike friend Sasha.

I dug the photo out and wrote on the back identifying when and where the photo was taken. Then I took the photo with me to the party, intending to give it to Lloyd Bridges.

Dress was semi-formal. Lavelle was elegant in a sleek, form-fitting gown. I wore the best sports jacket I owned and dress slacks.

Entering the Bridges' home that night felt like stepping into a castle. It was a mansion perched high on the mountainside in Montecito, with a gorgeous overview of the ocean below.

As I walked in, my eyes were drawn to an ornate, wooden staircase to the right, which ascended by a wall displaying three large portrait paintings of the Bridges' three beautiful princess daughters, all of them blonde and blue-eyed like their parents.

Then I started recognizing some familiar faces among the guests. I identified the actor Tim Matheson, the frat house leader in the John Belushi-classic movie "Animal House." I did a double-take at another famous face, speculating, *"I'm pretty sure that's David Crosby,"* the rock star of Crosby, Stills, Nash and Young fame who was still letting his freak-flag fly.

A huge buffet awaited in the large party room with lacy curtains on ceiling-high windows looking out to the large backyard. A band consisting of seven musicians and a singer was performing under a party tent outside. A dance floor was laid out over the lawn.

Lavelle and I mingled and soon engaged in conversation with Bud Cort, the actor who played Harold in the movie "Harold and

414

Maude," one of my all-time favorites. He was very friendly, very chatty. We were standing at the entryway from the backyard.

Our conversation was momentarily interrupted by a soft, feminine voice, stating, "Excuse me." We turned around to acknowledge the woman.

Lavelle, who never had a problem blurting out what was on her mind, spontaneously exclaimed, "Oh, I love your dress, Barbra!"

I turned around to look and thought to myself, yes that is a lovely dress, *Miss Streisand*. Then we all stepped back to make way for Barbra — *Mother Mary!* — Streisand to pass by in her lovely, long lacy white gown.

It was no big surprise she was invited to the party. Maybe it was a surprise she showed up. The movie "The Mirror Has Two Faces," starring Streisand and the host, Jeff Bridges, had just recently played out in theaters that year.

I usually try my best not to appear star-struck, but being in the presence of Barbra Streisand, forget it. I only hoped my mouth wasn't too wide open when I gawked. Later in the evening, when Lavelle and I were dancing a slow dance, we were in close proximity to Barbra dancing with her then-new boyfriend, James Brolin. I couldn't help noticing, dangling from the arm that she wrapped around his shoulder, a diamond-studded bracelet that glittered from the backyard lights illuminating the band stage. It felt like she had illuminated the whole night.

Lloyd Bridges was at the party, as expected. He was sitting quietly next to his wife in the backyard, listening to the band, when I struck up the nerve to approach him. I pulled out of my breast pocket the photo I had of him reaching back to return a lob shot on the tennis court from 12 years earlier in Aspen. I kept my story brief, then handed him the photo. He graciously accepted it. I don't know if it meant much to him, but it meant a heckuva lot to me. Mission accomplished, after 12 years.

Actor Lloyd Bridges playing at celebrity tennis tournament in Aspen, Colo. in 1984

Lavelle and Julian moved out after a few months, finding another place of their own. So the roommate roulette was set in motion. They were followed by Andy and Jim. Andy was a friend of mine and a colleague at the News-Press, working as an editor in the editorial department. He recruited Jim, a young friend of his who was about 22 at the time.

Andy was a close friend with whom I had confided my marital issues, both past and present. He took an interest in my screenplays I was working on at time. He had some graphic design artist skills that he put to good use designing a script cover for my screenplay, "The Big Lie," which contains some tangental connection to my marital experience.

Andy was a happy-go-lucky kinda guy. He loved good music, he had a good sense of humor. His passion was frisbee golf, and he helped organize tournaments locally. I was hoping he'd stick around a lot longer than he did. He and Jim lasted almost a year.

Jim was a just a kid who had recently lost his dad. Andy, who was closer to my age, took him under his wing like a big brother.

Meanwhile, I became acquainted with and became friends with Jim's recently widowed mother, Michele.

I was attracted to Michele. So was Andy. She was adorably cute. She was a no-nonsense, straight-talking, honest woman, but was very guarded with her feelings. Given she was a recent widow, I didn't think she was ready to jump into any relationship with another man. While she masked it well, I think she was in a state of shock over her husband's passing, which came by way of a sudden, tragic accident at their home. He was electrocuted while changing a ceiling light fixture. She really didn't talk about it much. Jim didn't talk about it at all.

Michele and I became good friends. She invited me for an overnight visit in the guest room of her home in Santa Cruz. She was frequently commuting down to Santa Barbara for business and visit friends. I was one of those friends for a while. We had a few casual lunch dates and shared a couple of pow-wows in my backyard hot tub with wine on balmy nights, waxing philosophic and cracking jokes. She had a good sense of humor. She was a good listener, too.

416

She much preferred me talking about myself and all my relationship dramas than talking about herself. I fear I may have overwhelmed her with all my stories and divorces.

———————◆◆◆◆◆———————

Following Andy and Jim in the roommate rotation was another single mom, Cynthia, and her teen-age son Jared.

Cynthia was a tall, statuesque blonde who used to be married to a surfer, and Jared was like-father-like-son; all he wanted to do was surf and skip out on school. He wasn't my kid, so it wasn't my problem. He was quiet and showed me respect, so that was good enough for me.

They lived with me for well over a year. It was Cynthia's idea to convert the back TV room to one big bedroom, despite the inconvenience of having the washer/dryer off to the side in the same room. Jared had his own separate room in one of the spare bedrooms. After a few months, Cynthia helped choose another roommate for the remaining spare bedroom. We welcomed a young woman named Karen.

I will always associate Cynthia with the death of Princess Diana. She and Jared moved in on August 25, 1997. Five days later, it was Cynthia who broke the tragic news out of Paris to me when I came home that dreadful night of August 31. So Cynthia's place in my memoir is forever locked.

———————◆◆◆◆◆———————

I was still recoiling from Maggie's announcement that she wanted a divorce so she could marry Bill, when I met the woman who would be the next significant relationship in my life a couple months later.

Since she had the same first name as another woman of significance in my life, I will give her a fictionalized name for the sake of storytelling. I will call her Gayle.

I met Gayle at the Irish pub Dargan's in downtown Santa Barbara one night. She was with a girlfriend. I was alone, probably feeling sorry for myself. Our eyes met. I remember locking in on those beautiful, big green eyes. She flashed me a big smile. She had a couple drinks in her by then, which put her in a happy mood.

We introduced ourselves. She was a nurse by profession. She's the one who couldn't bring herself to call me "Chic," so she asked if she could call me "Charlie." It was a momentous name-change.

Besides her green eyes, I loved her long, wavy golden hair that cascaded over her shoulders. She was small in stature, but big-breasted. She had a commanding voice and a hearty laugh. And she was pretty.

That meeting at Dargan's launched a dynamic but dysfunctional relationship that spanned over seven years, with several significant break-ups. It was Romance Roulette for all the wrong reasons.

What kept us going for so long was the sex and the travel. We shared a passion for both, and they both tended to go hand-in-hand. The sex was outstanding on its own. Gayle spoiled me, she gave me what any man would want. "You're a lucky man," she kept reminding me, and she was right.

What drove us apart was her distrust of my past — those four marriages, compared to only one for her — and Vern, an old boyfriend whom she couldn't let go of.

Gayle's lone divorce was messy. The mother of three daughters, Gayle had an idyllic life with her seemingly true-blue husband when it came to an abrupt, shattering end with the revelation he had been carrying on an extramarital affair for years. That was about 12 years ago. She never did overcome the sense of insecurity derived from that experience. So, as much as she loved me — she did love me — she never felt wholly secure with me as a four-time divorcee. Holding onto Vern was her safety net.

Gayle was a wreck from the divorce, very angry, and probably drank too much for a while in the early stages of the divorce. She still liked her wine; I noticed that from the get-go that first night at Dargan's. Alcohol made her happy and horny. In that way, I couldn't get enough of her.

She was a fiercely devoted mother to her daughters. She'd kill for her daughters — Clair, Jennifer and Amanda. She had to find a way around her Catholic upbringing to accept her youngest daughter when she "came out" as a young teen. She didn't just accept it, she openly embraced it. "A-man-duh!" she would jokingly proclaim about the revelation of her masculine daughter. Ultimately, she just loved her daughter that much more, and her chosen partners as well, and openly advocated for Amanda's right to love whomever she wanted.

There was a lot to admire about Gayle. Starting with her chosen profession as a nurse — a selfless, heart-rending, nurturing means to make a living. The passion it takes to devote one's self to that line of work was transferred to our relationship.

The relationship was cemented in the first trip we took together — to Death Valley in mid-April, the perfect time of year to visit one of the hottest spots on earth. It was comfortably in the low 80's when we were there. The spring desert flowers were in full bloom. The Death Valley trip set the tone for so many trips we took together, in which sex and adventure were the agenda.

We had one utterly unforgettable moment in Death Valley. We drove out in the desert night to take in the panoramic view of the billion stars in the sky. We parked the car off the side of the road, nestled between hills in the still of the night, and were listening to a cassette of Chopin music on the car stereo. There's something about Chopin with his effortless archipelagos that glide across the keys, change in moods, sudden surges, and exquisitely placed trills, that can bring out the romance of any moment.

But Gayle and I could not possibly have been prepared for what Chopin brought out on that night. Suddenly, out of the jet-black night, a huge dark wave swooped down, swirling directly at the front windshield of the car. It came within an inch of crashing into the windshield before rising just as suddenly over the roof of the car. A second wave, then a third wave followed in close sequence. We had to squint to focus on the dark waves against the black background of night to finally recognize that the waves were flocks of bats!

We were certain the bats were reacting to Chopin. Bats, I learned, rely on "echolocation," a system that allows them to locate objects in the dark using sound waves. There had to be something about Chopin that disturbed their sound waves and drove them to distraction, mounting a kamikaze dive toward our windshield. It was freaky and beautiful. We watched in awe. The spectacle lasted a little over a minute but was lodged forever in my memory.

Gayle and I talked openly about Vern during that Death Valley trip. She made it sound as if they were parting ways, but she wanted some wiggle room to let him down easy. We were just starting out and I had every reason to believe her. Boy, was I a fool. This was a problem that wasn't going away.

About a month later, I found out she was still seeing Vern. I should have gotten out right then and there. But she coaxed me into not breaking up with her. Ok, the sex was *that* good.

So were our subsequent travels. That's what made it so vexing for me. We were so good together as travel partners, experiencing places and adventures together, that I made excuses in my mind to accept that she was seeing another man.

I managed to forget all about Vern on another adventure early on in our relationship — a river rafting excursion in Idaho. We were in Twin Falls, visiting Gayle's brother Mark and his second wife. After a few days in their home, we took off for a river rafting guided tour down the Snake River. A staff of four young guides took a party of 15 of us on three inflatable rafts on a ride that proved to be wild and wooly, a little more than we bargained for.

It was early summer and the Snake River was running at full speed. It was more agitated than any river Dan and I had tried in our varied river trips.

We got our fill of whitewater thrills, nearly bouncing off the raft through some rough patches. The rafts were sturdy enough to take the punishment and absorb the massive blows of the current. It was wild and adrenaline-pumping fun.

Then when we rested at our campsites, the guides did all the work — what a deal! They set up the tents, cooked all the meals, did all the clean-up afterwards. This was the kind of lap-of-luxury-treatment-slash-love of-nature experience perfectly suited for Gayle and me.

But we lasted only halfway through the scheduled five-day excursion. After our third day of whitewater rafting, the action proved to be too volatile for Gayle's delicate composition. She became too ill to continue.

We were in the middle of the wilderness, so an early departure from the trip required an exceptional solution — by helicopter, which was dispatched to our campsite to airlift us out. The flight out was an adventure in of itself.

Then we were put up in a nice hotel, where we basked in

heavenly warm showers and were treated to a mouth-watering steak dinner that evening. The hotel bed was a lot more comfortable for our nighttime play than inside a tent.

The Snake River was not our last helicopter experience together. The second vertical flight was planned, during our Hawaiian vacation on the Big Island and Kauai. The chopper ride came on the Big Island, over the active volcano Kilauea that empties hot lava out into the sea in an eternal cloud of steam. We stayed overnight at the renowned Volcano House on the rim of the volcano, which made for a lovely evening.

The next day we hiked into the volcano crater, once we got our bearings straight. I was so disoriented that I started leading us "up" instead of "down" the trail, insisting that was the way to the crater below. Gayle wouldn't let me forget that one for years, dubbing me "Wrong Way Charlie."

Hiking was a major activity on all of our trips. In Hawaii, we took an ambitious 15-mile round-trip hike on Kauai, along the breathtaking Napoli coast and then deep into the rainforest. The trail dead-ended at a dreamlike waterfall, which required slipping and sliding the last couple of hundred feet or so on a narrow, muddy path to reach. It felt like our version of the movie "Romancing the Stone." I have a passion for waterfalls; I felt exuberant and alive under the thundering spray of water while wading in the pool below. We labored long and hard just to experience that feeling.

One of my favorite photos of Gayle on our Hawaiian trip

Gayle also hooked me on skiing in the winter months. I had skied only a couple of times in my life before I met Gayle, and wasn't very good at it. But with her, I became proficient quickly enough to handle intermediate slopes without hurting myself. It turned out to be another adrenaline rush I never thought I'd get into.

We crossed the northern border for one ski trip to Whistler Ski Resort in British Columbia. We spent some time in Vancouver first, before heading for the slopes at the resort. Just being in Canada gave an extra charge to the trip. It was cold, but the skiing was heavenly.

We were accompanied by Dan and Tami on another ski trip, to Mt. Baker in central Washington. This was simply an exquisite experience. For starters, there was little ski traffic to deal with the day we went, so we had lots of room to roam. A fresh snowstorm had blanketed the mountain and it continued to snow lightly while we were skiing, providing fresh powder that felt pillow soft and produced an easy glide to the skis. Dan was the only one who chose to snowboard, which wasn't a good idea. He kept falling down all day and the pillow soft powder likely saved him from serious injury.

Gayle met Dan and Tami for the first time on that trip. We all got along great, and Gayle seemingly felt at ease with both of them. But it would become apparent that she was internalizing some insecure feelings that didn't surface until more than a year later, when all of our lives was altered.

———————◆———————

Insecurity worked both ways in Gayle's and my relationship. The worst part about Gayle continuing to see Vern was that he and I lived in the same neighborhood, about a half-mile apart. This made it all too convenient for me to drive by and see Gayle's car parked on the street in front of his house. For the life of me, I don't know why I subjected myself to this self-torture.

Vern and I knew each other; our paths crossed several times shopping at the same grocery store. We both avoided making direct eye contact and the smoldering between us was perceptible.

The agony was insufferable. I had gotten myself in too deep. Vern and I both pressured Gayle to make a choice. I can't tell you how many times she chose me, only to find out she started seeing Vern again. I guess I put up with it so long because I was just tired of riding the relationship merry-go-round.

I stopped seeing her a few times. During one time-out, I got back on the merry-go-round, very briefly, with a fling with another woman tenant at Mom's house – Dahlia, a buxom blonde from South Africa. She could have made an interesting travel companion had we stuck it out. She was a businesswoman on the move who didn't last long at Mom's. Too bad.

Meanwhile, I always made time to spend with my kids. I mixed in some travel with each of them. I took Kasey on a camping trip to Big Sur, and I took Tessa to Universal Studios when she was about four and barely tall enough for the scarier rides. Then all three of us all took a train ride from LA to San Diego, where we did all the touristy things, including Sea World.

That was my lot in life — weekend dad. It was hardly what I had bargained for, I was stuck in this uncomfortable, in-between gap role of sometimes-I'm-a-parent-sometimes-I'm-not. I missed out on the day-to-day upbringing with both of my kids. I always felt like they were pieces of the puzzle I was trying to fit into the larger picture.

I often had Kasey and Tessa together on my scheduled visits to LA — the beach, parks, movies, lunches. It was a concerted effort on my part that they connected with each other as brother and sister. I had both of them some weekends in Santa Barbara as well. Those occasions presented the opportunity for a family favorite at dinnertime, when I'd make them the chili spaghetti that I learned how to make from my mother. The recipe for chili spaghetti reputedly originated in Cincinnati, Mom's hometown. I loved my mother's chili spaghetti, so did my kids, who came to calling it Dad's chili spaghetti.

One common link the kids shared was their devotion to Max, my goofy, adorable boxer. Both my kids loved Max, and I frequently brought him along to LA. I have one utterly priceless photo of three-year-old Tessa crouched on all fours on the grass lawn in Mom's backyard, facing off with Max. They are both biting down on opposite ends of an eight-inch twig in an intense tug-of-war. While I was taking this photo, it never entered my mind that I'd have to worry about Max biting Tessa. Max was extraordinarily gentle with and protective of both of my kids.

With Max, Tessa was in Santa Barbara every year for the

annual Dog Parade. That became a big Dad-and-Daughter event, for which we'd tie a red bandana around Max's muscular neck and parade him down State Street, the main drag in downtown. He was a handsome dog and we loved showing him off.

———————◆•••◆•••◆———————

I don't know if it was a coincidence, or self-conscious serendipity, but I noted the significance of the date in which I sat down to write this segment — May 17.

I'm pretty good with significant dates. I recently wrote this date down for its significance 21 years earlier. I had called my childhood buddy, Wayne, to talk about this milestone event in my life — one of those markers that tells you life is indeed passing you by and childhood is just a fading memory.

Wayne's younger brother Rod died at the age of 42 on May 17, 1999.

I never lost touch with my childhood roots growing up on Rossburn — growing up with the Ely boys, the Gerke boys, the Chadwick boys. As we all grew into men, with wives and kids and dogs, we all got together once a year to play like kids again in a rough-and-tumble flag football game. It was our Super Bowl. But we gave it a title worthy of its esteem —Dog Bowl.

It was an annual event, usually held in January before the real Super Bowl. We gathered at the football field at our old alma mater, Hawthorne High. We brought along all of our wives, kids and dogs to watch, with plenty of coolers stocked with beer. Then this rag-tag, out-of-shape, beer-bellied, joint-toking, boys-to-men group would divide into two teams, one wearing custom-made "Dog Bowl" yellow shirts and the other similarly designed red, to play out this festive match that, miraculously, didn't result in any trips to the ER over the years. There were plenty of icepack applications and ibuprofen popping for various aches and pains over the recovery weeks after the games.

All the boys I grew up with participated — Wayne, Rod and Brett Ely; Bruce, Joel and Doyle Gerke; Jim and Tom Chadwick. So did a host of friends who were mostly connected with Wayne — he was the central figure in all of this. Wayne was a popular and likable guy.

I bring up the Dog Bowl in the context of Rod's passing because every single person who played in the Dog Bowl showed up at Rod's memorial gathering at the Ely vacation house on the shores of

Lake Elsinore. It was a gathering like no other I had ever attended.

Rod was every bit as popular as his older brother. He was the ultimate pot-smoking, laid-back, "Hey Dude" surfer guy who, as Wayne succinctly put it, "Kept looking for the next good time."

Rod, the middle-aged Ely brother between Wayne and Brett, had leukemia. He underwent months of chemotherapy treatment. Wayne, who turned out to be a perfect match, donated his bone marrow in a transplant operation to help keep Rod alive. It might have worked, too, if Rod hadn't been Rod.

As Wayne told it, Rod, in his endless pursuit of a good time, engaged in reckless activity during and just after his chemo treatments that compromised his immune system. Rod didn't die from leukemia, he died from a lung virus. Wayne's tone barely masked the pain he felt when relating to me the sacrifice he had made for his brother that had gone wasted.

But in 1999, at the Ely's Elsinore pad, Rod's exuberant life was celebrated in a big way, by so many who loved him. The party was an all-day, all-night, overnight affair. Red eyes from tears only got redder as more beer was consumed. But it was a party that Rod would have loved — everyone was having fun, playing horseshoes and ping-pong, water skiing and jet skiing on the lake, pigging out on the food and drinks.

Speaking of pigs, the Elys had three potbelly pigs roaming freely around the property, Sweetpea and her two youngsters, Liberty and Ham. They got along harmoniously with their canine kin, who were also in attendance in abundance.

Jim Chadwick, who was something of a video wizard, put together a long video, compiled from old photos and film clips, with an amazing accompanying music soundtrack, as a moving tribute to Rod. On the basis of his inspired work for Rod, everybody should be so lucky to have Jim Chadwick make a tribute video when their time is up.

A big part of Rod's life were the two beautiful, blonde, blue-eyed kids who looked like him that he left behind, a son and a daughter.

Wayne and his wife Jeannie also had a son and a daughter, Matt and Kristen, both of whom I got to know at the memorial. Wayne married a woman who had the same name as his mother.

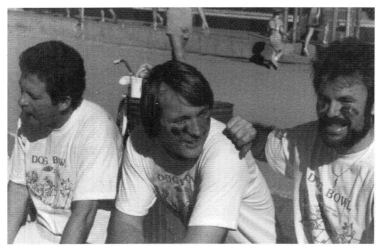

Bruce Gerke, center, and I chat on the bench during a Dog Bowl flag-football game

Wayne Ely and Jim Chadwick at memorial gathering for Wayne's brother Rod at Lake Elsinore

Nobody grieved over Rod more than his mother Jeannie, who was a larger-than-life figure in my childhood. As mothers go, I always thought she was pretty. The clearest memory I took away from the party was that of Jeannie, at mid-evening when everyone was mellow and sad, bellies full of beer, rum, hot dogs and fried chicken. A 60s music soundtrack was blasting into the night and Jeannie led everybody in a full-throated, heart-felt, rendition of Neil Diamond's "Sweet Caroline."

426

"Sweet Caroline,
Good times never felt so good..."

———————————•‧•‧◆‧•‧•———————————

I gained a roommate out of the Rod Ely memorial. Wayne's son Matt moved up to Santa Barbara the following fall to attend Santa Barbara City College. He needed a place to live. I lived just a couple of miles from SBCC and I had vacant room to rent in my home.

Matt was just like his dad — easy-going, affable, good-natured, family oriented. And he possessed the most prominent Ely family trait — profound dog-lover. Matt instantly bonded with my dog Max. They were inseparable. Matt took him for walks and to the park. He even let Max sleep with him, which was more than I could do for my own dog because of his pungent penchant for flatulence when he slept.

Matt was a roommate for a full school year.

The roommate roulette was in full swing after Cynthia and Jared moved out. I had a few tenants live under my roof who made things interesting. A sampling from the early years:

• Derek was a tall young man with a wisp of a goatee on his handsome face who I knew at work, at the News-Press. He worked in the paste-up department downstairs. Derek was quiet and thoughtful. He was an artist who had a painting-in-progress on a large canvas for most of the duration of his six-month stay. It was fascinating to see the development of his creation — an abstract shape of a beautiful woman surrounded by soft blues, greens, lavenders and yellows. I'd sneak peaks when he wasn't around just to see what he had added to the painting. I watched the painting evolve as Derek kept filling it with more colors, a privileged witness to a beautiful creation blossoming from the imagination of this artist in my midst.

• Michael, another connection from the News-Press paste-up department, followed Derek as a roommate. He wound up being my longest roommate, spanning about eight years. Michael was very smart, of German descent, who was full of "ideas." I used to refer to him as "Dreamin' Man," like the Neil Young song. One of his most ambitious dreams was to open a social-gathering cafe club, in which he imagined offering expanded activities beyond the typical

Starbucks or local cafe. He had written up an extensive portfolio business plan and had conducted conversations with a few people on financing the project. Unfortunately, his "dream" social cafe never materialized as he hoped.

Michael left an indelible mark at my house. He was quite the handyman and was responsible for turning three-fourths of my garage into a bedroom in ingenious fashion. He constructed a couple of large removable bookshelves which, side-by-side, walled off the front of the garage that remained intact as a mini "garage;" ergo, storage space. It rendered the garage illegal because a car could no longer fit inside. But his book-shelves idea was designed for easy removal in case I ever wanted to restore the garage to its original size. (Hmm, wonder why I'd ever want to do that?) Then in the bedroom, he installed dimmer ceiling lights and built in a couple of high beams that supported an artsy cloth ceiling banner he created, rendering a soft lighting effect. The dimmed lighting gave the room a certain ambiance. Michael was clever, and an artist as well.

Then, for a dramatic change, I commissioned Michael to rip out all the carpet in the living room and hallway and replace it with wood laminate flooring. With so much roommate traffic moving about, my carpet days were over.

As an artist, Michael had innate graphic design skills. He designed a cover page for my Nicaraguan screenplay, "Santiagatita."

One year, he landed a side job to design the program flyer for the annual Fiesta event that Santa Barbara puts on to celebrate its Spanish heritage. Fiesta, arguably one of Santa Barbara's most celebrated events dating back to the early 1900's, is a five-day party highlighted by numerous activities and entertainment all over town during the first week of August. When the party ends, downtown streets and sidewalks are littered with confetti spread from filled eggshells that are smashed open on the heads of unsuspecting victims in one of Fiesta's most honored baptismal traditions.

My favorite Fiesta event is the "Noches de Ronda" staged over three nights outside the Courthouse, featuring three hours of traditional Spanish folk, salsa and flamenco dancers wearing gloriously colorful dresses, mariachi bands, and singers belting out traditional Spanish songs. The programs, illuminated by the romantic lighting from the Courthouse perimeter on warm August nights, are free to the public gathered on lounge chairs and blankets on the Court-house lawn.

Michael, who knew Tessa and Maggie well, came up with an innovative idea for the program cover. He asked me if my ex-wife and five-year-old daughter would like to dress up in traditional, colorful Fiesta gowns and pose for a photo to be featured on the cover. Maggie loved the idea, so she brought Tessa up to Santa Barbara for a photo shoot in which they got all dolled up in full make-up and dresses, from which Michael caught the perfect image he wanted for his cover design.

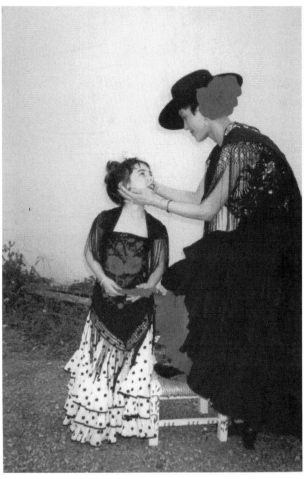

Tessa and Maggie in costume during photo shoot for Santa Barbara's annual Fiesta program cover, which my roommate Michael was commissioned to design

• Pieta was a good-looking young Brazilian man, just 21, who Michael had recruited as a roommate. Pieta was a muscular fellow who practiced ju-jitsu, or the Brazilian equivalent. A few months later, at Michael's behest, Pieta's attractive mother Lizia also briefly moved in, creating a full house.

Pieta will forever be remembered as the hero in the only "rat crisis" I've ever had to deal with in my home. Michael, who occupied the garage bedroom he had created, excitedly emerged from his room one night reporting that he had seen a rat roaming around on one of the shelves in his room. He was freaked out.

Pieta offered to help me eradicate the problem. Michael led us to the room just long enough to point out the shelf on which he had spotted the rat, and then he hurriedly left the room for Pieta and I to deal with it. The shelf was stacked with a pile of folded bathroom towels, so we presumed the rat was hidden behind the stack.

Pieta retrieved his BB rifle from his room. The plan was to shoot and kill the rat with the BB gun. I retrieved a broom, which I intended to use to remove the folded towels one by one until we uncovered the rat. Then, hopefully, Pieta would get a clear shot at him. Sounds like a good plan, huh?

Using the broom handle, I lifted the top towel from the stack and away from the shelf. Nothing. Slowly, I lifted the next towel in the same manner. Still no rat sighting. Then, just as I lifted the third towel, the rat suddenly leaped out from the shelf, front paws fully extended like wings, kinda like SuperRat, startling both Pieta and I as we jumped as far back as that rat leaped forward. He was huge! The rat landed on the carpeted floor and scurried under Michael's bed frame. That was friggin' great.

Pieta and I crouched down on either side of the bed frame to see if we could spot the damn rat. There was an eight-inch clearing from the floor under the frame. Michael, the computer whiz, had a couple of computer components under the bed. We carefully pulled those out of the way so they wouldn't get plugged with BB pellets.

I then stood back while Pieta took his best shot. He missed, and the rat flew out like a bat out of hell, heading straight for the closed bedroom door. It made a couple of frantic leaps at the door — measuring at least two feet in the air — before it scampered back under the bed for cover.

My nerves were completely shot by this point. But Pieta, ever composed, repositioned himself, crouched down on the other side of the bed, and fired away again with the BB gun. This time the rat staggered out bleeding, collapsing in the corner. Pieta took aim and plugged one more BB pellet into him to finish him off. Thank God! I then scooped up the —ugh! — remains.

- Reo joined the household sometime after Matt moved out. As a roommate, he was a "piece of work." Reo was a couple of years older than I. He had a slim, strong, muscular build, with a well-chiseled face set off by a double-cleft chin, piercing blue eyes and short-cropped blond hair. He was a housepainter by trade. He was hyper by nature, with this nervous energy about him that made me nervous sometimes because I was afraid of what he might do if he got mad.

I had to be careful in the way I dealt with Reo, because we occasionally clashed. He was often late with rent or scrambling to come up with the full amount. But most of the time I was able to keep him calm and avoid calamity. Most of the time.

The best thing about Reo as a roommate was his dog Dugan, who was half-Rottweiler, half-German Shepard. He was a gentle giant, weighing about 90 pounds. Dugan got along great with Max. He had an obsession about retrieving tennis balls. He would chase down a tennis ball all day if you were game.

I put up with Reo for about a year. It did not end well. Reo's exit went down as the most bizarre I had experienced with a roommate, by far. Naturally, we were fighting about rent, which got so bad that I had to issue eviction proceedings against him.

The matter came to a head one day and I told Reo that I wanted him to move out sooner rather than later. We became engaged in a loud argument. Pieta was part of this story, too. He was home at the time, outside on the backyard patio sunbathing in a brief Speedo bathing suit. Pieta was quite the specimen in a Speedo.

Reo, ever unpredictable, stormed out of the house in anger. I then noticed, to my shock, that he took my cordless telephone with him. *What the...?*

I had a second phone in the bedroom, so I used it to call the cops. Two police officers arrived within minutes. I tried my best to explain the situation, telling them about the fight I had with Reo. The officers were very nice, but I was very amused by what came next.

One of the officers pointed to Pieta sunbathing on the backyard patio, wearing nothing but the Speedo that highlighted his buff, sun-tanned body.

"Is he the reason why you two were fighting?" the officer asked, referring to Pieta. The officer, no doubt, was a veteran of every domestic relationship crisis in the book.

I had to think for a moment what he was implying. "Oh God, no! It's nothing like that!"

The officer accepted my answer. He then called Reo on my cordless phone that he was carrying while wandering somewhere in the neighborhood. The conversation did not go well. Reo started arguing with the officer, who was yelling in the phone, commanding Reo to return the phone he took.

In the end, I got my phone back and Reo was out by the end of the month. I lost a month's rent. Worse yet, he did something really shitty as a parting shot — he called city officials to report that the converted garage bedroom was an illegal unit. Wasn't that special?

Michael was soooo clever to build those removable bookshelves. We took out the bookshelves, moved out his bed and emptied his room, hoisted up the removable carpet, and basically re-converted the whole garage just for the city inspector to come by to see that the house was up to city code. Then we converted the garage back into Michael's bedroom right after the inspector left.

We needed to eradicate a rat named Reo. We could've used Pieta's BB gun.

CHAPTER 24
Motorcycle Stories

My love affair with motorcycles spanned more than four decades. This collection of stories is spread over that span of time. As with most of my love life, my experience with motorcycles is also filled with frustration.

———————•◆•———————

The first motorcycle I ever owned was a bit of a rarity, an odd model. Would I have it any other way? It was a Honda 305. I was a teenager when I got it. I think the Gerkes were my contact through which I bought it from a private party.

This was the bike with which I impressed the kids at the Children's Baptist Home where I worked while going to college. They were easily impressed. It looked bigger than it sounded and it was pretty cool looking — black and silver.

This was also the bike that inspired my "Easy Rider" short story about two guys riding to Las Vegas and getting stuck with a bike breakdown in Baker, the last town before reaching the state line. To refreshen the story, the two buddies compete for the attention of the beautiful daughter of a tavern owner. The conflict sorta replicated the real-life drama of my losing a short-term girlfriend to my best friend Phil at the time.

The Honda 305 was big and sturdy enough to comfortably support both Dorrean and I for a ride all the way from LA to Montecito to visit Mimi, my grandmother. It was a 100-mile drive, one way, representing the longest drive I've experienced on a bike. Our butts were a little sore and our nerves were a little frazzled from the hum of the engine by the time we got there. But we were young.

We made it to Mimi's little house nestled among the trees and just past the creek in its idyllic setting. We had a lovely visit with the Lavender Lady and her two cats, including the big Siamese she named Ping-Pong in honor of the ping-pong diplomacy the United States was engaging in with Communist China in the late 70s. We spent the night there and survived Mimi's burnt toast and burnt bacon for breakfast; cooking was not her specialty. Then we made the long ride back to LA.

Dorrean and I rode my very first motorcycle, a Honda 305, 100 miles to and from Santa Barbara to visit my grandmother Mimi.

Dorrean and I were not yet married when we made that trip. It was our first road trip together early in our courtship. Times were good for us then.

———————◆———————

The Honda 305 served as my main source of transportation when I was attending Cal State Fullerton. I regularly rode it on weekends down the 91 Freeway west toward LA, headed to my parents' house.

The bike was usually reliable, but it let me down on one ride home down the 91. It was choking up pretty badly and I had to pull off the freeway — in Compton, which wasn't the safest place around. Compton was notorious gang turf in those days.

The bike just died when I pulled off the freeway onto a side street in Compton in broad daylight. Futilely, I tried numerous times to restart the engine, with no luck. The frustration mounted with each unsuccessful attempt, and my uneasiness with the dire situation grew.

When I reached the breaking point, I did not handle it well. I got so mad that I started picking up stones from the ground and throwing them at the bike. It was not a highlight moment for me. I lost all awareness of how my irrational behavior was attracting unwanted attention in dangerous territory. A young white guy tossing stones at a motorcycle in the middle of Compton in the 70's was a recipe for trouble.

A few minutes of stone tossing magically re-started the bike. The engine evidently had just choked on an overflow of gas and needed to sit for a while to clear out. Compton was spared any further spectacle of my shameful tantrum.

The 91 Freeway was the scene of a calamity of a different sort on another homeward-bound trek to my parents' house for the weekend. This time the motorcycle was not at fault.

I was working on my novel, "Last of the Orange Groves," not long after my tenancy with the gay gentlemen and roommates in my college days. I was at the height of my inspiration writing about this experience in the story.

I had 105 typewritten pages of my only copy of the novel — representing many months of work — stacked inside a loose-bound folder. The folder was strapped to the back of my motorcycle seat by a bungee cord during the ride home, down the 91 Freeway.

I was mindlessly humming along, the wind cascading over my helmet, when I suddenly heard a flapping noise behind me. I cranked my neck back and noticed a couple of pages of my novel sticking precariously out of the folder under the grip of the bungee cord. I immediately pulled over to the shoulder of the road and parked the bike to check it out.

I unstrapped the bungee cord, opened up the folder, and to my utter dismay, identified pages 104 and 105 as the two pages that were flapping in the wind. The remaining 103 pages? They were missing!

I turned my gaze back at the freeway and my heart nearly stopped in horror at the sight of white pages flying every which way — like scattered leaves caught in a brisk breeze on an autumn day. Except the brisk breeze was generated by traffic zipping along at 65-to-75 mph.

The trail of flying pages representing my inspired work appeared to extend as far as the eye could see.

I panicked. How could I possibly salvage this, months of hard work at the typewriter, on a body of work in which I had poured out my emotions, my inner thoughts, my soul, in a young life I wanted to share with the rest of the world? Did Hemingway or Twain ever experience such a colossal loss? The next "For Whom the Bell Tolls" or "Huckleberry Finn" could have been out there floating in space, causing a sig alert on the 91. I was delusional, of course, and not thinking coherently in my naivety.

But hope sprung eternal when one of the missing pages landed softly just a few feet away from me. I immediately snatched it up. Then I peered father down the expansive asphalt and noticed floating pages settling off to the side of the road.

Casting away all thought of peril to my safety, I took off running like a crazed madman along the shoulder of the road, against the flow of oncoming traffic. I was still in great running shape, fortunately, having kept up my running regimen ever since my cross-country career ended. Slightly altering my stride when needed, I swept up pages within my grasp on the shoulder of the highway, clinging to bushes on the perimeter, and right out of the air.

There were a few moments when I dodged cars in the slow lane in pursuit of pages that didn't quite make it to the shoulder. Drivers in those cars had to think I was nuts. From the perspective of someone who has committed more than his share of crazy acts in his life, this episode rated right up there as one of the craziest. Hemingway or Twain would have done the same.

At one point I came up to a 12-wheeler freight truck that had pulled over to the shoulder of the road. I noticed one of my pages pinned under one of the big fat tires. Pressing the crumpled stack of pages I had already collected against my chest with one hand, I pried the pinned page from under the tire with the other hand, tearing off the corner to free it. The page was all wrinkled and grease-stained, but I got it, by golly.

I imagined that I would recall that humbling moment years later as a renowned best-selling author. The pains we artists suffer for the sake of our art.

I must have run back a good half-mile or so up the freeway

trying to retrieve my "lost" masterpiece. When all was said and done, of the 103 missing pages, I recovered 73 messy, greasy, torn, wrinkled pages. That meant 30 were gone forever, aflutter somewhere where freeway debris eventually ends up.

In order to restore the original 105-page manuscript, there were gaps from the missing pages scattered throughout that taxed my memory to fill. I labored for six months to get it back to the place I was before I made the knuckle-head decision to strap the manuscript in a loose-bound folder on the back of my motorcycle while hauling down the 91.

———————————◆◆◆◆———————————

The Ely and Gerke gangs that I grew up with loved the outdoors and they loved motorcycles. They were all off-road trail-riding enthusiasts, and they recruited me for one of their weekend rides at Kennedy Meadows in the Mojave Desert. Leading the pack was Mr. Ely, in between beer breaks, partaking in a risky activity usually pursued by men half his age. I still have harrowing memories as a little kid of Mr. Ely strapping me in a go-kart for a rollicking ride down Rossburn, which ended prematurely crashing into the curb. Based on that memory, what did I have to fear?

My off-road comrades convinced me that my Honda 305 was designed for off-road riding as a street-legal vehicle. This would have been a stretch for an experienced rider, given the relative weight of my Honda compared the lighter, nimble bikes everyone else was riding. As a novice rider, I was in for a helluva ride. They all told me not to worry, which was probably the first clue to start worrying right away.

Throughout the ride, I was pretty much helplessly on my own. I had a real hard time keeping up with the gang, given how many times I crashed. But they were patient with me, and I'm sure they were enjoying the comic relief I provided with my pitiful struggles.

Setting the tone for the day, my first crash came when I slid out of control turning a corner and ran into an unforgiving boulder. Ouch!

Next, while zipping along through a small grove of trees on an extremely narrow path I leaned ever so slightly and clipped a tree trunk, which sent me careening into a soft patch of dirt and leaves.

Then, while gingerly easing down a steep hill on a rock-laden trail, I had to plant my foot on the ground a few times to keep from falling, exposing both my inexperience and the lack of nimbleness of my 305.

Then we came upon a fallen tree obstructing the trail. My companions displayed their expertise by dismounting, tilting their lightweight vehicles at a horizontal angle, and juicing the throttle to power-walk their bikes underneath the tree trunk to get past it. Trying to duplicate that maneuver with my beast of a bike was a bitch. It took me eight attempts with an abundance of grunts and groans, much to the amusement of my companions.

But the fitting finale came in classic "How-can-Chic-possibly-mess-this-up" fashion. I was way behind the pack, as usual. I just needed to cross about 50 yards of wide-open meadow to catch up. Setting my sights on my riding party waiting for me at the far end of the meadow, I gassed full-throttle and started making a straight bee-line toward them.

About midway through the meadow I saw a small "puddle" of water ahead. Well, I'll just power right through that, I thought. So I went at it full speed ahead. Funny thing — I miscalculated; that body of water was slightly more substantial than a puddle. As soon as I hit the water my trusty 305 stopped dead in its tracks, stuck in the mud. But I kept projecting forward, flying over the handlebars, crotch bouncing off the front fender and face landing flat in the mud, body spread-eagle.

I was dazed for a few seconds before raising my face out of the mud, which formed a perfectly round happy-face imprint complete with a hole created by my nose. Crutching my dull-aching balls, I slowly turned around to see my bike standing in a complete upright position in that foot-deep "puddle" I tried to power through. Well. that was nice; the bike was spared from getting waterlogged and muddied, while I wallowed in the mud.

Then I heard the sound of a motorcycle approaching; it was Doyle Gerke riding up to check me out.

"Hey, you Ok, bud?" Doyle said with a concerned look on his face.

My face was covered with mud. I wiped the mud from my eyes, picked myself up, and doubled over in pain.

"Yeah, I'm fine," I lied.

The rest of the posse rode up to see if I was all right. Then I recognized Wayne's hearty laugh that I knew so well.

I wore spots of dried cake mud on my face the rest of the day, as a badge of honor for a "Here's-mud-in-your-face" moment.

<hr />

I got it all backward again with my next motorcycle. I acquired a Yamaha 275 two-stroke, which came about on a deal that Brett Ely fixed me up with. This bike definitely was designed to run in the dirt, but the opportunity never came up for another off-roading venture with the Ely and Gerke gang after my inauspicious riding display at Kennedy Meadows.

So, I rode the Yamaha exclusively on the street, where it didn't do so well. Riding that bike on the freeway, headed home from work after 2 a.m., got a bit hairy.

I never felt completely comfortable on that bike, with its high-pitched wheeze that gave you the impression that at any moment you'd hear the loud clunk of a part falling off. The Yamaha was designed for short speed spurts, which was ideal for dirt riding. But on the open highway, it labored to get up to 65 mph.

This was the bike I rode into the Her-Ex sports department, carrying my helmet, that persuaded Allan Malamud to offer me the motorsports beat. The irony goes beyond the fact that I knew nothing about cars or auto racing, like Allan thought, just because I had a motorcycle helmet. It's also the bike that I rode that woman named "Chic" late at night from a Chinatown bar to her car in Montebello where we had sex after she broke off her cop date.

I love motorcycles, but I didn't love that Yamaha. To be fair, I was still on the rebound from the break-up with my 305. We had a great relationship while it lasted. Sure, we had our fights, like that explosive stone-tossing spat we had in Compton. But we always made up afterward. It was important to learn how to forgive in any relationship. Admittedly, the 305 was showing its age in the latter years, so the attraction waned a bit. The big tear in the leather seat exposed some unflattering glucose, err, I mean weather-stained padding underneath. An unsightly wrinkle, or rather a leaky crack on the upper crust of the gas tank, was covered up with a piece of gum, my substitute for costly cosmetic surgery. But beauty was in the eye of the beholder, and I stayed true to my 305 'til the end.

Let's face it, the relationship with the Yamaha was hurtful from the get-go; it was basically a non-starter. I mean that quite literally, because it was a bitch to start the sucker with the kick starter, which was the only option available for turning the engine. I had to stand straight up and jump down as hard as I could muster on the starter foot peg. That stinkin' foot peg would instantly snap back up and smack me hard on my shin, which hurt like hell. Then, when I had to repeat it over and over again — because that Yamaha could be a stubborn one — I'd grimace in anticipation of tortuous pain each time that damn foot peg smacked my shin. There's only so much pain a guy can take. I'm one of those guys who doesn't seem to learn their lesson when it's in their best interest. When you keep repeating the same mistake over and over in a relationship, that's when you know you have to go your separate ways.

———————◆———————

Speaking of repeating the same mistake over and over and not learning my lesson, this next motorcycle story was experienced with Gayle.

It didn't happen on a bike that I owned. But it did happen on a two-wheeled vehicle, so it qualified for this chapter.

The location was a big part of the story. We were vacationing on the Greek Island of Mykonos, a small segment of a much larger trip that will be detailed in a later chapter.

We decided to explore the island on a picture-perfect day by renting a little motor scooter, which was barely big enough to support both of us.

No sooner than we headed out, I looked down at the gas gauge and noticed it was near empty. First order of business was to stop and refuel.

Fortunately, we made it to a gas station without running out of gas. With a full tank, we were on our way. There was something so liberating, humming along in open spaces in such an exotic location.

At one point during our trek, we sped along a road that was parallel to the runway for the Mykonos airport. For a few seconds, we coasted side-by-side with a midsized plane taking off, triggering a heightened sensation created by the sheer contrast in body mass between the two moving vehicles.

With a local map as guidance, we were seeking a particular beach with a particular reputation. Making the climb over a hill that overlooked an intimate azure bay, we found the beach.

Parking our little motor scooter, we joined a large gathering of sunbathers — several hundred people with golden tans. The beach's reputation was intact— nobody was wearing clothes.

We're talking about bodies that Greek sculptors would have used as models. We were in the midst of the beautiful people, mostly young and in the prime of life. A fair percentage of them were young gay couples. Genitalia and breasts were out in the open, free as the air. We freed ourselves from our clothes and joined in. It was a large gathering on a fairly small beach, so there was no room for shyness.

The smell of tanning oils integrated with the smell of money. Anchored close offshore were a couple of large yachts. A cabana nearby offered alcoholic cocktails that were priced for those who could afford them.

Swimming bare naked in the warm Mediterranean water felt like an experience I had to hold onto. I could not imagine coming back to such a dream-like place again.

———————◆◆◆———————

The real love of my life with relation to motorcycles didn't come until I moved to Santa Barbara. It had been a good 10 years or more since I had owned a motorcycle, I was missing having one and I wasn't getting any younger. So, one day, in a casual conversation with a woman who worked in the composing room at the News-Press, she mentioned that her boyfriend had a motorcycle for sale.

It was a 1982 Honda Hawk 450.

She showed me a picture. It was love at first sight. It was another black beauty, with orange trim. It was the perfect size. I didn't want something too big that I couldn't handle and I didn't want something too small that would be too wimpy. This just felt so right, a match made in heaven. I instantly proposed — sorry, no more wedding metaphors — I meant, made a bid.

So, I was back on two wheels and loving it. This was my version of dealing with the proverbial mid-life crisis. This was the start of a 20-year relationship, longer than all of my marriages combined (oops, did it again on the marriage theme.)

The Hawk came in handy around town for large events at which parking was scarce. But my favorite destination for a ride was heading over San Marcos Pass, either to the top of the mountain ridge overlooking Santa Barbara and the ocean out to the Channel Islands, or on the other side in the Santa Ynez Valley. I often stopped at the campgrounds at Lake Cachuma.

On Sunday afternoons I liked riding up to the top of the Pass and turning off Stagecoach Road to the historic Cold Spring Tavern, a former Pony Express outpost in the 1870s. The Tavern's rustic, weathered log structure evokes an Old West feel and ambiance. Most of the Sunday crowd that usually gathered there arrived on Harleys. They came to enjoy live music and the Tavern's irresistible tri-tip sandwiches and beer. I'd park my little ol' Hawk next those muscular Harleys, and join in with the crowd. Local bands played at Cold Spring — the duo of Tom Ball and Kenny Sultan were regular performers on Sundays — and were typically either folk or country. They would play outside on the front porch of the Tavern, creating a scene that felt like a backyard party. The tri-tip was grilled on an oversized barbecue off to the side of the building, offering a flavorful aroma from the smoke wafting in the air.

Whenever the chance presented itself, I liked taking people for rides up to Camino Cielo Road as it snaked along the top of the mountain ridge to see the magnificent view. I took my sister Pam up there once. The Hawk had one minor glitch that got us in trouble that day. The gas gauge didn't work, so I got in the habit of constantly peeking inside the tank and wiggling the bike to hear the swishing sound of gas to make sure it wasn't empty. I forgot to peek and wiggle for this trip. Oops.

We were done taking in the spectacular view as the sun was slowly descending on the ocean horizon. We climbed back on board the bike and had made it only about a half-mile on the descent back down the mountain when the engine started to chug.

I quickly turned the gas switch to the auxiliary option, but that carried us for only another mile or so. Hopelessly, we coasted to a stop, completely out of fuel. With the sun starting to set and the closest gas station located at the bottom of the basin, a good eight miles down, we were in a predicament.

But the solution was all downhill from there. I geared the bike in neutral, Pam and I together gave it a little push down the hill, then we jumped on board. It was a gamble, but we proved it could be done — we silently coasted in neutral all the way down the mountain on my Hawk for about eight miles without the engine running. We were within about a half-mile of a gas station when the road finally flattened out. I was able to push it myself from there. We refueled and rode home the rest of the way, just before darkness set in.

———————•••◆•••———————

I've often been told that I was pushing my luck every time I rode a motorcycle.

I was never the kind of guy to push his luck. (Smile.)

Not counting Kennedy Meadows, I went down on the street only once while riding a bike.

It wasn't very eventful. I was in the left-hand turn lane, waiting for the light to change. When it turned green, I hung a left onto a small side street. I hit a large patch of loose gravel in the pedestrian cross lane and the back tire lost its grip and slid out from under me. I did a side slide under 10 mph for about 12 feet, landing pretty hard on my left shoulder. I scraped my left knee up pretty good, too.

But other than that, I was none the worse for wear, and neither was the bike. I did have to straighten out the gear shifter a little bit. And it took a little more than a week for the shoulder to stop hurting.

———————•••◆•••———————

This next story was saved for last, as a lead-in into the next chapter. This story was specifically crafted to read before a live audience, which I was privileged to do one night. The story recounted a very special day, on one of those beautiful rides on my Hawk up to the top of San Marcos Pass, for a very special moment in my life.

———————◆———————

At first the rays took on the shape of a giant monarch butterfly, no shit. Yeah, you would've wanted to be smoking what I was smoking.

———————◆———————

One Of Those "I Saw God" Days

December. 23, 2001. As I accelerated my motorcycle up the San Marcos Pass highway on this gorgeous, crisp December afternoon, I pictured this day's date in my own obituary. The thought that this could be the day I die was enough to keep my focus on the road so that my thought didn't manifest into a self-fulfilling prophesy.

That thought took on a whole new meaning when it turned out I saw a glimpse of heaven this day. But to get there felt like defying death. A little paranoid, yeah, maybe. But I was taking some risk on that ride in the late afternoon sun. I wound up climbing a winding, severely cracked and marbled one-lane road while passing through alternating patches of bright sun and dark shadows. To add to the risk, I was high as a kite on pot, with more packed away in a pocket on the full-bodied ski suit that my roommate Reo gave me. It kept me warm in that icy air.

Cruisin' Santa Barbara in a ski suit. Yeah.

But the perceived danger pervaded, so I kept telling myself I had to pay attention. And to expect the unexpected. And the unexpected kept coming in surprising but harmless ways. I traversed up the extremely narrow, twisting Painted Cave Road, taking it to heavenly Camino Cielo Road at the top of the mountain ridge that overlooks Santa Barbara. "This is unbelievable," I said to myself, my senses hyper heightened, as I stopped to sit at a grassy ledge overlooking the city extending out to the sea, with sun drops sparkling like diamonds. I was reminded how thankful I am living in this paradise, devoid of deadly ice and snow, in which a ski suit would be suitable attire.

The unexpected kept coming in various forms — like, the two life-sized dummies dressed as farmers in blue-jean suspenders and straw hats, stationed at the front gate of a mansion I passed on Painted Cave Road; like, the young woman riding a horse with her dog at her side, which took some careful maneuvering with my motorcycle so as to not spook either the horse or dog; like, the pack of young BMXers just finishing a fun ride on Camino Cielo, which may have been problematic had we crossed paths moments earlier.

I stopped at a turnout on Camino Cielo, dismounted my beat-up old bike and took in the view from either direction. A sense of utter peace swept away the sense of peril. First, I looked north toward the

Santa Ynez Valley where shadows began growing longer on the sun-facing, color-drenched mountain range in the distance. I saw two magnificent hawks floating in unison down the canyon in full wingspread. I was looking down on them, following their effortless glide. Then suddenly they both accelerated downward like a couple Kamikaze bombers until they swiftly disappeared from view in the recesses of the canyon. Then, I looked south toward a blue-gray Santa Barbara spreading its wings out to the ocean where the steadily sinking sun sprinkled its glitter.

I noticed a path from the turnout, leading up to some pink rocks about 100 feet higher up. I ventured up the path, which first curved toward the valley side, then within a few strides, reached the top where the ocean side reappeared. A little further I came upon a splendid, slanted, smooth rock standing about 12 feet high. I easily scaled up the ragged edge of the rock and sat on its perfect perch, facing the sun in a meditative state.

From my perch, I could see down below a black Mercedes pull up and park off to the side of the road. Three elderly people emerged out of the car. One of them, a woman whose perfectly-coifed blonde hair was set off by her long, elegant red gown and black stole, turned toward the ocean view, and in an operatic soprano voice that reverberated down the canyon, suddenly started belting out:

"The hills are alive with the sound of music." Hearing that woman in red's beautiful voice fill the space in this beautiful place was pure joy.

After the Mercedes drove off, I cast my gaze at the sun. The glow of the sun at first was a comfort to my eyes through my sunglasses. Then it became much, much more. The longer I stared, visions appeared before me in the sun's rays, no doubt the Mojo Risin' effect taking hold. At first the rays took on the shape of a giant monarch butterfly, no shit. Yeah, you would've wanted to be smoking what I was smoking.

Then I saw something that blew me away. I'm not particularly a religious man, but for a moment I swear I recognized the face of Jesus in the face of the sun.

"I saw God," I thought to myself.

Captivated, as I scrutinized the light show on the water, I saw a pattern that at first I likened to a stream. Then I thought for a moment and decided, "No, it's a path." From my view the path was ascending upward toward a ribbon of haze hovering just under the face of Jesus, like a final crossing before reaching heaven. The haze, I thought, represented the Great Unknown.

That's when I thought of Dan, my best friend in life who had unexpectedly departed for the Great Unknown 11 months and a day before. Dan frequently flirted with his fate in self-fulfilling prophesy fashion, as he had predicted long ago he would never make it to the age of 50, and he was right. So it was, at a time in his life when he had everything to live for, on that early morning drive last January on a rural road in snow-covered northern Washington, he likely pushed it too far, as he was inclined to do, on the gas pedal in his Mazda Miata that caused his tires to lose traction on black ice, slip-sliding him into the broadside of another car, and taking another life with him.

Dan appears as an eery ghost-like figure in this photo that I weirdly captured (no Photoshop magic here), highly likely during a Mojo Risin' moment

I will never truly know if Dan really knew when he would die, much less project the date in his own obituary that shared space with that of the other driver, thus deepening the mystery of the Great Unknown. But there were a whole lot of strange circumstances surrounding Dan's death, none stranger than something waiting for me that shook me to my core, when I visited his girlfriend Tami in Washington a few weeks after his death. She gave me a cassette tape that Dan had compiled for me over the Christmas holidays, on which he recorded 40-some rock 'n roll songs from the 60's that he personally selected, a soundtrack of our youth. After four songs into the recording, Dan interrupted to say this: "Taking a little break from the music. I'm thinking of you, my friend, hope you're thinking of me. Bye."

Just like that, an abrupt "bye," then back to the music. Then Dan made a particularly vexing choice with the very next song he recorded, which was bone-chilling to hear, to say the least, when one-hit wonder Norman Greenbaum started singing:

"When I die, and they lay me to rest, I'm gonna go to the place that's the best, when they lay me down to die, I'm goin' up to the Spirit in the Sky."

I felt like the Spirit in the Sky was speaking to me on this day, Dec. 23, 2001, on that pink rock. I allowed myself to think that maybe it was Dan's face that I was seeing in the sun instead. Regardless, I knew he was watching me, probably chuckling at my marijuana-induced state that we had shared together way too often.

That's when I came up with a new plan for Dan. Dan's ashes, that is, the ones that still resided in my bedroom, in the paper vase that Tami constructed out of a thick sheet of plain off-white canvas paper by way of thirty-something folds. I'd wait for another day just like this –- and you know Santa Barbara will have a day just like this soon, one of those days only God can create. A handful of his ashes would be saved for Deep Creek; I hadn't forgotten my promise. But I'll take the rest of Dan with me on my rusty but trusty motorcycle to return to this slanted pink rock, and cast Dan out, from which he could scatter every which way. A whiff of him could wind up on the valley side, whooshing down with the hawks. And a cloud of him could carry out and settle at sea, and flicker like diamonds. And a pinch of him could sprinkle the ground and nourish the neighboring bushes that I truly believed were waving at me in the breeze. Or, flippin' me off, as my contrarian friend would have it. I think that meant he approved of my new plan for Dan, and that I could finally let go.

Finally heading for home, I was racing against the setting sun before my ride would be completed under darkness. I lost that race, because I couldn't help making several more stops to marvel at the beauty that was unfolding before me. At one point I looked to my left to see the green mountainside become awash by a red glow.

I thought, "Hmm, green and red. It's looking like Christmas." Santa Barbara-style.

My pink rock atop Camino Cielo overlooking Santa Barbara area and Santa Ynez Valley, where the paper vase containing Dan's ashes is perched

CHAPTER 25
Black Ice

It was just one game on the road in an otherwise dismal 2000-2001 season for the UCSB men's basketball team, in the dead of winter. It was the post-holiday blues, in mid-January. Our esteemed sports editor Mark Patton, who also was the beat writer for Gaucho men's basketball, took one look at the calendar and decided, nah, he didn't have to go to that game at the University of Idaho. It took a lot for Mark to miss a Gaucho men's basketball game. But this one, he could skip.

So, he sent me instead.

No matter how bad the team was, it was Gaucho men's basketball, the most popular team in town for Santa Barbara. So, coverage was mandatory. The boss didn't want to go but I was more than willing to take the assignment.

It was a quick weekend trip: Fly into Spokane, Washington, which was the closest available flight to Moscow, Idaho, where the University of Idaho was located, on a Friday. Make the 90-mile drive south down to Moscow, just on the other side of the Idaho border, for an overnight stay. Game on Saturday night, drive back to Spokane right after the game, and fly home late Saturday night. That was the itinerary.

I booked the same round-trip flight as the team. But I rented my own car for the drive from Spokane-to-Moscow and back. The drive back after the game on Saturday night was the tricky part for me — the team bus wasn't going to wait for me to write and file my game story. So, with my own ride, I took some pressure off getting my story done without holding up the team, and the flight was still late enough to get to the airport on time. The News-Press traveled on the cheap, so I rented a sub-compact car.

We arrived in Spokane at mid-afternoon that blustery Friday in January. It was lightly snowing. There was already enough snow on the ground to bury a good-sized basketball player standing upright.

The UCSB team bus pulled away from the airport well ahead of me by the time I picked up my tiny rental car. I climbed in and turned on the wipers to wipe away the slushy snowflakes on the wind shield, and an annoying squeaking noise from the wipers set in immediately. I braced, waiting for the noise to go away once the wipers warmed up. But it wasn't going away. Oh great, I was going to have to listen to that on the whole drive to Moscow. I decided I'd have to keep turning them on and off to minimize the distraction.

I headed out on the two-lane "highway" that would lead to Moscow. As soon as I accelerated to more than 35 mph, I could feel slippage on the tires as the car started to swerve out of control. I gripped the steering wheel, backed off the gas and gathered the car back onto a straight line.

"What the hell?" I thought. Then I remembered what Dan told me a couple of years ago about "black ice" that was prevalent in Northern Washington this time of year. He described the obvious dangers of black ice on asphalt, the fact that it was much more dangerous than slushy snow, which you could actually see. But black ice was invisible, because it was a clear frozen sheet on top of black asphalt, thereby camouflaging the slippery conditions.

I tried locking my speed in at 35 mph but even that was too fast heading into a turn. The first turn I came to scared the living bejeezus out of me, as a huge Mack truck came barreling around the bend. There was no divide separating me from oncoming traffic; all that lay between me and that huge truck was a three-foot wide path of slush. The truck's massive tires sprayed some of that slush onto the side panels of my tiny rental car as it roared by.

Oh my God. That was enough for a guy who lived all his life in sunny Southern California to say, "Get me outa here! Where's the turnoff for the beach?" But I had no choice. I had 89 more miles to go to get to Moscow. This was Gaucho men's basketball, after all, and I had a duty to perform.

I looked around and saw nothing but 15-foot-high snowbanks on either side of the road. I imagined that this is what Siberia looked like on a road to Moscow, Russia.

More large trucks and more blind curves were to follow. As I crept along a little further at about 30 mph, darkness descended quickly with daylight shortened in the peak of winter. It was nerve-wracking enough turning the squeaky windshields wipers on and off, which intermittently clouded my view. But all of a sudden, entering a bend, my eyes were blinded by red flare-lights spread out on the shoulder of the road. My foot hit the brake. The flares were placed to protect rescue workers helping a car that was stuck in the deep ditch off to the side of the road.

No sooner than my eyes adjusted back to black of night, another flash of red flare-lights sent my brake foot into action. Another car in the ditch. Then came a third set of flares, same story. The flares and cars in the ditch kept a-comin'.

As I precariously drove on, I was desperately looking for some sign of civilization, because I was getting hungry. Driving slowly through the bleak vastness, I was losing hope.

A good hour-and-a-half into the drive I saw a sign of life, approaching a small town, with darkness closing in at about 4:30 pm. I spotted an Arby's sign on the left side. Choices were very limited so I went for it and pulled into Arby's.

Inside, while waiting for my order, a large radio on the front counter broadcasting a local music station had the volume cranked up. I perked up when I heard the DJ interject between songs, talking about the weather, basically describing how god-awful it was.

"Folks, if you needed any excuse to stay home tonight, anchor down and stay put! This is no night to be out driving. The roads are very hazardous with black ice conditions and we're getting numerous reports of car accidents out there! So, don't venture out, unless it's for an extreme emergency!"

Calm my beating heart! That was all I needed to hear with another 50 miles and who-knows-how-long-of-a-drive to go. I hurriedly gulped down my roast beef sandwich and fries, got back into my car, turned on the squeaky windshield wipers, and headed out with frozen fingers crossed. As I crossed the mid-stripe slush on the street to get back on the right track, the car started to fishtail and shake violently for a couple seconds. That frazzled my nerves to no end, slushing my Arby's-stuffed stomach around a bit, with that momentary feeling of helplessness.

I passed more cars that had landed in the ditch parallel to the road along the way. At one point, I approached a police car parked in the middle of the road to block traffic for a tow truck to haul a car out of peril in the ditch. Two cars were idling in front of the police car blockade, so I attempted to slow down to fall in line behind them. Funny thing, my car kept sliding forward and I had to swerve left into the lane for oncoming traffic to avoid rear-ending the second idling car. Holding my breath, I managed to bring my car to a stop dead-even with the lead car. I managed to resume breathing, then I patiently remained frozen in place for another five minutes, waiting for the police to signal us forward.

When the police finally waved us on, I looked at the lady in the SUV next to me and gestured for her to go ahead of me. But, oh no, she wanted no part of taking the lead. She gestured for me to go first. Well hell, why not? So me and my little sub-compact inched ahead of her giant SUV and I turned the steering wheel over to my Guardian Angel.

Over the next excruciating 25 miles, all the way into Moscow, I led a caravan of about 14-15 cars on that wicked road. As a laid-back Californian I was probably the worst candidate to be leading the pack safely through. My speedometer never pushed past 25 mph and none of those cars were in any hurry to pass me.

I was the Pied Piper for a long, slow train of headlights dimmed by the mist of light snowflakes. I wound up counting *two dozen* cars in all that landed in the ditch amid Siberia West territory. How I managed to avoid joining them in the ditch, or something worse, was nothing short of miraculous. That black ice was nasty. There's nothing like it that I could compare it to living all my life in Southern California. Nothing comes close.

Somehow, by the grace of God, I finally was barely able to read the blurry sign for the hotel in Moscow where the team was staying. I completed the 90-mile drive just under four tortuous hours. That cheap Arby's roast beef sandwich didn't settle well in my gurgling stomach.

I made a decision as soon as I checked into my hotel room. I booked a second night at the hotel and changed my flight home for early Sunday afternoon. The weather report forecasted blizzard conditions for Saturday night after the basketball game. There was no way in hell I was going to make that 90-mile drive back to the Spokane Airport in a blizzard.

I attended the UCSB-University of Idaho men's basketball game that Saturday night with some peace of mind. The Gauchos lost a one-point heartbreaker, with Idaho scoring the winning basket with 4.3 seconds remaining. That was cold, really cold. Hmm, look what you missed out on, Mark Patton. But I slept well that night on my second night in my hotel room.

The drive back to Spokane Sunday morning was lovely. The storm that had blown through the night before had passed and the sun was shining through scattered clouds. I enjoyed a leisurely drive. The difference between the drives that Sunday morning and hellacious Friday night was *literally* night and day.

I made my flight in plenty of time. On my flight home, I reflected long and hard on that arduous drive on Friday, when I was really scared that I could've easily died somewhere on that road, a victim of black ice. Truly, I had my Guardian Angel watching over me. I was so thankful to be back in mellow, mild Santa Barbara on Sunday night.

As I stood in the auxiliary parking lot at the Santa Barbara Airport loading my suitcase into my car that Sunday night, I could have kissed the non-black ice asphalt I was standing on.

———————— ◆ ————————

The very next morning, Monday, the phone rang, unexpectedly and very early. It awakened Gayle and I, who were sleeping in her bed at her house.

Gayle answered, then handed the receiver to me with this strange look on her face. She was speechless, unable to get any words out. My mind raced with what possible terrible news awaited on the other end.

Please God, not one of my kids!, I thought, as I took the phone. Instead, I heard:

"Dan's dead!"

It was Tami. I wasn't quite connecting how she would have known to call me at Gayle's. Then I went into that momentary shock phase in which I couldn't transmit the reality of those two words. Dan's dead. Dan died. Gone.

In a flash, with those two words, the world seemed so different.

I flashed on a momentary feeling of relief that it wasn't one of my kids. But my mind spun instantly on the dreaded realization that it was my best friend instead. Finally, I was able to respond somehow.

"Whaaa? What happened? How did he die?"

"Car accident." Tami's meek, shaky voice displayed a controlled manner under the duress of a complete breakdown. "Black ice got him."

Now, the reality of *those* two words hit me like a ton of bricks, or worse yet, a Mack truck slip-sliding on *"black ice"* on Deadman's Curve.

I was trying to wrap my head around what Tami was saying. The conjunction of two events separated by a mere 60 hours — the frightening drive I had just gone through on Friday, within the same state boundaries and virtually the same storm that created the black ice conditions that killed Dan that morning — was too weird. This was one of those moments when your mind plays tricks on you, when you get these crazy thoughts in your head. Thoughts relating to your gratitude for your Guardian Angel's intervention that decides your fate, but in exchange a sacrifice is made at the bidding of black ice that claims the life of your best friend. That's messed up, thinking that way. But emotion rules the mind. You own it.

So I quietly listened.

"He was driving the Miata, on his way to work. He was driving too fast. It's freezing cold here. He lost control on black ice, slid into another car. Killed the other driver.

"I could hear the sirens from our house, but I had no idea they were for Dan!"

Listening to Tami describe the fatal accident reminded me of describing to Dan the fatal accident that killed Fred, falling off the cliff on Yosemite's Half Dome. The parallels were creeping up. It was an eerie feeling, to be on the receiving end of that exchange, the same position I was with Dan on my call fifteen years ago. It wasn't exactly deja vu, but maybe deja vu *flipped*, a mirror image reflected back on me.

As Tami talked more, her voice began to crack. I hung onto every word, my gut tightening in a gripping knot, my head spinning with all sorts of thoughts. But mostly, I ached, every fiber in my bones.

"You know what, Chic," Tami intoned, the borderline hysteria immediately dissipating into mournful realization. "Today is January 22nd, the same day my grandmother died. The two people I loved most in this world!"

454

Finally, she couldn't hold back the tears.

Tami had called my house and got Gayle's number from the roommate who answered. It was evident that she went out of her comfort zone to reach me. She needed to talk to me that morning. I felt suddenly very close to her.

Tami tearfully told me about having to visit the morgue to identify Dan. She took Agnes, their dog, with her. Instead of telling me how she reacted seeing Dan's body, all crushed and bloodied from the accident, she described Agnes' reaction. That was so *totally Dan* coming out of her, describing something from a dog's point of view. Agnes extended her nose to get a whiff of Dan lying on the slab. Then she gave Tami a quizzical look, knowing something was different about Dan. He didn't smell right. Dan, the way he was with dogs, would understand Agnes' agony.

When I finally hung up the phone, I collapsed in Gayle's arms. She tried to kiss my tears away. When I caught a glimpse of those beautiful green eyes of hers, I could see she looked very, very afraid.

———————◆———————

Tami and I had so much more to talk about that couldn't be covered in that call that Monday morning. For starters, we both knew we had to do something for Dan's mother, Mrs. Levandowski, who lived in Long Beach. I always called her "Mrs. L." She was old (80) and in poor health and she was living with her 90-year-old sister Beatrice, who was only slightly healthier.

Both Tami and I felt an obligation to arrange a memorial so Mrs. L could properly mourn the loss of her only child — her adopted son. We knew she and Beatrice were members of a local church in Long Beach. I called the pastor to set something up in which the whole congregation would be invited. He fully cooperated.

Tami, meanwhile, had called Mrs. L initially to break the terrible news to her. I followed up with a call to Mrs. L to let her know that everything was being taken care of by her church. She was so grateful. She was a sweet old lady whose Midwestern roots made her humble toward the spirit of generosity.

"Chic, Dan always loved you," she told me over the phone. I knew that, but was grateful to hear it from her.

I paid a visit to her and Bernice later in the week at the Leisure

World senior living complex where they resided. They had been living together for a quarter century after Bernice's husband died. Mrs. L's husband died when Dan was 12. He didn't talk much about that, but I knew it made the mother-son bond stronger.

During my visit, Mrs. L was sitting comfortably in the lounge chair that Dan had bought a couple of Christmases ago. It had a mechanical switch that lifted the chair to make it easier for her to stand up. She was very fragile. Dan had related to me last summer that he didn't expect his mother to make it to another Christmas.

"This chair is one of the best presents Dan ever gave me," Mrs. L said in a rare moment of glee.

Both she and Bernice expressed their grief in their simple, Missouri farm-upbringing sort of way.

"I can't believe he's gone, Chic," Mrs. L said. Her voice sounded tired, weak, bereft of the strength to weep.

I also had to call Leo, Dan's college buddy who lived in Long Beach. Leo was a cool dude — lanky, curly-haired, easy smile, studious-looking with his wire-rimmed glasses. He was the epitome of laid-back. This call was a chilling reminder of the one I made to Dan 15 years earlier when Fred died.

"Aw geez, good 'ol Dan is dead," Leo said, simply.

Leo wanted to attend the memorial, for sure. It was set up for Tuesday, January 30, a mere eight days after the accident.

Tami arrived in Santa Barbara on the Friday night before the memorial. She was waiting for me to pick her up at the airbus drop-off at the beach-front Ramada Inn. She was sitting on a bench, bundled up in a warm jacket and wool cap on a chilly, clear evening, waiting about 10 minutes longer than expected because I went to the wrong spot at first.

But when I got there and jumped out of my car, she stood up to greet me. I took her in my arms and held her for a good 10 minutes while she quietly cried into my shoulder. I never felt so bonded with someone as I did with her during those 10 minutes. Not a word was spoken between us. We just held each other. My heart melted for this scared, pretty, shattered young woman, all of 23 years old, less than half my age. She was 17 when she met Dan. She grew up with Dan. He was the only man she ever loved.

Gayle was waiting for us back at my house. In her endearing, motherly fashion, she offered Tami as much comfort as she could.

Gayle knew Tami and I were both grieving. That was a topic for discussion between Gayle and I on the night before Tami's arrival. Gayle was worried about the night following Tami's arrival. Gayle had to work that night and she didn't want us to be getting too close.

"I don't want you doing anything with her that might impair your judgement," my insecure girlfriend was telling me. Yes, the trust issue was being raised again.

In other words, she didn't want me to do any pot smoking or drinking of alcohol with Tami — like we customarily did on all of my summer Washington visits when Dan was alive — before Gayle arrived from work that night to join us.

This was just a prelude to greater friction to come.

———————◆————————

The memorial service was lovely. It was everything Tami and I could hope for Mrs. L. and Beatrice.

There were about 40 people in attendance, all of them near or about the same age as Mrs. L. It was a senior crowd. None of them knew Dan. They were just there for the free food. But that's OK, Dan would've been fine with that, as long as his mom was comforted.

When I reflect back on Dan's memorial, l always relate it to Elton John's heart-rendering song "Daniel," with Bernie Taupin's haunting lyrics:

"Daniel is traveling tonight on a plane…"

Tami elected not to say anything to the congregation. But Leo did; it was short, but sweet.

So did I. I had a long speech all typed out that likely put a few octogenarians in the audience to sleep. I acknowledged Dan's mom — her name was June— and Tami, and how much each of them meant to Dan. And Beatrice, how much she meant to her sister. Then I told all of my best Dan stories— how we met in high school, the tackle football games, the Mother Puckers, our days as college roomies, working at the Children's Baptist Home.

"After college, Dan, of course, stood by me as my best man at my first wedding," I told the gathering. "He was my best man at my second wedding as well. After that I think I just dreaded the idea of asking him. The point is, I've been through a lot of rocky relationships and Dan saw me through all of them. Even though we lived a thousand miles apart the last 20 years or so, he was always a phone call away. And every time he allowed me to vent, air things out, help me sort out what was really important and usually, find a way to get me to laugh when I needed it most.

"If he wasn't home when I called, I could usually count on some sort of funny phone message for which he was notorious. One recurring example had something to do with leaving Oreo cookies and a flashlight for space aliens who might want to make human contact; the flashlight, of course, was left for the aliens because, as he'd say, 'We know it's dark up there.' That just gives you some idea of Dan's sense of humor."

"Oh I miss Daniel, I miss him so much"

I talked about our river trips, Bark Too Eat Too, Rogie, Solomon, Godiva, Agnes, my excruciating call to him when Fred died, and the parallel I drew to the call I got from Tami.

Then I finished up with: "In closing, I just want to say that if any of you are looking up at the sky one of these nights and you see a blinking star, Dan would want you to know that it's him, with a flashlight, sharing Oreo cookies with space aliens."

"Daniel, you're a star in the face of the sky"

Tami and I felt good about the parting gift we gave Mrs. L. Three weeks later, she passed away and joined Dan in the face of the sky. She lived just barely long enough to see her only son die.

———————◆———————

Tami had another memorial service for Dan in the works up in Washington a couple of weekends following the Long Beach service. It was set for a Saturday with the school where Dan worked. Dan was revered by kids and parents alike at that school.

But Gayle couldn't go that Saturday because she was scheduled to work again. As a nurse, her work schedule was inflexible. I had no problem getting the time off from my work. But she let me know she didn't like the idea of my going up there without her. She knew how much I wanted to go, to visit Dan and Tami's house one more time.

Gayle saw Tami and I bonding over a shared love for Dan and it scared her. Tami was very pretty and very vulnerable. And me? How was I feeling?

We went a bit deeper on my feelings for Tami, farther than a little impairment of my judgement from pot and alcohol. I was flabbergasted. I admitted to some genuine feelings for Tami and I wanted to be there for her to comfort her, to share our mutual grief. But Gayle's mistrust in me was a bit off-putting. This was Dan's girlfriend, and ethically, I would never go there with Tami on a physical level. That would feel like a manipulation on my part, to exploit her vulnerability. She was very young. I had to be the strong one here, just in case — hypothetically — there came a point where we both fell into a sentimental trap that we might regret later.

Gayle wasn't the only one challenging me on my feelings for Tami. I had someone else push me into an extended dialogue on the same subject. I am speaking of Frank, who was another longtime tenant at my mother's house and became a virtual family member, forging ties with both my mother and sister. I considered him a friend.

Frank was a couple of years older than me, born in Brazil but raised in the U.S, and graduated from Hawthorne High. He was also a journalist and a writer like me; he had professional ties with NASA, which he reported on extensively. Through his work he met some well-known people in the space industry; he forged a personal friendship with moon traveler Buzz Aldrin.

Frank was a large man with a large personality and ego. He loved instigating philosophical discussions. He was a deep thinker and was not afraid to express his opinion.

He barely knew Dan, but his death greatly intrigued him. Frank often talked about his own mortality. He had met both Dan and Tami when they had come to LA for the holidays a year earlier. Frank had a thing for pretty young women, and I sensed that he was attracted to Tami.

I instigated the discussion when I told Frank about Gayle's jealousy over Tami. In the turmoil of my grief, I admitted that I had this thought buried in the back of my mind that I could be attracted to Tami. But Frank coerced me into bringing those feelings to the forefront, acknowledging them and analyzing them.

"Tami's a beautiful young lady," Frank said in his open, candid way. "And she's very vulnerable right now. As Dan's best friend, you'd be a natural person she would turn to for support. I'm sure you want to support her emotionally, as much as you can. But that could get dicey. If I were I in your shoes, I could see how that would be very tempting for the possibility of it evolving into something a little more compromising. No wonder Gayle is jealous."

"That all may be true," I said. "But I would never act on those feelings, just out of respect for Dan."

"Are you sure? What about your screenplay based on Dan and Tami?"

Ahh yes, my screenplay, "The Big Lie," which exposed a veiled envy of Dan's relationship with Tami. Was I lying to myself?

"That's a work of fiction," I told him.

So, no matter how much it hurt, I did what I thought was the right thing to do; I acquiesced to Gayle's wishes. I did not fly up to Washington for Dan's memorial. We agreed to go up together a couple of weeks later when Gayle was free from work.

———————◆•••————

Three weeks after Dan's death, in mid-February, was the running of the Daytona 500, NASCAR'S season-opening auto race. Gayle and I were still a week away from our planned trip up north to visit Tami.

Up until then, I really hadn't expressed my grief in any overt manner. I had been pretty numb the whole time, bottling up my emotions. I got choked up at the Long Beach memorial, but there were no outright tears.

Then it happened, while I was watching the Daytona 500 on TV. Dale Earnhardt, the NASCAR legend nicknamed "Ironhead" for his fearlessness on the racetrack, was trying to hold off Sterling Marlin for third place in the fourth turn of the final lap.

Earnhardt's car made contact with Marlin's car, spun out of control and slid off the track. As he veered back on the track, he crossed directly in front of the car of Kenny Schrader, who collided with him. Earnhardt was dragged a short distance down the track until he smacked head-on into the retaining wall at about 160 mph. The front of the car collapsed upon impact.

Less than two hours after the accident, NASCAR announced that "Ironhead" had died.

The moment I heard the news, I started bawling like a baby. My body shook uncontrollably as I cried. Grief presents itself in peculiar ways sometimes.

I held no particular affection for Dale Earnhardt during my years of covering motorsports, but I respected the man and what he represented to millions of race fans. His reputation on the racetrack was that nothing would stop him from going all-out in pursuit of taking that checkered flag. Race fans loved that about him. So, the idea that he would perish, just like that in a flash…A momentary tap between two race cars… a momentary slip on black ice.

Dale Earnhardt's death was truly a shock, but my tears were for Dan. The tragedy at Daytona set off a violent emotional release in me that had been delayed three weeks. An incredible burden was unleashed, as I linked the pain that a legion of race fans would feel over the loss of Dale Earnhardt with the pain I felt over the loss of Dan.

Earnhardt was 49. Dan was 48. Neither of them would reach their 50th birthday.

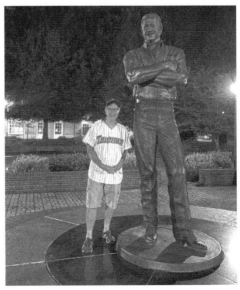

Twenty years after his death, I visited the Dale Earnhardt tribute square in his hometown of Kannapolis, N.C., while visiting my friend Paul

It was still the dead of winter in late February when Gayle and I finally made it up to Sedro Woolley to commiserate with Tami and Agnes. It was snowing, very gray, very cold.

Tami described for us all that had transpired at the memorial at the school. The entire school was in mourning. Students were grieving over losing their favorite teacher. Parents were grieving over losing a teacher who had made a dramatic impact on their kids. It sounded like a highly emotional gathering that I regretted not attending. I felt a little resentment toward Gayle for not trusting me enough to go without her.

Tami walked us out to the scene of the accident, which was only about a quarter mile from their home. The accident occurred at the intersection of a rural road passing through grazing pastures for horses and cattle.

At one of the corners of the intersection, Tami set up a little memorial site for Dan. The centerpiece was a cross, constructed out of plastic tubing and wood. The horizontal wood bar had inscribed on it: "Take Care My Friend" on the top and "Soar With the Eagles" across the center. The vertical plastic tube was filled with colorful rocks and marbles and other shiny objects that Dan liked to use in art creations.

Directly behind the memorial, in a corner of the grazing pasture, stood a rusty, metal frame of an old-fashioned plow with oversized wheels and a central driver seat. It was on display like a museum relic from a by-gone era. I took several photos of the memorial site, with the plow in the background, on that gray, moody morning.

It was such a strange feeling to be standing at that intersection, in front of Tami's lovely memorial, picturing Dan's final moment. I shuddered; I silently wept.

Tami gave me a copy of a local newspaper article reporting the accident and fatalities. The other driver was a respected 72-year-old retired school teacher who was "running down to Seattle to baby-sit her grandchildren," a friend was quoted as saying. The article stated that Dan slid on black ice and broadsided the other car. "Neither driver was wearing a seat belt," the article noted.

Like his buddy Fred, Dan perished along with another soul.

*Tami and Agnes on a bleak, snowy day at Dan's memorial that Tami
set up at the corner of intersection where Dan died in a car accident
in Sedro Woolley*

Over the next several days, the mystery surrounding Dan's
death intensified. Starting with the cassette tapes of songs from the
60's that Dan recorded for me over the holidays. My body tempera-
ture felt like it dropped a few degrees in a rush when I first heard
Dan's voice in the recording: "Taking a little break from the music. I'm
thinking of you, my friend, hope you're thinking of me. Bye."

Just the way he said "Bye," there was a tone of finality to it. Dan
was saying "Bye" for good. That's what it felt like. I was haunted by the
idea that that would be the last word I heard him say. He wanted me to
be "thinking of" him. Because he knew by the time I heard the recording it was "Bye" forever. How did he know that?

How does anybody know when they're going to die? That was
the thought running through my head 10 months later, when I was
picturing the date on my obituary on my motorcycle ride on my "One
Of Those 'I Saw God' Days." If Dan knew, could I have possibly known?
Thank goodness, I didn't. I'm sure that Fred's fickle fate shaped Dan's
sense of his own mortality.

Dan left all the clues to what he knew. When the familiar guitar rift of Norman Greenbaum's "Spirit In The Sky" kicked in right
after his "Bye," a lump clogged my throat. Tami and I looked at each
other in a shared state of shock, as the song intoned *"When I die and
they lay me to rest..."*

His message was clear. Then, just in case we didn't get it the first time, Dan recorded "Spirit In The Sky" a second time later in the two-cassette collection. It is the only song repeated among the 40 or so songs he recorded. He was writing down the title of each song he recorded on the cassette insert cards, so he *knew* what he was doing. Why did he do that?

Dan was prophesying at Deep Creek twenty years earlier that he wouldn't make it to age 50. He may not have known he was going to die when he started up his engine in the Miata to drive to work on January 22, but he knew his time was up.

It wasn't as if he *wanted* to die. True, Dan had been suicidal twice in the past. But he and Tami were in a good place at the time of his death; he had everything to live for at the time. In my last phone conversation with him during the holidays, he was talking about his and Tami's grand plans to pack up, buy a boat, and sail to some place in the Caribbean to start a new life, maybe in a year-and-a-half. Like, right before his 50th birthday, coincidentally, or not. He was excited about the plan, but he mentioned Tami's apprehensions, her fears about being in the open seas. He thought he would be able to help her overcome her fears.

All of that didn't sound like someone who wanted to die. But it did sound like someone who told me once that he never could see himself growing old.

"Dan died during the happiest days of our lives," Tami said ruefully. "And now, I feel like I have nothing to live for."

Yikes. Her time was far from over.

The way I knew Dan, I suspect he was too devious for irony to appear accidental in his actions. I think Dan left a clue that he wanted to live, in his choice of song to immediately follow "Spirit In The Sky" on the cassette, with Rare Earth belting out, *"I just want to celebrate another day of living."*

Beyond the cassette tape and utterance of "Bye," Dan left more evidence about knowing something about his own mortality. He was working on a large painting, a vertical canvas that stood eight feet tall. It was a shadowy figure of an older man resembling him, or maybe it was more like his buddy Mike, whom Dan had befriended during his days in Bremerton. From afar, it wasn't noticeable. But if you got up close to the painting, you could make out a faint, scrawled message that stated: *"You will know his name by its sound. It is Death."*

A secret death wish, maybe? What would possess Dan to paint such a message, in such a cryptic manner?

Tami was freaking out over the whole scenario. She and I were smoking pot together late one night. She told me that she *swore* she could still feel Dan's presence in the house. She cited several examples for me that sounded convincing. It wasn't just the pot.

Then Tami presented one more prescient piece of evidence that Dan's death was preordained. Just a couple days after he died, Tami received a package in the mail. It clearly was mailed out on Monday, the day Dan died. It was from the car dealer where they had bought the Miata. The package was an appreciation gift from the dealer, acknowledging the anniversary of their purchase just one year earlier. The package contained a miniature version of the Miata that they bought, in the exact cobalt blue color of the car that Dan was driving when he crashed on black ice and entered the Great Unknown. Also included in the package were two watches, a 'his' and 'hers' set. The 'hers' watch, obviously intended for Tami, was ticking away. The 'his' watch, intended for Dan, had stopped.

"Time had stopped for Dan," Tami mused.

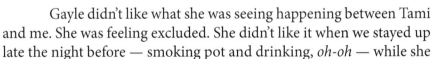

Gayle didn't like what she was seeing happening between Tami and me. She was feeling excluded. She didn't like it when we stayed up late the night before — smoking pot and drinking, *oh-oh* — while she went to bed early with a headache, from drinking too much wine.

We argued. About Tami. We chose a time when Tami was away from the house doing errands. The gist of the argument went something like this:

Gayle: Tell me you haven't thought about having sex with Tami.
Me: Thought about having sex? Are you going to hold me accountable for what I'm thinking?
Gayle: So you do admit you have thought about having sex with Tami.
Me: No! Well, wait... well, maybe. I can't say that the thought didn't cross my mind...
Gayle: Oh God! So, it's true! My worst fear!

You'd think, after all these years and all of my experience with women, that I would've gained some understanding of how they think. But once again I was failing miserably with Gayle at Tami's house in the wake of the...*death*...*of*...*my*... *best friend*.

I'll say it one more time, just to be clear — I may have *thought* about having sex with Tami, but I would never have acted on that thought. And I never was presumptuous enough to think that Tami was physically attracted to me. She never gave any indication that she felt that way. I was old enough to be her father. My affection for her was primarily paternal.

To make a long story short, Gayle and I wound up breaking up over this, for the third or fourth time. Well, it wasn't *exactly* because of Tami. Gayle's trip to Ireland a few weeks after our Washington trip, and her admission that she fucked two Irishmen when she was there, had something to do with it.

Oh, I get it now. I thought about having sex with Tami; Gayle had sex with two Irishmen. Call it even.

This break-up lasted a lot longer than the previous ones— almost two years. It took me a *loooonng* time to get over Ireland.

God works in mysterious ways; He has a way of giving you exactly what you need when you need it the most.

In my case, in the spring of 2001, I needed the UCSB Gauchos baseball team.

College baseball season gets underway every year just as February rolls in. I needed a diversion in the worst way during the 2001 season, in the aftermath of Dan's death, then my break-up with Gayle.

I was entering my fifth season of covering UCSB baseball in 2001. Up until then, the teams ranged from fair to mediocre. But the 2001 team was special. It was a group that gelled and put together a magical season, a 40-win season, the second-best in school history. They were ranked nationally in the top 15 most of the season. I loved covering that team, the players on the team. Watching them play — and enjoying the success they experienced — was just the tonic I needed for a heavy heart.

The Gauchos qualified for the collegiate national regionals. They were expected to be slotted in a Western regional, like Stanford, or Arizona State. But it was a pleasant surprise when the tournament drawings were announced and UCSB's name came up for the four-team regional hosted by iconic Notre Dame in South Bend, Ind.

I will save details of what happened in that regional for a later chapter. But it ended in very dramatic, emotionally-draining fashion, with an extra-inning loss, 11-10, in an elimination game. It was a barn-burner of a battle, against the host team, Notre Dame, before a hostile crowd, and it ended well after midnight. The schedule got pushed way back because of rain and the Gauchos had to complete a rain-delayed game earlier in the day. So it was an extremely long day, with lots of baseball.

There were a lot of tears among players wearing Gaucho uniforms that night, a team that was described by head coach Bob Brontsema as the closest bunch he had coached in his 20-some years. A dream season ended in such tumultuous fashion. After the somber post-game interviews, lingering condolences with family members who had made the trip to South Bend, and long showers in the locker room, it was a very sad group that boarded the team bus approaching 3 in the morning.

I was feeling a lot of emotions in that moment as well. I felt compelled to share my feelings, because I felt they would resonate with those young players at the time. So, I asked Coach Brontsema if I could address them briefly just as the team bus was idling, warming up the engine to return to the hotel.

Standing at the front of the bus, in front of those weary players, I thanked them for providing one the most rewarding highlights of my 24-year career as a sports writer. I told them that even though their dream season had ended, they were taking away golden memories that couldn't be reversed. More importantly, they were taking away friendships with each other that they would cherish long after the season was a distant memory. I told them they shouldn't take for granted the bonds they created. As I was giving this speech, in the back of my mind I was thinking, of course, of the special bond I had created with Dan during my college days.

I realized then that I was processing my grief through these young men, that I was channeling the formative college days I shared with Dan that shaped a lifelong friendship that meant so much to me. All those feelings were gushing forward in the tears swelling in the eyes of those emotionally-drained players, sitting passively on cold bus seats in the pre-dawn hour.

They just lost a baseball game. But they had won so much more.

———————◆•◆•◆•◆•———————

I returned to visit Tami in early summer. It would be my last time to see that wonderful house she had shared with Dan the previous six years, during which I visited every summer. Tami simply could not afford to stay at the place on her own. She and Agnes were going to have to move to a cheaper place. It was with great sadness that I returned to bid good-bye to that house, brimming with Dan and Tami's artwork, overlooking the serene, blissful lake. I took one long, last look from the lookout deck.

View of lake from deck of Dan and Tami's house in Sedro Woolley, in a shot I took mimicking Dan's signature photo-shooting gimmick, by tilting the camera at a diagonal angle

Tami gave me a couple of mementos to remember Dan by. She gave me his hockey stick, and she gave me a sign — framed — taken from the shores of Deep Creek, posted by the state Fish and Game Department, declaring the creek "Open To Fishing." The sign was given to Dan as a gift from his second wife Elizabeth.

Tami also gave me a few handfuls of Dan's ashes. To contain the ashes, Tami constructed a paper vase out of a flat, 10X12 sheet of sketch paper that she artfully folded into shape. The vase itself was an amazing creation from the hands of an artist. I had my Deep Creek promise I had to keep for Dan, which I vowed to carry out. Six months later, on my "I Saw God" day, I made the decision to scatter a portion of those ashes atop my pink rock.

But Tami held on to the biggest portion of Dan's ashes for a memorial event we planned with Leo, who was a skilled sailor. We decided that the three of us would meet in Santa Barbara on September 5 — Dan's birthday. We would rent a sailboat, and take his ashes to cast out to the sea. This would serve as the substitute journey for the sailing trip Dan and Tami were planning to take together to the Caribbean.

I wasn't the only one who came up to visit Tami that summer. Frank, for reasons that seemed somewhat mysterious, found his way to Sedro Woolley for a couple of days while I was visiting. He evidently had some "other" reason to be in the Washington area, and he was able to swing a side trip to join us.

I was somewhat dubious of Frank's motives. Our frank discussion months earlier shed some light on a possible hidden agenda he may have harbored toward Tami.

But Frank was no fool; he behaved himself at Tami's. He may have invited himself over just to satisfy his curiosity. He was curious about Dan's death. He got caught up in Tami's stories about feeling Dan's presence around the house. Frank claimed he could feel him, too. With Dan's artwork still on display everywhere, maybe Frank was feeling something. I wasn't feeling it; I just missed him terribly.

Frank's the kind of large personality who usually fills the room. In Dan and Tami's house, he was dwarfed by Dan.

We revisited the accident scene. Tami had modified the cross from the corner memorial, and she planted a couple of sets of flowers since the weather warmed up. It was a more life-like scene; colors had returned, minus the snow and gray.

Tami and I got high one last time at the house and had another talk. I told her about my break-up with Gayle, but I didn't tell her why. I hadn't dated anyone for a while. I didn't feel like it, didn't feel that need to be with anyone. We talked mostly about what she was going to do, how she was going to move on. This was a scary time in her life.

She had gone from 17 to a young woman in her prime at 23 with Dan. But now she had to adjust to life without him, all of a sudden. The best role I could play was that of a father figure for her.

We set our sights on when we'd meet again in a couple months in Santa Barbara.

<hr />

Tami drove down to Santa Barbara with Agnes, on the first week of September, as planned. With a home full of tenants, the best I could offer her was my bed to sleep in, while I slept on the living room couch. This was the same arrangement we had when she'd come to Santa Barbara seven months before for the Long Beach memorial for Dan's mom.

Tami had a pleasant visit. Agnes and Max hit it off. We took them to the beach for a romp. She and I took the dogs for a hike on Rattlesnake Trail in the local mountains and took a swim in Mission Creek that crosses the trail. I took Tami for a motorcycle ride up to Camino Cielo, enjoying the same gorgeous view that I would gaze at in the maze of marijuana, mesmerized on that pink rock on my "I Saw God" day two-and-a-half months later.

Shy Tami, in this shot I caught of her during her return trip to Santa Barbara in early September, 2001

Tami and I aboard the sailboat off the shores of Santa Barbara where we cast Dan's ashes out to sea for a final farewell

Then, on September 5, Leo drove up from Long Beach to join us for a short sailboat ride out of the Santa Barbara Harbor. Tami had brought her portion of Dan's ashes. She had made another one of her precious paper vases.

It was a gorgeous Santa Barbara day, just like the "I Saw God" day. Leo guided us out on our rented vessel about a mile out to sea, where we cast Dan out on his next journey. It was a somber moment. Tami was fighting back the tears. I felt a hollowness in my gut. But everything went as we planned it. We had made our final farewell to Dan.

From there, Tami had plans. She was driving back to LA for a few days to visit a couple of friends, then she was heading south for Arizona and the Grand Canyon for some sight-seeing and camping.

That following Tuesday morning, I got a call from Tami in Arizona. It was September 11. My eyes were glued to the TV all morning on the live news telecast of the two planes crashing into the Twin Towers in New York City. Tami's plans for Grand Canyon suddenly were canceled because the national park was shut down because of a frantic nationwide security alert.

"Can I come back and stay with you a couple days?" she asked.

"Of course."

The world seemed so different. Again.

Cass, looking hot on a warm Hawaiian night

Cass caught me taking a dip in the water after a memorable moment we shared on a beach in Kauai

CHAPTER 26
Roommate and Romance Roulette - Part 2

Nothing remotely romantic happened between Tami and I when she returned to Santa Barbara on September 11.

I saw her one more time the following summer, when she was living in Bellingham with her new boyfriend Omar. He was very close to her age, very age appropriate. It was a nice visit. But the dynamics had changed. Omar wasn't Dan.

Tami and I lost touch with the exception of one brief email exchange years later. Tami wrote that she and Omar were recently married, had just bought a house, and were into their dogs. They sounded happy. I couldn't ask for anything more than that for her well-being.

That's all I got. The connection with Tami went dead. She never responded to my email response.

She had moved on.

I had to move on, to life without Dan, life without Gayle (again), life with a rotating roster of roommates. That's what life does, it moves on. Relentlessly.

Living with roommates complicated my life in a number of ways. For starters, I had to live with them, which took some adjusting.

I had to share space. Luckily, I had my own bathroom, but sharing my tiny kitchen with three or four other people proved to be challenging. Not everybody had good cleaning habits. That went for the rest of the house, too.

Then, the cast kept changing; as I called it, Roommate Roulette. Every time I had a vacancy, I had to go through the interview process with potential new tenants. I never had a problem with attracting interest — my room rates were attractively low for Santa Barbara. But while I had the luxury of a plethora of candidates to choose from, that also meant a lot of extra work sorting it all out. I put a lot of thought on whom I wanted to live with.

Living with roommates also complicated my situation with my ex-wife and daughter. After four years of driving down to LA weekly to see Tessa, I determined she was old enough by age five for overnight stays at my home in Santa Barbara.

Not so fast, Maggie said. Not with all those roommates I was living with.

We were headed for a court battle. The drives to LA were killing me. I wanted my daughter in Santa Barbara. I was already missing Kasey, who was still living in Boston at the time.

I filed for visitation rights in my home in LA court, and won.

Having Tessa in my own home opened up a whole new world we could share that became part of our evolving relationship.

For starters, what five-year-old daughter doesn't love baking brownies? This became a required task for us for years. The requisite licking of the bowl that ended up with chocolate smeared all over my daughter's face got baked into our traditions.

Maggie wound up divorcing Bill shortly after the court battle. I decided to increase child support for Tessa to $550 per month, matching what I was paying Gail for Kasey.

------◆------

It took me a few months to start dating again after Gayle and I broke up over Tami and Ireland. But when I did, it was with a classy lady named Cass.

What started out as a friendly working relationship at the News-Press turned into something much more with Cass.

Cass worked in the graphics art department at the News-Press. She was an artist, with a talent for drawing and painting. She gave me a memento that I treasure — a picture of a wolf she drew in pencil. I think the wolf was meant to symbolize my furry coat (chest).

Cass had come a long way from her conservative upbringing in Boston, though she still retained a heavy New England accent. She was also a single mom, with a teen-age daughter, Tatiana, who was smart, talented, and troubled.

Cass had an exquisitely beautiful face with her round blue eyes and high cheekbones. Petite in stature, she had distinctive, short-cropped blonde hair. She loved good music (huge fan of Sting and Sarah McLachlan), a glass of wine with good food, and fun travel.

My daughter Tessa adored Cass. Winning the visitation rights for overnight stays in Santa Barbara afforded my daughter the privilege of knowing Cass.

Cass and Tatiana lived in a funky rented old house on the east side of town, and Tessa and I made a point to visit them on her weekends in Santa Barbara. The house reeked of Santa Barbara fifty years ago. Cass always had some sort of treat for Tessa. She found creative ways to entertain my daughter — games, books, puzzles, baked treats. Music was always present. Incense was always in the air. Tessa was enraptured in her presence.

Cass and I took one memorable trip together to Kauai. We explored all over my favorite Hawaiian island. We discovered the idyllic Queen's Bath natural pool, formed by lava rock along the shore, buffered from the crashing waves a few feet away. It made for perfect, undisturbed wading.

We gazed at the edge of Kauai's breathtaking Little Grand Canyon. I wanted to capture the view in a photo in a unique way, which is another way of saying that I came up with this idea that was pure nuts. I willingly put my life on the line by dangling from the edge of the cliff for the simple purpose of getting a great photo. I really wanted that photo, and boy, it was going to be worth it.

By the end of the day, boy, was I in for a huge disappointment. I had finished off the roll of film, or so I thought, and I popped open the back of the camera to remove the film. Dang, was I ever surprised to discover there was no film in the camera! Well, this was embarrassing. Somehow, I was snapping away at photos all day, and saw my photo count advancing on each shot. A whole day's worth of awesome photos were non-existent.

So, you're just going to have to take my word for it that the photo of me hanging from the cliff at Little Grand Canyon was *really* spectacular.

We didn't even try to capture our most memorable moment of the trip in a photo. We found a secluded beach that was "clothing optional." We opted to go without. We thought we had the beach all to ourselves, because nobody else was in sight. One thing led to another and the next thing you know, we were making love on that beautiful secluded beach. We nearly got away with it undetected. But in the afterglow, I looked up to see a guy walking by along the shore, giving me a "thumbs-up" sign.

Cass and I created some good memories for over a year, then sort of drifted apart. No drama, no bitterness. We remained friends.

The roommate juggle continued. One good-looking young man named Robb moved in for about six months. He had a bitchin' bike — a massive Kawasaki — that he liked to ride way too fast. He was a nice guy, so I put up with his occasional after-midnight hot tub parties with young ladies who thought his bike was bitchin' too.

Robb was followed, briefly, by a young Hispanic couple with an infant baby whom I was trying to give a break by renting them an affordable room. They lasted only a couple months due to extenuating circumstances.

Then I welcomed a roommate who made a major impact on my life — Theo. Theo was from Cyprus, that big island in the middle of the Mediterranean, just south of Turkey. Theo was in his early 20's, a big, burly, round-faced guy with a boisterous, youthful, extremely likable personality. He was a Greek Cypriot and he looked "Mediterranean" — olive-colored skin, jet-black hair, bushy eyebrows. He was a big kid who treated me with a lot of respect. I loved Theo like a little brother... until he broke my heart.

Theo moved in with two notable four-legged companions. Boris was a skinny, skittish Italian greyhound (I guess all Italian greyhounds are skinny and skittish), and when he ran at full speed, he was a bullet. Then there was Buffy, an adorably cute, fluffy Shih Tzu who was white-haired with traces of gray and brown streaks, and had the Princess attitude down to a capital "P."

Boris and Buffy got along great with Max. Meanwhile, my cat Thomas barely tolerated them.

Thomas was the cat I wound up adopting from Tessa and Maggie, who had raised him as a kitten, but had to give him up when they moved into a rental house that wouldn't allow cats. Tessa, a first-grader at the time, named Thomas after a boy crush in her class.

So, Thomas was barely a year old when I took him in, and had been ruling the house for a couple years when Boris and Buffy arrived. Thomas was a handsome gray-and white-patched cat who lasted longer with me than any roommate, or wife for that matter. He lived more than 16 years with me.

Theo's tenancy stretched nearly four years. Tessa embraced Theo, calling him "Uncle Theo." Tessa's arrivals at the house were always greeted by a big hug as Theo wrapped those big thick arms of his around her. Kasey was a little shier around Theo, but he embraced him, too.

Boris, Max and Buffy in front of my backyard redwood hot tub

I have to admit, the affable Theo brought "life" to the household. His presence meshed well with my other two roommates at the time — "Dreamin' Man" Michael, and Sarah, who was a cute, bright, personable young lady in her early 20's. The roommate chemistry hadn't been this good in the house since Andy and Jim.

Theo's backyard barbecues were legendary. He loved to barbecue — it's evidently a very Greek thing to do. He knew exactly how to season chicken and pork while patiently char-broiling them on a skewer over the coals. He took his time, sitting 30 minutes at the fire, adding seasoning, and lemon, intermittently, while cracking jokes with Michael. Then came the eating — Oh! So good! Lip-smacking good.

———————◆·•·———————

After a break-up that lasted nearly two years, Gayle drew me back in. She had dumped Vern — again. The same ol' relationship issues that I won't go into. But she knew how to win me back.

It was pretty simple, because I decided that I was in love with her. The clincher, to be honest, was when I chose her over Maggie. You heard that right. Briefly, I had a choice. Maggie and I were talking about getting back together. I was seriously considering it. The emotional pull was extremely high.

By this time in my long chain of relationships, I had pretty much accepted a change in partners as no big deal. I usually found ways to justify the changes.

I could have easily broken up with Gayle again and run back to Maggie. But she hadn't budged on the Kasey issue. She still sounded rigid in her stance, as in "No, I don't think I can put up with Kasey in our home" way of thinking. What it really came down to, she really didn't want to deal with his mother. I can't say I blame her. But that pretty much was the deal-breaker for me.

Besides, I didn't trust myself to resist straying back to Gayle if I had gone back to Maggie. I couldn't live with myself if I put Maggie through that. Maggie would have made sure of that.

I blame Neil Young. Whenever I heard his sweet love song "Harvest Moon," it made me think of Gayle. *"Because I'm still in love with you... on this harvest moon."* I was in love with Gayle. End of story.

———◆———

A few months after Gayle and I had reunited, Theo set us up for the vacation trip of a lifetime. It was the summer of 2003, and he invited us to join him on a trip to Cyprus. Theo was accompanied by his girlfriend at the time, a beautiful young Black woman with hazel eyes named Sabrina.

We were guests at the home of Theo's parents in Nicosia, the capital city of Cyprus. Evidently, American tourists were a rarity in Cyprus. A bartender at a resort hotel we hung out one day in the coastal city of Agia Napa clued us in when he told us we were the first Americans he had ever met.

I was surprised to learn that most Americans are unfamiliar with the charms of the enchanted island that Leonardo da Vinci coined "The kingdom of the Goddess Aphrodite" after his visit in 1481. Aphrodite, the Greek goddess of love whom the Romans later named Venus, is the official patroness of Cyprus. Her reputed place of birth, where she drifted ashore on a seashell, is enshrined at Aphrodite's

Rock, also known as Petra tou Romiou, located south of Pathos. According to one Greek myth, Aphrodite was born out of sea foam formed from the severed testicles of her father that had been tossed out to sea. No reason to doubt that the water off Cyprus is safe to swim.

I wrote a travel article on this memorable trip for the News-Press. Explaining the graphic origins of Aphrodite's legendary birth, I wrote, *"If this kind of stuff fascinates you, Cyprus will satiate your appetite. If you're a history buff, there are ancient sites and monuments aplenty that chronicle the turbulent regimes of this strategically located island."*

The Greeks, Romans, French, Turks and British had all occupied Cyprus at one time or another over the past 2,500 years. The island is currently divided between Greek and Turk territories. British influence remains intact on the island with driving on the left side of the road and steering wheels on the right side of vehicles.

As guests at the Vounoitis family home, we ate like the Greeks. Which meant lots of barbecues. Theo's father barbecued one meal for us that included seven different types of meat. I'm not sure I can name seven types of meat. Added in were an abundance of wine, fresh vegetables and fruit, in particular exceptionally sweet watermelon, which the Greeks typically serve at the end of every meal to cleanse the palette.

At one restaurant, we ate an incredible meal called Kleftiko, which was a deliciously tender lamb flank that was baked all day in a special stone oven. That's what living is all about — experiencing a meal like that.

Sabrina, Theo, Gayle and I at a restaurant in Cyprus

Theo was our personal tour guide, chauffeuring us around the Greek portion of the island. Aphrodite's Bath, on the remote northwest corner of the island, was the prettiest beach. Its crystal clear water was a few degrees cooler and more refreshing than the warmer waters along the southern coast, where the resort-laden Agia Napa and large port city of Limassol were located.

Theo took us to the quaint town of Lefkara, renowned for its elegant hand-embroidered lace that the local women have been stitching for hundreds of years. The narrow streets are lined with intimate shops pedaling lace as well as elegant, hand-designed glassware and silverware.

I was already acquainted with Theo's older brother Angelo, who had come to visit Santa Barbara about six months earlier to set up business contacts there. It was Angelo who served Gayle and I as our guide on a very special side trip crossing the contentious border separating the Turkish-controlled strip of Cyprus. Five months earlier this would have been impossible, because the border — heretofore known as the Green Line — had been closed off, heavily guarded and planted with land mines for thirty years dating back to 1974. The Turks and Greeks haven't liked each other for thousands of years. But they managed to finally come to an agreement to put aside their differences and join sides in a long overdue truce.

That made our day trip with Angelo to the Turkish side along the northern coast all the more fascinating. The highlight of the excursion was a visit to the huge, stone Kyrenia Castle that dated back to B.C. times.

The Turkish lira used for currency was interesting; I bought a blouse for Pam for about 25 million lira. I didn't have to mortgage my house to buy it; $1 million lira was worth about $1.

Cyprus wasn't the only island Gayle and I visited on this trip. Theo helped us book a six-day cruise, launching out of Limassol, to five Greek islands— Kos, Spetses, Tinos, Mykonos and Rhodes. Gayle and I were the only Americans on the ship. Out of hundreds of passengers, only about 30 spoke English, all Brits.

The cruise afforded plenty of land time on the islands. Kos was the first stop, where we took the tour excursion to the Ascyplion of Hippocrates, an ancient hospital grounds built in the honor of the Greek physician who created the Hippocratic oath that established ethics in the practice of medicine. The Ascyplion was an awesome spread of ruins on an open hillside that required three levels of stairs to cover the entire grounds.

Spetses, a little-known tiny island near the mainland of Greece, was a no-car zone. Horse-drawn carriages and mopeds were the lone options for transportation on the single-lane road in the tiny town. We rented a gutless moped that could barely make it up-hill with two of us aboard. But it got us to a scenic, secluded cove that we had all to ourselves just a few miles out of town.

The island of Tinos had basically one attraction — the richest Greek Orthodox church in Europe. Worshippers make pilgrimages to this church from all over the world to be blessed. We felt blessed just to take it all in, after reaching the top of three long, ascending blocks to the church perched at the top of a hill. A red carpet was laid out the entire length of the three blocks for the truly devoted who wished to do penance for their sins by crawling on their hands and knees all the way up to the church. I can't say Gayle and I remained sin-free after our pilgrimage.

Mykonos, meanwhile, brought out the sinful pleasure we craved. This was the most exotic of the five islands, with its classic, bleach-white buildings and brightly colored doors painted in blues, oranges, reds and purples. We got lost in the veritable maze of cos-mopolitan shops, restaurants and bars in the harbor area. We made the most of our 12-hour shore time with our motor scooter ride to that unforgettable nude beach. Then we finished off our satisfying day by drinking strange lime-green mojitos at a chic bar.

Rhodes, the closest of the five islands in proximity to Cy-prus, finished off the cruise excursion. We passed into Rhodes' en-trance at Mandraki Harbor, which used to be the site of a 75-foot-tall bronze statue of the warrior Colossus, holding up a torch. Ships would pass under the parted legs of Colossus to enter the harbor during the third century B.C. Considered one of the Seven Won-ders of The World at the time, the statue stood erected just over 100 years until an earthquake brought it crumbling down. The harbor resembled the medieval town that was originally constructed during the Crusades, lined by massive stone walls protecting shops and eat-eries awaiting tourists. We took the tour of the Acropolis at Lindos, a restored fortress that required a 365-step stair climb which afforded views of beautiful beach coves below.

I had to write two separate travel stories for the News-Press to cover everything on this utterly memorable trip.

There was a significant Part 2 to my brief News-Press travel writing career.

The following spring, in 2004, Gayle and I did our epic Southwest Hiking Tour, which merited a four-part traveling series in the News-Press.

It started in Sedona, Arizona. We stayed at the Desert Quail Inn, which added its own irony to the story. I committed a regrettable act of deadly recklessness when I accidentally ran over a squadron of baby quail while driving around looking for ... the Desert Quail Inn. Gayle would not let me off the hook for this egregious episode.

"I didn't see them!" I yelled in my defense.

"You didn't see them?!" Gayle repeated in disbelief. "There were twelve of them, and you wiped out about *eight* of them. How could you not see them?"

It was awful, believe me. I felt bad. Gayle exaggerated, it wasn't eight, more like four. But that was bad enough, admittedly. To commemorate the event when we returned home, she bought me a ceramic knick-knack of a mother quail leading a row of her of chicks, resembling the row that I didn't see and ran over. I was looking for the Inn, I swear, and wasn't focused on what was crossing in front of me on the road.

Moving past the quail massacre, we launched our Hiking Tour with a trek up to the vortex point in Sedona's famed Cathedral Rock. It was an arduous climb on the last leg. But once we got there, it was surreal. Peace, serenity, a sense of euphoria; all that meditative stuff applied. The vortex was a veritable V-shaped space between two magnificent spheres, sticking up into the sky like two plump, pink fingers in a giant peace sign.

That was the warm-up for the next stop — a three-day, two-night, guided hiking tour to Havasu Falls, a few miles out from the Grand Canyon. The hike consisted of 10 miles *down* into the Canyon, then 10 miles back *up*. In between the time was splendidly spent languishing in what felt like heaven. We needed to be in good shape for this tour. Gayle and I did a lot of hiking at home on Rattlesnake Trail along Mission Creek to train specifically for this part of the trip.

Not including the two tour guides, we were among a party of eight, including an inspiring man celebrating his 70th birthday. We figured if he could survive the 20 miles of hiking, so could we. We started from the rim of the Canyon, at Hualapai Hilltop, heading straight down on a mile of switchbacks. Going down wasn't so bad, other than getting out of the way of a pack of mules that Indian guides were escorting on the way down. But hiking back up the switchbacks, which accounted for the 10th mile on the way out and up on the final day, was a lot more challenging.

The 10-mile hike passed through Havasupai Indian Village. Towering over the Village were the imposing Man and Woman rocks, rectangular spheres arising about 50 feet high and about 15 feet thick. They were perched atop the 200-foot-tall cliffs that surrounded the Village. The Indians believed the precarious positioning of the Man and Woman rocks controlled the destiny of mankind, According to Havasupai lore, if the rocks toppled, that would signal the end of the world. Fortunately, they were still erect.

The Havasupai Village was home to a general store and Mule Train Express, one of only two Pony Express outposts remaining at the time. Gayle and I mailed postcards to ourselves from the outpost. We completed our 16-day trip before they arrived back home in the mail.

After six-and-a-half hours of hiking, we finally reached our campground destination at Havasu Falls. The Falls, measuring 160 feet, filled a gleaming turquoise pool in which campers frolicked.

Again, Gayle and I and our tour compatriots paid good money to have the tour guides do all the work in the campsite.

We spent the next day-and-a-half enjoying the Falls and surrounding area, which included two more falls nearby. Mooney Falls was about a mile hike from camp and well-hidden from the camping crowd at Havasu. Mooney Falls was a 200-foot-long cascade bordered by stunning red travertine, which was a craggy, moonlike rock formed from limestone deposits that had collected and hardened.

These falls were named after some poor sucker who was part of an exploration party in the 1800s. This Mooney guy was being lowered down the falls by rope, but the rope wasn't long enough to reach the bottom. As his colleagues tried to pull him back up, the rope rubbed against the travertine and broke, and Mooney fell into the travertine below, trapped on a ledge presumably unconscious or dead. Inclement weather forced the party to evacuate. By the time they returned to the scene, his body was encased in travertine build-up. There are a couple of other versions of what happened, both involving guys named "Mooney" and both of whom met their fates at the falls on two different dates in the 1880's. The story I'm relating is the version one of our guides told us.

Breath-taking Havasu Falls just outside the Grand Canyon that Gayle and I hiked 10 miles with a guided group to reach

Mooney Falls was not easy access. We had to climb down a vertical cliff, hanging onto chains, iron pegs and wooden ladders. A portion of the descent required passage through a narrow, vertical miner's tunnel. But once we reached water level, it was well worth the effort. Numerous peaceful, crystal-clear pools made for a refreshing swim.

On Day 2, we hiked about a half-mile upstream to Navajo Falls. These falls were much different than the first two, wider in expanse. Water spilled through trees at the top and over big, smooth boulders. Off to the left, water gushed out of a huge hole. It all emptied into another serene pool, perfect for swimming.

For someone who relished waterfalls as much as I did, this Havasu hiking excursion was paradise.

Moving forward on our Southwest Tour, Gayle and I headed further east on I-40 and stopped at Meteor Crater, which was created by a meteor crashing into the Earth about 50,000 years ago. It was a huge gray hole about three-quarters-of-a-mile wide and 550 feet deep at the time.

Further down I-40 was Petrified National Forest, a barren, treeless desert covered with 200 million-year-old tree chunks that had turned to stone.

We pushed further east into New Mexico and then north to the southwestern corner of Colorado. That's where we stopped at Mesa Verde, site of the famed cliff dwellings of the Ancestral Pueblo Indians dating as far back as 500 A.D.

Mesa Verde, which means "Green Table" in Spanish, is situated on a large plateau covered by small green trees and shrubs, overlooking the steep, multi-layered rock canyons that house the cliff dwellings.

We stayed two days to take in the best of well over 600 dwellings carved into the walls of rock cliffs. The Spruce Tree House alcove was the site first discovered by ranchers Richard Wetherill and Charles Mason, quite by accident, in 1888. The restored, squeaky-clean beige, stone-box structures took my breath away. The Spruce Tree House encompassed about 114 rooms, some stacked three stories high. The circular, perfectly symmetrical rooms carved deep into the floors, called kivas, were particularly fascinating. They were typically 20 feet in diameter, primarily used for spiritual and family gatherings.

The Balcony House site presented a bit of an obstacle course that required climbing down a 20-foot wooden ladder, then crawling on hands and knees through an eight-foot-long tunnel.

We also made time for a two-mile hike along a canyon rim trail featuring fascinating petroglyph carvings on rock walls.

From Mesa Verde we headed back west on Highway 160. That took us to Four Corners, the spot where four states — Arizona, New Mexico, Colorado and Utah — all converge. The spot is marked by a bronze circle inside a 40-foot-wide concrete square, with flags from all four states flying in the wind.

Next stop was Monument Valley, in late afternoon, when the low-lying sun brilliantly intensified the orange hues of the gorgeous rock monuments. We took the 17-mile drive through the park to see rock formations given names such as "Elephant Butte'" "Three Sisters" (appearing as a huge "W"), "Rain God Mesa," and "Thumb" (appearing exactly as its moniker.)

The last two stops on our amazing tour were Bryce Canyon and Zion National Park, a mere 78 miles apart in southern Utah. I had consulted my mother about Bryce and Zion, which she had visited many years earlier. She broke down the two parks in simple terms —in Bryce, she was always looking *down*, and in Zion she was always looking *up*.

Bryce's grounds are distinguished by its hundreds of amazing pink "hoodoos," which are veritable ragged rock columns pointed skyward. They are situated on a plateau at elevations as high as 9,000 feet. A winding, 18-mile drive along the top of the plateau offers splendid views of the hoodoos looking down.

Zion, in contrast, is comprised of massive rock mountains that you have to crane your neck to see along the seven-mile ride through Zion Canyon.

Gayle and I did everything we could to reverse my mother's perspective of the two national parks.

At Bryce we started with the customary downward viewpoint at Sunrise Point, crawling out of bed before 6 a.m. to catch sunrise casting its rays on the spooky east-facing, slender rock spheres.

But later in the day, we took hikes on the popular Navajo and Queen's Garden trails to get up-close views of the hoodoos at base level. From upward angles, the hoodoos took on more life-like appearances, resembling loopy creatures out of a Dr. Seuss book.

We entered Zion from the east side, passing through a narrow, mile-long tunnel that was burrowed through a mountain back in the 1920s. The tunnel had three "windows" cut out along the way, offering glimpses of the glories of nature that lie ahead.

We stayed at the Zion Mountain Resort just outside the park's east entrance. The appeal of this resort was the buffalo range that sprawled in full view from its private cabins. We leisurely gazed at the beasts while passing the time sipping on deep glasses of wine on our front porch swing.

Inside Zion, we took a couple of ground-level hikes. But the most adventurous — and dangerous — hike led us straight up the 5,990-foot-tall Angels Landing. This hike was not for someone with a fear of heights. It required scaling nearly 1,600 feet over two-and-a-half miles, beginning with two sets of switchbacks that seemingly never ended. The second set of switchbacks ended at Scout's Lookout, which Gayle and I mistook for the top of the Landing.

But then we saw hikers in the distance and realized we still had a good half-mile climb to go to reach the top. The last leg was truly a "climb," in which we had to pull ourselves up by safety chains. This definitely gave the faint of heart pause. There were a couple of precarious spots where we were holding onto the chains, looking straight down a vertical drop of several hundred feet. Beware, visions of vertigo.

If that didn't trigger light-headedness, the view at the top sure did. What a rush! We enjoyed a picnic lunch and looked *down* on Zion, in direct contrast to Mom's viewpoint. Our heads were literally in the clouds.

By the time we arrived back home, we had completed a 2,400-mile "grand" circle of the Southwest, serving as fodder for the four editions I wrote for the News-Press Travel section, each of which I dedicated to four dead baby quail.

———————————◆———————————

Amidst all of this travel, I found time for my kids. A few months before the grand Southwest Tour, I arranged a memorable life experience for my nine-year-old daughter. I took Tessa to a live speaking engagement at the majestic Santa Barbara Arlington

Theatre presented by Jane Goodall, the gift-from-God primatologist and anthropologist who related her remarkable intimate contact with chimpanzees by living in their midst for decades in African jungles. It made an impression on Tessa, who proclaimed she wanted to be like Jane Goodall when she grew up.

Tessa with Jane Goodall after Mz. Goodall's presentation in Santa Barbara

I also infected my kids with the travel bug by the summer of 2004. Tessa and I drove up to Cambria for a couple of days and toured Hearst Castle.

I followed that up with a return trip to Zion with Kasey. I braved another hike up to Angels Landing with my son. Then we descended from the heavens at Angels for a visit to Sin City —Vegas — for a couple of days. I decided Vegas merited an encore, so I returned there with both kids during the Christmas holidays.

This was a particularly difficult period for my son, who had moved back to L.A. after two years in Boston to start middle school. Kasey and his mother were allowed to move into the back unit of the Santa Monica house at a cheap rental rate on the good graces of my father.

I had watched Kasey growing up with obsessive attention spans devoted to a range of animated, fictional combative gangs — Ninja Turtles, Power Rangers, and Japanese Dragon Ball Zee, which involved an extensive collection of trading cards. But Kasey's intense, singular focus didn't carry over to school studies. He was crashing in high school. He was either falling behind or neglecting to turn in homework assignments. He had shown prior signs of struggle in middle school, during which his mother and I had invested in a remedial home reading program to get him on track.

By his junior year in high school, it was clear he wasn't going to complete enough classes to graduate. His mother and I formally requested to have Kasey tested for learning disabilities. The tests showed he exhibited some symptoms of ADD, and accommodations for class tests were recommended. It was not enough to save him in his senior year; he did not graduate with his class.

Kasey was a bit of an enigma as far as gauging his intellectual capabilities. While he never excelled in school, he was a helluva chess player. So, he had some intellectual skills with respect to chess that weren't transferring to his class studies. He became an obsessive student of chess, reading up on strategies and classic games. He became good enough to compete in tournaments. Playing chess had served as the link that forged the friendship between his mother and me, but neither one of us were good enough to beat him.

———————◆◆◆◆◆◆◆———————

Early in 2005, Gayle and I tried living together, at her house. It lasted about six months. Theo took over as custodian of my house while I was at Gayle's.

Gayle and I picked up on our travel adventures that year — a five-day ski trip in Tahoe, a three-day camping trip on Santa Cruz Island, and a 10-day trip back to Sedona, Grand Canyon, and New Mexico in late October.

New Mexico was a rush because it was all new to me. We passed through Roswell, the town famous for its alleged UFO sightings in the 1950s. Roswell was on our way to Carlsbad Caverns, the awesome caves that go as deep as 750 feet below the ground. We visited Santa Fe and Taos, too; both were pretty towns. Santa Fe featured the museum of acclaimed artist Georgia O'Keeffe, known for her paintings of enlarged flowers and Southwest landscapes. Taos reflected its artistic hippie leanings.

But the highlight of the trip, for me, was White Sands National Monument, situated in the middle of the expansive White Sands Missile Range and Air Force Base, located in the middle of the state. We arrived in late afternoon, perfect lighting for picture-taking. White Sands is miles and miles of eerie white gypsum sand dunes. The sand was cool to the touch and extra fine, more so than sand on a beach. The sand looked more like snow. It was — sorry, gotta say it — surreal.

We drove eight miles to reach park picnic benches, and we had the place just about all to ourselves. We ventured out to embrace its vastness. A professional photographer was there to shoot and he told us our timing was perfect for photos with the sun lowering closer to the mountain ridge on the horizon. He was right. Ripples in the sand formed by recent rains and devoid of human footprints created the illusion of water. Long shadows from long-stemmed cacti stood out as natural works of art. It was all simply breathtaking.

The loveliness of that New Mexico trip was the last hurrah for Gayle and I. A month later, right after Thanksgiving, I discovered that she had wandered back to Vern. This was a mis-step too far. When we had reunited from our previous break-up she had promised me Vern was finally out of the picture, no going back. I let her know then I couldn't take it if she let me down again. She did, and I couldn't.

White Sands National Monument, during precious pre-dusk lighting from the lower sun, rendering an uncommonly beautiful landscape. The sun set on my and Gayle's relationship after this trip

It ended a really good thing we had going. I could've married her. I was crestfallen. I had broken a few hearts. What goes around comes around, I guess.

———————◆•◆•◆———————

I went with a safe choice for a girlfriend after Gayle — Buffy. She had put her claim in for me long before I had officially broken up with Gayle anyway. She was sleeping with me. She was greeting me at the door every time I arrived at home. There was no question she was my girl.

Long before my break-up with Gayle, Buffy was serving the role as my replacement dog for Max, who succumbed to cancer at age 12. My beautiful, muscular brindle boxer had withered away in the clutches of that merciless disease in his final days. I likely held onto him a little longer than I should have; it was hard to let go.

Both my kids were heartbroken as well. I brought both of them together in Santa Barbara for a little memorial service for Max, just the three of us.

RIP, my dear Max.

With Max out of the way, That made my house Buffy's castle.

But Buffy wasn't just content to restrict herself to a stay-at-home companion. She loved driving in the car when I went out for errands. She would stand up in my lap in the driver's seat, with the window rolled down, and stick her face into the headwind. I admit that I got a kick out of putting my doll on public display.

Buffy was fearless, but unfortunately, not too bright. Once, when I took her with me to my local pharmacy, I had neglected to have her on a leash. My bad, not too bright. We started to ascend some stairs up to the sidewalk along the street when Buffy got ahead of me.

At the sidewalk above, she immediately charged at something, yapping away. I dashed up to try to catch up to her. To my horror, I saw her in attack mode headed straight toward two huge dogs, a Rottweiler and an Australian Shepard, both on leashes held by a woman. If the Rottweiler had chomped down on her, Buffy would have been a goner. But luckily, it was the Aussie Shepard who gently clamped down on my hot-headed mistress. I instantly grabbed Buffy and profusely apologized to the woman for not having my dog on a leash like a responsible dog owner. My Guardian Angel was watching over my ill-tempered Princess.

━━━━━◆━━━━━

My Guardian Angel accompanied me on yet another road trip.

In the summer of 2006, I made a solo driving trip through the Deep South.

The trip was structured around planned visits with two people I knew. The first was with Sherill Ann, Janice's longtime friend who I had met at the Vicksburg farmhouse 10 years earlier. Sherrill Ann and I had been in contact via e-mail. We had made a connection in that one conversation at Janice's farmhouse. Janice, meanwhile, had since fallen on hard times.

Sherrill Ann was living in Jackson, Mississippi, in the summer of '06. I flew into Jackson with plans to rendezvous with her. I don't know what happened, but she was a no-show. I don't know if she got cold feet, maybe out of loyalty to Janice, or what.

I was disappointed, but it wasn't a completely wasted trip. I moved on to my second agenda, which was to drive a rental car through four states in the Deep South all the way to South Carolina to visit Nipa, my Thai sister, along with her husband Harrison and 11-year-old daughter Beatrice. I cruised through lots of farmland, rolling green hills and pastures. The South definitely felt like a completely different world than where I came from.

Nipa and her family lived in Sumter, located in the middle of South Carolina. It had been about 35 years since I had last seen Nipa when she was a foreign exchange student living with our family. We had a good laugh at how much older we looked. I was her elder, by two years and a couple of days, since our birthdays were only a couple of days apart in June. I could still make her laugh.

Meeting Beatrice and Harrison was a treat. Beatrice was beautiful, very bright and precocious. Harrison was truly a gentleman, very kind and gracious with me.

During my visit we took a side trip to charming Charleston. The Old South was on display with the pastel antebellum houses that marked the city's distinct architecture. We visited Fort Sumter, site of the first shots fired in the Civil War.

Posing with my Thai sister Nipa and husband Harrison during my visit in Sumter, S.C.

After a few days with Nipa and family, I had to drive all the way back to Jackson for my roundtrip flight back home. It was a long drive back — 650 miles, about nine-and-a-half hours. I left Nipa's home in late afternoon, figuring on driving all through the night to Jackson for an early morning departure. I planned to sleep on the flight home.

The drive got off to an ominous start. Somehow, I got off-track near dusk while driving through a neighborhood in a little town in South Carolina. Searching to make my way back on the highway, I may have been distracted by glancing down at a map on the passenger seat. Suddenly, a cat darted in front of my car, and I hit it.

I immediately pulled off to the side of a the road to check on the cat. It was writhing in the gutter in the throes of near-death. I helplessly looked on; I wanted to cry. The cat was as good as gone, and there was nothing I could do to relieve his misery.

The horror of my karmic past with respect to running over cats and dogs in my younger days re-emerged in that moment. I had gone through a horrible streak, starting in my teens when I first started driving and extending into my college years, during which I accidentally ran over — I don't know — six or seven cats and dogs. I don't remember exactly how many, because the memories were too horrific. It was mind-boggling; I felt cursed. I confessed my sins to my friend

493

Phil, the big animal lover, and he mercilessly condemned me for years, which I wholly deserved.

It had been over a couple decades since I had run over a poor creature, not counting baby quail. But while I helplessly stood on that neighborhood street in South Carolina, it all rushed back to me as if it were just yesterday. I didn't know what to do. I wondered if I should wait for the cat to die, then scoop it up and try to find the owners. The thought of that was just too reprehensible. So, I did nothing.

After about fifteen minutes, I drove off. I was really shook up. The image of that poor cat stuck with me as I drove on. Soon I was out of South Carolina and entering Georgia. Night had fallen.

I pushed on after stopping for a bite to eat. It was getting late. I was about 25 miles out of Atlanta at about 11:45 p.m., cruising along on a three-lane highway in the pitch black of rural territory. Traffic was sparse.

Then, all of a sudden, I had to pull to an immediate stop behind cars lined up at a standstill for some obvious emergency ahead. I was in the fast lane. I watched a bunch of police cars and an ambulance pass by on the middle emergency lane to the left, which was a clue that not much time had elapsed since the accident occurred.

We were at a dead stop for a good ten minutes before we started to slowly crawl forward. That must have been some nasty accident, I thought.

As I inched closer, the darkness of night was disturbed by bright lights surrounding the accident scene. In the distance, it looked like quite a commotion. As I peered ahead, I noticed an indistinguishable, large black figure lying in the emergency lane. I couldn't make out what it was until I was about 20 feet away, at the stroke of midnight.

That's when I saw those big, dark eyes staring right at me. They were the eyes of a huge black cow, lying in a big puddle of blood. As my car rolled past that very dead cow, I could make out the tire tread pattern imbedded in its hide. Some car had run into that black cow as it loitered on that dark highway in the fast lane to nowhere.

Then, about thirty feet farther ahead, I saw the car that hit the cow. It was a small compact, much like my small rental car, resting upside down in a completely demolished heap. My immediate thought was, there was no way the driver survived.

That was a daunting thought. Because, I made an educated guess that the accident must have occurred about fifteen minutes before I arrived on the scene.

Fifteen minutes. That was pretty darn close to how much time I had spent back in South Carolina agonizing over that near-dead cat I had run over. That meant, if I hadn't *run over that cat,* I would have been fifteen minutes farther along in my drive. Which potentially meant, if I hadn't *run over that cat,* it could've easily been me in the fast lane colliding with fate and that black cow. One could argue that *running over that cat* might have saved my life.

Was I just weird to be thinking like that? Or have I been conditioned to think like that, based on how many times I have gotten lucky in potentially dire circumstances, thanks to my Guardian Angel?

If I was right, what the hell did it all mean? God bless that poor cat, that poor cow, and that poor driver who hit the cow.

———◆———

Theo had become a trusted tenant and good friend after nearly four years living in my home.

When I needed someone to sign as a witness to my living trust I was setting up, I asked Theo to sign. He was the big-hearted guy that both my kids adored. He was the guy who busted down my beloved hot tub and concrete slab foundation after the tub became infested with termites and beyond salvaging, which he did as a favor to save me from the back-breaking task. He was a sympathetic confidante during my final break-up with Gayle. It was Theo who drove me past Vern's house to see Gayle's car parked out in front — again.

So when Theo announced that he and his brother Angelo had to return to Cyprus for business early in the summer of 2007, I feared I was going to lose someone who felt like a brother to me. Boris was going with him to Cyprus, but he asked if I could take Buffy permanently. I couldn't break Buffy's heart, so I said yes.

Theo didn't know how long he'd be gone, but he said he planned to return. He and Angelo had been running an "import-export business," called AMT Management, in Goleta the past eight months. While they had a business associate to keep AMT running in their absence, their intent was to return because of the business.

It all sounded legitimate. Then I found out that girlfriends and ex-wives weren't the only ones who could break my heart.

Theo sat me down for a "serious" discussion. "I'm in trouble, and I need your help," he pleaded to me.

He said he had borrowed a huge sum of money from his current girlfriend, Lana, a young woman from Syria. He said she needed him to pay her back before he departed for Cyprus.

So, when he asked me if he could borrow money to pay back Lana, I trusted him when he said he could pay me back as soon as he closed some real estate deal back in Cyprus.

I asked him how much he needed to borrow.

"Twelve," he said.

"Thousand?" I asked, gulping.

"Thirteen… Fifteen."

"Hold on!" I held up my hand. "Jeesuz, that's a lot. I can't go any higher than that. And you're sure you can't get the money any other way?"

He shook his head. He had tears in his eyes, lamenting that he was being treated "like a common criminal." He told me that Lana was shocked to find out he was married to Sabrina. He told her that he and Sabrina had separated, but Lana was hurt. So that's why he needed to pay her back, to make good on a promise he made to her.

So, like an idiot, I wrote out a check to him for fifteen grand.

That was just the beginning of the nightmare. But then, if you're familiar with my story by now, you saw this coming.

What transpired over the next year-and-a-half was a little hard to believe. Theo — of course — never came back from Cyprus. Something started to smell when I began receiving dozens of notices in the mail from collection agencies seeking payments for credit card and other debts owed by AMT Management.

Then, I gradually became acquainted with a small circle of other people who had been "ripped off" by the Vounoitis brothers.

It began with Soteris, another Cypriot Greek who thought Theo and Angelo were his friends. Having met Soteris through Theo, I had contacted Soteris out of desperation months after Theo fled the country. My only means of communication with Theo was by e-mail. I was hoping Soteris would be able to trace Theo in Cyprus. That's when I found out Soteris was a victim of the brothers' scam practices.

Soteris was a decent family man, with a wife and kids and a respectable job as a chef at a cafeteria at UC Santa Barbara. Soteris was lured into buying an apartment, as an "investment," in Kiev, Ukraine, where Angelo had supposed business connections. Soteris put up $40,000 for an apartment that Angelo lived in, then sold without telling Soteris, who never saw a penny on his "investment."

Soteris then introduced me to two other victims of Theo and Angelo's misdeeds, both also Cypriot Greeks. Nina was the unsuspecting business partner who got stuck with all of ATM Management's unpaid bills when they bailed for Cyprus. Then, a young woman named Maria had sold Theo a car, a Cadillac, that he promised to make payments on, but — surprise — he never did.

We all met — Soteris, Nina, Maria, and I — like a club, on a couple of occasions, to formulate a strategy to solve our common problem with the Vounoitis brothers. Months of planning and strategizing disintegrated when we were faced with the realization that the brothers were beyond the reach of local law enforcement by remaining in Cyprus.

Then there was Lana. I contacted her to find out the truth. I was the one to break it to her that he was married, which I knew about because I saw the ceremony at the Courthouse. Theo and Sabrina never lived together, so the marriage may have been for nefarious reasons, too. Lana did lend him money, but she said she demanded to be paid back after she caught him red-handed on a hidden camera digging into her aunt's purse trying to steal cash in her home. She had threatened to file charges with the District Attorney's office if he didn't pay up. She was the smart one to not trust him.

Boy, you think you know a guy…

Theo wound up wiring two payments totaling only $2,200 to me from Cyprus. But as the issue dragged further toward the Great Recession in the fall of 2008, reality set in that no more money was coming out of Cyprus. I was left hung out to dry for nearly thirteen grand.

————————◆————————

Theo's departure set the Roommate Roulette back in motion. Troy, who was an earnest young pharmaceutical salesman and a true-blue Republican, replaced Theo in the summer of 2007. Troy and I got into some lively political debates during his six-month tenancy.

Troy triggered another theft in the wake of Theo's thievery, a couple of months after Troy had moved in. He left the front door unlocked one night when I wasn't home. According to police reports, two young white males broke into several homes in my neighborhood. My home was one of those homes when Troy left an opening. The intruders stole five laptop computers — two belonging to Troy, and one each belonging to Michael, Sarah and me — in addition to $600 in cash I had left in a drawer that Sarah had paid in rent. The two thieves were arrested within 24 hours, but only two of the laptops — Michael's and Sarah's — were recovered.

I shrugged off the whole unfortunate incident by figuring the house robbery was a small price to pay — OK, we'll throw Theo's treachery in the deal, too — if it meant, karmically, I wouldn't run into a black cow on a dark highway.

The roommate era wound down in the last months of 2007 and early into 2008. Michael and Troy had moved out by then, so the tenants accounting for the Roommate Roulette in those final months were: Sarah, who had been there long enough to feel like a pseudo-daughter to me; Joe, a tall, lanky, good-natured Italian guy in my age bracket trying to make ends meet as an independent contractor, who replaced Michael; and Caleb, a young college student who briefly replaced Troy.

I was ready to end the roulette games on both roommates and romance, and cash out.

CHAPTER 27

-- 30 --

In the olden days, when we proofread stories typed on paper, the symbol that designated "end of story" in journalistic copy was "—30—".

The "—30—" symbol dated back to the Civl War days, from the 92 Code of telegraphic shorthand, to signify the end of a transmission. The Associated Press wire service adopted this editing shorthand to message "end of story" and the practice was widely used by newspaper editors until the digital age rendered hand-written editing obsolete.

Coming from   the old school, I have a "—30—" to my News-Press story, a story that lasted 15 years.

My tenure at the News-Press started with a blaze of glory with lingering ties to LA, as told in a previous chapter about my spot coverage of motorsports events, the LA Lakers, the 1993 NFL Super Bowl, and particularly the LA Raiders. But overall, aside from the rare motorsports event assignment in LA, my writing opportunities waned in the mid-90s when the Raiders left town to return to Oakland.

Article I wrote on the 1993 Super Bowl XXVII game between the Dallas Cowboys and Buffalo Bills for the Santa Barbara News-Press, published February 1, 1993

Working the sports desk most of the time in the mid-90s, I was forced into a whole new way of thinking with the introduction of pagination. Gone were the days of designing pages with pencil and ruler drawing lines on paper. I had to learn how to map it all out on a computer screen, then make everything fit down to the line. Pagination required a computer mindset not suited to my generation and it was generally a struggle for me in the beginning. Given no formal training, I had to learn everything in pagination by trial and error. Fortunately, I did have some of my father's math skills that came in handy calculating font sizes and headline counts. I eventually mastered all the pagination skills required for layout responsibilities, which I was randomly assigned to as a fill-in.

It actually was an exciting time, working in a newsroom adapting to modernization.

I fondly recall my early years at the News-Press as the best, primarily because the paper was still owned by the New York Times, and Alan Parsons was Executive Editor. Alan was a smart, progressive-thinking, considerate leader. And he had a mean hook shot. He stood a lanky 6-foot-6, and played in pick-up basketball games at the Goleta Boys and Girls Club. He was a few years older than I, but he had no trouble keeping up while running up and down court. We made a pretty good tandem, too, on the give-and-go interchange when we played on the same team together, which we often did. That's what made Alan unique — an Executive Editor who was just "one of the guys" on the weekend playing in pick-up basketball games.

While pagination made desk work more appealing, I still yearned to do more writing. When I started covering UCSB baseball in 1998, I began accumulating more article clippings for my personal files.

In journalism classes, it is generally taught that the lead paragraph to any newspaper story is always the most important. One of my favorite lead paragraphs appeared in an article on a Gauchos baseball game in 1999, reporting on a wild game in which they lost to the University of Nevada-Reno, 19-11. The Nevada team outhit Santa Barbara 20-16, which I played off in my lead, reading: *University of Nevada's baseball team, hailing from a town where blackjack rules, hit on 20 and won. UCSB held at 16 and lost.* You'd have to know the intricacies of playing blackjack to appreciate that lead.

I wrote numerous features on local citizens who participated in motorsports in one fashion or another. One feature that stood out appeared in 1998. A local guy named Ron Cook had survived a 200-mph crash on a motorcycle in an attempt to break his own land speed record. The whole accident was caught on TV cameras filming a segment for the show "Extreme Machine." Cook was attempting to become the first rider to eclipse the 200-mph barrier in his racing class. He was grateful to live to talk about it and I wrote about it.

Mark Patton started utilizing me as his back-up for UC Santa Barbara men's basketball in 1999. He sent me to Stockton and Las Cruces, New Mexico, for a two-game road trip with the team that year.

Nothing was bigger than high school football for our sports department. It was all-hands-on-deck for everybody on Friday night during the fall for high school football, either covering a game or working the desk. It was a major staff production and a madhouse to make deadline. I primarily worked the desk for Friday Night Football in my early years with the News-Press. But starting in 2000, I was sent out to cover games.

Nothing was more stressful than covering a high school football game. I quickly learned the mind-boggling task of keeping my own stats during the games; you couldn't blink or else risk missing a single play. The games typically ended after 10 p.m. That didn't leave much time to scramble for quick quotes from the coach and a couple of key players. With precious time ticking away, I was usually forced to wait out the post-game team huddles and coaches' pep talks before I could talk to anybody. If the game was in town, it was a hustle back into the office, and if the game was on the road, I'd write the story from a lonely, chilly press box and send the story via teleprompter. Either way, before writing the story, all team and individual stats had to be tallied up, which required some lightning-quick math. Then the detailed line score and stats box had to be typed out first; I had to get that nerve-wracking, stressful task out of the way. By the time I was ready to finally work on the story itself, I had one eye on the clock as critical deadline approached.

———————◆———————

I wrote earlier about the 2001 UCSB baseball season standing out as a highlight of my sports writing career. Given the success of the team, coverage was extensive that year.

During that season I wrote a complex feature story on the entire Gaucho infield — Tyler Von Schell` (first base), Chad Peshke (second base), Jeff Bannon (shortstop), and Dave Molidor (third base). I cite that story as one of my finer accomplishments because it was a challenge melding four subjects together in a cohesive manner and maintaining a flow to the overall story in transition.

UCSB had a memorable late-season home series with the nation's No. 1-ranked team, Cal State Fullerton, my alma mater. Covering that series was definitely the highlight of the regular season. UCSB won the first two games and came darn close to completing the series sweep. Donovan Warrecker's dramatic run-scoring double in the 10th inning to win the second game, 7-6, was as good as it gets for baseball excitement.

Fullerton still edged UCSB for the 2001 Big West Conference title. But the Gauchos earned an at-large bid to the college baseball national regionals that season, drawing an unexpected slot in the four-team regional grouping hosted by Notre Dame.

A precursor of ill-fortune for the team occurred just a week before regional play was set to start. James Garcia, the team's best pitcher, was injured in an altercation with campus police who were responding to calls about a loud disturbance at the dormitory in which he resided. Garcia and his sister Melisa were arguing outside the dorm. The police arrived, and according to several eyewitnesses, the officers beat Garcia up with batons. Melisa jumped on the back of one of the officers to try to stop him, according to authorities. Garcia was cited for public intoxication and released, while Melisa spent the night in jail for assaulting an officer.

This was a big story. Garcia suffered bruises on his right leg from the baton beating. The incident beckoned scrutiny of excessive police force, which was a delicate subject to report on. Garcia was Hispanic, bringing to bear underlying systemic racism within law enforcement with respect to the incident.

It was clear Garcia wasn't the same pitcher he had been all season the following week at Notre Dame. He started the opening regional game against Florida International and pitched poorly. He had three balks called on him and didn't make it out of the fifth inning en route to the Gauchos' worst loss of the season, 17-4.

Facing elimination with one more loss, UCSB recovered to win its next game, but just barely. The Gauchos had a 12-7 lead over Wisconsin-Milwaukee after four-and-a-half innings when rain halted play. The game resumed the next day and Wisconsin-Milwaukee rallied to tie it at 12-12. But Jed Stringham's home run in the ninth inning saved the Gauchos from total collapse, breaking the tie for a 13-12 win.

That set up another elimination game against the regional host, Notre Dame, just a few hours after the Wisconsin-Milwaukee game concluded. The Gauchos and Irish staged another epic battle that saw five ties and six lead changes. Santa Barbara took the fifth lead change in the bottom of the eighth, 10-9. Skip Schumacher's double started the two-run rally, giving him 100 hits on the season and tying a school record. (That gave Schumacher an even .400 batting average for the season. He would go on to play several seasons in the major leagues, mostly with the St. Louis Cardinals).

But Notre Dame rallied to tie the elimination game in the top of the ninth, then won it in the 10th on a home run off a pitch by… James Garcia. The Gauchos, as the designated home team in that game, left the tying run at third base with two out in the bottom of the 10th.

The magic that propelled the whole Gaucho season seemed to have petered out in the previous inning, the ninth. In the previous two games, UCSB sophomore Ryan Spilborghs had extended his school-record consecutive hitting streak to 34 and 35 games by getting singles with two outs in the ninth inning each time. Could he repeat that one more time? As luck would have it, he stepped up to the plate once again with two outs in the ninth against Notre Dame, needing another hit to extend his amazing streak to 36 games. He meekly grounded out.

The Irish followed up with their turn at bat in the top of the 10th, and promptly produced the game-winning home run. Spilborghs' hitting streak, and the Gauchos season, were both done. That's baseball.

The gut-wrenching loss was tough enough to take. Making my emotional speech to the players on the team bus at 3 o'clock in the morning — with Dan clearly on my mind — was my own personal stamp to the whole experience.

I was given free rein to write occasional sports columns for the News-Press whenever I came up with creative ideas. In 2000 I wrote a column about how covering UCSB had restored my love for baseball. The professional game, particularly when the LA Dodgers broke my heart by trading away Mike Piazza, had jaded my interest.

In that column, I wrote about the intimate atmosphere of UCSB's Caesar Uyesaka Stadium. *"There's no more beautiful, laid-back setting than Caesar Uyesaka for baseball on a clear, sunny Santa Barbara day, with the local mountains serving as a majestic backdrop,"* I wrote.

Watching Gaucho baseball filled the void left open by my 12-year-old son, who I lamented *"would rather practice karate than play baseball."*

At the UCSB baseball awards banquet after the heralded 2001 season, I was accorded one of the greatest compliments of my sports writing career. It came from Fred Warrecker, who was the legendary baseball coach at Santa Barbara High seemingly forever. It was his son Donovan who cracked that memorable game-winning double against Cal State Fullerton. No one knew the game of baseball better than Fred Warrecker, so his perspective as a reader carried considerable weight. He told me that my coverage of the team not only brought out the personalities of the players in interesting ways, but it reflected the nuances of the game that went beyond the stats and cliches of play-by-play. Coming from Fred Warrecker, that meant a lot to me.

I think every parent at that season-ending banquet thanked me for my coverage of their sons that season. There was never a moment in my sports writing career comparable to that banquet when I felt more personally rewarded for my work.

———————◆———————

Kasey was the subject of another column I wrote in September 2002, when he was 14. The column expressed how I rejoiced over a phone conversation I had with him, during which he was telling me about his very first race as a member of his high school cross-country team. Out of over 300 freshmen, he finished 36th overall, and first among his 10 freshmen teammates.

I was so thrilled to think that my son showed the potential to follow in my footsteps and develop into a cross-country star. I could see the potential was there. His finish was impressive, to be sure, but

I knew it could have been better because he ran the race in clunky *basketball shoes*.

"I need to buy you running shoes," I told my basketball-crazy son over the phone.

Kasey may have had running prowess, but he enjoyed playing basketball more, which was why he was running cross country wearing basketball shoes. He was a 5-8 freshman — not exactly tall enough to stand out under a hoop — and we played one-on-one basketball together all the time. His greatest potential wasn't on the basketball court.

I wanted so much for him to experience what I experienced as a cross-country star in high school, the prestige and self-esteem it afforded me. The column didn't mention how my broken toe shattered my cross country dreams in my senior year, but I'll admit that I held out hope that Kasey could recapture some of that luster long lost.

Having the proper, lightweight running shoes would give him that chance.

My son Kasey running in a high school cross-country race as a freshman

So, we had one of those classic father-son moments. I drove all the way to LA to buy him running shoes, which became the gist of the column. I picked him up after school, after cross-country practice. He was all sweaty, which brought back memories of my smelly high school locker room scenes.

The column detailed how Kasey tried on a bunch of different shoes in a sporting goods store. Finally, he held out a pair, asking "How 'bout these?"

I looked in disbelief at my teenager, incredulous that he had no idea that he was holding up a pair that was an exact replica of the basketball shoes he was already wearing. The column went on a diatribe in which I imagined whacking my son on the side of the head with those shoes he held out after his *"How 'bout these?"* comment. Name me just one teen-age boy who couldn't use a good whack on the side of the head by a basketball shoe once in a while?

I'm sure the whacking-on-the-side-of-the-head idea for my son was a rub-off from the phone conversations I was having with my Spanish lady friend Ana in Washington. Her son Lance was close to Kasey's age, and we shared our frustrations on how to knock some sense into our wayward, aimless boys. We posited the whacking solution as our desperate fall-back remedy.

Ana and I were kidding, of course, just as I was in my "whacking" reference in my column. I light-heartedly wrote about joking with Kasey that we needed to take into consideration the "whack-ability quotient" in deciding which shoes to buy. He thought that was funny. That's my boy, same sense of humor.

But my heart was in the right place. I wanted to help my son become a star in cross country. I decided to drop the whacking idea, concluding the column with: *"So better yet, let him wear the shoes and win races, and watch a father swell with pride. Maybe I've been whacked in the head, 'cause I'm seeing stars."*

——————◆——————

I wrote another outside-the-box type column in 2003. It was my attempt at a parody feminist column, exploiting an innocent misunderstanding over my name "Chic." The misunderstanding came up when I was coaxed to join an NBA fantasy league by my News-Press sports desk colleague, Rudy. I joined 11 other males in the league.

Rudy, who left a newspaper in Tucson to join the News-Press, recruited three of his former colleagues in Arizona for his internet NBA fantasy league. None of the Arizonans knew me or had ever seen me. They only knew me by our league's internet correspondence.

The only name the Tucson fantasy owners knew me by was my team name, "CluelessChic." I had no intentions of casting aspersions on feminine intellect regarding the NBA, but rather on my own "cluelessness" with respect to the basketball league. I further clouded my gender by assigning my team manager the name of "tessakasey," after my kids Tessa and Kasey.

So, early in the season, I had a head-to-head fantasy match-up with one of the Tucson guys, whose team was called "Watermelon Bullfighters." In advance of our match-up, he dispatched a message on our league's website, confessing that he wasn't sure if I was a male or female.

It occurred to me that maybe this guy thought my name was Tessa Kasey, who considered herself a "CluelessChic."

So, as I re-told the story in the column, I decided to have some fun with this guy, with a response to his message that I labeled "Sexist Bullfighters." In the message I feigned indignation over his raising even the slightest doubt of the existence of a female member. I wrote: *"You pig men are all alike. You think that just because the league is pertaining to sports, it must be an all-male gig."*

I played up the ruse further, claiming to alert "my bosom buddy," women's rights activist Martha Burk, who was waging a war at the time on the all-male membership at the famed Augusta National Golf Course, home of the PGA Masters Tournament. Then I laid it on thick with a reference to the best player on my fantasy team, Baron Davis, calling him *"my cute little Baronmeister."*

The poor guy sent a response, which he labeled "Raising a Ruckus," and he stated, *"Damn, calm down, oh mighty female in the league. No disrespect intended."*

I felt bad, realizing this guy welcomed a female member in the league and didn't deserve my tongue-lashing. But then I confessed in the column about the "rush" I felt from having convinced him that I was a female. I likened it to the movie "Tootsie," in which Dustin Hoffman, in his gender-reversal role, declared to Jessica Lange's character, *"I never felt more like a man than when you thought I was a woman."*

I then downgraded my ruse in comparison to Tootsie. I also questioned, *"What in God's name is so great about knowing anything about sports anyway?"*

Then I surrendered to my ultimate "maleness" with my participation in yet another mindless fantasy sports league. With a war in Iraq, pollution, poverty and corruption rampant in the world, my biggest concern at the moment was worrying how many games a knee injury would sideline *"my cute little Baronmeister."* Any respectable female would laugh at the frivolity of that mind-set.

————————◆————————

My coverage assignments became more diversified starting in 2002. Mark Patton dispatched me on another Gaucho men's basketball road trip to Logan, Utah, and Moscow, Idaho, again that season. No black ice road trips to Moscow on this occasion.

Logan was another matter altogether; the thermometer registered 26 degrees below zero the night before the scheduled game. As a native Southern Californian, I had to find out what negative 26 degrees felt like. So, I stepped out of my hotel room at midnight to find out and my face nearly cracked smacking against the frozen air.

I enjoyed covering novelty sports such as beach volleyball. The American Volleyball Players (AVP) tournament had returned to its roots in Santa Barbara in 2002. Santa Barbara had earned the rightful reputation of being the "birthplace" of beach volleyball. One of the biggest trailblazers was Karch Kiraly, the local Santa Barbara High and UCSB star alum who went on to win Olympic gold medals in both team and beach volleyball, and then coached the U.S. women's team to a bronze medal in 2016. He was one of the AVP's winningest stars, and I got to see him in action in '02.

Another novelty event I covered was the State Street Mile Run in 2004, in which hundreds of runners stormed down the main downtown street on a Sunday morning.

Covering polo matches at the Santa Barbara Polo and Racquet Club diverted me into unfamiliar territory, away from the path of mainstream sports. I was rubbing elbows with the rich and well-heeled in attendance, dressed in sports jackets and ties and elegant summer dresses and bonnets. Watching the magnificent horses gallop from one end to the other on the vast, well-manicured green field was like witnessing poetry in motion. Had I not covered polo, I would have never known what a "chukker" was; it's polo's word for a period of play, lasting seven-and-a-half minutes between time-outs to bring in fresh horses. Not only was it a rich man's sport, but it was an international sport; I did a story on four Argentinian brothers who came to Santa Barbara to play.

One inspiring story I took particular pride in writing was on Dr. Lindsay Blount, a local 47-year-old cancer doctor who overcame colon cancer to resume his amateur road cycling career. The story drew parallels to Lance Armstrong's rebound from testicular cancer to win six Tour de France cycling titles. Armstrong's admission to illegal doping and disgrace that disqualified all of his Tour titles was still years away.

I also wrote stories for the News-Press' weekly special section focused on the Santa Ynez Valley. One distinguished subject I wrote about was artist Merv Corning, whose walls in his expansive ranch home displayed 25 years of commemorative Super Bowl posters and portraits that he painted, dating back to the first Super Bowl in 1967.

But baseball remained the staple of my writing. The 2002 UCSB baseball team lost nine players from the illustrious '01 roster. But they still had Ryan Spilborghs, the player who hit safely in 35 straight games to break the school hitting streak record in '01. Spilborghs was a homegrown talent who attended Santa Barbara High before going to UCSB. He was a natural for a feature story and I couldn't have picked a nicer kid to write about. His high school coach, the legendary Fred Warrecker, preached about Ryan's numerous admirable qualities. Warrecker made it part of his coaching regimen to tell his players, "Be like Ryan Spilborghs." Spilborghs went on to play a few seasons for the Colorado Rockies in the big leagues.

In '02 I started covering the Santa Barbara Foresters, who developed into a dynasty in the summer collegiate baseball league. The Foresters went on to win an all-time high seven National Baseball Congress titles under Manager Bill Pintard between 2006-18, an era that evaded my sports writing career.

———————◆———————

When ownership of any business changes hands, it's scary.

In the fall of 2000, we had no idea what we were in for when local billionaire Wendy McCaw bought the News-Press — and it's stately downtown building — from the New York Times.

The New York Times was a good company. It paid staff reasonably well, offered good benefits, and even had a pension plan for employees. The pension plan ended under Wendy McCaw, which wasn't a good sign.

Worse yet, Allan Parsons resigned. He turned in his resignation on Day 1 of Wendy's regime. Newsroom morale took an instant nosedive. No amount of the caviar she ordered for the free buffet she served up for staff on her first day could cover the odious projection of things to come.

Parsons was revered in the newsroom. We all felt deeply wounded by his departure. We braced to meet his replacement — an elderly, short, bespectacled man with a graying goatee and large ego named Jerry Roberts.

Roberts was coming from a distinguished journalistic career and dubious departure from the San Francisco Chronicle. That pretty much summed up the duality of Jerry Roberts.

Roberts was made out to be some kind of cultish hero when the News-Press newsroom's war with Wendy exploded in the summer of 2006. I avoided that mess by a full year, when I was unceremoniously terminated by a very cocky and hypocritical Jerry Roberts.

Did I mention Jerry Roberts was short? He stood about 5-foot-6. In my experience with him, Jerry Roberts came off as very small.

My last three years at the News-Press, under the guidance of Roberts, were not pleasant. I was working my ass off, pumping out far more stories than I had time for outside of my desk shifts. On many occasions I was forced to write stories while working desk shifts.

Working the desk shift was not the most conducive environment for writing a story. *Imagine you're at the computer, typing out a story, reviewing your interview notes, then the phone rings. A high school coach is calling in a basketball score. Gotta takes notes from that call to write a little roundup blurb. Make sure you spell everyone's name right. God forbid if you spell somebody's name wrong. Then you look at your working queue — ah, something just came up from the layout editor, a story you have to jump on. Edit and headline.*

It'll be a few more minutes before you get back to that story you were writing. Where the heck did you leave off reviewing your interview notes?

Some nights, I was the layout editor, filling in when needed, running the show on the desk. Calling the shots that would appear in the sports section the next day was a big responsibility. But I enjoyed doing layout. That's where my creativity was allowed to shine in a more graphic way than my writing. Playing with variations with photos, headlines, fonts, type layout, all on pagination, was mind-expanding.

There was nobody else on the News-Press sports staff who filled multiple roles like I did — covering live events, writing features, working the desk, *and* providing spot duty as layout editor. For 28 years in the business, I had prided myself on being a jack-of-all-trades in the sports department for two newspapers. I think that starting out as a lowly copy clerk had something to do with drilling into me the idea that I had to work a little harder than most of my peers to earn some respect.

I was relatively happy with what I was doing and felt appreciated when John Zant and Mark Patton were my bosses. Then Jerry Roberts arrived in 2002 and made two managerial moves in sports. He named 27-year-old Gerry Spratt as Sports Editor, moving over from the news desk; and six months later Roberts hired 25-year-old Nick Masuda as Assistant Sports Editor.

Those two twenty-somethings were overseeing a very veteran, aging sports staff that had remained intact as an efficient entity for many years. Among John Zant, Mark Patton, Barry Punzal, Dan Shiells, Dave Loveton, and Ken Noe, I was still the "new guy" in sports for years, until "youngster" Mike Traphagen joined the staff. The old gang ranged in age from late-40's-to-50's, and earned top salaries, with maxed-out vacation benefits; in other words, the "expendables."

Wendy, for all her billions, was a penny-pincher when it came to running the News-Press. It was bad enough she was an arch conservative — she would go on to publicly endorse Trump for President in 2016, marking the News-Press as one of only six newspapers in the entire nation to back Trump. She had very little appreciation for experienced, dedicated, committed staff of a certain age if she could replace them with younger, less expensive talent.

Roberts, assigned to do Wendy's bidding, decided that the newsroom had to become younger in order to attract younger readers. The News-Press was not unique in its thinking. Marketing studies clearly showed newspaper readership was in a state of decline in general, mostly because the younger generations weren't using newspapers as their main source of information.

The irony is that Roberts was part of the older generation he sought to replace. The sports department was the primary target on his list. For all our collective experience, it was somewhat galling that Roberts would install two young, relatively inexperienced guys half our age to call the shots and, under Roberts' direction, determine our fates.

Spratt was a tall, lanky, quiet, introverted type behind glasses that accurately conveyed his well-read intellect. I was the guy primarily responsible for initially integrating Spratt into the sports staff by inviting him into the fantasy football league that I started. I admit it, I was so obsessed with fantasy football that I was involved in two leagues for several years, counting the old Her-Ex league that continued long after that paper went out of business. The News-Press fantasy league was terminated when Spratt became the boss on the sports staff.

Spratt was promoted to Sports Editor very capriciously, replacing Mark Patton, who didn't ask for the demotion. As a boss, Spratt generally was an enigma. I never knew where I stood with him because he wasn't particularly friendly. But I caught on that he had it out for me, virtually as Roberts' puppet. I didn't trust the guy.

Then there was the insufferable Masuda. He was the young, highly ambitious, very cocky type whose status as Assistant Sports Editor went to his head. He was hired when Rudy, whom we hired out of Arizona three years earlier, left to work for another paper in LA.

Masuda clearly was the main cog to Roberts' agenda in sports. Spratt actually was too nice of a guy to carry it out on his own. Masuda, on the other hand, was the ultimate "brown-noser" with respect to Roberts, all too willing to play as his lap dog. If Masuda's cocky attitude wasn't unbearable enough, he was also dishonest; he was fine with lying to your face about what was going on in the department.

Over the final two-and-a-half years at the News-Press, I knew

I was being targeted. I could tell by what was expected of me. No matter how hard I worked, I was expected to do more. My jack-of-all-trades pride was thinning out when I was expected to write more stories with less writing shifts. With some lingering resentment, I took note of another sports writer half my age producing roughly the same amount of stories I was without ever having to work a single desk shift.

I had always scored well on job performance reviews when Mark was reviewing me. Then in 2003, my first yearly job performance review under Spratt was dramatically different. On almost all categories he graded me "1" or "2' for *"improvement required"* or *"substantial improvement required."* His comments were like reading a work of fiction splattered with unbelievable outright lies. I wrote an extensive rebuttal to all of Spratt's spats in my review, and hashed it out in a face-to-face discussion with him. I'd like to think the rebuttal stalled management's concerted efforts to get rid of me.

Scores on my second yearly review, for 2004, were slightly better, in part because Spratt knew I'd call him out for his BS. But that review still had factual lies that rankled me. I was particularly appalled to read that Spratt stated I was spending too much time on writing stories while working the desk. That was utter bullshit, given that I was forced to write 80 percent of my stories on desk shifts. I felt I should have been praised for my productivity under those circumstances. Instead, I was seeing my boss using it against me in my job performance review in an Orwellian twist. Again, I wrote a lengthy rebuttal.

After that review, I documented everything I did in e-mails to Spratt. In effect, I was filing my factual documentation to counter their "fictional" narrative against me.

Nevertheless, I had already been set up for failure. Management had laid the foundation to terminate me. Within the first six months of 2004 I received two "write-ups" for three-to-four random published mistakes that they cherry-picked and magnified. Write-ups were presented by Roberts' second-in-command, Assistant Managing Editor Linda Stern. I had no chance to defend myself. Judge and jury was Jerry Roberts, with the verdict delivered by Stern.

Everyone made mistakes working the desk, none more so than Gerry Spratt and Nick Masuda. Both of them were spared from taking calls from local coaches reporting game results, easily the most stressful task working the desk. I couldn't tell you how many times I caught mistakes Spratt and Masuda had made while proofreading pages and corrected them before they made print.

But management was specifically signaling who they were keeping tabs on for committing mistakes. Dan Shiells was the first in sports who faced heavy scrutinization until he decided not to put up with it. His sudden departure cast a pall over the whole staff. Dan had been at the News-Press for over 20 years. He was Mr. Prep Football on the staff and had earned legendary status in the community. He decided to resign because he saw the writing on the wall. It wasn't worth his while to prove his worth. He was in the fortunate position to make that decision because his wife was making good money with her job, so he didn't really need the job.

Dave Loveton, my "extra" companion as the limping cowboy in the movie "Steal Big Steal Little" a few years earlier, wasn't in the same fortunate situation. He became the next man targeted a couple months after Dan's departure. His tenure at the News-Press nearly matched Dan's. He did not choose to leave.

I was already on the hit "list." The News-Press supposedly was operating under a "three strikes and you're out" policy— three write-ups and you're gone. After my second write-up, I was paranoid about getting the dreaded third strike, so I was double- and triple-checking my work to make sure my work was clean. It was a very stressful time, knowing that you were under the gun, that the slightest mistake would likely cost you your job.

Finally, my turn was up on May 4, 2005. It came in the same way that Dave received the news. Yolanda, the HR Director whose office was downstairs, came upstairs, walked up to my desk, and said the chilling words:

"Can you please follow me to my office? Now?"

With my throat tightened in a knot, I followed her down. Waiting for me in her office, sitting at a large desk with my personnel file in front of him, was Jerry Roberts. He proceeded to tell me that I was being terminated from my position, immediately.

I was given my entire personnel file to take home with me. There was no third write-up in that file. That's because there was no justifiable write-up since receiving the second one some ten months

514

earlier. They had nothing on me. Jerry Roberts just decided it was time for me to go.

I have no recollection of his explanation for why I was being terminated. My mind was in a fog when he spoke. It was a bunch of general gobbledygook predicated on the fictional and cherry-picking documentation they had assembled just to set the table for this day.

The utter sense of doom that set in at that moment was indescribable. My whole world collapsed. I stared in silence at the contemptible lowlife with the gray goatee telling me I wasn't good enough to work on his sports staff after a 28-year sports writing career I was proud of. I already hated him for doing this to Dan and Dave. Now I had every reason to despise him for terminating a memorable, fulfilling chapter of my life. I was devastated by the realization of how hard I had campaigned to keep this job, and it wasn't enough to persuade this small man.

Roberts laid out a severance package that was, to be honest, fairly generous. But it was generous for a reason. It came with a signed agreement preventing me from suing the News-Press for age discrimination, which was exactly what was going on here. Dan and Dave were victims as well. There were two other 50-somethings in the newsroom who were swept up in the same scheme — a news reporter and the Entertainment editor.

The News-Press wasn't the only paper guilty of this crime. I read about papers all over the country applying the same practice in a desperate aim to reach younger readers. It was hard to swallow, to be perceived as dinosaurs, doomed for extinction.

The experience was humiliating. After the meeting downstairs concluded, I was escorted by Yolanda back up to my desk, in front of my colleagues, to collect whatever personal items I had in a box that Yolanda provided. I looked at my colleagues as I cleared my desk. They knew exactly what was going on. No words were spoken. Then I was unceremoniously escorted out of the building, banished forever. After fifteen years.

Jerry Roberts would get his comeuppance a year later. That's when the infamous meltdown of the News-Press newsroom bubbled over because of Wendy's heavy-handed editorial intervention. The proverbial you-know-what hit the fan after Wendy's ridiculous staff reprimands that resulted from her objections to the publication of actor Rob Lowe's personal address, which was disclosed in a story regarding a public city council meeting. This episode exploded into the national media spotlight. The newsroom revolted in defiance and six editors, including Spratt, resigned out of principle. Roberts, who was publicly propped up as the renegade ringleader, was unceremoniously fired, and he got escorted out of the building just like I did a year earlier. Many of my former peers made him out to be a hero. Gag me.

————————◆————————

On the day of my termination, a story was just emerging from my UCSB baseball beat that had to be told.

Since I could no longer write this story for the News-Press, I pitched it to the Santa Barbara Independent, a weekly publication.

Chris Malec, the senior leader and heart of the Gauchos baseball team, was having a stellar season mid-way through to cap a brilliant collegiate career, when suddenly, he was diagnosed with testicular cancer.

The team had been hit by the injury bug all season long. But this was the last straw. It didn't get any worse than this.

It was assumed that Malec was lost for the season, after he underwent surgery and chemotherapy treatment. But, miraculously, he got his doctor's clearance to return to play baseball by Mother's Day weekend. It had been just 23 days since the surgery.

Malec's return to action was announced on the Tuesday before Mother's Day, That was May 4, the day I was asked by Yolanda to follow her downstairs.

UCSB was hosting Long Beach State, ranked No. 10 in the nation, for a three-game series over Mothers' Day weekend. Suddenly working for the Independent, I had prearranged to sit in the stands with Chris's mother during the Mother's Day game on Sunday. That lent a poignant element to the story.

When Chris stepped up to the plate for his first at-bat in the game, LuzAnna Malec looked up and smiled at a four-year-old boy who had stood up a couple rows above her. The little boy held up a little-boy-sized, hand-painted sign that read: "Chris, we are praying for you."

"It's a gift," LuzAnna Malec told me simply when I asked her what she was feeling on Mother's Day. She had made the four-hour drive from her home in Laguna Niguel to watch her stricken son play baseball. She was rewarded for her efforts.

The outcome of the game was irrelevant. "Just putting on the uniform on Friday morning was a blessing," Chris told me.

The whole weekend was a crescendo of dramatics for Mrs. Malec's son. Coach Brontsema didn't push Chris into action right away, inserting him as a late-inning defensive replacement at shortstop in the first game of the series on Friday. As if it was scripted, the very first batter in that inning hit a ground ball to him, which he fielded flawlessly. The Gauchos won the game, 8-6, snapping a seven-game losing streak in Malec's absence.

Bronstema put Malec in the starting lineup for Game 2 on Saturday. When he stepped up to the plate in the first inning, marking his first at-bat since the cancer diagnosis, the bases were loaded. On the second pitch to him, he cranked the ball over the fence in right-center for a grand-slam home run. If I was writing a movie screenplay depicting this scenario, critics would have cried out "Corny!"

The Gaucho bench poured out of the dugout to give Malec a hero's welcome at home plate. The entire stadium went nuts. UCSB won Game 2, 7-6.

Malec's grand slam had an eerie sense of déjà vu. One year before, in the Gauchos' three-game series against the same Long Beach team at the 49ers' home field, Malec smacked a game-winning grand slam against heralded pitcher Jered Weaver, who went on to be named 2004 Division 1 College Pitcher of the Year. Weaver would go on to an illustrious major league career with the California Angels.

The Chris Malec story, with parallel grand slams, drew parallels with a testicular cancer case that struck cyclist Lance Armstrong, long before his fall from grace for his doping scandal that wiped away his racing career accolades.

Malec had cited Armstrong's "It's Not About The Bike" as his favorite book, which recounted Armstrong's recovery from testicular cancer and remarkable rebound to win the Tour De France six straight times. LuzAnna bought Chris the book two years earlier in part because of a cancer-surviving episode for the son of a friend of hers. Chris acknowledged that the book helped him face his own dire diagnosis and gave him hope that he could recover. Armstrong's eventual disgrace years later didn't wipe that away.

The Independent gave the story a big spread. It far overshadowed the meager coverage the News-Press accorded the Malec story. I felt some sense of vindication in the face of Jerry Roberts' false indictment of my journalistic record of service at the News-Press.

I wound up accepting the severance package and I filed for unemployment as well. Between those two income sources I could afford to remain unemployed for the next seven-and-a-half months.

I made the most of my time off. I took a couple of months to paint the outside of my house, which was quite an undertaking. I felt a keen sense of accomplishment.

The uncertainty of unemployment didn't change my big plans for a summer vacation trip to Maui with my kids.

My kids and I had an absolute blast in Maui. We hiked to waterfalls; frolicked on a black sand beach; scuba-dived with exotic fish and large tortoises; drove to a mountain top for spectacular views of a multi-cratered volcano; got doused by voluminous sprays of water from a blowhole in lava rock at a beach; swam at lots of other beaches and one cozy lava pool. My kids both agreed it was the best trip ever.

Later in the fall Gayle and I made our farewell bon voyage trip together to New Mexico, preceding our final break-up. I had wondered if my lingering unemployment had put pressure on the relationship.

Regardless, the writing was on the wall. It was time to put a "—30—" on both the relationship and my 28-year newspaper career.

CHAPTER 28
Making a Hard Left Onto a New Path

It was clear there was no future for me in the newspaper business at age 52. I had to think long and hard what I wanted to do after 28 years as a sports writer. It was tough to swallow, having to give up on a career I loved so much. But it just seemed so futile to even try to seek a job in a profession that was facing its own survival issues in the digital world.

The unpleasant end to my sports writing career was cause to think about how my life might have been different had I not broke my baby toe twice during my senior year in high school, effectively derailing my promising running career. Had I pursued the running to its fullest potential, who knows where that would have guided me more than thirty years later?

Following my departure from the News-Press, I was lured back into sports writing for a while. Barry Punzal, my friend and colleague from the News-Press sports department, had lasted a couple of years longer than I before suffering a similar rude fate at the paper. He then found work with a fledgling local sports website that provided online coverage of local Santa Barbara sports. High school football was the primary sport in town and Barry hired me as a "stringer" for Friday night games in the fall. I lasted three seasons before giving it up for good.

By then, I was entrenched in my new career.

The old adage "When one door closes, another one opens" rang true for me at this juncture in my life. After being unemployed for seven months, I left myself open for another door to lead me in a different direction. I responded to a small classified ad in the Santa Barbara Independent that caught my eye.

It read: *"Looking for people who are compassionate, patient, reliable, responsible, trusty-worthy."* I thought those traits generally applied to me. It was with an agency that provided support services for people with disabilities, called Work Training Programs. I thought I'd apply for a part-time position, try it out, see if I liked it.

A young woman named Melissa Waites, a very cheerful and earnest woman from the Midwest in her mid-twenties, interviewed me.

She was Program Coordinator for Individual Supported Employ-ment (ISE) services. The pay wasn't great, but I accepted the job offer.

Melissa played a part in an important decision — what name to call me. I was thinking that my new profession required a new identity — "Charlie," the name that Gayle had called me the past seven years. "Chic" was the byline I was known by in the public eye as a sports writer, so I decided to retire that name, professionally speaking. Melissa thought the name "Chic" wasn't a good fit, professionally, for this job. She liked the idea of calling me "Charlie."

So, I became, Charlie, the job coach.

———————◆———————

I started work at WTP on December 12, 2005. I was quickly lured into a full-time position, padding my hours by working in residential (SSP) services. Medical insurance, paid vacation and sick pay were added incentives.

I was added to an older, veteran ISE staff of six other job coaches, all except one of whom were over 40. The exceptions were Melissa and her second in command as the Lead Job Coach, Laurie Furuta, an Asian American woman in her twenties. It was not lost on me that the hierarchy in ISE had a striking similarity to what I had left at the News-Press sports staff — two young people directing an older staff. But I was a "rookie," I had no misgivings about the generational divide at my new job. Melissa was a great boss.

I had a lot to learn. I was immediately put to the test, assigned to cover an extremely autistic young woman who was completely non-verbal working at a pizza parlor. She had a habit of swaying back and forth in an apparent innate coping mechanism that wasn't an ideal optic at the workplace. Unfortunately, the job proved to be too stressful for her.

This came to bear just three days on the job. She was cleaning tables outside in the patio area when she inexplicably tossed a napkin holder and parmesan cheese dispenser onto the ground. Then, while bobbing back and forth uncontrollably, she grabbed a knife as if she was going to cut her wrist. Instinctively, I grabbed her by the wrists to keep her from harming herself. Normally, using physical force on a client would be strictly forbidden. I managed to call Melissa right away, who immediately rushed to the work site. In this case, she validated that the aggressive action I took was appropriate. As a "rookie" job coach, I needed assurance for trusting my instincts in an extremely challenging moment.

———————•◆•———————

Cyndi, one of the veteran job coaches whose ranks I was joining, took me under her wing and became my mentor. Cyndi was a slender, attractive woman with neatly cropped, shoulder-length, blondish-brown hair. She wore glasses over her blue eyes that conveyed an intellectual persona. When I first met her, I assumed she was 10-12 years younger than me. Her cute, youthful-looking face fooled me; I learned much later she was a lot closer to my age.

We quickly became friends, meeting for lunch and coffee. We flirted. Something was brewing between us. But she was married. Her marriage was going on 32 years and was on the rocks, for reasons I won't go into, because that's not my story.

Cyndi was the antithesis of the type of woman I had always been attracted to. She was quiet, reserved, bashful. Her life experience obviously was completely different from mine. But we were drawn to each other by our shared passion for our work.

She had an extended medical leave coming up, and she entrusted me to take on her most challenging participants on her caseload while she was out. She was expected to be out from work for three months.

It took a measure of trust on her part to place this much responsibility in the hands of a newcomer. The stage was set for my knight on a white horse role. I think I needed this, after my self-esteem took a hit from the final break-up with Gayle.

———————•◆•———————

Work Training Programs changed its name to PathPoint not long after I was hired. PathPoint, nee WTP, is a non-profit agency that is contracted to provide support services for people with disabilities, as funded by the state. The state agencies that authorize our services are the Tri-County Regional Center (TCRC) and Department of Rehabilitation (DOR), both with operating offices in Santa Barbara.

Working with people with disabilities pushed me into utilizing people skills I didn't realize I had. The closest I could relate to it were my jobs working with kids way back during my college days. Patience is definitely a virtue required for the job. So is compassion, which is a basic component to the agency's core principals related to treating the individuals we serve with dignity and respect.

PathPoint is very conscious of the words we use. "Respect" is the "R" word that we emphasize to counter the other taboo "R" word — "retard." Our clients stage campaign rallies once a year against the use of that "R Word."

Also, we stopped calling our clients "clients" — the word was considered too clinical. Instead, we adopted the word "participants," and then eventually changed that to "persons served." Words in this field can be tricky in the pursuit of showing respect.

As job coaches, we are not expected to tell our "persons served" how to do their jobs. We can advise, suggest, and give them choices with variable outcomes laid out in an understandable manner. The standard form of support is carried out during work-site visits — observing, and documenting what we observe. We are expected to understand every aspect of their jobs, including tracking their work schedules, identifying exactly what their tasks are, getting acquainted and serving as communication links with their supervisor(s) and coworkers, and knowing what safety protocols are in place at the work sites. Safety is a big part of PathPoint's emphasis.

We apply a person-centered approach to our support, which is facilitated by showing an interest in the personal lives of the people we support. Personalizing our services helps build trust, and projects dignity to their lives. I've always considered that their personal lives have a direct impact on their jobs, so the more I know about them on a personal level, I am better informed to advise them on matters related to work.

———————◆———————

I have worked with hundreds of interesting people with disabilities spanning over 15 years. There is a core group with whom I've worked for a long time, so I've gotten to know them pretty well. These are the relationships I've cherished the most.

Using fictitious names for privacy reasons, I offer a sampling of a few of their stories:

- Howie was added to my caseload when I was just a couple of months on the job. Jessica, the job coach who had been supporting Howie at the time, suggested that he would respond better to a male coach, so she recommended that I take over. I've been working with Howie ever since. I eventually expanded my role with Howie as his case manager. My Howie stories are among my favorite.

Howie had worked over 15 years in the mail room at a business office when I took over as his job coach, and he really didn't need on-site support at the work site. Assessing his shy, reclusive personality, I determined that I could better support him with weekly off-site meetings away from the work site. I arranged to pick him up after work to go to Starbucks, Coffee Bean and Tea, or McDonald's, every Wednesday. Howie and I are the same age, and he had virtually no friends, no social life other than his karate classes. He clearly enjoyed the companionship I provided.

I tended to bend the rules a bit on setting boundaries with Howie; we could be "friendly," but not friends in the real sense. But I had gained Howie's trust in a way in which I never would have otherwise if I hadn't allowed him to think of us as friends. He was very suspicious, sometimes paranoid, by nature. He didn't like crowds, in general. He was an odd little guy, who could get emotional. There were moments when he exhibited a bit of a temper, and he had a stubborn streak, which resulted in a few spats over the years because he didn't like what I was telling him.

But I feel genuine affection for Howie. I tried to bring him out of his shell, which wasn't easy. I encouraged him to pursue interests that he really enjoyed. He enjoyed cooking, had a collection of cookbooks that he occasionally took a crack at recipes that typically, as he would put it in a melancholy tone, "didn't turn out too well." He enjoyed working on computers, exhibiting a persistence in attempting to self-teach himself by trial and error from instructional guides he'd find online. He wasn't always successful at cooking or computer skills, but he liked the process of trying. He had already given up trying to take adult ed classes in both endeavors; classroom settings had intimidated him.

Howie's father was a decorated World War II Air Force pilot who was stationed at Vandenberg Air Force Base in Lompoc, where Howie grew up. His father left him a sizable trust that his sister

Sandy manages. Howie had mentioned Sandy, who lives in the Seattle area, in passing a couple of times.

But after 12 years working with me, he never bothered to mention to Sandy anything about me. When I finally decided to reach out to her, and call her, she had no idea who I was, and was astonished to find out somebody in Santa Barbara had been looking out for her brother all those years. She was so grateful to finally talk to me; it was a heartening conversation that I wished I had initiated much sooner.

Howie did have one friend among our persons served, a woman named Maura, who attended the same church as Howie, even though she was Jewish. One time, Howie was thinking of inviting her out to dinner with the holidays approaching, a bold move given his shy nature. But Howie was adept at making creative excuses to wiggle out of doing anything that made him uncomfortable. Our conversation went like this:

"I'd like to take Maura out to dinner for Thanksgiving. But I don't think she celebrates Thanksgiving."

"She doesn't?" I questioned. "Why not?"

"Well, you know, because she's Jewish."

I stifled a laugh, realizing he was confusing Thanksgiving with Christmas. I assured him the likelihood that she celebrated Thanksgiving, and then I delicately persuaded him to invite her to dinner. Knowing how stingy Howie was with his money, I strongly advised him to pick up the dinner tab.

When Maura had to move out of the area to Grass Valley a few hundred miles further north to reside closer to her brother, I worked on Howie for a couple years to summon the courage to board a plane to go visit her. Sandy, who paid for the trip with Howie's trust money, coordinated the complicated logistics of getting him there. We didn't want Howie to get lost along the way.

Howie has had his moments of confusion over the years. I went to great lengths to avoid confusion for him in an effort to get him out of his apartment by pursuing entertainment activities in town. I was proud of him when he bought a ticket to an Asian acrobat show at the Granada Theatre downtown. I took Howie on a drive-by a few days before showtime to make *sure* he knew where the Granada was from the downtown bus Transit Center, just a couple of blocks away. He knew how to take the bus to the Transit Center. But when we met up off-site at Starbucks on the Wednesday following the show, I had a sneaky suspicion something went wrong when Howie, in his usual roundabout manner, vaguely explained that he wasn't watching the acrobatic show that he expected at the Granada Theatre. After some artful digging, I finally figured out he was watching a classical orchestral concert at the *Lobero Theatre*. Somehow Howie took a wrong turn walking from the Transit Center and wound up at the wrong theatre. He sat in that audience a full hour before it sunk in that he wasn't watching the right show. Oh my. I had no problem granting Howie benefit of the doubt, but it left me wondering who was the numbskull who allowed him to enter the Lobero with a ticket for the Granada show.

• Walt was my very first client, and became a permanent fixture on my caseload all these years, well past his 70th birthday. Because he was my very first, I hold Walt dear in my heart. Walt is a gentle spirit of a man. In all the years I've worked with him, I've never seen Walt get mad. He has held the same job at an escrow company, scanning escrow documents into the company computer system. My support has gone beyond the scope of his job, helping him through a lot of financial and medical issues. I've always been there to explain things to him, and help him understand his options, because he sometimes got confused.

Walt is a big baseball fan, who closely follows his favorites teams, the St. Louis Cardinals and LA Dodgers. He also has been a long-time participant and ambassador for the Special Olympics, serving as an athlete, coach, committee member and fund-raising volunteer. That links him with a lot of our people who are also Special Olympic members.

Walt is very popular among his expansive social circle, which I have exploited to gain valuable information on his long list of friends in the service of support we provide. I couldn't tell you how many times I've gained tips from Walt pertaining to critical issues related to his friends. Walt's good-nature qualities also sets him up to be unwittingly taken advantage of by some so-called friends, particularly when it comes to footing the bill for social activities that he couldn't afford on his shoestring budget. I've often had to work out the math on entertainment and travel costs on road trips to Anaheim for Disneyland and Angel games, to be equally divided among all those aboard. Walt, who is one the few people we work with who has a driver's license, typically pays for the rental car up front, then I'd come in to help him figure out what he is owed by each of his tag-along friends.

- Lance is, hands down, the sweetest participant in ISE. Every job coach who has worked with Lance loved working with him. And with Lance, there is no such thing as a job coach he doesn't like; he wants to work with everybody. He typically asks to work with every new hire that comes around. An army of coaches have come and gone working with him because he is one of just a few persons served who have required 100 percent coaching on the job because of his limited work skills. Before Covid hit, he was working at a local coffee shop, performing general clean-up tasks (restroom, table-tops, trash take-out, floor sweeping), but he required a lot of hands-on coaching.

Cyndi has served as Lance's long-time lead coach, and I've been his only other reliable mainstay over the years.

Lance is eternally playful, very childlike, and he has a mischievous streak in him. I've had a running joke with him that he *never* gets tired of playing along. I came up with a silly tactic to keep him focused on his task, or keep him from doing something he wasn't supposed to do, by sternly warning him: "Don't make me wag my finger." Lance always reacted by breaking out with that goofy smile of his and proclaiming, "I don't want make you have to wag your finger," knowing full well that was his intention all along. I would start wagging, heed to his baiting by telling him, "I'm getting it warmed up." If he persisted, I'd tell him, "My finger is worn out today. Please don't make me wag it anymore."

Lance is also a local legend for his "rain dances," for which he proudly touts whenever Santa Barbara gets a much-needed drought-busting shower. Climate change has made us beg for more rain for years, which has prompted me to admonish Lance many times to get his feet moving.

- Bruce is a participant about 15 years younger than me who was diagnosed on the "spectrum," but he projects as someone who has no disability. Because Bruce possesses an ability to reason, analyze, and assess as well as somebody of high intellect, I sometimes forget that he has a disability. The inappropriate social tendencies associated with autism as related to Bruce do arise. I am always counseling Bruce on making appropriate behavior choices, and he readily seeks my advice, a reflection of self-awareness on his part. Despite his intellectual level, Bruce's biggest struggle is containing his emotions. He has anger issues; he easily builds resentments. He isn't always in control of his impulses, which makes him an interesting case study to work with.

But Bruce is personable. He is a huge sports fan, which makes him an easy participant for a former sports writer to support. He loves talking about sports with me. He is a fanatic about his favorite teams, and he has strong "hates" for teams he roots against, none more so than the New England Patriots.

One of my success stories resulted in getting Bruce a much higher paying job. He was working in maintenance at a print shop when he first landed on my caseload. When somebody else on my caseload vacated a higher paying maintenance job at an eatery for medical reasons, I recommended Bruce as a worthy replacement to the supervisor with whom I had built a rapport. Then, I worked to get another participant hired to replace Bruce at the print shop, promoting the interests of both employers whose partnerships Path-Point coveted.

Bruce's personal life with girlfriend relationships became a frequent topic of discussion between us. Relationship issues often affected his motivation at work, so I considered this topic to be work-related. I helped him through a break-up with a longtime relationship and the fallout with bouts of depression that followed.

Then, I guided Bruce through a crisis that turned out to be the most intense, time-consuming case I ever had to handle, spanning nine months. We initiated a very controversial grievance against another support vendor. Without going into detail, the grievance involved intimate, private details of Bruce's relationship with a girlfriend and a major intervention by the vendor on behalf of the girlfriend's protective parents that effectively broke up the relationship. The grievance basically addressed alleged violations of both Bruce's and the girlfriend's HIPAA privacy rights. The case was gingerly handled by TCRC and was elevated to very high channels; TCRC had never had to deal with a case quite like this one before. It was an *extremely* sensitive matter; the parents were quite upset. Ultimately, after considerable deliberation, the matter was not resolved in a satisfactory manner, as far as Bruce and I were concerned.

- Julia was just 18 when she got her first job as a courtesy clerk at a local grocery store. Besides her intellectual challenges, she has a high level of ADD. But she is a really hard worker. We've come a long way together over the years. When I started working with her, I overlooked her annoying habit of not making eye contact with me and ignoring me when I said "Hi." It took a while to win her over. Now, I feel almost paternal in my support role for her. I helped shaped her into a mature young woman who always showed the potential to rise above her level of disability.

But she does show exhibit obsessive tendencies with her ADD. Such as calling me, for instance, over and over. I made it OK for her to call me, even if that bended PathPoint's rules a bit. I made this concession with the realization that she was not any different from young women in her age group attached to their smart phones.

I've worked with her on ADD, which was fueled by her sugar habit, especially drinking sodas (a common tendency among our participants). She was a typical teenager who likes to drinks sugary soft drinks, but it fueled her ADD which affected her focus. When I make work-site visits, the first thing I assess is how hyper Julia is. If she's bouncing off the walls, a half-empty bottle of Coke likely lurks in her vicinity.

As years passed she grew older and more mature and made an effort to eat healthier meals, and reduce her sugar intake by drinking more water instead of soda. I was so proud of her.

I supported her for years when she was taking classes toward the commendable goal of earning her GED degree. I helped her arrange her work schedule to accommodate her class schedules. When she finally graduated, I was in attendance for her ceremony, feeling like a proud parent.

I love explaining things to Julia that she doesn't understand. There have been some moments when I got through to her and a light went on inside her. And I could see it. And I lit up every time I saw it.

◆

The roommates had to go. When Cyndi had filed for divorce, we officially became a couple. I wanted to clear the way for Cyndi to move in with me.

Joe, the tall, lanky, older Italian roommate, was a very nice guy and an ideal   roommate. He took it well when I asked him to leave.

It was much harder to part with Sarah. She was very cute, sassy, and had a playful personality. She had been living with me for a good five years, and she felt like a permanent attachment to the house. I even got used to her habit of falling asleep on the living room couch with the TV on late at night. Kicking her out of the house felt like I was clearing a daughter from the nest. She begged both Cyndi and I to let her stay, but I knew it wasn't a good idea. After some gentle prodding, Sarah finally gave in and moved out.

So when Cyndi finally did move in, the big test was, how would Buffy react? Because now, all of a sudden, she was going to have to contend with Cyndi for my attention.

Sadly, the competition did not last long. Buffy suddenly started acting very hyper and agitated one night, just one month after Cyndi had moved in. Something wasn't right, so I rushed Buffy to an emergency pet hospital. The vet wanted to keep her overnight for observation.

At about 3 in the morning I got a call from the pet hospital with the shocking news that she didn't make it through the night. Heart failure claimed my little Princess. I couldn't believe it. She was only 8 1/2 years old. My sweet, sweet Buffy was gone.

———————◆◆◆———————

That left Thomas as the last pet in the household. Cyndi is a lifelong cat lover, so Thomas served as a bond between us. Cyndi was mourning the two cats she left behind with her ex-husband. We formed a family unit with Thomas that lasted nearly a decade.

Thomas didn't just belong to us; he had reached legendary status in the neighborhood. "The Neighborhood Cat," as he came to be known, sometimes disappeared for days in his wanderings. On a couple of occasions, neighbors taking walks past my house saw Thomas hanging with me out front, and they shouted out: "Is that *your* cat? I know your cat!"

Meanwhile, Thomas the Hunter ruled over his home territory. He was my best weapon for combating my perpetual gopher problem on my lawn. I wasn't crazy about how he'd bring the wounded gophers to me to finish them off; drowning them in a bucket of water was the least messy way I could think of to handle that unpleasantness. Mice, meanwhile, didn't fare so well in comparison. Thomas liked to eat mice; I often found detached tails behind on the backyard patio. One night while Cyndi and I were watching TV, he proudly dropped a decapitated body in the middle of the living room. But birds were easily the messiest of his prey. I was mystified how Thomas dragged one bird into the dining room where he left feathers scattered everywhere.

But his most infamous kill left a legacy that lasted for years. Somehow, Thomas managed to ground a huge crow in our driveway. His prey came from a flock of crows that had been circling our neighborhood as long as I've lived in it. For years that flock demonstrated its scorn toward Thomas for killing one of their own, squawking up a storm every time he came into view.

Our beloved cat Thomas laying out on the living room carpet

As Thomas got older, we had to convert him to a permanent indoor cat after he got torn up pretty bad from a much younger male cat. I couldn't afford any more vet bills like that one. Then, when a pack of coyotes moved into our neighborhood and made their presence known by baying at night, that sealed the deal. Thomas's "Neighborhood Cat" days were over.

Cyndi and I actually allowed one rent-paying tenant to live with us, for a few months. The experience reminded us why we didn't want to live with tenants.

Her name was Irene (pronounced Iren-eh). She was the teen-age daughter of Soteris, one of Theo and Angelo's scam victims. Irene was starting school at SBCC. We decided to give it a try for one fall semester. She seemed like a bright, quiet, polite young woman.

She turned into a not-so-polite, spoiled teenager on us. We clashed. We argued. We mutually agreed to part.

Our self-imposed ban on tenants didn't last long. About a year later, we agreed to take my son Kasey in to try to kick-start him toward getting a driver's license and finding a job. I put him to work around the house, too; mostly house-painting jobs.

Kasey, in his early 20's at the time, lived with us for 14 months. I paid for professional driving lessons and tried to instruct him myself. He passed the written test but flunked the driving test three times. He kept getting distracted behind the wheel and making silly mistakes.

As for the job hunt, I took him to interviews all over town. I had to teach him how to interview for jobs and act like he really wanted the job. The only place that would hire him was Chipotle. He lasted all of five days in training. They let him go, stating that he couldn't multi-task. Needless to say, all of this was troubling.

We were supporting and feeding him the entire 14 months. When Kasey went back to LA to visit his mom for the holidays I told him he'd have to contribute something toward rent — $200-$300 — when he returned. It was time. He was 24 and I felt he needed to take on some responsibility for himself. I was facing the classic parenting struggle.

He never returned from LA.

————— ◆ —————

The hierarchy at PathPoint changed quickly during my first few years, and I was a part of that change.

Alana Walczak, a bright, very principled young woman with strong leadership qualities, was hired as Division Director. Coinciding with Alana's hiring, Jaime Rutiaga was brought on board for a long stint as Program Manager overseeing all employment services.

Melissa had resigned during my second year after becoming pregnant, and Laurie replaced her as ISE Program Coordinator. I was elevated as Laurie's second-in-command to ISE Lead Coach. I dropped out of residential services altogether to accommodate this move.

But Laurie left after about a year and I succeeded her as ISE Program Coordinator.

The position was modified so I could continue to provide direct support to participants out in the field roughly 50 recent of the time. This was my choice and management accommodated it. I also handled the monthly billing, staff caseloads, and staff productivity chart; tracked DOR and TCRC authorizations; coordinated and ran staff monthly meetings; approved staff timesheets; interviewed and hired new coaches in coordination with Jaime; trained all the new hires; and carried out staff job performance reviews. I was working harder than ever. But it was rewarding work.

I enjoyed the staff I oversaw and they responded well to me. Cyndi was on staff, but since we were in a relationship, Jaime was designated as her supervisor to remove any perception of conflict of interest. A core grouping of older, veteran coaches comprised most of my staff. Besides Cyndi, there were Kerry Shaughnessy and Joan Patchett, both close to my age who I regarded as friends; Yifat Nahmias-Rogner, the indefatigable Israeli native who offered an intriguing perception and became Cyndi's close companion; Judy Jimenez and Cynthia Wyatt, both young moms in their early 30s.; and Andrew Vail an earnest but troubled young man in his late 20s who I took under my wing. As Program Coordinator, I hired John Walker, a returning American ex-patriot who had carved a life in Brazil after taking in a Brazilian bride. John was a couple of years older than I was, and we became fast friends.

Turnover on the ISE job coaching staff was common as new hires over the next decade trended toward younger and female, which as a whole, was an attractive group. The list seemed endless over the years — Christine, Muneerah, Karin, Karalea, April, Kristen, Carla, Liz, Nicole, Shannon, Becky, Natalie, Stephanie, Iris, Madeline, Julia, Anna, Debbie — I'm sure I'm leaving some names out. Liz Crain, who I trained, eventually was promoted to ISE Program Coordinator when the position was reinstated, and she became my supervisor.

I took one of those young female coaches under my wing, and she stood out as my favorite— Felicia Garcia. First off, she is gorgeous, with her light-complexioned face set off by her dramatic dark eyes and brows. She has long, naturally curly black hair that is just divine. Like so many of the young coaches we hired, I trained her, and she evolved into one of our best and reliable coaches in the five-plus years she worked for us. We shared many of the same participants and collaborated on support for them. She respected my way of coaching.

Felicia, who like my dad, graduated from UCLA, was also a big sports fan. She was a die-hard Lakers (and Kobe) fan. In her spare time she served as a volunteer basketball coach with the Special Olympics. She truly shined in so many ways.

Out on the town with Felicia, one of my favorite job coaches whom I trained

My short tenure as ISE Program Coordinator was the one and only experience in my life as a boss overseeing a staff. It wasn't something I had strongly aspired to do, but in this case, I was passionate about the work. I relished being in charge and dictating how ISE provided its support services.

That was, subject to Jaime's approval. He was my boss.

Altogether, I wound up working with Jaime for about 12 years that turned out to be one of most dynamic working relationships of my life. We went from clashing on policy and participant issues to a mutual respect and admiration from both professional and personal standpoints.

There is no one I knew who is more devoted to the cause of serving and supporting people with disabilities than Jaime. Jaime, roughly 10 years younger than me, was a verified workaholic. In his over-arching role at PathPoint, he was already working entirely too much. But beyond that, he was involved with Special Olympics and Best Buddies, both social outlets for our core group.

Jaime wound up taking my job as ISE Program Coordinator while remaining the overall program manager for employment services. After a couple of years at the job, my position as ISE Program Coordinator became a victim of the 2009 recession. Employment services did not fare well at all in a downward economy and Path-Point downsized by eliminating the ISE Coordinator position. Jaime absorbed the responsibilities because he didn't have enough to do, I guess.

Jaime — a big ice hockey fan— during his grand farewell from PathPoint surrounded by well-wishers, when he finally decided to leave the agency in the summer of 2019

I dropped back to the ISE Lead Coach position, taking a substantial hit in wages, but I was content. I wasn't really cut out to be anybody's boss anyway. Jaime and I ultimately formed a productive team together. I held the Lead Coach position for 10 years until I decided to go to part-time. I followed the lead of Bob Voorhees, a refined elderly gentleman who resigned as a well-paid bank exec to provide us a few years of elegant, sage service until he was ready to retire.

━━━━━━━━ ✦ • • ◆ • • ✦ ━━━━━━━━

There was a time when ISE provided job coaching for mental health participants, representing a very small percentage of our support roster. It was a whole different animal than our regular services for people with disabilities, largely because of the maddening documentation and billing criteria demanded by the Medi-Cal county department to justify our services.

It was enough to place my "mental health" in jeopardy. Jaime had designated me for a trial effort to write Medi-Cal case notes to see if they could pass muster. No one in ISE writes more copious case notes than me, but my notes didn't measure up to Medi-Cal's approval. So the county made our entire staff sit through a yawn-inducing, three-hour training class at the Alcohol, Drugs and Mental Health Services (ADMHS) center to learn how to write case notes to their liking.

It got drilled into us that our case notes were expected to read like technical "clinical" actions and skills that had virtually little to do with what we were actually doing with our participants. In other words, our case notes were effectively reduced to works of fiction, under very specific categories entitled "What You Do" and "What Kind Of Skills." The trick, evidently, was to throw in a few clinical words to authenticate whatever the heck was expected of us in our support services for our participants.

To save my own sanity, I exposed my rebel roots by creating my own fictitious "cheat sheet" glossary of terms to facilitate case notes for Medi-Cal.

The "What You Do" List was composed of proactive verbs to describe job coaching actions. My tongue-in-cheek list included words like: reject, plot, exasperate, resist, agitate, fabricate, defy, twist, exaggerate, make up as I go along, mock, ridicule, irritate, wishfully think about, and f...k up. You get the idea where I'm going here.

The "What Kind Of Skills" List took a little more creativity: maintain sanity skills; rebel against authority skills; overmedicate on clonazepam skills; bomb-ADMHS-building skills; (wasting) time management skills (by writing Medi-Cal notes); nose-picking skills (variation on previous listed skill); coming-up-with-clinical-phrases-with-lots-of-hyphens-so-that-no-normal-person-would-understand skills; navigating Medi-Cal Clinicians Gateway to Hell website skills; punching-fist-through-computer skills (if previous skill fails); and turning "Give-me-a-f...king-break" into "I-can-do-that" skills.

Fortunately, Jaime eventually got us out of having to provide these services, turning them over to our Mental Health Division. I utilized my Consume-As-Much-Alcohol-As-Possible skill to celebrate.

———————◆———————

Medi-Cal wasn't the only agency that placed unattainable demands on us poor job coaches. DOR pushed a specialized service on us that required an awful lot of extra work. The service was given a mouthful of a name called External Situational Assessment (ESA), and the job coaches for this service were called "ESA Specialists." We felt special.

Jaime was PathPoint's point man dealing with DOR, and ESA's were his cross to bear with DOR. They were a bitch. But we provided the service in order to stay in good graces with DOR. Cyndi and I, the two veteran coaches with the most experience on the staff, drew the short straws as the "chosen ones" to serve as ESA Specialists.

The ESA service entailed finding work situations for "potential" job sites to assess the participant's work skills, and interests, as a precursor to actual job development. The ESA Specialist had to "sell" the service to up to three employers as an opportunity for free labor provided by the participant, paid in full by DOR, and supervised fully by the ESA Specialist. But it was a hard sell because the labor was being provided by an unknown entity to the employer. Essentially, ESA Specialists were job developers and job coaches rolled into one.

A lot of responsibility was placed on the ESA Specialist. ESA sessions each typically lasted up to three full, boring hours, which were much longer than the regular work-site visits. The ESA Specialist was responsible for the participant's safety at all times. Then DOR required a bunch of documentation reports on poorly-designed forms for the overall assessment. It was a major pain-in-the-ass. Cyndi and I dreaded ESAs, but we did them knowing Jaime wouldn't be able to find any other coach willing to do them.

Seven out of eight ESAs usually ended up as busts.

But I had one successful ESA that I was extremely proud of pulling off. Going in, when I met Faith for the first time, I assessed this ESA as a surefire bust. "Good luck," Jaime said to me, knowing full well I would need a lot of it.

Faith was 60ish, wheel chair-bound, a Vietnam War vet. She had half of her teeth missing. She had a hole in her stomach from an old war wound, requiring a tube to empty out secretions into a body waste bag. She was a survivor of six or seven heart attacks. She had an assigned special needs dog companion named Rudy. Oh, and she was homeless.

Faith had this scratchy, tangy, irritating voice that she would give you an earful of if you got her riled up. Her cantankerous attitude and pessimism resided just south of "Go Fuck Yourself."

Go for it, Charlie. One decisive break — DOR decided only two work sites were needed to complete this ESA instead of three. But it was still a tall chore —finding two employers willing to let someone like Faith work at their place of business.

DOR approved volunteer work as an acceptable option for ESA sites, even though that wouldn't ideally produce potential paying jobs. I knew going in that Faith loved dogs because of Rudy, so I arranged for her to volunteer at the local dog shelter. Faith worked as a greeter for the public coming in to see the dogs. Turned out, she was a natural for the role; she loved talking up the dogs to folks.

Then, I didn't have to search far to find the second job site — PathPoint. This was a stroke of genius; I put her to work performing one of my hellish tasks as Lead Job Coach. I had fallen way behind scanning staff monthly case notes into our computer files. This was an arduous task that Faith, surprisingly, excelled at doing.

The task called for rearranging the voluminous, hand-written pages of case notes turned in monthly by an expanding staff of 16 job coaches, documenting support for approximately 90 participants.

Faith seemed to enjoy redistributing the notes alphabetically by participant.

Then Faith was equally as eager to show off her computer skills by scanning the case notes for each participant, retrieving each file in email, properly renaming the file, and re-routing the file to the corresponding computer folder. Faith was smart enough and organized enough to carry out every step independently without my help. I was so proud of her. It gave her a huge sense of accomplishment.

Jaime and I were high-fiving each other when we were able to put a "completed" stamp on that ESA. I only wished we had the budget to hire Faith.

———————◆———————

As ISE Lead Coach I continued doing all the billing, caseload management, and staff productivity charts. Staff billing was a bear, an intense 10-hour task spread out over three days that I took a lot of pride in completing. I did billing for 12 1/2 years. I was accurate and meticulous at it, catching 99.9 percent of the numerous staff mistakes that landed on my desk. Those precious math skills I inherited from my Dad paid off.

Caseload management, which was like re-juggling a massive puzzle every month, required an intrinsic knowledge of almost all 90-plus participants who were served in ISE, which I found invigorating. I turned into a walking Google search of fun facts on nearly everyone served in ISE, which is how I accumulated so many stories about them. Caseload management involved parcelling out participant support equitably among all job coaches. But with the frequent turnover in staff, I often had to take on more of my share of participants onto my caseload, which usually ranged between 25-30 people.

———————◆———————

Job coaches are human, therefore imperfect, and I certainly qualify in that category. Over the years I've had a few dark moments in which I lost patience and control of my temper, and had to deal with immense regret in the aftermath. One glaring example involved a hyper and eccentric woman with whom I had worked for years. While I generally enjoyed working with her because of her quirky personality, she required 100 percent job coach supervision and presented immense challenges keeping her focused on her tasks. My patience with her started running on empty after all those years, reaching the point where I finally lost my cool, and in the guilt-ridden aftermath decided maybe it was better if somebody else worked with her.

But I would not have stayed with this line of work if my success stories didn't outweigh my failures. Over the years, some of my more triumphant positive outcomes emerged from some pretty knotty cases that I prevailed with unwavering determination.

One extremely sensitive case involved an autistic person who raised serious security questions by making one ill-advised comment he meant to be a joke that made his supervisors very uncomfortable. The case expanded to such an extent that I wound up in a large conference room in a meeting of 20 people representing various involved parties, engaged in an intense discussion seeking to resolve the issue. This ranked as one of the more intimidating scenarios that I had experienced. But it produced a happy resolution for that participant in the end.

I handled another complicated case in which I diverted a near-disastrous move to save a participant's valuable pension plan. Months of considerable effort went into reducing the participant's weekly work schedule to salvage his qualification for a Section 8 Housing subsidy voucher. The participant was one week into his reduced weekly schedule when I dug further and became apprised of the lucrative pension plan. It turns out the participant was just one month away from reaching his 20-year milestone that qualified him for the pension benefit. He wouldn't have qualified if he continued working at the reduced weekly schedule. The participant's brother, who was a lawyer, was pushing to save the Section 8 Housing voucher for retirement. I had to make the case to the brother to convince him that the pension was a much better deal than the Housing voucher. The brother approved, setting off a mad scramble to reinstate the participant's original weekly 20-hour schedule, and his pension benefit was salvaged.

I cherished the rewards my job produced from the tangible impact I made on the lives of those whom I supported. Do I have more stories to tell? I thought you'd never ask:

- Miriam was a sweet, endearing Jewish lady in her 60s who was set in her ways and habits, carried a strong sense of pride, and had no problem speaking her mind. She was practically blind in one eye and her "good" eye was starting to blur on her, too. Her hearing wasn't very good, either, so she was forced to make some adjustments just to function. I was her job coach until she retired at age 69.

She grew up on the East Coast, where she was taught proper manners and an old-school education. As a young adult she was transferred to the West Coast through a nationwide agency that provided residential services for people with disabilities. The agency also gave her a job as an administrative office assistant, but as she approached retirement, some of her office tasks were reduced because of her failing eyesight. I was on hand to negotiate the accommodations.

For someone with an intellectual disability, Miriam always had a natural curiosity for learning how to master computers. Hannah, one of her two sisters who lived on the East Coast, bought her a 27-inch desktop Mac, and emailed me with a request to set it up for Miriam at her apartment. She could barely make out the computer screen with her one good eye, but we implemented the Zoom lens so she could read the screen. She figured out how to "google" all on her own, by memorizing her password on the keyboard to log on to Google to access her g-mail account.

As her job coach, my way of supporting Miriam was to visit her weekly at her apartment and teach her computer skills. The idea was that maybe she could apply some computer skills to her job. Miriam either had a specific request to help her with something, like using clip art to design birthday and holiday cards for her sisters, or I'd think of something new to teach her, such as copy-and-paste, changing fonts, and attaching e-mails. She experienced such joy in learning and I got a kick out of teaching her.

Miriam flew back east at least a couple times every year to visit family. Hannah always booked her flights to the East Coast. Miriam then would write out her itinerary multiple times (copies for each member of her support staff) in full detail in her exquisite, perfect handwriting, which was remarkable for someone who could barely see.

Hannah parceled out a weekly allowance to Miriam, who always grumbled how Hannah controlled her money. I occasionally drove Miriam to the bank so she could make cash withdrawals. The tellers all knew Miriam well. They were familiar with her routine of asking for $30, to be dispersed in thirty one-dollar bills. Miriam, who couldn't read the bills, was clever enough to figure that when she needed to make a cash purchase, she could count the bills out one-by-one to approximate the amount owed. Miriam had her own unique ways of functioning in the world.

- Benny was one of my favorites. He was a funny little guy who worked at a skateboard factory, assembling boxes in the wheel department. He also did basic maintenance — taking out recycling and trash, sweeping the floors in the large warehouse. He was my age but had the energy of somebody half our age, as he cranked out boxes at a manic pace because that was the only speed he knew how to operate.

Benny didn't know how to read, so I was available to read any important work-related documents to him. Growing up in the pre-digital age, he also didn't know how to read time on a standard, old-fashioned clock. But he could convey the time visually, by identifying, say 3:30, by stating: "Little hand on the 3, big hand on the 6."

Benny didn't like missing work; he had a wild streak of anxiety when it came to missing any work. This became an issue every time one of his sisters — one in Arizona and another in Texas — tried to pull teeth to get him to fly out to visit for the holidays. I had some epic debates with Benny trying to convince him the shop wasn't going to turn in to "a complete disaster" like he thought if he missed one day of work. He would get so worked up that he'd throw up his hands and proclaim, "Then I might as well retire!" I'd call his bluff and persuade him to make the trip by reassuring him that I would visit him on his first day back to work to help him cope with the anxiety of "a complete disaster."

- Finally, a fictitious name is not needed to relate my stories on the dearly departed Timothy Kriedman, who was loved by everyone who knew him, this little man with the giant heart.

As his job coach, I supported Timmy for many years at jobs at two restaurants in which he worked as a host and dishwasher, and as a volunteer worker at both Cottage Hospital and the local Red Cross office.

Timmy was an original. He was a funny, little guy, with a large head crowned by a shock of wavy red hair attached to his tiny, skinny body. His "family" consisted of two saintly women — whom he considered his sisters — who evidently adopted him and integrated him into their respected families. One sister lived in northern California, the other in Oregon. Timmy's annual visits to each of them — usually during the holidays — were epic events for him.

I believe the sisters adopted Timmy shortly after he had open heart surgery to insert a pacemaker at age 2. His heart was a health issue his entire life.

Timmy was a regular member of the large Calvary Chapel Church in downtown Santa Barbara. He would refer to the pastor, Brett, as "Daddy" Brett. There was no real father that I was aware of in his upbringing, so this was his openly transparent way of filling that void in his life.

Timmy's intellectual disability never got in the way of his often humorous, inflated sense of authority. He loved being in charge. His home telephone voicemail message was priceless. Every Sunday he voluntarily directed cars into the large church parking lot prior to Sunday mass. For this, he assigned himself his own imaginary title by proclaiming in his voicemail greeting, "You have reached Officer Timothy Kriedman, Chief of Security, Calvary Church, Santa Barbara."

At the Red Cross office, Timmy answered the phone and manned the reception desk. Through his connections with the Red Cross, firefighters in the local Fire Department adopted Timmy as one of their own. Timmy reveled in this honorary inclusion, referring to the firemen as "my boys." Whenever a disaster emergency broke out, like a wildfire or earthquake, Timmy reported to the Red Cross office to take phone calls. As one of the "boys," he wanted to feel part of the action by declaring that he'd been "deployed."

Once a year the Fire Department came out to our PathPoint office to put on a demonstration on fire safety, including proper utilization of fire extinguishers. These demonstrations were a big deal for Timmy, whom PathPoint ordained the unofficial honorary title of "Safety Monitor" at our office. The firefighters always included him in the demonstrations, so he would show up, decked out in a full-on, yellow firefighter's protective uniform and hat, all of which were five sizes too big for his diminutive body. He was such a precious sight, standing so proud dressed up like one of "my boys."

Timmy's giant heart finally gave out on him at age 47. A memorial service was held for him at Calvary Church and its large gallery was packed, including a dozen or so of Timmy's "boys" from the Fire Dept. I asked Pastor Brett if I could give a commemorative speech at the service.

In my speech, I told my favorite "Timmy story," related to his volunteer work at Cottage Hospital. He worked the patient courtesy service desk, helping dispatch hospital assistants for incoming and outgoing patients. He also served as an unofficial "information director" for visitors who passed his desk once they got past the reception desk where visitor passes were dispensed. But as a self-appointed "security guard," Timmy often took it too seriously by admonishing visitors who didn't have their visitor passes fully displayed. His supervisor Pat had to ask me to talk with Timmy about toning it down.

My "Timmy story" at the memorial service involved this funky tool belt that he loved to wear, equipped for any manner of imaginary "emergency" that might arise. The tool belt was well-stocked and, consequently, sagged heavily on his skinny waist.

One particular "tool" became a sticking point when I received a call one day from Pat.

"Charlie, could you please talk to Timmy," she said in her straightforward, calm tone that she usually spoke with on issues regarding Timmy.

Pat got straight to the point. "Could you please ask him if he could leave the *hand-cuffs* at home and not bring them to work?"

◆━━━━ ◆ ◆ ◆ ◆ ◆ ◆ ◆ ━━━━◆

I've had the privilege to work with so many decent and dedicated people at PathPoint. Besides all of the great job coaches in ISE, there were myriads of amazing people in the office with whom I interacted— Brad Hunt, Becky Spadoro, Ross Godlis, Tana Wilcox, Paul Ganaway, Liliana Ramirez, Patty Alvarado, Debbie Merriman, Diane Coulter, Lucia Rushton, Bev Barry, Patience Ncube, Carmen Navarez, Pearl Moratilla, Scott Myrvold, Seth Miller, Tasha Addison, Cristina Cunningham; the list could go on and on. I have to single out PathPoint's now-defunct Opportunity Shop operator Cindy Williams, a colleague and friend who projected a captivating sparkle in her gorgeous green eyes every time she laughed. And a special nod to Ellie, the beautiful red-headed receptionist with the hearty laugh I never tired of hearing.

My work at PathPoint, and the professional and personal rewards that have come with it, serve as an ultimate redemption for the manner in which my sports-writing career had ended. I will always consider myself very fortunate and blessed by one of life's wonderful surprises.

Group gathering at Mom's (around table, counter-clockwise): Frank, Pam, Gloria, Dad, Mom, Jana, Kasey

CHAPTER 29
Family Matters

Watching my dear grandmother Mimi slowly wither away the last couple years of her life while battling cancer, in 1980-81, was my first experience dealing with the mortality of a family member.

Mom had moved her into the Rossburn house so she could take care of her. My mother had the good fortune of meeting a new roommate who was willing to nurse Mimi as part of her tenancy. That new roommate was Janice, my Mississippi Queen who became family and my longtime lover.

Mimi's final few days were spent in a nursing facility when she required round-the-clock care and the end was inevitable.

I was fortunate to be with her on her final night. Just me and her, alone.

Mimi was heavily drugged with morphine during our final conversation. She was pretty much incoherent; not much was being said that was making any sense.

But she uttered something that night that caught my attention and stayed with me.

She said, "Beth didn't have to give up the baby."

"Beth" was obviously my mother, Mimi's only child. But who was this "baby" that my mother gave up?

I perked up as soon as I heard Mimi say it. I wondered if it was just the drug that was doing the talking, and that she was hallucinating. Or, was she referring to some real truth that had been kept secret? Mimi, I remembered, had worked for years at an adoption agency as a social worker.

My first thought was, since I was Mom's first-born, maybe I was the "baby" she was thinking about giving up. Then maybe she changed her mind. That was plausible.

But then I wondered, is it possible that I might have another sibling somewhere in the world?

Mimi, bless her soul, passed away the next day. So, I never got an answer out of her. I thought about asking my mother if she had given up a child in adoption. But then I thought better of it, deciding to let her ultimately decide if she wanted me to know.

Flash forward twenty-six years later — 2007. A stranger appeared at my mother's front door at the Rossburn house one day. Frank, my mom's longtime tenant and the friend who shared an interest in Dan's death and his girlfriend Tami, responded to the knocks at the door.

"Does Maribeth Perkins live here?" asked the large, burly man whom Frank didn't recognize.

"Maybe," Frank said, looking the guy over skeptically. "Who's asking?"

"Well, I have reason to believe that I may be her son," the man answered.

Frank stiffened. "I *know* her son, and it isn't you."

The stranger politely responded, "What I do know, is that I was put up for adoption at birth by a woman whose maiden name was Maribeth Crawford, and that she went to school at Northwestern University."

Holy shit! The stranger was talking about my mother! The mysterious words Mimi uttered to me on her death bed turned out to be true!

Say hello to my half-brother, Pat.

The evidence that Pat had presented for Frank was enough to summon Mom to confirm. Reluctantly, she did.

Mom was somewhat sheepish when the truth was finally brought out in the open. It was clear that if it were her choice, the secret would have remained hidden. But once Pat had left her no choice, she reacted the way she did with everybody — she embraced inclusiveness. Faced with the full-grown version of the life she had given up for adoption 56 years earlier, she invited Pat to join the family gathering for Easter the following weekend. Pat, who lived four hours away in Paso Robles, was willing to make a return trip for the occasion.

I didn't learn about Pat's existence until I arrived at Mom's for Easter Sunday. Pam greeted me right away when I stepped inside the house. I was an early arrival, beating most of the attendants, including Pat.

"Mom has something she wants to tell you," she told me.

I found Mom in her bedroom, watching an NBA basketball game. She gave me the basics to the story — she gave birth to Pat and turned him over for adoption where Mimi was working as a social worker. This was a couple of years before I was born. The father was another member of the folk dance group at UCLA in which she and my father met. She was adamant that she and the father both had no interest in marrying each other. She admitted that she didn't want the truth to come out, but she more or less accepted her fate and let me know that Pat was invited to join us at Easter dinner.

Now, our family holiday gatherings always tended to be a bit unusual, but this one took the proverbial cake, with the icing piled on a mile high. Add a cherry on top, courtesy of Pat. He brought a big box of cherries that he grew in his nursery as a contribution to the Easter feast.

Dad and Gloria always attended our family holiday gatherings. Mom would have it no other way. So, they were at the house before Pat arrived. I hadn't quite connected the dots yet, but if Pat had been born a couple of years before I was, I figured out that Mom had to have given birth to him just a couple of months before she married my father. I knew their wedding date (April 1951). I had to wonder, how would my father react to the question, "Guess who's coming to dinner?"

When Pat finally arrived, Gloria, who was *always* pleasant with everyone, had no trouble introducing herself in the front living room. But then the awkwardness flooded into the large family room where Dad was sitting, when she buoyantly announced to him:

"Look who's here, Wes! It's Pat, the son that Beth gave up for adoption!"

Dad couldn't have possibly looked less thrilled. Pat represented a reminder from the past that Dad didn't want to remember. "Oh really?" he said, barely looking up. "When are we going to eat dinner? I'm hungry."

He got grouchy when he was hungry.

Meanwhile, I couldn't have been more thrilled to meet Pat. First of all, I was just flabbergasted to know I actually had a *brother* in the world. Pam was equally thrilled. And Pat was ebullient over meeting both of us. He couldn't have been nicer, or more gracious about being invited to the dinner.

I looked him over with keen curiosity. We don't look much alike. Pat is much taller, six-foot-three, with a much broader body structure. He doesn't have what I would call the "Crawford eyes" that my mother and I shared. His eyes are more rounded. His other facial features are decidedly different — larger nose, distinctive squared chin. He still has a full head of hair, which was just beginning to gray when I met him.

Pat was charming in our first meeting. I was taken by his strong, commanding voice. He filled me in on the rest of his story. He was born on February 12, the same birthday as Mimi's. He grew up with his adoptive parents in nearby Glendale about a half-hour's drive from where we grew up. Both of his parents were recently deceased, which partially motivated him to find out who his natural mother was. So, he started doing some digging, through the internet.

My mother told me that Mimi was considering adopting Pat herself, especially since he was born on her birthday. Mimi was, after all, overseeing her daughter giving birth to her grandson. There had to be a load of emotion running through her when she had to give up on the idea. Maybe it just wasn't financially feasible for her to take the child. Maybe Mom's impending engagement to Dad put Mimi in an uncompromising position in relation to bringing the baby into the family circle.

But Mimi didn't cut the umbilical cord completely. When she was delivering the month-old baby to Pat's adoptive mother, she gave the new mother a hand-written note that contained two clues that would one day ultimately help Pat trace Mom's whereabouts — the name "Perkins" as an aside to "Maribeth Crawford," and "Northwestern University." Mom maintained the Perkins surname after divorcing Dad.

In re-telling the story to me years later, Pat noted that Mimi would have had to drive 11-12 hours from LA back in 1951 to deliver him to his presumptive adoptive parents, who were living in a small town called Angwin in Napa County. The early days of Highway 101 and 1 were much more primitive back then, so driving was arduous and slow.

When she arrived at the address with the baby in her arms, Mimi was presented with an abrupt surprise at the door. The prospective mother told her she was too "sick" to take in the baby. It turned out, she wasn't sick, she was pregnant. But then the woman offered that "the couple across the street" were interested in adopting a baby.

The "couple across the street" would wind up being Pat's parents. My resourceful grandmother, faced with the prospect of driving 11-12 hours back to LA with a baby — her grandson — that she thought she had found a loving home for, crossed the street and knocked on another door.

This time she wasn't turned down. Mimi left the baby with the new mother, who presented Pat's prospective father with a nice surprise when he arrived home from attending classes all day at Pacific Union College. "Look what we got today, honey! *A baby!*"

Then Mimi had to make a return trip on another day to complete the paperwork for the adoption, for which Pat's new parents hadn't yet applied.

I think Mimi would be smiling to see where Pat had ended up 69 years later. He has a wife, an adult son (Steven), and an adult daughter (Cambria). His wife's name is Louise, which — I'm not making this up — was Mimi's name.

Back to the fateful festivities. The Easter dinner was a delightful and robust affair, after we recovered from the customary announcement that happened at every family holiday meal, that "Mom forgot the rolls again!"

It was years later, when I pieced it together, that I realized Dad must have proposed to Mom only on the condition that she gave up the baby. She was pregnant with another man's child during most of their courtship. That realization gave me a perspective on the dynamics of their relationship. It was a different time back then. Mom was much younger then. Knowing how independent and free-spirited she became later in life, I can't help but wonder if she might have chosen differently in a more leveraged position.

She made a choice based on the convenience of the moment. Hmm, who does she remind you of?

Oddly, Mom seemed emotionally detached from Pat. She didn't make much of an effort to continue the relationship with him after that initial Easter dinner. He was invited to a few more family holiday gatherings, of which he attended a couple despite the long drive. Mom's detachment may have been an early sign of decline in her mental health, a prelude to a precipitous slide into dementia that kicked in less than two years after Pat's emergence into our lives.

It became incumbent on me to maintain the family tie. Pat and I forged a close relationship. Cyndi and I have met Pat and Louise for dinner a couple of times in Paso Robles on our drives to visit Cyndi's family further north.

Me and my half-brother Pat

Pat and I engage in long phone conversations a few times a year, sharing our respective stories. Pat, it turns out, is a pretty good storyteller, too.

———————◆◆◆◆◆———————

Our family gatherings were held together solely because of my mother. As I mentioned, she always included Dad and Gloria. Pam and I were mainstays, but over the years the wife who accompanied me would be subject to change. Depending on who it was, that tended to change the dynamic of the gathering somewhat. Jocelyne was welcomed with open arms by Mom; Lizamara and Maggie, not so much.

The open-arms welcome extended to Gail, Kasey's mom, as well. She became a permanent fixture in the family once Kasey was born. That setting tended to make things awkward for a few relationships that followed her. Maggie and Gail; 'nuff said.

Kasey was always in attendance with his mom. I managed to include Tessa as often as possible.

Our family gatherings extended beyond family. Mom always had roommates and she always included them. In fact, she liked to think of her roommates as "family." There were quite a few who stuck around long enough to feel like family.

Merrie Smith, Pam's bosom buddy and Gail's metaphysically and astrologically-connected mate, started the trend. She lasted a good 10 years at Mom's house until she moved to New Mexico.

Donnie was another long-time tenant who spanned a decade in the early years of Mom's roommate experience. Donnie was a sweet, amiable, middle-aged alcoholic. He was a tiny man, with a boyish face that made him appear about half his age, until he grew a reddish-blonde beard to match his long reddish-blonde hair that promoted the caveman look. I got along with him. Old photos rekindled memories of a day trip I took to Deep Creek with Donnie and my Irish setter Trig. Eventually, his chronic lateness with rent — Mom basically forgave his last few months — and chronic dives to the bottom of the bottle finally forced him to move out.

Jana left her mark as a tenant for over seven years, during the final leg of Mom's roommate run. It was no accident that she drew striking comparisons to Janice. Like Janice, Jana was from the South — Texas — and she had the accent that gave it away. Like Janice, Jana was adorably attractive; she had a wild bouquet of reddish-blonde curls that framed her angular face. The thought had crossed my mind to make a romantic pitch with her, but it wasn't meant to be.

Then there was Frank. He preceded Jana by a few years in moving into the Rossburn house, and remained a household fixture for over ten years. Frank felt a close connection with my mother. He was always present at our family gatherings and customarily held court over them.

Frank and me, with framed photo of my young mother on cabinet behind us

No one commanded the room like Frank did at our holiday meals. He loved to stir things up by bringing up controversial political topics. That usually got my Dad riled up. Everybody participated, even mild-mannered Gloria. Mom got into it. Pam usually bickered with Frank at the dinner table, and that set a volatile dynamic between the two of them that exists to this day.

There was a long succession of tenants at the Rossburn house over the years who sat in at our family holiday meals. Mom also occasionally invited friends of hers from her social circles to join us.

Something new — or someone new — always came up every year at our family gatherings. The only constant you could count on was that Mom would forget the rolls.

———————◆———————

Father Time took its toll on the Rossburn house family gatherings. The first person we lost was Gloria. She suffered from emphysema the last year-and-a-half of her life and needed to lug an oxygen tank around everywhere she went. She finally succumbed in August of 2007, leaving behind an unhappy, sad widower in my father.

Gloria was the perfect antithesis mate for my Dad from my mother. Gloria was perfectly content to stay at home with him, the lone exception being his revered weekly nights out at his folk-dance gatherings. I don't think Gloria danced much herself; she mostly watched Dad dance up a storm with a collection of women who took turns partnering up with him for decades.

Gloria was an indomitable spirit. She was a writer herself and she joined a writers' group in her later years. From her participation with that group, she produced a collection of stories which Dad compiled — out of a labor of love — into a memoir book after she passed away. Dad titled the book "Jezebel," named after a hit song composed by Gloria's first husband, Wayne Shanklin. Frankie Laine recorded the song that turned into a huge hit in 1951. Royalties from "Jezebel" sustained Wayne and Gloria's expanding family for years.

Wayne was a cocky, two-timing, son-of-a-bitch who had five children from a previous marriage. He seduced Gloria, born into a poor family from Chicago, when she was 17. He surprised her with three of his children when she moved in with him, then added the last two after she got pregnant at 18. She became his teenage bride and mother of three more kids making the count nine children that she wound up raising.

Gloria's memoirs related this hard-to-believe tale about how Wayne, convinced that nuclear war with Russia was imminent, cast out Gloria with six of the kids — ranging from ages 10-to-15, minus three older daughters who married in their teens — to live in the middle of the Mojave Desert for nearly a full year in 1957. The family dog was thrown in for good measure. In early October, they were left stranded on the top of a mesa, camping out on cots and a mattress, with a water tank and nearby reservoir for sources of water. They managed to construct a dilapidated shack, consisting of a corrugated metal roof, one wall, and half of a wooden floor for shelter during the harsh winter months. Gloria had a rifle for hunting rabbits, ducks, chukar and quail. Wayne left them an old Chevy that the 15-year-old son could drive. Wayne, meanwhile, remained back in Hollywood to — "wink-wink" — continue recording his music, while cavorting with his mistress. He'd rejoin the family on weekends, gradually equipping them with a generator for electricity, and an oven and stove. The whole story read like something out of a "Mad Max" movie.

It was no wonder she eventually left that bum. By the time Dad came along, he looked like a veritable prince in comparison.

Gloria and Dad at one of our family gatherings at the Rossburn house

Gloria's passing removed any question about the inheritance of the Santa Monica house she and Dad resided in, which Dad had gained control of after Aunt Evelyn died in 1993. I highly doubt Gloria would've fought me for the deed on the house had Dad passed before she did, but it might have created yet another complicated legal hurdle with respect to her spousal rights. Certainly she would have been allowed to continue to live in the house, and I may have been stuck with maintenance costs and property tax bills. But it all became a moot point when she passed away.

———————◆•◆•◆•◆———————

Dad's health started to deteriorate right after Gloria's passing. He was in his late 80s and was a quintuple-bypass survivor. So, after Gloria died, I made a concerted effort to drive down to Santa Monica to see Dad more often. I knew he would be lonely. He looked forward to my visits and genuinely enjoyed my companionship.

The last couple years of his life were definitely the closest between us. In his declining years, Dad felt his own mortality closing in and we often talked about getting his matters in order and passing the mantel on to me.

When I was growing up, my relationship with Dad was ambiguous. He was a loving, caring father, and I clearly looked up to him respectfully as the head of the family. But he generally seemed aloof to me with his introverted personality, so recollections of early father-son moments appear hazy.

What stands out in my mind is that Dad's tutoring was the main reason I passed my high school algebra and calculus classes. And I do fondly remember the very distinctive way he routinely sneezed, which in the act he would unleash a very loud "Horseshit!" I always wondered if that was intentional on his part, because it seemed so out of character for my highly intellectual, serious-minded, nuclear physicist father to purposely blurt that out for humorous effect. On the other hand, if it was me, you knew I was purposely doing it just to be goofy.

Generally, Dad amused me in ways that weren't intentional. When I drove down from Santa Barbara to see him in his remaining years, we usually went out for lunch, and he insisted on driving in his beat-up, old '88 Datsun. It was pretty funny riding in that classic, twenty-year-old clunker that had relatively low mileage and was still running because Dad wasn't driving much. But even funnier was when we'd arrive at the restaurant, Dad would reach under his seat and pull out "The Club" anti-theft lock to apply it to the steering wheel. Dad's peace of mind from knowing that his twenty-year-old clunker was secure from car thieves was assured.

But our lunch dates were no laughing matter when Dad started to experience health issues with his stomach and esophagus. Eating became an increasingly unpleasant task. Dad was thin to begin with, but when he started eating less, he took on an emaciated look.

I felt so bad for my poor dad, complaining how much his stomach hurt and lamenting how he couldn't get any food down without suffering pure misery. Toward the later stages, he often ordered a beer to sip on, which evidently settled his stomach a bit.

Meanwhile, his weight continued to plummet. Dad stood just a shade less than 6 feet, and I got really worried when he reported his weight as 129 pounds. One day, when I arrived at his doorstep to see him, I got a clear, unflattering visual of what 129 pounds on him looked like. Dad greeted me butt-naked from the waist down, as he had —according to the explanation he offered— gotten straight up from the toilet to answer my knocks on the door. Good thing it wasn't Girl Scouts selling Girl Scout cookies at the door.

Dad went over all of his financial accounts and records with me in preparation for the inevitable. Having lived through the Great Depression at a young, impressionable age, he had the Depression mentality with respect to hoarding money permanently implanted in his brain. So, he showed me the secret hiding place in his house where he had stashed an old cigar box containing a thick, sealed envelope and a pound of gold coins. He wrote on the envelope, "To Be Opened By My Son Chic After I Die." The envelope contained sixty one-hundred dollar bills — $6,000 in cash. Depending on the going rate for gold, the coins were worth somewhere in the range of $15-$18,000. Dad had another $2,500 or so in cash in the top drawer of his bedroom dresser.

By the summer of 2009, Dad's health had deteriorated to the point where he needed to be placed in a nursing facility. Since Pam lived only 10 miles away, she was checking on him almost daily. I made the 100-mile drive down to see him at least every other week. Pam was freaking out about the care — or lack of care — Dad was getting in the facility and kept harping on me to make more frequent visits. I did the best I could around my demanding work schedule, but there really wasn't much I could do to improve the situation for Dad.

Dad must have had a near-death experience near the end. He lived to tell me about it. He described it as if it were a peek into the after-life — a bright light experience, as if he was transformed onto another plane of existence. He didn't quite express it that way, but he did talk about it in a way that I had never heard him talk before. He scribbled on a piece of paper, "I Died," after waking up from the experience. He spoke about it in awe. Dad was an atheist. He didn't believe in the after-life.

I do. When I think about my Dad and his mortality, I vividly recall a dream I had years ago when I was a teen, and it has stayed with me to this day. In the dream, I was a young teen and I was in a rowboat with my dad. We were in the ocean, which was very still, about thirty yards away from a small, wooden pier. We weren't going anywhere, just sitting in the water, as Dad read passages from the Bible to me. The water was very shallow, maybe 15 feet deep. But then we rowed toward the pier and the water gradually became deeper as we drew the closer to the pier. When we pulled up next to the pier, I peered down past the edge of the boat into the water. The water was clear and about 40 feet deep. I could see down to the bottom, which was covered by hundreds of dead fish — small perch — with their heads severed. We climbed out of the boat and up onto the pier. I noticed one headless dead perch, identical to the hundreds I saw in the water, laying on the pier. I picked it up, and it started pulsating, like a heartbeat.

I still don't know what all that was supposed to mean, if it means anything at all — my atheist dad reading the Bible, moving from shallow to deep waters, headless fish, then a pulsating headless fish. This sub-conscious experience just felt soul-piercing, and made me think there is more to our existence than what we see and feel on the surface— much more. I think Dad felt that in his near-death experience.

<hr />

Dad died on November 11, 2009, a little more than a month shy of his 90th birthday. I wasn't there when he died because I had just had a hernia operation the day before and was still recovering. Pam, much to her consternation, had to handle all the matters related to transporting Dad's body to the morgue.

I submitted a nine-paragraph obituary to the LA Times. I covered the cost for cremation from Dad's estate. Then Pam and I planned a little memorial service at the Rossburn house. It was attended by about twenty-five people including seven women from Dad's folk-dance group who were his regular dance partners.

Dad , at age 20, posing with pride over his very first car, his significant status acquisition rising out of the Depression

I mourned Dad's passing much like I mourned the passing of my two grandmothers. I cherished our bonding in his final years but seeing him suffer had prepared me for his fate. I wanted his suffering to end.

Attention turned toward the Santa Monica house. I commissioned my all-too-willing sister to direct the massive renovation required to get it ready to rent. Again, Dad's estate was more than sufficient to pay for it. I was willing to look the other way when Pam cleaned out Dad's bedroom dresser of the cash he stowed there. But I was able to remove the hideaway cigar box of gold and cash before Pam could find it.

It took more than two months to get the front unit in shape. Then we settled on a family of five to move in. The choice could not have been more fortuitous; I don't think I could have found better tenants. Twelve years later, husband and wife Ady and Ashley and their three beautiful daughters, Lilly, Talia, and Nela, were still residing in the front unit, establishing themselves as mainstays in the neighborhood. I have enjoyed a warm and amicable relationship with them, which made my life much easier as a landlord.

As for the back unit, I allowed Gail and Kasey to remain for a bargain rent price, because I knew Gail couldn't afford much more. After three years, she couldn't even afford the bare minimum in rent I was charging, so they had to move out. More renovation to that unit followed.

Then I found another pair of ideal tenants— sisters Erika and Vanessa. Vanessa eventually moved out and Erika's boyfriend Brandon moved in. Erika and Brandon got married, then had a baby, and finally moved on to a bigger house. Then I lucked out with another ideal tenant in Sara, from Austin, Texas, who moved in after a major renovation of the unit.

I found out something about Dad years after he died through an unlikely source — Ashley's father, Devin. The obit I had written on Dad for the LA Times mentioned his military service in the Navy during WWII. But it didn't tell the mysterious complete story.

Devin and Ashley's mother, Carol, lived in New Mexico, but often made the drive out to California to visit Ady and Ashley and their three grandchildren. Devin told me about a conversation he had with an elderly neighbor who apparently knew my father while serving in the Navy at the same time.

My dad was a nuclear physicist who worked for decades at Hughes Aircraft. He didn't talk much about his work. He most certainly didn't reveal anything about his experiences in the Navy during WWII. According to Devin, this elderly neighbor of Dad's met him as a co-worker at Los Alamos, New Mexico, where the atomic bombs that were dropped on Hiroshima and Nagasaki were developed. My dad, as Devin told it, was there when all that happened.

I don't think Dad wanted us to know anything about his involvement at Los Alamos and the atomic bomb. This was just another example of the curtain being peeled back to a secretive past in my family — a half-brother put up for adoption as a precondition to my parents' wedding; a father who contributed in the creation of mankind's most destructive weapon, something my pacifist dad would not be proud of.

Life — it never ceases to surprise.

———————◆◆◆◆◆———————

Mom's health was already in decline when Gloria and Dad were experiencing their medical issues. Mom had a cancerous kidney removed in 2006. From that point on, it just seemed as if her health problems snowballed.

Mom battled with her weight and she was diagnosed with early signs of congestive heart failure. She was supposed to adjust her diet; Pam was constantly harping on her to make healthy eating choices. But Mom occasionally broke the rules.

Exercise was also lacking in her routine, but Mom kept up on her yoga. When she turned 80, her flexibility waned, so she modified her yoga regimen from a sitting position in a chair, which was better than nothing.

Besides the heart and cancer issues, Mom began to exhibit some cognitive challenges in her later years. She had a reputation for absent-mindedness, but the cognitive slippage unfortunately developed into real signs of dementia.

One of the sadder developments which Pam had to enforce was to restrict Mom from driving. Mom had always been a notoriously bad driver, but it got worse in her later years with her habit of abruptly applying the brake, jerking the car to a stop. I had always counted on a ride to the airport from Mom for flights out of LAX, which was just ten minutes away from her house. But that ten-minute ride became a harrowing experience as Mom got older, especially when she navigated around the airport circle to the departure terminal in wall-to-wall traffic.

The driving ban was a crucial blow for Mom; she always coveted her independence and mobility, which enabled her to stay active in her social circles. Her social activities consequently were drastically reduced to Pam's availability to chauffeur her around. The lack of social interactions only accelerated Mom's deteriorating cognitive functioning.

The dementia got progressively worse during Mother's final two years. In conversation she fell into a pattern of repeating the same question over and over again. At first it was amusing, as I would make light of having to repeat my answers. But that got old real quick, as it became evident her memory was slipping so badly that she was unaware of how she kept asking the same question repeatedly.

To complicate matters, traces of Mom's cancer had returned. It had been localized in another part of the body and potentially could be surgically removed. But her doctor ruled surgery out because of Mom's heart condition. She was given medications for maintenance control.

Pam put Mom on a bus for what turned out to be her last visit at our Santa Barbara home for a few days in the fall of 2010. Pam wrote out an extensive "care list" with respect to Mom — medications, what to feed her, what *not* to feed her, assisting her for bathing, assisting her to dress, etc.

I screwed up and let my guard down when Mom and I set out for a ride around town. I was thinking about taking her to the Santa Barbara Mission. I asked her where she wanted to go.

"I want ice cream!" she announced.

Ice cream was on Pam's list of what not to feed her, but I foolishly decided there wasn't any harm in letting Mom enjoy a rare treat. But I made the mistake of dropping her off at the local ice cream shop, to save her from a long walk while I looked for a parking spot on the street. When I caught up to her at the ice cream shop, she was sitting at a table, licking at a humongous, double-scoop cone. Pam would have had a fit.

I saw Mom a couple times after that when I drove down from Santa Barbara, for the holidays and one more visit in mid-January.

On the first Saturday of February, Pam left me a voicemail expressing concerns about Mom. She was urging me to come down to see her right away. The next day was Super Bowl Sunday; I left Pam a message saying I could plan a visit in the next few days, but not on Super Bowl Sunday.

The following day after the Super Bowl, Monday morning on February 7, Pam tearfully called me to say Mom had died. The cause of death was heart failure.

With a huge lump in my throat, I made the drive to LA that day. I went straight to Torrance Memorial Hospital, where mother's body had been taken. I asked if I could see the body. I was allowed in the morgue, where I found my dear mother lying lifeless on a cart.

The luster of her trade-mark orange hair — routinely restored in her beauty salon visits that extended well into her final days — was lacking.

It was one of those surreal moments in which I suppressed the pain, forcing myself to see her one more time, just because *I had to*. I had to see her, with my own eyes, to believe that she was really gone. But it wasn't suppressing the guilt I felt for not coming down on Super Bowl Sunday to see her one more time. My sister would make sure I didn't overcome the guilt for that egregious decision.

Yet another memorial service was conducted at the Rossburn house. About sixty people attended, packing the house. There were quite a few former tenants who came to pay their final respects to my mother. Members of her church group, her book club, the old folk dance club that had been around forever were all represented. I invited all of my closest friends and their respective wives — Phil and Sharon, Rich and Emily, Rich and Sharon, Jim and Diane.

Both of my kids were there, as well as Kasey's mom. I also invited Maggie, who was fashionably late. She arrived just in time for the moment when I gathered everyone in the backyard to present my prepared speech honoring my mother. I was just about to start when Maggie walked into the backyard. All eyes riveted on her, because she was dressed in a body-tight, leopard-skinned, mini-skirt and matching blouse. Cyndi was appalled by its fashionable inappropriateness. In contrast, my fantasy football buddy Sean, who always had a thing about Maggie, hilariously relived that moment for years.

But once that brief distraction passed, we settled into an appropriate appreciation of my mother. I set the mood first by performing Mom's favorite piece from my compositions on the piano, entitled "Brook." I was still trying to come up with a title of the piece when I first played it for her. I asked her what it made her think of when she heard it — a peaceful, meandering melody. Her response: "A brook."

My backyard speech acknowledged how Mom had embraced so many people into her life, into her home — all the European travelers she redirected to her home from her information desk at the international terminal at LAX; then the countless number of roommates who lived with her over thirty years. All told, over 100 people shared space under the same roof at the Rossburn house that Mom presided over.

A reflection of Mom in the prime of her life

Mom loved people. And people loved her.

———————◆◆◆◆◆———————

I won't mince words — this next story is laced with immense regret.

It is another story about Janice, who I included in this chapter because I considered her family. Her relationship with my mom, dating back to their first meeting at that NOW convention in the late 1970s that led to Janice moving in as Mom's first tenant; her relationship with Mimi, who Janice nursed over the last two years of Mimi's life; and her relationship with my sister, who she embraced as a sister, entitled her to inclusiveness with our family.

It goes without saying, my relationship with Janice went beyond family boundaries. The truth was laid out in three letters she sent me. I live with the regret every time I sit down and read the flowery words that Janice wrote in those three letters. They are love letters, pure and simple.

I'm ashamed to admit that I only got around to reading the letters in depth after it was too late. If I had read them more fully earlier in real time, I might have acted on them. Maybe...because, it was Janice, after all.

It's odd, sometimes, the moments in which I find myself when writing certain segments of my memoirs. For this particular segment

I was alone during the time of coronavirus, purposely stowed away alone in a hotel in a northern California beach town to focus on writing. I had just re-read Janice's letters and drove down to the beach prior to sunset to reflect. I popped in a Diana Krall CD and the first song that came out was her sultry, melancholy rendition of "California Dreamin'." The song invoked reflections on Janice, as so poetically expressed in her letters.

The first letter was postmarked in June, 2006. I was unattached during the summer of 2006. I had met Cyndi in my new job at Path-Point, but she was still married at the time.

Janice started out with *"Hello Sweetheart, how is Santa Barbara?"* She lamented that her daughter Cori had left home, possibly for college. Janice was yearning to return to California.

She asked me for money — $300. Other than love, she never asked me for anything else. Then she reminisced about time we had spent together, declaring *"I've always loved you, 25 years later, The Song Remains The Same," Led Zeplan (sic)."*

She mentioned missing my mom, then my sister. *"Pam is Pam. I love her, too."*

She was torn, admitting *"I don't know what to do,"* because on the one hand she wanted to lure Cori back home and on the other, she wanted to come West. *"You could come for me. I could take a bus."*

At the time, I thought the situation would resolve itself by Janice showing up in California.

At the end of the letter she wrote: *"There's an aftermath from Katrina, a flood of people, crime and craziness. I would like to help with your novel, maybe we could write one together. Some time together could be wonderful.*

Love, Janice"

Her reference to helping me write my "novel" rings with irony now.

That letter contained two mini cassettes that I've never listened to. I have nothing to play them on now, so I still have no idea what's recorded on them. Back in 2006, I remember reading the letter, and never getting around to listening to the tapes. Overall, there was an indefinite tone to the letter. I didn't know what to make of her reference to "crime and craziness." That gave me pause, so I didn't know what to do, either. Was that in reaction to Katrina, or in her own life?

So, sadly, when the opportunity presented itself, nothing was done. Other than I did send her $300.

Five years later, I was living with Cyndi. We had been together for over three years. I had not heard anything from Janice in the interim. I had heard some vague reports about Janice regarding problems with drugs and problems with the law, presumably connected with her ex-husband from years ago.

Christmas in 2011 was the first Christmas without Mom at the Rossburn house. She had passed away nearly eleven months earlier. There was no family gathering. But I did drive down for Pam's birthday three days after Christmas.

It was during that visit that Pam gave me two letters Janice had mailed to me, addressed to the Rossburn house. The first letter was dated August 26; the second had three entries with separate dates, on September 1, then continued on September 15, then again on October 6. So I was getting them more than three months after she wrote them. The second letter had a return address for a P.O. Box in Alabama. From the gist of her letters, I understood Janice was in jail.

The August letter started off by speculating, *"I bet you are confused,"* then explained she was indeed in jail on charges related to a stolen car back in 2005 that she claimed she didn't steal. She said a cousin of hers loaned her the car, which she left at a friend's house, and it was subsequently stolen while she was in California. Years passed, the cousin died, a warrant for the theft remained outstanding, and Janice got nabbed for it on a routine ID check as a passenger in a car with another friend who got pulled over by police officers. Oh my.

In the letter, Janice stated she had already served five months of a seven-month sentence. Then she knocked me over with what she wrote next:

"So, my next trip to California has been delayed. Not forever. Chic, I don't think I can wait much longer to get to you. I can remember the feel of your kiss by the ocean. Walking, holding hands in New Orleans, cuddling with you on the farm, your are warm, Hollywood Nights, Hermosa. I am ready, Chic, and have been waiting for 25 years. What man could resist Liza, I loved her, Gail and Kasey came along, Cori was born, and then your daughter."

Janice laid it out — there was always something, or someone, keeping us apart.

"What man could resist Liza, I loved her..." Janice wrote about my third wife

"Things you should know; I can feel your presence when you park the car. I know you are near. I love listening to your stories; your music is delightful to me, I can spend hours on end by you while you play. I like it when you organize a ball game, watch football on TV, a Dodgers game or play tennis. These are a few of my favorite things. I love making love to you by the ocean on the beach. Hermosa, Santa Barbara, El Segundo. I love you being furry. Let's drink some wine, walk on the beach and take it from there. A good beginning, don't you think. I've fallen in love again with you. I love you, Chic.

"I love you, Chic. I don't think I ever told you. Although it has always been true. Since the days in your little room in Hawthorne. It is a great feeling. I love you, it feels good to say. I believe you have always known. We deserve a River of Pleasure, our lives overflowing with tenderness and joy. Check yes or no. That's a song, Country song. Cori likes the idea of me with you. She trusts and likes you. I don't mean to overpower you with these feelings, but if I don't say something now, then when? I'm here in my head and my heart's with you.

Love, Janice"

Janice had encapsulated our thirty-year relationship succinctly, in her words; thirty years of raw emotion laid bare, beginning with our first intimate moment together in a parked car when she shared her grief over a brother who committed suicide. Janice knew what made me tick, like nobody else, with her list of "favorite things." That's what made her so desirable, and why her words painfully stir a longing. Re-reading these letters years later, I can't fully express the feelings they instill in my heart. Still.

The August 26 segment also contained a separate letter for Pam. Janice and Pam evidently had spoken by phone shortly before the letters were written, when Pam broke the news to her of Mom's passing. In the letter, Janice was expressing her shock, commiserating with Pam's grief, and ticking off memories she had with my mother (*"Go Greek dancing at Cafe Danza and drink plum wine, Big Bear retreats, she gave wonderful parties, candlelight and wine, champagne brunch on Sundays. I want to get married at the Unitarian Church in Santa Barbara."*) Since she declared earlier in the letter, *"I love your brother,"* it was obvious who she intended to marry.

Mimi was a longtime member of the Unitarian Church of Santa Barbara. Janice could not have picked a better place for a "family" reunion.

Janice wanted matrimony to finally legitimize our relationship. It wasn't Janice's manner to make a declaration so bold as to want to marry me, so you knew it was genuine and coming from the heart, and not from a sense of entitlement. But beneath the surface of that declaration was a hidden hurt from decades of no open acknowledgement of our true relationship among friends and family. In Janice's Southern upbringing, this would have manifested at the discretion of the gentleman — me — and she quietly waited for me to publicly claim her. My indiscretion was inexcusable.

Nevertheless, she proclaimed her love for me profusely. And so poetically.

Her intentions became more obvious in the last dated section of the letter chain with three different dates. They read more like journal entries from jail. She cited a hurricane blowing in from the Gulf of Mexico that she could see from her window, and her allergies acting up. Then she segued to: *"I long for the oranges of California poppies and the steel blue of the Pacific Ocean. I would be there, I will be there, on the Wings of the Wind & God's Speed ASAP."*

She wrote about how there was nobody left in Vicksburg for her to go home to — Cori took off to nursing school, her brother

Stevie died, her surviving brother Keith was gone most of the time working on a riverboat.

She reiterated dreams of a life spent with me. *"Chic, I don't want to live alone anymore. Honestly, I do not want to be by myself, it's old. I want a companion, someone to love and care for. Someone to be tender with, someone to laugh with, someone to sleep with, this will be heaven to me. Chic, do you think and want us to work, be a couple. Your Mom always did."*

Mom would have been pleased to see Janice and I together.

I admit when I first received those last two letters from Pam, I read them hastily, feeling a tinge of guilt. I hadn't allowed the passion of Janice's words to sink in like they have now. I think I avoided the letters out of fear of the feelings they could unleash. I was conflicted back then, because I was in a relationship with Cyndi. I'm married to her now, but it doesn't change how I felt then, or how I feel now.

I had it all wrong about Janice with respect to the movie, "The Unbearable Lightness of Being." I thought she was my Sabina, the "lightness," when she was my Tereza all along. The burden of heaviness as associated with Tereza in the movie lends added weight to my life with Janice in it. My *"How wonderful life is, when you're in the world"* girl.

My sense back then, after Christmas of 2011, was that Janice was in jail, or did she get out? I didn't know for sure. But I thought it best to wait and find out what might happen next. She tried to call me a few times over the next year-and-a-half on our landline and it was generally awkward with Cyndi around. Janice gave me a number to call her back, which I did on a couple occasions. I promised her that I would come east to visit her.

In the back of my mind I always intended to keep my promise. Go back where was not clear, though. Was she back in Vicksburg? Or still in Alabama? I wasn't sure. The uncertainty stretched the contacts between us further apart.

Then, in January, 2014, I suffered my two strokes. Clearly, they had brought Cyndi and I closer together, and any thought of reuniting with Janice was dismissed.

But I wasn't abandoning her. In the summer of 2014, I had recorded the first CD of my music. I was able to get a mailing address for Janice — in Vicksburg — and I mailed her a copy of the CD.

On August 18, 2014, Janice texted: *"I got my gift today it is fantastic a flood of memories I will call"*

She never called. I kept meaning to reach her, but time slipped away. I didn't realize at the time, so was she.

Two years later, in late September, 2016, I received a call, out of the blue, from Sherrill Ann, Janice's longtime friend who was a no-show for a planned rendezvous in Jackson, Mississippi, 10 years before. I hadn't heard a word from Sherill Ann since, until this chilling call to tell me that Janice had died, in a hospital, from a brain aneurism, the same ailment that killed Aunt Evelyn. Sherrill Ann said Janice had been in poor health for a while (COPD), perhaps the price she paid for years of drug abuse.

But Janice wasn't on drugs when she wrote me those last two letters in the summer and fall of 2011. She had already spent five months in jail when she wrote them. She was of clear mind, and she had a clear vision of what she wanted in her life at that point in time. I didn't.

Would she have stayed clean from drugs if her letters had swayed me to marry her? Or would have I committed to the despair of caring for an addict? Whenever she was with me, I never saw evidence of her drug habit. When I read those letters now, I wistfully see the possibilities.

But when I skimmed through those letters after receiving them following Christmas of 2011, I didn't see it. Instead, the letters disappeared into a drawer. Until I got that call five years later from Sherill Ann.

"I thought you would want to know," Sherrill Ann told me.

I definitely wanted to know. Sherrill Ann gave me a number to contact Janice's daughter Cori, who I called right away. Cori is my last remaining link to Janice, and I've kept that link alive with regular contact to this day.

I don't think I will ever get over it, the Unbearable Lightness of Being In Love With Janice. Her letters haunt me. Yes, they were a cry for help, but they were also harbored in credible hope, given our history. She described what heaven would be like for her, married to me. I wasn't able to deliver. It wasn't meant to be.

Why?

CHAPTER 30
Home Sweet Hell As My Sister's Keeper

It was only a matter of when, not if.

"When" came on November 17, 2017. Pam received a Notice of Foreclosure on the Rossburn house. Frank tipped me off first with a call, then e-mailed me copies of the notice.

Nine months of silence between my sister and I regarding the house was about to end. And I was about to be forced to take action that I really didn't want to take.

If the two strokes didn't kill me, surely this would.

It all began on a wintry day in the first week of January, 2017, at a table in the lobby of the Manhattan Beach Bayclub spa and gym that was costing Pam $160 a month in membership fees. Sitting around that table were Pam, myself and Julie, a real estate agent Pam had been engaged with for a couple years consulting on the prospect of selling the house. Julie lived in the same upscale Holy Glen neighborhood where the Rossburn house was located, so she was well-acquainted with the market value for that area. She would turn out to be a godsend.

She was the only reason I agreed to step into this morass in the first place. She was the sea of calm in the eye of an approaching hurricane. We were three weeks away from a Trustee Sale on the house – January 26 – and I was prepared to let the house go. Say bye-bye to the $20,000 I loaned Pam on the house in April 2015. It was too late. Pam let it go too far.

She owed nearly $550,000 on the first mortgage and another $131,000 on a second. She never resolved probate, which meant the deed on the house was still in our deceased mother's name. Our dear mother had passed six years earlier, on February 7, 2011.

Pam kept making mortgage payments under Maribeth Perkins' name for five years. She stopped making payments starting the sixth year, the beginning of 2016. She was in default for 13 months, which was why the lender, Ocwen, was calling in the loan on the first mortgage. Well, imagine that.

Pam was reasonably contrite sitting at that Bayclub table, as she should have been given her desperate circumstances. But this would be the last time the word "reasonably" would apply to Pam.

Julie laid out her informed estimate for what the Rossburn house was worth, to help me determine whether or not I should stick my neck out. The numbers were stunning. There was hope I could avoid the executioner's axe.

The house was in pretty bad shape. But the property's massive lot size of 9500 square feet gave it lucrative marketing value. Dwarfing most other houses in the neighborhood, the house could command a selling price as high as $850,000, according to Julie. The house consisted of four bedrooms, three-and-a-half bathrooms, a living room, a huge family room with large fireplace, and a laundry room. She estimated that escrow could close within six months.

Since I had inherited Dad's Santa Monica house, I had no claim on Mother's house, other than what would be owed to me. Pam was the lone beneficiary. Crunching the numbers, Pam could walk away with about $80,000.

Pam brought some interesting reading material to the meeting — Mom's Will. I was reading it for the first time. Fun fact in the Will – Mom established me as Executor of her estate. Pam didn't want me to know.

What I read was only a copy of Mom's Will, because Pam didn't actually have the original. Now, I already knew this part of the story well before the meeting took place, because it was Pam's excuse for not taking care of Probate, besides the fact she couldn't afford the estimated $20,000 cost. A few years back she entered into talks with a woman lawyer to start the probate process and gave this woman the original Will. In typical Pam fashion, she balked when the woman billed her a few hundred dollars for consultation and started talking to another lawyer. Pam then told the woman lawyer she no longer needed her services, but the lawyer still demanded to be paid for services rendered. Pam refused and the lawyer –- just a little pissed off, ya think? -- held onto Mom's Will. As Pam vaguely told it, her second lawyer vainly tried to get the Will back in a tug-of-war that continued for years, leading into our meeting that January morning with no resolution. Pam's last hopeless report was that the woman lawyer had gone into hiding because she had been diagnosed with some form of cancer.

Well, *that* complicated things considerably, as I contemplated my potential involvement with the Probate issue. Classic Pam setup.

Was I nuts to say "Yes" to all of this? Yes.

Then Julie added a big tease. She said her office's loan depart-ment did some checking and, curiously enough, there was a chance the second mortgage on the Rossburn house might have been "re-conveyed." In other words, excused. Meaning there could be an extra $131,000 in it for Pam.

I mean, that was a *lot* of money to walk away from.

So, I took a deep breath, looked into my sister's pleading eyes, and swallowed out a "Yes." And only after she agreed that I would be in charge of everything -- all of her finances, all of the monthly rent she was collecting from her tenants, all of the mortgage payments. She agreed to add me to her checking account. And everyone, including her, Kasey, Kasey's mom, and Frank, would have to be moved out by closing sale of the house within six months.

This would go into effect immediately after I made payment on the $35,000 due to hold off the January 26 Trust Deed auction. Gulp!

So, I jumped right in with Pam on budgeting, going over all of her bills. I started with that $160 Bayclub membership fee. And then her student loan. I didn't bother asking her how much she owed on her student loan; she had been a "student" forever.

Then came the income part of the budget — how much rent she collected from each of her tenants. She had four paying tenants — Frank, Sam, Derek, and Gail, Kasey's mother. Then there was Kasey, who was a non-paying tenant who slept on a futon bed in front of the fireplace in the large family room. Usually he shared the bed with Negrita, Frank's dog. That was kinda par for the course for how living space was occupied at the Rossburn house.

Frank was in Mom's old bedroom, which had an adjoining, large, private bathroom that he shared with Pam. She gained entry into the bathroom through a side door leading out to the backyard. Frank paid the highest monthly rent among the tenants at $1,000 be-cause of the private bathroom.

Added all up from both ledgers, Pam was short about $1,100 on the expenses side. Guess who was going to have to make up the difference over the next six months? I cautiously broached the topic of Pam finding a job to help out on expenses and sustain herself for the long run. Pam talked the talk, but she hadn't had a real job for years and made an art out of avoidance.

Her biggest monthly bill was the first mortgage, amounting to nearly $2,800 per month. Back when Mom was still alive, it was around $2,200 per month, as I recalled. The adjustable rate had ballooned the payment since then, which was partly what drove Pam under water. At any rate, I was going to have to make sure this payment was paid each month to keep the loan from defaulting again. Julie assured me that I wouldn't have to pay anything on the second mortgage; that if anything were owed on it, escrow would settle it.

Sam, Derek, Gail and Kasey were all kept in the dark about the dire straits Pam was in over the house, and, it goes without saying, the foreclosure notice. Frank was the only tenant who knew. So, that was a delicate piece of news I was burdened with disclosing, before segueing into the more crushing news that they were all going to have to move out by the end of June.

I left that meeting with Pam and Julie at the Bayclub with so much uncertainty. That's not the state of mind you want when you're wiring a check of $34,789.49 to Ocwen just a few days later in order to reinstate the loan and keep the house off the auction ledger. There was no turning back after that.

———————◆———————

I had taken a leap of faith with Julie. But I needed further reassurance. The next order of business was a meeting with my paralegal aid, Victoria, in Santa Barbara, who had done a lot of work on my living trust. She also did probate and, fortunately, she was able to do it a lot cheaper than the lawyers Pam had been talking to.

Of course, nothing was going to get done easily and Pam made sure of that with the minor detail about the original Will being in the hands of somebody else. Victoria informed me that the court would not accept a copy of the Will, which may have rendered the probate process dead in the water.

If we cleared that hurdle, there was the troubling matter regarding Mom having departed this life six years ago. Would the court question why probate hadn't been processed sooner? As Executor of the estate, I had to prepare myself to explain to the judge that it had been only a week since I learned I was Executor of mother's estate, and thus wasn't aware of my responsibility regarding probate any sooner. Hopefully, that would be enough to spare my neck.

Victoria gave me a full rundown of how this was going to proceed. I was going to file the petition as Executor of mom's estate. A hearing would be scheduled in about six or seven weeks in which the judge would declare me Executor in a Court Order, as stipulated in Mom's Will. In the meantime, the Probate proceedings on the Rossburn property would be publicized in a notice in some daily publication (Victoria chose the LA Daily Journal.).

That was Phase 1. Phases 2 and 3 would follow later, assuming Phase 1 fell in line without a hitch.

Which it did. Starting with the news that mom's original Will was miraculously returned by the AWOL lawyer with cancer. Bless her. Julie picked it up from Pam and then sent it on to Victoria. That eliminated a huge nerve-wracking issue.

Then the loan was reinstated by Ocwen after the $34,748.49 payment was accepted. I was sweating that one out.

Then came my hearing date on March 1 in LA County Superior Court. I left Santa Barbara at 6:30 a.m. thinking I could get to court by the 8:30 appointment time. What was I thinking? Downtown LA traffic was horrible, of course. Then I sabotaged myself by calling up the map app on my IPhone to determine whether I exited left or right off the 101 to get to the Courthouse. I was not aware of any audio instructions available on the app. I had the phone lying on my passenger seat and looking down I could see the flashing red light on the phone signaling that it was located to the left of the freeway. I was in that same Courthouse 24 years before for a custody battle over my son, so if memory served right, I could have sworn it was to the right of the freeway. But the app flashed left, so I deferred to the app over my unreliable memory and exited to the left.

Mired in street traffic, I took a closer look at my phone and realized it was *upside down* on the seat. Damn! It was a right turn and my memory wasn't off after all.

I arrived 25 friggin' minutes late to court. But by the grace of God, my name hadn't been called yet, or else I would have made the trip for nothing. When my name was called the judge asked me a couple of basic questions, tapped his hammer on the desk and declared me Executor.

If only things would go this smoothly from here on out.

———————◆———————

Next on the agenda was notifying the tenants with a 60-day notice. I talked to Pam about this. She tried to get me to hold off. After all, she had held them off for six years, what was another few months?

Frank was in a different category than the rest because he was still talking as if he could potentially buy the house himself once his latest Brazilian business investment came through and made him millions. He was on his third or fourth investment over the past several years. First, it was some connection with a Chinese investor, I think involving motor scooters. Then it was cocoanut water. The latest was a vaccination for the Zica virus. Based on that dubious track record, I had little faith on literally betting the house on Frank's prospects. I was particularly gun-shy about money for friends after my experience with Theo.

Every time I talked to Frank, his timeline for when he thought he could cash in changed. First it was mid-April. Then mid-May. Then...

Pam and Frank had a very dysfunctional and, in many respects, weirdly co-dependent relationship. Their fights were epic. In the beginning of this saga, Pam was leaving me voicemail messages telling me horror stories about Frank. He was verbally abusive. He was selfish. He was thoughtless. She needed him out of her life. All of which sounded true. Then a week later, Pam would turn all sweet on Frank –- she loved him like a brother. He was going to save the day. So, I didn't know what to make of Frank.

As for the others, Derek sounded very problematic. Pam warned me about him right off the bat. She had been trying to kick him out for about a year for chronically falling behind on rent, and for smelling up the house with marijuana smoke. Derek, who was in his mid-60s, sold a variety of marijuana products for a living. *Well, that doesn't exactly sound like a model tenant, now does it?* Pam warned that he might be the most resistant to moving out; he may not have any place to go. *Well, hell, give me something positive about this guy.*

Sam seemed like a decent guy. I wasn't worried about him. He supposedly had a decent job. He had a Yorkshire terrier, which probably made him a good guy.

Then there was Gail. And my son Kasey. I had already evicted both of them four years earlier from my rental home in Santa Monica.

Now, I had to do it again. I tried to imagine what reaction I would get addressing a convention of home rental owners with this question:

"Let me see a show of hands. Among the men out there, how many of you have evicted your grown sons, *and* their mothers, at least twice?"

The first time I evicted them, Gail was in such dire financial straits that I offered them five months free rent to ease them out. Kasey was unemployed, so he wasn't contributing anything toward rent. The key question with Gail this time around was, could she afford to find a two-bedroom apartment for her and Kasey? Probably not. She probably could afford a one-bedroom place for herself. But where did that leave Kasey? Moving back up to Santa Barbara with Cyndi and me was not an option.

As for Pam, I did not write her a notice, thinking at the time I didn't have to. After all, she was going to cooperate because she was going to get all this money from the sale of the house, right? Right!

So, these were all the thoughts in my head as I was writing this very thoughtful eviction letter, which was more than a straight-forward notice. In the letter, I discussed the uncertainty and stress among tenants about the future of the house, the financial stress which the house had been in for some time and was no longer sustainable, and that I was the Executor of the family estate who had no other choice but to sell the house.

I explained further how the house would be put up for sale by early April, that their privacy would be respected, and I apologized for any inconvenience, blah-blah-blah. I mean, I don't think I could have been any nicer, as eviction notices go. I was really going out of my way to break the news gently.

I didn't want to freak anybody out, so I decided to make a trip down to Hawthorne to personally hand the letters to everyone on March 19, which would have given them a 60-day notice, plus a two-week bonus, effective on June 1. I was prepared to give Frank a verbal exception potentially through the end of June because he was still talking as if he could make a bid on the house. That was contingent on how he stood with Pam, of course. Would she be on lovey-dovey terms with him or ready to kick him out? It could go either way.

When I first arrived at the house on March 19, I decided to

take inventory of the *incredible* amount of junk on the property. First, the driveway was lined on both sides with furniture, kitchen ware, gadgets, books, clothes and exercise machines; just tremendous amounts of shit Pam was convinced she could sell in the imaginary garage sales she kept talking about having someday. There was a temporary aluminum storage unit in front of the garage with more crap inside.

In the backyard, she had six more large exercise machines in the side patio, a hot tub, and another storage unit on the side of the house with lots of half-empty cans of paint, weed killer, various other hazardous waste, and rusty garden tools. There was also a storage room behind the garage, filled to the max, and the garage itself, which Pam had majestically converted into her makeshift bedroom and filled it with her voluminous personal belongings up to the rafters. Among this morass were about 20 years of National Geographic magazines, another six-foot long shelf of Dad's ancient Physics Today magazines, four other book shelves with several hundred books, and her very large rock collection from her years of working on archeological digs.

I made a mental note of all the stuff in its totality on the property, calculating that most of it had to be thrown out. Moving the rest of it still figured to be monumental.

Driveway at Rossburn house cluttered with Pam's
"garage-sale" junk prior to selling the house

That wasn't counting the people, which I addressed with a presentation of the letters to each of the tenants. The reception was pretty cordial. No one was too surprised. Right off the bat I had one less person to worry about; Sam was moving out at the end of the month. That was OK, except it meant I would have to cover one tenant's rent for the remaining months. Derek was a bit of an enigma, but he sounded like he would cooperate. He just wanted to be assured he could stay at least through June 1 and not be forced to move sooner. I promised him that much. Gail was very cooperative, though she was not at all sure about finding a place for her and Kasey.

Pam wasn't home.

Then there was Frank. He was starting to worry me. He definitely did not want to move out by June 1. I told him he could possibly stay longer, at least to the end of June, but I explained that I hoped to have the place sold by then unless, of course, he was the buyer. But the way he was talking about his investments, the prospect of him buying the house sounded more and more remote.

He was also starting to sound like a stick in the mud about moving his stuff out of the house, starting with the quagmire he had turned the family room into as his personal office space. The family room, which would have otherwise been Julie's featured showroom for prospective buyers, was horrifically cluttered with piles of paper, books, magazines, and newspaper articles, all belonging to Frank. Nothing in the room was untouched by something belonging to Frank, including the '60ish, psychedelic, spinning-wheel colored, round dining table that had occupied the same corner of the room since the 60's. The only non-floor space in the room that wasn't filled with Frank's crap was one of the naugahyde chairs to the table, and the futon that Kasey and Negrita slept on.

Julie had seen the state of this room and expressed her concern to me. "Do you think Frank will be willing to clean it up so we can show the place to buyers?" she asked.

In March, my hopeful answer was "Yes, I think so." But Easter was right around the corner, and by then it had become abundantly clear that the resurrection of Jesus might be the only miracle on record that could top the prospect of Frank cleaning that room.

Julie was very involved in the 60-day notice plan targeting June 1. That projection was based on when she could put the house on the market, show it to prospective buyers, and get an acceptable bid. She sincerely thought it would sell relatively quickly, given the active market and the house's appeal because of its sheer lot size and location. She had one young couple as clients who expressed early interest – Fabio and Grace. Fabio was Brazilian, like Frank. I wasn't sure if that was a good sign or bad.

———————•·•◆·•·•———————

Julie had hoped to start showing the house by early April. Fabio and Grace were eager to see it, but Julie wasn't getting any cooperation from Pam, nor Frank, who wasn't making any effort to clean the family room. Fabio and Grace were willing to see the house as is. But it seemed Pam had to get Frank's permission before allowing Julie to show the house, because — God forbid — his personal belongings in the family room might get disturbed. Frank always acted like he ran things around the house and he definitely had his way of controlling Pam.

Julie thought she finally was given a green light from Pam to bring Fabio and Grace for a showing on a Saturday afternoon at 5 pm. When Julie knocked on the front door, she was greeted by Frank, in *his bathrobe*. In living color.

It was not a pretty site. Frank did not lay out the proverbial welcome mat. In fact, he was upset, because evidently Pam neglected to tell him that Julie was coming with Fabio and Grace. Julie was embarrassed. You would have thought Fabio and Grace would have walked out of the deal right then.

But miraculously, they didn't. Frank managed to calm down and Julie was allowed to show Fabio and Grace the house, god-awful cluttered family room and all.

This was the beginning of Pam and Frank's collusive obstruction campaign against getting the house sold. They both wanted more time. Frank was unusually sentimental about the house, saying how I had to keep it in the family, that it would be a shame to let it fall into the hands of someone else. He acted like he was more attached to house than I was, attributing this to his supposed close relationship with my mother all the years he had lived with her while she was alive. It was a major motivation why he wanted to buy the house in the first place.

But then he started showing signs of paranoia about the idea of moving out for more basic survival reasons. The first sign was on full display in a call I received from him on a Saturday night, April 29, just as Cyndi and I were about to sit down for dinner at our favorite Italian restaurant in downtown Santa Barbara.

Frank was very direct. "I have something very important to discuss. Can you talk?"

"Well, Cyndi and I are just about to sit for dinner at a restaurant," I told him. He dismissed that information immediately and launched into a speech that went something like this:

"I'm about to go Brazil for some very important business matters. I don't know when I'll return. A lot is hinging on what happens on this trip. I may, or may not, have some good news when I return. But it is imperative that you agree to this. I want a binding, signed agreement between you and I, in writing, that will stipulate that I'm allowed to stay in the house at least through the end of June, and possibly longer. I need the time to tie up business matters. I'd like to have the agreement in place by Monday, if possible. Or, we could do it by e-mail. Whichever is easier."

So, it struck me how Frank was presenting this as a *demand* and not as a *request*; a demand for a *binding* agreement in writing, in other words, as in *legally* binding, because I knew the way Frank thought and talked. Frank continued with his relentless pressure tactics.

"As a measure of our friendship, will you give me your *word* that you will agree to this?"

In that moment, sitting in my restaurant chair, seeing Cyndi's annoyed look as this uncomfortable conversation with Frank dragged on, I couldn't tell you how fogged my brain had become. I could only say that I wanted to get off the phone as quickly as possible and order my lasagna. So, inexplicably, I said, "Ok, Frank." Big, BIG mistake.

That following Monday morning was May 1. The next mortgage payment of $2,785.37 was due. I had been transferring funds from Pam's Wells Fargo account to Ocwen on the first of every month to pay the mortgage. I looked into Pam's account that morning and saw that the only rent money she had collected in April was a $1,000 deposit, presumably from Frank, because he was the only tenant paying that amount for rent. So, I was going to have to cover the rest.

Monday mornings were bad enough when trying to start the work week, much less dealing with a mortgage payment to keep one's sister's house from foreclosing. But on this Monday morning, I had a ramped-up Frank to deal with through another call.

"Did you have a chance to send me that e-mail yet?"

"Whoa! Hold on Frank! You're asking me to agree to a binding signed agreement. I've got to think about this. Now, there's a possibility that I can give you some extra time in the house. But you can't be rushing me into this."

"As my friend, you gave me your word the other night. I expect you to live up to your word. What good is your word, if you don't live up to it?"

"Oh, come on Frank! Are you going to hold me to that? I was just trying to get you off the phone. Cyndi was getting irritated."

Frank's next line showed just how diabolical he could be.

"I'm not saying I would do this, but technically I don't have to pay rent, with the house up for sale. Pamela has my security deposit, and I'm entitled to that as a refund, which could be used toward my final rent, should I decide to move out by the end of the month, which I may or may not decide to do. That check I gave to Pamela in April hasn't cleared yet, so I could still cancel it."

I literally hit the roof when I heard that. This was pure blackmail from someone who was purporting to be my friend. This was the beginning of an all-out war with Frank and Pam.

Two days later, I sent Frank an e-mail, but not the one he was expecting. He did not cancel his rent check, but I had plenty to say about his tactics. I started out by putting an end to the charade that Frank was going to buy the house. Not going to happen. Not on his endless timeline. Maybe if and when he does strike it rich, I suggested, he could buy another house in which he and Pam could live. But I didn't have the luxury of time to wait on him, I had to get the house sold while the market was hot and without draining my savings to get the best possible deal for Pam. Then I addressed the family room and offered a proposal; tendering a break in rent and an extended stay in the house if he would *just please* clean up his shit. Then, finally I gave him a piece of my mind about his manipulations in his attempt to pressure me, telling him in no uncertain terms, "What the fuck, Frank, chill."

The unintended consequence of my e-mail to Frank was an out-of-nowhere response from Pam. A couple of days later she left me a voice-mail saying: "You blew it with Frank. He doesn't want to ever talk with you or see you again. You are screwing everything up and ruining my life. I don't want to deal with you again any longer with the house. Anything you need to say about the house to me, you can go through Ralph. Julie and I will handle everything."

———————————◆———————————

Julie, the professionally trained real estate agent with the patented mantra to every crisis — "Everything is fine," no…matter… what — was starting to show a few cracks when it came to Frank. You couldn't blame her. It was the bathrobe.

"You know Charlie," she started, "it's Frank that's starting to worry me, not Pamela. I can handle Pamela. But Frank, he scares me. And I don't scare easily."

Undaunted, Julie had good news. Fabio and Grace had put a bid on the house — $875,000! She said they had solid financing in place, their credit was great, and they were really sold on the house. She also said that Pam had met Fabio and Grace, and she *really* liked them.

This sounded too good to be true. But there was more. Julie had at least two other offers. She had been busy! One was for $750,000, in cash, which is why they low-balled. The other was for $900,000. Yeah, it topped Fabio and Grace. But, (it came with a "but") it was contingent on the sale of the bidders' current home. Hmmm.

Julie and I decided it would be best if we met with Pamela to discuss the three offers. I had already made up my mind on Fabio and Grace and Julie concurred that that was the best and safest offer. It was higher than we had originally projected and with highly motivated buyers.

So, how hard was it going to be to set up this meeting with Pam? Climbing Mt. Everest comes to mind.

———————————◆———————————

It was panic time. I needed to talk to Victoria to get my house in order, so I met with her within a week of hearing about the house offers from Julie. Victoria wanted to see my eviction letter.

"Oh no. This won't do," she told me straightforward.

She handed me a short, terse, cookie-cutter eviction notice she had on file. I read it over. Oh God, it sounded very intimidating.

"Do I have to give them this?" I meekly asked.

"Yes."

Then she added the coup de gras. "And I strongly advise you give your sister one, too."

A deep chill ran down my spine. How the hell was I expected to hand one of those notices that basically threatened legal action over to my sister? Evict her out of the home that had been in our family for 62 years? I just couldn't fathom how that was going to transpire in any way, shape or form. Never mind the rest of the lot. Pam mentioned Ralph. That was her alcoholic, chain-smoking, Vietnam vet buddy who was battling colon cancer. I couldn't picture handing Pam's eviction notice over to him, either.

As for that timeline that Julie and I were planning on to wrap things up by the end of June, kiss that goodbye. This required some careful strategizing and meant pushing everything back another month. Which meant another month that I'd have to pay for everything to keep things afloat.

But wait. Maybe that was a good thing. Pam and Frank wanted more time and now I had no choice but to give them more time. So what if I was going to have to put out a little more money? If it meant a little peace with those two, maybe it would be worth it.

By using that terse, terrifying, template eviction notice, I established July 20 as the new move-out date for everybody. Hopefully that would make everybody happy.

So, I had two important agendas to cover in one trip down to 13707 Rossburn in mid-May -- five eviction notices and three offers on the house, for those of you keeping score.

I had Mother's Day weekend in mind at first. But Pam said no in her text response, because she was having her garage sale (wink-wink—yeah, and hell was freezing over that weekend too). Wait another week. So we were meeting the following week, OK Pam? No, she insisted I come the week after that, to which I told her "No! That's Memorial Day weekend, and I'm not driving down to LA on a holiday weekend!"

Besides, the longer we pushed it back, the further back we were pushing the move-out date, because I had to give everyone at least 60 days. Memorial Day weekend would have virtually pushed the move-out date to August 1.

Pam turned nasty in our text exchange over this meeting. She went off the deep end again and took it out on me. I was "ruining" her "peaceful plan" for the house, and I was causing her undue stress, and I was "harassing" her. She was claiming I freaked out Frank with my e-mail, that I owed *him* an apology. She was totally freaking out about Derek because he had just stopped paying rent, and we at least agreed on one thing — giving him notice. But everything else was off the rails. I targeted May 21 as the day to go down to Hawthorne, with no assurance I would get any cooperation from Pam.

I wanted to be totally prepared, from a legal standpoint, before I made that trip. So, I met with Victoria three days before with plenty of questions. I asked questions like, "Do I have the authority to sign a purchasing agreement on the house without Pam, and what legal recourse do I have if Pam doesn't sign?" Followed by, "What documents, if any, does Pam have to sign toward selling the house?"

I wrote down Victoria's answers in a journal I was keeping on this entire ordeal. The answer to the first question was "Yes." The answer to the second question was, "Pam signs a Waiver of Accounting & Receipt of Distributee Check once the house is sold." That was it. Julie and I wanted to know the answers to these questions to make sure Pam couldn't block the sale of the house on her own.

———————◆———————

With scary eviction notices in hand, I entered 13707 Rossburn Avenue tentatively on that Saturday, the 21st of May. Kasey greeted me at the door. Derek and Gail both were in the kitchen. They both accepted their eviction notices gracefully. They seemed a little relieved to have the extra time to move out and they both sounded like they were going to cooperate, though Derek's plans sounded very vague. He likely would end up living out of his car.

. Frank, surprisingly, was home too, and came out of his room to accept his notice peacefully. He made no mention of my e-mail that pissed him off. He was short with me, telling me that he thought he could be out by July 20, probably sooner. The family room mess hadn't been touched yet. And then he said to me:

"I'm worried about Pam. What's going to happen to her?"

"Believe me, I've been worried about her from the start."

"I don't envy your position, Chic."

Pam, of course, wasn't home. Her excuse for not being available to meet with Julie and I to discuss the offers on the house was that she had an appointment to meet a couple at the Bayclub to negotiate a weekly Air B&B rental in Sam's vacated room. This was Pam's latest big idea for creating some income for herself. Julie wasn't so hot on that idea just as she was trying to prep the house for a sale.

So, I left Pam's eviction notice in her garage bedroom on her bed, right underneath the American flag she draped for a canopy. Then Julie and I huddled at a patio table in the backyard and weighed the three solid offers. Without Pam's input, we were already sold on accepting Fabio and Grace's offer of $875,000. Julie said she had told Pam about the three offers, so my sister knew about the higher offer of $900,000. But since she had no power to change the decision, and she had refused to meet with us, we were in the clear to accept Fabio and Grace's offer without her approval.

Julie brought up how much Pam liked Fabio and Grace, so she thought Pam might be OK taking their lower offer over the $900,000 bid. But, (and you knew there would be a "but"), Pam, umm, had this idea in her head that Fabio and Grace might let her stay in the garage a few months after the sale.

"Oh no," I said in disbelief when Julie laid this on me. "She can't be serious."

"Well, you know how your sister can be," Julie spelled out the obvious. "The thing is, she's kinda scaring Fabio and Grace. They are really nice people and they like Pamela, but they have no intention of carrying her as a tenant in the garage beyond the sale."

After filing that one away in the "Duh" file, I drove home escaping from Pam's fantasy, only to dive right into her hell via text. Our nasty text exchange that began earlier in the day turned worse bleeding into the night. Receiving the 60-day notice was the deal breaker. "This ruins our relationship & I will never talk to you again. Maybe I'll forgive you after the sale but Frank is my brother now," she wrote in one stinging text. I have to admit, that hurt a lot.

I got very angry with her, unleashing a bunch of family history with respect to Mom and Dad's intentions with their respective estates, my authority as Executor for both of their estates (which I'm sure she deeply resented), and Pam's long history of lying to me. She became more and more acrimonious, finally concluding with, "After my heart attack you'll have a stroke. Thank you." Finally, I got a "Thank you" out of her for something.

The text war continued for a couple of days after that, with no positive results. I finally told her, "No more texts." All communication between us was off. Thank you.

———————•·•·◆·•·•———————

Julie called me the next day on Monday, with some not-so-good news.

"Fabio and Grace asked me to show them another home on the market today."

"Why?" I asked anxiously.

"Well, Pamela is making them nervous."

Julie described the house she was going to show them that day –- in Palos Verdes, on the cliff with gorgeous ocean views, with asking price of $875,000, matching the price they bid on our house. Shit. We were doomed. We were going to lose them.

"But," –- oh good, there was a "but" –- Julie said the house was precariously close to the cliff, so it was a bit of a risky buy.

So, I decided to place a little bet to win them back.

"Tell Fabio and Grace we'll accept an offer of $850,000 from them," I told Julie. I calculated that if our house was cheaper than the Palos Verdes house, maybe that might sway them.

Julie was going to call me at the end of the day to let me know what Fabio and Grace's response was. I sweated it out all day waiting for that call. But she sent me a text instead, and it wasn't the news I was expecting. It was a bombshell, a low left hook I didn't see coming that cold-cocked me.

Her text said: "I got this strange message from Victoria saying that Pamela has to sign a letter of approval on any offer on the house. Were you aware of that?"

I called her right away.

"WHAT!?!?"

This just *had* to be a mistake. I went over my notes again from my meeting with Victoria on May 18, three days before I went down to Hawthorne to serve the second round of 60-day notices. I reviewed the answer to my question, "What documents, if any, does Pam have to sign toward selling the house?" Over and over again — nothing about a letter of approval on an offer on the house. This changed *everything*.

Victoria has never done me wrong. Somehow, I must have screwed up. This just couldn't be happening! I was flabbergasted. I tried so *hard* to make sure I had the right information going into this. And somehow, I still got it wrong!

With Julie on the other end of the line, I had to face the reality that the deal with Fabio and Grace was probably dead. Pam was never going to sign a letter of approval for an offer of $850,000. I told Julie to explain to Fabio and Grace how our circumstances had changed and that we had to fall back to the $875,000 offer because of Pam. Oh God, this was going to be awkward.

So, here is yet another reason why I may be the luckiest ordinary man. Two days later, Julie called and told me that Fabio and Grace were ready to make a formal offer on the house – for $875,000! It defied logic. I couldn't explain it. Maybe that Palos Verdes house fell off the cliff. By the grace of God, and Grace and Fabio.

Now, Pam's signature was the only obstacle left to a done deal.

———————————◆•••——————————

On June I, I docusigned the Purchase Agreement for the $875,000 purchase price with Fabio and Grace. Victoria provided me the Letter of Approval, or more accurately the Consent Form for Proposed Action, that Pam had to sign. Julie then worked on setting up an appointment with Pam to sign it. We decided I should stay away. Smartest move of this whole ordeal, right there.

Five days later, Julie coaxed Pam to sign it. In a stroke of genius, she invited Fabio and Grace to meet with Pam during the signing. Hallelujah!

"Pamela was still hoping she could stay in the garage for a while longer," Julie related to me. "Fabio and Grace were very sweet with her, and they were open to giving her maybe a couple more weeks to move out. We'll have to check with the Escrow manager to see if we can move back the closing of escrow to accommodate. Their loan has a lock-in date on the interest rate up until August 1, I think. But I think Pamela was starting to see the overall picture that this was finally coming to an end. It was very sad."

Now came the heavy lifting. Since Pam still was not talking to me, I wrote a long letter laying out a plan for moving. We had to lot of planning to do, whether she wanted to talk to me or not. I left no stone unturned.

First, I itemized all of the money owed to me that was coming out of the sale of the house. This included the $20,000 loan Pam owed me from two years ago, the $34,789.49 I paid in January for Reinstatement to avoid foreclosure, all money I paid toward mortgage payments since January, all money I was paying Victoria for her services on probate and court filings, all moving costs I was going to have to cover including movers and dumpsters, and an Executive Director fee of $10,000. Victoria advised me that I could have charged twice as much.

There was plenty left for Pam, as it turned out. The Escrow officer confirmed what Julie was saying all along, that the second mortgage of $131,000 had been re-conveyed, which meant Pam was gaining that amount in full. Minus what I was owed, the $520,000 remaining on the first mortgage, and closing and real estate costs, Pam was going to walk away with more than $214,000, tax-free. Damn.

The letter pushed back the moving date a week, to July 28. I proposed making a visit a couple of weeks before to help her and Kasey start packing things in boxes and to check in with the other tenants to see where they were at in terms of moving out. The letter addressed renting dumpsters, a minimum of at least three large ones. The letter addressed hiring movers, setting a reservation for July 28. The letter addressed Frank and the family room, which still was strewn with his crap, but he was in Brazil with a return date unknown.

Then the letter addressed the great unknown— where would Pam be moving? Julie had been telling her all this time that she would find a rental home where she, Frank and Kasey could move. Gail and Derek presumably would be finding their own places.

I made another trip back to Hawthorne on Father's Day. I had lunch with my son and talked quite a bit with him about what his plans were. I asked him what he would do if neither his mother nor Pam had any room for him. His answer was he would ask his friend George if he could move in with him. I gave him the kind of father-son speech you normally give a 22-year-old college graduate –- that he had to find a way to support himself, that he couldn't count on someone to provide a roof over his head the rest of his life. Kasey was 30. I was very worried about him.

Despite all that had transpired in our rocky past, Gail had become my lone confidant in the household. She had been keeping me abreast on what she knew about Pam and Frank's status of the moment –- were they getting along, or not? Gail was no fan of Frank's. She clearly resented his authoritative rule on the house and felt he was abusive toward Pam, whom she considered a friend. Gail had been vigorously searching for an apartment, and prospects looked bleak that she was going to be able to afford a two-bedroom for her and Kasey. She was hoping Kasey would be able to hitch onto wherever Pam ended up.

I got a chance to talk to Derek, too, on the Father's Day trek. He was quiet, seemed resigned to his fate. He had finally caught up on rent. I could see a deposit in Pam's checking account that likely came from Derek. There were a couple of other deposits that caught my eye, too; they were earmarked "air b&b." I didn't happen to sneak a peak to see if Sam's old bedroom was occupied that weekend.

I also met Fabio and Grace for the first time that weekend. That was an enlightening experience. They were a young couple in their early 30s. Fabio was very charming, enthusiastic, with a lot of energy, and had big ideas for the house. Grace, who was gracefully pretty, was the more reserved, practical one. Julie had indicated Grace was a little more worried about the Pam factor than Fabio was. She also was worried that there was a lot more work to be done on the house than they had bargained for. An inspection on the house was expected any day.

I took a more in-depth inventory of the stuff all around the house with Fabio. He gave an indication of what he thought he might be able to keep. Hint—not much.

The house inspection report came through the next day and Julie sent me a copy. It included about 150 photos. Oh my God! According to this report, the house was a wreck— roof over Frank's room was shot, major leak underneath Frank's bathroom with possible mold problem, Frank's bedroom floor was off level, another leak under the kitchen sink, and termite infestation everywhere. If I were Fabio and Grace, I would have been horrified seeing this report.

Instead, Julie came back to me with a reasonable request from the buyers for a $5,000 house reparation inclusion in the purchase agreement. I felt like I was getting off easy. That brought Pam's take-away to "only" $209,000.

In a related matter, Victoria gave me my next probate assignment -- getting a tax ID for my mother's estate. I also opened a new estate account at my bank specifically to deposit all the money from the sale of the house.

Within the next week I was in direct contact with Diane, the escrow officer. She mailed me a huge packet of escrow documents that I had to sign. There was one small hiccup regarding a tax matter that could have been easily resolved by a letter from my tax guy, who didn't seem to get it. So that meant a little extra work for me, instead, but I somehow got it done.

All the other legal matters were in place by mid-July. All that remained was the moving out part, which was sort of like watching for a huge chunk of a massive glacier to finally fall after thousands of years of frozen stillness.

———————◆◆◆◆◆———————

Julie and I made a gallant attempt to meet with Pam on July 16, two Sundays before the move-out date. Pam had not acknowledged my letter at all, so we thought it would be a good idea to go over it with her in person. The way it came down was disastrous. Julie thought Pam had agreed to meet with us at the Bayclub at a certain time that Sunday. Julie and I were sitting in the lobby waiting for her for a half-hour when she sauntered out from the gym. When Pam set her eyes on us, on me in particular, she flew into a rage, and the screaming commenced.

She obviously was in no mood to meet with us.

The screaming carried out into the parking lot as we (mostly Julie) tried to plead our case for the need to talk. But Pamela would have none of it. Again, I was ruining her life and she just wanted me to leave her alone; that was the gist of her tirade. Nothing was accomplished there.

But, that Sunday added other moving parts to the process. I learned that Gail had found a place by then, just for herself. She was moving in with somebody else, but there was no room for Kasey.

I also spoke to Frank and cleared the air on the fallout from the e-mail I sent him back in May. It turned out the most upsetting part of the e-mail was the "What the fuck Frank, chill" phrase. He was insulted. I had no idea how sensitive he could be. As for the family room, there was still no progress on his shit spread out everywhere. Every slip of paper was still in place. He promised to have it all out by the moving date.

A week before the moving date (Friday, July 28) I thought I better call the moving company just to make sure I had that date confirmed, because in the back of my mind I wasn't so sure. And sure enough, in some sort of mix-up, I was told it wasn't confirmed and they were all booked up for that day, which sent me into a panic. Damn!

My wheels spun for an immediate remedy. "How 'bout Thursday?" I spurted out.

"The 27th? Yes. We could schedule you in that day."

Fortunately, moving the move-out date a day earlier did not set up another round of screaming from Pam. She had gotten past her manic episode that exploded on the 16th and had calmed down enough to accommodate a planned trip on the weekend prior to the 27th, to help with packing things up.

So that weekend produced the first moment of actual cooperation I got out of Pam... sort of. Actually, compared to what had transpired up to that point, it was a minor miracle. But, it provided a preview of how the actual move-out a few days later would go. *Heehee.*

Did I mention how much of a control freak Pam is? She had to be in control of everything, especially as it applied to the house. The bickering began in earnest when I informed her I had ordered two mid-sized dumpsters, even though I had wanted to order three large dumpsters but couldn't because there wasn't enough room due to all the stuff in the driveway that Pam never sold in her non-existent garage sales.

Her response on the dumpsters? "Cancel one of them. We only need one."

"Are you kidding me?" I asked, flabbergasted. "Pam, you've got so much crap around here that's got to be thrown out, you can't *possibly* take all of this stuff with you."

"No, I'm going to have my garage sale. And whatever I don't

sell, Miguel and I will take to Goodwill.""Miguel? Who's Miguel?"

Miguel was somebody I would meet later. But I stood my ground on the dumpsters. My sister was exhibiting more signs of her vision of la-la land when it came to this whole scenario of moving.

So it went. Kasey and I tried to get as much packing done as we could despite Pam's interference. We got *maybe* one-third of the stuff packed away. As I took a closer look at some of the incredible junk in the storage units that would easily fill multiple dumpsters, I caught on pretty quickly when I asked Pam for her assessment. In her view none of it was junk and she was planning on holding onto most of it. I did a lot of head-shaking that day.

But by the end of the day I had regained my sister's profound love and gratitude. What sudden turn of events could have miraculously reversed my sister's affections towards me? It was the one-year lease I signed on a three-bedroom rental home Julie had found in the neighborhood for Pam, Kasey and, as it turned out, new roommate Miguel. It did not include Frank, evidently. He was headed back to Brazil, and typically, his long-term plans were up in the air.

Pam had no source of income or credit, so her signature on the lease was useless. She needed me to sign. Was I crazy? With Julie present, I did it only on condition that Pam agreed to allow me to take out a full year of rent money from the sale of the house. Monthly rent was $3,100, so the total was $43,400. The first six months were due in advance. I controlled the purse strings as Executor, so Pam pretty much didn't have a choice.

So all was good. I was again Pam's brother, not Frank, and she wanted me back in her life …at least for a day to get my signature on that lease.

———————◆◆◆◆———————

July 27 – moving out day was really happening. Gail was already moved out by then. Derek had his room emptied, believe it or not, and was gone. Frank had finally cleared the family room of all his crap, as well as everything in his own room, and transferred it to a rental storage. He was sleeping on a mattress sprawled out in the living room when I had arrived at 9 am that morning, an hour before the scheduled arrival of the moving van.

At about 9:30 there was a knock at the front door. I thought maybe it was the movers arriving a bit early. Instead, it was a middle-age woman with some form of accent with two pre-teen daughters. I answered the door. The woman mumbled something I didn't quite understand at first through her accent. I heard the second try much more clearly:

"We are renting the room, air b and b."

I can only imagine what my facial expression must have looked like to that woman and her daughters in reaction to what she said. They all could have been standing there naked and I couldn't have been more surprised. My sister decided it would be no problem to have air b&b renters around on the very morning we were moving out of the house. Just add that to the long, long list of things to move out.

Getting over the shock, I finally was able muster up a response. "Did my sister tell you we were moving out today? I mean, like, *today?* Like, in a half-hour? More… or less."

"Yes, we are leaving soon."

Moving day at the Rossburn house

The mom and her daughters were gone within the next half-hour, thankfully, just before the arrival of the movers. The moving crew was comprised of four young men, all of them foreigners. The foreman of the group was Stas, from some eastern European country, I'm guessing. Then there was the imposing Alex, who was definitely Russian, and who had biceps thicker than my thighs. The other two were quiet and I forgot their names, but I think one was Irish and other Hispanic.

I was paying them (and getting reimbursed out of the estate sale, so effectively, Pam was paying them) an hourly rate. When I booked them I had estimated four hours for their services.

But I had neglected to add in the "Pam" factor. These four young men, all very nice and polite, showed tremendous patience under incredible duress under the direction of my sister, who undermined whatever instruction I gave.

Example:

Me: "That's trash. Goes in the dumpster."

Pam: "That's going to the new place."

Even Fabio didn't have the final say. A couple weeks before the move-out date, he put in a claim on a weather-worn, wooden counter along a backyard wall that I thought for sure was junkyard-bound. But when he appeared on moving day to check on how things were going, he reminded me that he wanted that wooden counter as we strolled through the backyard together.

"Yes, I think I could do something with that counter right over..." he stopped, pointing to the wall where the counter had been. "Hmm, the counter doesn't seem to be there now."

I looked over to the wall, aghast. "Oh my God, it looks like Pam had the movers pack it in the truck." Yes, she took that, too.

When it came time to move Pam's voluminous stuff in her garage room, the movers seemed to be throwing their arms up in the air in frustration. At one point Alex said to me, "Sir, your sister tells us to do one t'ing, then tells us to do another t'ing. It is all very confusing."

At the other end, in the rental home Pam was moving into, the owner was changing the locks on the door and performing some other odds and ends. I made the short trip there to meet him. He seemed very nice.

But later, Julie told me he was freaking out about the piles of stuff Pam was cramming into the place. She filled the two-car garage to the ceiling, assembled all her exercise equipment, two complete sets of patio furniture and dozens of potted plants in the backyard, imported her line of garage sale items onto her new driveway, and filled every room in the house so that it was hazardous to navigate through it. At the end of the day, Julie told me the owner was already thinking it was a big mistake taking Pam in as a tenant.

It made for a very long day overall, seven hours total, three hours over budget. I tipped Stas, Alex and crew members 20 bucks each; they earned it.

Pam had pushed it to the limit. She and all of her belongings needed to be out of the house by August 1 by the very latest, or she would have had to cover penalties on extensions on Fabio and Grace's loan. With Kasey and Miguel working around the clock, she got everything out literally by the stroke of midnight on August. 1. They left behind two overflowing dumpsters.

Miguel turned out to be something of a lifesaver, a much-needed bundle of energy for a 40-something individual who was about to become Pam and Kasey's new roommate. Plus, he had a much-needed pickup truck for hauling stuff over to the new house in a hurry. He was a man of considerable charm and character who I couldn't come close to sizing up in one day to ascertain if I could trust him.

Escrow closed on August 2 and the money was in the Estate account that day. Julie and I arranged to meet with Pam the following Sunday, August 7, when I cut her a check for $166,556.04, which was what was left over, minus security deposit, first six months rent paid, and the second six months rent that I retained. Pam signed the Waiver of Accounting & Receipt of Distributed Check; you know, the only form that Victoria told me that Pam had to sign... once upon a time in a land long forgotten.

I paid myself back every penny I accounted for in the letter I sent Pam back in June. The extra ten grand I awarded myself almost made the seventh months of migraines and bouts of heartburn worth it. I said "almost." But the streak of the Luckiest Ordinary Man Alive lived another day.

CHAPTER 31
Travels and Travails with Charlie

I inherited my passion for travel from my mother. She went to many places around the world on her own, once she was unencumbered from marriage to my dad.

I had an ideal travel partner for a while with Gayle. But when that relationship ended, I was pretty much on my own. Unfortunately, Cyndi, my current wife, is unable to travel any long distance comfortably due to various health issues. So, I have her blessing to fulfill my international travel dreams alone.

Every trip offers adventure and often misadventure, both of which make for good stories.

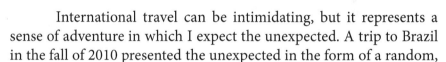

International travel can be intimidating, but it represents a sense of adventure in which I expect the unexpected. A trip to Brazil in the fall of 2010 presented the unexpected in the form of a random, extraordinary act of kindness from a complete stranger.

My friend John Walker was offering my favorite way to travel internationally — visiting friends in faraway places. With John, an American ex-patriot who knew the country and customs, and spoke fluent Portuguese, the spoken language in Brazil, the intimidation factor was minimal.

We planned to unite in September, springtime in the Southern Hemisphere, in a Brazilian town of Araxa, where John had reunited with his wife Lucilia, from whom he was temporarily separated while living and working in Santa Barbara. Araxa was slightly larger than Santa Barbara, with a population of around 105,000.

I was on my own to reach John in Araxa, located a couple of hundred miles northwest of Rio de Janeiro. I was flying out of LA to Miami, for a connecting flight to the massive Brazilian capital of Sao Paolo. Those two flights combined would account for 18 hours in the air. Then I had another connecting flight from Sao Paolo to Araxa, another two-and-a-half hours on a small, domestic airline. The options for completing the last leg were very limited.

When I booked my flights I had consulted John via email. I was due to arrive in Sao Paolo at 5 a.m. and had two hours to catch a

7 a.m. flight to Araxa. *Plenty of time*, I thought. "Hmmm, I'm not so sure," John wrote.

It was critical that I didn't miss that 7 a.m. flight to Araxa because the next available flight was 7:30 p.m. After a full day and night of travel, I couldn't bear the   thought of waiting 12 1/2 hours for the next available flight to Araxa, I imagined myself passing out in the terminal (snore!), and I would have missed *that* flight as well. God only knows the peril that would have awaited me then.

So, there was *no way* I was missing that 7 a.m. flight to Araxa.

The flight into Sao Paolo arrived on time at 5 a.m. I felt *very* confident following my fellow passengers to Customs, walking along a circular hallway, and walking, and walking some more as that damn hallway kept curling to the left. My confidence waned as that hallway was my first clue that this Sao Paolo Airport was friggin' huge!

Finally, we were herded down some stairs, where a mile-long line snaked its way to the six Custom guard stations. It took nearly an hour before I got my passport stamped and pointed to the exit door.

Which led to *another* line. An attendant at the front was waving two out of every three passengers — on average — to exit left, which bypassed some sort of detailed baggage check to the right. I anxiously noted the time and wondered, what were the chances of my getting directed to the *right?*

I looked at the guy immediately ahead of me and felt pretty good about my chances. He had a *huge* box that was big enough to house a nuclear bomb; so surely he'd be the unlucky bastard directed to go right, and I'd get the easy way out to the left with my tiny carry-on suitcase.

But, no, what was I thinking? The guy in front of me got waved to the left and I got pointed to the right. *"Damn, the guy with the nuclear bomb gets a free pass and I get the shaft!"*

Precious minutes ticked away while waiting for my tiny suitcase to pass through an x-ray scanner. But just as I thought I was free and clear, I walked out and saw another long, snaking line. Hmm. That line couldn't have been for me! So, I walked right past it.

Truth be told, I had no idea what I was doing or where I was going. I tried asking a woman in a uniform if walking straight ahead would take me to the main terminal. She answered in Portuguese, which I assumed meant "Yes." So, I walked straight ahead... into a duty-free shop that dead-ended.

As tempting as those duty-free bargains were, I made a hasty retreat and unwittingly found myself back at the start of that long line I had ignored. I showed the attendant standing there my itinerary print-out. Big mistake. She pointed for me to get in line.

I couldn't tell you what that line was for, but it moved along pretty quickly. But now it was getting close to panic time. I had to find the ticket agency for the domestic airline flying me to Araxa to get my boarding pass. John had told me that it was located on the second floor.

Ascending an escalator, I looked up to read a large "Arrivals/ Departure" monitor hanging from the ceiling. I located the latest update for my flight. It stated, in English, "LAST CALL."

"Last call for alcohol," I was thinking in my rising delirium. I hastened my stride, looking left and right for the ticket booth that I needed for my connecting flight. I kept walking, and walking, and walking. Did I mention how huge this airport was?

I became so desperate that — I don't know what possessed me to do this — I spotted a pretty, young woman ticket agent standing off to the side at a booth for an airline that had nothing to do with my flight. The point was, she wasn't doing anything at the moment.

I caught her attention by frantically waving my itinerary at her. I blurted out something about how I was going to miss my flight and I needed help!

I now know why she was standing there. She was waiting to serve as my Guardian Angel.

She took one look at my itinerary and passport that I handed her, and without saying a word, started marching forward, beckoning me to follow.

We walked at a brisk pace for what seemed like a mile to reach the ticket booth for my domestic flight. There was yet another line, but she bypassed it, and handed my itinerary and passport to another woman ticket agent, who quickly processed my boarding pass. That agent handed the pass and itinerary back to my G.A. (Guardian Angel). As we started to walk away, I glanced back and noticed the ticket agent waving my passport I was leaving behind. *"Oh yeah, guess I'll be needing that."*

We made another long trek before reaching the security check for the boarding gates, where another long line awaited. But my G.A. wielded her clout — we advanced straight to the front of the line.

It was flat-out frantic time at this point. I had to empty the contents of all the pockets in my pants, shirt and jacket. I'm one of those nerds who stuffs all sorts of stuff in his pockets. The last thing I added to the pile was the belt to my pants, which were a little loose on me. I purposely chose to wear those pants for comfort, and uhh, bladder control, on the long flight.

Oh Lordy. I piled all that stuff into the tray for the x-ray scan. After a quick pose in the x-ray scanning booth, I made my classic move — in a hasty swipe at the tray, I dropped it.

My stuff spilled all over the floor— a bunch of change, cell phone, comb, reading glasses, sunglasses, pen, my belt. Loose change ping-ponged every which way, and in the corner of my eye, I saw a rolling quarter making a beeline for the boarding gate. Completely crazed, I tried sweeping up the important stuff within reach. *Screw it, I'll buy another comb.* My G.A. stooped down to help, but then she sprung up and took off like that rolling quarter, and I scrambled to keep up.

The next image is forever etched in my mind — watching that beautiful, smartly-attired young woman three strides ahead of me, with her raised right hand, holding up my passport, my boarding pass, … and my belt. There was no time to spare, certainly no time for me to put my belt back on at the security check.

Take it from me, if you think it's easy running at full speed wearing belt-less loose pants, weighed down by all that crap I stuffed back in the pockets, while dragging my carry-on suitcase with one hand and clutching a smaller travel handbag in the other, think again. I desperately flung the handbag on top of the suitcase, to free up one hand I needed to hold my pants up and keep them from sliding down to my *knees.*

It was not a pretty sight.

I huffed and puffed for 50 yards or so trailing my G.A. until we reached the boarding gate. I lost track of time, but it was at least 15 minutes past the 7 a.m. scheduled departure. But the flight miraculously hadn't departed yet.

In fact, there were about a dozen people standing in line at the gate counter. I have no idea if they were hoping to get on the flight I was catching. But we weren't standing in any *line*, my G.A. was seeing to that. She guided me straight to the glass doors leading outside to the tarmac.

In full view of the passengers waiting in line, this was where she handed me my belt. I think that's the first time I saw a little smile on her face. I put my belt back on my pants, then sheepishly looked up and briefly waved at the *very* curious audience at the counter. I remembered thinking, what were those people thinking? What possible scenarios could they imagine to explain why this pretty young ticket agent was handing over a belt belonging to this old-fart American?

With the belt back on, I profusely thanked my Guardian Angel. Words were impossible to express my gratitude. With that, she disappeared from my life. But I'll never forget her.

A van awaited me on the tarmac. Four other late passengers were aboard that van; oh good, I wasn't the only one. The van caught up to our plane, which had stopped about 30 yards away. Somehow, I walked onto that plane only by the grace of one extraordinary Guardian Angel.

I boarded a small plane that contained seats for less than 50 passengers. I plopped into a window seat, totally exhausted. I was going on 21 straight hours with little or no sleep, so I was hoping to stretch out a bit and catch a nap on the two-and-a-half hours flight to Araxa. But fat chance of that happening when a man weighing about 270 pounds took the seat next to me. In the next beat a mom with a crying baby settled into the seat directly behind me. I don't make this stuff up.

I slept really well when I finally arrived at John and Lucilia's lovely home.

Araxa is a pretty little town. John showed me around; he was proud of his adoptive Brazilian hometown. He showed me his language school that he had run for decades as proprietor, teaching Brazilians how to speak English. His son, also named John, ran the business when his father moved to Santa Barbara to be with his daughter. It was John's intention to eventually move back to Araxa to reunite with his wife.

Lucilia was comfortably settled in Araxa, with her four fluffy white poodles, her caged parrots, and her cigarette habit. A housekeeper cooked wonderful meals while I was their guest — fabulous

Brazilian dishes with plantains (fried banana), seasoned rice, boiled tomatoes, black beans, and a variety of seasoned beef and pork entrees.

John, who was an American, met his beautiful Brazilian bride when he was dispatched to the South American country as a young man working in the Peace Corps. He fell in love with Lucilia and the country, learned to speak fluent Portuguese, and never left, until his grown daughter migrated to Santa Barbara decades later.

John and I had forged our friendship through playing tennis. In Araxa, I played on a clay court or the first time. I quickly found out it was a lot different from asphalt, struggling to adjust well to the slippery surface. John beat me pretty handily.

John treated me to a tour of an old coffee plantation on the outskirts of town. It felt like a step back in time.

But then came our big side trip — a two-hour flight to Rio for a three-day, two-night stay in one of the more amazing cities I've ever experienced. Flying high above Rio was an introduction to the sheer audacity of the city, the density and sprawl of ultra-white, high-rise buildings that cast shadows over enclaves of abject poverty-stricken neighborhoods tucked away in hideaway valleys descending from the mountain range. A vast link of jaw-dropping beautiful, crystal-blue ocean bays embroidered by white-sand beaches are nestled between a series of prominent, cone-shaped mountain peaks. The one peak that stood out was Mount Corcovado, crowned by the iconic, nearly 100-foot-tall statue of Cristo Redentor (Jesus Christ), with his hands majestically extended, overlooking the city.

John and I rode a tram up to the Cristo to see it up close. It was an imposing, awe-inspiring sight. The view of the city below was equally breathtaking.

We stayed at a modest hotel just a couple of blocks off the beach in Copacabana Beach. We spent a couple of hours on the beach, enjoying the view of scantily-clad bikinis adorned by tanned young ladies. We boarded a bus and trekked the coastline for about eight miles for a joy ride. We enjoyed a magnificent feast at a restaurant that kept bringing skewers of different assortments of grilled meats, and we stuffed ourselves until we cried *"No mas!"*

On our second night we stopped for beers at what we thought was a patio restaurant along the beach. We were hoping to order food, but no one seemed to be interested in taking our order. Finally, John summoned a waiter to ask if they served food.

The waiter gestured for John to look around the patio to recognize what the place was "serving." We glanced around and noticed the tables were fully occupied by gorgeous women in alluring outfits. It suddenly dawned on us — we were surrounded by prostitutes.

At one point John excused himself to go to the restroom. That was when I caught the eye of a beautiful young woman with long blonde tresses and a perfectly shaped body in a tight-fitting, ocean-blue dress, sitting a table away. She moved over to sit next to me. She got close enough to where I got a whiff of her light perfume.

She introduced herself as Shauna. She spoke English. She was incredibly sexy, with an air of sweetness to her. In John's absence for several minutes, this would turn out to be the only conversation I had with a native Brazilian by myself on this trip. I could only imagine what sort of erotic fantasy she could fulfill for a couple hours. Ultimately, John returned, and the fantasy ended, as she parted with a light kiss on my cheek.

Being in Rio felt like a fantasy.

Aerial view of Rio de Janeiro

When Tessa was just three years old I was driving her around the neighborhood near my mother's house on one of my visitation visits. We were driving down Rosecrans Avenue, a busy street that borders Manhattan Beach, just east of Sepulveda Blvd that parallels the coastline and serves as a demarcation line for residential neighborhoods unofficially classified as "beach property."

We were headed away from the beach and approaching the intersection of Rosecrans and Aviation Blvd., headed back to my mom's house about a half-mile away. The intersection is distinguished by an imposing, arching, metal-constructed railroad bridge crossing diagonally.

My three-year-old daughter pointed to the massive metal structure and shouted, "Paris!" I was instantly struck by this. I suddenly realized that Tessa was relating the metal bridge to the Eiffel Tower, which is of a similar metal construction.

Following that episode, Tessa and I always talked about going to Paris one day to see the Eiffel Tower. Over the years, this became a reoccurring theme between us. What started off as something of a joke evolved into a serious vow.

Fifteen years later, after Tessa graduated from high school, we finally made it happen. A trip to Paris, just the two of us, was my graduation present for her.

I planned the 10-day trip for July well in advance. I made sure Tessa renewed her passport, which she hadn't updated since her mother took her to Honduras as a young child.

With all my careful planning, you'd think I would have thought to check my own passport to see if it was up to date. One week before our scheduled departure I finally decided to take a look, and golly gee!, sure enough, it had expired on my birthday just a couple of weeks earlier in June. Oh shit!

I couldn't believe it. In total despair, I called Tessa and told her that I feared we may have to postpone the trip because of this monumental goof. She was all set to start college at Azusa Pacific in September, so that was going to complicate things, if not make it impossible to reschedule. I felt absolutely horrible.

But my fantasy football buddy Sean, who lived in L.A., saved the day. The next day he told me about a place in Beverly Hills that specialized in renewing passports within 24 hours. It was going to cost extra, of course. But I drove down that same day to get it done. The trip was salvaged and I was so relieved.

So, Tessa and I were on our way to Paris. Would you be surprised to know that the goofs didn't end with the passport snafu? Expect nothing less from Mr. Mistake.

As luck would have it, Paris was mired in a heat wave during most of our 10-day stay. When I was booking our hotel accommodation through my travel agent, she was set to reserve a room at a pricey hotel with air conditioning. But then she quoted me a price for a place that was $600 less, *without* AC, so I opted for that choice instead.

Mr. Mistake had struck again. Regret reared as soon as we stepped in the room. It was late afternoon when we arrived, the hottest time of day, and our tiny room felt like an oven. The room was so small, barely large enough to contain the two thin twin beds separated by only a couple of feet. The open window offered little relief since there was virtually no breeze. The lone saving grace was the tiny shower in the bathroom. Taking a cold shower and drip-drying was the only way to beat the heat.

We searched the city far and wide for a fan, but every store was sold out. It got so bad that, midway through our stay, I booked us a room in a hotel across the street for one night just so we could enjoy the luxury of air-conditioning. I kept our original hotel accommodation open, which we returned to after our one-night reprieve.

The best part about our hotel was its location — it was a mere seven-minute walk to the Eiffel Tower. After fifteen years of talking about it, we finally saw the Eiffel Tower in person on our first night, walking out after 10 pm on a balmy night when it was still 85 degrees outside, under a full moon. It was a true threshold moment for us, seeing the Tower lit up in all its glory. Scores of people were out, sitting on the lawn in front of the Tower, drinking wine and eating late-night picnic meals. Tessa and I were so jet-lagged we just laid out on our backs, looking up at the sparkling metal monument.

Over the next nine days, we packed in a tour de force of the city. The best decision I had made was buying Paris Passes for many of the countless museums that Paris has to offer. That allowed us to cut to the head of the lines, avoiding standing in the sweltering heat. The museums, with air conditioning, were ideal places of refuge.

We started with the Louvre. Mona Lisa painting, check,

Venus de Milo statue, check. Hours gazing at Renaissance art. Then we walked a couple of hundred yards over to the Musee de l'Orangerie, featuring four panoramic, thirty-foot-long Monet masterpieces in a pair of oval rooms that were a feast for the eyes.

It took us a little while to figure out Paris's confusing metro subway system to navigate around town. On a couple of occasions we realized we were headed in the wrong direction, because all those damn stops with long, hyphenated French names were hard to keep track of on my little metro map. Call me Mr. "Wrong Way" Mistake.

But over 10 days, we managed to cover just about all the requisite tourist sites that world traveler guru Rick Steves recommended in his top 10 Paris "must-sees": Napolean's Tomb massively on display in an imposing, ornate, oval building; Rodin Museum with the artist's world-renowned "The Thinker" bronze sculpture and many other impressive sculpted artwork; old, old Notre Dame Church with its prominent gargoyles watching over on its outer walls, centuries-old stained-glass windows, and Joan of Arc statue inside; the Arc de Triomphe that we scaled 265 steps to the top for breathtaking overviews of Paris' heralded Champs-Elysees shopping district; the luxurious Luxembourg Gardens and Palace bursting in colors on a sun-drenched day; St. Chapelle Cathedral with its vast array of stained-glass windows in homage to the immortal St. Francis; Pere LaChaise Cemetery, where we located gravesites for the Doors' wild front man Jim Morrison, classical composer Chopin, and French songstress Edith Piaf; the panoramic city view from the steps of Sacre Coure Cathedral, where we were warned to look out for pickpocket thieves; and a riverboat ride at dusk on the Seine River, under a picturesque, illuminated cloudy sky, taking in all the sights that included an iconic scene of a group of Parisians ballroom dancing on the river boardwalk.

Tessa had one specific request — a stop in Paris' famed Chanel store. This was a promise to her mother that she would do. When we were in the store, a nattily dressed security guard kept a close eye on us, making us feel as if we didn't belong there. That didn't deter us from gazing at perfume, toiletry and accessory items that were way out of our price range.

The food in Paris was fabulous, of course. Our favorite place for dinner was a pizza restaurant a couple of doors down from our hotel. Not only did it have great pizza and pasta, but it served a delicious vanilla-amaretto ice cream dessert to die for. We went back three times.

We feasted on a wonderful meal at a restaurant in the shadows of Notre Dame, during which I ordered a bottle of French wine. In France, the legal drinking age is 18, so I had planned to share the wine with Tessa. But she ordered herself a beer, so I had to drink the entire bottle myself. I suffered an exploding hangover the next morning, painfully jolted awake at 5:30 a.m. by a very loud thunderstorm that finally broke through the week-long humidity.

Tessa posing in front of Chanel store in Paris

We ventured outside of Paris only once, aboard a 30-minute train ride to the Palace of Versailles. We set out for a 9 a.m. start — early by our standards — to try to beat the excessively large crowd. We hoped to avoid standing in a long line on another hot day. Our Paris Passes were no good for the Palace.

I swear, something always seemed to screw things up with the best-laid plans. The train boarding platform nearest to our hotel was located underground, with two tracks side-by-side. There were no visible signs signaling which track was headed for Versailles, which raised a little bit of a panic in me. Having guessed wrong twice on groan-inducing occasions with the city metro, I wanted to make sure we boarded the right train for Versailles. We waited for a train that pulled into the station clearly heading in the direction of Versailles, so we boarded that train.

We comfortably settled in our seats as the train pulled away. Within a couple of minutes the train started bearing toward the right, which threw me for a loop. I looked outside the window at the next few stops to catch the posted signs to see if we were headed in the right direction. In short time, I got the sneaking suspicion that we were headed in the wrong direction.

A nice young French woman was seated in front of us. *"Parlez-vous Anglais?"* I anxiously asked her. Yes, she spoke English.

"Is this the train to Versailles?" I followed up.

"Oh no."

I could barely contain my frustration. Damned if that train hadn't made a U-turn a couple of minutes out of that station where we boarded. What were the odds, like we were supposed to know that, standing helplessly on the boarding platform all alone?

Tessa and I hopped off at the next stop, which placed us god-knows-where in Paris, frantically looking for a train station that would direct us back to the original station where we started. I was dragging my poor daughter around on a hot day in a futile search, until I flung a *"parlez-vous Anglais"* at a young man carrying a briefcase. He finally directed us to an underground station another block away and we made it back to the original pick-up station to board the right train to Versailles. *Merde!*

Tessa napped on the train ride to Versailles. It was another ten-minute walk to the Palace, then an hour-and-half wait in line that we had tried so hard to avoid, baking in the sun.

Once we were inside the Palace, all the trouble we went through to get there was worth it. I had never seen anything like it — King Louis XIV's collection of exquisite 17th century artwork, statues, furniture, painted ceilings and ornate hanging chandeliers, and the awe-inspiring, rapturous Hall of Mirrors. The opulence of the place was overwhelming.

There was much more beyond the Palace walls. We rented a golf cart and took a ride through the expansive, beautiful outdoor gardens. I was particularly taken by Neptune's Fountain, a large greenish oval pond with a bronze statue in the center. The statue emerging out of the water depicted a caped, bearded Neptune guiding a chariot powered by three hard-charging horses, surrounded by four muscular males swimming forward in looping dives, alongside four dolphin heads bobbing out of the water.

When we had finished our exceptionally long day, I asked Tessa what she thought of the Palace of Versailles.

"No more museums, please!" I got the message loud and clear.

Our final night in Paris was the perfect finale — an elevator ride to the top of the Eiffel Tower at night to see the City of Lights all lit up. I don't know if I can describe how perfect that scenario felt, looking out and seeing the glitter of the city with my daughter; how the realization of a 15-year dream we shared was capped in a truly magical moment.

Eiffel Tower at night

We were ready to go home after 10 days. We were in for one more surprise when we arrived at Charles De Gaulle Airport for our Air France flight home. Through no fault of our own, we were among the last passengers arriving at the boarding gate after delays on our taxi ride to the airport and a long wait in line to get our boarding passes. We still got to the gate in plenty of time for boarding. But no legitimate reason explained "Why?" when we were told that our seats had been given to another party.

I wasn't quite believing what I was hearing. Tessa was ready to burst out in tears. I bitterly complained, shouting that I had made reservations five months in advance. The woman at the counter was sympathetic to our plight, frantically typing away at her keyboard to see if there were any seats left to squeeze us on the plane.

That's when I noticed a distinguished, uniformed Air France manager who obviously had some clout standing nearby. Then, shortly after everyone else boarded the plane, I saw three cheerful people waltzing toward him pulling small carry-on bags, waving at him, and shouting *"Merci beaucoup!"* as they walked on past us through the boarding gate. The manager waved back, smiling. The woman at the counter nervously looked up, then avoided making eye contact with me.

I put two-and-two together — I just saw *who* got our seats! Now I was really pissed.

But I couldn't stay too mad at the woman at the counter. Especially after she offered us a 1,600 euro (about $1,200) refund, an overnight stay at an airport hotel with free dinner and breakfast, and tickets for a flight out the following morning. *Merci beaucoup!* So Tessa and I had one more night in Paris. We enjoyed our free dinner and slept, with a big bundle of cash to ease the inconvenience.

Best of all, our room had air conditioning.

Unceremoniously, and without fanfare, Cyndi and I got married in early spring of 2017.

Then— this is going to sound a little strange — I departed for my dream trip the next day to Italy, by myself. It was a trip I had planned five months in advance without Cyndi because of her various health issues. I had her blessing.

I joined a tour group, through Insight Vacations, for a 10-day excursion to Rome, Florence and Venice. I had some reservations about being tied down to a tour group. But it wound up being a divine experience.

I was one of only two people out of 40 on the tour who was traveling alone. The other solo traveler was Erica, a young black woman who worked as a doctor at a military base in Florida. So we wound up sitting next to each other on the tour bus.

Our tour guide was Daniele, who was a 40ish Italian man who definitely made the tour worthwhile. The tour guide could make or break the success of a tour. Daniele was charming, affable, had great stories to tell, was knowledgeable enough to provide just the right amount of information, and he threw in a couple of audibles along the way that provided very pleasant surprises.

I got along great with the tour group as a whole. It was mostly an older crowd, as expected, although there were two young, honeymooning couples in the mix.

I have to admit, I was pretty much gob-struck by the sights in Italy as a whole. In Rome, we opened with a tour of the Vatican — oh my, its vast artwork reminded me of the Palace of Versailles. Michelangelo's masterpiece on the ceiling and walls of the Sistine Chapel, and St. Peter's Church, with the famous statue of Mother Mary holding baby Jesus, were both "Wow" moments. Then on to the Roman Coliseum. It was as ancient and historic-looking as I had long fantasized about, with its crumbling outer walls and inner stone maze on the ground floor. Then we took a short walk from the Coliseum to the Roman Forum area, another remnant of the ancient past plopped in the middle of the modern world.

The next day we took an hour's drive to Pompeii to see its excavated streets and ruins, which were eerie. The prostitutes' stone quarters with drawings on the walls were particularly interesting. However, I was disappointed that the entire exhibit featured only one encased, ash-hardened body on display; I expected to see a lot more. Then we stopped in Naples, a city that is 2,800 years old, as Daniele informed us, on the way back to Rome. In full view from Naples' vast harbor stood mighty Mt. Vesuvius that leveled Pompeii 1,900 years ago.

Moving north toward Florence, we stopped to see the Leaning Tower of Pisa — which was pretty awesome, just like it appears in the postcards. Then, in the heart of Tuscany, Daniele diverted the tour to a winery and olive oil farm. We all got a mellow buzz from the local wine, mixed in with fresh baked breads dipped in olive oil along with sun-dried tomatoes, salami, and olives.

Florence was enchanting. Walking the streets felt like reliving the Renaissance. There seemed to be an old church at every corner. We saw Michelangelo's iconic nude statue of David during a guided tour of one museum. On my own, I reserved time to visit the Uffizzi

Museum that houses many famous Renaissance paintings, including Botticelli's Birth of Venus, depicting the nude Aphrodite standing on a seashell in her mythical birth off the shores of Cyprus. I related the painting to my visit to Cyprus 13 years earlier.

We took a side excursion to the fortressed Tuscan village of San Gimignano, surrounded by luscious rolling green hills populated by sprawling vineyards. The village looked like a blast from the Middle Ages, featuring numerous round, stone towers that were used to store saffron, which Daniele said was as good as gold back in the day.

I missed out on possibly the best meal on the whole tour — a Tuscany-style feast at a ranch house — when I misunderstood the pick-up time to board the bus. I noticed a piano in a secluded side room adjacent to the lobby where we were supposed to wait for the bus, and got distracted while playing it. Daniele tried calling my room several times before the bus departed without me. I wound up eating by myself at a nearby restaurant that night, which was so depressing. This was Mr. Mistake's lone mis-step of the entire trip.

But Venice was still to come, which fulfilled a lifelong dream of mine. On the drive there, we made a touristy stop in Verona to gaze at the balcony immortalized in Shakespeare's "Romeo and Juliet," with gift shops peddling "love" souvenirs.

My heart swooned the moment we boarded the boat taxi headed toward our hotel in Venice. We stayed at the Stucky Hilton, which was by far the nicest hotel of the tour. When we first entered the fancy lobby, my eyes immediately dialed in on the beautiful black grand piano, which would provide an exquisite moment for me on the tour's final night. Entering my classy deluxe room, I marveled at the comfy king-size bed and pillows, the ornate light fixture hanging from the high ceiling, and the luxurious marble bathroom and tub.

Daniele introduced us to St. Mark's Square on our first night in town, where he treated us to Venetian Spritz drinks while listening to a lovely live concert by a classical quartet comprised of piano, sax, violin and cello. We sat in the shadows of the medieval St. Mark's Basilica, the wild-looking Doge's Palace, and landmark Campinile Tower that chimed bells every hour.

Our three-day stay in the celebrated city of canals was full of highlights. We were given a walking tour of hideaway corridors hidden away from the tourists, guided by an older local woman who lamented about how longtime Venetians like her were trying to hang on in their iconic neighborhoods that were being increasingly overrun by tourism. We picked a good time of the year to avoid the heavy tourist crowds — late March.

The tour included a visit to the venerable Murano glass-blowing shop, in which we were given a demonstration by a glassblower who fabricated a colorful glass figure of a horse. I made a spontaneous purchase of a very expensive wedding gift for my new bride back home — two glass figures of a man and woman in 17th century-costumes, gleaming with speckles of real gold visible through the transparent bodies.

We were accorded the requisite gondola ride through the canals — a half-hour of pure bliss. I was going nuts with my camera as we floated under the arching walkway bridges that distinguish Venice's waterways, and meandered past the rows of multi-storied, centuries-old apartments.

Later, we took a 25-minute boat ride to a nearby island called Burano for a spectacular early dinner featuring a variety of fish dishes. Burano is a small fishing town also known for its lace-making. The town dazzled in an array of bright colors from the row of houses aligning its canal.

Late on our second night at the Hilton, I wandered down to the lobby and sat at that magnificent grand piano and started playing a couple of my own compositions. I attracted the attention of two older couples from the tour, Jay and Judy, from North Carolina, and Gavin and Jennifer, newlyweds from Australia, who were all very impressed, evidently. Jay video-taped me playing, and the secret was out.

We were given free time to ourselves on our final day in Venice. I ventured out on my own, walking leisurely all over town, crossing bridges, and taking respite at the Point Academie (academic center) at the end of an isthmus jutting out from the harbor.

We had our final meal at a restaurant next to Venice's famous opera house. That's when Daniele surprised me with a request in front of everyone at the dinner table— would I be willing to perform a couple of pieces on that grand piano in the hotel lobby for the entire tour group? Evidently, Jay's video of me playing the night before had gone viral.

I had never performed my own music before a large audience

like that in my life. Of course I said "Yes," but boy, was I nervous! The first piece I played was given a name change for a reason — I call it "Comfort Zone" now because it was the perfect first piece to help me get over my nerves and perform in front of that audience. It was a catchy melody that won over the crowd. Then I followed up with one of my pieces with a little pizzaz and little out of my comfort zone — "Butterfly." And well, let's just say I was richly rewarded by the kind words from everyone who approached me afterward.

Playing on the grand piano at the hotel in Venice, Italy, performing for two of my tour companions, Australian newlyweds Gavin and Jennifer

Following that incredible high in Venice, I said *arrividerci* to the tour and thanked Danielo for the enriching experience. I wasn't done with Italy yet. I hopped on a train for a four-and-a-half hour ride to the western coastline, where I spent the next four days all on my own in heavenly Cinque Terre.

Cinque Terre is composed of five tiny, picturesque villages along the rocky coast. They are linked either by convenient, five-minute train rides, or by boat, or by foot on breathtaking hiking trails along cliffs bordering the shore.

Because it is my nature to go against the grain, I chose to stay in the least popular of the five towns, Corniglia, the town that PBS TV tour guru Rick Steves called "the Ringo Starr" among the five villages that compose Cinque Terre. Worse yet, Steves said Corniglia would appeal only to "hermits, anarchists and billy goats." So, when I finally got off the train with my 60-pound suitcase (stuffed with added gifts at this point), looking up at a long, steep, winding road into town from the train station, I had absolutely no idea what I was in store for.

I had booked my accommodations in Corniglia online, without the benefit of a recommendation by any credible source. By chance I found a listing for a place called "Angela Apartments," with a rather unflattering photo of an ocean view from a distance high up from the mountain-side plateau. The photo appeared as if it was taken about a mile from shore. I was curious to see what exactly constituted an "apartment" in Italy.

I was set up for the most pleasant surprise of my Italian experience. The "apartment," as it turned out, was a delightfully charming cottage with cheerfully bright yellow walls, a full kitchen, a separate dining room, a serviceable bathroom with a small sit-in bathtub, and a small washer/dryer. The ocean was a lot closer than that website photo implied. On my first night I captured a wondrous sunset shot over the water from my balcony. From my apartment, I took a short walk down some steep stairs the following morning and reached an intimate cove within a few minutes.

Angela Apartments was owned and operated by a charming middle-aged Italian couple, Agnese and Fabrizio. The cost for this treasured find? A little more than $80 per night. I felt like contacting Rick Steves to pass on that hermits, anarchists and billy goats know a thing or two that he might appreciate. But Steves is a good-hearted, progressive-thinking, ol' stoner, so I'll cut him some slack.

Part of the logic behind choosing Corniglia was that it was situated in the middle of the five little villages, which I thought would make it advantageous for exploring the other four. That proved to be an asset to planning my excursions.

Steves was correct in implying that tiny Corniglia didn't have much of anything to offer in town. But I was completely content getting breakfasts at the intimate Caffe Matteo, and dinners at the Bar Nunzio with outdoor seating in the tiny, quiet town square.

"Quiet" is what I liked most about Corniglia, because there weren't many people in town, mostly hikers passing through. Maybe that was the "hermit" in me.

But I managed to visit all four other villages from my central locale, either by foot or by train. I discovered why Cinque Terre is a hiker's paradise on my first full day. I made the two-mile hike on a trail along the cliffs to reach the next town south, Vernazza. It was an arduous hike, with steep changes in elevation up and down. But the views were spectacular, reminiscent of the drive along Highway 1 between Cambria and Big Sur in California. It helped that the weather was very Santa Barbara-like as well— low 70s. A remote, tiny bar cafe located about two-thirds of the way to Vernazza offered a much-needed rest stop, during which I took in the view from a breezy open window while slowly sipping on a wonderfully refreshing lemon slush.

Descending from the cliffs into Vernazza, I had to concede it was as beautiful as Steves described. A castle prominently stood out at the entryway into the harbor, lined by its wall of Italian-style apartment buildings and shops. I stopped at a restaurant perched on the hillside and ordered a fresh tomato salad with a glass of the local Vermintino white wine that had been recommended to me by the taxi driver who gave me a ride to my hotel on my arrival in Rome twelve days earlier.

Looking down on Vernazza in Cinque Terre, Italy

While I was sitting at that restaurant, basking in the glory of my two-mile hike, taking in the beauty of Vernazza below and enjoying my solitude, I reflected on my mother and her profound passion for travel. She had pursued the bulk of her travels when she was about the same age I was at that moment, and I reflected on my gratitude for her passing on that passion so I could experience moments like this one.

I spent a couple of hours in Vernazza, then hopped on the train for the five-minute ride back to Corniglia, at the cost of three euro. The next day, I opted to take a train further north to visit Riomaggiore and Manarola. The "Via dell Amore" (Pathway of Love) trail linking the two towns was closed, but I did enough walking around both villages to get my exercise in. Both towns were quaint and pretty. I ended the day gazing down from the elevated rim of a secluded harbor, transfixed on a lovely redhead young beauty wading topless in the harbor water.

The last day was spent in Monarosso, which is the largest of the five Cinque Terre towns. It is the only town among the five with a large sandy beach. I went in for a swim, feeling safe enough to leave my handbag with my wallet inside unattended on my beach towel. While I thrived in my solitude most of the time, it was moments like that in which I felt disadvantaged traveling alone.

I wandered to the Old Town side of Monarosso, finding a very old cemetery on a hilltop that offered 360-degree vistas. From above, I watched a young man serenading his girlfriend on a guitar while standing by a statue of a friar, which triggered long-ago memories of young love.

I visited a church built in 1307 and walked in on a ceremony led by a priest, being followed by about twenty children reciting biblical verse in Italian. Then I capped my Monarosso visit with a late dinner with a beachside view, ordering an entree of mussels sautéed in a tomato sauce, washed down by a half-bottle of chianti.

Boarding the train on my final morning in Corniglia, I arrived six hours later at the Rome airport. I stayed one more night at a quirky bed and breakfast place in a residential area near the airport. I took a relatively short walk down to the beach after eating dinner at a pizza place, my last memory of my dream trip to Italy.

<hr>

I formulated a trip to Europe — Switzerland, Vienna, and Germany — in the summer of 2018 around people I knew. I had a standing invitation to visit Switzerland through my long-time tenants in the front unit of the Santa Monica house. Ady, the father of the family, was from Switzerland. He and his American wife Ashley, and their three daughters — Lily, Talia and Nela, ages 15, 12, and 11 — traveled to Switzerland every summer to visit Ady's widowed mother. Then I planned a three-day stay in Vienna, a city I had wanted to visit ever since seeing the movie "Before Sunrise," followed by a train ride to Germany to visit my German sister Janni and husband Tetsu.

This trip almost didn't happen. I tore a minuscule ligament in my left knee playing tennis a few weeks before my scheduled departure and arthroscopic surgery was strongly recommended. But my departure date was too close to risk scheduling the surgery before the trip, so I postponed it until I got back. I took the calculated risk that I could hobble around Europe without making the knee worse. The surgeon gave me a cortisone shot for pain the week before.

The more problematic issue was a large cyst on my back near my right shoulder that suddenly became horribly infected. The cyst had been dormant for years, which was shrugged off by at least two doctors. With less than four weeks prior to my departure, the infection became unbearably painful, and I rushed to the local Urgent Care. I suffered the worst torture of my life as the nurse practitioner cut open the cyst with a knife and squeezed out gushes of puss. I went in every other day over the next 20 days to repeat that act of torture under extreme duress and pain, finally completely draining that cyst dry on the final visit on the very morning I was driving down to LAX to catch my flight to Europe.

I flew in on a connecting flight out of Manchester, England (with an eight-hour layover). I arrived in Zurich about 10:15 p.m., with Ady and Ashley waiting outside to pick me up. I ran into trouble right away in Customs when I vainly tried to go through the automatic gates by scanning my passport, mimicking what other passengers ahead of me had done. I noticed that passengers posed for a full-body photograph at the second set of gates. So in anticipation of that photo, I removed my favorite blue golf hat and $250 sunglasses and laid them down on a stand next to the first gate.

But the first set of gates wouldn't open for me like they had for everyone else. I panicked and moved down the line, trying without success to scan my passport at each of the other six gates. When I returned to the first gate, my hat and sunglasses were gone! Those sunglasses were in reality my anti-glare glasses to avoid headaches from indoor lighting. Without them, a full-on headache began to emerge.

Frantically, I looked around for help and saw a customs agent in a booth off to the left. No, my hat and sunglasses had not been turned in to him, which was severely disappointing. I concluded somebody walked off with them. Then when I told the agent about my problem at the gates, he looked at my passport and calmly explained that those gates were for European passports only. Oh. That, umm, explained it.

I was supposed to go directly to his booth all along, but you know me, where was the sign to tell me that? It only cost me a really nice hat and very expensive sunglasses to find out. Really...annoying.

I got over it, thanks to Ady and Ashley and Ady's lovely mother, Lonny, who lived in a charming large house in a farming community called Selzach, about a 45-minute drive south of Zurich. I joined a large household that included Lonny's two male tenants.

Lonny grew her own fruits and vegetables, which she harvested every morning for meals she prepared every day. She loved to cook. I loved to eat her meals, so we got along great. In Lonny's eyes, I couldn't eat enough to satisfy her. One day she prepared a fresh fruit salad of blueberries, strawberries, peach, banana, apple and some other berry I didn't know, that was simply exquisite.

Ady and Ashley planned a fulcrum of activities for me over four full, lovely days. We took a hike along the edge of high hills overlooking the farmlands that felt like a Von Trapp family moment with my host family, as I watched Talia chase butterflies, and we stopped to pet grazing cows along the way. They showed me a 600-year-old church in Solothurn, scaling 11 symbolic quarry steps at the entrance to memorialize the year 1411, when the Swiss overthrew the Hapsburg rulers from Austria.

They drove me to the town of Interlaken at the base of the Alps where they had lived for 13 years and where all three of their daughters were born. While they had their own agenda in town, I was dropped off at the pick-up point for a ride on a 125-year-old cable train to Schnige Platt at the top of a towering mountain. I spent the next two-and-half hours hiking a six-kilometer loop at the top of the

Alps on my bum knee, overlooking awesome panoramic views of snow-capped mountains and a pair of lakes and villages below. I was literally, and figuratively, on top of the world. When I returned to ground level, I managed to follow Ashley's detailed instructions to navigate through three train changes to reunite with Ady for pick-up in Solothurn.

On my hike in the Swiss Alps, wearing the hat and sunglasses I bought to replace the ones I lost in Customs

I took a stroll through Lonny's farm neighborhood, coming across a stunning, large crop of seven-foot-high sunflowers. At one point I decided to *lay down to rest in a big field of tall grass, where I felt the sun caressing my face*, experiencing my own "Spill That Wine" moment as sung by Eric Burden and The Animals in the 60s.

Ady, Ashley and I made the two-hour drive to Montreux for the famous Montreux Jazz Festival, along the shores of Lake Geneva. At lakeside, we paid respects to the statue of the late Freddy Mercury of Queen, immortalized in the movie "Bohemian Rhapsody." Then we bought tickets for a three-hour live concert in the famed Stravinsky Auditorium to see headliner Jamiroquai, a '90s electronic funk band. Ady told me the story about the famous fire in the 60's that broke out while the rock group Deep Purple watched from a boat on the lake and came up with the song, "Smoke On the Water." My knee held up standing up on the dance floor all three hours, while being goaded to dance by the pretty red-headed woman less than half my age directly in front of me, while her mother who was my age tried to keep up.

Bidding farewell to my Santa Monica tenants and Lonny, I caught a flight to Vienna to lap in the next three days and nights. I stayed at an elegant hotel. The nights were warm and breezy; it felt lighter than air walking in downtown Vienna the first night. People were in a festive mood, celebrating all over town France's just-completed World Cup soccer final victory over Croatia.

I used the Hop On Hop Off bus tours to get around to tourist stops. I stopped at Prater Park and took a ride on the famed Giant Ferris Wheel. I ate a Vienna specialty, veal schweineschnitzel, for lunch at a restaurant on the top of the Danube Tower that rotated 360 degrees and overlooked the river. I went to the vast Schonbrunn Palace and Gardens twice. In the daytime I toured the Palace interior (the "Millions" room with its gold-embroidered walls was my favorite) and walked the expansive grounds offering vast displays of flowers, sculptures, and fountains. Then I returned to the Palace at night to be mesmerized by a beautiful classical operatic concert. I toured Vienna's famed Operahouse, after which I stopped for lunch at its cafe, where I enjoyed a sumptuous order of Vienna beef and noodle soup, apple strudel, and Baileys on ice. Then I walked over to Stadtpark to see the magnificent gold-plated statue of Austria's heralded classical composer, Johann Strauss. I capped my walking tour with a stop inside the ancient, majestic, massive St. Stephens Cathedral.

Then I boarded a train for Germany. I was the first person to board, 30 minutes in advance to get all settled in, only to get chased out of first class because I didn't have a first-class ticket, even though I had specifically asked the lady at the station ticket booth if my ticket was first class. (You'll be surprised to know this wasn't the first time I had been kicked out of first class aboard a train.) I reluctantly paid the extra 38 euro to remain in first class. Then I was shocked to find out I needed to fork over an additional 71 euro to stay in first class as soon as the train crossed the border from Austria into Germany. The hell with that; I moved down to the very last car to find the last remaining open seat in second class. In a word, I was put off.

My mood changed once I arrived in Rothenburg — reputedly the oldest medieval town in Europe — for an overnight stay. The Hotel

Eisenhut where I stayed was originally built in 1873 as a family-run tavern, then converted to a hotel in 1890. It was very interesting and very funky in its decor, reflecting its history.

Exploring the town the next day, I discovered a pretty park that contained a small building that commemorated Jews who died in Nazi concentration camps during World War II. I found a really old church, and a museum with lots of medieval stuff (weaponry, pottery). Then my gimpy knee made it up 200 steps to the top of a really old Town Hall Tower. The knee was fine, but the climb was a killer. The view was spectacular.

Then I boarded another train for Kassel, where Janni was waiting for me. It had been over 20 years since we last had seen each other when she had visited me in Santa Barbara in the mid-1990's. Janni, who was a hearing specialist as a doctor before she had recently retired, diagnosed within the first twenty minutes of speaking with me that I had suffered a thirty-percent hearing loss.

We had so much to catch up on. She heard all about my fallout over the Rossburn house with Pam, with whom Janni was close when she was staying with us as a high school foreign exchange student. Janni recalled how shocked she was by the bickering she witnessed between my parents. She recalled a horrible fight between my parents that I didn't recall that occurred during a family outing we all took to San Francisco. Janni said the fight broke out while we were driving and I got out of the car and started walking. I laughed because I didn't remember any of that, but she did.

Janni and Tetsu live in a large house that Janni inherited from her parents. A month earlier she and Tetsu, who owns a separate apartment, used both residences to host a Jewish family of 25 visiting from Canada. The family came to Kassel to partake in a ceremony in front of a house where the wife of Janni's father's best friend used to live. During the ceremony, seven gold plates bearing the names of a mother and each of her six children were cemented in the sidewalk in front of the house to commemorate their "escape" from Kassel just before the Nazis swept in to clear the Jews out.

My visit with Janni and Tetsu was splendid. They were into eating healthy and harvested their own fruit and vegetable garden in their backyard, which housed the large pen that contained their three noisy pet ducks.

They showed me around town, including Kassel's most prominent landmark —the Hercules stone monument high atop a long hill overlooking the city. A life-sized statue of a naked Hercules stands at the top of the monument, hovering over a large fountain. Every Wednesday and Sunday residents come out to watch the spectacle of water released from the fountain into a canal cascading down the hill through a series of pools. It takes an hour-and-a-half for the water to complete its full run to the bottom, emptying into a large pond.

I was taken to a town about 20 miles north of Kassel called Grebenstein, which reminded me a lot of Rothenburg with its old, medieval-style homes and towers. I was taken to an art gallery exhibiting paintings by a pair of friends of Janni and Tetsu, Maya and Ingo. Maya, who is Japanese, primarily paints portraits of Japanese children with priceless expressions on their faces, against interesting textured backgrounds of tiny squares shaded in lightly-hued colors. Ingo's detailed, life-like paintings of an elephant and an orangutan on large canvases were particularly impressive.

Janni, Tetsu and me in Kassel, Germany

Janni and Tetsu enjoined me in more of their favorite activities. We drove a short way out to the countryside to pick fresh blueberries and raspberries off the vine from an orchard. We went to a nighttime concert featuring a charismatic young Portuguese woman singer backed up by three guitarists, singing songs from the heart. We feasted on lamb kabob at an Iraqi restaurant. We took a bike ride to the park at the base of the Hercules monument and toured a palace there. We took a swim in the public pool where Janni regularly goes.

Then I boarded another train for a six-hour ride back to Zurich. When I finally arrived at the airport, I would have never found the airport hotel in which Janni had booked a room for me without her online research. Online research, hmm, what a concept.

The following morning, at 6 a.m. at the Zurich Airport, I ran into trouble again at Customs. I headed straight for the manned booth, thinking that's where I was supposed to go, as I had painfully learned on my arrival at the airport two weeks before. But the agent admonished me, informing me that I was at the wrong booth designated for Swiss travelers only. Well, shoot, I *knew* that. He said he'd let me pass this time, but "next time" go to the right booth. *Yes sir.*

I'm guessing that the agent was tipped off about my misguided entry into Switzerland two weeks earlier; maybe he had a posted photo of me accompanied by instructions to "get this goofball out of the country as fast as possible."

CHAPTER 32
Odds and Edds . . .

Right off the bat, I'm gonna confess that "Edds" in the chapter title is a typo; I meant to type "Ends." But then I pondered it a little further, and decided I liked the sound of "Edds" and kept it in. I thought that was a great metaphor for my life — an endless series of typos that I just brushed off and accepted as reality. My life was too messy for spellcheck to correct.

There is no particular theme tying the stories in this chapter together, other than they are the latest stories leading into ascension into my twilight years. A mixed bag here, of laughter, luck and loss.

———————◆———————

This story made me laugh. Maybe it shouldn't, because it was a very *painful* experience. But I can laugh about it now.

I got bit by a dog. Not that big a deal, right? And really, how funny could that be? Maybe it's my warped sense of humor. But here's how it went:

One Sunday morning, I stepped out into my front yard to let Thomas, our elderly, sick- and indoor-bound cat, wander out and lay in the garden bed for a while. He was weak and wasn't going to go far. When I opened the door for him, he turned right, heading to turn the corner of the house.

That's when I heard the yapping of the two dogs that lived next door. Except, instead of the yapping coming from the backyard where they were usually cooped up behind a locked gate, it was coming from the sidewalk directly in front of my house. They were on the loose when they shouldn't have been.

One of the dogs was an old measly mutt that I had seen out front before, alone. She was cantankerous and never very friendly toward me. The other dog was a young bulldog that was never allowed outside the backyard. So clearly someone goofed, maybe by leaving that backyard gate open.

When I set eyes on the dogs, my first concern was for Thomas. I was afraid they might dash up toward the front and charge after my old cat.

Those two dogs did start dashing up front, side-by-side, full speed ahead. Only they weren't charging at Thomas; they had their sights set on me.

I had less than three seconds to react. My eyes darted off to the left to focus on the bulldog, calculating he would be the most likely to launch an attack.

As luck would have it, out of my peripheral vision I saw the measly mutt leap in the air directly at me, and in an instant chomp at… my groin.

Doubling over in pain, I immediately scrambled to my right to collect Thomas before the dogs had a chance to turn their attention on him. The canine pair ran off back toward the house next door.

After stumbling back inside with Thomas secured, I pulled open the front of the sweat pants I was wearing to assess the damage done by the measly mutt. Aghast, I saw I was bleeding pretty badly. Ever since I started taking blood thinner after my strokes, I've been a bit of a bleeder.

Rushing to the bathroom, I dropped the sweat pants, spread my legs and gazed down for a closer look. There, in living color, was a gash about an inch long, just a half-inch below my left testicle. If that damn dog had bit me just a half-inch higher up, I would have been looking at a lot more damage than just a bloody surface gash, and this would have been a much different story.

Now, I'm thinking that's pretty damn funny. Back then, not so much.

Cyndi rushed me to Urgent Care. I applied a paper towel to the wound to absorb the bleeding. I had to drop all pretense to propriety at the door when I walked into Urgent Care clutching my crotch to hold the paper towel in place under my sweat pants. I felt a little self-conscious that I might have been perceived as some kind of pervert as a few eyes cast my way in the waiting room.

My clutching remained intact as I presented myself to the front counter. The woman receptionist at the counter didn't bat an eye as she blandly asked, "What is the reason for your visit?"

"A dog bit me in the balls," I told her. "And I'm bleeding pretty badly."

I expected a more animated reaction to my "A dog bit me in the balls" declaration. But the "I'm bleeding pretty badly" comment was taken seriously, and I was rushed into an exam room ahead of everybody waiting. I was spared the awkwardness of waiting with them with unwanted attention directed toward my wounded groin.

Once inside the exam room, I stripped into a white gown and spread my legs for the doctor to assess. She determined stitches were needed. She gave me a tetanus shot in the arm and an assistant cleaned the wound. Then came the shot "where the sun don't shine" to numb the pain for application of the stitches.

Later, I had a talk with my neighbor about her dogs. The measly mutt showed no remorse. I'm happy to report that both of my balls are still attached.

———————•·•·◆·•·•———————

I count my blessings every day since I had my two strokes. Those strokes changed my life. They did bring Cyndi and I closer together. I indicated in my "Stroke Of Luck" chapter that I was motivated to write these memoirs because of my stroke experience.

The strokes also inspired me to record my music. It struck me that my compositions — over 40 years of creativity — were heard only when I sat at the piano and played them. They existed only in my head. I realized that if I didn't record them, they would die with me.

This idea got a push start when I crossed paths with Gregor, a former colleague of mine on the sports desk at the Santa Barbara News-Press. Gregor had quit the News-Press because he had the luxury of an abundant family trust that allowed him to pursue his dream — as a musician-songwriter.

I bumped into Gregor at the Montecito YMCA where he was a member, and I was supervising a participant working in the maintenance department. In a conversation at poolside where Gregor was laying in the sun working on his tan, he told me he was recording his music at a local studio owned by this really cool guy named Nik. He gave me Nik's number.

Life blessed me with Nik for the short time he was in my life.

Nik was one of the more gifted and giving persons to ever grace my life. I was so grateful that Gregor guided me to him. Nik was an expatriate Brit, a former rocker who used to play with the likes of Jimmy Page in his youth, and in the late 1980s and early 1990s he toured with a band called Blue Murder. Nik moved on from there to form a dynamic singing-songwriting duo with his wife Penny, called The Away Team. Penny, every bit Nik's equal in talent on so many levels, composed the songs and sang on all their collaborations, while Nik did most of the arranging and accompaniment.

Nik performed his musical magic out of his Santa Barbara studio, Black Cat Studios. It exists as a tiny sound room in the basement of a large building in downtown, full of recording equipment from which Nik produced his abundant palette of instrumental sounds. It was in his studio that I started working with him on my music in the spring of 2014, just a few months after my recovery from my strokes.

Nik's genius was as eclectic as his personality. He was very tall and thin, with stringy, shoulder-length blonde hair that exuded his rocker look. He usually was dressed in skimpy denim shorts and blousy tops that were effeminate, and he typically wore a shawl around his neck. He kept in shape as a long-distance runner and he and Penny both ate an all-healthy diet. Nik never did drugs.

His manner was always polite and enthusiastic. He was wholeheartedly engaged in my project and very supportive. The recording experience was new to me, so I was very nervous at first and often butchered my first few takes on pieces I played on his Yamaha piano in his studio. It took me a while to get comfortable playing on a foreign keyboard. But he was very patient with me and reassured me that it wasn't crucial if I didn't get it exactly right. That's because he had amazing editing abilities to correct my mistakes after recording, to make me sound like I could actually play the piano as well as two fingers on Jon Batiste's right hand (that's as close as I'm ever going to get to Jon Batiste, which is still pretty darn good). I marveled how Nik could cover up my mistakes.

Then, if I had an idea for some kind of accompaniment to my pieces, Nik was all too happy to oblige. He added arrangements that transformed my pieces. He added orchestral strings to quite a few of my pieces that enriched the sound. For years I had envisioned a saxophone accompaniment in one piece, called "Candlelight," and asked Nik to add a sax track. What he came up with was pure bliss and it took the song to another level. When I first heard his added track mixed in, my heart soared! It completely surpassed my expectations. When Nik, always a model of modesty, offered to bring in a real saxophonist to record a track instead of the one he came up with, I said, "No way! Are you kidding me? This is perfect!"

Nik made my dream come true. He produced my first CD, "The Key Of C," which was completed by August of 2014. It contained 15 tracks, including four vocal tracks, on three of which I sing. Singing was a weak spot that I had to work hard to get right and again, Nik's patience and tutoring made me a better singer. He used his editing abilities to cut from numerous takes and amplify the sound to make me sound better. He pumped up my confidence by telling me that most recording stars receive this fine-tuning treatment in recording studios.

I was really proud of "Key Of C." The multi-talented Penny designed the cover, employing photo-shop creativity with a sunset shot on the front and a shot of me at the piano at home on the back. It was a real glossy, professional piece of work. She also set up a website for me to launch the CD online through CD Baby. I showed little motivation to market the CD; I was just content to distribute it to friends and family members.

Then Nik and I started working on a second CD, choosing from about 45 tracks of my compositions Nik had recorded. Several pieces needed to be re-recorded, mostly because my performance was not up to par the first time through. Accompaniments were added to a few others.

Midway through the project, Penny dropped the devastating news regarding Nik— He had cancer. There was a reason why he always wore shawls around his neck; they were hiding an ugly growth on his neck. By February of 2015 it had developed into multiple, grotesque formations of a Stage 4 cancer tumor.

Nik steadfastly worked with me through the next eight months as he fought his incessant disease. He wanted to live. His valiant battle against cancer finally ended on March 13, 2016. I last saw him at the hospital two days before he died. He was only 61, much too young. I grieved not just for my loss in having so little time with him, but for the world that was deprived of what he had to offer with his immense talent. Penny, his wife, his soulmate, was devastated. After a prolonged period of mourning, she processed her profound grief by creating music in honor of Nik's legacy.

Penny, who has now become a good friend, kept Black Cat Studios running and helped finish my second CD, "Arabesque." She laid out arrangements on a couple of pieces, including one dynamic violin accompaniment to a new composition. Then, according me the same care and editing skills that Nik provided, she also helped me produce a third CD, entitled "Songs of My Youth," virtually completing recorded tracks of nearly all of my compositions, so that they now have a permanent existence outside of my head.

Nik and Penny

It was Nik who heard a Middle-Eastern sound to the title track of "Arabesque," and he produced that sound by adding an utterly stunning accompaniment with stirring strings, a hypnotic choral hum, and crashing cymbals. Hence, I came up with the title as a play on the word "Arab." Then Penny clued me in that "Arabesque" is a term for a distinctive ballet pose. I did not think it was pure coincidence that "Arabesque" was the piano piece which Janice, who passed away only six months after Nik, declared that she could see herself dancing to the music so many years ago. So I've dedicated that composition to her. But Nik's imprint on the recording renders a wonderful remembrance of his brilliance.

Losing a beloved pet always sucks. Cyndi and I had to put down our cat Thomas on September 20, 2017 after he suffered through 10 months with pancreatitis and cancer. He was 17.

It took us nearly a full year to come around to taking in another cat, provoked by a casual conversation I had with a plumber fixing a leaky bathroom faucet at our house on September 12, 2018. He mentioned in passing that he and his wife had just welcomed a litter of kittens in their home, born the day before, on September 11. I was immediately drawn to the idea of having a kitten with a September 11 birth date, so I told him we wanted to adopt one of his kittens.

So we adopted Micha, a beautiful, adorable, sandy orange and white tabby male. He lit up our lives with his very sweet nature and wild, high-flying playfulness, which reminded us of the balletic leaps of Baryshnikov, who was called Misha. Micha (we chose to spell it differently, but pronounce it the same) had a couple quirky habits. He was the only cat I've ever witnessed who braced his front paws on the upper edge of his litter box so he could stand up while pooping — no shit. Then, he liked to show me affection by getting in my face to lick my lips, and I was weird enough to grimace through it and let him at it for a couple minutes.

Micha standing up in his litter box to take a poop

But Micha's time with us was cut much too short. He had just passed his first birthday when he suddenly stopped eating and was running high fevers up to 105 degrees. He was diagnosed with a rare fatal disease called FIP (Feline Infectious Peritonitis), which typically affects younger cats about Micha's age. He deteriorated quickly and was obviously suffering. We were given no hope of saving him and couldn't stand to watch him suffer any further, so we put him down within two weeks.

That just about killed us. The lone saving grace was that we already had taken in a second kitten we had adopted as a playmate for Micha. Quincy is a gray and white, black-striped tabby male who was eight months younger than Micha. Micha and Quincy were inseparable for three months, seemingly bonding together as mates, turning our household into their own chaotic playground, until Micha's sudden downfall.

About a month prior to Quincy's first birthday our worst fears started to materialize. Quincy was showing a drop in appetite in the same fashion Micha had. A woman who was actively involved with the agency that processed Quincy's adoption had warned us ahead of time that two of his siblings had come down with FIP. We agonized over this news on two fronts— that we were going to lose Quincy in the same manner as Micha, and that Micha had caught FIP from Quincy.

There was nothing we could do to reverse that latter reality, however horrible that made us feel. But there was hope for Quincy, who was diagnosed with early stages of FIP. Avery, the woman who broke the news to us about his siblings, also alerted us about a new drug that had proven to cure FIP, which until then had been an automatic death sentence. She told us both of Quincy's siblings were miraculously cured of FIP under treatment with this drug.

The drug wasn't cheap and it was available only on the black market, coming out of China. But we were on board. We put Quincy on the 12-week treatment. Thank God, he quickly recovered.

Micha will forever be in our hearts, with regret that we didn't have access to this miracle drug in time to save him. But the angels gave us Quincy to keep Micha's memory alive, and for that we are grateful.

———————•◆•———————

This is another drug-related story. I have been seeing my neurologist, Dr. Karen DaSilva, for years to treat my migraines. In the fall of 2018, she prescribed a new medication, Topamax, that proved effective in drastically reducing the frequency of migraines.

Topamax clearly worked. But it triggered a couple of other strange reactions. Dr. DaSilva had warned that I might lose a little weight from Topamax, maybe five or six pounds. Well, I wasn't expecting to shed over twenty pounds that incrementally dropped over two years without really trying. The weight loss, scaling in on a number I haven't seen since my 30's, has made me feel younger.

But I had a much more bizarre reaction that was mind-boggling in the first two months of taking Topamax. The prescription called for a double dose after the first week.

Doubling the dosage did something strange to my brain. We're talking about a brain that had suffered a couple of blood clots that caused strokes a few years earlier. I was feeling an utter sense of euphoria. I was suddenly seeing the world in a much lighter frame of mind; everywhere I went, I was cracking jokes. Out in the public, I'd pop out witty remarks to waitresses, baristas, retail clerks. My mind felt like it was working so much quicker, on a whole different plane than it used to. I interacted with strangers in playful, but respectful ways — completely unfiltered. I couldn't turn it off.

Exhibit A of this new behavior streak came during an interaction with a waitress at one of our favorite seafood restaurant in Santa Barbara. The waitress was six months pregnant with a Christmas holiday due date. As was my custom with restaurant food servers, I asked her for her name, which was Sandy. She had the prettiest open smile. In my unfiltered fashion, I told her that she reminded me of my cousin Sherrie when she smiled.

Sandy first asked my wife what she wanted to order. She gave the usual spiel about the two choices on how their fish entrees were cooked — grilled or pan-fried. Cyndi ordered the salmon.

"How would you like that cooked?" Sandy asked her.

Cyndi asked Sandy what she recommended. "Most people like their fish grilled, but I prefer pan-fried."

Cyndi went with Sandy's recommendation. Then when it came to my turn, I ordered the sea bass. Sandy asked me how I wanted it cooked.

"You recommend pan-fried?" I asked.

"Yes."

"OK. I'll have it grilled then."

Did I mention how this drug made me a smart-ass? My response threw Sandy for a loop, but she politely and graciously laughed. She left to put our orders in. Then she returned to our table a few minutes later with a question for me.

"I just wanted to make sure I got this right. You ordered the sea bass, not the swordfish, right?"

"Correct," I told her.

But I couldn't let it end on that note. Mind you, I never would have gone this far in my normal state of mind; it was the drug. So, when a young male busser brought our orders to our table, I said to him:

"This is just a joke. Would you please tell our waitress Sandy that I thought I ordered the swordfish?"

Evidently, the young man didn't hear the "This is just a joke" part, as he immediately jerked my plate away thinking it was the wrong order. Sandy, meanwhile, overheard my comment while passing by and busted out laughing with that pretty smile of hers, reminding me of my cousin again.

I made amends when it came to paying the final tab. I threw in an extra $10 over my usual 20 percent tip and wrote a note on the bill: "Sandy, a little extra added here for your holiday arrival."

So that's how it went with me for a couple of months, starting the double dosage on the Friday before Labor Day weekend. We held our annual fantasy football league draft on that weekend at Gary's house, and I must have been extremely manic. I was in charge of writing down the draft picks for each of the 12 owners over 14 rounds, and I made numerous goofy mistakes on the list, notably mixing up the two Garys and two Seans repeatedly. Later that night I went totally off the wall while writing up a tongue-in-cheek analysis of the league's draft, which Gary had encouraged. This bizarre diatribe had me rolling on the floor in uncontrollable hysterical laughter at 3 o'clock in the morning. Trust me, it wasn't *that* funny.

Under the influence of this drug I noticed that I'd talk *very* fast, my mind racing a mile a minute. As my normal self I'm inclined to stumble a bit in my speech — a little stutter every now and then, mixing up cliches, and notoriously mispronouncing words. But under the spell of Topamax, I flummoxed two of my long-time friends Phil and Rich W., both who made comments about how different I sounded over the phone, "What's up with Chic?" they were telling each other.

I was acutely aware of how different I sounded. I swore that it felt like my brain had been re-wired somehow.

Feeling euphoric all the time was awesome, but something was off when I returned to work after the three-day holiday weekend on the double dose. I had to start on monthly staff billing that Tuesday morning, and suddenly, math equations that I had been doing automatically in my head for years were being completely miscalculated. I was screwing up so badly that I went home early, determining that I could not function at my job. I finally figured out it must have been the double dosage causing this reaction, so I dialed it back to one pill. By the next day, I was able to think clearly again and focus on the billing.

While the euphoric cloud lingered on a little longer on the single dosage, another disturbing side effect emerged. Something was terribly wrong every time I sat down at the piano to play my music— I was screwing up. I was forgetting how to play my own music, music that I had been playing for *decades*. This scared the shit out of me, after what I went through a few years earlier when I couldn't remember the name of the woman I had been living with for six years because of a stroke. What the hell was going on with my brain? For all that clear-minded, good-feeling, euphoria stuff I was getting from the medication, this memory issue offset all that. My bubble burst.

Alas, the euphoria phase was short-lived. It faded out after a couple of months and that quick-witted guy with the waitresses, baristas and retail clerks was gone. In some respects, I missed that guy. As for my music, that came back, too, fortunately, but it took a while, with a few months of practice.

The weight loss had finally leveled off, but then the Topamax was causing some digestive problems, too. It reached the point where I had to discontinue it altogether. Fortunately, my migraine problem had been minimized by then.

I had returned to being the same goofy, absent-minded, tongue-tied guy I had always been.

———————◆———————

After more than 18 years, I decided it was finally time to fulfill my Deep Creek promise to Dan.

I did release some of his ashes from my pink rock up at Camino Cielo, as I had decided I would do on my "I Saw God" day on December 23, 2001. But I held onto a handful of his ashes in the small paper vase his girlfriend Tami had constructed, tucked away on a bookshelf in a back "junk" room. I hadn't forgotten the promise I had made during our camping trip back in our mid 20s at Deep Creek, located in the Angeles Crest Forest above the greater LA basin. I hadn't forgotten Dan's stunning premonition that he wouldn't live past the age of 50, and that he wanted me to spread his ashes at Deep Creek.

I set out to do that on September 5, 2019, which would have been Dan's 67th birthday. I was driving my wife's new Prius; I needed a reliable car that could handle the long dirt road that led to the trailhead to the creek. That trailhead opened up to a trail that Dan and I had hiked down about a mile-and-a-half in length to reach the pristine stream of crystal clear creek water snaking through sun-baked, smooth boulders that served as our camping playground.

To refresh my memory of a place I hadn't been to in nearly 40 years, I did a Google search of Deep Creek. I came across a crude, sketchy map identifying a "Deep Creek" running just above the town of Arrowbear, midway between Running Springs and Big Bear. The map showed the creek emptying into a "Deep Creek Lake" in close proximity to Arrowbear. In fact, a very short "Deep Creek Rd" off the Rim of The World Highway dead-ended at the lake and creek. That gave me a vague game-plan to go by.

So, on a very warm day I drove out from Santa Barbara. It was 100 degrees driving through San Bernardino, but temperatures dipped slightly as I climbed up Highway 33 that would turn into Rim of the World Highway.

I recognized Running Springs when passing through it. My first in-laws, parents to my first wife Dorrean, owned a cabin in Running Springs in which we frequently spent weekend retreats. Arrowbear was a few miles further up the road. I happened to notice "Blondie's Bar" in town, on the highway, just a stone's throw from Deep Creek Rd.

I drove about three miles past Arrowbear and came upon Green Lake Road. Yes! This was it, I was sure. I turned left onto Green

Lake Road and ventured on in search of a turnoff to the dirt road leading to Deep Creek.

About five miles further, lo and behold, there was a turnoff to a dirt road off to the left. I was banking on a vague memory, but it definitely looked familiar to me, after all these years. I noticed a direction sign at the entry of the road and got excited. It stated "Crab Flat Campground 4."

I clearly remembered a campground on the dirt road headed toward Deep Creek. I clearly remembered that we had to drive four or five miles to get to the trailhead we needed to hike to get to Deep Creek. The Crab Flat Campground sign was all I needed to know.

I was so excited that I pushed forward on the dirt road, neglecting to read the second entry on the direction sign. That couldn't have been very important (snicker). I shrugged it off.

The dirt road was pretty smooth and well-maintained, not nearly as rough as I remembered it 40 years ago. But I drove slow in my wife's Prius, heading downhill at no more than 25 mph, because the road was often narrow with many twists and turns and the occasional surprise bump in its path. I drove cautiously for 40 minutes, encountering no on-coming traffic. Then, the campground suddenly appeared.

The campground was completely empty — no campers. I parked in one of the camping slots and got out of the car. It was still hot outside, in the high 80s. I was immediately accosted by an annoying swarm of gnats flying around.

Vainly trying to swat the gnats away, I ventured out on foot to see if I could find any sign of the trailhead leading to Deep Creek. Nothing was looking familiar. I noticed the dirt road that had gotten me this far continued on in the distance past the campground. I hadn't bothered to go that far, taking my chances in the campground.

Futilely, I climbed back in the car, trying to escape from the gnats. I decided to head back to Blondie's Bar and ask for help to find the "Deep Creek Lake" that I saw on that sketchy Google map. I figured a local would have to know about the lake. It's a lake, for crying out loud.

So I drove another 40 minutes back up the dirt road to the entryway at the main road. When I got there, I glared at the direction sign, and this time I bothered to read the second entry below "Crab

Flat Campground 4." My jaw dropped. It said "Trailhead 5." Oh no! The trailhead I was looking for was just one more mile past the campground up the dirt road! But of course. My memory kept telling me the drive on the dirt road was four, or *five*, miles. I felt pretty stupid in that moment, classic block-headed blunder on my part. Why, oh why, didn't I read the entire direction sign at the entryway? Oh, that's right, I'm a man, and *real* men don't actually read directions.

So, what do I do? Do I make that 40-minute drive back down to the campground, then 10 more minutes for the extra mile, just to get to the trailhead? Then make the 50-minute hike to Deep Creek? Or, do I go to Blondie's and carry out Plan B?

It was still early afternoon, plenty of time. I ultimately decided I owed it to Dan to drive back down and make one more attempt to find Deep Creek. I wasn't going to give myself an easy way out just for being an idiot.

So, 40 minutes later, I was back at the campground, only this time I didn't park. I sure as hell didn't want to deal with those gnats again. I kept going further — not a good idea. When I exited the campground, the road narrowed considerably, just wide enough for the width of the car, and it got considerably bumpier. I bounced very slowly down the suddenly treacherous road for about 20 feet, the bottom of the car smacking against one large bump along the way. I stopped and decided, no way. The car couldn't take the punishment. (Sigh.) Four months later, I learned through my insurance company that I had caused $4000 of damage on the bottom of the car.

But fortunately the car was still drivable during my predicament in that campground. In total frustration, I reversed the car and backed out onto safer ground. Back to Plan B. I grumbled the entire way back out to the main road.

I drove all the way back to Blondie's Bar. I walked into the bar at about 3:30, which wasn't exactly peak hour for business for a bar. It was completely empty, except for a 50ish blonde woman behind the bar who I assumed was Blondie. The only other person there was a Hispanic guy in the kitchen. I took a seat at the bar and, deciding I was hungry, opened up the menu. I ordered a chicken melt sandwich and a draft beer. Blondie obliged, giving the Hispanic cook something to do.

Then I asked her, "I was wondering if you could help me out. Do you know anything about a Deep Creek Lake around here?"

A quizzical look crossed Blondie's face. "A lake? No, I don't know of any lake here. There is a creek up in the hills that people fish."

"Is that Deep Creek?"

"Yeah, that's it, I think. There's a Deep Creek Road just across the highway."

"Yeah, I saw a Google map showing the road dead-ending into a creek, emptying into a little lake."

Her face contorted again. "A lake," she said, doubtfully. "No, wouldn't know anything about a lake."

Just then two young men, with soot all over their clothes as if they had been digging up dirt somewhere, wandered into the bar. Blondie perked up when she saw them.

"Why don't you ask these fellas. They'd have a better idea."

The two guys sat on the bar stools next to me. I turned to the guy sitting closest to me.

"I'm looking for a Deep Creek Lake. Would you have any idea where I might find it?"

The guy gave me the same contorted look that Blondie gave me at the mention of a lake.

"The only lake I know of is a few miles thataway," he said, pointing in the direct opposite direction of where this alleged Deep Creek Lake was supposed to be.

I gave up on the idea of finding Deep Creek Lake. I don't know what the hell I was looking at on that Google map, but if any such lake existed, none of the locals seemed to know about it.

'Well, how 'bout Deep Creek? Is there a creek nearby?" I queried.

"Well, yeah, there's a creek just up at the end of a road about a block down," he said. "But this time of year, I don't think there's much water runnin' in the creek."

"Well, that's OK, as long as I can find the creek," I said. "I think I know what road you're talking about."

A creek that didn't have much water running in it didn't sound ideal. But if it was the same Deep Creek, damn it, at least I could keep my promise to Dan.

I ate my sandwich, washed it down with my beer, and felt refueled for my search for Deep Creek.

I got in my car and found Deep Creek Road easy enough. My pulse was racing. I was sure I was getting close. About a half-mile up, I came to a stop sign and a road crossing. I looked directly ahead and saw the road ahead was no longer paved, but rather a wide path consisting of dirt and bark. Worse, I saw a sign posted stating "Private Property — No Trespassing." This was a bad sign, both literally and figuratively.

Well, I did what I usually do and ignored that sign, too, and trespassed right past it. Driving cautiously down the private road, I noticed a chain-link fence to the left. Peaking through the bush and trees along the fence, I caught a glimpse of what appeared to be a possible "creek." The question of whether there was any water in the creek was another matter.

I ventured a little further, where there was another sign clearly stating "No Trespassing," just in case I missed the first sign (confession: I didn't). The road came to a dead-end at a chalet-like house. With a deep sigh, I turned around, and headed back out.

When I reached the road crossing I had passed earlier, I turned right and immediately parked off to the side of the road. Another chain-link fence paralleled the road. I looked past the fence and saw a tiny dry lakebed, with a couple of rotting rowboats that hadn't seen water for *years,* stuck in the cracked dirt.

Then I turned my gaze up ahead at a large, barn-like building on the shore of the dry lakebed. There, in all its glory, was a big, crude sign on the barn: "Deep Creek Lake."

Well, I'll be dammed, I found it. This was it. A bone-dry patch of cracked dirt. Well, hell. My sources at Blondie's were right. There was no existing lake anywhere near these parts. The "Deep Creek Lake" on that Google map could have just been a coffee stain blotch for all it was worth.

Damn.

To wrap up my pitiful story, I carried Tami's lovely paper vase with Dan's ashes down that "No Trespassing" road looking for an opening in the chain-link fence off to the left to get to the creek that I thought I saw. But then I took a closer look from the fence and it was confirmed. There was just as much water in that damn creek as there was in Deep Creek Lake — not a drop. Deep Creek and Deep Creek Lake were one in the same — a mirage.

I decided the hell with it, Dan didn't want his ashes spread over dried mud. So, I drove my wife's bottom-damaged Prius all the way back to Santa Barbara, with Dan's ashes in Tami's pretty vase on my passenger seat, to wait for another day when I could fulfill that promise I made. I knew Dan could wait.

◆◆◆◆◆◆

As a self-professed storyteller I admit that I crave an audience. I saw an opportunity after attending a performance at Santa Barbara's Center Stage Theatre presenting "Personal Stories" as told by local storytellers. The director was Maggie Mixsell, who was the same instructor for the acting class that I had enrolled in twenty years earlier at Santa Barbara City College during my mid-life crisis. After the performance, I approached her and expressed interest in auditioning for future performances.

When the next round of auditions came up eight months later, I signed up and was selected for a reading of a condensed version of my "Stroke Of Luck" chapter. The next "Personal Stories" performance was scheduled in October, 2019. I was pretty excited.

And nervous. Maggie Mixsell slotted me to open the program among eleven storytellers, so the pressure was on.

To get it within the 10-minute time limit, I used a gimmick to condense my stroke story. I retitled the story "Stroke of Luck— Part 2." The first stroke was told in a rapid, stream of consciousness fashion as "scenes from the previous episode — Stroke of Luck, Part 1." I had to nail this segment smoothly in under two minutes, so I committed it to memory, which was kinda risky. If I muffed the opening out of nervousness, the rest of the story might have fallen flat.

As I sat waiting behind the curtain side stage, hearing the crowd settle into their seats, I was rehearsing the memorized opening section several times inside my head. I was seated next to the woman who was slotted to go third in the program. The odd-numbered storytellers in order of the program were on one side of the stage, and the even-numbered storytellers on the other side. We were waiting a good half-hour before the program was set to start.

Well, about ten minutes before I was set to go on stage, the inconceivable happened at the worst possible moment. I removed my reading glasses from my glass case and dropped them on the floor.

When I picked them up, one of the lenses popped out of the rimmed frame. These were my $300 bifocal reading glasses. I couldn't believe it.

Frantically, I tried popping the lens back in the frame. It was loose as hell. I did not like my chances that it would hold, not exactly what I needed to calm my nerves. I didn't know it at the time, but the frame was loose because it had cracked. Uh-huh, ten minutes before I was supposed to read my story in front of a live audience, I had broken my reading glasses.

"This is what I typically do to myself in these situations," I jokingly told the woman next to me, but I really meant it. It was absolutely true. This was by the script. You heard of Murphy's Law — what *could* go wrong *will* go wrong? Substitute "Perkins" for "Murphy."

Maggie had each of us storytellers select a lead-in song for our stage entrance. When the first few bars to The Bee Gees' song "How Deep Is Your Love" kicked in, I swallowed hard and walked out on stage. The second line in my memorized "Part 1" gimmick related how I was falling off to the left at the early onset of my first stroke. In a bit of performance art, I jerked slightly to the left to re-enact that moment.

Maybe it was the bright lights shining on me on stage, I don't know. But I was completely oblivious to what had evidently transpired in that jerking moment. Somehow, though, I got through my memorized spiel and then the rest of the story without a hitch. The audience reaction was really positive; they laughed at all the funny parts.

Then I retreated back to my seat behind the curtain side stage, feeling pretty good. As the next storyteller was entering the stage from the opposite side to read her story, the curtain in front of me was parted open by a polite elderly gentleman.

"You dropped this," he said to me, holding his hand out toward me. Then he handed me… one of the lenses to my reading glasses.

Oh my God, I had no idea! The lens must have popped out when I made the jerking gesture. The kind gentleman evidently had retrieved it from his front-row seat. Then I must have read my entire story on stage with just one lens in my reading glasses. It seemed that everybody else in the entire theatre was aware of this; family members and friends clued me in after the performance. How goofy did that look? It was probably a good thing I didn't know, a very good thing. I stayed calm by not knowing.

The evening turned out all right. But I'll say it again, sometimes it's tough being me.

—————————◆ ·◆· ·◆·—————————

After the sale of the Rossburn house in August of 2017, I drove by the house a few times over the next two-and-a-half years to see how far the new owners, Fabio and Grace, had progressed converting it into something I didn't recognize.

On one occasion, I stopped to get a closer look. I walked down the driveway and took a sneak peek through the skeleton walls. The whole house had been gutted or stripped down.

Fabio and Grace were building their dream house. As the project slowly evolved I could tell that they had expanded it by a couple of feet along the driveway and raised the roof in the central section of the house. I had remained in contact with Julie, the real estate lady who had sold the house, and had become a good friend. She had been giving me updates on what Fabio was doing with the place.

It had been a good eight months since I had seen the place when I inquired with Julie in February of 2020 if Fabio and Grace had finished rebuilding the house. They had, she said. And they were putting it up for sale… because they were getting a divorce.

I was shocked and sad for them. Then Julie told me she was having a big open house, and it just so happened I was planning a trip down to LA that day, to settle a lingering matter with Pam. It had been a year-and-a-half since I had last seen —or talked with — my sister. Julie encouraged me to come by that evening to see what Fabio and Grace had done to the place, so I did. Pam declined to go with me.

I walked into a party, with about fifty people mingling about. They had been wooed to the open house by the free taco bar Julie had served up in the backyard.

I stepped into a showcase home displaying state-of-the-art interior design. It was utterly stunning and nothing at all like the home I had grown up in and existed in our family's hands for over 62 years. There was only one element from our old house that remained intact— the huge fireplace in the family room.

Literally, everything else was different. Every single wall, cabinet, door, window, ceiling and flooring space had been changed, removed and/or reconfigured. While I was in awe of the sheer elegance of the look and admiration for Fabio's work — he had done almost all of the work himself — I couldn't help feeling tremendously saddened.

I looked into my old bedroom. The window through which I had climbed out for my hormonally charged naked run through the streets late at night as a young teen had been replaced. The front porch which I had blindly raced to and tripped in a spectacular crash when my third-grade classmate embarrassed me by disclosing that she liked me was totally rebuilt. The family room where live bands rocked during our epic high school parties, where we had held our family holiday meals spanning decades, where the iconic 60's, rainbow-colored, round metal table sat in the corner in a test of time, where Mom conducted her nude massage parties, and where Frank's shit was spread all over up until escrow closed, had been re-leveled and merged with the front living room, with the dividing wall removed. Pam's psychedelic shack behind the garage, where Kathy and I had our all-day sex marathon, was gone. The backyard where I swung my baseball bat and broke my sister's nose had been completely re-landscaped. The row of camellia bushes alongside the driveway that I watered with a hose as part of my weekly chores while growing up — *go up and down three times and spray underneath the leaves,* like my dad instructed — were all cleared out.

I saw Fabio at the open house. I expressed my condolences over the break-up with Grace. Julie had been dropping hints that Grace's patience was growing thin living out of a camper for so long while the rebuilding process dragged out, and it obviously reached a breaking point in the marriage. Fabio was sad and I felt sad for him. He was hoping he could break even on the sale of the house after all the expense and labor he put into it.

I left the open house feeling sad as well for the memories I was leaving behind. Time was marching relentlessly onward.

Life is a continuous chain of changes.

CHAPTER 33
. . . And Life Extends

The Coronavirus pandemic of 2020 effectively ended a 40-year streak of the exalted annual poker games with my old high school buddies— Phil, Rich W., Rich B., and Jim.

We had managed to get together at least once a year for hours of four-four-two, no-peek-fours-wild-eights-extra-card, seven/twenty-seven, jacks-or-better-to-open-trips-to-win, three-across, screw-your-neighbor, seven-card-stud-high-diamond-split, spit-in-the-ocean, don't-forget-to-flush (a Phil original), and a few other wildly named card games we made up along the way. It was never high stakes — the big winner and big loser walked away with $50-$60 or minus the same amount by the end of the night. No one was surrendering any keys to a car.

A major theme to my memoirs is how lucky I've been; I declared myself the Luckiest Ordinary Man Alive and I meant it. Although each of my high school poker buddies could lay claim to the same title. As a collective group, we've all been pretty damned lucky. Phil and I often acknowledge that very point as we enter our senior years in a state of relative comfort, financial security, and good health.

But when it came to playing poker with my buddies, it didn't seem like we were playing on an even playing field, from my perspective. I gained a reputation for usually winding up woefully short when it came time for counting chips to divvy up the cash pot. My buddies always wanted to make sure that I made it to the party because they could pretty much count on profiting at my expense, so the joke went.

Some of my bad luck was self-inflicted, which is another way of saying I'm not a very good poker player. In one of life's ironies, my half-brother Pat happens to be a great poker player; he's a big-time player in the casino near his home in Paso Robles, and he claims he makes good money. I'm sure my high school poker buddies would wonder how we could possibly be genetically linked.

But luck in poker derives considerably from an innate confidence in the cards you draw, which has been my greatest challenge. I venture to say that I had more than my share of bet-the-house poker hands that somehow, some way, somebody at the table miraculously managed to beat, which tended to suck the confidence right out of me.

I was usually the guy holding four natural kings losing the hand to the guy —more often than not, that guy was Phil — who laid down four natural aces. Sometimes my losses defied the odds.

My life-long high school buddies and I during one of our recent annual poker games

Which brings to mind an article I read in the New York Times' Sunday Review Section on June 21, 2020, written by Maria Konnikova. The article was headlined "Dealing With the Hand of Fate," derived from her book "The Biggest Bluff: How to Pay Attention, Master Myself, and Win."

The article discussed being lucky in life. *"Luck surrounds us — from something as mundane as walking to work and getting there safely to the other extreme, like surviving a disease when someone just like us wasn't spared,"* Konnikova writes. Hmm, a sobering, relevant point in the age of coronavirus.

Then she writes about the game of poker, and how it relates to luck. *"Poker is a game of incomplete information. There are the cards I hold, known only to me. There are the cards you hold, known only to you...I can make the best decision possible and still lose. And I can make a horrible mistake and luck out. The process and the outcome are not equivalent."*

Ultimately, Konnikova concludes, *"In many ways, poker is a poor metaphor for life."* But she drives home the point that poker can teach us good lessons about luck in life. No matter how much skill or talent we possess, we have no control over how lucky we might be. We have no control over what cards we're dealt. *"No one is asking that poker replace life,"* Konnikova continues. *"You don't want to eliminate uncertainty — it's presumptuous to believe you can. You want to understand it."*

As I've gotten older, I feel like I've gotten closer to understanding uncertainty. Lord knows, I've had more than my share of circumstances where uncertainty hung in the balance. But I've been lucky by how those uncertainties balanced out in my life and I've learned to accept that. Uncertainty makes life interesting.

But it still pisses me off when Phil lays down those four aces over my kings.

———————◆•••——————

I've made reference to "The Unbearable Lightness of Being," both the movie and the book on which it's based, numerous times throughout my memoirs. When I saw the movie as a young man, it held particular fascination over me in its depiction of life and love, which resonated a harmonic chord within me.

While researching a review of the 1988 movie that Roger Ebert penned for the Chicago Sun-Times. I noted a line he wrote that could have been written about my memoirs:

The Unbearable Lightness of Being' carries the feeling of deep nostalgia, of a time no longer present, when these people did these things and hoped for happiness, and were caught up in events beyond their control."

That seems to parallel the story I've been telling, a life full of unexpected twists, rendering it unpredictable. Whether that defined my destiny or not is another question, in a universe that is either cosmically planned or haphazard, but clearly there were forces that have been utterly beyond my control.

In the novel "The Unbearable Lightness of Being" by author Milan Kundera, "lightness" is presented as a contrast from love in the characterization of Tomas. In his pattern of womanizing, Tomas is able to separate love from sex, and therefore embrace the "lightness of being," or freedom from the burden that love presents. I could never do that. Lightness never came easy for me with my sentimental nature. As applied to Tomas in the movie, he falls in love with Tereza and gets trapped in the "heaviness" that is metaphorically represented by the 1968 Russian occupation of Czechoslovakia. So ultimately, when he has the chance to escape, Tomas chooses heaviness by returning to Czechoslovakia to be with Teresa.

That's why I likened my relationship with Janice to Tomas and Sabina at first. Like them, Janice and I were "lovers" with the freedom to love others; hence, we were experiencing the "lightness." But in the end, after she was gone, I realized that my love for Janice was not without "heaviness," or weight, which I equate to meaningful substance. That was how I now interpret Sabina's unspoken "unbearable" feelings at the end of "The Unbearable Lightness of Being" when she learns that Tomas has died. She mourns Tomas' passing in the same regretful way I mourned Janice's.

I'm not implying that Janice was some sort of exclusive "soulmate" for me. I could make the same case for my first true love, April, who has never escaped my heart, and has never left me. Or maybe it was Katya, however short-term our ill-fated passionate affair burned. Or maybe it's Cyndi, my wife now, who may be the last person I see when I exit this life. Or maybe I've just been lucky enough to experience a collection of "soulmates," who form the puzzle that Dan once artistically created out of clay to represent the wholeness of my life.

This memoir is an attempt to assemble the pieces of that puzzle to present a complete picture.

The bottom line is that I love women, and I have been truly blessed to be loved by many women. I am eternally grateful for all the women who have touched my life in one form or another — Doris, Lizette, Laura, April, Kathy, Sandy, Dorrean, Karen, Jocelyne, Carolyn, Lizamara, Janice, Teri, Jeannette, Katya, Gail, Jeri, Sophia, Maggie, Gayle, Dahlia, Cass, Cyndi.

While I may have not always "understood" women in some of my various relationships, I've always respected women and their feminine perspective. I frequently felt like I got along better with women than men, in general, which may sound weird coming from a guy who made a living writing about male-dominated sports. Women may have served as means of balance to the masculinity reinforced in sports.

I don't mean to slight the many women who have excelled in athletics, but looking back it occurred to me that the vast majority of my sports reporting was on men. (Drag racer Shirley Muldowney was an extraordinary exception.) But sports writing was my chosen profession, and when I sought out personal relationships with women, I clearly gravitated toward women who weren't into sports. (My wife Cyndi, whom I met through my female-centric second profession in social work, has zero interest in sports. I get absolutely no sympathy from her when I try to tell her about my rotten luck in fantasy football.)

I've had plenty of male friends who were into sports, so I got my sports fix through them. The women in my life — either romantically linked or "just friends" — tended to be non-sports fans. I think subconsciously there was a "need' in me to relate to women who weren't into sports. Maybe women were my means to break from the structure and rules that come with sports. Maybe that's why some of my romantic relationships broke the rules.

My male friendships tended to provide more structure in my personal life; my relationships with women certainly leaned toward more uncertainty. I am blessed to have really close male friends who I've known most of my life — Phil, Rich W., Rich B., Jim, Wayne, Paul. No break-ups among this group.

While I was a baseball nut in my younger days, no one is more passionate about baseball than Paul, another life-long high school buddy of mine. We recently attended a minor league baseball game in Columbia, S.C. wearing jerseys and hats from Paul's vast collection of baseball apparel

I have another group of male friends from our shared years working together at the Santa Barbara News-Press sports department — Dan, Barry, Dave, Mark, John, and Mike. Fifteen years after my last day working at the News-Press, we've gathered for a few reunions that have strengthened our bond.

In more recent years I have forged friendships with my tennis buddies — Tony, Phil, Rolando, Bruce and Cesar.

I struck a gender balance that somehow guided me through the chaos that has been my life. When things got way out of control, which was often, I seemed to possess an innate knack to find balance to right the ship. I fell down a lot, but more often than not, I regained my balance just in time to catch my fall.

———————•·•·◆·•·•———————

"The Unbearable Lightness of Being" also deals with themes on the afterlife, presenting an alternative to Friedrich Nietzche's "eternal recurrence," which posits that events have already occurred and will recur ad infinitum somehow in the vast universe. "Lightness of Being" implies that we are all only given one life to live. That's what my atheist father believed.

But my beliefs are more in line with Nietzche's. I believe in love, and I believe God is love, in all of us, some more than others. And therefore, that implies some sort of "eternity" that possibly is recurring forever. Or maybe recurring with slightly different alternatives, based on the choices we make, opening up the possibility of infinite alternative consequences.

Or maybe our souls are reborn in the energy within us that never dies atomically and we are allowed to live again. I don't pretend to know the answers to the Great Unknown.

But this represents how I *feel*. I distinctly remember a dream I had when I was very young; I'm not sure how old I was. I think I was young pre-teen. But when I think about it now, I clearly understand it presented a vision of a "rebirth," or reincarnation, if you will. In the dream, rain was pouring heavily for a long time, long enough to instill the fear that the earth would be flooded and drown out all life. So, in the spirit of community, all the neighbors on my block, on Rossburn Avenue— the center of my universe back then — gathered up in the middle of the cul-de-sac street. We huddled in blankets, and bunched up close together to stay warm as sheets of rain poured down from dark gray skies. Ultimate doom prevailed. Then the dream suddenly shifted, in which I was swimming through a large "tube" of some sort (a fallopian tube, perhaps?) Then I burst up in a cloud of tiny bubbles at the surface of a large swimming pool of clear blue water. The storm of doom clearly had washed away, as the water was gleaming in bright sunshine — light that illuminated a ray of hope; hope in a new world reborn.

As unconventional as it has played out, my life has been fulfilling in so many ways, as the title "Luckiest Ordinary Man Alive" implies. If my soul is "reborn" and I am granted another life to live, I can only hope that if it comes anywhere close to being as fulfilling as this life, I will be one lucky woman, indeed.

Livin' life to the fullest

EPILOGUE

I wrote the bulk of my memoirs in the first year of the Age of Coronavirus. I think writing my memoirs served to save my sanity. To reflect and languish in the past during lockdowns and extreme social distancing — recalling how life used to be — is what got me through trying times.

Writing memoirs during a massive virus pandemic also forced me to reflect on a past that truly felt more distant than ever. It made me wonder if the experiences I lived through represented a way of life in a bygone era that will never return. It made me sad to think my collection of life experiences may not be available to the average person today, whether it's due to the dying newspaper industry or social media's impersonal dynamic, which has impacted the way relationships are formed, or worse, avoided.

Certainly, my future will be a lot calmer and less exciting than my past, but age may be more of a factor than the coronavirus in that respect. But I am even more thankful for having these memories to treasure. They have made me realize just how lucky I've been.

Meanwhile, I live on:

• My daughter Tessa graduated from Azusa Pacific University with her B.S. degree, then went two more years to earn her Master's Degree in Business Psychology by the spring of 2020. I could not be prouder of her. She's on her way to a promising career with a good-paying job working for an HR department for a start-up business. With me and her gushing proud mom Maggie looking on, she also managed to marry her longtime boyfriend, Tanner, in the summer of 2021, after the Covid pandemic finally abated. They got married in Santa Barbara, where Tessa chose to get married in an intimate family gathering at the Santa Barbara Courthouse on Fourth of July weekend. Santa Barbara was significant for Tessa because she was born there, and she targeted Fourth of July weekend to honor the day she and Tanner met at a BBQ party. A bigger destination wedding bash that included Tessa and Tanner's friends was held a few months later in Puerto Vallarta.

- While I felt like I lost a brother in Dan, I gained one back in Pat. We've only grown closer since the day he came knocking on my mother's front door.

- There were times I felt like I was losing a sister ever since the sale of the Rossburn house — my relationship with Pam was strained. I finally reached out to her by inviting her to Tessa's wedding, and she showed up. By then she was homeless, living out of her car, after she had burned through all her money from the sale of the house by the summer of 2020. She could no longer afford the high rents she had been paying on a couple houses she shared with Frank and Kasey, neither of whom were contributing to rent for the better part of two years. They were all finally evicted out of the last house, and Kasey and Frank paired up on their own, hop-scotching around in air b&bs in a search of a permanent apartment. They left Pam to fend for herself, ostensibly because of her bad credit. Pam had loaned Frank a good chunk of her money when he was freeloading off of her. He keeps saying he will help her find a place to live. We're still waiting.

- Cyndi and I did welcome Pam into our home for a couple of months after Tessa's wedding, until — supposedly — she returned to LA to take a job as a senior caregiver. She left behind a bunch of family photo albums and mementos at our house. The mementos included a revelatory letter that our dad had written to our mom when we were just toddlers. In the letter, Dad accused Mom of having an extra-marital affair prior to Pam's birth and questioned whether he was Pam's real father. That may have explained why her blond, blue-eyed features were so different from mine. This revelation could not have been beneficial for the mental health of my struggling sister, who harbored lifelong psychological struggles trying to gain the approval of the father who raised us. It also brought into question our sibling link — the possibility that she may be my half-sister.

- In the process of writing my memoirs, I renewed contact with Janice's daughter, Cori, who is a traveling nurse. She was in Arizona during the Covid outbreak. We connected when I e-mailed her excerpts from my memoirs on my long relationship with her mother. I believe my stories about her mother had a profound effect on Cori. In honor of the memory of Janice, I made a pledge to add Cori as a beneficiary in my living trust. I think it's fair to say that I feel like I have gained another daughter. I texted her on the day Kamala Harris was sworn in as Vice President, stating how both our mothers would have cherished that moment some 43 years after meeting at the National Organization of Women convention.

- I never lost contact with April. We engage in long, rambling phone conversations about once a month. She has always been someone whom I can easily talk with, a bond that I can always count on. I wrote a song about April, called "That Yesterday Feeling," a feeling that remains alive and well today. April was in her fourth marriage, to Archie, and living in Virginia, at the time of this writing. I spent an extraordinary weekend as a lucky houseguest at their mountainside home atop five acres overlooking breathtaking 360-degree views of lush green countryside. Their household included four dogs, a cat, and at the time "Baby Bird," as April gushingly called her. Baby Bird was an adolescent crow April had been nursing back to health for three months after finding it as a helpless fuzzy chick abandoned in the wild. April's heart saved that bird. It reminded me of my lifelong friend Phil when he nursed that hawk he rescued off the TV antenna of the Rossburn house when we were kids. Besides their love for animals, April and Phil are very much alike in their ethical, down-to-earth, no-bullshit, personable personalities. I realized that April and Phil had supplanted Dan and Janice as the ying-and-yang best friend components that helps me keep it together in my senior years.

- I also retained a friendship with Gayle, who is married now to another guy. She found someone with whom she could break her Vern habit. She's a full-on endorser of CBD for whatever ails you or keeps you up at night. Full disclosure: So am I. She was pissed off at me for not telling her about my strokes. As a nurse where I was hospitalized, she lamented that had she known I was a patient, she would have checked in on me to assure I was getting the best care possible. I promised to call her next time a medical emergency visit comes up.

- Nik Green's widow Penny has become the one friend I can count on as my creative collaborator. She produced my third CD, "Songs from My Youth." The last track on the album is my most recent composition, my pandemic piece that I entitled "Covidual Consciousness." It represents a fitting "epilogue" on a collection of songs from my past.

- On the subject of youth, playing tennis is what keeps me feeling young. About 12 years ago, I started playing with a large contingent in my age group on Saturdays, rotating server-out on two or three courts at a time.

- For the last five years I've been playing Tuesday mornings with a foursome composed of a rotation among Rolando, Tony, Phil, Bruce and Cesar. I'm the youngster of the group. Tony and Bruce are my aspiring role models — they were still going strong at ages 80 and 82. So, I've got a long way to go before I'm done hanging up the racket.

- As hard as I try to defy the aging process, I've been given sobering reminders of how I'm growing old. During the coronavirus pandemic in the summer of '20, the reality of time passing was personified by somebody from my youth — Bruce Gerke. Bruce, who is a year younger than me, was the youngest of the four Gerke boys who grew up next door to me on Rossburn. He suffered a debilitating stroke in his early 60's. He was living in Nipomo, some 80 miles north of Santa Barbara, with his ex-wife Kathy, at the time. In the summer of '20, he was transferred to a nursing facility in Goleta, much nearer to me, for cost reasons. I attempted to visit him a couple of times, but because of Covid I could only talk with him over a fence that contained a patio, where he sat in his wheelchair with partial left-side paralysis that resulted from his stroke. That could have been me six years earlier. There was nothing wrong with Bruce's memory; he and I relived some nice memories — our off-road motorcycle adventure at Kennedy Meadows, as well as our harrowing brush with the *Federales* in Ensenada. Seeing Bruce was yet another affirmation of how blessed I am with my good health.

- R.I.P.: Dave Loveton, a k a "The Limping Cowboy," from the movie "Steal Big, Steal Little," who succumbed to his three-year battle with cancer on April 28, 2021.

- I finally edged closer to retirement by stepping down to part-time status with PathPoint in the summer of 2019. It remains to be seen how much longer I'll work; Covid pretty much gave me a reason to continue working because there was little else I could do with my time. My wife Cyndi has a similar decision to make, and she's been doing this job coaching thing a few years more than me. As for Cyndi and I, we have found contentment in our marriage without the drama, sharing a life of comfort. What a concept.

- I want to publicly thank Jim Short, long-time motorsports writer for the Riverside Press-Enterprise, and my driving buddy in the wild ride we shared in the 1985 Mint 400 off-road race, for editing and fact-checking my memoirs. Jim noted that he and I are the last two survivors among the Big 5 of LA motorsports writers during the 1980s. RIP Shav Glick, Tim Tuttle, and Allan Wolfe. Jim has lived the life my dad had in mind for me — married 40 years to his sweetheart Lynne.

• I offer special thanks to my son Kasey for designing my memoir website and posting excerpts to lure in readers. Kasey is self-taught in website design, a skill I can't relate to, proof that my son is a lot smarter than I am in today's tech world.

• I also want to publicly express my gratitude for the multi-talented Penny Little, who provided some memoir editing, then formatted the entire text and photos, and designed the book cover. Penny knows me cover-to-cover after her work on my book. This book would not have been possible without her friendship and support.

• I also want to thank the handful of friends who agreed to read along on chapters while I was in the process of writing my memoirs. They include: my tennis buddy Tony, who reminisced about his own variety of life experiences while reading about mine; April, who saw me through many of my stories as my high school sweetheart and dear friend who knows me as well as anybody; Paul, with whom I've become much closer since he suddenly lost his wife — the beloved matriarch of his expansive family; and finally, my everlasting best friend Phil, whom I've known since our hop-scotching days in fourth grade, who exulted in learning what he didn't know about the many gaps in my life, and who provided reams of helpful, thoughtful feedback, and sincere, emotional parallels to his own life. After he's read this, Phil won't say it to my face, but I know he's thinking, "I'll never understand how in the heck you are still alive."